BOLLINGEN SERIES LXXXVII:2

Alexis Leger at Monhegan Island, Maine, 1954

St.-John Perse

LETTERS

TRANSLATED

AND EDITED BY

ARTHUR J. KNODEL

BOLLINGEN SERIES LXXXVII:2

PRINCETON UNIVERSITY PRESS

Copyright © 1979 by Princeton University Press

Published by Princeton University Press, Princeton, New Jersey
In the United Kingdom: Princeton University Press,
Guildford, Surrey

All Rights Reserved

THIS VOLUME IS NUMBER LXXXVII:2
IN BOLLINGEN SERIES
SPONSORED BY BOLLINGEN FOUNDATION

The letters are translated from the Pléiade edition of
Œuvres complètes of St.-John Perse published by Editions
Gallimard, Paris © 1972, which copyright also pertains
to the poems quoted in the original French

Library of Congress Cataloging in Publication Data will
be found on the last printed page of this book

This book has been composed in Linotype Granjon
Printed in the United States of America
by Princeton University Press, Princeton, New Jersey

CONTENTS

INTRODUCTION

In an unpublished letter to Archibald MacLeish dated February 21, 1967, Alexis Leger, better known in the world of letters as St.-John Perse, wrote:

> From Paris I'm being asked to make a selection from my personal letters to be published along with a critical edition of my [poetical] works in the collection of the Classics of the Bibliothèque de la Pléiade (Gallimard), and I am at the moment supposed to track down whatever letters I can get hold of that I wrote during my long period of exile in America. Might you, by chance, have kept a few of my letters that could give some idea of that phase of my life, even if only psychologically, should the literary side be lacking?

And then, farther along in the same letter:

> But I wouldn't want you to go to too much trouble or waste too much time in the search. And in the event that you can unearth something without too much trouble, I'd like to request, in order to make things a bit easier for you, that you leave the business of reproducing the originals, whether by typist or Xerox, to me; and then I'll send back the manuscript-letters to you after I've had them copied.[1]

---

1. The original text of this letter is in the MacLeish Papers (Container 45) deposited in the Manuscript Division of the Library of Congress. The original letter is in French; the English translation given here is by A. J. Knodel, as are all translated passages occurring in the footnotes, unless another translator is specifically indicated.

The Gallimard publishing house, with whom Leger had had relations for many years, knew that he had known many famous writers, and many more famous public figures, both in France and abroad, and that he had maintained a correspondence with many of them. The interest of the letters was evident. So, many requests like the one to MacLeish went out—not only to correspondents of the "long period of exile in America" (1940-1957), but likewise to correspondents of the preexile years or to their survivors. Copies of many letters were thus obtained; but, of course, many had disappeared over the years. There were, however, quite enough to fill a sizable volume, and it was from these that Alexis Leger made the selection that was published in 1972 in the Pléiade *Œuvres complètes* and that is here presented in English translation.

The letters extend well over half a century, the earliest dating from 1906, the most recent from 1966. They begin in those years preceding World War I that the French refer to as *la Belle Epoque* and then continue through World War I. They then skip to World War II and the period since then. Only a very few of the letters date from the period between the two wars (1919-1940). The dearth of letters for that period is significant in more than one way.

First, the years 1922-1940 were the period of Alexis Leger's most intense diplomatic activities—activities that culminated in his seven-year tenure as Secretary General of the French Ministry of Foreign Affairs (1933-1940). Leger certainly had less time then for writing personal letters than he had had before or was to have afterwards. Moreover, such personal letters as he did write during that period were, in many instances, lost or destroyed. But the virtual omission of the Between-the-Two-Wars period is also a clear indication of Leger's intention in selecting the particular letters he did for publication. He wanted them to concern St.-John Perse much more than Alexis Leger—a very meaningful distinction. The continuing drama that underlies almost all these letters in one way or another is the running battle Alexis Leger waged, from adolescence on, against the poet within him, the poet to whom he finally gave the name St.-John Perse and who was to receive the Nobel Prize for Literature in 1960. In the prolonged struggle, Alexis Leger would win occasional skirmishes, even important major engagements; but, fortunately for us, St.-John Perse finally won out. The victory came in 1941 with the composition of the poem *Exil*. But even after that date there are sudden displays of recalcitrance and many a sharply "anti-literary" moment. For literature exercised a simultaneous fascination and repulsion for Alexis Leger that is evident in the earliest, as well as in some of the most recent, of the letters printed here.

What this collection presents, then, is primarily an inner record, a kind of epistolary private journal. Its autobiographical character is heightened by the omission of all the letters to which these are responses. This is not a Leger-Rivière or a Leger-Gide or a Leger-Biddle correspondence; it is a series of letters, all by Leger, that gives us an insight into his inner struggles and profoundest traits of character. Dag Hammarskjöld, in his poignant *Vägmärken*, approvingly quotes a line from *Exil* that begins: "Il n'est d'histoire que de l'âme. . . ."[2] Embedded in the present selection of letters is such a chronicle of the soul. Yet, while the *histoire de l'âme* is the chief interest of the letters, they also tell us a great deal

2. *Vägmärken* (Albert Bonniers Forlag, 1963), p. 121. An English translation by Sjöberg and Auden entitled *Markings* was published by Alfred Knopf in 1964.

about the external details of the life of Alexis Leger at various periods; and there is a wide variety of materials to be found in them. There are the intellectual strainings and adolescent effusions addressed to a schoolmate, but there are also letters in the grand manner to elders such as Philippe Berthelot and Joseph Conrad. There is a humorous "Chinese" chronicle addressed by the young diplomat to his chief; and then, from the same period, the easy confidences, the loving concern, and the incidental minutiae of a family exchange (the letters to his mother). There are elaborate discussions of literary matters suddenly interrupted by a personal confidence or by descriptions that recreate a whole setting or countryside. But throughout, the "dual" personality of Leger-Perse is present on every page.

The recipients of these letters are present only as shadowy figures whose features we reconstruct sketchily from the tone and manner that Alexis Leger adopts in writing to each of them. Were it not for the fact that many of these correspondents are well-known literary and political figures, we would really know very little about them. The very character of the correspondents here represented is, however, in itself indicative. Only a very few are diplomatic or political figures (Philippe Berthelot, Francis Biddle, Dag Hammarskjöld); almost all the rest are writers or friends of writers (Rivière, Jammes, Gide, Larbaud, Frizeau, MacLeish, Tate, Caillois, Paulhan—with Claudel figuring in both groups). Once again, it is the poet St.-John Perse who is in the foreground; and his hesitations, misgivings, revulsions, and final surrender are the chief matter in these letters. Even the most "political" ones—the extraordinary letter to Berthelot and those parts of the letters to his mother concerned with China's role at the Paris Peace Conference—even those

are as much from the pen of the poet as from the pen
of the diplomat.

The letters fall quite naturally into three groups. The
"Early Letters," corresponding to the adolescence and
early manhood of Alexis Leger, are centered on Pau—
that most British of all French cities at the turn of the
century. The Leger family, which for generations had
lived on the French Antillean island of Guadeloupe,
where Alexis was born in 1887, had to return to France
in 1899 as a result of the economic and social crisis in
the islands. The immediate family consisted of the father,
mother, three daughters, and young Alexis. The boy
was scarcely twelve when he had to leave the islands,
and the memory of them transforms more than one of
the earlier letters into poems of penetrating nostalgia.

Alexis' father developed an important law practice in
Pau but died suddenly and prematurely in 1907. This
circumstance forced Alexis to abandon a dream he had
of becoming a planter in some far country—Borneo or
Brazil, for he was now the only remaining male in the
household, and he took his new role as head of the
family very seriously. He wrote poetry, but for himself
and almost in spite of himself; and the thought of a
literary career was repugnant to him. Above all, he was
determined to succeed in practical terms as a family pro-
vider. From this determination, difficult to maintain,
arises the tension that runs through these "Early Letters"
as the solitary young man, at once athlete and esthete—
a most unusual combination for those days—groped his
way towards a diplomatic career. All these early letters
—even those that are immature and over-elaborate—ex-
hale a subtle bouquet of that legendary *Belle Epoque*,

which, for Leger's generation, must have embodied the *douceur de vivre* that Talleyrand, at an earlier date, attributed to pre-Revolutionary France.

In 1914 Leger entered the French Foreign Service, and it was not long before he was sent off to China on his first assignment abroad. The second group of letters, the "Letters from Asia," have Peking as their "axis." These letters—especially those to his mother and the two long ones to Philippe Berthelot and Joseph Conrad, respectively—are perhaps the most continuously fascinating of the whole selection. They were written during the period immediately following the end of the Manchu dynasty when the war lords were rampant, when Sun Yat-sen was establishing himself in southern China, and when the Great Powers were shamelessly exploiting a nation that had remained ritualistic even in the way it waged wars. The "Letters from Asia" give us a first-hand picture of this strange and remote world from which, nevertheless, the China of Mao Tse-tung was already beginning to emerge. But there is more. The poet who wrote *Anabase*—the poem that T. S. Eliot was to translate into English, thereby introducing St.-John Perse to the English-speaking world—is here revealed in all his solitary pride and secret tenderness. The very human underpinnings of that vast poem are very much present in these letters. But the "Letters from Asia" end on a somber note, since the hope so carefully nurtured by the young diplomat for the integration of China into the world community was brutally dashed to pieces at Versailles.

No sooner did Leger leave China in 1921 than he was made a member of the French delegation to the Washington Conference on the Limitation of Armaments as an expert on the politics and economics of the Far East. It was in Washington during that conference that Leger attracted the attention of Aristide Briand, the great exponent of international collective security who was head of the French delegation. An intimate association between the two men began almost immediately and was to end only with Briand's death in 1932. Leger's rise in the French diplomatic hierarchy, from 1922 on, was steady, even phenomenal. He remained close to Briand and to Berthelot, and in 1933—the year Adolf Hitler took over in Germany—Leger was promoted to the rank of Ambassador and named Secretary General of the Ministry of Foreign Affairs, a post that had for many years been held by his friend and sponsor, Philippe Berthelot. Leger held this high office until May 18, 1940, when he was forced out by the intrigues of Paul Reynaud's notorious busybody of a mistress, the comtesse de Portes. Leger, thus, had the thankless task of maintaining a semblance of continuity in the French Foreign Office during the last seven tragic and chaotic years of the Third Republic. The Fall of France less than a month after his forced resignation obliged Leger to take refuge abroad, first in England, and then in America. He landed in Halifax, Nova Scotia, on July 14, 1940, and shortly thereafter took up temporary residence in New York.

These few details on the 1921-1940 years are essential to the understanding of the third group, the "Letters from Exile." In fact, the first letters of this group—those to Mrs. Francis Biddle—are scarcely comprehensible if one is not aware of what happened to Leger in the years between the two World Wars. The anguish and the loneliness that pervade so many of the "Letters from Exile" are the direct result of Leger's political and personal tragedies. The Fall of France completed the destruction of the diplomatic edifice that he had so devotedly helped Briand and Berthelot to construct. On the personal level, Leger found himself cut off from his mother and two of his sisters who were stranded in Occupied France, where he could not assist them, since the very mention of the name "Alexis Leger" would have meant reprisals from the Nazi authorities.

But if the "Letters from Exile" mark the beginning of the most acutely painful period of Leger's life, they also mark the beginning of his return to literature, which he had resolutely set aside during the "Quai d'Orsay years." He was never to return to public life, but he was now to become a widely recognized literary figure almost in spite of himself. As we have pointed out, 1941 —with the publication of his poem *Exil* in French in an American periodical, *Poetry*—is the date of the beginning of the final victory of St.-John Perse over Alexis Leger. His actual "exile" lasted from 1940 to 1957, when Leger finally made a return trip to France. During those seventeen years his most permanent *pied-à-terre* was Washington, D.C.; but he traveled a great deal on the American continent and in American waters. In 1958 he took an American wife, Dorothy Milburn Russell. He and his wife thereafter divided their time between Washington and a house on the southern coast of France, "Les Vigneaux," which is so vividly described in some of the letters to Mrs. Mina Curtiss and to the Biddles. These "Letters from Exile," thus, trace a graph: first a rising curve of mounting despair, anxiety, and tension, and then a downward curve of joyous acceptance and "resolution"—in the musical sense.

But from the earliest letters to the last—even bridging the hiatus of the 1921-1940 years—the story is a continuous one, told in considerable detail and with occasional repetitions, since the same events are sometimes recounted to different correspondents, but usually with interestingly varied emphases.

❖

It is probably inevitable that, sooner or later, a whole series of volumes will appear: *La Correspondance Rivière-Leger, Lettres d'Alexis Leger à sa Mère, The Leger-Biddle Letters*—to suggest only a few of the possibilities. When such complete texts are published they will be of great interest, but in a limited way. They will be read chiefly by specialists in twentieth-century French political and literary history. But such complete two-way correspondences will surely not have the general appeal, nor give so well-rounded a picture of St.-John Perse, as this unilateral but highly diversified selection does. My hope is that the letters here presented will induce readers to explore the poetry and will help them realize how completely "lived" all the poems are, despite any contrary impression that their sumptuous and singular style may at first make. In spite of the determined effort that Alexis Leger made to keep himself and St.-John Perse apart, they are intimately one. There is no better record of that strange relationship—unique in so many ways—than these letters.

Even their style is testimony to the fundamental oneness of the man and the poet. The pen that wrote the letter to Joseph Conrad from China was obviously the same pen that wrote *Anabase*. But that does not mean that the letters are uniformly written in a "grand style"—as the letter to Conrad, however, *is*. The style of these letters varies not only with the recipient of each, as one would expect; it also changes "diachronically" over the years. The earliest letters, dating from Leger's late adolescence, have the strained, unsure, and frequently pretentious quality that one expects from a very literate, intellectually alert, but basically solitary young man. The rather amusing imperious tone and display of paradox in these early letters disappear entirely in the letters from China. Intellectual and emotional maturity are reflected in a new

easy, flowing style. The busy young Foreign Service
Officer does lapse into elegant but conventional diplomatic formulas on occasion, especially in the shorter
notes begging indulgence for not having written. (It was
undoubtedly such a note that, some years later, elicited
the now-celebrated reply from Colette: "Cher impossible
ami—'Le temps n'existe pas'—parole d'ambassadeur!")[3]
But such devices disappear in the "Letters from Exile,"
where the intense loneliness is palpable in the very formality and hyper-correctness of the first few letters to
Mrs. Biddle and to Archibald MacLeish. The style does
not relax until Alexis Leger feels sufficiently at ease with
his new American friends to express his loneliness and
anguish unabashedly—a release that also makes it possible for him to speak once more of his surroundings and
of simple daily concerns, as in the wonderful letters from
Seven Hundred Acre Island. That same elegant informality reaches its climax later in the letters from "Les
Vigneaux" to the Biddles and to Mrs. Curtiss. These
major pieces among the "Letters from Exile" are, of
course, liberally interspersed with missives that concern
purely literary matters. In fact, certain of the letters to
Mrs. Biddle, MacLeish, and Tate, to Max-Pol Fouchet,
Caillois, and Paulhan, contain the most fully developed
formulation of Alexis Leger's concept of poetry and the
role of the poet that we possess. That concept is a very
special one, equally far removed from the *fin de siècle*
estheticism fashionable in Leger's youth and from the
various kinds of "committed" literature that became
dominant from the thirties on. In addition, since his literary activities were now as much a public concern as his
diplomatic activities had once been, he had to attend to

3. Colette's note is printed in *Honneur à Saint-John Perse*
(1965), p. 798.

the practical demands of publishing; but the "semi-business letters" are, like all the others, always impeccably correct in style and tactful in tone. In fact, *all* the letters merit the qualifier "patrician." Crudity, slovenliness, incoherence, off-handedness are all conspicuously absent.

✧

The present translation is based on the French text found in the 1972 Pléiade *Œuvres complètes*, as prescribed by Alexis Leger himself during the years immediately preceding his death in 1975. All the letters in the section of *Œuvres complètes* entitled "Lettres" (pp. 643-1083) are here translated, plus thirteen additional ones that appear elsewhere in the same volume.[4] These additional letters are concerned chiefly with literary matters and have been inserted in their proper chronological place in the present volume, with a note indicating where each of them can be found in the *Œuvres complètes*.

The only departures from the original printed text are corrections of a very few obvious errors in transcription or printing and, in even fewer instances, of errors in

4. The thirteen letters are:
   1. to Gaston Gallimard. 23 Apr. 1924.(146)
   2. to Paul Valéry. 26 Nov. 1922. (151)
   3. to Archibald MacLeish. 9 Sept. 1941. (223)
   4. to Archibald MacLeish. 23 Dec. 1941. (224)
   5. to Roger Caillois. 26 Jan. 1953. (252)
   6. to Roger Caillois. 10 Feb. 1954. (260)
   7. to Adrienne Monnier. 26 Mar. 1948. (289)
   8. to Jean Paulhan. 12 June 1963. (315)
   9. to Dag Hammarskjöld. Sept. 1958. (356)
   10. to Dag Hammarskjöld. Feb. 1959. (357)
   11. to Dag Hammarskjöld. 16 Aug. 1959. (358)
   12. to Dag Hammarskjöld. 3 June 1960. (359)
   13. to Igor Stravinsky. 2 Mar. 1958. (365)

chronology. Such modifications are clearly indicated in the footnotes. The bracketed three dots [. . .] indicate omissions that exist in the printed text of the letters and that were effected by Alexis Leger himself.

In order to make the letters as immediately comprehensible as possible, it was necessary to identify the recipients and to explain, as succinctly as possible, the allusions to people, events, and literary and artistic works. This is done in the footnotes, many of which are drawn directly from Leger's own copious addenda to the *Œuvres complètes*. The usual problem of not-too-much-and-not-too-little had to be confronted. The best that can be hoped for is that the notes will serve as a help, and not a hindrance, to the uninterrupted reading of the text— for the letters speak for themselves, and the notes should do no more than establish acoustical conditions that make the voice of Alexis Leger clearly audible at every moment.

Of the many persons who assisted me in translating the French text and completing the explanatory notes, none has been more vigilant, helpful, and forthcoming than the poet's widow, Mrs. Dorothy Milburn Leger.

For help in clearing up obscure passages and references, I owe special thanks to my friends Monsieur Etienne-Alain Hubert of the Sorbonne and Monsieur Marcel Ruff, Honorary Dean of the Faculty of Letters of the University of Nice.

To Mr. William McGuire and Mrs. Arthur Sherwood of the Princeton University Press, I am indebted for their patience, encouragement, and wise counsel. Working with them has been an uninterrupted pleasure.

Arthur J. Knodel

Leger's handwriting in 1909. Fragment of a letter to Monod. (*See p. 28 of text.*)

LES viandes grillent en plein vent, les sauces
se composent et la
fumée remonte les chemins à vif et rejoint qui marche
Alors, le Songeur aux joues sales
se tire
d'un vieux songe tout rayé de violences, de ruses et d'éclats
et orné de sueurs vers l'odeur de la viande
il descend,
comme une femme qui traîne : ses toiles, tout son
linge et ses cheveux défaits.

Leger's handwriting in 1911. Manuscript of "Eloge I," sent to Gide. (*See p. 193 of text.*)

À la question Toujours posée :
« Pourquoi écrivez-vous ? » la réponse
du Poète sera Toujours la plus brève :
« Pour mieux vivre. »

St. John Perse

Leger's handwriting in 1955. Answer to a questionnaire.

CHRONOLOGY AND ABBREVIATIONS

(N.B. The following list of dates is purposely synoptic, since it is intended solely for rapid consultation to facilitate reading of the letters.)

1887   May 31. Marie-René Alexis Saint-Leger Leger is born in Guadeloupe, French Antilles.

1899   The Leger family moves to Pau in southern France.

1907   AL's father, Amédée Saint-Leger Leger, dies suddenly.

1911   *Eloges* is published.

1914   AL passes the Foreign Service Examination.

1916-1921   AL is Foreign Service Officer in China.

1921-1922   AL participates in Conference on Limitation of Armaments at Washington, D.C., where he meets Aristide Briand.

1924   *Anabase* is published; first use of the *nom de plume* St-J. Perse.

1925-1932   AL serves as Aristide Briand's *chef de cabinet*.

1933-1940   AL is Secretary General of the French Ministry of Foreign Affairs with the rank of Ambassador.

1940-1957   Prolonged voluntary exile in the United States.

1942   *Exil* is published.

1946   *Vents* is published.

1957   *Amers* is published; AL makes first return trip to France.

1958   AL marries Dorothy Milburn Russell in Washington, D.C.

1959   *Chronique* is published.
1960   AL is awarded Nobel Prize for Literature.
1962   *Oiseaux* is published.
1972   *Œuvres complètes* is published in the Biblio-
        thèque de la Pléiade series.
1975   Sept. 20. AL dies at the age of eighty-eight in
        his home, "Les Vigneaux," near Giens on the
        south coast of France.

Abbreviations Used
in the Footnotes

AL   Alexis Leger
OC   Saint-John Perse, *Œuvres complètes* (Paris:
     Gallimard, 1972), i.e., the poetry, prose, and
     correspondence of Alexis Leger as published
     in the "Bibliothèque de la Pléiade" series.
NRF *La Nouvelle Revue française* (the magazine,
     as distinct from the publishing house).

LIST OF ILLUSTRATIONS

*All but those otherwise indicated are printed
by courtesy of Mrs. Alexis Leger*

EARLY LETTERS

LETTERS TO GUSTAVE-ADOLPHE MONOD
(1906-1911)

1

To Monsieur Gustave-Adolphe Monod[1]   *Pau, May 1906*
(Paris)

My dear Monod,

Your letter radiates health; it oozes that delight in work, that complete confidence that fires your enthusiasm. [. . .] I don't know what your metaphysical or moral beliefs are, but I have the distinct feeling that you have strong ones, or that you feel yourself capable of acquiring such beliefs. In that sense you are "dogmatic," for dogmatism can be a perfectly natural attitude; and in that sense, it is altogether rational that, where you are concerned, it should be, as you say, "anti-rational and anti-scientific," since it then becomes a belief. . . .

I like it, my friend, that you broaden or limit the meaning of the words "to live" in this way. But isn't that going somewhat further than you did last year? Or did I misunderstand you when, at your house at "Park Lodge,"[2] you seemed to be protesting against any sort of inner life? And yet, I would often think of you while I suffered the torture of a prolonged and needless strain, during which I managed to exhaust, inside myself and with only myself as witness, a sincere and deep longing for death. I would think of you when I read your letters and feel very sure that I sensed your healthy, outgoing curiosity. I felt that you would be incapable of saying, as an old Flemish mystic did, "Why should I be concerned with what is outside of me?"[3] I recalled our talks at "Park Lodge," your great preoccupation with social issues, your interest in every matter of earthly economics, and your relaxed manner and enthusiasm, which the active life and physical training of military service may have brought out in you. And it is just those aspects of your conception of life that struck me, and still strike me, as, at the very least, "Goethean" in the widest sense of the term.

—Your way of understanding altruism interested me. But nothing could be further from my mind than a rejection of that "category of the ideal" that your beloved Milhaud[4] adds to the other categories. All this may simply be a question of terminology.

—I like your hatred of the bourgeois spirit, your confidence in the possibility of improving the lot of the common people [. . .]; but isn't the "bourgeois" mentality also an intermediate stage through which, as a matter of fact, the common people will pass as they rise to a higher level? Aren't you setting up your own desires a little too hastily as beliefs, in the face of the unresponsiveness and stagnation of the masses?

—You don't define religion for me, as you understand it; but you tell me enough just by saying that you refuse to see it as an end in itself and want to see in it only "the means of attaining the moral ideal." If I were genuinely religious, for me religion would not be the means of fulfilling earthly wishes; it would be a real goal insofar as it was a striving towards the absolute. Its demands are wholly metaphysical.

—I never suspected that the Master's Degree in Philosophy would require you to work so hard. You don't even have time to investigate the Greeks more thoroughly! No matter how broad "and enriching" your program may be, aren't you already beginning to suffer somewhat from specialization?

—Some unpleasant things in your letter: After talking to me about altruism, your self-concern turns into selfishness; you reject friendship not so much because it is unattainable—which is true, though, since every human being is totally cut off from every other, and since "souls," according to you, "are like monads"—but mostly because you "don't feel the need for friendship"; your solitude is not simply forced upon you—you delight in it. And what is more, you seem to consider all relationships only from a utilitarian point of view. ("I don't need others to help me develop. . . . If I concern myself with others, it's not in order to receive anything from them, but to improve the material side of their lives . . ." etc.) Your letters are replete with a rationalistic rigidity and dryness. Your brains are there, but not your nerves. In the very quest for truth as you see it, in your social pre-occupations, I don't really feel that you take your sensitivity—your "inner feelings," as the old Flemish mystics in love with Plato and Plotinus say—into account. I thought you were less cerebral. Maybe you'll turn out like those individualistic young fellows in Barrès, who start out from a bookish cerebralism but—through the awakening or, perhaps, hypertrophy of their sensitivity coming in contact with human suffering, or under the influence of a feminine sensibility—are led to the point of responding only to what arises spontaneously within their total, and no longer merely rational, selves. And their final word is that they want to be guided solely by truths that make them weep. "What! Always things that appeal to our intelligence!" says one of these fellows who has vainly questioned contemporary logicians. "Such things don't overwhelm me! . . . I want to be overwhelmed! . . . Oh for something that has the power to change our hearts! . . . You're fed up—aren't you?— with understanding devoid of feeling. You'd rather weep. . . . To have a taste for tears!"—And if you've read *L'Ennemi des Lois*,[5] how you must have disliked the fellow who asks his lady-friend's dog to restore his confidence in spontaneity. According to him, our collegians, overloaded with an intellectual baggage of mere concepts, and not modes of feeling—weighted down, as it were, with opinions that don't really touch the core of their being—these schoolboys would relearn from the dog how to listen to their instinctive selves.

But what am I doing? I've let myself go to the point of talking to you about feminine influence, and all you talk to me about is "mingling with the profs . . . !"

You scold me for not writing to you. . . . But isn't any letter that goes beyond one's true feeling an absurdity?—just as a discussion becomes absurd when the collision of two strong ideas never does anything but reinforce each of them?—the inevitable disagreement of two minds that have not shared the same associations, definitions, terminology over a long period of time. . . .

—You ask how I'm making out in uniform.[6] I often manage to forget I'm wearing one. I go over the wall as often as possible. Outside of my family, I see hardly anyone but Jammes[7] in these parts. I think of you when I come back from maneuvers and catch sight of the firs of "Park Lodge" from the highway. There is peace there of a kind you no longer enjoy. But perhaps you like your new life; and perhaps, in Paris, you're already subjugated to ideas and books. The concerts have been very fine this winter; I missed very few of them. More than once I've found myself liking *Tannhäuser* and *Tristan*. I make a point of telling you this because you used to be over-fond of Wagner [. . .]. The one thing this year of military service may do for me is to make up my mind to learn to play the violin. And now that "graduation" is approaching, it occurs to me that, having enjoyed for some time now the stultification, even the utter emptiness, of barracks life, I may at least have profited from it to the

extent of no longer believing in the possibility of renunciation, fakirism, or oriental nihilism, which for a while
had a vague attraction for me through my memories of
an Asiatic nurse who looked after me during my childhood in the Islands. I may also have profited by realizing,
through reading of Seneca and the *Encheiridion*,[8] how
Stoicism may lead in a sinister way to self-absorption—
a wretched state. And also the realization that an unfettered sensibility must be respected, and that, in all
things and always, there is a need (even an urgent need)
for immense freedom.

Until July then, my friend. I don't know whether I'll
be seeing much of you, because that's the period of large-
scale maneuvers; and in my company they've discontinued Sunday and midnight passes for one-year en-
listees. After that, if "graduation" isn't put off too long,
I am determined to go to Egypt for a month. (I've an
uncle there who is Chief Engineer for the Suez Canal.)[9]

We won't talk about Lévy-Bruhl, or Durkheim, or
Rauh,[10] but about the simplest things of everyday life.

Yours truly[11]   Alexis L.

1. Gustave-Adolphe Monod (1885-1968) was the son of a
Protestant pastor, Ernest Monod, and a classmate of AL at the
Lycée de Pau. AL's letters to Monod are the only ones in which
the familiar *tu* is used throughout, indicating the early close
friendship of the two men. Monod became an *agrégé* in philosophy and subsequently rose to very high positions in the French
Ministry of Education, from which he was dismissed in 1940 for
refusing to comply with an anti-Semitic decree; he was reinstated
in 1944.

2. Park Lodge was the private residence of the Monod family.
Its English name reflects the strong British presence in Pau,
which was a favorite wintering spot for well-to-do Englishmen
and for refugees from various other countries at the turn of the
century.

3. Jan Van Ruysbroeck (1293-1381), the Flemish prelate and

mystic. In his last mystical treatise, entitled in the French translation *Le Livre des douze béguines*, one of the twelve *béguine* nuns, in a verse passage, says of Christ:

> Je suis englouti dans sa bouche.
> Je n'ai rien à faire du dehors!
> [I am swallowed up in His mouth.
> What is outside does not concern me!]

See Maurice Maeterlinck's introduction to his French rendering of Ruysbroeck's *L'Ornement des Noces spirituelles* (1891). Cf. letter to Claudel of Nov. 1906. (52)

4. Gaston Milhaud (1858-1918), French philosopher. Author of several philosophical treatises, among them *Essai sur les conditions et les limites de la certitude logique* (1898).

5. Maurice Barrès' novel, *L'Ennemi des Lois*, was published in 1893. A poodle, "Velu," is an important character in the novel. The lines quoted here by AL are spoken by the novel's hero, André Maltère, in chap. 5, entitled "Velu II confesseur et martyr."

6. AL did one year of military service, 1905-1906, volunteering as a student to begin his stint before actually being called up. This arrangement apparently precluded any possibility of his serving in the cavalry, as he would have preferred. He spent the last three months of his service at the Fort du Portalet near the village of Urdos, very close to the Spanish border.

7. Francis Jammes (1868-1938), the Béarnais poet, became acquainted with AL's family shortly after they moved to Pau from Guadeloupe (French Antilles). See letters to Jammes. (81-92)

8. Seneca the Stoic (4 B.C.-A.D. 65), author of several Latin tragedies and moral treatises; and Epictetus (1st and 2nd c.), the Greek freedman, author of the Stoic breviary, *Encheiridion*.

9. Emilio Dormoy (1869-1927), one of AL's maternal uncles, who was chief engineer of the Ateliers et Services Techniques de la Compagnie du Canal de Suez. See AL's letter to his mother of 10 Jan. 1917. (154)

10. Emile Durkheim (1858-1917), noted French sociologist. Lucien Lévy-Bruhl (1857-1939), French sociologist and anthropologist, disciple of Durkheim. Frédéric Rauh (1861-1909), French philosopher and sociologist who taught at the Sorbonne and the Ecole Normale. (*OC* has "Rank,"—an undoubted faulty transliteration or misprint.)

11. English in original.

2

To Monsieur Gustave-Adolphe Monod   *Pau,*
(Paris)   *October* [1], *1906*

My dear Monod,

I could use some advice from you at this moment. I'm appealing to your own personal experience.

Here's the situation:

I've decided to go on with Law Studies, but I'd also like to get a Master's Degree in Philosophy. Do you think that, in view of this double preparation, it would really be to my advantage to go to Bordeaux? Would the courses in the Faculté des Lettres be more profitable to me than my working alone, right here in Pau and in my own house, where I can continue my Greek studies in my own way? At least here, in spite of the loneliness that is sometimes depressing, and in spite of the torpor and stultifying emptiness, my life might be broader and richer, and in any case more demanding, than the daily vulgarity of student surroundings. But take into consideration that, if I want to finish up in one year, working alone and far from a university environment may not provide enough stimulation and practical training. And bear in mind too that I am very serious about the law studies. Finally, I must tell you that, in addition to all this, I'd like to take courses in a third Faculté: the Sciences.

I'd never have confided like this in anyone but you.

Affectionately yours.   Al. Leger

3

To Monsieur Gustave-Adolphe Monod   *Pau,*
(Paris)   *October 1906*

My dear Monod,

I'm going to take your advice and go study in Bordeaux.

So now I'm beginning to feel a little regretful about leaving the unrelieved mildness of the Béarn, the wayside shelters in the high mountains, the friendly nearness of Jammes; and also a solitude that has become a part of me—and above all the physical life that is so necessary to me, now that I've developed the soul of a pantheist in these last two years. And I'll miss the violin, which I was just going to take up, and which would certainly be more useful to me than the philosophy taught at the universities.

After all, I might very well come right back here in January, at least if I decide to give up that absurd Master's Degree in Philosophy.

For the moment, it's still autumn here—an autumn that is turning out to be beautiful—moving and beautiful as a piece of music that would mingle the austerity of a d'Indy with the divine sincerity of Schumann, the man who "confides in you."

I suffer with you, having now to think of you in the chaotic midst of studying for examinations. Maybe pure speculation has opened the doors to real exaltation for you— But no!—"pure" is an ironic word when we talk about studying for exams.

I wish you good luck, even though, to judge by what your father says, you're not running any great risk. Soon you'll be letting me know about your success.

Yours truly[1]   Leger

1. English in original.

4

To Monsieur Gustave-Adolphe Monod   *Bordeaux*
(Paris)   *January 1907*

Dear friend,

Here's my Bordeaux address: 6, rue de Roquelaure—
a neighborhood of pitiful tarts, fortune-tellers, and un-
healthy students.

The sight of your handwriting will always give me
pleasure. I hardly go out at all any more. I'm just not
made for city life.

It's really good of you to take an interest in my plans
for going to Chile. My father doesn't want me to give up
my studies before I'm entirely free of my military obligations. (You know that I anticipated the draft when I
was eighteen by volunteering as a student.) So I still
have four years to go in France, if something doesn't
come along to change my lot—four years of working
for a law degree in some university town.

And what are you doing? What are you "living on?"
I can't quite imagine what you hunger for. I'll probably
be hearing less and less from you, if friendship is merely
an angle or a parabola [. . .].

Tell me what your parents have decided about leaving
Pau.

Affectionately.

Yrs. truly[1]   Leger

1. English in original.

5

To Monsieur Gustave-Adolphe Monod   *Pau, March 1907*
(Paris)

Dear friend,

Thank you for thinking of me. My grief is great. Your Pastor father was more than Christian to me when my father died.[1]

So I'll be here in Pau for a long time to come. I can't leave my family. And I can't think about the future yet; there are too many other pressing matters to be looked after.

You understood perfectly that the hardest thing of all is to keep alive in those around us the strength it takes to get through each day, each hour. But do you have any idea what a burden the mute suffering of women can be?—what torture this ever-present exhaustion is?

As for me, I have a solid constitution and a few well-established habits. I won't know the relief that fatigue can bring.

I loved my father too much not to have thought very often about his dying. —I really believe we loved each other to the point of suffering from it. We were so completely alone when we were with each other.

I don't know what you're doing now—nor what your philosophers bring you—suffering or peace.

Yours, dear friend, most affectionately.   L.

1. AL's father, Amédée Saint-Leger Leger, died suddenly on 12 Feb. 1907, at the age of fifty-six. AL, as the only remaining male member of the immediate family, took over as head of a household that included his mother and three sisters. He was not yet twenty years of age.

6

To Monsieur Gustave-Adolphe Monod   *Pau, May 1908*
(Paris)

My dear friend,

Write to me, tell me about yourself whenever it doesn't require a special effort on your part. You know that there is a very real friendship between us, and its naturalness is today much to my liking. Every affection begins with a getting down to essentials and then is "simply there."

I don't have much to tell you. My home is still filled with sadness—and preoccupations that I must bear alone.

But the light is becoming beautiful!

I hope to see you in July [. . .]. I'll be in the Pyrenees with my family; but you'll come to see me up there.

You have music, there in Paris. To think that you heard the *Eroica* last month! It makes me happy for you and for myself. To grieve for something or someone great! To grow and to feel deeply! (Grief = capacity.) (And I note that in the old editions, the 3rd Symphony was given its full title: "Heroic symphony to *celebrate* the memory of a great man.") —But can you imagine the funeral march, or even the allegro, in a simple piano reduction?

All the best, my dear Monod. With a heartfelt handclasp.   Alexis L.

You may keep my books as long as you like.

7

To Monsieur Gustave-Adolphe Monod   *Bielle (Vallée d'Ossau)*
(Paris)   *[Basses-Pyrénées]*
                                            September 1908

My dear friend,

If you're in Paris at the moment, can you do me a favor?—find me a copy of Spinoza's *Tractatus Theo-logico-Politicus*? You know how long I've been looking for it.

Write to me once in a while; tell me about yourself. Aren't things easy enough between us for that?

Did you read that Turkey is setting up an advanced and secondary teaching corps that is to be recruited in France? Would there be anything in it for you?

I'm still at Bielle. The light, all of a sudden, has become very lovely; the nights, for the time being, are extraordinary. But why are *you* in Paris?

Warmly.   Leger

—Jacques Rivière[1] has just become engaged, to the sister of one of his friends.

—Claudel[2] has announced to me the birth of a son. What a prey for that man!

—Are you familiar with a philosopher named Georges Dumesnil,[3] whom several people have spoken to me about and whom Frizeau[4] has gone out of his way to see? F.[5] sent me one of his books, *Le Spiritualisme*. To me it's a bowl of lymph. An elliptical writer would be a lot easier for me to follow than this explicit one. Ah yes, ellipsis! that's what we all lack, in every field. Even our Bergson, couldn't he use a good, stiff physic?

—I'm sending you—with a few corrections however—a very bad poem from our *lycée* years.[6] I let it be quite seriously published in the review *Pan*. It was a joke!

(They could at least have been a little suspicious about my Late Latin epigraphs, authentic though they are.) It's no good at all, seeing that I let it be published. Because anything that would really mean something to me, as you well know, I would never allow to be published. Well, that's literature for you! . . . It will remind you of some of the better mischief we got into at the *lycée* —and remind me, with no hint of mischievousness, of everything "literary" that I was already learning how to disclaim. (Which is about the only good I got out of our miserable year in the "Philo" form, with good old Thomas,[7] the disciple of Renouvier; he was as bad a 'cellist as he was a philosopher.)

Towns, in Three Keys[8]

I

> Quies inops vitae exsilium. . . .[9]
> Hilarius, *Trin.*, I, 1

Towns more absent than a mirror once used by women now dead, towns more servile than a candle at morning, towns more absent, where the door stands ajar. . . .

The sound of sandals accompanied the steps of the Capuchin friar; the din of cicadas exploded in the gardens of wild pinks, and at poolside the still water reflected light on the widows.

For the silent child behind the Venetian blinds, the Goatherd made his ocarina weep; and the goats, rearing on their hind legs near the rose trellises, come down on all fours with a sharp, resounding hoof.

If the fountains abase themselves at dawn, as do the doves, and again the fountains—that is simply the better to share the secret of the young girls' boredom.

If the anvils are silent, and the kitchens, it is because of the children's dreaming, so they will forget to wake up—for the children, in the kitchen where the pink fire glows, shell peas as Werther did.

On Bell-Sunday the flowers wilted in the cemetery where the birds with the purple-red spots take their dust bath. And the hour, its bloom gone, abandons the round-dance and, in the glow of false winters, sheds its leaves, panting. And there's a tremendous crash, if the Servant-girl happens to drop the silverware. . . .

O towns where fruits rot in the rain-gutters, where time is worn down as by a donkey's nibbling, O indigent towns not worth pillaging! Here below let the mule-teer's smile rest upon you. . . .

II

Aperiam, inquit, horrea mea! . . .[10]
AMBROSE, *The Book of Naboth*

Companions of the Three Seas, Extortioners and Pirates, may the Devil light my way! And on the flat canvas, for pillage and rape, casually, I'll draw you the City, sprawled like a beast, on its back. Sail up the estuaries as fast as your frigates will go. Here is wealth for the taking, abundant as fish-spawn, Masters! Here is gold heaped pellmell, grain on the threshing-floor, and the good salt taste in the districts where anything goes. I'll tell you about the painted city, the houses like young girls' trinket-boxes full of new-minted pennies, scraps of material, and needles; and then the Law Courts, the Poor House, the Prison, and the shut-down Theaters, the Gardens and the iron palings. And the Church Ladies (honor of the Almighty), the midget Scribes, the Gravedigger and the Midwife. . . . All that! we come,

*wearing our red jerseys, but idly rich, as befits a child
who simply refuses or takes what he pleases. —The
crafty Bankers are locked in cages, and the City Fathers
are beaten up. As for Art, whether on cardboard, canvas,
or even stone, we'll trace its lines with the cutting edge
of our rapiers!*

Our leering monkeys will prowl in the Marketplaces.

III

Per quinque sensus quasi per quas-
dam fenestras. . . .[11]
JEROME, *Contra Jovinien*, II, I

*Because I have slept in widths of raw canvas, I know
of a distant port where the brutal sunlight makes a
metallic sea leap from its bed; I know the strident sky
where the glowing clouds are torn asunder.*

*Rumblings of a sky held up by volcanoes, tumult of
perfumes in the eternal slack, O glory upon the waters,
luminous cadence! —Gleam of naked torsos and rolling
of haunches,*

*And shouts! in the midst of this joyous streaming. . . .
I know the explosive soul of tar, the complaisant oils,
the green tafias on the famous wharf where the sluts
will choose their man by flipping a coin.*

*Free-living sons, put down your cutlasses. Here there
is nothing but laughter and ecclesiastical curses, and
every man will ply his arms and legs as he sees fit,
renegades from Jesus, Mahmoud, or Buddha!*

*You, Swashbucklers, around the peak time of fevers,
go caress the mestiza and pay up in gold nuggets, snap
your fingernail, and play at cork-penny with goldpieces
on the doorsteps—*

The holds of the pot-bellied caracks are swaying for you in the basins of shimmering water where the sharks swim about, and for you the satin-slippered Chinese girl will arouse agile vice in her loins.

Saint-Leger Leger

1904

1. Jacques Rivière (1886-1925), the future editor-in-chief of *La Nouvelle Revue française*, married Isabelle Fournier, the sister of his close friend, Henri Fournier (who wrote under the name Alain-Fournier), future author of the novel *Le Grand Meaulnes* (1913). AL first met Rivière in 1907 at the home of Gabriel Frizeau in Bordeaux. This was the beginning of a lifelong friendship. See letters to Rivière. (17-49, 184)

2. Paul Claudel (1868-1955), the diplomat and well-known Catholic poet and dramatist, was to become a lifelong friend of AL, who met him for the first time at the home of Francis Jammes at Orthez (near Pau) in 1905. See letters to Claudel. (52-66, 302-305) Claudel's son, Pierre, was born on 23 Sept. 1908 in Tientsin, China.

3. Georges Dumesnil (1855-1916), French Catholic philosopher and teacher at the University of Toulouse. Author of several books, including *Le Spiritualisme* (1905), and founder, in 1906, of an orthodox Catholic review, *L'Amitié de France*, to which Francis Jammes, Paul Claudel, François Mauriac, and many other Catholic writers contributed.

4. Gabriel Frizeau (1870-1938), the enlightened wine-grower of Bordeaux who became an art collector and patron of literature. He was one of Claudel's first notable converts to Catholicism and a close friend of Rivière and Jammes. AL met Frizeau in 1906, thanks to Claudel. (See letter to Claudel of Nov. 1906.) AL soon became a close friend of Frizeau. See letters to Frizeau. (67-80)

5. Frizeau.

6. The poem, "Des Villes sur Trois Modes," was published in the July-Aug. 1908 issue of the ephemeral little magazine, *Pan*, published at Montpellier. The text in *Pan* is full of errors and bears 1906 as the date of composition for the poem. Actually, it had been written considerably earlier, while AL was a pupil at the Lycée de Pau. Though AL had sent the poem to *Pan* for publication, he never authorized any subsequent reprinting of it. It

was reproduced without the author's permission by Maurice Saillet in his *Saint-John Perse: Poète de Gloire*, published in 1952. (See letter to Adrienne Monnier of 26 Mar. 1948.) The text that appeared in *Pan*, however, is AL's earliest published poem.

The English translation of the poem follows the letter immediately. For original French text, see below, note 8.

7. A. Thomas taught at the Lycée de Pau from 1902 to 1906.

8. The original French version reads as follows:

DES VILLES SUR TROIS MODES

I

> *Quies inops vitae exsilium...*
> HILAIRE, *Trin.*, I-1.

Des villes plus absentes qu'au miroir des mortes,
Des villes plus servantes qu'un cierge au matin,
Des villes plus absentes, où bâille la porte...

Les sandales sonnaient au pas du Capucin,
La cigale éclatait aux jardins de silènes,
Et l'eau calme éclairait les veuves aux piscines.

Pour l'enfant silencieux derrière les persiennes
Le Chevrier a fait pleurer son ocarine
Et les chèvres debout vers les rosiers des grilles
Avec un sabot net sont retombées, sonores.

Si les fontaines à l'aurore s'humilient,
Si les colombes, si les fontaines encore,
C'est pour mieux se confier l'ennui des jeunes filles.

Si les enclumes se sont tues, si les cuisines,
C'est pour le songe des enfants, et qu'ils oublient
De s'éveiller: car les enfants dans la cuisine
De feu rose écossent des pois comme Werther.

Au Dimanche des cloches, sont mortes les fleurs
Du cimetière, où les oiseaux tachés de lies
Prennent leur bain de sable. Et l'heure défleurie
Qui délaisse la ronde, au feu des faux hivers
S'effeuille, à perdre haleine. Et là, c'est un grand heurt
Si la Servante laisse choir l'argenterie...

O villes où les fruits pourrissent aux larmiers,
Où s'épuise le temps comme un broutement d'âne,
O villes d'indigence, indignes du pillage !
Sur vous soit, ici-bas, sourire de l'ânier...

II

> *Aperiam, inquit, horrea mea!...*
> AMBROISE, *Livre de Naboth.*

Compagnons des Trois Mers, Rançonneurs et Pirates,
Que le Diable m'éclaire! et sur la toile plate,
Pour le sac et le viol, je tracerai de haut
La Ville, là, comme une bête sur le dos.
Remontez l'estuaire au vol de vos frégates:
Voici le bien livré comme frai de poisson,
Maîtres! voici de l'or en vrac, le grain sur l'aire
Et la bonté du sel aux quartiers débonnaires.
Je vous dirai la ville peinte, les maisons
Qui sont comme des boîtes de petites filles
Avec les sous neufs, les chiffons et les aiguilles;
Et puis les Tribunaux, l'Hospice, la Prison,
Et les Théâtres clos, les Jardins et les grilles!
Et les Dames d'église, honneur du Tout-Puissant,
Les Scribes nains, le Fossoyeur et l'Accoucheuse...
Ça! nous viendrons vêtus de nos rouges vareuses,
Mais riches à loisir, comme il sied à l'enfant
Qui refuse ou qui prend. — Les Banquiers avisés
Sont mis en cage, et les Notables sont rossés;
Mais l'Art, sur le carton, la toile ou bien la pierre,
Nous en suivons le trait au fil de nos rapières!

— Nos singes ricaneurs rôderont aux Marchés.

III

> *Per quinque sensus quasi per quasdam*
> *fenestras...*
> JÉRÔME, *Contra Jovinien,* II, 1.

Parce que j'ai dormi aux lés de toile crue,
Je sais le port lointain où le soleil brutal
Fait jaillir de son lit une mer de métal,
Je sais le ciel strident où rompt l'ardente nue.

Sonorité du ciel étayé de volcans,
Tumulte des parfums dans l'éternel balan,
O gloire sur les eaux, lumineuse cadence!
— Eclat des torses nus et roulement des hanches,

Et cris! parmi tout ce ruissellement heureux...
Je sais l'âme explosive des goudrons, les huiles
Complaisantes, les tafias verts au quai fameux
Où les garces joueront leur homme à croix ou pile.

Fils de gracieuse vie, posez les coutelas:
Ici tout n'est que rires et jurons d'Église,
Et chacun remuera ses membres à sa guise,
Renégat de Jésus, de Mahom ou Bouddha!

Vous, Capitans, vers l'heure où les fièvres s'irritent,
Caressez la métisse et payez en pépites,
Faites claquer cet ongle, et jouez au bouchon
Avec des onces d'or sur le pas des maisons:

Les caraques pansues pour vous bercent leurs cales
Aux bassins d'eau lucide où naviguent les squales;
Et pour vous la Chinoise en souliers de satin
Suscitera le vice agile dans ses reins.

    9. An indigent quiet, exile from life. . . .
   10. I shall open, he says, my granaries. . . .
   11. Through the five senses, as through windows. . . .

8

To Monsieur Gustave-Adolphe Monod   *Pau, May 9, 1909*
(Paris)

   My friend, I'm glad you wrote to me [. . .].
   People move about before my eyes or call to me from afar—my elders. But you, I'm happy to know you're there, closer to me, my own age. Perhaps the only real friendship is one we have not purposely cultivated. At least that's the only kind that can remain silent. Silence is the essence, the most mysterious form, of affection.

Mon cher, when I think of you, it makes me glad to think that we'll never write real "letters" to each other, "letters" in the hateful sense of the word, things that begin to sound like "literature."

[. . .] But I'm eager to hear your news.

I believe you're really in line for your *Agrégation de Philo*[1] this year. Your next-to-last letter was sad; yes, I recall that. You're suffering from Paris. And if I tried to imagine you fully yourself, I'd imagine you so far from any big city! . . . a real storehouse of shabby wares! . . .

I can't imagine anything more frightful than having to fight for "silence" or than the torture of coming to grips with one's self surrounded by "hubbub." What an absurdity, when you already don't have enough strength to fill out *your own* dimly perceived pattern, to have to make the additional effort, negative and costly, of fending people off, of getting off by oneself, of being alone! when all is said and done, of becoming unapproachable! —What a waste *there*, where this duty *must* be fulfilled, and at the same time, *to be*, with propriety.

(I think there is a sentence in Nietzsche's *Ecce Homo* on this subject.)

Yours, cordially.   L.

About Rivière: Yes, it's possible I misjudged him the first time we met,[2] in Bordeaux, before I had read anything of his. I got an initial bad impression, I think, on hearing him express himself a little bit too "Parisianly" about everyone and everything, in present-day literature, and in small talk. He showed off his cultural acquisitions much too much as the day wore on, and he somewhat gave me the impression of a person who simply can't neglect whatever is "the last word." I realize now that it was all just timidity. His study of Claudel was a revelation to me. Strange, though, that the article in

L'Occident,[3] which I so greatly admired for its literary dignity, was judged by Claudel to be full of heresies and too lacking in comprehension of his work. (Don't tell that to our friend, if you see him these days. I got it from Jammes, who is with me in recognizing Rivière's intelligence. Moreover, Claudel surely has a great deal of admiration for him.) —What's he doing? Is he working on something? I'm afraid lest his excessive fervor and fever in "the literary life" leave him impotent, to begin with. He must do like the admirable, incomparable Jules Laforgue: "learn to forget everything and everybody, once having known them all."[4] Because one must know everyone—or no one. And admiration is harder on "civilized persons" because of the very quality of their admiration: dirty hands soil things less than clean hands do.

—*La Phalange?*[5] —Yes, a rather strange review that struck me at first as being suspect of miscegenation; but now it seems to be of purer strain under the direction of Vielé-Griffin. V.-G. wanted me to publish in it; but instead I got myself excluded from it by withdrawing a manuscript.

1. The strenuous competitive examination given yearly by the French Ministry of Education. In recent years the *agrégation* has been considerably modified, but before World War II only a very few of the many candidates who took the examination were passed and declared *agrégé*. They were destined for the best teaching posts in the lycées and universities of France. Monod failed the examination on the first try but succeeded the second time.

2. Cf. letter to Rivière of 13 Sept. 1909 (17), written shortly before this first meeting.

3. "Paul Claudel, Poète et chrétien." See letter 52, note 1.

4. Jules Laforgue (1860-1887), the symbolist poet who was to become one of T. S. Eliot's favorites. Quotation unidentified.

5. *La Phalange*, edited by Jean Royère, was a literary review of post-symbolist tendencies to which Vielé-Griffin was an important contributor. It lasted from mid-1906 to 1912.

9

Monsieur Gustave-Adolphe Monod   *Pau, June 26, 1909*
(Paris)

My dear friend,

May I come right out and ask you to lend me your copy of Spinoza's *Tractatus Theologico-Politicus*? You can take it back when you come to visit me at Bielle.

I'm taking the family up there in July. I certainly hope you'll be able to give me a few more hours there than you did last year. I'm hoping to organize a mass in Gregorian chant there with Maufret.[1]

Claudel talks about not arriving in France before September 20. He's planning to spend the winter in Italy.

I'm sending you a little monograph on Jammes[2] to give you a taste, if you don't have it already, for this very attractive figure. He's a pure enough poet so that one can not help liking him.

I talk on. But what about you? Are you still suffering because of all the things you just "refuse to accept" and because of all you fear losing? Will you ever forget your most personal grievance against schoolbook philosophy?

Affectionately yours.   Leger

If you get the chance, have your sister play you d'Indy's Piano Sonata. It was composed one or two years ago, I think. It has a precise beauty [. . .]. And have someone play you Franck's Sonata for Piano and Violin too (particularly good in the third movement).

1. Paul Maufret (1881-1916), pianist and composer. He was a pupil of Vincent d'Indy at the Schola Cantorum. For reasons of ill health he moved to Pau. He and AL became close friends. AL wrote occasional reviews of Maufret's concerts in the bilingual weekly, *Pau-Gazette*.

2. The "little monograph on Jammes" is probably the booklet by Edmond Pilon entitled *Francis Jammes et le sentiment de la nature*, which was published by the Mercure de France in 1908.

10

To Monsieur Gustave-Adolphe Monod   *Pau, [beginning*
(Paris)   *of July 1909]*

My dear friend,

[. . .] I wish I could at least have talked music with you. It's my surest respite here.

With two very good pianists, and in strictest privacy, we manage to see quite a number of things done. Maufret and his friends, through the Schola,[1] get hold of new scores for me, and they're always expensive. Without Bach being neglected, our parade includes Chausson, Debussy, Ravel, Roussel, Séverac, Albeniz, Ladmirault, the whole "class."

I see a lot of Brunel,[2] on a personal basis—the old Hoffmannesque master against whom the whole town seems to be in league. This great conductor is not at all an intelligent man, nor always even a man of very sure taste—but what a wonderful passion for music!

—By the by, the d'Indy sonata I mentioned to you and which I've made my Baruch,[3] dates from 1908: the Sonata in E Major, opus 63. Try to hear it.

The Franck Sonata for Violin and Piano? Yes, it's a beautiful, and painful, thing. There is some padding in the third movement; and yet I never hear it but it moves me deeply, perhaps because my sister used to play it for me whenever things were difficult. (And then there's that calm interlude of the central song coming between the two passionate outbursts. Finally, the fugue in the allegro movement is unforgettable.)

I've just heard the Symphony in D Minor for orchestra again. There again one finds padding, the moment the sincerity becomes too immediate (the belief-motif developed by the whole orchestra in the "lento"). But what a wonderful thing—and what a moving work the whole finale is! You'll never hear it without being enthusiastic, I'm sure!—or without a few furtive tears even [. . .].

Yours affectionately.   L.

1. The Schola Cantorum. See above, letter 9, note 1.

2. Edouard Brunel (1844-1921), an orchestra leader who retired to Pau where he conducted yearly concerts. AL became one of his admirers and friends and even wrote reviews of some of his concerts in *Pau-Gazette*.

3. "My Baruch": A proverbial way of designating one's prevailing enthusiasm. La Fontaine, the seventeenth-century writer of fables, became pious in his later years and "discovered" the text of a prayer attributed to the Biblical figure, Baruch. He became so enthusiastic about it that he would ask everyone, "Have you read Baruch?"

11

To Monsieur Gustave-Adolphe Monod   *Pau, [July 1909]*
(Paris)

My dear friend,

[. . .] To come back to our Spinoza: I always pick him up again with the same fascination. He opens vast arenas for us, charged with meaning, unforgettable even after one has touched their limits. And more particularly in the *Tractatus*, there is an extraordinary "etymological" delight, even though it does not attain verbal mysticism. It's a sublime "Word-for-Word," even for one who could never admit such literalness. Don't you find that there is in this Jewish bargaining, which defends the divine, foot by foot, against encroachment by the human (unless it's not already everything human pitted against the divine), something of that prodigious Jewish "speculativeness" that was the final outcome of Abraham's intercession in favor of Sodom (in Genesis)?[1] —Abraham outwitting his God, pressing Him hard, or even striking bargains with Him! (No, I can't think of a more extraordinary page in all human history—or a more complicated, more humbly haughty or sublimely base one!)

—You ask me about Rivière again. Well, here goes! I get the impression that he has real intellectual distinction. I especially like his sincerity and will always like it so long as it manages to spare me all literary "ascesis." Through Frizeau[2] I have learned how courageous and strict he is in his private life. In short, I really like him immensely. But obviously we'll never make our respective litters out of the same straw. There is a sort of ravenous hunger with regard to one's self as a living being that he cannot admit. Who knows? Maybe he even sees it basically as a sign of literary impotence. Valéry,[3] one of the few "figures" who still interest me, has so often been suspected of just that.

—No, you don't have to wonder about the matter at all; you can be sure of it: there is no "art" without *some* falsehood (initial or incidental, but always present); or at least, in art, it's from falsehood that sincerity borrows its most sublime maieutics. And another fine falsehood is to label a book "First Edition." I can't remember just what I wrote to Rivière,[4] but I had to tell him what I believe—that, in art, sincerity can never use the immediate; that it can never come out but involuntarily, by transparency, or even negatively; that what is "essential" here can never become its own object without cheating. The "essential" is never said, and what is even more, never wants to be said. And it's a madman, atrociously symbolical, who, in Edgar Allan Poe's tale,[5] wanted to make clothing out of the thing clothed.

After all, if we all had the courage to seek our genius first of all in the act of "living," maybe the mouth of man might open a little more widely—and at least, with no goal set, it would yawn when there is nothing to seize upon.

But no teacher, not even far-off Emerson, has ever taught, or even dreamed of teaching, how to acquire a taste for burning everything without leaving any remains or ashes. —And maybe, in that case, Rivière is right—for himself, and in literary terms—in loving his art "as a mason loves his craft." That's what he tells me, and I see that he is entirely in possession of his "art." But let him never put any of that mortar into his mouth! for the artist—and he knows it—never mixes anything but ashes.

You will, please, thank him most warmly for sending me his note on Rameau's *Dardanus*.[6]

—[. . .] Under the heading of requests:

—When the February issue of the *NRF* appears, copy out and send me a dozen or so verses that Claudel is contributing about Charles-Louis Philippe:[7] I'm rather curious about them (a letter from Prague).[8]

—Could you find out for me where I could pick up, and what it would cost me, the Bergk *Poetae Lyrici Graeci*, the first edition of which came out in Leipzig in 1878? (The fourth, which is not the latest, came out in 1884.) Dupuy, the Pau bookdealer, has never been able to find it for me. Do you know of a good rare-book dealer in Paris?

[. . .] Excuse me for not having talked about myself. I have weighty problems on my mind, too weighty for me, perhaps, but problems I have to bear all by myself in a household of women. I'll soon have to hurry and make up my mind, somehow, about what I want to do with my adult life. [. . .]

L.

1. See Gen. 18:22-23, where Abraham seeks to intercede with Jehovah on behalf of the inhabitants of Sodom.

2. See above, letter 7, note 4.

3. Paul Valéry (1871-1945), the famous poet and essayist, was subsequently to become a personal friend of AL. See letters to Valéry. (150, 151)

4. See letter to Rivière of 13 Sept. 1909. (17) There seems to be an error in the conjectural date assigned to the present letter to Monod. AL's first letter to Rivière contains the ideas here expressed, but, as indicated, that letter to Rivière is dated 13 Sept. 1909, and there was clearly none *before* that date, whereas the conjectural date on the present letter (July 1909) would indicate that AL *had* written to Rivière before September.

5. Unidentified. No Poe character quite fits this description.

6. Probably the manuscript text of *"Dardanus* de Rameau, à la Schola Cantorum," a brief music review that was published in NRF, Jan. 1910, pp. 552-554. See letter to Rivière of 17 Feb. 1910. (19)

7. Claudel, "Charles-Louis Philippe," a short poem first published in NRF, Feb. 1910, and later incorporated into the collection *Corona Benignitatis Anni Dei.* Philippe, the author of *Bubu de Montparnasse* and several novels about very poor people, died prematurely in 1909.

8. Claudel was French Consul General in Prague from 1909 to 1911. Prague was the principal city of Bohemia, at that time a part of the Austro-Hungarian empire.

12

To Monsieur Gustave-Adolphe Monod   *Pau, [July 1909]*
(Paris)

My dear friend,

Still another hasty note. (Taken up night and day with Civil Law: debasement, pure and simple, "Privileges and Mortgages" even haunt my dreams. . . .)

I don't need either the Schröder or Bergk Pindar. Three years ago I managed to get hold of the Heyne text (Oxonii ed.), which strikes me as the masterwork and preserves the pre-Dissen metrics[1]—the only correct metrics, to my mind. But I really would like to have either

Crusius (*Poetae Eleg. et Iambogr.*) or Bergk (*Poetae Eleg. et Poetae Melici*). I'd go as high as 25 francs. Unfortunately I can't go any higher, unless I go to Paris and kill off one of those forebears that call me a ne'er-do-well.

Your letter, my friend, is heartbreaking. Couldn't you come down here this summer? If only you could see how beautiful the light is at the moment, and what a help it is, and how "solid" it is!

I'm going to take the family to Bielle as soon as I've finished my exams. (Have to move the piano up there!) May my fate and my examiners decree that my vacation will permit me to do anything but law!

Let me hear from you when you're far from Paris.

Affectionately.   Leger

1. Georg Ludolf Dissen (1784-1837), the German Hellenist who became an accepted authority on classical Greek metrics. "Pre-Dissen" editions would presumably be those of such earlier classical scholars as Boeckh and, especially, Heyne. See letter 61, note 3.

13

To Monsieur Gustave-Adolphe Monod   *Bielle, Monday*
(Paris)   [*July 1909*]

My dear friend,

You have a purchase-order, "quotation limited" to 20 francs. (Can you believe that's how we talk in "Phynance," at which I'm becoming a past master?)

I'm sorry I have to limit you to a one *louis* maximum; but my most carefully concealed purse contains only three of them at the moment, and I'm really committing a folly in spending that—now that I control the purse-strings, in the best "noble father" tradition, of the family exchequer.

I'd like the edition to contain Bergk's Latin translation. I don't want it as a textbook for study purposes, but as a book for easy reading that I can carry around.

Up here, I can't give you from memory the exact information that I gave you from the Tauchnitz catalogue. I think it was a matter of choosing between a problematical re-issue of the Bergk and a revision by Crusius that I'm not familiar with. But I can't recall very clearly any more just what the choice was. After all, whatever edition has to be picked out, you can always guide the bookseller according to the "hierarchy" of my wishes:

   I. *Iambici et Lyrici* (excluding Pindar)

   II. *Elegiaci.*

Affectionately.   Leger

14

To Monsieur Gustave-Adolphe Monod   *Bielle, canton*
(Paris)   *of Laruns (B.-P.)*
                                            September 14, 1909

My dear friend,

I'm happy to have your letter, which I ought to have answered sooner. Let's not lose sight of each other too quickly. Life is already parabolic.

But where are you? —The Landes would be far worthier of you than Saint-Jean-de-Luz.

I've been here in Bielle since July. I had a piano carted up here. I probably won't return to Pau until the end of October. Come see me up here any time you wish. You know that you'll always find a more straightforward welcome in my family than people may think [. . .].

(I learned from the newspaper about your failure and Rivière's. But, when it comes to the *agrégation*,[1] a "flunk" the first time round seemed to me so normal that I really didn't get upset for the two of you. [. . .])

This last year I've had—and still have—worrisome concerns that I want to bear alone, without involving the rest of the family. I haven't had time to prepare thoroughly for my law exams. That puts off for one more year the time when I'll have to leave my mother and sisters.

It's not hard for me to understand how the question of choosing a "career" can bother you so much. And I like it that you are still worked up about it, because one of the things I like you for is the fact that the poet in you won't die. I think I understand the way you're trying to achieve an inner balance: to be essential and central, if one can really be that way and at the same time "panic," I mean without spreading thin!

At this end, in spite of all the sacrifices, a tremendous joy every morning at getting up a new man and, generally, a better man. But the end result is already evident: a hatred of talk. Surely that's the real reward—the reward that we have to be most wary about and that makes us the most headstrong, in a furtive way, like wine, almost—if riches exist only in the here-and-now.

Do you want to have a good laugh with me? A chap from the Goncourt Academy, a friend of my father's younger days, Léon Hennique,[2] in a letter to me talks about "the admirable career of letters!" Do you think that any man of that generation (Maupassant's), even supposing that he happened to be born for it, was ever capable of being alone? And won't I have to reply—in a few minutes, after I've taken leave of you—that our generation will always prefer raising rabbits or ostriches or bombyx-moths to the "career" he talks about?

If you're at Saint-Jean-de-Luz, don't leave without knocking at the door of my friend Gayac's[3] studio at Guéthary. He's a rare artist, an engraver who is highly esteemed—I know it for a fact—by Odilon Redon[4] himself. And he's a hermit—a timid and very gentle, very simple wild man, though people don't suspect it, even though he doesn't care if they do. But the least sign of real sympathy has enormous consequences for him; it makes him aware of his own potential. Because he's a long way from being "able to cope" with his solitude, and he suffers long stretches of impotence, either out of indifference or out of dissatisfaction with his work. Jammes, to whom I introduced him, likes him very much. Just present yourself in my name. I really feel that your curiosity will do him good.

Did you meet Charles Bordes?[5] Did you get to the festival at Saint-Jean-de-Luz in which he was supposed to put on the Third Mass by Lassus? I've just heard that he's now at Mauléon.

Most cordially.   Leger

I don't know to just what extent this first setback at the *agrégation* may be a real nuisance to you. In the event you give up the *agrégation*, let me know if you'll have to think about something else in the same line. And you mentioned a sojourn in Italy. (But that's idiotic; a sojourn in Croatia or Arabia Petraea would be more profitable to you.) [. . .]

1. Rivière took the examination for the *agrégation* twice, in 1909 and 1911, failing both times. See above, letter 8, note 1, and letter to Rivière of 8 Aug. 1911. (31)

2. Léon Hennique (1851-1935), novelist and dramatist of the naturalistic school. One of the original contributors—along with Maupassant, Zola, Huysmans, Céard, and Paul Alexis—to the famous collection of short novels entitled *Les Soirées de Medan* (1880).

3. Ernest Gayac, painter and engraver admired by AL, Jammes, and Frizeau. Influenced by the art of Bresdin and Odilon Redon. See letter to Frizeau of Mar. 1911. (79)

4. Odilon Redon (1840-1916), the celebrated symbolist painter and engraver, was among the friends of AL.

5. Charles Bordes (1863-1909), French composer and one of the founders of the Schola Cantorum. He was active in reviving sixteenth-century polyphony, whence the interest in the great Flemish polyphonist, Orlando di Lasso (ca. 1531-1594).

15

To Monsieur Gustave-Adolphe Monod   *Bielle, Vallée d'Ossau*
(in Paris) [to be forwarded]   *[late September 1909]*

And now, dear friend, it gives me pleasure to think that you are finally enjoying a real vacation.

May you, wherever you are, have more light than I have now in Bielle!

Here it's the usual silence: two of my sisters and my mother with me. Health good, at least. And as much music as possible: a little Gregorian and, on the piano, the second series of Bach's Preludes and Fugues, which is to the first series what an isolated tree is to a tree planted in a border-row.

[. . .]

I think of you affectionately.   Leger

16

To Monsieur Gustave-Adolphe Monod   *Pau, May 10, 1911*
(Paris)

My dear friend,

This note is being delivered to you by Rivière. My room is in such disorder that I simply can't find your present address; it has dissolved into thin air. (And why don't *you* write more often? Do you want to force me to buy Writing Pads and Big Address Books like an inveterate stay-at-home?)

Yes, I did talk to you about the poet Jammes. You know (my respect for Art is so great!?!) how I like to act as a traveling salesman of my friends' works! . . . (Don't you remember when you got this same insistent treatment from me about Claudel, and how we loitered along the highway so late that your worried father came looking for us with a lantern? All that is a long way off now, eh? Farther off than Charles Renouvier and my bicycle with the red tires that used to shock you when I leaned it against the iron fence of "Park Lodge"; farther off than our arguments about Spinoza or Nietzsche, under the magnolia tree with its falling leaves in the pathway to the left at the far end of the park. . . . Naturally, I never turn my head to look back: for hygienic reasons, to begin with, and then for fear of running into Emmanuel Kant, along the road to Tarbes, with his slippers stuffed with postulates.)

Please remember me cordially to your family.

I don't know whether I should be imagining you at Chatou or Paris now. As for me, commercial law and civil procedure are still my regular diet. I don't even have time any more for a little mountain-climbing. I wander off, pockets filled with study-outlines, to all those insipid places around Pau, so brimming with loathsome - Second Empire promises, where you wouldn't even bend down to pick up a little bit of meteorite. No acid anywhere.

Let me hear from you.

Nothing here, really. . . . But always plenty of music at my house. And I'm becoming more and more of a big financier. It's about time, because I'm having all sorts of trouble keeping the family going. Will I end up buying lottery tickets? At least I've won all the lawsuits undertaken for the family!

I'm not taking the family to the Vallée d'Ossau this

year, but to the Basque mountain country instead, probably around Tardets, that poor Bordes[1] loved so much.
Will you be going to those parts?

Cordially yours.   Leger[2]

1. See letter 14, note 5. Bordes, who had died in 1909, had done
a great deal of research on songs of the Basque country.

2. For an additional letter to Monod. (183)

To Monsieur Jacques Rivière
c/o Mesdames Fernand
domain of Saint-Victor,
Cenon-la-Bastide
near Bordeaux (Gironde)

Bielle, canton of
Laruns (B.-P.)
September 13, 1909

Dear Sir,

I thank you for your letter.

To speak as you do to a person unknown to you is an *act*, and one that may be courageous.

So I want to reply to you dispassionately and honestly,[1] because I have felt in sympathy with you for a long time already [. . .].

You must believe what I am going to tell you. I've also told it to Jammes, who persists in expecting too much from me: Literarily, there is nothing to be expected from me.

[. . .] Exactly one year ago I defined the words "useful" and "useless" to myself. And even had I not yet done so, my friends, by their exaggerated expectations, would already have put me to flight. For I think it is better to stay home and twiddle one's thumbs than to disappoint one's friends.

Nor, of course, do I think that it is possible to predict anything on the basis of a few pages of literature by reason of their date. "Puerility," defined by the very fact of its being unconscious, is what one gets over in the silliest, but most decisive, way. And perhaps we take less and less pleasure in writing the more voluntarily we do it: syntax has its hidden snares.

What souvenir should one keep of those years when we had not yet exhausted a delight in language? —I don't know. —Remember that at my present age it takes only a little bitterness to make one try out various kinds of cerebral asceticism and achieve dryness in a search for "the essential". . . . Ah, what fine phrases we used! —I can't recall allowing the least luxury. . . . Moreover, a bereavement in 1907 really brought to a close the years of play, self-indulgence, and picture books. Now, anything I might undertake in a strict, bare vein—an art the exact opposite of all that—would be so subjective, and above all so negative, or else it would register a curiosity so discreetly silent that no one could possibly take any interest in it. It would really amount to giving up the struggle with the key-mechanism of solitude: the ellipsis —which gradually makes what we write more and more obscure without our realizing it. —But there is more: before achieving the goal of silence, which is the consummation of sound—if lyricism itself is not simply a special way of feeling joy within one's self, a sort of private pretext—then lyricism must finally resolve into the inertia of utterance or of statement, as music, potentially, is already present in the statement of the theme.

But from beginning to end, I would have experienced nothing but loathing.

And at present, my efforts are exclusively metaphysical, and the only thing that I would really like to have leisure time for is music. . . . And then, I have a responsibility to my family which, I fear, I'm already not up to. . . . And has my friend Monod[2] told you that I'll have to go off, in two or three years, to God only knows what colony? . . .

And yet, I haven't been able to bring myself to destroy *everything*, as was reported to you. I put aside (why?) two notebooks, after I received a letter from Frizeau.[3]

The poems in them, as I recall, seemed to me better than the ones that you liked. —I don't like these either, unfortunately. But maybe you're right; maybe we have to make up our mind, once and for all, about the insurmountable physiological distaste for all literary work.

I may try to publish these poems some day (if I can afford it, and if I ever really feel like it). To risk making a mistake would at least force me to take a stand. —But I really can't think of doing that yet, for very material reasons. (There's enough mutual respect between us to permit me to say this to you matter-of-factly.) But even should I overcome the material difficulties, I feel so "unliterary" that the problems of publication would strike me as very complicated and very disconcerting.

There is, Sir, no coquetry in any part of this long letter. You must believe that any such intention is far from my mind as I speak to you. I assure you once more of the admiration and esteem I have had for you ever since I chanced upon a remarkable article of yours in the *Nouvelle Revue française* (which I no longer receive). [. . .] I recall speaking to Jammes, at whose home I read it, about the strict beauty of your language, about its propriety.

Perhaps I'll run into you in Bordeaux, where I have to register for courses during the first days of November.

I am happy to have the names of Messieurs André Lhote[4] and Henri Fournier,[5] who are your friends [. . .].

I remain, Sir, most sympathetically yours,

                                        A. Saint-Leger

1. This first letter to Jacques Rivière is a reply to one AL had received from Rivière who, at the behest of a group of friends including André Gide, urged AL not to abandon literature and not to destroy his youthful manuscripts. Rivière was scarcely known to AL at the time, though AL was shortly to meet him at the home of Gabriel Frizeau in Bordeaux, where Rivière had been born and where he resided at the time.

At the time this letter was written, AL had published only the series of poems entitled "Images à Crusoé" (in NRF, Aug. 1909), and a poem in regular alexandrine verse composed while he was a *lycéen*, entitled "Des villes sur trois modes," which appeared in the ephemeral Montpellier review, *Pan*, July-Aug. 1908. See above, letter 7, note 6.

2. Gustave-Adolphe Monod. See above, letter 1, note 1, and letter to Monod. (4)

3. Gabriel Frizeau. See above, letter 7, note 4, and letters to Frizeau. (67-80)

4. The painter, André Lhote (1885-1962), of Bordelais origin, was a friend of Rivière and Frizeau and, ultimately, of AL. Lhote became associated with the Cubists in 1910. He is the author of numerous books and articles on painting.

5. Henri Fournier ("Alain-Fournier"), Rivière's brother-in-law. See above, letter 7, note 1, and two letters to Fournier of Sept. 1911 and Jan. 1912. (50, 51)

18

To Monsieur Jacques Rivière   *Pau, December 19, 1909*
c/o Monsieur and Madame Fournier
24, rue Dauphine
Paris

Your letters, here, before me [. . .].

My friend, —surely I may so address you—I am still not sure I understand your attitude in this dazzling night we call life. All I know is that this life can be utterly beautiful the moment that it goes to extremes; for the only decent stance is an excessive one. Delighted that I can admire your integrity and clarity in matters where I feared I might find the smugness and mutilations of culture [. . .]. But tell me, don't you think that the surest way to combat pride would be to merge it, at the point of infinity, with humility? Aren't they one and the same thing, the moment you are obliged, without reservations, to follow the simple cosmic paths?

Humble one's self because one has been humiliated?—
Oh! I can readily grasp the logic there would be in learning from the fact, in drawing sustenance and growth
from it, if that really meant persevering in one's own
mode of being—a mode of being that is ever willing to
learn, that never cheats, and that never has its fill of
honesty! . . . But are you sure you were humiliated? And
how can humility be humiliated—humility which con-
sists in inventing, at every turn, a formidable sufficiency,
that is to say, greatness! In your eyes, perhaps, one "dis-
qualifies" life by wanting it to be neutral as a flame,
meaningless except in terms of intensity, like a huge,
blind, luminous docility. But, stay as far as you can from
the paths of pride—I still can't see how weakness can be
humiliating so long as it does not keep from collaborat-
ing with strength in the very act of celebrating total
anonymity!

"People around me," you keep saying? —Oh, what a
luxury! a luxury!!! The invention of the monstrous
treasure would surely worry me as it does you, although
I have not lived as much as you nor been surrounded by
as many people. But I feel no embarrassment in telling
you: I have never come across such brilliance, *I have
never met with it!*[1] Only a kind of *bovarysme* could lead
me to embrace this anguish of "the crowd," if the word
means anything more than physical "mass." There are
"Personal Rights" that will always strike me as too private if the term does not also mean "The Rights of
Things." And the tortures occasioned by affection may
even arise from a communion that is less strictly human
and more humbly inclusive: [. . .] I covet only the weakness of being *totally* affectionate. "The people who surround me" are not distinguishable from "*what* surrounds
me." And I never have thought that our ways of looking
at things in this world must converge; they should

rather pursue desires along parallel lines. What goal could I expect to achieve by dispersing myself in "them," when the goal can only be within myself?

Besides, empty spaces are the only thing that gives me a feeling of being strangled.

You really can't criticize my solitude, which is no more my "attitude" than it is yours. Because it is merely "legal," neither I nor you could make solitude a talking-point—any more than we would the laws of silent breathing or digestion. We're confronted with the inert presence of fact.

But my friend Monod deceived you and deserves to have the big toe of his right foot cut off if he let you imagine that I harbor the slightest cultural or dilettantish design. I still know how to hate, and there's nothing I hate more! —I don't think I'm over-indulgent toward myself. And I swear by all races that no longer go about barefooted that I care only for getting things straight before seeking out subtleties. . . .

And now, should I reply to your letter at greater length? —As friend to friend, why do you want me to yield—when it's already only too easy!—to that frightful taste for writing, more "luxurious" than all the other vices, since it brings with it (and at least *you* know this) nothing but food for disgust and no respite with regard to oneself? —I make no distinction between art and a nervous twitch. And so long as I am unable to acquire a lasting taste for make-believe, I might even say that I hate "art" for being an end and no longer a means. Might I not even hate it finally, in itself, for being unable to confront what is unresolved, and for requiring its own extinctive prescription? —The whole business involves, in a terribly sensual way, an indirect giving of one's self, a kind of turning aside, when lyricism can be an immediate and unpremeditated thing. —It's simply that I would like to be healthy, and that means, avid to possess. Art = onanism. Only by running away from himself can a man write, and clandestinely, with his mouth full of saliva, the way one discovers some nasty, solitary pastime as a child. By "art" I mean the only relevant sort, the sort that submits to the rules of games that are useless, secondary, and incomplete, and that shuns as if it were an indecent, vulgar outburst, the saying of anything "essential."

"Write in order to be less strong?" you say. (And I read, "Publish in order to. . . .") —Ha, but don't you know that means obliging oneself to go on writing *forever*? For it's possible that one might not feel the intolerable pressure until one has published, and that means creating the obligation of justifying oneself, of justifying those pages that were simply waiting to be published in order to infect things hopelessly, *to be stinking*![2]

Won't you understand that I am even more afraid of any tie than I am of myself?

At the very moment when tiresome logic makes a frightful corollary of "living" and, even worse, when I am taking an enormous pleasure in living—wouldn't I choose this primordial force in preference to literature?—which I fear like the threat of having to wear false teeth? For one is *honor bound* to write only after the first dental cavity. —I keep thinking about all that.

And . . . and . . . ! if I could only make you feel how far, and unhampered, I would like to drift [. . .]. There are tribes, there are still tribes in which art is limited to mutilating the flesh of the fingers or nostrils. And I don't pack my gods along with me nor ever again expect to. Do you understand? It took my family an endlessly long time to learn a little about sunlight. I had to come home today in order to thank you at last for your two letters; for I live only to be outdoors.

Is there really any of that "conceit" in me that you say there is? —I don't know! —I don't quite see what conceit is. I'm not too fond of analysis. I do remember one thing: the Late Latin language, which isn't lacking in beauty, once revealed this point of grammar to me: the word *inutilis* meant "harmful," quite apart from any Christian context.

I'll go down to defeat, you say? —Sometimes I fear I will. That's what makes me want to fight!

In the same forthright way as you, I ask you to believe in my deep friendship. And when I hasten to underscore the word, you must understand how much I want to make it "fraught with meaning." For I've never thought that sharing friendship was a trifling matter.

If neither your luck nor the quality of the light will ever bring you down here to see me—I who can get no nearer to the Great Bear than Bordeaux—rest assured, since you ask, that I will always be happy to receive a letter from you.

I would be really grateful if you were willing to tell me about the work that commands your attention, and to let me be taken into your confidence as of now. Should you publish the least page in a magazine, please remember to send it to me yourself, since I don't read magazines any more.

Truly yours[3]   Leger

Since you're in Paris, would you be able to tell me if there exists a piano-reduction for four hands of the great Mahler symphony[4] that has just come out? —And do you know if Florent Schmitt has already published (conductor's score) his symphonic poem on a tale by Edgar Poe?[5]

A very affectionate thought for Monod, to whom I am sending some books—at your address, since I don't know his. Tell him again, please, on my behalf, that he must at all costs find someone who will play for him (all the way through) d'Indy's 1908 Sonata for Solo Piano— tell him that every day I'm surer of it: it's a real event; it breaks through the sonata framework and achieves, in the variations, what Franck was only able to dream of doing [. . .].

Tell him I have news of Duparc.[6] There's no hope. But he hasn't yet been able to destroy the great opera he was working on when he was stricken. His son keeps it hidden from him; his friends keep an eye out: an amazing conflict, for his health may depend on the destruction of his work!

Cordially yours.   A.S.L.

1. English in original.

2. Rivière had written: "You must not be so contemptuous of us—you have no right to be—that you give us only the part of yourself for which you feel contempt. Give us, first, those works that you disown, because they are surely good ones. But then go on to give us the rest, which expresses your true self as you presently are. Give it to us not simply as a work of art, but so that, after you've done it, you no longer belong wholly to yourself, *so that you are less strong* [Rivière's emphasis], so that you feel less inviolate in your solitude." The text of the first draft of this letter of Rivière's, dated 1 Nov. 1909, was printed for the first time in the St.-John Perse commemorative issue of the NRF, Feb. 1976, pp. 158-162. The last three words of the paragraph in AL's letter ("to be stinking") are in English and underscored in the original.

3. English in original.

4. Gustav Mahler's *Third Symphony*, performed for the first time in 1910.

5. Florent Schmitt's *Etude symphonique pour le "Palais enchanté" d'Edgar Poë*. The poem in question is "The Haunted Palace," which occurs in Poe's tale, "The Fall of the House of Usher."

6. Henri Duparc (1848-1933), César Franck's favorite pupil and the composer of many well-known songs. Duparc was stricken very early with a mysterious and debilitating disease and ceased composing in 1885. He was a friend of AL's friend, Francis Jammes.

19

To Monsieur Jacques Rivière   *Pau, February 17, 1910*
c/o Madame Fournier
24, rue Dauphine
Paris (6e)

My friend,

I am annoyed with myself for not having thanked you yet for your *Dardanus*.[1] Yes, I'm annoyed with myself. You mustn't hold it against me, though. Worries. . . . My life mocks me a bit sneeringly at the moment.

What you wrote is very fine; and your language is grave and beautiful, remaining aloof, but with precision. Even when you permit yourself lyrical passages, even the last one, that doesn't spoil the piece. Your thought? It never ceases to satisfy and to fulfill expectations, right up to the last smile over a job well done. It may even be that its chief quality occasionally suggests its one defect, namely, being too assiduously consecutive and going too far along the path with the reader. For it sometimes seems that, by reiteration, it assumes inertia on the reader's part, eating the whole meal by itself before the invited guests arrive.

But, I beg of you, please don't take as reservations what is really admiration on my part. It's just that I don't want my letter to strike you as if it came from a stranger. I'm forcing myself to be critical, and that's all I can find to criticize. Having said that, let's both say that art is ennobled through egoism, not politeness; and that it's obvious that while one must invite people, one must do their eating for them, letting them look on as you do it. Art has the head of an Ubu.[2] The sheer delight of expressing oneself is absolutely the only "pretext" that might be unfailingly self-sufficient. And that's why I say one must be wary of it. I know I am much too partial not to be afraid of the least "entelechy" (horrible school-word!).

But where does Rameau come into my letter[!?]! (Rameau, who appears so precisely concerned with exhausting every possibility open to him!)

And what business did I have telling Monod that you seemed unaware of a consuming hunger with regard to oneself? I obviously was not thinking of the diligence you apply to your art!

I regret that I don't know any part of *Dardanus*. All I know is *Castor et Pollux*. But that's enough to make me think, as you do, that the name of Rameau could become a kind of rallying cry today.

Dramatic modes of expression? I wish you would write a note on Monteverdi. He's my great passion at the moment. Maybe we'll have a chance to hear the *Incoronazzione* at the Schola! Down here, quite humbly, I've persuaded a musician friend of mine[3] to put on *Orfeo*.

I mustn't forget to thank you for the information you were able to give me in spite of the vagueness of my questions. The Mahler symphony[4] I was curious about is indeed the Third (and so there must be a piano-reduction of it); it took up one entire concert at Geneva this season, and I'm told that Weingartner wants to do it in Vienna. The work by Schmitt[5] has only just been published by Durand ("Étude symphonique pour le *Palais enchanté* d'Edgar Poe"). Obviously, that can only be the poem "The Haunted Palace" (which is also found inserted in *The House of Usher*). Schmitt wanted to have it played at Pau; and one of his friends asked me to talk about it to the Conductor of the orchestra, Edouard Brunel,[6] whom I know. But Schmitt blundered by sending along only the four-hand piano-score, and my very touchy old friend refuses to open it.

Should I go still further in answering your letter?

I've learned, through Frizeau, with what firmness you act in private life. I detest unfleshing a man too much (a way of saying that I've flayed Art too often) not to take an interest in your private life.

I've also thought about your intellectual attitude at times. —Art, cruelty towards oneself, as the only "consequence" or conclusion. But in your very flight, your headlong flight, toward what is imperfect, disheveled, imprecise, I can't help still finding your incurable quest for perfection. I'm thinking of the double meaning of the word "impatience."

You want to include in your book *everything* that is most *vital* to you? In that case, how strongly I insist on your telling me about it!

I was delighted to learn that you will be in the Pyrenees this summer. I'll be very happy to visit you and pay my respects to Madame Rivière. But why do you say that "you are a little afraid of me?" You must forget the impression of me that you carried away if it isn't a good one. When I met you at Frizeau's house,[7] maybe I was unwittingly a bit distant and bristling, as one always is before the age of twenty. I was in a turmoil, and, outside of me, I was also faced with having to make a big decision at that moment—a decision that was resolved shortly thereafter by a death in the family. But I assure you that my feelings may be hurt if I find any hesitation where I have decided, suddenly, that I have found friendship.

As for me, I'm slitting the throats of a whole herd of cattle, on the spot, and I remain yours, in friendship,

Leger

1. See above, letter 11, note 6.
2. The reference is, of course, to the main character of Alfred Jarry's play—originally a puppet-play—*Ubu Roi* (1896). King Ubu is the embodiment of everything that is cruel, stupid, and grotesque in people occupying positions of authority.
3. Probably Paul Maufret. See above, letter 9, note 1.
4. See above, letter 18, note 4.
5. See above, letter 18, note 5.
6. See above, letter 10, note 2.
7. See above, letter 7, note 1.

20

To Monsieur Jacques Rivière   *Pau, Saturday*
24, rue Dauphine   [*March 12, 1910*]
Paris (6e)

My friend, your note goes straight to my heart! I have understood your friendship [. . .]. I had never given a thought to how simple a thing friendship is. And suddenly, what do I discover?

Leger

I haven't said anything to you about the news you broke to me (the publication of my poems in the next *N.R.F.*).[1] Nor was that the "main thing." But don't go thinking that I'm all that aloof. I'm happy about it; you can be sure of that. The only trouble is—can you understand?—that down here we've been wearing straw hats for a week already.... (And then, you and Monod are the only people I know in Paris, and I'm afraid the two of you won't like the poems, they were so purposely limited!)

[...] —I have heavy family responsibilities that necessitate my going to Bordeaux very soon to confer with a notary. I regret very much that the trip won't coincide with Easter vacation, which might possibly bring you back to Bordeaux.

The strikes in Guadeloupe are a very serious matter for any number of families from the Islands. I had bad news just this morning. I'd like to be on the spot, but I don't have the money to take a fast packet, and a freighter would arrive too late.

Just this moment received a letter from Gide[2] announcing proofs. He says that he "likes my poems," and that I am going "to frighten some readers and cause a few subscriptions to be canceled; but it's good from time to time to shake the subscribers in order to make a few fall. . . ." At least the image is a good one, for one can't help thinking about the cochineal harvest![3] But I really can't imagine what is frightening about those few pages. I recall that I strove for exactly the reverse.

All this to be kept *entre nous*, please.

Very cordially yours,   L.

1. The poems by AL published in the Apr. 1910 issue of NRF were: "Ecrit sur la porte," "Pour fêter une enfance," "Récitation à l'éloge d'une reine," and "Histoire du Régent."

2. André Gide (1869-1951). AL's first contacts with Gide were made through Rivière and remained exclusively epistolary until late in 1911. (See note to Gide of Nov. 1911. [108]) At the time of this letter, Gide was the chief moving spirit of the newly founded NRF, of which Jacques Rivière was the editor. Though AL did not see a great deal of Gide, he was to remain a very loyal friend of Gide until his death in 1951. See letters to Gide. (93-120, 186, 291-301)

3. The dye-bearing cochineal insects were collected, usually from cactus blades, in various ways, one of them being to start a small fire at the base of the plant, thus killing the insects, which were then shaken or scraped off.

21

To Monsieur Jacques Rivière   *Pau, March 14, 1910*
24, rue Dauphine
Paris

My friend, let me tell you right off what pleasure I derived from your *Cézanne*.[1] You've written a beautiful piece, with a few real groundswells in it. I was especially delighted that you used very forceful language in talking about the beauty of the "movement" beneath the immobility. That's really what we look for in everyone.

I especially prize what you wrote on "locality"; it overflows and has implications for much more than just the painter's art.

Even finer, to my mind, is the way you identify color, that "duration" which you have managed to express so movingly in your almost figurative exposition: "Aussi se passionne-t-on . . ." etc.

With all my heart.   Leger

1. Rivière, "Cézanne," NRF, Mar. 1910, pp. 366-370. The passage referred to farther on in the letter reads, in English translation: "And one is fascinated to discover these landscapes persistently enduring. They are completely absorbed in the day's passage; they expect nothing. They have become so completely imbued with the uniform movement of time that they let themselves be carried along by it. They drift along with the hours, and during the night they will still be obscurely there." (p. 369)

22

To Monsieur Jacques Rivière   *Pau, July [8], 1910*
c/o Monsieur and Madame Fournier
2, rue Cassini
Paris (14e)

My friend, I know friendship; I know affection even better. I don't have—and you don't have—to find reasons to explain my silence. Perhaps there is no more affectionate word than "far away."

You are often in my thoughts. And both of us like the expression "to endure." But I'm studying law—do you understand that? Can you picture what that means? Two exams to prepare in haste: brackets, outlines that make a place, as in entomology, for "privileges" and "mortgages"—and then the urge to get away. . . .

I'd like a little more respite—will I ever find it?—so I could talk to you about all the things by you that I've read and liked, ever since our first meeting. About your *Gauguin*[1] especially, as I don't see things in that area exactly as you do, at least I don't delimit things in the same way as you do. But your six pages are very fine; your poem, internally, emerges; and I love the distinction of your language; in my eyes, it relates you to an even more ancient lineage.

To my way of thinking, you speak about Dukas[2] with a great deal of tact; about his bloodless, but not meager, honesty. Dukas is obviously totally lacking in genius, in the strict sense of the word. But you shouldn't seek him in *Ariane*, which gives us the craftsman more than the artist, but in his Symphony in C Major, and even in his two piano works: his 1900 Sonata and the Variations on a Theme by Rameau. I've heard his symphony twice; I assure you that it contains an intricate clockwork that allows one to overlook the passages imitative of Franck and d'Indy. (I believe the work dates from fifteen or twenty years ago.)

I'm waiting for you to give us a piece on Roussel.[3] I've been told that he's returned from India. I've managed to get his symphony, *The Forest*, which I've not heard, programmed here for next winter. I know only what he has written for piano and his chamber music: a remarkable Trio in E-Flat Major for piano, violin, and 'cello.

But won't you get around to d'Indy some time? His art is pure, luminous, and forthright as a lobed forehead. I admire more every day, to the point of amazement, how inexhaustible such an "art" is—inexhaustible precisely in that it leaves almost nothing to chance [. . .].

You spoke about the few pages by me that you've had a chance to read; nothing could have given me more pleasure than the way you are able to read them aright.

I must have expressed myself awkwardly, that you could, even for a moment, have thought that I wanted to merge the musical and the verbal methods. It would, of course, never occur to me to deny a certain mysterious musical "contribution" to the poem (if it is not consciously planned)—the unconscious utilization of verbal timbres, and the very way one distributes or "composes" the whole mass, once it has come to life. But I shall never admit that the poem can ever elude its own inherent law, which is the law of the "intelligible" theme. The art of writing, which is the art of naming or, even more generally, of designating, will never function except through words, which make up a kind of society, and that are further entailed by etymological meanings. I see here an exclusively analytic art, for the most "musical" verbal material is radically subject, at the outset or in the end, to special laws of "propriety." (And has propriety ever had anything at all in common with "rightness" in music?) This confusion, which was good enough for a generation that was half musician, has, with its taste for crude approximations, too often debased our language. In the last analysis, it means one really doesn't love music enough, doesn't love the prodigious power of such an art, if one can not understand what is irreducible and recalcitrant in it. The moment one feels it impossible to avoid such a trap, there's nothing left but to devote oneself exclusively to music.

Rimbaud,[4] whom you spoke to me about, is precisely the most a-musical, if not anti-musical, of our true poets. I know few others that are as precise. There is, in the divine spareness of his cursive language, the whole nonsonorous and blindingly bright sense of the abstract.

Please thank your brother-in-law[5] and Copeau[6] for their kindness to me; and remember me to Lhote. Tell André Gide that his good will means a great deal to me. But how can one get accustomed to publishing in a review? The only thing that could be more irritating would be to play piano on shipboard. I've been told Gide has a rather yellowish skin and has never managed to be a good pianist. He'll understand.

I'd like to get rid of all these poems[7] at one stroke, that is, in a book. I've inquired, indirectly, about prices; the sums are such that they would pay for a trip around the world on oxback.

[. . .]

Affectionately, my friend; I wish I could see you again. My most respectful regards to Madame Rivière —and my warmest too, for I was so happy to have been introduced to her.

Leger

1. "Paul Gauguin," NRF, June 1910, pp. 738-743.

2. Rivière, "*Ariane et Barbe bleue* de Paul Dukas à l'Opéra Comique," NRF, May 1910, pp. 686-689.

3. Albert Roussel (1869-1937), the composer who spent his early years in the French Navy and subsequently joined d'Indy at the Schola Cantorum. The work referred to here by AL is Roussel's first symphony, "Poème de la forêt," composed in 1904-1905.

4. Arthur Rimbaud (1854-1891), the precocious genius who abandoned literature by the time he was twenty and ended up as a trader and gun-runner in Abyssinia. In 1910 the only readily available editions of Rimbaud's poems and prose pieces were the various editions overseen by Rimbaud's pious brother-in-law, Paterne Berrichon. But the notorious *Œuvres de Arthur Rimbaud (Vers et Prose)* that was revised and "put in order" by Berrichon, and to which Paul Claudel wrote a "Préface," did not appear until 1912. Claudel's "Préface" is referred to by AL in his letter to Rivière of 18 July 1913. (147)

5. Henri Fournier. See above, letter 7, note 1.

6. Jacques Copeau (1879-1949) was one of the original founders of the NRF in 1909. In 1913 he created the famous Théâtre du Vieux Colombier. He was a close friend of Gide and Rivière.

7. The poems in question are the *Eloges* that actually were later published in book form. See the letter to Rivière of 2 June 1911 (28), and the notes to it.

23

To Monsieur Jacques Rivière   *Bielle (vallée d'Ossau)*
15, rue Froidevaux   *Friday [October 21, 1910]*
Paris 14e

My friend,

I'm disappointed that I did not see you this summer —I had so wished to.

Please don't be annoyed with me because of my silence of several months. These months contain only one day: summer. In the country, simply going in to one's room to write becomes a problem. [. . .] Please believe

—you must believe—in my affection; it is unwavering and rejoices in itself, because now I deeply want friendship not to be a game.

I remember your last letter very well. Always remember, when you write me, that I eagerly welcome everything you tell me about yourself and about your writing, as well as about your daily tasks.

I'm happy for you over the job at Stanislas[1] that liberates you somewhat from the "literary life." And you gave me such good news about your real work that I'll be joyously looking forward to your book.

You must not doubt your own abilities. *I* have confidence in you on your own behalf, since I know there is in you a poet who is ever alert; even better, I know there dwells in you the "grammarian." Now is there anything at all more essential and more urgent?—since that is the very thing a poet is, in the last analysis.

I still recall a sentence from your letter. It was not my intention last April in Bordeaux to restore "criticism" in your eyes, but the "critical poem" as you conceived of it and which, as we said, has never existed, except perhaps latently in a few English-language essayists. I'll never bring myself to believe that the Michel Arnaulds[2] of this world are readable. But the critic I dream of, the critic who takes on the task of restoring and recreating (which, in simpler terms, means to situate and interrelate)—a critic withdrawn, turned in upon himself, and "making finds" the way a poet makes finds, and like the poet, in touch with the unconscious and the mysterious, a "seer" if you will, but with the right to say more than the poet, because, being less elliptical, he brings out and fills in all the suppressed connections—that critic is himself a poet, or he risks being nothing at all. He "imagines" no less than the poet, since he must restore to the work its entire careening, that is, the whole world that supports it; nor can he avoid personal revelation, since he, too, "investigates" from within. It is in that way, it seems to me, by the use of interrelating and by a play of analogies, that criticism can accomplish a unique service and cease to be parasitism, becoming instead an itinerant apprenticeship; an "anabasis,"[3] if you will, or return to the sea, to that all-embracing sea whence the work was drawn (in its definitive, and perhaps cruel, uniqueness).

Remember the meaning that the word χρίνειν takes on in Alexandrian Greek (and always in Plotinus): "to call forth, provoke a crisis"—isn't it wonderful—this contribution that may come from medical language (always so sharply precise)?

All this chatter, my friend, in part because I was so happy, in the last issue of the *Nouvelle Revue française*, to come across the admirable pages that you gave us on Claudel.[4]

But tell me about the writing you're now doing. Is it the play you spoke to me about in Bordeaux?

I didn't say anything about your *Voyage à Reims*[5] because I didn't like it. But nobody is more prompt at making a mistake than I am. I'd also read, at a painter's house, your study of Besnard:[6] beautifully written, but really to no avail!

You spoke about Dostoievsky. No, I haven't really read him. I haven't "run across" him. But there was nothing silly about your question [. . .]. I know the Russian soul only through its composers, whom I like. I know it's a strong soul, because it goes naked; and free, because it delights in being of service. It knows what "wariness" is, like a child who has witnessed a murder. —Is that it? It lives at the crossroads and, were it Latin, would not enroll in the Rhetorician's school. Didn't our marvelous Moussorgsky like *The Idiot* too?

I liked what you wrote, my friend, about thinking of
me when you heard *Prince Igor*.[7]

Tell me what you'll be hearing this winter.

I'm working at getting a symphony by Magnard[8]
played by the Pau orchestra.

Mahler, whom I spoke to you about,[9] is to me now
nothing but a gray elephant swollen with lymph. I'd
give the 30,000 instruments on his title-pages for one
little "Song of Death" by Moussorgsky.

If you've finally come around to d'Indy,[10] don't bother
with his music for the theater, which is an error. Leave
out all his symphonic work before *Istar*, which is sheer
beauty; you might even go so far as to downgrade, in
a general way, all the work he's done of a plastically
imaginative sort, because d'Indy, who is very short on
"phantasy," is neither imaginative nor sensual, and in
the works I refer to, all the beauty of his craftsmanship
won't succeed in making us forget the pure weavings
of the unconscious that are so liberally given to Debussy. But please, approach without preconceived notions those pure cerebral feasts called Symphony in
B-flat; the second, and even the first, String Quartet,
and finally, the sonata for solo piano: Sonata in E
Major, [. . .]. The first time I heard it at a private performance, I recall that an Englishman among us, forever bored, it seemed, by anything but the Bach of the
Clavichord II, to which he had devoted himself, began
to sniffle because he was actually crying like a young
girl. And my sister, who is not a great pianist, herself
admits that the work is, basically, very simply fingered.

[. . .] I'll be staying at Bordeaux during the first days
in November, on the way back from La Rochelle, where
I'm going to hear two masses in Gregorian chant.

We won't be able to stay much longer in this part
of the country; it's already quite spoiled by winter.

Everything is dying or going awry, even to the piano strings. And you can't sleep out on the mountainside any longer.

Yours affectionately, my friend. Remember me to Madame Rivière. I hope I'll see both of you this year in Bordeaux. I'll stop by there four times, for my last Law, and some other, registrations.

Your friend.   Leger

1. Shortly after his marriage to Isabelle Fournier, Rivière accepted a post at the Collège Stanislas in Paris where he taught students preparing for entrance examinations to Saint-Cyr, which was then the principal military academy of France. Rivière, who was nearly the same age as his uncontrollable students, did not stay long at the Collège Stanislas; in fact, he quit his job in Oct. 1911.

2. Michel Arnauld was the pseudonym of Marcel Drouin (1871-1943), a professor of philosophy at the University of Bordeaux and frequent contributor to the NRF and other periodicals. He was the brother-in-law of André Gide.

3. This is the earliest of several mentions of this Greek term ("expedition into the interior"), which was to become the title of one of AL's most celebrated poems. See letter to Claudel of 10 June 1912 (63), and to Larbaud of 13 Oct. 1923 (143), and notes thereto.

4. The only piece on Claudel by Rivière published during this period is "Les Œuvres lyriques de Claudel," which appeared in the magazine *Art Libre* of July 1910, pp. 361-366, and not in the NRF, as AL here indicates.

5. Rivière, "Voyage à Reims," NRF, Aug. 1910, pp. 169-175.

6. Rivière, "Albert Besnard, décorateur," *Art et Décoration*, May 1910, pp. 153-170.

7. A few months later Rivière was to publish a short piece, "Les Scènes Polovtsiennes du *Prince Igor* [de Borodine] aux Concerts Colonne," in NRF, Jan. 1911, pp. 172-173.

8. Albéric Magnard (1865-1914), the pupil of Vincent d'Indy who produced numerous symphonic works and was killed by the Germans in 1914 at his country home.

9. Cf. letter to Rivière of 19 Dec. 1909 (18), and above, letter 18, note 4.

10. AL's admiration for Vincent d'Indy (1851-1931) and his work in the Schola Cantorum was unflagging. Several of d'Indy's pupils became personal friends of AL. See above, letter 9, note 1 and letter 14, note 5.

24

To Monsieur Jacques Rivière   *Pau*
Paris   [*December 1910*]

My friend,

I've just put down your study of Baudelaire,[1] which I read.

I am delighted, delighted that you wrote it. Your smile shines through everywhere, my dear Rivière.

There is always something sensitive and "integral" in your criticism; and, without your ever slighting the rights of analytical intelligence, there is still that intimate outpouring that lets one glimpse, now and then, a bit of the sacramental host. . . . And then your language, which never goes astray and rejoices in simply being what it is and saying just what it wants, once and for all. A priceless remark (p. 724)[2] on the modesty of language, which only a French writer of thoroughbred stock, like yours, could have written.

(Just one thing: when you reprint these pages on Baudelaire, you should eliminate the note by Ch. Péguy[3] about confession, which doesn't belong there. Péguy doesn't move in the same circles.)

Warmly.   Leger

1. Rivière, "Baudelaire," NRF, Dec. 1910, pp. 721-740.

2. The passage in question reads, in English translation: "This carefully marshaled poetry carries all words along in its rhythms. The rarest words are here alongside the commonest ones, the humblest along with the most audacious. But, submerged in the sure but delicate overall movement, not one of them shocks us.

A strange flow of words. Now and again like a voice suddenly
grown tired, like a sudden reticence that seizes the heart, like a
gesture of submission—a word charged with sudden weakness.
. . ."

3. The note in question was retained by Rivière in later reprintings of the article. It reads, in English translation: " 'The
function of Confession,' said Péguy, 'is, preferably, to bring to
light unseen items, and to say especially what ought not to be
said.' " (*Victor-Marie, Comte Hugo*, p. 14.) Charles Péguy
(1873-1914), the Catholic Dreyfusard, poet and editor of *Les
Cahiers de la Quinzaine* in the years immediately preceding
World War I, was never one of AL's great admirations.

25

To Monsieur Jacques Rivière   *Pau,*
c/o M. G. Frizeau   *December 21, 1910*
17, rue Régis
Bordeaux (Gironde)

My friend,

I won't see you in Bordeaux. I'll miss you by a few days.
My Registration begins January 4, and at that moment
I'll be so busy with a lawsuit in which I am a plaintiff
for my mother, that I may not be able to go to Bordeaux
before the 8th or thereabouts. I'm very sorry about this,
because this is the last year that I'll have to go to Bordeaux. Won't I be seeing you around Easter?

Your letter gave me great pleasure, with all its news
about your work and your daily life. [...] When I think
of all that you have already published or are tempted
to publish, I am struck with genuine admiration for the
way you have so happily organized things for your work.

Did I give you the slightest pleasure by entrusting to
you that new manuscript for Gide, and for him alone?[1]
Consider only the *act*, because, as a piece of writing, it's
not good; that is, it doesn't have any "literary" interest,

properly speaking [. . .]. Besides, it is not really a poem.
Why did I choose these pages? Somewhat for that
very reason—and for their literalness; and because they
amused me and are not for publication [. . .]. All it is,
is an enumeration of sea-birds that provided me amusement during a convalescence that really made me hate
this part of the country. (I had caught cold in the
mountains.)

You chide me for my persistence in wanting to return
to the Colonies. There may be a certain cowardice in it,
but it's not just an idle fancy. Careers in the Colonies
are more accessible, more rapidly achieved, and more
ample. And I must now assume the burden of a career.
I would never accept this if I were going through life
without ties, because you may be sure that I recognize
nothing in that area worth taking the trouble to achieve.
But I have sisters and a mother—sisters for whom nothing is too good so far as I am concerned, even to puerile
things. A mother who is scarcely twenty years older
than I am, and whom I cannot bear to see grow old
without my being able to supply a little of the comfort
she was deprived of by my father's death.

You can judge how fond I am of you, my friend, to
talk to you this way. But now you understand why I
must go off to the Colonies; or abroad, if my circumstances allow me to go to Paris to prepare for a consular
career, as Claudel would like me to. I can't see any
future for myself in France. I absolutely could not coun-
tenance working seven or eight hours a day. I would
die of boredom in this country—of boredom, cold, and
impersonality. Today I want to *live*, do you see? (—
which is exactly what sets me apart from the others.)
I want to live every day, every morning when I get up,
forcefully and almost vehemently. There are too many

reasons, and even material ones, that daily make me believe strongly that I was not born for art, that I manage perfectly well to forget about it, and that I do myself not the slightest violence in all this, contrary to what several of my elders think, with an obstinacy that I find unbearable (I'm not talking, my friend, about anyone you know.)

All this unburdening of myself merely to tell you that I want to live in a warm country where I shall never again hear talk of winter, nor of the rains that eat up eight months of the year here. Claudel says that the *artist* is the person who prefers his work to his life. You won't find a *man* to deny that!

Before I gallop off, let me beg of you, my friend, in the friendliest way, not to speak to me about that Gauguin-like poem,[2] nor to allow Frizeau ever to read it to you. That would be the first wound inflicted on my friendship. (With the possible exception of one page, not only was the poem bad—it was written in a language that is absolutely not my own and is foreign to me.) It's unbearable to think that I have not yet been able to retrieve the manuscript and destroy it.

What's all this about Péguy?[3] The note was simply superfluous; and in art what is superfluous is harmful. I know nothing about Péguy, except for the admiration with which Jammes speaks to me about him. To which I add yours.

Won't you be annoyed at my reading so few contemporary authors? Don't think this is just a pose on my part. My isolation, and the limited facilities we have down here in the bookstores stocked for foreigners, have made me have recourse to a few *textbooks* that don't ever leave me short of reading material.

I was overjoyed to learn of your admiration for one

of the Brandenburg Concertos. Tell me which one. They are all worth knowing. It's something you will carry everywhere with you.

I like the way you talk about your novel: to recount artlessly.

I leave you with the reassurance of my affection. [. . .]

Leger

COHORT[4]

Innumerae comitantur aves, stipatque
volantum
Alituum suspensa *cohors.* . . .
Claudius Claudianus[5]

We used to talk of them on shipboard and on the empty verandas, not far from the low-lying, very porous islands or the crumbling shores where the sea grumblingly rolls its coral dolls:

Birds! Birds! Of every sect and every clan! pelagic or riparian, resident or nomadic, starvelings of a night, fanatics by the year, a great chosen people!

They came on, wings trenchant and brief, plumage very subdued, the tragic beak grafted onto the narrow mask. . . . ah! on they came, on and on, this chosen people,

in great warrior-fraternities, like the sacred Herman-dades, *just so! more prolix and vain than any genealogical tree, just so! more adventurous and vain*

than last-born sons and gentlemen of fortune: Birds! Birds! guests for a day in the pre-evening hours. —And here we are, standing on shipboard and on the wooden verandas,

pushing back our rattan chairs, glass in hand; and the cry is on our lips, all of us drawn, by the sudden clap of

*the tradewinds in the canvas of our awnings, to the bar-
riers and handrails,*

*we hailed you, Passers-by, and we named you; we
called aloud your everyday names and your names from
other sources. Or else we named you on the spur of the
moment with a new name, more fitting than that bestowed by the Learned.*

*Ten names, twenty names thrown overboard, as if to
kennelmen for the baptism of the pack! . . . Ah so! will
you tell us the truth about your appelation? living parcels torn from the vast Unnamed. . . .*

*And the wing that fluttered in us, and flapped wildly
for us in the awnings (may the madman possessed of
God be with us!) would not let us be, nor have patience
until we had found the new name!*

*To name, to create! Who was it that created within
us, shouting the new name? Language at the forkings of
language. . . . from the deeps, rising, bubbling among
the pockets of blue salt. . . . (May the madman possessed
of God be with us!)*

*Thus did childhood stamp its feet on the highest heir-
loom-chair! Thus was childhood elevated for us to its
highest calling, which has always been to give names,*

*and the word panted within us at the traps and fork-
ings of language, like the green-skirted flame of the
ghost that haunts the great pans of white rum.*

*Let the evening take its due, let man's one-night
dream squander its holdings: repopulated sky! seeded
sky! the god's endless squandering, and the thing itself
dispensed to the four winnowing-baskets of the sky. . . .*

*And there is no traffic in spices nor fabrics, no cowries
on the trading-counters, no Senegambian gums; but instead, commerce in living things and live currency,*

Birds! birds! currency forever valid, forever payable!

*a wandering people, a chosen people! . . . Let the sky and
the sea draw up our accounts,*
  and the madman possessed of God spell them out!

We begin with this one: the "Ethereal Phaeton"[6] *(and
let its old name stand!),*
  *Prince of a fairy-tale era, mime of lordly grace, the
most decked-out of the high-flying birds, the Ethereal
One lives its name. Brooding is not its concern, but
flight, to go on, to go on and on. . . . like one who says
of a work and of himself, "You are no longer my concern. . . ." To go on, go on and on, O marvelous flesh,
the lowest*
  *in oil-content, requiring it only in thin layers that
line the dihedral bone-structure of its sternum. . . .*

*You have guessed it: the Tropic Bird, the most aerial
of our sea-birds, (the only one that rows with its wings
as does our Island Dove). One could weigh less only in a
dream—a mass of luminous essence, a phantom with
grafts of feather and bone. The headdress is of white
faille; a lacquered stripe passes through the eye; the
white-satin mantle is spangled with thin black crescents
—all washed with pale salmon-pink, and the tail marvelously thin-tapered, the two central rectrices trailing like
two wisps of fresh straw, yellow or white. Preposterous
feathers that are too much for it; they cross when at rest;
the bird does not know quite what to do with them, they
are such a luxury! . . . Ah, this one can afford to lose a
few of his feathers. —I am on his side!*

*Of the same family is the "Anchises" (a borrowed
name), which makes its nest of three pebbles and a
splinter of wood. A lover of barren isles that are more
notched than a great fossil's crest, it is not—indeed, far
from it—the most chaste of birds. . . . But the*
  woman-eyed "Bilimbe," the gentle denizen of sheltered

shores, if it does not manage to hatch its eggs, ends up starving, obsessed with laying. . . . And the "Minime" lays its eggs

on the sonorous isles, living there in great colonies. We provision a canoe for a pleasure-jaunt: here is a whole basketful of their rusty-spotted green eggs—they taste like hazel-nuts.

The "Dadou" has to its credit a good memory: it returns to us before the rains; it recognizes its particular isle from a hundred others, and its nest among a thousand others—cheating on the nearby nestings.

An old bird of the South Seas that paints its nape with cinnamon—its breast and lores a fine black, the wings reddish with white bars trimmed with chamois-colored curls—is surely the most giddy to be found. "I left you there, camper on the high seas, and this season is still yours, in that other latitude, that same seaweedy spot! . . ." Perhaps its memory is nothing but a flurry of snow-pellets and sticks bobbing up and down in the intoxication of foam. —Envy him.

There are several species of Crab-eaters, all equally notable for the plumage of their backs. The Skuas are well known: the Jaegers, the Boobies, the Catharactas. . . . It is customary

to speak of the Albatross. We have no regard for it. It is the largest of our Sea-Birds, and it is stupid. It is caught with a fish-hook, as Bustards are in the snowy season on the plains of the Old World. —The Albatross is voracious and lays only one egg. (A nest made of grasses matted with dirt and excrement.)

A Giant Petrel of the southern seas comes all the way to see us one evening. He is the Inspector of the flowing seas swollen with the ferment of obese refuse that they carry along. . . . He goes after whatever is dying; he

*befouls his beak with the whale's carrion; he wallows in
whatever is soft, stinking, and warm. His job? — to
undo! . . . He splatters himself with pus, ah! a frenzy
of tarsi and wings, ah! a kind of demented celebration;
and childhood is capsized by the look in his eye. . . .*

*An "Abraha" comes down from the North, thanks
to a cool current: its head still circled with the sparkling
of ice, the cumbersome bird, over-feathered, fattened on
flounders, ends up in the smooth plains of our seas; in
the late afternoon, color of fresh salmon-flesh; there,
silent, it draws from the tired waters an astonishing fish,
black and tufted as a fresh-water chub. It is snatched
from his beak! —For I forgot to tell you about*

*the effrontery of a pillaging gull: the Stercorarius that
lives by attack and rapine.*

*(A different variety is cowardly: though cruel to the
unspiny conger, it takes fright at a fish that suddenly
spreads out a fin.)*

*The "Krahak" with its great gular pouch and its face
of grainy blue skin (crest curly at the occiput and an
iris of tarnished yellow, like the old gold in churches),
with its high well-constructed hull, shaped like a rustic
sledge or a poor man's cradle, does not spend all its time
fishing: he delights, with furled wings, in drifting on
the water for a whole day and night: he is at ease, he's
done enough, he floats and puffs up under his plumage,
his head resting on a curved neck— By dawn an island
is nearby under the mangrove-trees.*

*And others move about, their long legs in the reddish
water, like mosquitos over our ponds. . . . Others wait in
the harbors for the boats to put in and for the load of
bruised entrails to be thrown overboard at one fling. —
He is mad who would count them! they are more numerous than were*

those Birds of Islam that one night attacked the army of the Prince of Ethiopia![7]

. . . And we, what do we know of the Terns, diminutive race? —That on the calcined shores they hold conclave for a whole month. Much good may it do them! but the ship-following "Cobre" and the "Corale" of the lagoons,

gluttons for the ambiguous, choose to foregather at the river-mouths. Two days from land they utter their itinerant's cry; and perhaps then

the silky female, feeling in her womb the ovum's ferment, begins to dream of puddles becalmed, of the fresh water of ponds cut off from the sea, where the male goes, filled with the knowledge of how to plait his floating nest.

Similar are the ways of the "Supercilious," which is very slow and travels in droves, by tribe and cohort. At night it flies over a great, ghostly river that is humped with beasts and filth; and at daybreak it plummets, suddenly shattering the slate of a great lake.

The "Ajaia" has a spatulate bill. . . . O warmth beneath the slime, intimacy of mud! . . . To reach our shores, it unerringly detects a wind that will blow for six days, entrusts itself to that wind, falls so dead-tired, on seeing the coastlines, that we row out to it, and it lets itself be taken.

Another migrant, whose nose sticks from its beak in tubular nostrils, is infested, even though it is a diver, by a copper-blue insect.

And here are the "Coasters," familiars of the rock and flailers of cliffs. The "Utter-male," a sea-eagle also called "Erne," chooses the loftiest site looking out to the open sea. It veers in circles above the roadstead, which is un-encumbered; it plummets—the water is blacker here.

This Osprey is not alone in picking up fish in its talons: one kind of "Peque" (the others are web-footed) comes to us from the West and on sighting our keys releases its free toe—the fish are quicker here.

The adventurous "Vindi" rises from the forests. And even though it feeds on fish, it smells bad on its breeding-grounds, smells like the mouth of a carnivore. I have seen it advance inward over our lands, a threat to iguana and armadillo.

A word or two about the "Pitul," a giant of our highest reefs; he has the horned bill, reinforced with a spur, that has earned him the name of "Bone-breaker."

The "Arenaria," O futile one! is nothing but the turn-stone; you have seen it restless and fretful along our shores at low tide. It knows that in the islands, from where I speak, an old green-skinned tree containing red tannin is loaded with oysters as if with gills; and it knows that on the sloping sides of wreckage one finds the sea-acorn. . . .

But enough about precedence; make way for the Lord of the Domain!

Here, here is the one who never was and never shall be named, the one who always was, and ever shall be for us, "The Unnamed One!" (for others, the "Frigate Eagle" or "Fregata magnificens").

He has the proudest prerogatives of all the Lords of the Sea: High Constable of the Empire and Overseas Provost, Pirate turned Commodore and Commissar of the Islands, God's Condottiere in his most ancient Sea-Marches and Maritime Provinces. . . .

May he deign to set for us the tone of his high and mighty ways: the wings honed to a scimitar, and the immense spread of his authority—sovereign arrogance of flight under the immobility of the gesture.

All-powerful Governor of the Ocean Vineyards, Steward and Regent of fabulous Indies; he draws honor and pleasure from occupying in turn, on the sky's twin slopes, the two alcoves of a single dais. He lives only on the wing and inhabits the air all day, wing moveless and tail free, thin-drawn, that he folds to a point or opens as he sees fit.

Thus he goes to his most prolonged pleasure, clothed in black luster with green highlights, or purplish blue, metallic; and the jabot a lubricious red, swelling with the breath of desire.

He is the finest of our great sea-birds. I have waited until last to speak of him:

". . . He comes, he comes, we are not sure from what parts, and rises silently with the day from a very distant island that is a stranger to all names. He comes via the channel of the great, overheated celestial roadways; he leans against the calm and dazzling South; and as he descends and finally deigns to use his eyelids, assailed by fame's sheerest trials, behold

he feels something give way, in the warmest, most secret of the sky's smooth waters, something like a stubborn torment that at last dissolves in tears. . . .

Or else he has misgivings about his power; and his tail, deeply forked, takes a wind-reading by means of two long quivering feathers and the angle they make. . . ."

He is the finest of our great sea-birds; I awaited him at the end of my poem:
". . . He comes, he stays aloft for more than a day; he is alone, he stays

in the country of soul-stirring expanses, there where dawn is duration and space, a habitable country. . . .

None knows better how to use the rose of the winds.

*With his own head—it is easy—he determines his
route; he has made his the secret of the fault along
which the roadway lies, and now it is his turn to yield;
and on nonpareil wing never bent like a finger, even at
its tip, my friend seeks his fortune!"*

*Or else the air is emptiness, and I have seen his wrath
struggling against absence.*

*. . . Even better, he rides the wind, and it is fine to see
how expertly and cleverly he knows how to rise against
the wind. . . .*

Never does he resort to a wingstroke,

*but drifting toward our islands, along a safe cleavage
in the air, he glides, with consummate ease, over the
smooth layers of space,*

and veering on his curve into pleasure's widest arena,

*he approaches the ship in full sail in a leisurely way—
and everyone is on deck: the sailmaster, the ship's monkey, and the black cook;*

*he approaches the semaphore on the cape in a leisurely
way—and everyone comes to the door, with the goat, the
yellow dog, the tame gull, and the domestic fowl;*

*he approaches the Governor's mansion in a leisurely
way—and everyone is on the terrace near the flagpole:
the white women, the prelates, the admirals in white
duck, the white-helmeted guard on duty, the servants
in white surah, and the child who is master of a piebald
pony with red and white spots,*

*and suddenly this cry, this cry in chorus: "He has seen
us!"*

*His presence betrayed by a continuous whistling sound,
feathers tightly inlaid, and the neck frenzied, he goes by,
quivering like a hurled weapon. It is he; I hear him and
am filled with his strange vibration! . . . In the country*

of soul-stirring expanses, he goes by, visited by terrible delight. . . . He vibrates along the whole length of his iron wand. The wind's hearty laughter carries him out to the open sea,

and you yourself, O Teller of Tales! coming to the end of your recital!—with the onrush of your speech and the migration of words, with your host of living people, with your shock-troops, ah! the whole onrush of your legions, ah! the whole onrush of your season, and suddenly, the beauty of the word "cohort"! . . .

These are the Birds—unslaked, unenslaved—that I have praised. I could tell you the plumage of each; I have seen it.

By chance, it may happen
that a stray, if
his territory is on other Waters,

will come to us in heavy weather, violently torn away from his proper place. I look him straight in the eye: I've never seen him before.

Saint-Leger Leger
1907

1. This was the manuscript of a poem entitled "Pour fêter des oiseaux," which was an abridged version of a longer poem in manuscript entitled "Cohorte." Gide had "Pour fêter des oiseaux" printed in the NRF without AL's knowledge. When, to his surprise, AL received the proofs of the text for correction, he appealed to Gide to withdraw the poem, even though it had already been set up in print. Gide was able to get AL's request granted. The famous thank-you letters to Gide of April 1911 (96, 97) were for this favor, and not, as is usually thought, for the special edition of *Eloges* paid for by Gide some months later. See letter 97, note 1. A translation of the original complete text, "Cohorte," immediately follows the letter. For the French text of the poem, see below, note 4.

2. The "Gauguin-like poem" remains unidentified.

3. See above, letter 24, note 3.

4. The original French version reads as follows:

COHORTE

Innumerae comitantur aves, stipatque vo-
[lantum
Alituum suspensa cohors...

CLAUDIUS CLAUDIANUS.

Nous en parlions sur les vaisseaux et sur les vérandas désertes,
non loin des îles basses, très poreuses, et des rives croulantes où
la mer roule en maugréant ses poupées de corail:

Oiseaux! Oiseaux! de toutes sectes et de tous clans! pélagiens
ou ripuaires, familiers ou nomades, faméliques d'un soir et
fanatiques à l'année, très grand peuple d'élus!

Ils s'en venaient, l'aile tranchante et brève et la livrée très
sobre, le bec tragique enté dans l'étroitesse du masque...ah! s'en
venaient et s'en venaient, peuple d'élus,

par grandes confréries guerrières et comme saintes herman-
dades, ça! plus prolixes et vains qu'aucune souche d'ancêtres, ça!
plus aventureux et vains

que cadets de famille et gentilshommes de fortune: Oiseaux!
Oiseaux! hôtes d'un jour dans l'avant-soir. — Et nous voici
debout sur les vaisseaux et sur les vérandas de bois,

et repoussant nos sièges de rotin, le verre en main, le cri aux
lèvres, au claquement soudain de l'alizé dans la toile des tentes,
nous portant tous aux lisses et rambardes,

nous vous hélions, Passants, et vous nommions! vous appe-
lions tout haut de vos noms de toujours et de vos noms d'ailleurs.
Ou vous nommions, soudain! d'un nom nouveau, plus vrai que
chez les Doctes.

Dix noms, vingt noms jetés par-dessus bord, comme aux
valets de chiens pour le baptême de la meute! ... Ah ça! nous
direz-vous le vrai de votre appellation? parcelles vives arra-
chées au tout de l'Innommé...

Et l'aile qui battait en nous, et s'affolait pour nous aux toiles
de la tente (le fou de Dieu soit avec nous!) ne nous laissait de
cesse ni patience que nous n'eussions trouvé le nom nouveau!

Nommer, créer! Qui donc en nous créait, criant le nom
nouveau? Langage aux fourches du langage...montées d'abîme
pétillant parmi les poches de sel bleu... (le fou de Dieu soit avec
nous!)

Ainsi l'enfance trépignant sur sa haute chaise de famille!

Ainsi l'enfance en nous promue à sa plus haute vocation, qui toujours fut celle de nommer,

et la parole en nous haletante aux pièges et fourches du langage, comme la flamme en jupon vert du spectre aux grandes bassines de rhum blanc.

Autant en emporte le soir, autant en dissipe le songe d'une nuit d'homme: ciel repeuplé! ciel de semailles! dissipation sans fin du dieu, et la chose même dispensée aux quatre vans du ciel...

Et ce n'est point trafic d'épices ni d'étoffes, cauris sur tables de comptoirs ni gommes de Sénégambie, mais commerce de vivants et vivant numéraire,

Oiseaux! oiseaux, du plus long cours et du plus long débours! peuple d'errants, peuple d'élus! ... Le ciel, la mer nous en tienne le compte,

et fou de Dieu qui nous l'épelle!

Nous commençons par celui-là: « Phaeton Ethéré » (et le nom vieux lui soit laissé!),

Prince d'une ère de féerie, mime de grâce seigneuriale, et le plus affublé des Oiseaux de haut vol, l'Ethéré vit son nom. Son affaire n'est point la couvée, mais le vol, et d'aller! ô d'aller... comme celui qui dit d'une œuvre et de soi-même: je n'ai plus soin de vous... et d'aller, et d'aller, ô chair insigne, la plus pauvre

en huile, et qui l'invoque en couches minces sur l'ossement dièdre du sternum...

Vous l'avez reconnu: c'est « l'Oiseau des Tropiques », et le plus aérien de nos oiseaux de mer (seul à ramer de l'aile comme un ramier des Iles). On ne pèserait moins qu'en songe: masse d'essence lumineuse, spectre greffé de plume et d'os. La coiffe est de faille blanche et l'œil barré d'un trait de laque, la mante de satin blanc pailletée de minces croissants noirs; le tout lavé de rose pâle saumoné et la queue s'effilant en merveille, les deux rectrices médianes à la traîne comme deux brins de paille fraîche, jaune ou blanche. Plumes extrêmes, et qui l'excèdent: elles croisent au repos, il n'en sait plus que faire, et c'est un luxe!... Ah! celui-là peut perdre de sa plume. — Je prends parti pour celui-là!

De la même famille est l' « Anchise » (nom d'emprunt), qui fait son nid de trois cailloux et d'un éclat de bois. Amant des îles désertiques plus ébréchées qu'une crête de grand fossile, ce n'est pas, il s'en faut, le plus chaste... Mais le

« Bilimbe » aux yeux de femme, le doux longeur de rives

sous-le-vent, s'il ignore de couver, s'abîme dans le jeûne et l'idée de la ponte... Et le « Minime » pond

sur les îles sonores; là vit en société. Nous armons un canot en partie de plaisir: voici un plein panier de ces œufs verts tachés de roux — le goût est de noisette.

Le « Dadou » a pour lui une bonne mémoire: il nous revient avant les pluies; il reconnaît son île entre cent autres, entre mille son nid — fourbe aux nichées du voisinage.

Un vieil oiseau des Mers du Sud qui peint sa nuque de can-nelle — gorge et lores d'un beau noir, l'aile rougeâtre à baguettes blanches bordées de mèches chamoisées — est bien le plus écervelé qu'on ait pu rencontrer. « Je t'avais laissé là, campeur de haute mer, et cette saison encore est la tienne, en cet autre parage et même lieu de sargasses!... » Peut-être sa mémoire n'est-elle qu'un pur grésil où des verges s'ébrouent parmi l'ivresse de l'écume. — Envie-le.

On compte plusieurs espèces de Crabiers, également remar-quables par les plumes du dos. Les Squas, les Labbes sont connus, les Jaegers et Sulas et les Chatharactas... Il est d'usage de citer l'Albatros. Nous n'avons point d'égard pour celui-là. C'est le plus grand de nos Oiseaux de Mer, et il est bête. On le prend à l'hameçon, comme l'Outarde en temps de neige aux plaines d'Ancien Monde. — L'Albatros est vorace et ne pond qu'un seul œuf. (Nid d'herbage pétri de terre et d'excrément.)

Un grand Pétrel de mer australe remonte un soir jusque vers nous. C'est le Voyer des mers fluentes, soulevées du ferment des pourritures obèses, charriées... Il s'en prend à qui meurt; il s'empêtre du bec dans la charogne du cétacé; il fait ventre du mou, du puant et du chaud. Sa besogne? — délier!... Il s'écla-bousse de sanie, ah! c'est une frénésie des tarses et de l'aile, ah! comme une fête de démence, et qui fait chavirer l'enfance de son œil...

Du Nord, un « Abraha » descend à la faveur d'un courant frais: la tête encore ceinte de l'étincellement des glaces, l'oiseau balourd, outré de plume, engraissé de flétans, échoue aux plaines lisses de nos mers, dans l'avant-soir pareil à de la chair de sau-mon frais; là, silencieux, il tire des eaux lasses un étonnant poisson, noir et touffu comme un chabot d'eau douce. On le lui prend au bec! — Car j'oubliais de vous citer

l'effronterie d'une mouette pillarde: le Stercoraire qui vit de l'attaque et du rapt.

(Un autre est couard: cruel au congre inerme, il prend peur d'un poisson qui ouvre une aile brusque.)

Le « Krahak » à grande poche gutturale et face de peau bleue grenue (crête frisée à l'occiput et l'iris jaune usé comme du vieil or d'église), de sa haute carène carrossée en forme de traîneau rustique ou de berceau de pauvre, ne fait point que pêcher: il s'éprend, l'aile ferlée, de dériver sur l'eau tout un jour et une nuit: il est aise, il est quitte, il flotte et s'enfle sous sa plume, la tête reposant sur une anse du col — A l'aube, une île est proche sous les palétuviers.

Et d'autres vont, les pattes longues sur l'eau rousse, comme les maringouins au-dessus de nos mares... D'autres attendent dans les ports le bateau qui relâche, et qu'on leur jette à la volée tout un paquet d'entrailles avariées — Fou qui les veut compter! plus nombreux qu'on n'a vu
ces Oiseaux de l'Islam qui assaillaient un soir l'armée du Prince d'Éthiopie!

...Et nous, que savons-nous des Sternes, menu peuple? — qu'aux rives calcinées elles tiennent diète tout un mois. Grand bien leur fasse! Mais le « Cobre » voilier, le « Corale » des lagons,
friands de l'ambigu, choisissent de frayer aux bouches des rivières. A deux jours de la terre ils poussent leur cri d'itinérants; et peut-être qu'alors
la soyeuse femelle, éprouvant à ses flancs le ferment de l'ovule, commence de songer aux flaques pacifiées, à l'eau douce des mares retranchées de la mer, où va le mâle plein de science tresser son nid flottant.

Pareilles sont les mœurs du « Sourcilleux », très lent, et qui voyage en foule, par tribus et cohortes. Il survole de nuit le spectre d'un grand fleuve bossué de bêtes et d'ordures, et s'affalant soudain, avec le jour, fait voler en éclats l'ardoise d'un grand lac.

L' « Ayaya » a le bec en spatule... O tiédeurs sous la vase, confidence des fanges!... Pour venir jusqu'à nous, il discerne sans méprise un vent qui soufflera six jours; s'y confie; tombe si las en vue des côtes que nous ramons vers lui et il se laisse prendre.

Un autre migrateur, dont le nez fait saillie sur le bec en naseaux tubulaires, abrite, bien qu'il plonge, au plus fin de sa plume un insecte bleu cuivre.

Et voici les Côtiers, familiers de la roche et fouetteurs de falaises. Le « Mâle-Fini », aigle pêcheur, que l'on appelle aussi « Pygargue », fait choix du plus haut site en vue de mer foraine. Il vire en cercles sur la rade; elle est franche, il s'abat — l'eau est plus noire ici.

Cette Orfraie n'est pas seule à choisir le poisson par la main: une sorte de « Pèque » (les autres sont palmées) nous arrive de l'Ouest, et en vue de nos cayes délie son libre doigt — le poisson est plus prompt par ici.

L'aventureux « Vindi » s'élève des forêts. Encore qu'il soit pêcheur, il sent mauvais sur l'aire comme une bouche de carnassier. Je l'ai vu s'avancer sur nos terres, menace pour l'iguane et pour l'armadillo.

Deux mots sur le « Pitul », géant de nos plus hauts récifs: il a ce bec corné, renforcé d'un ergot, qui le fait appeler « Briseur-d'os ».

L' « Arinaire », ô futile! n'est que ce tourne-pierre, tu l'as vu, qui, mobile, inquiet, prend souci sur nos grèves par temps de basse mer. Il sait qu'aux îles d'où je parle, un vieil arbre de peau verte, à tannin rouge, est chargé d'huîtres comme d'ouïes; et qu'au biais de l'épave on trouve le gland-de-mer...

Mais trêve à toutes préséances et place au Maître de céans!

Voici, voici qui ne fut point, qui ne sera point nommé, celui pour nous qui toujours fut, et sera, « l'Innommé »! (pour d'autres, la « Frégate-Aigle » ou « Frégata Magnificens »).

C'est le plus fier apanagé de nos Seigneurs de mer: Connétable d'Empire et Prévôt d'Outre-mer, Pirate fait Commodore et Commissaire des Îles, Condottiere de Dieu dans ses plus vieilles Marches et Provinces maritimes...

Veuille celui-là nous dispenser le ton de ses hautes façons: l'aile acérée en cimeterre et l'envergure immense de son autorité — arrogance souveraine du vol sous l'immobilité du geste.

Tout-puissant Gouverneur des Vignes océanes, Régisseur et Régent d'une Inde fabuleuse, il tire honneur et jouissance d'épouser tour à tour, sur deux versants du ciel, les deux alcôves d'un même dais. Il ne vit que sur l'aile et tient l'air tout le jour, l'aile immuable et la queue libre, suraiguë, qu'il effile ou qu'il ouvre, à sa guise.

Ainsi va-t-il à son plus long plaisir, vêtu de lustre noir à reflets verts, ou bleu de pourpre, métallique, et le jabot, rouge lubrique, qui s'enfle au souffle du désir.

C'est le meilleur de nos voiliers, j'attendais d'en parler:

« ... *Il vient, il vient, de contrées incertaines, et silencieux s'élève, avec le jour, d'une île très lointaine, étrangère à tout nom. Il vient par le canal des grandes voies célestes, surchauffées; il s'appuie sur le Sud éblouissant et calme, et à mesure qu'il descend et reconnaît l'usage des paupières, assailli des plus purs sévices de la gloire, voici*

qu'il ressent fondre, au plus tiède et secret des eaux lisses du ciel, comme un fixe tourment qui trouverait ses larmes...

Ou bien s'inquiète de sa puissance, et sa queue, très fourchue, par deux longues plumes vives et leur angle, docile, prend conscience dans le vent... »

C'est le meilleur de nos voiliers, je l'attendais au bout de mon poème:

« ... *Il vient, il tient l'air plus d'un jour; il est seul, il se tient*

au pays d'émouvante largeur, là où l'aube est durée, et l'espace, contrée...

Nul ne sait mieux s'aider de la rose des vents.

De sa tête, facile, il invente sa route: il a séduit la faille du chemin; à son tour d'y céder; et d'une aile émérite et dont le bout jamais ne se recourbe comme un doigt, mon ami tente sa fortune! »

... *Ou bien l'air est vacance, et j'ai vu son courroux en lutte contre l'absence.*

... *Ou mieux, il vente, et il est beau de voir*

comme savant et plein de ruse il sait monter contre le vent...

Jamais il n'userait du battement de son aile,

mais dérivant jusqu'à nos îles à la faveur d'un sûr clivage, il glisse, à très grande aise, aux couches lisses de l'espace,

et virant sur sa courbe au plus grand cirque du plaisir,

il s'approche à loisir du navire sous voiles—et tout le monde est sur le pont, le maître-voilier, le singe du bord et le cuisinier noir;

il s'approche à loisir du sémaphore sur le cap — et tout le monde est sur le seuil, avec la chèvre, le chien jaune, le goéland apprivoisé et la volaille domestique;

il s'approche à loisir de la maison du Gouverneur—et tout le monde est aux terrasses, auprès du mât de pavillon, les femmes blanches, les prélats, les amiraux en toile blanche, le factionnaire

*casqué de blanc, les domestiques en surah blanc et l'enfant maître
d'un poney pie, taché de rouge et blanc,
    et soudain, là! ce cri, ce cri de tous: « Il nous a vus! »...*

*Ainsi trahi du sifflement qui dure, la plume étroitement sertie
et le col frénétique, il passe, frémissant, comme une arme de jet,
et c'est lui, je l'entends, plein de sa vibration étrange!... Au pays
d'émouvante largeur, il passe, fréquenté du terrible délice... Il
vibre tout au long de sa tige de fer... Le plein rire du vent l'emporte à ses eaux libres,
    et toi-même, ô Conteur! courant la fin de ton récit! — avec
l'afflux de ta parole et la migration des mots, avec ton peuple
de vivants, avec ton peuple d'assaillants, ah! tout l'afflux de tes
légions, ah! tout l'afflux de ta saison, et la beauté, soudain, du
mot: « cohorte »!...*

*Inassouvis, inasservis, j'ai loué ces Oiseaux. Je dirais la livrée de
chacun: je l'ai vue.*

*De fortune il arrive
qu'un étranger, s'il a
sur d'autres Eaux son aire d'évolution, nous arrive par gros
temps, disputé violemment à son lieu. Je le regarde au nez: je
ne l'ai jamais vie.*

SAINT-LEGER LEGER.

1907.

5. The Latin epigraph, meaning "Innumerable birds accompany
his flight and form a cohort suspended in the air. . . ." is taken
from a poem about the Phoenix by the late classical Latin poet,
Claudius Claudianus, active at the end of the fourth century.
The Koch edition (1893) of the *Carmina* gives a slightly different reading:

> Innumerae comitantur aves stipatque volantem
> Alituum suspensa cohors. . . .

6. The names in this "enumeration of sea birds" are of three
sorts: (1) scientific, (2) popular, and (3) purely fictive. Sometimes both the scientific and popular names are given, as in the
case of the Ethereal Phaeton (*Phaethon aethereus*), which is also
referred to by its popular name of Tropic Bird. In either instance,
the bird is easily identifiable. That is not true of the birds for
which AL coined names of his own, though all the birds mentioned are real ones AL had actually seen in the Antilles. In a
letter to Valery Larbaud dated Dec. 1911 (128), AL writes

that this text "would have struck me as the outpouring of some ornithological crank or pedant, if most of these birds had not received from me, without any deception on my part, the baptism of their names. Yet I was thoroughly familiar with all of them, with the real birds as well as with their scientific nomenclature and classification."

The names that AL himself coined include: Bilimbe, Minime, Dadou, Abraha, Krahak, Cobre, Corale, Sourcilleux, Pèque, Vindi, Pitul, and—in another poem, "Pour fêter une enfance"— the Annaô (128). In many instances, the particularities of the fictively named bird are so clearly stated that it should not be too difficult for a qualified ornithologist to identify some of them. See also the letter to Frizeau of 30 Apr. 1911. (80)

7. In the "Elephant Sura" of the *Koran* (traditionally Sura 105) there is an allusion to an army sent by the prince of Ethiopia against Mecca. Referring to the Almighty's intervention, the *Koran* says:

Did he not hurl flights of birds against them who threw claystones at them . . . ?

These birds, in some translations of the *Koran*, are called "Ababils," and AL, referring to them many years later in his poem "Oiseaux" (1962), uses that name: ". . . ces oiseaux Ababils dont il est fait mention au livre de Mahomet" (canto xii) [". . . those Ababil birds mentioned in the book of Mohammed." (Fitzgerald trans.)]

Blachère, in his French translation of the *Koran* (1949) has the following note on the passage in question:

ṭ ayran 'abàbîla—"des oiseaux par vols." Ce second mot arabe est un thème de pluriel. Comme le sens n'en est pas sûr et que le terme est rare, K[azimirski] et M[ontet] y voient un nom propre. (*Le Coran*, vol. 2, p. 115.)

AL very probably had read one of the editions of the Kazimirski translation—Montet's was not published until 1929—in which there appears:

N'a-t-il [le Seigneur] pas envoyé contre eux les oiseaux ababils, . . . (*Le Koran*, trad. par Kasimirski, ed. de 1844.)

26

To Monsieur Jacques Rivière   *Pau, April 30, 1911*
15, rue Froidevaux
Paris

My friend,

You will recognize true friendship in this: I can't manage to write you. One has to sit down at a table. It's too easy. . . . I would do that for others.

My affection for you is something ever-present.

[. . .] There is no time that is really long. There is only one day to a year, one year to a lifetime,[1] and this single, terrible pursuit of *being*: a pursuit I want always to enjoy.

[. . .] I admire how courageous and free of all negligence your life is. Tell me what you are doing now. I have put my faith in you. I have read everything you have published in the *Nlle R.F.* Many issues of it are cut only where your name appears. [. . .] I ought to have told you right away what gave me special "pleasure." I can think of only one thing that annoyed me, a rare word, "*alliciantes*,"[2] in the pages you devote to *Tristan*.

I pay the closest attention to everything you tell me about your literary torments. Ah, my friend, you are going to suffer! You'll have no more respite, nor pure joy in just being you. You have been poisoned—forever discontented and at odds with yourself. . . . eager to be reassured—for henceforward you live with that fear, the most "obsequious" and grotesque of fears—the fear of not acquitting oneself well. My eye goes straight to what you analyze so well, literarily: "At every moment it seems to me that everything is senseless!"

You insist that I read Dostoievsky. I feel hostile without even knowing him. Tell me which is the best translation. I insist on it now. I hope he's as far removed as possible from all that Russian Christianity I so loathe. Excuse me. I read Tolstoy one day—a most unpleasant memory.

No, Rivière, I never for a moment doubted that the work of Bach was in your eyes a powerful aid in keeping us alive and healthy. To the first three Brandenburg concertos can be limited much of the joy—and a formidable joy it is—that the Occident has given to the world.

If you run into Monod, tell him that I ask him quite simply to return only the Jammes and the Elskamp[3] from among the books that he made off with last November—because they weren't mine; I filched them from one of my sisters for him. He may keep my Locke, my Alexandrians, but not Philo. Have him send back my Hegel, too.

What else is there to tell you that may be told? I heard the *Saint John's Passion*[4] again and reread Archilochus.[5]

And maybe I should go on to tell you, just as I am about to close, that there have been times when I hated your ideas because they are a last tie still linking me to art [. . .]. Perhaps you think I can strike some sort of balance. Yet I live far from everyone, as simply as I can, and as immediately or strictly as I can. And with no other concern, once I have taken care of my family, than to indulge in any excess but that of making my life an "act." And when it happens, as it did recently, that someone passes through and talks to me about art, I feel vaguely annoyed with him without really knowing why, [. . .].

Yes, I did withdraw from the *N.R.F.* the poem[6] that had been printed in it, unknown to me, in this month's issue [. . .]. The whole thing bores me, when all is said and done. I have no intention of hunting up something else for the Review to take the place of the manuscript that I had to withdraw. Besides, at the moment I'm swamped preparing for examinations. So tell Gide, when you see him, that it would be best for him not to publish any more of the other manuscripts he has on hand. Say that I simply "gave" him, as a personal gesture, the final *Eloges* that he got from me. Nor will I remind him of the printing in book form that he so kindly spoke about.

All this annoys me without my knowing exactly why. Maybe it's uneasiness about a literary commitment. Yes, that's it.

But tell Gide, on the same occasion, that his kindness has always touched me deeply, more than I'll ever be able to tell him. Besides, Gide wrote me the one thing in the world that could make me even more attached to him than I am: he said that his affection for you keeps growing. Although I have never met him, I know that I will always remember him in a very personal way when I have left France.

Tell me all about yourself, my friend, about your life, your work.

Don't scold me for not knowing what I want, but only for not knowing what gives me "pleasure" (if you can excuse me for always wanting to limit everything to that word, in spite of all the ways it is misused!).

And tell me—it would make me so happy—that maybe I'll see you down here this summer, where I am not likely to be by the summer of next year [. . .].

Yours, from the heart.   A.S.L.

1. The "one long day" formula, which occurs here for the first time, became a favorite one of AL's when seeking to excuse a long silence. See letters to Monod (1-16, 183), to Rivière (17-49, 184), to Gide (93-120, 186, 291-301).

2. In the magazine printing of Rivière's article on Wagner's

Tristan und Isolde (NRF, Jan. 1911), he speaks of the musical phrase thus: "Elle est faite de flammes soumises, alliciantes . . ." (p. 29). Rivière seems to have taken AL's comment seriously, as the word "alliciantes" does not occur in the text of the article as printed in the book *Etudes* (p. 144). The word is derived from the Latin *allictens*, "enticing."

3. One cannot be sure which books by Francis Jammes and by the Belgian symbolist poet, Max Elskamp (1862-1931), are here referred to.

4. Of Johann Sebastian Bach.

5. Archilochus (712-644 B.C.), Greek lyric poet, author of *Iambics*.

6. "Cohorte." (25)

27

To Monsieur Jacques Rivière   *Pau, Wednesday*
15, rue Froidevaux   [*May 10, 1911*]
Paris (14e)

My friend, how close to you I feel, and how moved I am, all smiles, by the news that you imparted only at the close of your letter—a little child, a little bit of man. . . . Yes, indeed, your life may be radically changed now, and greatly enriched. Please transmit all my best wishes to Madame Rivière [. . .].

I shall think of you most warmly in September, and from now until then.

Heartfelt wishes. I clasp your hand.   L.

I was going to write you a few lines to talk to you about your piece in the last issue of the *N.R.F.*[1] I read it first for what it said, and then looked for you in it. What a joy it is for me to follow this ascending progress. Joy in the thought that my confidence will continue to increase where I have already bestowed my affection.

You are visibly divesting yourself of non-essentials, your language is more and more naked, achieving the leanness that confers authority. And without losing any of that inner urgency or that intimate inventiveness (if only we could say "ventilate-iveness!") which, even as each idea takes shape, remains the essential mystery of artistic intelligence—you now give us an immediately achieved whole, rather than a succession of discoveries. And what a wonderful thing a "final resolution" is in art (without in any way excluding further development)! One can even add to the word its chemical meaning: a precipitate. In the people I like, what pleases me more than anything else is the cruel inflexibility that precludes elaboration, which is downright cowardice that implies something more than just "letting one's self go" —something that may turn out to be the vice of great "artists" like Suarès.[2]

It makes me so happy, my friend, to be able to write to you this way. I still had in mind a page about Moussorgsky[3] that was over-written, that was rather embarrassing in its outpouring of explanations. There, it seemed to me that you occasionally did beauty the disservice of glutting it.

Tell me about your novel.[4] I am eager to read a work that you are so keen about. If the article on Gide appears in some other review than the N.R.F., please send it to me.

I am your affectionate friend.   Leger

1. Probably "Reprise de *Pelléas et Mélisande* à l'Opéra Comique," in NRF, Apr. 1911.

2. André Suarès (1868-1948), French essayist and critic.

3. "Moussorgski," NRF, Feb. 1911; reprinted in Rivière *Etudes*, pp. 167-172.

4. Unidentified. One can only say, negatively, that it was not *Aimée*, Rivière's only complete novel, written in captivity in 1915-1916 and published in 1922, nor the fragment, *Florence*, on which Rivière was working at the time of his death in 1925.

28

To Monsieur Jacques Rivière   *Pau, Friday*
15, rue Froidevaux   [*June 2, 1911*]
Paris (14e)

My friend,

Later on I'll speak about your "Ingres",[1] when I've read it a second time—and when I am able to look at that issue of the *N.R.F.* without getting angry. [. . .]

Even though I thought I was completely detached, when I glanced at the first insane page[2] printed there above my name, I wanted to shriek like a child. No, I'll never forget the low trick that has been played on me, in this magazine for stupid pedants, put out by people who are so ill-bred they allowed publication of a manuscript of over twenty pages without so much as looking at my proofs, which I corrected and carefully sent back, by registered mail, within the three days allowed. If these people have no compunction about making a contributor look ridiculous, at least politeness to the readers (and I'm one of them, since I'm a subscriber) might have kept them from insolently serving up to us pages that only someone out of his mind could have written. Last year they told me that I was the cause of subscriptions being canceled. I didn't believe it; but this time I'm sure of at least one canceled subscription—my own.

I hardly need add that I don't hold Gide in any way responsible. Please tell him that I hold nothing against him. Nothing will ever make me involve the name of Gide in such a "mess."

If I didn't prefer never to hear of the *N.R.F.* again, I would demand a full listing of errata at the end of the next issue, along with a full correct printing of the liminary poem. That is strictly my right. And that's why I won't avail myself of it [. . .].

Three days ago I wrote to Verbecke, and I'm waiting to hear what his conditions are for printing the text in a separate booklet—at my own expense—so I'd be exonerated in the eyes of a few of my friends. My intention is not to add anything else at all from among my manuscripts, except for reprinting, if Verbecke's conditions allow it, two of the *Eloges* (the first and the last) submitted to that Review last year.

That will make a booklet of some fifty-five pages, which I'll have to have printed in a very limited quantity, since Verbecke is not a book publisher. It will be something clandestine, stored at my house, not for sale commercially; and it will end up—if I don't use them all up right away for my friends (a short list!)—in my cellar.

I can think of only a few immediate friends. For those beyond my reach, well, it's just too bad. I'm not going to put myself out. But just to think of all those who, seeing my name, will carry away the impression of all the extravagances and mad nonsense that the *N.R.F.* attributes to me—ah, that alone is enough to make me more disgusted than ever at the thought of publishing [. . .].

Excuse me. Let's talk about something else.

This is not an answer to your letter, which I very much enjoyed. And here are still more wishes for Mme. Rivière. And I've asked one of my sisters to embroider something for my friend's child. She is happy to do it. She herself tells me so. I thank her for that. [. . .]

My heartfelt wishes are with you.   Leger

Claudel has sent me the new edition of his *Tête d'or* and his *Propositions sur la Justice*, put out by "L'Indépendance."[3] Do you know if he's already returned to France?

1. "Ingres," NRF, June 1911; reprinted in Rivière, *Etudes*, pp. 35-40.

2. The May 1911 issue of the NRF contained the first printing of eighteen poems by AL collectively entitled "Eloges." The text is full of egregious typographical errors—a circumstance that produced the violent reaction expressed by AL in this and subsequent letters. See those to Claudel of 1 June 1911 (60), to Gide of 1 June 1911 (100), to Jammes of June 1911 (88). The incident was to have a good many repercussions. It is now possible to reconstruct fairly completely the sequence of events leading up to and following the publication of this first defective text. AL, earlier in 1911, had sent a handwritten manuscript of the eighteen "Eloges," later renumbered to make a series of only sixteen, to André Gide for publication in the NRF. "Images à Crusoé" had appeared already in the Aug. 1909 issue of the NRF, as well as several other poems by AL in the Apr. 1910 issue of the NRF ("Ecrit sur la Porte," "Pour fêter une enfance," "Récitation à l'éloge d'une reine," "Histoire du Régent"). All these poems, including the eighteen "Eloges," appeared over the name "Saint-Leger Leger."

André Gide himself, almost forty years later, gave an account of what happened after he had received AL's manuscript:

I have before my eyes the very precious manuscript of those first poems. The handwriting is as disconcerting as the text. In those days we didn't attach such great value to autograph texts; often we simply let the printer keep them without bothering about what might become of them. They were promptly replaced by galley-proofs and page-proofs which became the author's only concern. But the handwritten pages Leger had sent to me struck me, quite apart from their content but simply in themselves, as so beautiful that I just couldn't bear to part with them. I decided to send only a copy of them to the printer. So the first thing to be done was to have a copy made by an ill-starred secretary—a deplorable bit of imprudence, since the secretary in question was quite impervious to Leger's charm. I didn't realize this until later—much too much later, alas! Frightful "typos" disfigured the text of *Eloges* in that first printing in the NRF. I felt personally responsible for these errors; I should have kept a closer watch on things. I could recover peace of mind only by proposing to Leger that I assume all the costs of a special separate printing of the text. I've saved all of Leger's letters: numerous are those concerning this friendly act of reparation. (Gide, "Don d'un arbre," in *Cahiers de la Pléiade*, Summer-Autumn 1950, pp. 24-25.)

(The letters Gide refers to form part of the present selection. See pp. 199-207.)

The special edition in book form was printed by the NRF later in the summer of 1911 under the title *Eloges*; but it included, in addition to the eighteen "Eloges," all the poems previously printed in the Aug. 1909 and Apr. 1910 issues of the NRF. (See above.) The edition bore the name "Saintleger Leger," but only on its title page, not on its cover.

3. This prose piece, dated "Prague 1910," was first published by *L'Indépendance* in 1911 (with the note: "Marcel Rivière pour M. Paul Claudel"). It was reprinted much later—in 1934—in *Positions et Propositions II*, pp. 37-44, which contains the additional note, in French: "After reading Proudhon's book, *De la Justice dans la Révolution et dans l'Eglise*." (p. 37).

29

To Monsieur Jacques Rivière   *Pau, Wednesday*
15, rue Froidevaux   *[June 14, 1911]*
Paris

My friend,

How can you say such things to me? And how can you, of all people, have the least fear of having displeased me in any way in all this business with your friends of the *N.R.F.*? [. . .] Please spare yourself such misgivings [. . .]. I've already felt so bad about all the trouble I've caused you over it; I feel that deeply. And you'll never know how annoyed I am with myself for having momentarily lost my self-control to the point of having written to you as I did. You must certainly think I set great store by those poems! Yet I can assure you that I now scarcely think at all about the misadventure.

If I haven't written to you, that is because, first of all, I had to be away (registration at Bordeaux); second, because you must picture me with my head buried deep in preparations for my law exams for at least another month. I've discovered I'm way behind (one is always

behind in that pernicious school of inaccuracy known
as an examination).

I would have preferred to put off a little longer talking
to you about what you wrote on Ingres,[1] so great is my
fear that you might take my spontaneous appraisal as an
exchange of compliments. The beauty of those six pages,
the severity of the first few, were brought off the way
Ingres himself might have done it. Above and beyond
the intelligence exhibited in your study, I like its sense
of neatness and propriety—yes, propriety—and, in places,
that sense of what is definitive, which helps us to understand what Ingres discovered and captured in his work:
that very presentation of figures within definite limits
that constitutes Ingres' absolute, his "geometry" or "geog-
raphy," his "living" style. For his art makes one think,
at the end of a long afternoon, of the early *sententiae*—
of Solon!

But how wonderful it is; I mean, how good it is, my
friend, that at your age you have hit upon phrases that
sum up all Art, phrases that "take the place of all the
rest": ". . . With a passionate sureness and sublime sense
of choice, replacing the object at one stroke. . . ."[2] Intuition has perhaps never produced, in criticism, brief
statements so far-reaching and so general in their appli-
cation.

I must leave you. . . . At the moment I'm working at
changing my handwriting,[3] so that nothing about me,
even at first glance, may make me appear peculiar. (And
then, I'll be called on to take several competitive examinations.) But for the time being, this makes my hand
hurt quite a bit [. . .].

—I'm eager to read your study of Gide, who is so hard
to pin down that, I imagine, you have given up any
thought of a synthetic presentation (the very expression
is such an insult to someone who is really alive!). Yes,

Gide must occupy a very important place in the work you are preparing, for he is certainly the person who, one day, will show up as the truly "French" figure of his period, when people have come to realize what little bits of dry wood the mime Barrès is made of, and what limp bits of nansouk Anatole France is made of. (But it's Barrès who breaks all records at self-deception.)

Since I've mentioned Gide, I must confess to you how very embarrassed I am about his last two letters. I tell you this quite openly. Now he's talking about a book edition of *Eloges* at *his* expense, whereas, up to now, I'd understood it was "at the expense of the *N.R.F.*" (Verbecke having notified me textually that this was the case, citing a letter from Jean Schlumberger, and Gide himself having at first used the expression "at our expense.") So now what am I to understand, and how can I ask questions about all this? Is Gide speaking for the *N.R.F.*, or is he speaking for himself? Could *you* find out the answers for me? Please do. Please be understanding and don't be hard on me. It's an entirely different matter, letting a review—which was responsible, and did wrong by me in doing wrong by itself, a review, moreover, that doesn't pay its contributors—pay these costs and, on the other hand, letting a private party defray them—a private party who, besides, was in no way responsible for the mishap. You can't imagine how intolerably embarrassed I am right now. (Please understand that all this has nothing to do with presumptuousness.)

And in addition, how can I go counter to all the agreements that have been made with Verbecke? Or just how is one to talk to Gide about all this without fear of hurting such rare considerateness?

I'll never extricate myself from such an embarrassing situation. Please advise me about it, if you can.

Yours.   Leger

1. See above, letter 28, note 1.

2. The quotation is from the closing sentence of Rivière's piece on Ingres, which reads in English translation: "Indeed, it is not with painstaking patience, point by point, that Ingres pins down the movement of the bodies and the object that he is painting; instead, with one stroke, passionately decisive and unerringly sublime, he catches the movement."

3. AL's handwriting up to this time had been small and vertical and not easily legible. Realizing the disadvantages this might present in his various written examinations—especially the big competitive examination for entry into the Foreign Service —AL went to work methodically reforming his handwriting, soon achieving the large flowing, sloping hand which became his hallmark. See handwriting samples, pp. xx-xxi.

30

To Monsieur Jacques Rivière   *Pau, June 23, 1911*
15, rue Froidevaux
Paris

My friend, you'd be doing me a great favor by letting me see a picture of André Gide, if that is possible. I'd send it back to you by return mail. That would be very helpful to me when I do or do not accept what he wants to do for me, at his own expense, at the *N.R.F.* publications. I simply have to know what a man looks like when I have to deal with him about anything at all.

In haste.

Yours.   Leger

31

To Monsieur Jacques Rivière   *Pau, August 8* [*1911*]
15, rue Froidevaux
Paris, 14

My friend,

I've been away—at La Rochelle with one of my sisters [. . .]. I just got back to Pau, where I'm going to join the rest of the family in the mountains. Your letter is on my desk. And this is not an answer, but just a hastily written note to ask you to please let me know how you came out on your *agrégation*[1] [. . .].

In haste, most cordially.   Leger

Excuse me for the matter of the little volume of *Eloges* published by Gide.[2] I haven't yet done anything about it; I haven't even seen it yet. It's a little annoying to me, now that I've forgotten that it was intended to make up for damage done. But Gide must never suspect this. On the contrary, tell him that I'm very happy about it and that I'll busy myself with it during vacation, for a few friends.

—Yes, I finally got through the law exams. One of my Seven Old Men found that I had "an extremely juridical turn of mind!" If only he speaks the truth!

[. . .] Who is a Mr. André Baines[3] who has dedicated a poem to me in the *N.R.F.*? [. . .]

—I'm thinking about the beautiful "book" in which you serve your art by serving your masters [. . .].

1. See above, letter 14, note 1.
2. See above, letter 28, note 2.
3. "En Mer," the seventh in a series of eight poems signed "André Baine" in the Aug. 1911 issue of NRF is dedicated "A Saintleger Leger." André Baine was the pseudonym of André Benjamin-Constant (1878-1930).

32

To Monsieur Jacques Rivière   *Saint-Sauveur (H.-P.)*
15, rue Froidevaux   [*August 20, 1911*]
Paris

My friend,
   [. . .]
I have often reflected on the book you're preparing,[1] which will be a real "work"—yes, a book, and that very

rare thing in criticism: a unified whole. That's the way some hidden determining force decrees it to be in every writer who carries within himself the strength to see it through.

I've thought about your table of contents once again, with your sheet before my eyes. It is so important as a preliminary statement that, if I were you, I wouldn't hesitate putting it at the beginning of the book, the way the English do. Your "book" will really be well ordered and put together. The careful way you've distributed the materials is excellent; and the table of contents is as beautiful to look at as a map is, in astronomy —with its laws of gravity and compensation, its various "scale" relationships taken only as "values," and its magnetic pole: Baudelaire. One small detail struck me: even though your table of contents seeks to get away from chronological ordering, I would have preferred putting the Russians before Debussy and even before Ravel; Moussorgsky between *Tristan* and *Pelléas*. But you most certainly had your reasons, which escaped me, and this is a mere detail. I especially like the ingenious way you quote the three writers to prove your points.[2]

I'll answer you some other time about the photographs of Gide. This isn't a dodge, I promise you. I'm afraid I'll miss the mail pick-up today.

[. . .] As for your failing the *agrégation*, how the devil would it ever have occurred to me to "pity" you? There is no failure of will in all this, since you hadn't set your sights exclusively on that goal. And when, above and beyond that, you reassure me about your present position at Stanislas,[3] what importance do you imagine I assign the *agrégation*?! . . .

I think of you and of the little child that will be born to you; my affection for you is great, and I am your friend. Leger

1. Rivière was preparing a collection of his essays for publication in book-form under the title *Etudes*. The book appeared later in 1911 and was re-issued in an enlarged edition in 1924.

2. The three writers were Baudelaire, Claudel, and Gide. A long essay on each of them appears in *Etudes*.

3. The Collège Stanislas. See above, letter 23, note 1.

33

To Monsieur Jacques Rivière   *Saint-Sauveur (H.-P.)*
15, rue Froidevaux   *August 26, 1911*
Paris

My friend,

I was handed your letter out in the middle of the road at the very moment I was thinking of you [. . .]. I was greatly upset on reading the words "Caesarean operation" [. . .]. What torture that must have been for you! . . . But that is all over now! [. . .] It's finished. You have a little daughter that you carry in to her mother; and a great new thing is given you to share, wonderfully given to you [. . .].

There is a special kind of courageousness about your life that I like more than any other: the courageousness that knows how to see something through with the simplest kind of patience.

Heartfelt greetings.   Leger

34

To Monsieur Jacques Rivière   *Pau, 37, route de*
15, rue Froidevaux   *Bordeaux*
Paris   [*November 11, 1911*]

My friend,

Your letter has been re-forwarded to me here after having sought me out in several corners of the Luz valley. [. . .]

I think of you, I think of your courage and the way you will always be able to trust in life: to trust the mysterious forces that are present, eagerly waiting to watch over all human life. Embrace your little daughter for me and give Madame Rivière my most confident wishes [. . .].

You ask if I've brought my family back to Pau. — Yes. It had already snowed in the Luz valley.

I deeply appreciated your brother-in-law's visit to Saint-Sauveur.[1] Please be sure to remember me warmly to him [. . .]. I was especially grateful to him for the open manner in which he revealed something of his inner life to me.

I expect to see you soon in Paris, where I have business. You know, quite simply, that I shall be happy to take a chair in your house and sit down for a moment across from you.

Tell me if Gide is in Paris. I would so much like to go and thank him, even though the prospect of meeting literary people at his house doesn't at all appeal to me.

Speaking of Gide. —You've asked me several times for my impression of the photographs you sent me, and it seems as if I've always avoided answering you. Well then—

The image, so far as I am able to call it up in my memory, was finally that of a type of man who is basically "serious," incurably serious, much more serious than he would like to appear. I also think that there are, behind that intent kind of face (nose, temples, mouth, and chin) a more painstaking recourse to duplicity, more tentative probings and ruses, more solicitations, in short, than were ever attributed to the impatient Ulysses. The man with the calabashes whom you presented to me in one of the photographs—didn't he look a little as if he were putting something over on himself? Besides, it's quite possible that this sort of man starts out by lying in the same way that one may be imploring—in order to enrich oneself and be tempted on every side, so as to end up liberating oneself, by which I mean, remaining free. But I also think there is something else about Gide, if the photographs didn't betray him, a very methodical urge to charm, a kind of real "coquettishness"—mere subservience and politeness, maybe, in order to keep a safer distance. (I'd prefer it to be only that!) There is usually in the faces of these fruit-tasters a whole elaborate cultivating of instability, dissatisfaction, and irreducible loneliness. And in the Gide you showed me, there was something more, especially in the jaws and hands, which in my eyes is—quite unparadoxically—the highest and rarest quality, the mark of a thoroughbred, in an artist as in all other men—an enormous "good sense." —Stubbornness too, most unexpected beneath so much flexibility. —And sadness too, to be expected, beneath this art of yielding. Finally, this live human being will find out what it means to be abandoned along the way by all those who settle down; and perhaps he will nevertheless lead two generations of men toward their goals. But if what you wanted to know from me is this, I would trust in, but have little taste for, Gide's friendship—because I firmly believe that a man of this sort intoxicates himself with friendship more than he actually attaches himself to a friend.

I am affectionately your friend,   Leger

1. Henri Fournier (1886-1914). See above, letter 7, note 1. The visit to Saint-Sauveur mentioned here is described in detail in a letter of Alain-Fournier to Rivière of 9 Sept. 1911. See Rivière-Fournier *Correspondance, 1905-1914,* pp. 400-402, and also AL's letter to Alain-Fournier of Sept. 1911, in the present collection, p. 113.

35

To Monsieur Jacques Rivière   *Paris, Friday*
15, rue Froidevaux   [*November 17, 1911*]
Paris (14e)   *chez M. Monnerot-Dumaine,*
                                     10 avenue Victor-Hugo

My friend, if I'm free tomorrow, I'm going to see Isadora Duncan (Movement!). I'll look around for you under the peristyle of the Châtelet[1] [. . .].

Affectionately.   Leger

1. The tempestuous American dancer, Isadora Duncan (1878-1927), was at the height of her fame in Europe at this time. The "Châtelet" is the Théâtre du Châtelet.

36

To Monsieur Jacques Rivière   *Paris, 10 avenue*
15, rue Froidevaux   *Victor-Hugo*
Paris   [*November 27, 1911*]

My friend, I am most grateful to you for calling my attention to the performance of Bach's "Magnificat" in Paris.

Yes, unless something comes up (in which case I'll notify you by *pneumatique*), I'll be there. Tell me where to meet you.

Please continue, my friend, to believe in the daily simplicity of my affection, and be sure to express my affectionate regard to Madame Rivière [. . .].

                                                   Leger

37

To Monsieur Jacques Rivière   *Pau, January 1, 1912*
15, rue Froidevaux
Paris

My affectionate and attentive wishes for you [. . .].
I do not cease to think of you and the simplicity of
those hours when I sat with you in your house. Embrace your little daughter for me [. . .].

Tell your brother-in-law that I trust him completely.
And please take care of this letter for Monod which
didn't reach him. Tell your friend Jacques Copeau,[1]
whom I find congenial and about whom Gide spoke to
me, that at any other time I would very much have
liked to meet him. And make my excuses to Gaston
Gallimard, who is a friend of Larbaud's[2] [. . .]. And
finally, I send my best wishes to the Lhotes[3] through you.

Please, my friend, never entertain the least suspicion
that I harbor the slightest bit of hidden conceit. Every
time I try to get rid of that aftertaste of smugness, I
laugh uncontrollably inside me. Otherwise, it would
mean I'd never seen the word "man" written across
my face while getting dressed [. . .].

I am affectionately at your side.   Leger

It wasn't possible for me to see you before my departure. I had to devote all my time and energy to one
of my sisters in Paris.

1. Jacques Copeau. See above, letter 22, note 6.
2. Gaston Gallimard (1881-1975) took over the direction of
the publishing enterprise of the NRF that came to be known
officially as "Editions de la *Nouvelle Revue Française*" and that
was founded in 1911 by the editors of the magazine. In 1919
it took on the name of Librairie Gallimard and has ever since
remained one of the most important publishing houses in France.
Gallimard was a friend of Valery Larbaud, whom AL had met
in April, 1911. See letter to Larbaud of 13 Oct. 1923. (143)
3. André Lhote, the painter. See above, letter 17, note 4.

38

To Monsieur Jacques Rivière   *Pau, January 5, 1912*
15, rue Froidevaux
Paris

My friend,

Valery Larbaud writes me that he has published, in
the December 25 issue of *La Phalange*, an article[1] on
my little book of *Eloges*, and he didn't send it to me
[. . .]. Please do me the favor of buying a copy of that
issue for me. I don't know whom else I might ask.

[. . .]   L.

I have just put your "Essay on Sincerity toward Oneself"[2] at my bedside, so I can read it whenever the spirit
moves me.

  1. Larbaud's article had indeed appeared. It was the first public
recognition of AL's poetry ever to appear in print. See letter to
Larbaud of Dec. 1911 (128), and also letter 128, note 1.
  2. "De la sincérité envers soi-même," NRF, Jan. 1912, pp. 5-18.

39

To Monsieur Jacques Rivière   *Pau, January 10, 1912*
15, rue Froidevaux
Paris

My friend,

[. . .] Believe me, I have thought things over thoroughly.

I don't wish to do anything more in France but prepare for a diplomatic and consular career that will one
day permit me to get away, and preparing for that
career is now precisely my one all-consuming concern.

Thanks for the issue of *La Phalange*. A much too
favorable article. It's already resulted, in the Paris press,
in a number of stupidities that, in a way, affect me more

than have all the eulogistic letters from Claudel. It isn't possible for anyone to think more meanly of my poems than I do, but I'd like to be alone in thinking that way. [. . .]

Tell your brother-in-law, please, that I am really embarrassed at not having yet been able to write him about the two prose pieces[1] he was kind enough to let me read. I scarcely have a quarter of an hour to myself each morning before I have to bury myself in my work [. . .].

Don't let yourself feel any remorse over your friendship, and don't think either that a letter from me could contain the least hint of those little reticences that seem to alarm you. I am your friend, period.

                                            Alexis Leger

1. Unidentified. AL also refers to them in his letter to Alain-Fournier of Jan. 1912. (51)

40

To Monsieur Jacques Rivière   *Pau, February 11, 1912*
15, rue Froidevaux
Paris

Thank you, dear friend, for my copy of *Etudes*[1] and for its inscription [. . .]. Your book has to be a great success, I want so much for it to be! That's not just a wish; for even though I think that a book of such quality would have been better appreciated in England, I'm also sure that justice will be done to it here.

Cordially by your side.   L.

I'll be in Paris in two days, but I'll only be spending 24 hours there and very busy ones at that. It's about a job in finance that has been offered to me, and I have to consult with one of my relatives before taking a decisive step in my life. One does not sit easily in the presence of money.

1. A collection of the essays that Rivière had published, chiefly in the NRF.

41

To Monsieur Jacques Rivière   *Saragossa*[1]
Rue Froidevaux, 15   *March 21, 1912*
Paris (Francia)

My friend, I got your letter. Thank you. And I also learned, through a letter from my mother, that two weeks or so ago a magazine arrived at Pau for me, bearing your name. Excuse me for not being able to have it forwarded. I had no permanent address. And I'm traveling down here practically without baggage [. . .].

It never occurred to me to tell you that you could call on my old cousin, Olivier Sainsère[2] (30, rue de Miromesnil) in my name, to see his Gauguins and his whole modern collection [. . .]. I could drop him a few lines, if you wish [. . .].

I'll be in Spain for six more weeks, I imagine. I'll return before the first hot spells, for I sometimes have to lead a life of physical exertion here that tires me. But I couldn't abide Pau any longer; I had to come down here one way or another. I'll take off toward the Mediterranean next, and then linger a while in the south.

This address is good for six more days: Casa Doña Fernanda Carrizo, Calle Santiago, 22. Zaragoza.

A.S.-L.

1. AL had gone off to Spain in the latter part of 1911 for study purposes in preparation for a consular career.

2. Olivier Sainsère was a cousin by marriage of AL's mother. He had made a career in the Conseil d'État, which, at the time of this letter, performed legislative and administrative functions of the highest order.

42

To Monsieur Jacques Rivière   *Madrid, April 27, 1912*
15, rue Froidevaux
Paris

Dear Friend,

I'm taking the liberty of giving your address to one
of my friends, an American painter of English extraction. Please welcome him and take him to see Lhote,
who may be able to guide him around a bit. Gordon
Stevenson,[1] with whom I spent two weeks in Madrid,
has just come back from Morocco in order to go and
consult an oculist in Paris.

As for myself, I'm heading for the south, as I have
to catch a freighter for Genoa at Malaga; and from
Genoa I'll take a quick trip to Hungary—Agram and
Budapest.

Very affectionately your friend.   L.

1. Gordon Stevenson (b. 1892).

43

To Monsieur Jacques Rivière   *Paris, 176, boulevard*
15, rue Froidevaux   *Malesherbes*
Paris   *[June 6, 1912]*

My friend,

Tonight I'll be in London. I've had to devote almost
all my time here to my sister and have been unable to see
you.

But I must tell you how happy I was to hear you
talk about the feeling of security you now have as you
move forward.

With friendly regards.   A.S.-L.

44

To Monsieur Jacques Rivière   *London,*
15, rue Froidevaux   *October 14, 1912*
Paris

Dear friend,

A letter from my mother informs me that she is going to leave Pau, where I'll never again set foot.

I no longer have a permanent address in France. Will you please see that the Nouvelle Revue Française people note the following forwarding address, in Paris:

c/o Mme. A. Dormoy
176, bd Malesherbes

Affectionately yours.   A.S.-L.

45

To Monsieur Jacques Rivière   [*Paris, December 20, 1912*]
15, rue Froidevaux
Paris

Dear friend,

Please let me have the two following pieces of information:

—when is the next Schola Cantorum concert?

—when and where is Claudel's play to be performed?

Please don't forget to remember me to him, if I don't manage to get to the performance.

Your little daughter is really a very pretty little creature.

Affectionately.   A.S.-L.

46

To Monsieur Jacques Rivière   [*Paris*], *Sunday*,
15, rue Froidevaux   [*February 16, 1913*]
Paris

My friend, I know what friendship is. Please believe that my friendship is no less direct and real than yours; nor has it any more to say.

I won't be able to lunch with you for some time yet. May Madame Rivière be so kind as to excuse me. Two months from now I'll take the liberty of reminding her of her invitation [. . .].

It's been very thoughtless of me not to have asked you to take your little girl to my mother and sisters. If Madame Rivière were free next Sunday, you would make them ever so happy by simply having family tea with them. Come around five o'clock, you will find them alone (13, rue de Bruxelles, at the corner of Place Vintimille). Just drop me a line so that I can also arrange to be at my mother's. And will you let me ask you quite simply, when you get to know my family a bit more, never to let them hear the slightest word, where I am concerned, about literary matters?

Let me congratulate you, dear friend, on the lecture you gave in Luxembourg. You'll have to tell me about it when I next see you.

I really should look up a poem for you, a rather fine one, which I received not very long ago from your friend, René Bichet.[1] Believe me, dear friend, I was saddened by the news of his death, and I thought of the grief your friendship must bear.

Most cordially.   A. Saint-Leger

1. René Bichet (1886-1912) was a poet who contributed to the NRF and who became a friend of Rivière and Alain-Fournier. They referred to him as "le petit B." His poems were published posthumously in 1939, as were Alain-Fournier's letters to him.

47

To Monsieur Jacques Rivière   *Cernay-Ermont (S.-et-O.)*
15, rue Froidevaux   *route du Général-Decaen*
Paris   *Friday [July 18, 1913]*

My dear friend,

I've only just returned to France and merely passed through Paris. Could you tell me if Claudel is there at the moment? I was supposed to spend the last days of August with him in Frankfurt, and now I find a letter from him announcing that he is leaving and has to change all his plans, because the performances of *L'Annonce*[1] at Hamburg have been put off until September. If I can see him right here, let me know, please, before I leave again.

I think of you, my friend, and of your family. I now see you only through several thicknesses of glass and years of separation. I hope you will always look upon me as your friend; at least let my affection for you be the last thing about which you ever entertain any doubts.

Are you already in the country, and what will you bring back from it? I've been thinking about the study of Rimbaud you spoke to me about, because it seems to me that you will be able to say things that wouldn't have made Rimbaud himself too unhappy and which Claudel himself hasn't managed to say (for Claudel[2] didn't manage to speak about Rimbaud sparingly enough to bring out his absolute greatness). Perhaps you'll at last tell us the real truth about Rimbaud—all his "fever of intelligence," the genuinely spiritual breed he belonged to, the impatience that set Rimbaud apart, and the whole miserable but lucid way he lived his life— the leanness and the impatience, the whole striding spirit of this steadfast, overgrown boy who has first and foremost to settle accounts with himself. His disgust with the "genius" that he alone could gauge; his nausea at the spectacle of his tearing himself to pieces so as to give himself no quarter—his horror of human make-shifts, and the ordeal—eagerly embraced—of his inadequacy as a *man* and poet, which was the key to his secret greatness, both as poet and man. His genius, which he could not accept—doesn't it strike you that this is the ultimate shortcut of this poet of shortcuts and leaps—a poet of ceaseless action? And doesn't it seem to you that this is the source of his power as a writer?—his skill at eluding whatever does not belong to his breed, whatever is not part of his impatience? Which means everything that entices us into the ambush of form, everything that is attractively facile both literarily and spiritually, the artists' smugness and mere human smugness, and everything that has already been done and approved, and aiming at—and being satisfied with—momentary perfection: happiness, hateful cadences of the mouth and the soul—false grace, false grease!

It is the infinitely lonely hatred of all *that*, where Rimbaud is concerned, which makes the poet in him find fortune and ease, not in concrete fame, as has been commonly thought, but in the intellectual, Pascalian din. Rimbaud the man, in spite of himself, was less goaded by his imagination than he was harrowed by his soul. It seems to me that one can go so far as to think, paradoxically, that Rimbaud does not belong first and foremost and instinctively to the breed (which is infinitely heavier and stodgier, more passive and, above all, more colorless) of pure imaginative, or simple, visionaries. Vision in him seems to proceed from the nerves much more than from his frontal lobes; and what he has to say usually goes far beyond the sordid poetic adventure. Rimbaud's genius lies in his very partiality and in the human interest his fate holds for us.

But what a spate of words, my friend, especially when

there are so much better things to put into an envelope
when we write each other. At least you will find in this
one my affection for you, which is already well aged.

                                                    A.S.-L

1. Claudel's verse-play, *L'Annonce faite à Marie*.
2. Claudel had published an essay on Arthur Rimbaud in the
Oct. 1912 issue of NRF. It was subsequently reprinted as the
"Préface" to the Paterne Berrichon edition of *Œuvres de Arthur
Rimbaud* (Mercure de France, 1912). See above, letter 22, note 4.

                              48

To Monsieur Jacques Rivière   *Château de la Chaumette*
30 bis, rue Boulard   *Joué-lès-Tours (I.-et-L.)*
Paris (14e)   *July 21, 1922*

Dear friend,

I must tell you of the great pleasure I had on reading
the remarkable essay that you have just published on
"the dangers of excessive consistency in politics"[1] [. . .].

The evil that you denounce is no less dangerous in
things of the mind than in the realm of action. It is a
malady peculiar to Latins, who are grammarians and
rhetoricians, dialecticians and jurists, commentators and
writers of glosses. A malady of Mediterranean peoples
[. . .]. "Consistent politics": the abuse of it—an autom-
aton's bondage and mania—is where the difference lies
that separates genius from "uprightness"—separates the
groping, hesitant, empirical divination of genius, clair-
voyant and sensitive, from the humdrum "lucidity" of
talent, which is methodical and sterile. The grammatical
cast of mind of a Poincaré,[2] a bad "poet," is no less far
removed from the mysterious course of life than the
political turn of mind of certain writers, who are bad
"statesmen" in their own field. The most perfect masti-

cation with dentures is never the same as chewing with one's own teeth.

I suffer from a keen feeling of remorse toward you, my friend. I tried to see you in your family circle before I left Paris. You had already gone.

I have been down here on leave for a week, with my mother, at a place belonging to one of my sisters. I'm going to look for a big touring-car so I can once again assail the soil of France head-on. My Antillean grandparents,[3] who laid out this weird domain in the most enervating spot in France, would have done better to have left me enough money to buy a boat.

I'll telephone you when I return to Paris at the beginning of August [. . .].

I think of you with affection, dear friend, and say so quite simply. Please, always trust in my friendship.

My mother asks me for news of Madame Rivière. Please remember me to her and hug your two children for me.   A. St.-L. Leger

1. "Les Dangers d'une politique conséquente," NRF, July 1922, pp. 5-11.

2. Raymond Poincaré (1860-1934) had brought about the downfall of Aristide Briand in Jan. 1922 and once more become Prime Minister and Minister of Foreign Affairs.

3. The château of "La Chaumette" in the department of Indre-et-Loire at Joué-lès-Tours had belonged to the childless widow of AL's great-great-uncle, general Comte Alexis de Leyritz. The Leyritz branch of the family had close ties with the island of Martinique. AL's mother and older sisters, when they returned to France during the summer in AL's early years, would stay at this château, but young AL always stayed behind in Guadeloupe. In 1922 the property belonged to a brother-in-law of AL.

49

To Monsieur Jacques Rivière   *Affaires Etrangères*
38 bis, rue Boulard   *Direction des Affaires*
Paris (14e)   *politiques et commerciales*
                                     [Paris] December 21, 1922

Dear friend,

I have read *Aimée*[1] [. . .].

Nobility and purity: it is a beautiful work. It is "high-born" and of good lineage. It contains within itself the guarantees of its rightness: that pure aroma of a sensitive intelligence, and the natural spareness that transforms a work of the mind into a living, naked body in which we can see, transparently, the stream of life circulate. It is genuinely French in its abnegation and disdainful modesty—unbending in its invisible bonds and yet strong in its poise; neither facileness nor striving for effect. —Such modesty, or if you don't like the word, such restraint is hardly usual these days, when taste is no longer the natural extension of good breeding, but stems rather from acquired culture.

Dare I tell you? I was a little apprehensive about your excessive scruples and over-application in a work involving character-presentation. But your intuition, and the fact that you are a poet, always helped you to make the leap. Your innate sense of balance will always steer you towards the great simplifications of maturity.

And I love for itself, dear friend, the chasteness of the language you use; I find in it, as you clothe a thought, all the docility, fidelity, and unobtrusiveness of the most expensive linens.

Making such demands of yourself won't earn you any great popularity; but you, you must put full trust in the work that you know you can produce; treat it, as is said in the testament of a true Frenchman, Monsieur de Saint-Simon:[2] "with neither magnificence nor modesty." Affectionately yours. A. St.-L. Leger[3]

1. Rivière's only complete novel, published in 1922.

2. The exact wording of this formula in the holograph testament of the duc de Saint-Simon (1675-1755) is, "sans nulle magnificence ni rien qui ne soit modeste" (text as given in the Chéruel and Régnier edition of Saint-Simon's *Mémoires*, vol. 19, pp. 428-429, pub. 1875). AL's original reads slightly differently: "sans magnificence ni modestie."

3. For an additional letter to Rivière, see p. 376.

50

To Monsieur Alain-Fournier   *Saint-Sauveur (H.-P.),*
                                              [late September] 1911

Dear Sir,

I was delighted that the charm of this part of the country was sufficient to bring you all the way up here, not far from me, and I greatly appreciate your remembering me so graciously.

I regret that I was not able to extend to you a more fitting welcome into my family, and for a longer time. You were no stranger to me; the friend of Jacques Rivière and brother of Isabelle Rivière, Alain-Fournier in person could not be a stranger to me.

It is I, rather, who hope I did not strike you as too much of a stranger; I did the best I could in this regard. I trust you implicitly, and I am grateful to you for sharing such friendly warmth with me.

Saint-Leger Leger

The last issue of the *N.R.F.* was very late in reaching me here. I read with interest the "Portrait"[1] you spoke to me about. Though I did not forget that you were not very satisfied with it, I nevertheless liked the nakedness of its language, which I prize above all else, and which, I think, will, through the very pressures of life, become more and more pronounced in your work. I also think that you are incurring an obligation of the most redoubtable sort, but one you may come to like—the obligation of no longer having the privilege of writing just a little.

—I urged you to go see Francis Jammes at Orthez (who

is nearer to you than I can be). But I owe it to him, and to you, to warn you that he may still be preoccupied with his family in the aftermath of an invasion of whooping-cough that I know laid all of them low recently.

1. Alain-Fournier, "Portrait," NRF, Sept. 1911, pp. 309-319. A prose sketch of a former classmate who committed suicide because of unrequited love.

51

To Monsieur Alain-Fournier   *Pau, January 1912*
in Paris

Dear friend,

I've reread your two "prose-pieces."[1] I like them very much. I have no qualifications for saying more about them. But let me just add this: one likes the clarity of your vision, the sureness of a natural rhythm, and the fact that you write because you really want to—not just to be doing the fashionable thing, but, on the contrary, from a taste, very French and very demanding, for real discretion.

May you remember me with affection. I was happy to see you again when I was in Paris. The human voice has its mysteries for everyone, as you yourself know.

I send along my wishes most sincerely—for your literary endeavors and for yourself, and above all, for the conduct of your life.   A.S.-L.

1. Unidentified. See above, letter 39, note 1.

LETTERS TO PAUL CLAUDEL
(1906-1914)

52

To Monsieur Paul Claudel[1] *Bordeaux, November 1906*
Peking

Very dear Sir,

I thank you for your letter [. . .].

A long time has already gone by. —I haven't written to you because I have nothing to say. Nor can I have anything to say to you. I am alone, without wanting to be. As a child I thought that souls had neither doors nor windows, like the "monad" I later learned about in school. The only trouble is that I was too blundering to manage to take pride in this.

And then, you are very far away. Your kindness to me is remote—and I don't share the slightest bit of ordinary, everyday life with you, which alone creates ties.

What do I expect from you? —I don't know. I believe that I shall remain lonely.

When I think of you, it is with a little pang of resentment, which is surely selfish of me, because for me—and for Jammes as well, and for your friend Frizeau—you are the man who has reached the goal, who has "come through," who has "arrived," whereas I am just starting out. And I'll undoubtedly be alone to the very end. You are among those who have disappeared for me beyond that Brimstone Lake of your Holy Books [. . .]. Think back to your younger days and you will recall the desolate feeling that preceding generations always inspire in us.

Your letter made it possible for me to meet your friend

Frizeau. I have seen him only once. He has very kindly eyes, doesn't he? He lent me the Poe text[2] that you left with him, along with your translation of it. And he agreed to lend me your *Partage de midi*[3]—privately printed.

Jammes will be passing through here soon. He has not yet got over his suffering, for my mother writes me that he keeps asking questions about Ismailia.[4] He still keeps referring to you as "Alighieri." Perhaps he will come to see me here in this temporary room and make fun of my staying here, because he once introduced me to Ruysbroeck.[5]

I am talking to you about myself; excuse me [. . .].

I am at Bordeaux where I'm going on with law studies, instead of medicine. I had hoped that, once freed from my military service, I would be leaving for Chile to raise cattle. But here I am, and I am to remain here—in order to take a master's degree in philosophy [. . .]. I hate the philosophy of the philosophy professors, and they repay me in kind. I'll probably return to Pau, if I don't sail off before that.

The young men here are fine, healthy specimens; they know the value of money and their own value; they know how to consider men only in terms of the shoes they wear, and women only in terms of their vagina. Better that than to have to hear them, as one does in Paris, talk about Ibsen, maybe, or Bergson, d'Indy, or Carrière,[6] in some restaurant. And here they also participate in fine charity functions.

But what can all this matter to you, even if my letter does "come to you from France"?

I sometimes come across your name in the reviews. You're being sought out; you're admired; you're "understood." I saw, in *Antée*, I believe, that a lecture on *L'Arbre* was being given at the "Labeur,"[7] and it was in the *Mercure* that a critic explained your ideas about time and causality in terms of Bergson.[8] —But now you are printing your things privately.

I take leave of you, my dear Monsieur Claudel.

I don't know whether I shall ever see your face again, which grows dim in my memory—or even your handwriting.

I ask that you believe me quite simply yours: *truly Yrs.*[9]
Alexis Leger

(7, rue Latapie, Pau)

1. Paul Claudel (1868-1955), diplomat and Catholic poet, dramatist and apologist. AL met Claudel for the first time in 1905 at Orthez, where Claudel was visiting his friend Francis Jammes. At that time Claudel was on leave after two diplomatic assignments in China (1895-1900, 1901-1905). He married in March 1905 and returned to China for a third assignment (1905-1909). He corresponded with AL and was instrumental in steering the young man toward a career in the consulates. Claudel remained a friend of AL's to the end of his life, when AL wrote a moving tribute to him, "Silence pour Claudel" (reprinted in OC, pp. 483-486). Both men, moreover, shared an admiration for Philippe Berthelot and Aristide Briand. See AL's later letters to Claudel. (52-66, 302-305)

2. "Leonainie." Also mentioned to Jammes. See letter 81, note 3. This supposed "last poem" of Edgar Allan Poe, which Claudel found printed in the British periodical, *Fortnightly Review* (Feb. 1904), is in reality a pastiche by James Whitcomb Riley that first appeared in the *Kokomo* (Indiana) *Dispatch* on 2 Aug. 1877. The poem was reprinted in Riley's *Love-Lyrics* (1883). The English text of the poem, along with Claudel's French translation and a fulsome "explanatory" note appeared in the 15 Jan. 1906 issue of *L'Ermitage*.

3. Claudel's verse drama based on a crucial episode in his own life. *Partage de Midi* was printed for the first time, privately, in 1906 by the Bibliothèque de l'Occident. For Claudel's connection with Frizeau, see above, letter 7, note 4.

4. A young lady with whom Francis Jammes had fallen in love, and who is the subject of some of the somberest poems in his *Clairières dans le ciel 1902-1906*, married a young naval

officer attached to the Suez Canal Company and permanently stationed in Ismailia, where AL's uncle, Emilio Dormoy, also resided at the time. See above, letter 1, note 9.

5. See above, letter 1, note 3.

6. Probably Eugène Carrière (1849-1906), the painter.

7. *Antée: Revue mensuelle de Littérature*, a Belgian literary periodical that began publication in mid-1905 and lasted until 1908. The reference here is to a lecture on the plays Claudel published collectively in 1901 under the title of *L'Arbre*. The lecture was given by Georges Dwelshauwers at the *Labeur* gallery in Brussels on 18 Oct. 1906 and was commented upon in the Brussels press, as reported in the Nov. 1906 issue of *Antée*.

8. Jean Blum, in a footnote to his article, "La Philosophie de M. Bergson et la poésie symboliste," in the 15 Sept. 1906 issue of the *Mercure de France*, p. 207.

9. English in original.

53

To Monsieur Paul Claudel   *Pau, June 1907*
French Consul at Tientsin

Dear Sir,

You had the kindness to write to me—shortly before my father's death.

You spoke to me about the struggle that had saved you. I thank you for having told me about yourself.[1]

But why hurt my feelings with this fear of annoying me? It is quite impossible for you to do that. Won't you believe quite simply in my gratitude and affection?

I didn't understand everything in your letter—for example, when you said that we "make" ourselves deaf, whereas I simply believe that one grows deaf.

I was glad to hear you speak of that strength, in connection with life, that doesn't even need to be understood. (I was once delighted when you criticized Jammes for his *Existences*, those sulking pages.)[2]

When a young man "sulks" about life, it's not always a sign of weakness, but simply proof that at his age he expects so much more from life that he does not greatly prize it as such. For anyone incapable of illuminating it, as a Christian does, any grasping at life is doomed to failure—don't you think?—and life then becomes time that must simply not be wasted in trying to understand.

A refusal to become a lawyer or a doctor is not always a matter of wanting to do something better, but may perhaps be a duty to do less in order not to be one of those who "grow deaf." —From one of the Latin Fathers whom I have liked, I still remember the sentence, "*Fac, et tu homo, tibi thecam.*"[3]

You tell me that it is no fun being a consul, and I readily believe it—and that to have one's wife or baby daughter in Tientsin (and you will surely suffer even more, having a son there) is no fun either. But what can that matter to you, here on earth, if, Catholic that you are, you have the potential for joy? You work hard for the French government, and that surely means a loss to others; but for you, since you were eighteen, I believe, your time here below is not really of the essence.

Dear Sir, you are worried about the literary bent of our young men. You of all people must not harbor that fear about them. I don't know the young men of my generation very well, but I feel their "need" is for something more direct and that, above all, their lives make metaphysical demands.

To make them "incapable" of facing "life" is a result for which you Christians can not condemn the "villainous" philosophies of our time, when you think of the excruciating emptiness that young men find in them.

If a young man today tells you that he recoils at this or that calling in Europe, I beg you not to see in this any "scorn," as in the days when M. Barrès' young men were obsessed with "barbarism,"[4] but rather the profound desire to preserve that time, in all its mobility, when there is one all-important need—the *"fac tibi thecam"* [. . .].

Frizeau intends to go to the Pyrenees very soon. He showed me the picture of your child—a square little forehead on the photograph.

Truly yrs.[5]   Al. Leger

I give you my new address, which I'm told is impolite.
          23, boulevard d'Alsace-Lorraine, Pau

Excuse me for not speaking about the grief in our household, and about how great that other grief is—having to endure the weakness in the hearts of four women.

1. Claudel had undoubtedly written to AL about the inner struggle that culminated in his conversion to Catholicism on Christmas Day 1886. (See Claudel's text, "Ma Conversion," first published in the 10 Oct. 1913 issue of the *Revue de la Jeunesse* and subsequently reproduced many times.)

2. Jammes composed his collection of verse, *Existences*, in 1900. It was published, along with his *Jean de Noarrieu*, under the collective title *Le Triomphe de la Vie*, in 1902 by the Mercure de France publishers.

3. "You, too, man, should avail yourself of a casket . . ." from Saint Ambrose, *Hexameron*, The Fifth Day, xxiii, 80. (John J. Savage, trans.)

4. Reference to Maurice Barrès, *Sous l'Œil des barbares* (1888), the first volume of his trilogy, *Le Culte du Moi*.

5. English in original.

                          54

To Monsieur Paul Claudel   *Pau, December 31, 1907*
French Consul in Tientsin

Dear Sir,

My heartfelt greetings to you; it is New Year's. I can at least wish for health for you and yours.

I have not forgotten you. I have lost only the features of your face.

I recall your last letter. I have never "rejected" the Kingdom to which you invite me; and I sincerely believe I have "done" more—because it was said: "*Violenti rapiunt illud*"[1] (It that not so?).

I know it is wretched to be deprived of that "ecstasy," because then there is nothing more to "conquer." —That is my way of thinking.

Right now I don't want to "make" anything out of my life—if I cannot go beyond it. That has something laughable about it, I know.

It is not true that Art is a refuge—any more than thought as an end in itself is. Dead weight! There is in Art nothing but an unconscious means; and I laugh heartily at an Art, an instinct, which would be at one and the same time a way and the law governing that way.

Your Hermits must have declared that Art is diabolical, because it distracts. They were souls that plunged straight ahead; they disdained curves! This, in order to insure the very tension of their demands.

Don't tell me that I have a duty already laid out for me, if the benefit to me is merely a physical necessity.

And I can do nothing for the hearts of four women but to remain here, near them, in mutual love. We can't really fortify anyone; we simply become hardened, and we suffer on hurting someone else. And women are too little "capable" of their religion. You say that one must "cling." Ah! how *they* cling! And I am not the one to "tear them away." What armor could I, of all people, share? They pray, I know; and they ask for various "things," not for just one. While I tried to help my father, all alone, as he was dying, in their rooms they were praying that he would live; and now they will pray that I may succeed in this or that undertaking, in some financial arrangement, in an examination maybe! . . .

I haven't seen Jammes for a long time [. . .]. He came here to announce his marriage, at the very moment when you were telling me of your desire to see him happy and "settled down." He writes to me now from Bucy-le-Long.[2] At Orthez, he moved out of the little house.

From Frizeau I have only good news. —I ran across an article in *Occident*, an article about your work by a young fellow I met at Frizeau's.[3]

You must have received the book by Madame Burnat-Provins.[4] I think she is, rather amusingly, quite concerned about your opinion of it.

My heartfelt greetings, Monsieur.

I know you will write to me; you don't have to talk about me just because I did; but tell me all you want about yourself—and whether you are returning to France soon.

Yrs.[5]   Alx. L.

1. ". . . and men of violence take it [the kingdom of heaven] by force." Matthew 11:12.

2. Jammes had married Geneviève Goedorp at Bucy-le-Long (Aisne) on 8 Oct. 1907.

3. Jacques Rivière's "Paul Claudel, Poète chrétien," which had been serialized in the Oct., Nov., and Dec. 1907 issues of *L'Occident* and was later reproduced in Rivière's book of essays, *Etudes* (1911).

4. Marguerite Burnat-Provins, *Le Livre pour toi* (1907). Madame Burnat-Provins (1872-1952), an engraver and poetess, was a friend of André Gide, who had met her in 1906 when she visited Jammes in Orthez. See letter to Frizeau of Mar. 1910. (78)

5. English in original.

55

To Monsieur Paul Claudel   *Pau, December 10, 1908*
French Consul in Tientsin

Very dear Sir,

My letter will reach you in January. Once again I am happy to be able to greet you, to have the right to do so. My gratitude and my affection—if you will permit me to use the word—authorize it—and your good-heartedness too, [. . .].

I don't want the sad business of my having said too many silly things to you to keep me forever from speaking to you [. . .]. —At least you may be sure that you are liberating me at this very moment as I speak to you. Emerson uttered the word "liberator" sixty years ago.

I have news of you through Frizeau and Jammes. Great peace has settled on the Jammes household; I often see him in his family circle. You have undoubtedly heard with joy the news that Frizeau doesn't have to worry about his eyes any more [. . .].

As for myself, if I must speak to you of myself, in the midst of all the mourning, I nevertheless begin to feel more confident about my family. I have been able to put my mother's affairs in order, and I'll be able to remain with my family for another two years [. . .].

Before that time is up you will be returning to France, and perhaps I'll have the good fortune to see you once more. I am still no more worthy of listening to you than when I was seventeen years old. But I will be delighted.

I no longer complain that life is an act or a defense. And perhaps it will once more be you who tells me to ask life for its simplest terms—(I call this "the ellipsis").

Even though I still suffer, I have learnt that one can suffer without grieving. Hope is to suffer constantly, but

without having to remind oneself to think about it—
that is even more than hope; it is joy!

You told me that the person who has known thirst
would not have his thirst diminished. Were I certain of
this, it would assure me great reserves of strength. But
I think I shall have to be cautious—and that is a loss!

Perhaps you will think that I ought not to have written
to you, since I have so little to say. —Yes, that's true.

But I didn't start out far enough away, finally to come
around to Christianity [. . .].

I beg of you, excuse my letter [. . .].

And you, you do not have to answer it. I give you no
address. You have said to me all that is essential, and
only now am I able to thank you.

But please accept my very great respect.   Leger

56

To Monsieur Paul Claudel   *Pau, February 15, 1910*
French Consul
Prague

I am most, most grateful to you. Frizeau forwarded
your letter to me.[1] I thank you. I will not be embarrassed
over having appealed to you. I knew for a certainty that
I would have to ask you for advice.

[. . .]

I have thought your letter over and am still thinking
it over. I juggle figures. —I can't yet order my life the
way I would like to.

Will you excuse me for being so late in congratulating
you on your appointment to Prague? I am delighted,
as I think of you and yours, that you are finally back in
the West. —But it struck me that I owed it to you not
to write any more, drawn away, as I am, from Christianity.

But you must not think, on pain of causing me great sadness, that I treat my memories of you as just so much anecdote. —I have never thought that the human face, no matter whose, was something "literary."

Please think of me as preserving your memory faithfully and completely.   Leger

I read in the *Nlle Revue française* the three "Hymns"[2] in which you pray.

Dare I speak of admiration or tell you, though I am not qualified to do so, of the emotion and the wish, of the feeling of anonymity that permits one to surrender to immobile brilliance in your "Saint Paul," to weightiness, in your "Saint Peter," and, in the other, the "Saint James," to logic pushed to sublime extremes?

1. Claudel had no address for AL at that date, so he sent his letter to Gabriel Frizeau in Bordeaux. Frizeau was the friend who first introduced AL to Claudel's literary works.

2. The "hymns" referred to are the poems "Saint Pierre," "Saint Paul," and "Saint-Jacques le Majeur," all three of which appeared for the first time in NRF of Dec. 1909. Claudel subsequently incorporated all three in "Le Groupe des Apôtres" section of *Corona Benignitatis Anni Dei* (1915).

57

To Monsieur Paul Claudel   *Pau, 37, rue de Bordeaux*
French Consul General   [*December 1910*]
Prague

Dear Sir and friend,

I send you my very sincere best wishes—for your family, for your literary work, and for yourself.

I do not forget to think of you.

Rivière recently gave me news of you.

I know you will be pleased with the good news of Jammes I can give you. He radiates health all around him, and he tells me that he has never felt more strongly and fully involved in the work he is now engaged in,[1] having just begun the third canto. I see him often in the midst of his family at Orthez. His new work surprises me, but I like the man himself with as much affection as ever.

Please think kindly of me.   Alexis Leger

1. *Les Géorgiques chrétiennes.*

58

To Monsieur Paul Claudel   *Pau, May 17, 1911*
French Consul General
Prague

Dear Sir and friend,

I was deeply touched by your note and by what you were kind enough to say about an introduction to M. Berthelot[1] in Paris.

I put off writing to you until I was able to tell you something more definite about my plans, if not about my wishes. And I am still floundering in uncertainty.

Do you think it would be possible, without my being overly optimistic, for me to undertake on my own, here in Pau far from the Ecole des Sciences politiques, the preparation for the big competitive Foreign Affairs examination, which I could take only once, since I will be over the age-limit soon?

I do have a taste for this career, but I also keep thinking of everything that would be working against me if I entered upon it. The loss of my father, my lack of means, and my isolation here in France, far from all Parisian connections and without the possibility of spending time in Paris—all this is not designed to make things easier for me. My father, who was a lawyer in the

Antilles before bringing his family, of old French stock, back from the Islands, knew very few people in official circles in Paris. And I, who was not born in France, have studied only in Bordeaux. In July I'll take my final law examinations there.

If, between now and November, you conclude that, in view of the circumstances, I should give up all thought of the Foreign Service examination, perhaps you could, on a personal basis, give me some other friendly advice. In case I should not decide on the colonial magistracy, which doesn't at all attract me, any more than anything else "colonial," I've been offered a private career as a settler in Latin America (Chile), in South Africa, in New Zealand. But all this is not easily reconcilable, for the time being, with the obligations of a man who, even from far away, still has to look after the other members of the family.

I shall be grateful for whatever you may tell me as a friend. Moreover, I would understand quite well that you might not be able to judge any better than I am able to.

Very affectionately yours,   Leger

1. Philippe Berthelot (1866-1934), the famous career diplomat and associate of Aristide Briand, was at this time the Assistant Director of Asiatic Affairs in the Ministry of Foreign Affairs and, thus, Paul Claudel's superior. AL was to become a close friend of Berthelot almost as soon as he entered the Foreign Service in 1914. See letter to Berthelot of 3 Jan. 1917 (147), and note 1 thereto.

59

To Monsieur Paul Claudel   *Pau, 37, rue de Bordeaux*
French Consul General   *May 29, 1911*
Frankfurt-am-Main

I am overjoyed—really overjoyed—at receiving from you the two versions of your drama.[1] I thank you.

I admire, in this century, a work that has been twice written; and the greatly increased weight of the word *œuvre*. —I keep thinking about this.

In the introductory poem there were stanzas so beautiful (the third from the last, and the second one, also the first stanza with its second line) that I could wish Edgar Poe were still alive so that, of an evening, I could talk to him about them. (The beauty in the first "Pythian Ode" of Pindar of a pair of antagonistic words: κατασ-χόμενος ῥιπαῖσι . . .[2] [Antistr. I]).

As for your "Propositions sur la Justice,"[3] its admirable clockwork mechanism was already implicit for me in a letter you wrote to me once in reference to the word "just."

Please accept, along with my reiterated thanks, my most respectful feelings of admiration and affection.

A. L.

1. *Tête d'or*, first published in 1890, was reprinted in Claudel's *Théâtre 1ère série* along with a second, revised version (Mercure de France, 1911). In this 1911 edition Claudel included, as an introductory piece, a poem he had composed in 1891 that was eventually entitled "Chant à cinq heures" (see Pléiade ed. of Claudel's *Œuvre poétique*, pp. 7 and 8).

2. "restrained by impulsions" in the Pythian Ode I to Hieron of Etna.

3. See above, letter 28, note 3.

60

To Monsieur Paul Claudel   *Pau, June 1, 1911*
Consul General of France
Frankfurt-am-Main

Very dear Sir and friend,

[. . .] Will you please disregard an extraordinary text, published by the *Nlle R.F.* and attributed to me, and allow me to send you a corrected issue?[1]

There were, in that house, men sufficiently ill-bred to allow the printing of manuscripts that belonged to André Gide—without correcting any proofs. (Gide, moreover, is in no way responsible, and has written me that he himself went to the printer, in Bruges, in a last attempt to correct the proofs.)

I am quite willing to appear grotesquely impertinent to a public that is unknown to me and that I care little about; but where the few men whom I do care about are concerned, it seemed to me that it was a matter of elementary politeness to make amends for the extravagant or merely incomprehensible things appearing over my name, that they may have read in a text swarming with typographical errors.

With greatest respect, believe me affectionately yours.

Leger

1. See above, letter 28, note 2.

61

To Monsieur Paul Claudel   *Bordeaux, June 10,* [*1911*][1]
French Consul General
Frankfurt-am-Main

You will never know what solace your letter brought me [. . .].

You immediately put your finger on the desire I have [. . .] of one day finding the limits of a "work." Please believe me when I say that I've had quite enough of browsing around, quite enough of everything that then lies about in disorder—a disorder that one would so keenly like to clean up, were it only to keep from ever writing again. A base sort of courage, a sort of flight, and the solitary vice of brief self-indulgence—I'm familiar with it all; and all those poems that "form a sediment" in notebooks, after being transcribed—I'm unbearably sick of them, when all is said and done—to the point where I have neither the strength nor the desire to publish a book. I would simply like, some day, to have the privilege of leading an "undertaking" the way an *Anabasis* is conducted by its leaders. (That very word seems to me so beautiful that I should like to come across the work worthy of such a title. It haunts me.)

I must not forget to thank you for having drawn my attention to the exact spelling of the word "*poême*."[2]

Yes, I like Pindar; and his work, along with Bach's "Brandenburg Concertos," has been a powerful aid to me in living, ever since I had the rare good luck of running across the Oxford edition (Heyne's),[3] which preserves the old metrical distribution. Yes, I like in it just what you mentioned—that the "strophe" itself, or quantity of text recited in a single "turn" about the altar, forces us to savor what is preassigned in a free oral recitation.

I write to you in haste, on a restaurant table (I have to register for law courses here). I'll write to you in a more leisurely fashion to discuss with you once more my desire to prepare for the Foreign Affairs[4] as soon as I've finished off my last law exam. But I wanted to get this hasty letter off to you because I must ask your advice. Gide has taken it upon himself to publish in book form the few pages of mine that he gave to the *Nouvelle*

Revue Française. I'm wondering whether, at the moment the book is passed for press, it might not be wise, in view of the future, not to publish it under my name[5] [. . .]. Please let me have your answer. I'll try to hold off the printer until I have your reply.

Cordially, in haste, and surrounded by noise.

A. Leger

1. Erroneously dated 1912 in OC. AL's request for advice concerning the use of a pseudonym on the book edition of *Eloges* clearly indicates that this letter was written in the late spring of 1911. See letter to Gide of Aug. 1911. (105)

2. Claudel, at least as far back as 1903-1904 (the date of composition of his *Art Poétique*), insisted on the use of the diaeresis [poëte] rather than the standard *grave* accent [poète]. I do not find any example with the circumflex accent, as the text in OC has it. Probably a typographical error.

3. See above, letter 12, note 1. AL presented Claudel with this very rare edition when the two men met in Hamburg in 1913.

4. The competitive Foreign Service examination.

5. Claudel urged AL to publish under his own name. A sort of compromise was finally struck: the name "Saintleger Leger" appeared on the title page of the book, but not on the cover.

62

To Monsieur Paul Claudel   *Pau, June 23, 1911*
French Consul General
Frankfurt-am-Main

Dear Sir and friend,

A misunderstanding has deprived me, up to now, of the joy of telling you how proud I am of my copy of *L'Otage*.[1] The book was delivered to me without your card (you had not sent enough of them to the publisher); and on the heels of an exchange of letters with Gide at that same moment, I had been led to believe that it was he who had had it sent to me.

And it was already painful for me, when the work appeared in the review, to think that no correspondence afforded me the opportunity of telling you how much I liked, from the very first reading, this great, robust, and severe drama, prodigious in a very tight way and, out of urgent necessity, free. For I never cease liking, in your work, this enthusiasm for the "real," which always leaves you with such a solid base, and in this instance allows you to move about in the midst of contemporary history, to create, for our own time, something that is timeless, but accurately so.

The beauty of such a work [. . .] really strikes one as "feudal" in its very weightiness, so that it almost makes one wish it could be published in a "special edition for tax farmers."[2]

I like it for its shortcuts, which are grave and terrifying, and which you use as if you were playing a new instrument you have picked up at just the right moment —and that is not what is least astonishing to me.

With the greatest respect, as friend and admirer, please be assured that I remain your   Leger

1. *L'Otage* was first published in 1911 by the NRF publishing house.

2. The reference is to a much-sought-after 1762 edition of La Fontaine's *Contes*, with ornaments by the engraver, Pierre Choffard (1730-1809). The edition is often referred to as the "édition des Fermiers Généraux."

63

To Monsieur Paul Claudel   *Esquiez, near Luz (H.-P.)*
French Consul General   [*August 1911*]
Frankfurt-am-Main

Dear friendly Sir,

I've been a long way from Pau for some time now,

staying with a sister who asked me to come, and only when I went back to my own place did I find your latest book[1]—a great joy that awaited me.

And I still put off thanking you. —Here in this little mountain village where I brought a few books along with me, I've been waiting until I had read at leisure—and at leisure reread—the first version, with which I was not familiar, and the second, which I have always liked, of a work I so greatly admire that it sometimes strikes me as the finest hour of your whole theatrical output.

At this point I am moved when I think of this growing dramatic production in its totality, appearing in double-version editions. And I am moved by the thought of how hard and lonely it must be, in times like ours, to bring such a work as yours to completion. (Are we already in the period of universal mediocrity [. . .] predicted by Gobineau?[2] . . . the old age of the first era? [. . .])

And even to good artists, so selfishly taken up with their "lucky finds," you give a harsh lesson, with these "works" reworked, these double versions.

And to the others? . . . aren't you by the same token demonstrating the marvelous sense of balance that is present in all your work? [. . .]

I had the greatest pleasure comparing the two versions of *La Ville*, seeing what becomes of the crisis, so gravely developed and, in places, so smoothly elaborated, almost decanted—in the spacious and serene pulsation that opens the second version.

I admire the way the entire vast mural projection of the first version, pitilessly shorn of its happiest accidental details, of all side issues and unassimilable visionary insights, becomes something concentric: the conflict situated and circumscribed right from the first act, reduced to five characters; and finally, as we say in commercial law (I still haven't sloughed off all traces of my last examinations), the way you have there transformed "corporate capital" into a "corporation of persons."

Adding Lambert, combining Ly and Cœuvre in one character, so that the most searching exposé of the poet can this time be carried to its conclusion, the metamorphosis of Thali into Lala, the dancer enriched with a violinist, and this time in Cœuvre's own presence, raised to the height of the Cœuvre-Lala conflict; Avare given more relief in contrast to Lambert; Ligier swallowed up by Besme, and Bavon by Lambert. . . . All that is, quite simply, a source of pleasure for me, and I thank you for it.

There are good wishes for you in this letter, and my most affectionate respect.   Leger

—A young reserve officer named Alain-Fournier,[3] who had to come to the Midi for maneuvers, brought a copy of your *Annonce faite à Marie* to me here.

—Valery Larbaud, quite a long time ago, spoke of translations of Coventry Patmore[4] by you, about which I am most curious.

1. The second volume of *Théâtre Ière Série*, which contained only the first and second versions of the verse play, *La Ville*. The first version of *La Ville* was originally published anonymously in 1893. The second version appeared for the first time in 1901 in *L'Arbre*, a collection of some of Claudel's verse plays.

2. Joseph Arthur, comte de Gobineau (1816-1882), the French diplomat and writer whose theories of inherent racial inequality were seized upon by the Nazis long after Gobineau's death.

3. Henri Fournier. See above, letter 17, note 5, and letters to Alain-Fournier. (50, 51)

4. Claudel's translations of a group of poems by Coventry Patmore, the nineteenth-century English religious poet, appeared in the Sept.-Oct. 1911 issue of NRF. See letter to Larbaud of 22 Sept. 1911. (124)

64

To Monsieur Paul Claudel   *Paris, 176, bd Malesherbes*
French Consul General   [*December 1913*]
Hamburg

Dear friend,

Perhaps you have already completed moving into your new quarters,[1] started the pendulum of the clock going and set your watch on Greenwich time, at the moment when the "time ball"[2] is dropped from the height of the Free Port Tower. . . . If you've managed to find something better than what we saw together, you must be set up like a satrap. I hope it's in the same neighborhood, which is beautiful and resembles certain English cities in the tropics, where there are rain, gardeners, and the sound of women singing in open houses.

On leaving you, I took a train on which they forgot to paint an eye[3] and which acted up as it went through the Belgian countryside, to the consternation or amusement of the travelers of various nationalities.

I like your *Protée*[4] very much—a play that will get you in trouble with the intelligentsia and the Protestants. There's no one in your time to whom you could dedicate it. . . . not even (your) Romain Rolland! . . .[5] There is a starboard and a larboard of creative joy, and it is rare to find anyone who still knows how to roll from one to the other in full swing! (Wasn't the "paternal testicle"[6] cremated along with Moréas in Père Lachaise cemetery?)

I've gone back to work. My fate will be decided within five months. If I can be a consul, I'll be happy, feeling I've struck a true note in my life; and they can send me wherever they wish. —Meanwhile, I'd gladly install my desk under the Elbe.[7]

Give your little Chouchette,[8] on my behalf, the most

courtly old-fashioned kiss that she may consider worthy of her little feminine hand, and take your little boy to the zoo to see his "little Chinese brothers": there are three of them, black all over, that look like those young wild Guyanese boars that are still eaten on the oldest of the "Royal Mail" Lines, and for whom Audubon[9] sought his prettiest Yankee-from-Louisiana terms.

Affectionately.   L.

News from Jammes this very instant; his wife gets better and better.

1. During AL's brief stay in Hamburg, he had assisted Claudel in looking for an apartment where Claudel, newly appointed French Consul General in Hamburg, could install his family.

2. English in original.

3. A painted eye, as a charm to insure that a conveyance reaches its destination, is referred to repeatedly in Claudel's play, *Protée*. See Act I, sc. 3, and Act II, sc. 1 and sc. 5 of that play.

4. *Protée*, a two-act farce in verse composed in Hamburg in 1913, was published for the first time in the Apr. and May 1914 issues of the NRF. Either AL saw an advance copy of *Protée* or the letter is dated slightly too early. A second version of *Protée* was published much later (1927).

5. Romain Rolland (1866-1944), the French writer and pacifist, author of many works, including the long novel *Jean Christophe* (1904-1910). He was admired by Claudel but was never one of AL's literary passions. See letter to Larbaud of Sept. 1913. (138)

6. This reference to a private joke remains obscure. Jean Moréas, the turn-of-the-century poet and *boulevardier*, was indeed cremated when he died in 1910. It is also known that he underwent some sort of drastic operation in his younger days. But these facts scarcely suffice to explain AL's reference.

7. The reference is to a particularly memorable conversation that AL and Claudel had while seated on a bench in the long tunnel under the river Elbe at Hamburg. The two men were visiting the port on foot, and Claudel had asked to stop for a moment's rest in the middle of the tunnel.

8. "Chouchette," nickname of Marie, Claudel's oldest daughter, born 20 Jan. 1907. ". . . your little boy" is Pierre Claudel, born 23 Sept. 1908. It is hard to say what animals are designated by the "little Chinese brothers."

9. This is the first mention by AL of the famed early American ornithologist and artist. Later, Audubon is cited by name in the poem *Vents* (*Winds*, canto II, 1), composed in 1945, and is referred to in several letters. See letters to Caillois of 26 Jan. 1953 and Feb. 1953. (253, 254)

The Guiana boar here referred to is probably the "Collared Peccary" (*Dycotyles torquatas*) described by Audubon in *The Quadrupeds of North America* (1846-1850). Since Audubon (1780-1851) was the son of a "Saint-Domingue" planter, it is quite probable that AL, as a boy in Guadeloupe, heard about this famous "Antillean."

65

To Monsieur Paul Claudel   *Paris, 176, bd Malesherbes,*
French Consul General   [*January 1914*]
Hamburg

Dear friend,

I send my sincerest and most attentive wishes; you know that they are highly respectful of your works, and quite simply affectionate for yourself.

I've seen "no one" but Fontaine.[1] I haven't seen Berthelot[2] again, so as not to importune him, but I learned through Giraudoux[3] that your *Protée* slipped into France in the diplomatic pouch. (Will the pouch henceforth have an eye painted on it?)

I think of you. You live in a port city where the hammer-blows are marvelous! Soon they'll be taking the ice-breaker boat out of its shed—yet one more thing in this world that I wish I'd seen! The teeth of the Brazilian women in Cuxhaven must be chattering. And as for the river Alster. . . .[4] it must have been some time now since you took that path through the gardens and lawns to take the boat that deposited you in front of the Atlantic Hotel.

If you go into the little Hall of Noisy Birds at the zoo with your children some day, stop for a moment before the cage of the *Buceros elatus*,[5] the practical-joker

bird that plays dead, or else comes absurdly bounding up
to have its head scratched like a monkey—an odd little
fellow indeed, a disquieting and touching grotesque
from West Africa. I know of nothing more extraordinary than an animal that caricatures itself, and I wasn't
even aware that this lugubrious thing was possible. But
you have to go to Hamburg to see the African Carnival!

Maybe I'll see you soon, if the next run of *L'Echange*[6]
brings you to Paris.

Respectfully and loyally yours.   Alexis Leger.

1. Arthur Fontaine (1860-1931), a civil servant and future
director of the International Bureau of Labor in Geneva, who
was a collector of modern art and a man of wide culture. He
was a friend of Jammes, Claudel, Gide, and Valéry, among
others.

2. Philippe Berthelot. See above, letter 58, note 1.

3. Jean Giraudoux (1882-1944), the diplomat, novelist, and
dramatist, who was a close friend of the Berthelot family, which
he was to defend in a novel *à clef*, *Bella* (1926). As to the
"painted eye": see above, letter 64, note 3.

4. The Alster is a tributary that flows into the Elbe at Hamburg.

5. *Buceros elatus* is the elate hornbill, now called *Ceratogymna
elata*.

6. *L'Echange*, Claudel's verse play, which had had its première
in Paris at Copeau's Vieux-Colombier 15 Jan. 1914.

66

To Monsieur Paul Claudel   *Paris; 13, rue de Bruxelles,*
Paris   *[January 1914]*

Dear friend,

[. . .] Would you put my name in for the dress rehearsal[1] on the 22nd? I want very much to be there.

Cordially.   Leger[2]

1. For a dress rehearsal of Claudel's verse play, *L'Otage*, first
published in 1911.

2. For additional letters to Claudel. (52-66, 302-305)

LETTERS TO GABRIEL FRIZEAU
(1907-1909)

67

To Monsieur Gabriel Frizeau[1]   *Pau, March 1907*
Bordeaux

Dear friend,

What a very great source of strength for you it must be to partake of that "ecstasy," the etymology of which [ex-stasis] is so beautiful; and what an advantage to be able to transform your joys into joys of another sort, and your sorrows into joys!

I thank you for inviting me to participate in your Easter celebration. I have never spurned it.

But, please, don't think I smile as I write. Irony is either puerile or feminine; real irony is detestable and has made all of us suffer at precisely the times when we were suffering the least.

I am grateful to you for telling me about your children. It is so like you—and I am right there with you in your home; I've watched the flu take over. I don't have a very strong feeling about children, for it takes us a very long time to stop considering their lot in an abstract way. But I imagine that a little child's suffering must make a grown-up feel very helpless.

Even though so much is a matter of pure chance, I too keep thinking of your responsibility to Jean.[2] (When we want to tease Jammes, we tell him that a fear of children should keep all decent folk from getting married.) I understand your question about health, or rather, about my health. But I can't answer you briefly, for I wouldn't sound very scientific to you if I did. I came by my good health *above all* by willing it; that is to say, by autosuggestion. Consider that statement about as convincing and true as Goethe's quip: "We die only when we really want to." But I must add that I also had recourse to external measures.

My whole childhood was seared by attacks of malarial fever; and, unfortunately, I enjoyed these attacks so much that I would even pretend nothing was wrong just to avoid having to take quinine. Attacks of bilious fever, in spite of the accompanying delirium, had taught me to hate sickness and to dread having to stay cooped up, there in the Colonies (the boredom of a bird tethered by one foot); but later, in France, the feeling of not really belonging here, combined with pride and curiosity, were to plunge me into such an orgy of study that I almost did myself in by staying up late night after night. Later on, that came to an abrupt halt; I resolved once and for all to be physically strong.

At first I undertook a sort of health program, but in a haphazard way and without regularity, simply because I, more than anyone else, was incapable of sticking to it. I dragged my bed to the window, and from that moment on I've always slept with the window open, even in winter. I trained myself to wear less clothing more and more of the time and to go out in any sort of weather—thus eliminating colds and the like. I sought sunlight, instinctively believing, like the Malabars, in the "purification" of the body by the sun—(radiations); last but not least, I took to the mountains, with my father, in the beginning. That did so much for my physical well-being and had such a marked effect on my state of mind, that, in order to make the most of it, I refused a trip to Paris when school was out.

There were two basic functions that I re-educated: digestion and breathing. —Digestion, by complete mastication and insalivation (mental side-effects of this, very marked). That way I was able to eat much less and assimilate much more, with the result that I never have headaches or a sluggish feeling (time-wasters, both). —Breathing: *I learned how to breathe.* ABSOLUTELY BASIC! Proper breathing makes possible the control of one's *nerves*, balance, patience, confidence—in short, self-control—and above all, an *awareness* of all these acquisitions. (As a small child, I tried to overcome fear by breathing a special way.) The way I breathe, which has become second nature to me long since, has helped me to keep from getting irritated or losing my head in a number of very serious cases.

Finally, above all else, I am convinced that I fortified myself through autosuggestion—a formidable resource, the will asserting and reinforcing itself. The point of the following illustration is amusing and not really so silly. The tree that *wants* to bear fruit ends up fructifying. It became easier and easier for me to train myself—maybe even to the point of its becoming automatic (another resource!)—and to maintain a certain *mental* striving for physical strength, a self-affirmation on getting up and going to bed (and in this way I learned how to "adapt myself," even to store up a "potential" of strength). The moment the nerves act as an intermediary, the influencing of all physical functions is possible, indirectly.

I'm speaking solely about bodily health. Mental hygiene, disciplining the mind, and educating the will, are much more difficult and much less obvious.

And what can parental influence, passive education, be?—the only kind that is of interest to you in dealing with your son. That, I really don't know. You see what an important role I assign to awareness, to taking cognizance of things. One has to recognize and detest weakness on one's own. Fruitful action is the action a person effects upon himself. But I don't know how one would go about preparing a child to take such an initiative on his own.

I sound like a village schoolmaster; but, believe me, I more often blundered along, heedless and unaware. My parents, true Creoles that they were, never gave a thought to matters of health, and they let me grow up in my own way—a terrribly bad way. I owe my health to *my own* hatred of physical weakness. Physical superiority is something I *willed*, because it's the *only* superiority that has limits, and *the only kind of superiority that does not make one suffer*. When I was young, I wanted it for reasons of sheer brute force, and then, later on, in the belief that it determined so many things. I was afraid of my nerves, afraid—quite illogically—of a depression that would undermine the will, afraid of being carried away by dreams or music, afraid of losing control if I lost my balance, afraid—again illogically—of sickness, afraid of all the time-consuming little miseries, and afraid of *suffering*, which is detestable when it *demands* attention.

But first I had to reach a certain age. And telling you that my real tool was *willing*, constantly willing, is only begging the question, since what one really has to do is figure out how one learns to want to will something.

Still, where your Jean is concerned, you can "enforce" regularity—something I was never able to achieve for even a day when I was left to my own devices and will never really achieve. You can "enforce" the choice of food, which is so important. And you can also "do" a certain amount of physical training. Here, you should concern yourself SOLELY with the boy's thorax, because the lungs are the crucial organ, the actual reserve-potential of his future strength and of his stability!

—If mountain-climbing, for which there is really no substitute, is not feasible, have him do exercises at home.

My sisters benefited greatly from Swedish gymnastics (which involves special exercises for children).

There are also stretching apparatuses that are good for the thoracic cage.

Maybe he can already get started on fencing, which is also good for the chest.

You talked about going boating during your vacation. An oar once saved me when I was even younger than Jean, as I recall.

And have him sleep with his windows open, as English babies are made to do. Begin in summer. But I hope you'll put off buying him a bicycle as long as possible, and that you won't make him saw wood—Gladstone's wretched sport—though the old boy understood very well how to lead a healthy physical life.

Here is indeed enough, don't you think?, to anchor you to this earth "on which you are embarked."

Thank me for having chattered on, with your Jean alone in mind.

All yours
Yrs. truly[3]   Alexis L.

1. See above, letter 7, note 4. Gabriel Frizeau had been a schoolmate of Francis Jammes. AL had come to know him in 1904 during the early days of AL's studies in Bordeaux. It was Frizeau who finally persuaded young AL to send some of his poems to the NRF for publication.

2. Frizeau's health had never been very good, and he was much concerned to see that his young son, Jean, should be physically fit. He had consulted AL about AL's own experiences in improving his health.

3. English in original.

68

To Monsieur Gabriel Frizeau   *Pau, January 17, 1908*
Bordeaux

Dear friend,

[. . .] You ask me for my translations of the *Pythian Odes*.[1] I'll send you two or three of them when I have time to copy the notes I abandoned. Don't say, "your Pindar." What I have liked above all else, and for a long time, is an imaginary Pindar. Pindar is harmonious and moderate, terribly continent—taking his place with those who achieved perfection in the soulless centuries. But he's the greatest master of metrics in all antiquity.

I've read Rivière's first two articles in *L'Occident*, and I liked them.[2] He already knows how to strip down his language; his terms are precise. And that sort of criticism, which limits itself to restoring a work, is the only tolerable kind.

Th. Lovell Beddoes is the English poet whom Poe admired. (They died the same year.) A study devoted to him was written in 1894 by Mrs. Andrew Cross (in "Temple Bar").[3] I've only read one poem by him, a strangely and gravely ironical one.

I'm not familiar with this Dumesnil[4] you mentioned to me. But I do know of another mind that you would like for its lofty serenity: Lord Balfour, the Balfour of *The Foundations of Belief*.[5] He comes, I believe, from that admirable Scottish race, which gives us solid men, and would not give us the agility of a Gide.

I have word from Jammes, at Bucy. You must have seen him.   Al. L.

1. Pindar was one of AL's early passions. See OC, pp. 732-733, for a sample of the translations sent to Frizeau by AL.

2. Probably refers to the first two installments (Oct. and Nov. 1907) of his three-part article, "Paul Claudel, Poète chrétien,"

published in *L'Occident*. One earlier article by Rivière, however, had also appeared in *L'Occident*: "Méditation sur l'Extrême-Orient," in the July 1907 issue.

3. An article on Beddoes by Mrs. Andrew Crosse (OC omits the final "e") in the British periodical, *Temple Bar*, Mar. 1894, pp. 357-370.

4. See above, letter 7, note 3.

5. Arthur James Balfour (1848-1930), the British statesman who was Prime Minister from 1902 to 1905, was the author of several books, including *The Foundations of Belief: being notes introductory to the study of theology* (1895), which appeared in a French translation by G. Art in 1896.

69

To Monsieur Gabriel Frizeau   *Pau, March 23, 1908*[1]
Bordeaux

Dear friend,

You still question me about my translations of Pindar? No, they were not done with publication in mind; and I can't permit you to send them along to Claudel as you wanted to.

As I told you, they were simply a study-device for my own purposes—a study of metrics and verbal structure. Beyond that, my present knowledge of Greek, which is just about adequate for my immediate needs, is far from being sufficient to justify taking responsibility for a new translation as I conceive it, entirely independent of all earlier translations.

Basically, Pindar doesn't really fascinate me nearly as much as you persist in thinking; I find his themes tiresome. But, now that I admire him with more detachment, and from a more literal point of view, neither would I want to belittle this lofty, official figure as he has become enshrined in the Hellenic myth.

I don't know why, but when Pindar is mentioned,

and the moment the word *Epinikia* [*Odes*] is pronounced, people are always tempted to assume blindly some modern conception of great, individualistic lyricism, compounded of jubilation, exultation, and intoxication—a conception that has nothing to do with the moderation of the Greeks in their choral lyricism. There is nothing of this in even the most individualistic, the most unusual, and the loftiest of the great Greek poets, because Greek poetry for the lyrical poet is not a solitary, but a collective, even quasi-collaborative, phenomenon. We must not forget that the Greek "Lyric Poet" is a "Coryphaeus" ["Leader of the Chorus"].

In the commissioned art of a Pindar, the close collaboration of recitative and song, along with the dance, even, or the ritual movements of the chorus, subjugates him from the outset to a threefold discipline, which singularly increases the subservience of the analytical text. There is no true extravagance in this great respecter of rules, who was unjustly suspected in Athens of "sowing from an overflowing sack."

A three-dimensional poet, he is surely the one who does not write in profile; but there is in his lucid rapture, in his coolly conceived rapture, a great sense of unity that requires a withholding of the poetic afflatus. The very movement of his verse, the indispensable movement, is bound solely to the rhythm of a pre-assigned modulation.

"Pindaric intoxication"—an intoxication with rhythm and musical keys—all the keys manipulated like sluice-gates, to release a flood of sound rather than a distribution of verbal elements. It is the retribution of the Just Man. Yes, the poem of a Just Man. And from a man who was not by nature created for justice—which is parsimonious. The whole thing is saved by the authoritativeness of the tone, which is sustained from the outset.

(The individual verse and sometimes even the whole poem, in Pindar, seems to strike only a single note.) If he knows, or knew, what it means to be really intoxicated, he doesn't sit down to write until an hour later, faithful in this to the lesson taught him by Athens, whose prestige he had finally to submit to.

You already have a pretty good idea of what I think of "Atticism." Pindar, alas! remains for me a natural-born poet turned from his true bent by a culture foreign to him.

When I think of this Nordic from a great indigenous race, of this Theban, this Dorian, who by birth was backed up in some obscure way by the whole continental mass, well beyond the Cynoscephal Mountains[2]—a man of hardy patrician stock, from an ancient caste attached to the soil, a caste in which the priestly tradition of the family was still hereditarily practiced—in short, everything that was by nature farthest removed from the urbane spirit of an Athenian—when I think of all this I can't stifle still another grievance I feel against triumphant Panhellenism, whose parasitism may have cost us a vital element in Greece, an element perhaps much closer to the great Celtic substratum than to anything of Mediterranean origin.

The Macedonian, pupil of Aristotle, made no mistake, when, marching on Attica, he refused to do honor to anything along the way at Thebes except to the memory of Pindar. —A wonderful story.

Yours, dear friend, most affectionately.   Leger

—Do you know if Rodier[3] is still teaching in Bordeaux? (Alexandrian philosophy?)

—And can you also tell me when the next big fencing tournament will be held in Bordeaux? Will the Italian masters be there?

1. This letter is out of order in OC, where it appears on pp. 742-744, after the letter to Frizeau dated 27 Feb. 1909.

2. Cynoscephalos, a range of Thessalian hills whose summits resemble dogs' heads, whence the name. They were the site of several battles celebrated in antiquity, including one in which the Roman consul, Flaminius, defeated Philip V of Macedonia.

3. Georges Rodier (1864-1913), professor specializing in Alexandrian philosophy, who was the editor of the learned journal, *L'Année philosophique*, from 1904 to 1912.

70

To Monsieur Gabriel Frizeau   *Bielle (canton de Laruns)*
Bagnère-de-Bigorre   *Maison Henri Beyle*
                                  August 22, [1908]

Dear friend, another bereavement, a very heavy one—I have lost my father's mother, really my own flesh and blood, whom I still needed in order to understand myself. —But I don't want to be forever talking of bereavements.

I received your card. I am just close enough to you to realize that I'm far from you. I've conned the timetable; there's hardly any possibility of my going to see you from here. —But tell me when you expect to leave Bagnères, and if your itinerary might not take you near to Orthez, and then to Pau. Jammes must have his child as of yesterday;[1] maybe you'll go to see him.

I would be *delighted* to see you again. To me you are not a face stuck onto a detachable collar; I like to remember you, and you extended a helping hand to me.

I've been here since July. I can't believe that I've ever lived in a city. I'd like very much *not to be* convinced that living is an art, a profession, in our hands. To keep trying without a candle, *what a laughable thing*! . . .[2]

The mountains of Ossau are moderate ones, but they are the ones I first learned to love; and in them the wish, the *mortal* wish to live a thousand years—if not three thousand, as in the Antilles—grows on you. —But that's still simply living, when the important thing is to be lived.

I'm not familiar with Bagnères, where I try to picture you. I know the two big ranges of Bigorre, but I've always started out from Barèges.

Here, just as there, it's summer: warmth and light!

Light! after the inconceivable misery of one metaphysics after another, which can't even throw light on *dreams*!

Once again I've had to experience the horror of withdrawal after entertaining high hopes. —May I withdraw still farther! The nearest position is really the most hopelessly distant one. And whoever, in our day, would write the Mystical Book, should inscribe on it as an epigraph: Who comes from just across the way does not go far! —When I was little I used to cry at the thought of the inhabitants of the *rings* of Saturn. —No, that really wasn't so stupid. Think about the centripetal eccentric rings—satellites, but within the system; within the system, but satellites!

There's nothing more to tell you.

I'm in a terrible jam over an English edition of Pindar that was "lent" to me, because I couldn't afford it.

Did I tell you that *Le Mendiant ingrat*[3] was in Jammes' hands?

M. Dumesnil's[4] book is a bowl of lymph. An elliptical writer would be easier to understand than this explicit philosopher. It's the position he maintains that is admirable.

Mme. Burnat-P.[5] has published another book this year, very inferior to her *Livre pour toi*. —If it is of the least interest to you, let me know.

I'm sending you an issue of *Pan*, a rather stupid review, to which I submitted some verses.[6] —I can't abide them, and to *you* I say that just as frankly as I would say the exact opposite. But you know that we have to pay tribute to the reviews by being impersonal about them.

I'm sending them to you (still one more *act of faith*) so as not to seem to be skulking along the walls (it's a form my pride takes)—and because I won't be giving any more verse to the reviews—and *because* you live in Bordeaux (like sounding out Nassau or Puerto Cabello).

[. . .]

I am most cordially yours.   Alx. Leger

[. . .]

1. Jammes' first-born, his daughter Bernadette, who inspired the book of prose pieces, *Ma Fille Bernadette* (1910).

2. English in original.

3. The first of the eight volumes of the journal of Léon Bloy (1846-1917), the apocalyptic Catholic pamphleteer and writer. *Le Mendiant ingrat* (*The Ungrateful Beggar*) covers the period 1892-1893 and was published in 1898.

4. The book in question is Dumesnil's *Du rôle des concepts dans la vie intellectuelle et morale* (1892). See above, letter 7, note 3.

5. See above, letter 54, note 4, and letters to Frizeau of 19 Sept. 1908 (71), and Mar. 1910. (78) No book by Burnat-Provins other than *Le Livre pour toi* is listed for the year 1908. A novel, *Le Coeur sauvage*, is listed with the date 1909 in the Talvart and Place bibliography, with the note: "This book was withdrawn from circulation and the edition reduced to pulp on orders from the author a week after its publication." Could AL possibly have seen an advance copy?

6. See letter to Monod of Sept. 1908. (7)

71

To Monsieur Gabriel Frizeau   *Bielle (vallée d'Ossau)*
Bordeaux   [*B.-P.*]
                                      September 19, 1908

Dear friend,

Pantheism?—a tremendous question! Tremendous especially for someone who doesn't talk. This pantheism, which the critical side of me rejects, I carry it with me still in the innermost recesses of my body: that is the ineradicable contradiction.

But I'd prefer to answer you in a couple of days from now. I'm leaving in a moment and hardly have even a few minutes to spare.

Dear friend, I am sorry to hear that you are not well. I realize so fully what it must be for your eyes to suffer torture from light itself. Isn't the worst torture of all having to wish that winter were here? But the country around Bigorre was not good for you, so hot and bare, so pitilessly sharp in outline.

I hope with all my heart that nothing will keep you from coming nearer to Orthez within a month. If it's granted to me to see you in Pau, I'll take you to see a very beautiful Bassano,[1] and also, at the home of a priest friend of mine, some wonderful primitives, and then a Spanish *Christ with reeds* that Carrière[2] looked upon piously.

Claudel has announced the birth of his son to me. A son! . . . a God-given prey that he now has on his hands.

If you saw Jammes for a time, maybe he read you a fine prose-piece that he read to me in June or July: *Notes sur la pauvreté*.[3] In it, there is a poet of our byroads, bearing his knapsack, whom, as we leave, we are tempted to clothe in shreds of string, like a ragged angel. And the marvelous thing is that, out of this serene, ironic prose, soft-spoken and made up of details, one can achieve lyricism, by a curious process of introversion. Nothing could be more English: a poetic Wells[4] would admire it [. . .].

You mention Marguerite Burnat-Provins.[5] Judging by her last book and all her letters, she is heading straight for Christianity. (But she won't "get all the way there" precisely because she is a woman and hasn't covered enough ground.) I think she is just about the only woman, at the present time, who has true artistic temperament and integrity. It strikes me as a fine—and healthy—sincerity; and for once, there is more than a womb, really a lot more. —Having said that, I add that I don't like female ink any more than you do. Good God, no! That's the ink that supplies us with the most stupidities about the word "living." For there is not a single woman who understands the monumental stupidity of the three words to "live one's life" coming from her mouth! When all is said and done, the women who shout the Bacchantes' cry loudest live on a diet of paper flowers and bits of tapestry, like stray goats in the street. And their literature, like their art, always has something marginal about it, something slightly frilly; it doesn't look as if feminine taste will ever get beyond handkerchief-boxes or stationery. [. . .]

Most affectionately yours.   Leger

What gives your letters such a delightful smell of aloes or agave? Maybe you're using an exotic ink without realizing it!

1. Iacopo Bassano (1510- or 1516-1592), Italian painter.
2. Eugene Carrière (1849-1906), painter and lithographer who was a friend of Francis Jammes.
3. Unidentified. Jammes may have published the piece under some other title.

4. H. G. Wells (1866-1946), the English popularizer and science-fiction writer.

5. See above, letter 54, note 4.

72

To Monsieur Gabriel Frizeau   [*Pau*] *January 13*, [*1909*]
Bordeaux

Dear friend,

Toward the end of January you will receive a visit from a painter and engraver that I introduced to Jammes: Ernest Gayac.[1] He's a friend of Charles Lacoste, and Odilon Redon once made a very favorable comment on something of his. I'll be talking to you about him again soon, and so will Jammes, as I'm very eager that Jammes himself should tell you of the visit.

But what about you? Tell me, aren't you coming to Orthez, to Villeconstal? You promised us you would [. . .].

Your book, all marked up, tells me that your eyes are much better. Perhaps they even permit you to read the serial publication of Nietzsche's *Ecce Homo* in the *Mercure*.[2] Never has the Great Monkey let the sound of his chain be more clearly heard. How can one accept the word "free" from a seesawing mind that is strictly controlled by contradiction (even when it confronts itself!)? Free! I am, you are—that is the condition Nietzsche lays down; we all hold on to the other end of the chain. And what's most amusing is that such a genius cannot cut his teeth unaided, and that even he has a certain "altruism" in his make-up, since he needs all of us, without exception, so as to have opponents. I think N. is as simple, precise, and symmetrical as a cast shadow. His cleverness is mechanical; it's an inversion, a subversion— not even a real transformation of values, simply a "repetition." Let's give the word "succubus" a new meaning by applying it to him! . . . The Traveler proposes and takes the place of his shadow; if I take that place, he will insist on taking the place I originally occupied.

Three pages! . . . You can see, though, that I'm letting myself talk on . . . as on that second evening when I sat in your house.

For two months now I've been trying to track down for you, in Germany, the photograph of a portrait of Edgar Poe that exists, I believe, somewhere in Bavaria(!). If I can manage to find two copies, will you be so good as to send one to Claudel for me[3] [. . .]? I can't write to Claudel any more [. . .]. It was really only as a Catholic that he was concerned with me. And then, he would feel that he had to reply.

[. . .]

Always reserve some of your friendship for me.

Leger

1. See above, letter 14, note 3, and letter to Frizeau of Mar. 1911. (79)

2. A French translation of Nietzsche's *Ecce Homo* appeared in five successive issues of the *Mercure de France* beginning with the 16 Nov. 1908 issue. AL's critical comments disturbed Rivière and Monod. See letter to Frizeau of 27 Feb. 1909. (74)

3. The two copies of the photograph of Poe were finally obtained by AL and sent on to Frizeau. In a postscript that Frizeau added to a letter to Claudel dated 3 Feb. 1909, we read: "I am sending you a photo of E. Poe that A. Leger asked me to send. He wanted each of us to have his own copy." (Translated from the Blanchet ed. of *Claudel-Jammes-Frizeau Correspondance, 1897-1938*, p. 149.)

73

To Monsieur Gabriel Frizeau   *Pau, February 7, 1909*
Bordeaux

And I, too, dear friend, am being towed along by a
steamer. I'm following my cousin[1] as he is outward
bound toward those "climes" where we have never
ceased to live . . . the Islands! For ten or twelve days
already, it isn't here that I really go to bed or get up,
here where it is winter! —For my cousin, each day
dawns more luminous, more blazing, and in greater
haste. At the latitude of the Azores he puts aside his
steamer rug; the seagulls stop following the ship. Then,
three days later, a phosphorescent sea, and then the Sar-
gasso Sea; the first "frigate bird." . . .[2] The wind is west;
from far off, the plantation-smell, like Bermuda lilies
(from very far off, to the nose of a Creole!). Does my
cousin catch that smell? Day before yesterday he took
out his white clothes; yesterday he slept on deck (the
Southern Cross at spar-deck level, to starboard); and
today, just think! the course lies between the first islands,
with islets around the roadstead: my father's islet, Saint-
Leger-les-Feuilles, that we sold; and the other islet that
belonged to my maternal grandmother, where they sent
our family in the malarial season [. . .].

I, too, linger on. You can imagine with what obsession, what physical torture!

And yet, I sometimes say to those around me, exoticism is, in the last analysis, nothing but a horrible gri-
mace—a kind of satanism! a flight, a cowardly flight! yes,
a flight! (And that's the reason why, now, I recoil at the
thought of taking refuge this way—withdrawal, nonpar-
ticipation! Would I be less at odds with myself out there
than I am here? At least it would be only because of
mere things? . . . Still this same old cult of the faun-

man who stands just behind me, who will never cease standing there.

Ah, yes! one thing I understand very well—for you, it took nothing less than the Absolute Garden[3] to liberate you from exoticism.

I thank you for the welcome you extended to my good cousin. *He* belongs entirely to Europe and suffered on leaving it. He is not a weak sort, simply mistrustful, timid when alone with himself; he'll always need someone around, a helping heart. I'm a little uneasy about him because of the prodigious solitude of Marie-Galante, the little island that you have so vividly imagined. I've never been on it, but it was there in the distance, opposite the "Habitation" of my Uncles[4] where I grew up until I was twelve years old; from there, while I recited Greek declensions (ἡ τράπεζα, the table . . .) I recall watching the lives of the people across the way through an old telescope transformed into a marine spyglass. How well you grasped everything that the island means in terms of being cut off! "Se-creta" = "Se-clusa": whence "O-missa."

That "O," which is the very shape of an island, don't you find it everywhere in Gauguin?—and even in human forms, miraculously! as in the canvas you have in the drawing-room, to the right of a cartoon by an artist unknown to me (it's in a more or less symmetrical position to the "Cabaret").[5] The painting that I call "L'Animale" has haunted me for a long time. If you ever have it photographed, think of me, please. I even ran across a page I'd written about it, while I was putting things in order these days—or rather, alas! while I was weeding out a collection of prose pieces that I must destroy (because I was afraid, with two years gone by, that it was not all absolutely my own—exactly and solely my own) —in form, I mean [. . .].

Have I told you?—the only thing I really care much about here is music. This winter I've taken up with two friends of Vincent d'Indy[6] who really resemble men, or something very like men.

Claudel has written me a very kind letter [. . .]. A few harsh affirmations about Catholicism, which he says places man in the center of the universe, precisely and ever so rightly.

Yes, I had heard about this *Nouvelle Revue Française*.[7] A Belgian, André Ruyters, who is on the editorial staff, wrote to me in December, asking me, on behalf of his review, for a wretched manuscript of mine that the old review *Antée* still had [. . .]. I admit that such insistence prejudiced me against the new review, and I didn't answer. I'll have to send something else [. . .]. Besides, I feel that one should give to the reviews only what isn't worth printing in book form, and above all, impersonal things: if need be, rhetoric, professional exercises!

I don't want to pose as someone who rides serenely above all this, because you have to have found your wings to do that; yet I assure you that, for the moment, all this is very remote from me—very, very remote. (And I just wouldn't have the willpower to go poking my nose in manuscripts again, unless it would be to throw the whole lot out. Even the stuff I gave to reviews, I'm recalling from all sides.)

My cousin misinformed you if he told you that I was still working on literary projects. But it's awfully nice of you to take an interest in them.

Besides, I've just wasted three months learning one of life's harsh lessons, after a bereavement. And now that I've just about got over that, I'm going to have to get busy here with my law studies!—in the midst of family affairs that leave me an hour or two a day to give my body a workout.

But the light is rather beautiful this winter [. . .].
Most cordially.   Leger

1. This unnamed cousin of AL who was going back to "the
Isles" i.e., Guadeloupe, had been warmly welcomed by Frizeau.
2. Cf. the evocation of the frigate bird in "Cohorte." (25)
3. The "Absolute Garden" is probably a reference to some
Christian mystic—and certainly a reference to Frizeau's recent
conversion to Catholicism under the influence of Claudel. See
letter to Frizeau of Mar. 1907. (67)
4. The Habitation was one of the two plantation houses belonging to the maternal (Dormoy) branch of AL's family. It
was actually named Bois-Debout ("Standing Wood") and was on
a sugar plantation on the east slope of Basse-Terre, the moun-
tainous "wing" of the "butterfly island," Guadeloupe. It looked
out across the Caribbean towards the Îles des Saintes and the
larger island of Marie Galante. This is the house referred to in
the last lines of the poem, "Pour fêter une enfance."
5. This particular Gauguin painting remains unidentified.
There were several Gauguins in Frizeau's collection, the most
famous being "D'où venons-nous, que sommes-nous, où allons-
nous?"—which is now in the Boston Museum of Fine Arts.
6. One of the two men was certainly the pianist, Paul Maufret
(see above, letter 9, note 1). One cannot be certain of the identity
of the second.
7. The first "genuine" issue of the NRF appeared in Feb. 1909.
After a false start in Nov. 1908, the new magazine really "got
off the ground" with the Feb. number, issued under the names
of Ruyters, Schlumberger, Arnauld [Drouin], Gide, Copeau, and
Ghéon. The name of Jacques Rivière was soon to be added to the
list, because of Gide's promptings.

74

To Monsieur Gabriel Frizeau   *Pau, February 27, 1909*
Bordeaux

Dear friend,
    What's this? Irritation and indignation in Paris from
my friends Rivière and Monod just because of a simple

statement I made to you about the way Nietzsche's mind works: the automatic reflex of contradiction and his enslavement to it.

"Sacrilege, defamation!" . . . I like to see my friends so wrought up, and to know that such freshness of feeling is still possible even on the benches of the university. —Has the university ceased to be the university? Or has Kantian impersonalism finally taken a beating in that old Logicians' Lodge? In that case my Nietzschean friends would look like pilgrims in quest of a new Grail.

The most amusing thing about it is that, by nature, I go much farther than they do in my taste for Nietzsche. My only objection is that he doesn't himself go far enough into Nietzsche. It's not the fact itself of contradiction that bothers me in him, but his inability to pursue it all the way and finally exploit it to the fullest. A sudden break may be more productive than any logical chain of reasoning—scythe-strokes or thunderbolts of contradiction, risky as they may be in the restricted field of the mind, may open up more paths for man's desperate footsteps than they conceal from him. And since forces that act at a great distance seldom miss the mark, liberating them may be less destructive of new opportunities for the mind than generative or revelatory of such opportunities. The real inconsistency of Nietzsche, that Grand Inquisitor, is that he hasn't managed to carry the inquisition of his inconsistencies far enough—that is, to that final explosive flash-point where irrationalism might finally lay bare the paths to a super-rationalism.

Him, more than anyone else, we would like to see take that final leap, without losing his sandals, into the crater of the absurd.[1] But all his hatred of metaphysics doesn't even lead him to continue his forward drive. Instead, it's nothing but turning tail, a flight that, far from liberating him, will play him the ultimate dirty trick of bringing him back automatically, in circular fashion, to that other enslavement, that equally wretched obsession—the "perpetual return!"

Bankruptcy and shipwreck, that something in him that is frenzied and panicky, rather than truly elevated; an inability to take hold of anything—and on the part of the greatest marauder ever seen to have invaded the lands of Christendom [. . .].

But this compelling companionship still holds great attraction—a very lofty and stimulating course of hygiene for the living, combating every kind of laziness and quietism. And the man himself, to be sure, delights us, to the point of prejudicing us in his favor—for so much irreverence and initial animadversion, for such absolutely final disapproval of every sort of false conventionality.

But, much as he fascinates us, and as much as we like to stack the cards in his favor, how can one silence the great reservations that must be made in the face of such inadequacies? Admirable Nietzsche! provided we don't take this disquieting lyric spirit too literally as a true "philosopher."

But even of the "poet," don't force us to say aloud what we are silently obliged to think: a detestable poet, because, and in spite, of all the prejudices in his favor that could be brought to bear!

Besides, he isn't the only case of such an anomaly. Blake, Novalis, Nietzsche: three thoroughbreds of the "uneven" family. Their aphoristic thought strikes us right off with its initial grand manner and its unequivocal promise—daring of the soul or the mind; but their poetic performance, once they're in the harness, is, alas! terribly disappointing (even to the point of making us feel vaguely uncomfortable, vaguely nauseated in a way one hates to admit—*embarrassing*[2] as it can be better expressed in English).

Is that still more "blasphemy?" If so, tell Rivière I'm sorry. And you, dear friend, I hope you will judge all this fine indignation to be as healthy a thing as I feel it is.

Affectionately yours.   Leger

1. According to legend, the Greek philosopher Empedocles threw himself into the crater of Mount Etna, which then spewed forth one of the philosopher's sandals.

2. English in original.

75

To Monsieur Gabriel Frizeau   *Pau, March 9, 1909*
Bordeaux

Dear friend,

[. . .] Yes, I did receive the book by Chide.[1] [. . .] It contains some rather elegant, often even original, thought—not very forceful, but, what is rarer, suggestive, and interesting to me [. . .]. The subject-matter is, moreover, a synthesis—a rare thing these days.

I want to tell you still once more how happy I am, in my isolation, to receive books from you [. . .].

I ran into Jammes and his wife at a concert in Pau. I told him about your Blanc de Saint-Bonnet[2] [. . .].

And finally I must reply to you about my manuscript, "L'Animale."[3] Your letter was delivered to me one morning at just the moment I had decided, for a second time, on totally renouncing literature [. . .]. The precarious hour that my unskilled handling of family affairs left to me, I must now devote to law [. . .].

I am most truly yours.   Leger

1. Alphonse Chide (b. 1868) was the author of a philosophical study, *Le Mobilisme moderne* (1908), that had irritated Frizeau and Claudel, but interested AL.

2. Antoine Blanc de Saint-Bonnet (1815-1880), an arch-conservative French Catholic philosopher, author of *L'Amour et la chute* (1898), which Frizeau and Jammes admired, but which AL found insipid.

3. This problematic manuscript, which was apparently never sent to Frizeau, must have been inspired by the Gauguin picture referred to in AL's letter to Frizeau of 7 Feb. 1909. See above, letter 73, note 5.

76

To Monsieur Gabriel Frizeau   *Pau, Wednesday,*
Bordeaux   *June 2, [1909]*

Very dear friend,

Again a few hasty lines to ask you to extend a welcome to the musician, Paul Maufret, who is passing through Bordeaux and would like to call on you, and who has written just this morning to tell me so—(Thursday, the third—probably between two and three o'clock).

Maufret is a friend. And I must tell you that Jammes, to whom I introduced him, finds him most congenial and, well, in his own right, worthy of sitting down with you for a brief chat.

He is a wonderfully sincere artist who, in his earlier days, abandoned scientific studies for that other sort of mathematics which is music. And I admire the "training school" from which he graduated: d'Indyism.

He is also a man of great dignity who keeps to himself and is even timid to excess, but informed with seriousness and a fine simplicity. —I think he suffers somewhat from having had, for reasons of health, to abandon the Schola and exile himself in Pau. —He is quite curious about general culture and would be most grateful to you if you would let him see your pictures. I once told him about your Gauguins.

What else is there to say about him? —He's thinking of giving a concert in Bordeaux next winter, and maybe you would be able to give him a few pointers right on the spot about the choice of his program.

There! —I just hope he won't arrive at a bad moment for you. If you can spare him a moment, accept, as of now, a bit of my gratitude.

Very affectionately yours.   Leger

77

To Monsieur Gabriel Frizeau   *Pau, June 23, 1909*
Bordeaux

I've been away. But right off, dear friend, what a joy to be able to write these few lines under your very gaze![1]
I thank you.

I was afraid of being indiscreet. But, you see, in my friendly relations I have to combat a sort of amnesia where faces are concerned—an amnesia that afflicts me with a fear of some day not being able to recognize them. (I spent a whole day with Claudel, I *watched* his face; and, believe me, if I sat down next to him today, nothing would give me immediate assurance that it was not a stranger! A Villiers[2] would have seen smthg. diabolical in this, like real severance, like the damned who may never look upon God—and he would have said: When one falls away from God, one no longer knows how the men he created look!)

But now I have recaptured your look—that veiled, distant something that one can fleetingly discover in it. For you have the eyes of a man who hears weeping. And your face in this portrait doesn't convey all of you, but at least the refusal and the renunciation are there; and beyond that, a desire to keep one's "distance," a kind of "animal indolence" and "patience," something even more *lofty*, a sort of "musical slackness" that is the true, active goal. (Faith is a reign.) You back away.

(Don't bother with all these words used with their etymological meanings!)

You must indeed have "traveled" in some way, for I caught something of your look in those relatives of mine who had traveled a great deal. (Isn't that just another way of drifting?)

And now, please tell me that I haven't been indiscreet.

I understand why you hesitate in your choice of a vacation spot, if you have to combine taking the waters with simply getting out into the open air. I don't think you can really find, in the Pyrenees, a *mineral* treatment for the nerves. The waters are always more sulfurous than sodic there; or else, if they are desulfurized, as at Cauterets, their efficacy becomes purely imaginary. They'll tell you about Saint-Sauveur (where my mother conscientiously took baths for her nerves). But you can be sure that there, just as at Eaux-Chaudes, the cure is entirely a result of the climate. At least there is a spring there that is really a specific for the *stomach*. —You can see I'm not pleading my own case. For at Saint-Sauveur I wouldn't see you, whereas Eaux-Chaudes is 12 kilometers from Bielle.

Maufret came to tell me his great regret at not having been able to call on you, as he had hoped to. He'll be going through Bordeaux in August and late September. You won't be there. But he'll see you this winter, as he is supposed to give a concert in Bordeaux. Unless he sees you before then at Eaux-Chaudes. He is supposed to come here to Bielle to give me the treat of organizing a mass in Gregorian chant with three female voices. I really don't *know* what his standing as a composer is; I've never heard anything by him. All I know is that d'Indy, this year, did an orchestral work of his in Paris. But he's neglecting composition for performance—without our being able to dissuade him from it; for, even though he is very strong in technique, he seems totally lacking in imagination.

Very affectionately yours.   Leger

1. This letter was written shortly after AL had received a portrait of Frizeau.

2. Villiers de l'Isle-Adam (1838-1889), the symbolist writer, known especially for his posthumously published drama, *Axel* (1890).

78

To Monsieur Gabriel Frizeau   *Pau, March 1910*
Bordeaux

Dear friend,

For too long now my days have been snatched from me as soon as I get up, and I am constantly deprived of the pleasure of chatting with you. I am ashamed of having left your letter unanswered for such a long time. You have no idea how I break into a smile at the sight of your hyaline-blue envelope among all the letters from lawyers, notaries, or bankers!

My time is now as completely taken up as if I had a profession. I won't complain about it; but why do you think I should be "proud" of it? —My only consuming wish was to be able to live like a "grammarian!"

I haven't been to Bordeaux yet. I was able to put off my trip in order to steel myself here for a groundless lawsuit with which I am threatened. I have a young lawyer whose blunders I have to be continually on guard against. [. . .] I also had to take care of a citation to put a stop to a short-term prescription, and now my poor scum of a debtor is in the process of dying of typhoid fever.

I expect to be in Bordeaux right at the beginning of April. I'll certainly call on you and spend a little time with you. I'll return the books by Fabre[1] to you, which, I hope, you'll excuse me for keeping so long. I take good care of a book when it's a good one, and even when it's not a good one.

I'd like to arrange things so I could see Rivière too. I believe—I *know*—that there is now a very solid, warm friendship between us, and a lasting one, because it sprang up in the most natural way.

Gayac[2] must be in Bordeaux at the moment. His wife is here. I really think you should put pressure on him to keep him from committing the unthinkable blunder of doing an apocalypse! Even Albert Dürer's woodcuts on the subject are hard to accept. An illustration that is exclusively "beautiful" precludes, once and for all, its being "inexhaustible," kills its chances of holding boundless reserves! Gayac will get himself hated!

Which doesn't alter the fact that I greatly admire Gayac, but I'm not at all sure that he's the imaginative sort; or at least I'm afraid that his imagination follows the beaten track much more than it wanders off anywhere it pleases! There is in him, so far as I can make out, a whole fund of romanticism that he should get out of his system once and for all by illustrating Hoffmann.[3] After that, then, don't you think he ought to let himself be "reincarnated," to get a good healthy dose of humanity again by illustrating some broadly human document like Cervantes' *Don Quixote*? —Edgar Poe? I really don't know! Basically, Poe never grimaces; and will Gayac be able to see that, while in the tales of the "grotesque and arabesque," Poe has his back turned to us, with a mask at the nape of his neck, one can't for a moment neglect the other side, the watchful live presence of a sublimely ordered face!

Well, Gayac must be with you at this very moment, and I'm glad of that, for you've already helped him a great deal.

You ask me for news of Madame Burnat?[4] —The poor woman! She didn't undergo just one operation, but four; they took two hours, at the end of November. Since then her convalescence has been slow and difficult; she can't manage to rally and doesn't conceal her bitterness. She is in a terrible state of poverty, unbearable to contemplate. She wasn't the one who first told me. I don't know if she's been able to pay all her hospital expenses. She left Saint-Moritz a month ago and is with a woman relative at Cantin, in the North.[5] She sent me a poem that is *so* literary in the worst sense that I concluded from it that she was really suffering very badly! I think, judging by her last letters, that she would like to bury herself somewhere in the Pyrenees. Buy her album-books, which you don't have to read (there are always the pictures). She is dependent on book sales.

Am I writing a piece on the Pau Salon?[6] —No, dear friend, I'm being spared that this year—spared the task of finding a scapegoat to load down with praises and good wishes, like an obstetrician! . . . But you don't have any idea what a salon at Pau is like. (And obstetrics doesn't bring in enough to feed its practitioner!)

I don't read *La Phalange*,[7] but I did read it for a time. It's a rather shady outfit, very South American, a lower deck loaded with persons of all colors and crawling with "mestizos." But it's possible, after all, that one might have a little better chance of running across something interesting there than in exclusive, high-toned circles. —If, that is, one could believe that chance meetings take place in reviews! —I can't keep up with the reviews, not even with the good old *Mercure*,[8] which we ought to receive the way we do a "Dalloz publication"[9] — I'm too isolated here; I'd have to subscribe to too many things. —But why your question about *La Phalange*? —I recall that you once talked to me about submitting one of my manuscripts to it; if that is still possible, don't do anything of the sort, please. I don't like reviews. If I one day had what it takes to publish, I might again work over that ancient piece, along with some others, but in a more personal, more strictly personal way. I think that, these last two years, I can really write the word "*mine*."

But please don't take this for conceit! My intention is to come very close to renouncing literature for good.

You ask me if I'm going to be a consul. I haven't yet had time to put the question seriously to myself. Right now I have to devote all my energies to preparing for my law exam. I'm a long way from being ahead of schedule, in view of the little time I have left.

When I pass through Bordeaux, I hope you will give me some information about Spirito Santo (Brazil). I was *obliged*—I'll tell you how it came about—to keep 8000 in N.E. Spain; the rise is continuing and makes my mother's counselors jubilant. But if you feel a slump coming on one of these days, I'd be very grateful if you alerted me.

You'll be reading, I think, in the next issue of *La Nouvelle Revue française*, three poems[10] I sent to Gide four weeks ago (fifteen or so pages, I think, judging by the proofs). They're of no interest to me any more because I let them get discolored (and I now understand the danger you pointed out to me of waiting too long to publish = never publishing). But I do recall that in them I strove for a musical effect, using verbal material as if it were pure sound. It probably doesn't come off, but I had fun revising them, a long time afterwards, when I recopied them. I think it would be a grave mistake, even a mortal one, to confuse the two methods of composition: verbal and musical; and developing the verbally intelligible theme with the thought of musical instruments in mind, in a very literal way, would be ridiculous. But doesn't it seem to you, as it does to me, that tonal considerations may rightfully compete for the poet's attention, provided that they are first raised from an unconscious to a conscious level and then are once again reduced to the unconscious level (isolated words in different keys)?

Jammes is well now, after a bout of flu. He was here at the house recently. I hadn't seen him for several months. He has all sorts of projects. His book on Bernadette[11] is about to come out; the volume is on press.

Cordially yours.   Leger

1. Jean-Henri Fabre, *Souvenirs entomologiques (1870-1889)*.

2. Ernest Gayac. See above, letter 14, note 3. Gayac, who corresponded with Frizeau, often scandalized him by his bold and advanced ideas.

3. E.T.A. Hoffmann (1776-1822), the German romantic, especially celebrated for his fantastic tales.

4. See above, letter 54, note 4.

5. In Northern Switzerland.

6. On 28 Mar. 1909 AL had published a review in *Pau-Gazette* concerning a controversial painting by Georges Bergès (1875-1935) which had presumably been exhibited in the annual Salon de Pau.

7. *La Phalange* was a literary review created by Jean Royère in 1906, to which many of the "neo-Mallarmean" poets contributed, as well as others, such as Guillaume Apollinaire and Jules Romains.

8. *Le Mercure de France*, the famous literary review founded

by Alfred Vallette in 1889. It continued publication, with only brief interruptions, until 1965.

9. The Dalloz publishing house, founded in 1824, was a standard source of French legal books, as well as of standardized student outlines and works in economics.

10. "Pour fêter une enfance," "Récitation à l'éloge d'une reine," and "Ecrit sur la porte," which actually did appear in the Apr. 1910 issue of NRF.

11. Jammes' book about his daughter Bernadette. See above, letter 70, note 1.

79

To Monsieur Gabriel Frizeau   *Pau, March 1911*
Bordeaux

Dear friend,

You are doing me great service, and I congratulate myself on having turned to you. You remove any hesitation I may have had, because a doctor friend of mine, whom I first consulted, gave me exactly the same two names: Arnozau and Cassaït—with this slight qualification: that Cassaït might be less "official," though even better qualified, judging by the accuracy of his diagnoses, as a physician to be consulted.

So I'll see Cassaït right away on Monday, because I'll be arriving in Bordeaux before this member of my family does; and if Cassaït, after he has seen her, confines it strictly to something pulmonary, I'll take her to the specialist recommended by Dr. Mesnard.

News of the Jammeses? They have been back from Gers for several weeks already, because I've seen them twice here at the house, and they were in Pau again quite recently for a Maufret concert. Jammes is awaiting the first booklet containing the first two cantos of his *Géorgiques.* The second one, which he read to me from the proofs (*Wine—Corn*) was more open to intoxication, and within just as strict limits. He'd already started on a third canto.

My Pau friends? —Maufret fell ill, right in the middle of the concert season. He has to give up the trip to Bordeaux again and devote all his energies to his remaining concerts in Pau, both the piano concerts and the ones with the Schola.

Damelincourt is working very hard, too hard.[1] His haste has something tragic about it. And his mistakes are tragic, too, because I really feel that there is in this steadfast and rugged soul some of the mysterious gifts of the true painter.

Smith[2] has finally published his translation of *Don Quixote* into English. He is still very cool towards his compatriots.

Gayac's wife[3] stopped by. She's exhibiting five new plates, one of which, *The Miser*, is to me a work descended from good stock, of good lineage, in which Gayac has really outdone himself—it's the solidest thing of his I've seen since his *Satyr*. —His *Magician* seems to me strongly influenced by Redon. His *Concert*, if it had a different dancing figure, would really be a good piece, for the left-hand corner, with its alternating white masses, makes it a beautiful "composition."

I'm writing to you with an open suitcase next to me. I wish I had time to tell you at greater length how much your letters, even when hastily written, interest me and, in more than one way, set off trains of thought. —"*More leaven! More leaven!*"[4] . . . isn't that a much finer, and more general, rallying cry than Meredith's "*More brain!*"?[4]

The way you lay claim to Claudel, in the big-circulation French press, seems to me the most fruitful way.

Remind me to tell you when I'm in Bordeaux one of these days, the way Jammes took Claudel's "cynical" Crucifix in *L'Otage*.[5]

Yes, the verse form that Jammes is presently using simply betrays even more clearly the strict way his metrics fit his breathing, that is, fit the work he has assigned himself—and there's an open-road pace that is entirely different from a mountain-climbing pace, and that also differs quite as much from a normal walking pace. The only thing is that it seems regrettable to me to generalize as an *a priori* principle and dogma (an *ars poetica*) what is a purely accidental mystery. —The strictest laws of musical composition, though derived from mathematics, and though quite ineluctable, are none the less quite consistently experienced by, and revealed to, our inner beings by what is most *ancient* in them.

You mentioned Signoret[6] to me in connection with Pindar. I'm not familiar enough with Signoret to be able to answer you. All I've read is a few fragments in anthologies. I found there a fine classical nudity, but it too often came close to a kind of emptiness. So much so that it would seem to be less a genuine lyricism than an occasion calling for lyricism (less matter than mold), which must really be supplied by the reader. Signoret brings us the sacrificial stone, the altar, which is well-wrought, but he is not the only one present at the sacrifice. —One might be very enthusiastic about his work one day, and the next day find it distasteful, I think. And if it does happen that a verse of his is really charged, glutted with its own reality, as a result of continuousness and sameness, it is not long in sliding back, like the sound in a conch-shell, into a kind of soundlessness. Each verse of his, and sometimes the whole poem, strikes only a single note. A rather monotonous lyricism, it's seemed to me, really too uniformly lyrical, too musically lacking in relief—(doesn't a flame itself have its shading?). I think that it would require a real effort at being attentive to be able to read very much of such a pure poet extensively without letting whole sequences of verses escape one's hearing at first reading.

Musically, nothing could be less Greek, since the whole of Greek phonetics is based essentially on the multiplicity of "keys" on one and the same staff. And nothing could be less Pindaric—above all! For in Pindar (the most deliberately musical of all poets) the verse, indeed the whole stanza, is invaded (... "*invahi*"[7] would do better) by incidences that make the melodic line weave in and out among all the unexpected movements of the dance. The "Pindaric intoxication" you speak about is analyzed by me as follows: An intoxication with rhythms, in their purest form—nothing more [...].

Hastily, dear friend, I say *au revoir* to you and express the wish that I'll have the opportunity to greet Madame Frizeau and embrace your children. Yours, with all my heart.   Leger

1. Hubert Damelincourt (1884-1918) was a painter who had set up his studio in Pau. He was physically handicapped and finally took his own life. AL became a friend of Damelincourt, introducing him to Jammes and Frizeau and even writing an article about him in the 9 Jan. 1910 issue of *Pau-Gazette*.

2. Robinson Smith (b. 1876), whose translation of *Don Quixote* did appear in 1910 under the title *That Imaginative Gentleman Don Quixote de la Mancha* (London: G. Routledge; New York, Dutton).

3. See above, letter 14, note 3; and letter 78, note 2.

4. English in original.

5. Claudel's verse-play, *L'Otage*, had just been published in the three successive issues of the NRF: Dec. 1910, Jan. and Feb. 1911. One of the principal characters in the play, contemplating a restored crucifix in an old Cistercian abbey, says, in this original version: "Et maintenant le grand bon-dieu noir rongé par le soleil

et la pluie, le cynique supplicié." (Act I, sc. 1) ["And now the great black Good Lord, weathered by the sun and the rain, the cynical crucified victim."]

Francis Jammes, in a letter to Claudel of 8 Feb. 1911, praises *L'Otage* but adds: "So far as I am concerned, the only thing I find to criticize is the word 'cynical' applied to the Crucifix (First act). Whatever your etymological reasons may be, I don't understand them. That adjective *should not* be there." (English translation of French text in *Claudel-Jammes-Frizeau Correspondance 1897-1938*, p. 198.) Claudel defended his use of the adjective, but Jammes persisted in his objections. Claudel finally wrote: "No, Jammes, I don't understand your point of view about the word 'cynical.' But if it offends you in the slightest, I submit and cross it out. Let's say no more about it." (English translation of French text in *Ibid.*, p. 200.)

So Claudel's definitive version reads, "le scandaleux supplicié." Jammes, in his next letter to Claudel, thanked him for the alteration.

6. Emmanuel Signoret (1872-1900), a poet of Parnassian tendencies whose work was admired by Gide, who wrote the preface to the posthumous *Poésies complètes* of Signoret, published by the Mercure de France in 1908.

7. Normal French for "invaded" is "envahi"; "*in*vahi" restores the original Latin form of the prefix.

80

To Monsieur Gabriel Frizeau   *Pau, April 30, 1911*
Bordeaux

Dear friend,

I come to you as embarrassed as a child who dares not show himself.

I ought to have thanked you immediately for the financial sheet that helped me to arrive at a decision about my mother's Mexican shares. Since their steadiness in the market seems explicable only by the presence of old Porfirio,[1] I'm keeping my eye peeled for a good arbitrage so we can sell them before his death (not the whole lot, because these shares have been highly recommended to me, but rather the portion of them that makes the holding too large for a portfolio as small as my mother's). What is annoying is that the quotations on "Mexican Central" can not be followed in the French papers, since only the bonds are given there.

I've been able to make a nice profit for my mother on the last Moroccan loan, which I bought into when it was floated and sold just a month ago at its maximum exchange rate: 527.75. The news from there struck me as too unsettling.

In place of that, I bought some Buenos Aires Intern. at 6%, a little above par (s. at 111.25). I regret that this Buenos Aires stock, unlike the Argentine, can not bring in a surplus, but it seems to me that these are not bad stocks to invest in. Please tell me what you think about this. I vaguely remember your saying something to me about it.

I also bought some Banque Rouvier stock, the only "shares" that I allowed myself to take a risk on. Their too spectacular rise in value doesn't exactly reassure me. Maybe this is the moment to sell?

I tell you all this, dear friend, so you may be able, if the occasion arises, to help me keep from making a bad move. I am so clumsy, and so ill-equipped to cope with the *necessity* of buying unstable issues! And I have such a hard time training myself to handle this sort of thing, which is so harassing to me!

I hope the news at your end is all good. Write me that it is.

Here, for Madame Frizeau, is the musical information that I abjectly apologize for not yet having sent her! (Madame Frizeau is benevolence personified, so I ask her to pardon me for having buried my head in law studies.)

—The great d'Indy sonata, in my eyes his masterpiece for the piano, is his Sonata in E, opus 63, 1907. —I've just heard it again; Mme. Frizeau's piano technique will permit her to tackle, very patiently, the great difficulties of this work. But what strictness here, what severe constraint for a feminine sensibility!

—The most practical, most empirical method, if I may say so, on use of the pedals is Falkenberg's *Les pédales du piano*—available at Ménestrel, Hengel & Co., 2 bis, rue Vivienne (10e).

Lavignac's work would be of less immediate relevancy for a pianist.

Good news of Jammes, at whose house I lunched recently. They have reserved a house for the summer, along with the Goedorps, at Saint-Jean-de-Luz. He read his third canto to me and the beginning of the fourth. Very much between us, Claudel wrote him that, without understanding in any way his attitude on the subject of the word "cynical," he yielded to Jammes' insistence and withdrew it.[2]

Claudel wrote me a long, very careful letter, for which I am profoundly grateful to him. But he rightly says that he knows nothing about me—about my character, about my aptitudes, from a practical point of view. I know that he has written to Jammes for information on these matters. If he also questioned you, please insist strongly on this point: I am not in any way ill-adapted to life; my life is devoid of all vagaries, and I strive to make it regular, literal, and diligent. I will be able to give free rein to my private whims in other areas. Up to now my life has been nothing but one long, conscious effort at training myself for the most bourgeois kind of discipline and balance—with a deep hatred for any sort of "literature." I bear down a bit on all this because I'm afraid that Claudel may be tempted to see me through the latest poems of mine he's read, even though he spoke to me about them (but from an artistic standpoint) in very laudatory terms, of which I was proud.

While I think of it—my family is very satisfied, in the matter of our Creole friend, with the treatment or, even better, the influence of Cassaït. Thank you again for advising me.

Here Maufret has just put on, with a hundred performers, and soloists from the Paris Schola, a remarkable rendition of *The Passion according to Saint John*.

Do you know whether Schmitt was given Pennequin's[3] baton in Bordeaux?

I've had to set the whole *Nouvelle Revue française* against me these days by withdrawing a ten-page poem[4] already in proof, which had already been printed up for the May issue. That involved me in quite a correspondence; Gide wanted to prepare the readers of his review for a short sequence of *Eloges* that I gave him and that I had copied off for him personally. He wanted to turn them over to his review. I may even withdraw those, too. I get no satisfaction out of publishing, none whatsoever. It even annoys me without my being able to say just why. Nor do I like to acquire the reputation of being "peculiar"—peculiarity being a flaw, in my eyes. Well, it just doesn't give me any *pleasure*.

In addition, I live alone; my life is somewhere outside the *Nouvelle Revue française*.

But Gide continues to be very nice, even "affectionate."

One of his friends, a woeful figure of a traveler—Valery Larbaud[5]—spent a day here with me. Read, if you have the chance, his *Fermina Marquez*. It has real flavor and is exquisitely written, very thoroughbred, very French. A real talent as a storyteller (the most thankless and rare of talents).

Rivière doesn't say anything to me about his novel any more. I like the way he worries, indeed, even gets frightened about literary matters.

Give me news of your children.

Transmit an affectionate thought to Darbon;[6] and my respectful homage to Madame Frizeau.

Cordially yours.   Leger

1. Porfirio Diaz (1828-1915), the dictatorial president of Mexico at the time.

2. See above, letter 79, note 6.

3. Jules Pennequin (1864-1914), director of the Conservatoire Municipal de Bordeaux.

4. The text "Cohorte." (25)

5. See letters to Valery Larbaud. (121-145)

6. Perhaps André Darbon (1874-1943), a philosopher and professor at the Lycée de Bordeaux.

LETTERS TO FRANCIS JAMMES

(1906-1912)

81

To Monsieur Francis Jammes   *Saint-Sauveur,*
Orthez   *September 1906*

Dear Monsieur Jammes,

Here are two letters I have just opened; they are from the *curé* of Goyave,[1] where your grandfather is buried. Because I wanted some photographs and a few items of information for you, I wrote to the *curé*, though I can't any longer recall in exactly what terms. Here is what little I was able to get out of this priest, who seems almost to be suggesting that you "file a property claim." He is undoubtedly familiar with your name, since, judging by his letter, he knows you are a poet.

In any case, you really must admit that he is diligent and that he lost no time in cutlassing the thickets and brambles of the "Champ d'Asole."[2] I like it that it was the work of a priest; maybe now you'll be a little less annoyed with me.

I have just this very moment received a letter from your friend Claudel, who asks to be remembered to you. He doesn't have the text of "Léonainie"[3] any more and refers me to his "excellent friend Frizeau," to whom he gave a translation of the poem that is much better than the translation in *L'Ermitage*. —His letter is cordial in the most unaffected way. He says I should write to him; he refers to himself as a man in exile, congratulates himself on having a great deal of work, and complains about the ugliness of the country in which he is living;[4] but "the marvelous sky" nevertheless makes it possible for him "to do some writing." —In another place, I am happy to say, he calls Stendhal "odious," this Stendhal whose old papers are constantly being dug up by our reviews.

I take leave of you, cher Monsieur Jammes, I hope to see you again soon. I've been here in Saint-Sauveur since I was freed from Fort Portalet,[5] and I'll be returning to Pau four days from now. This transition will make my stay in town a little less disagreeable. I don't know as yet whether I'll be in Pau, Bordeaux, or Paris during the coming year. I've decided against medicine, as I have decided against many other things.

Very affectionately yours.   Alexis L.

1. AL, some time between 1900 and 1904, met Francis Jammes during an excursion to the Betharam caves in the Pyrenees. Jammes was curious to meet the other members of the Leger family, since his own grandfather had lived and died in Guadeloupe. AL then became quite friendly with Jammes, frequently visiting him at nearby Orthez, where the two often botanized together.

The reference here is to the grandfather in question, who was buried in the little village of Goyave on the coast of the island of Guadeloupe. Jammes refers to him in his "Elégie seconde" thus:

> Que ta main, en passant, frôle pour se bénir
> la correspondance grave de mon grand'père.
> Il dort au pied de la Goyave bleue, parmi
> les cris de l'Océan et les oiseaux des grèves.
> Dis-lui que tu t'en vas trouver son petit-fils.
> Son âme sourira à ta grâce un peu frêle.
>
> (III, strophe x)
>
> [Let your hand, so it may be blessed, touch lightly,
> as you pass, the grave letters my grandfather wrote.
> He sleeps at the foot of blue Goyave, amid
> the cries of the ocean and the shore birds.
> Tell him you're going to go see his grandson.
> His soul will smile at your rather fragile grace.]

2. Probably the name of the cemetery at Goyave.

3. Claudel's translation of "Leonainie." See above, letter 52, note 2.

4. In 1906 Claudel was stationed in Tientsin, China.

5. AL spent the last three months of his military service at Fort Portalet near the Spanish frontier.

82

To Monsieur Francis Jammes   *Pau, April 6, 1909*
Orthez

Dear friend,

I am sending you some manuscripts. I hesitated a long time. I have nothing that I like, or rather that I don't dislike.

Still, I'm sending you more pages than I did last year, for fear of making a bad selection; I've picked out those that differ the most from each other, and chosen them from different bundles.

It *seems* to me that I could do much better (but I really can't say), if I could only believe that it was still worth doing. Since my last vacation I've done no *re-working* of any of my notes, because I've lost confidence.

The page headed "Ulysse au bâton,"[1] which you will read, is the most recent. It seemed to me that there was more propriety in its language, which is less concrete. —But I really can't tell about that either.

Maybe it could be printed in one of the reviews you've spoken to me about. I'd really like to have something published at this time, because I've just had a regrettable mishap—which I'll tell you about—thanks to André Ruyters, in connection with a terrible schoolboy manuscript.[2]

[. . .]

Most cordially, I am your   Leger

I'm sorry I couldn't copy off for you the rather long

poem[3] that I sent to Frizeau. His excessive praise terrifies me a little, and I don't know just what to think about it. But I assure you that my rough draft is unusable. It's written in pencil, with footnotes and adjectives piled one on top of the other, and alternate wordings—and I can't even remember which ones I finally decided on.

1. A text that was destroyed, lost, or incorporated into some other poem.

2. Reference to a manuscript that AL had submitted to the review *Antée*, of which Ruyters had been one of the editors. *Antée* ceased publication in 1908, and many of its manuscripts were passed along to the newly established NRF. AL had wanted to withdraw the manuscript in question but did not act promptly enough. This was presumably the manuscript of "Images à Crusoé," which was printed in the Aug. 1909 issue of the NRF.

3. This poem has not been satisfactorily identified.

83

To Monsieur Francis Jammes   *Bielle, July 30, 1909*
Orthez

Dear friend,

Do you know approximately when Claudel intends to leave China, and can you tell me if there is time enough for me to send one last greeting to him?

Thinking of you and yours, with deep affection, and with my best wishes for the health of Mme. Francis Jammes.

                                                          A. Leger

I'm having lunch tomorrow with Maufret, at Eaux-Bonnes, and I'll speak to him about the Collet manuscript.[1]

1. Henri Collet (1885-1951), French composer, who was a friend of Francis Jammes. See next letter.

84

To Monsieur Francis Jammes   *Bielle, August 7, 1909*
Orthez

Dear friend,

Maufret can't say anything about Collet; he's not familiar with any of his work; he met Collet at Bordeaux when Collet was quite young, at a time when he didn't yet seem seriously concerned with music. I mentioned the manuscript of songs you spoke to me about. If you want his really frank opinion, send them to me, and I'll see that he gets them, and then he'll write to me [. . .].

I'm delighted to have good news of your family.

There's been a change of schedule these days that affects the stop at Bielle; we're studying it. My mother will write to remind you about the day you promised to spend with us.

It's through you that I have learned of the publication in *La Nlle Revue Française*,[1] which, they told me, would appear in the September issue. It does seem to me that they could have sent me a copy, since that review, according to what you said, is delivered only to subscribers! Some day at Orthez I'll ask to see the issue; that will make me happy, I think. —I thank you very much for your note and the way it helped. In spite of all the deletions I told J. Schlumberger to make, I was still afraid that there was nothing worth while in all that.

Most cordially.   Leger

1. The "Images à Crusoé," which appeared in the Aug. 1909 issue, rather than the Sept. 1909 issue of the NRF.

85

To Monsieur Francis Jammes   *Pau, January 13, 1910*
Orthez

Dear friend,

[. . .] I thank you so very much for sending me your
Elégie.[1] The down-to-earth cow-level diction, the earth-
colored faces, the birds of passage—and the amazing
sonorities in these long verses, their sustained quality,
from near and far—it all struck me as so many fine
things that I felt I must tell you about.

Affectionately yours.   Leger

1. "Elégie d'automne," which appeared for the first time in
the *Mercure de France*, 1 Jan. 1910.

86

To Monsieur Francis Jammes   *Pau, December 1910*
Orthez

Dear friend,

Thank you for the issue of the *Mercure*[1] that you had
sent to me. I'm reading your *Géorgiques.*[2]

I can't help feeling a little uneasy about this new preoccupation you have with the highroad of latinity.

What I like in a literary work is an inherent urge to
seek out the country and race to which it really belongs,
regardless of any of the accepted standards of the reign-
ing literati.

Any number of things would then shine as brightly
for me as do already "The Lark and its young with the
Teacher who knows but one song,"[3] or as a certain verse
that echoes Ovid: *Circus erat pompa celeber numeroque
deorum*[4]. . . .

I don't know just why, when one listens to you striking your surest notes—

"J'entreprends dans mon âge mûr ce grand
    labeur. . . ."

"Ainsi moi à mon tour. . . ."

"Après un grand combat où j'avais pris
    parti. . . ."[5]

one thinks, in spite of oneself, of the Roman rhetorician's
little school where, you must occasionally dream, it
would really be nice to have a child some day learn your
name.

Most cordially, dear friend. And remember me to your
family. My mother and sisters join me in assuring you
of our affection.   Leger

1. The *Mercure de France.*

2. The "Premier Chant" of the *Géorgiques chrétiennes* appeared in the *Mercure de France*, 16 Dec. 1910.

3. Quotation not identified.

4. "The circus will be thronged with a procession and an array
of the gods."   Ovid, *Fasti*, IV, line 391 (J. G. Frazer, trans.)

5. These fragmentary verses of the "Premier Chant" come
from the following lines of the poem:

J'entreprends dans mon âge ce grand labeur.
Il est le fruit que donne au bel été la fleur.

. . .

Ainsi moi à mon tour comme ces grands ancêtres
Et comme le chevreau j'ai vu naître le monde.

. . .

Après un grand combat où j'avais pris parti
Je regarde et comprends qu'on s'est peu départi.

[I undertake this great labor in my mature years.
It is the fruit that the blossom gives to a fine summer.

. . .

And I, in my turn, like my great ancestors
and like the kid, I have seen the world being born.

. . .

After a great combat in which I took sides
I look about and understand that nothing much has
    changed.]

87

To Monsieur Francis Jammes   *Pau* [*beginning of*
Orthez   *June 1911*]

Dear friend,

I did receive Canto III of your *Géorgiques*. I am
touched by your thinking of me. My profoundest thanks.

But I won't speak to you about it right now. I'm overwhelmed with preparing for my last law exams, which
this time involve a field that is perilous for me: actual
legal procedure, and financial legislation. I'll wait until
I'm on vacation in the Ossau countryside to write to you.

Please believe, as I do, that my affection for you is
great and steadfast.

Most cordially.   Alexis Leger

Valery Larbaud, from England, asks to be remembered to you.

Good news about Claudel, the latest comes from
Vienna.[1]

1. OC has "Vivien," an undoubted typographical error for
"Vienne." Claudel was in Vienna from March 9 to 13 in 1911.

88

To Monsieur Francis Jammes   *Pau,* [*June*] *1911*
Orthez

Dear friend,

I don't understand how you could write to me in this
vein over the mere publication, by André Gide, of a few
poems by me in the *N.R.F.*—poems published quite by
chance (and full of typographical errors at that).[1]

Without your knowing, you say? —You know very
well that between us, or at least on my side, it is never a

question of anything literary where I am concerned. That is not where the chief interest of my life lies; and I already find it hard enough to express myself about almost anything else, and more urgent matters, as I confront life itself.

And wouldn't it also be quite understandable that the affectionate concern of not wanting to displease you or disappoint you in any way makes me constantly a little mindful of the gulf, which is quite natural and which is perhaps widening, between our literary tastes, as well as between our philosophical or political convictions?— without this affecting in any way everything that I like about you as a poet and man?

If I really were the *kind* of poet that you may have wished me to be, would I really find any more pleasure in being so?

Believe me, dear friend, your letter was unfair and made short shrift of the profound sincerity that has always made me turn toward you, in mind and heart.

So do forget all the rest that really doesn't matter between us, and take me at my word when I say I am very affectionately yours.   Leger

1. Jammes felt quite hurt at not having been given advance notice of the publication of two successive groups of poems by AL in the NRF: The first group in the Apr. 1910 issue, comprising "Pour fêter une enfance," "Récitation à l'éloge d'une reine," and "Ecrit sur la porte"; the second group being the mutilated text of eighteen "Eloges" that appeared in the June 1911 issue. See above, letter 28, note 2.

89

To Monsieur Francis Jammes   *Pau, June 1911*
Orthez

Dear friend,

Why do you again write to me in this way, which is
surely the worst possible way between friends, and which
is over nothing but a mere literary matter?

If you intend to mortify me in a literary way, you
really couldn't have chosen worse grounds. If it is simply
that you were offended in any way by my letter, then
I'm sincerely sorry and have no qualms in expressing
my most deeply felt regrets to you.

It was never my thought to say that your letter was
"unfair" in any of its literary evaluations—how could
you impute such nonsense to me?—but simply that it
was "unfair" to think that I deliberately sought to conceal what I did from your literary view.

Once again, please forget all this, which sounds all too
literary, and let's not be too hard on the friendship between us when I have so little time left to spend in this
part of the country.

Yours, most faithfully.   Leger

90

To Monsieur Francis Jammes   *Pau, [end of]*
Orthez   *June 1911*

Dear friend,

In this same envelope, two letters from André Gide.
Jean Schlumberger has written to me in similar terms. I
shall accept this offer of *errata* for those massacred
poems.[1] But in what form? Should I accept the publication in booklet form just as it's proposed to me?

About the actual publication of these unfortunate poems, your letters have really hurt me—by the very fact that it was friendship, you tell me, that dictated them.

You can't really believe that I'm neglecting my situation and my family obligations just because I let a few old manuscripts, which I had sent to André Gide, be published in a review. Nor can you really suspect me of self-indulgence. And you will also see very clearly, in Gide's letter to Rivière, that I have never—far from it! —"secretly" nursed that eagerness to publish for which you criticize me.

In that, too, your letters were unfair. I do not harbor the arrogance nor smugness that you always seem to detect so readily. I live far removed from any young literary group, and if I occasionally indulge, quite in spite of myself, in writing poetry, it is without the slightest thought of publication, but simply to aid me in seeing things more clearly and vitally within myself, in this mystery of life through which I journey alone.

You know better than anyone else how pressed for time I am and how little inclined ever to be gravitating around literary reviews, or to be bothered with any Parisian circles. My life has other cares, of a much more basic sort, maybe even of a more commonplace—but immediate and urgent—sort, leaving no room for self-indulgence.

And that, too, I would have told you—not without sadness and heartfelt friendship.

Affectionately.   Leger

1. The "massacred poems" are the eighteen "Eloges" in the June 1911 issue of NRF.

91

To Monsieur Francis Jammes   *Saint-Sauveur (H.-P.),*
Orthez   *September 1911*

Dear friend,

This letter bears wishes for you and yours and for your work, as well as a thought for the little child that has just been born to you.[1]

No more talk between us, please, about the little book of *Eloges* put out by Gide at the *N.R.F.* publishing house. All that is a thing of the past. I am deeply appreciative of the way you now write to me. I was especially touched by the thought that you wanted to be the first to write something about me.

Thanks for the good news you gave me about Claudel. A young fellow from Paris, Alain-Fournier[2]—who, as a reserve officer, is taking part in large-scale maneuvers in the Gers—came all the way here to bring me a copy of the manuscript Claudel sent to the *N.R.F.*: *L'Annonce faite à Marie*. It's the transposition, which we had already heard about, of *La Jeune Fille Violaine*.

I think I'll be in Paris in about two weeks, to see Philippe Berthelot,[3] a few other people in various circles, and some of my mother's relatives,[4] before I make up my mind about a professional commitment. If it should prove necessary for me to give up all thought of a career in an embassy or consulate, I would have to fall back immediately on Egypt or Chile. I'll stay in Paris as long as necessary, if I am able to see people who may be able to help me get oriented a little through their first-hand knowledge. I should be back in Pau towards the beginning of October or November.

Affectionately,   Leger

1. Jammes' daughter Marie.
2. See above, letter 17, note 5.

3. See above, letter 58, note 1.

4. The relatives in question were Auguste LeDentu, a maternal great-uncle who was a surgeon and wished AL to take up medicine, and Olivier Sainsère, a cousin by marriage of AL's mother, who was a member of the Conseil d'Etat and who wished AL to follow *his* example. See above, letter 41, note 2.

92

To Monsieur Francis Jammes   *Pau, February 16, 1912*
Orthez

Dear friend,

Now that all the correspondence and all the reflections are over, I can give you my answer: negative.[1] (In this same envelope you'll find a copy of my letter to your financier friend, who had a far too favorable opinion of me.)

It's a matter of great sadness to me that, the first time I am offered a position, and through so friendly an intermediary as you, I have to decline. It is painful, in my relation with you, and in a family situation such as mine, to seem so hard to please. But after long and cold reflection, I still had to face up to the fact that it would be a grave mistake, in either a short- or long-term way, to commit my whole life to a career in finance. And it is not at all simply because I would be unhappy in such a career, but because I am sure I wouldn't find in it, on my own, the full measure of success as I understand it.

But above all don't think that in *any* career I want to have leisure for literary pursuits. Long ago I firmly resolved to resist any literary temptation, even were it marginally and with a good livelihood assured [. . .].

Yours, most affectionately,   Leger

1. AL had been referred, by Jammes, to a Paris financier.

LETTERS TO ANDRÉ GIDE
(1910-1914)

93

Monsieur André Gide
Paris

Pau, Monday,
[December 1910]

Jacques Rivière has written to me; he says I should send you poems for the *Nouvelle Revue française*. And it's obvious that I can't forget the very kind way you received my literary efforts last year.[1] But I was well aware that my poems might be disconcerting. Which is not at all what I would like, please believe me. The trouble is that I don't know what to choose.

I've picked out the enclosed pages. It seems to me that, short of being as explicit as a process-server, they couldn't have been written more literally, in a more "juxtalinear" way (for they just barely give way to song, and only towards the end).

At least, even to the most wary reader, they can't possibly seem tainted by peculiarity. (And I live too far removed from literature—which I am too eager to sacrifice to "really living"—ever to be pleased by that sort of misunderstanding.)

I address this note to you, Monsieur, as I would like to be permitted to sit and talk with you if ever I passed through Paris; what I mean is, as if it weren't already too cold here, and if Paris—I can whisper this into your ear—were not closer to the Pole than is commonly thought.

Please accept, Monsieur, my most devoted and respectful good wishes.

Tell Rivière, who will deliver this note to you, that my affection for him is very great.

A. Saint-Leger Leger
37, route de Bordeaux, Pau

1. Reference to AL's "Images à Crusoé," which had appeared in the Aug. 1909 issue of the NRF.

94

To Monsieur André Gide   *Pau, 37 route de Bordeaux,*
Paris   *[January 1911]*

I liked your letter very much.[1] I thank you.

The *Nlle R.F.* is the finest and most liberal of all the reviews [. . .].

Herewith, under the same cover, with the title of *Eloges* (the whole thing copied out, not haphazardly, but with the thought in mind of not becoming winded too soon), some short things—which were a bit free only in "phantasy" (if you will permit me to revive an outmoded spelling).

If these things don't really appeal to you, you must tell me so [. . .].

And now I pray you most respectfully not to be annoyed with me nor to mistrust or dislike me, if I take the liberty of noticing or feeling that your envelope, when I hold it, and without my knowing just how, is filled with sadness, fatigue, or boredom. Anyone but a stranger to you would have been quite upset by it.

Maybe you're still expecting a straw hat as a New Year's present [. . .].   A. Saint-Leger Leger

1. Gide's letter had praised those of AL's poems that had already appeared in the NRF and requested still more.

95

To Monsieur André Gide   *Pau, April 9* [*1911*]
Paris

Valery Larbaud paid me a visit;[1] he came with your friendship as a reference; and he himself is most likable and has the most natural way of being likable.

While we were chatting, he told me that you were soon going to print in the *Nlle R.F.* some poems that I sent to you in January: I beg of you not to do anything with them until I've received proofs.

[. . .]   Leger

1. This is the earliest reference to Larbaud's first visit with AL. Reference is made to the same visit in a letter to Frizeau of 30 Apr. 1911. (80). See also letters to Valery Larbaud. (121-145)

96

To Monsieur André Gide   *Pau, Saturday*
Cuverville, Normandie   *April* [*1911*]

Very dear Sir—I would like to be able to say "friend," for it is to your friendship that I am appealing—help me. I am terribly upset; I am obliged to ask a very real service of you. I am withdrawing, I am forced to withdraw,[1] the manuscript for which I have just now received the proofs. So help me, please help me, in getting the review to accept this withdrawal without their holding it against me too much; [. . .]; and tell them, in order to justify me, that I was never informed by the review.

Those pages on Birds[2] I picked out simply as an amusement, as you know; I[3] had immediately sent you something else, and there was no question of printing this earlier manuscript. I've just reread it. It is senseless; [...] it can't be published; no consideration, not even of being tactful towards the review, could ever make me accept the idea of letting it get into print.

So I'm appealing to you; I beg of you, please help me to withdraw it—I mean, please help me in getting the review to accept the withdrawal I am making.

I know neither M. Schlumberger nor M. Ruyters; but Jacques Copeau is, I believe, a friend of Rivière's; he will do his best to overcome any annoyance he may feel. It's not a matter of great importance to them; there is still time enough to re-do the make-up of that issue [. . .].

And you, *cher Monsieur*, if you are able in this way to help keep me from harboring bad memories of the *Nlle R.F.*, rest assured that I shall find some way to thank you;

most cordially.   Leger

I'm keeping the proofs. Please drop me a line telling me whether I myself should write to the review, and to whom.

1. From the NRF.
2. The poem, "Cohorte." See above, letter 25, note 1.
3. In the printed text of this letter in OC, AL has added, for clarity: ". . . as an amusement, *and for you alone*, as you know: *for the review*, I had immediately sent . . . ."

97

To Monsieur André Gide   [*Pau*] *Wednesday*
Paris   [*April 1911*]

I thank you.[1]
Here is a way I have found to thank you, and I think it will be a good one:

I am giving you this tree, the ninth from the left, which is one of the most inexhaustibly[2] beautiful things —I mean simply the most beautiful—that one can contrive.

A member of my family planted it—it really is of no importance to you to know where—on a little island that has only a local name.

I am familiar with this specimen. These trees are thoroughbreds. Here, tormented by the nearness of the sea, is the great species *Oreodoxa*.

I give you this tree, meaning that I'll have it named after you without explaining why; I'll write and tell them to give it that name. So your name will somewhere know the joy—of not standing for anything else!

Give its full weight to my letter. You must.

A.S.L.

1. This is the famous "thank-you note" to Gide for having successfully withdrawn "Cohorte" from the NRF. Gide based his 1950 tribute to AL (published under the title, "Don d'un arbre," in the Summer-Autumn 1950 issue of *Les Cahiers de la Pléiade*) on this note, which is reproduced in the tribute with one notable typographical error: *Oreodoxa* has become *Orcodoxa*. The note was accompanied by a snapshot of the trees.

2. OC has "incomplètement belle," and this reading is apparently in conformity with the autograph letter. Could it be that "*in*complètement" was a slip of AL's pen for "complètement"?

98

To Monsieur André Gide   *Pau, April 25, 1911*
Paris

[. . .]
You really shouldn't have told me about the gift of a star that has already been bestowed upon you! . . . By now you are probably feeling uneasy about having mentioned it to me [. . .].

As for what the botanists say about *Oreodoxa*: I know nothing about botany or any other science, but I'd like to shred the tongue of any man who thinks he can fix the height of *Oreodoxa*. This tree, which, in every location where it is found, is the most precise and unerring that may be singled out for praise, is the same tree that may reach a height of 1.5 meters on windy heights (in which case it is called a "cabbage-palm"); 10 to 15 meters on the slopes (in which case it is called a "straight palm"), and more than 20 meters in the lower regions (and then it is called simply a "palm"—though a scientist I came to know in my childhood, Father Düss,[1] because he was a Catholic, sometimes pretended to make the error of calling it a "psalm").

And have the botanists bothered to tell you that this palm tree, the most beautiful of its kind, is the one that is destined to die when its heart—to be chopped up and eaten in an extraordinarily good salad—is cut out?—the heart being the leaves, still white and tender, that form a bud at the center of the crown. —And two months later one can gather up a fine crop of "palm-worms," which are the fat larvae of a beetle (*Calandra palmarum*), which lays its eggs right in the pithy center of the trunk. You eat them live or slightly roasted, always as a salad, with lemon-juice, pepper, and salt. It's good. And then the tree dies. I have done [. . .].

Affectionately.   A.S.L.

1. The R. P. Antoine Düss (1840-1924), a French botanist-priest who compiled the classical *Flore phanérogamique des Antilles françaises: Martinique et Guadeloupe*, published in Mâcon in 1897. See letter to Marcel Raymond, 30 Apr. 1948. (286)

99

To Monsieur André Gide   *Pau, route de Bordeaux*
Paris   [*May 1911*]

I am most grateful to you for the way you accepted things.

I thank you for taking the trouble to write, telling me there will be proofs [. . .].

You ask me for a title that would include all three of these poems? —*Eloges*.[1] It is such a beautiful title that I don't think I would ever want any other, if I ever published a book—or even several books [. . .].

Please tell the Review that I insist on proofs—and that I would like to take advantage of the italics they used formerly instead of that face-powder they have begun to use that turns every poem into an embarcation to Cythera.[2]

Would you be so kind—I would be most grateful to you for it—as to give me a grammar lesson? In the third of these *Eloges*: ". . . . que le sang était beau et la main qui. . . ."[3] I wouldn't absolutely swear that I'm writing French. The thing wrote itself that way, and my instinct was not offended; and now when I analyze it, you can easily imagine how blindly I came up with a thousand good reasons and justifications in Latin (agreement of the active neuter? ellipsis? and I don't know what else?. . .). But in French, all this just doesn't really hold true, does it?

I am happy, Monsieur, and honored to have this opportunity to greet André Gide.

                                    A. Saint-Leger Leger

Subscribers? —The weather is not really bad enough down here to allow one to get to know many people, especially people who read. But here is one name (visiting-card herewith). You may tell the Review to open a subscription at that address—it is that of a talented musician.[4]

1. The series of sixteen poems (actually eighteen in the original numbering) that appeared in the June 1911 issue of the NRF. This printing provoked a violent reaction from AL because of the typographical errors. See the six letters that immediately follow, as well as the letter to Rivière of 2 June 1911 (28), and letter 28, note 2.

2. The reference is to Watteau's celebrated painting, "L'Embarquement pour Cythère."

3. The problem is the use of the masculine adjective *beau* to modify both the masculine noun *sang* and the feminine noun *main*.

The poem in question was originally Number III of the "Eloges," but was subsequently removed from the series by AL and given a separate title, "Histoire du Régent," to be included later in the group of poems collectively entitled "La Gloire des Rois."

4. Undoubtedly Paul Maufret.

100

To Monsieur André Gide   *Pau, June 1, 1911*
Paris

I thank you once again for your kindness.[1]

I am terribly embarrassed that you yourself were obliged to look over those sheets.

I shall always think of André Gide with affection and admiration.

[. . .] What can I say to you, finally? —That typography is a crude invention, a stupid pedant's invention [. . .] but that, otherwise, the weather is fine in June. May I never again recall the "*N*" "*R*" "*F*" . . . "dancing letters" that I would just as soon turn loose in a Carnival [. . .].

I won't send my corrected issue along to you—as politeness obliges me to do for Claudel, Jammes, and a few friends—because you might think momentarily that I am annoyed with you—you who could do nothing in this situation—or think that I am all that fond of my poems! . . . But if I did point out to you a few of the more horrendous misprints that run wild in the text, you would readily understand that, even were a list of errata published (which I have no intention of asking the Review to do), it would be unthinkable ever to present myself again to the readers who had to stomach so insane a thing as the whole first poem!—not to mention extravagant little details here and there, such as the "children who bear their eyelashes like umbrellas" (instead of "like umbels") . . .!

But enough of all this, which I shouldn't even have spoken to you about. Excuse me.

Some tiresome business makes it necessary for me to spend a fortnight in Paris this coming November. I'll pay my respects to you in person, should you be there [. . .].

I am respectfully yours, *cher Monsieur*, and shall always continue to be.   Leger

  1. See above, letter 28, note 2.

101

To Monsieur André Gide   *Pau, Thursday*
Paris   [*June 1911*]

I was up in the mountains; I really had to go. (And the weather was so beautiful that you could bed down in the open, but not sleep—too many crickets.)

But how close to you your letter made me feel!

I'm back now. I remember. I've thought it over. Yes, do for me whatever might have occurred to you [. . .].

Leger

I would like to be able—would it be possible?—to reprint (at my own expense) an additional ten pages that I gave to the *N.R.F.* last year[1] [. . .].

I wrote to the printer requesting his rates. M. Verbecke didn't deign to answer. What can I do?

1. "Ecrit sur la Porte," "Pour fêter une enfance," and "Récitation à l'éloge d'une Reine," all three of which had appeared for the first time in the NRF of Apr. 1910.

102

To Monsieur André Gide   *Pau, June 26, 1911*
Cuverville, Normandie

Dear friend, I don't want to argue with fate, but I shall never forget that André Gide, in France, has been kind to me, and that to my admiration for his art I have been able to add my affection.

[. . .] I'm delighted to see that your letters are at last dated from Normandie. And it's evident that even there you fear having to smile and be weary when, like Candaule,[1] you insert parentheses: "Too many roses here."

Ah yes, may there always be enough roses around (and I would want it that way)—when you have to drop me a line—enough roses to take your mind off writing well.

I'm terribly embarrassed at having made Verbecke lose so much time these days because I put off reading the last proofs—I simply forgot, because I didn't have a forwarding address. But I'm going to get at it this instant. And I want to do a thorough job; I must not let a single unexpected error crop out in all this typography [. . .]. I'm seated at a desk this time, and I've provided myself with everything—even bought the *Perfect Proofreader's Manual* and what else?—a bottle of red ink, like an ancient scholiast or a modern Hellenist, Didymus Chalcenterus or Theobald Fix.[2]

Verbecke said that he could print the copies on Holland paper in either of two formats: in the same format as those on ordinary paper, or in a larger format (19 x 21), and that I must let him know my decision, since he has no instructions one way or the other. But I suppose—not knowing anything about printing matters—that the second arrangement would mean more profit to him commercially, and I'm going to hurry and write him that he should stick to the ordinary format—which is really very good, and not at all bad looking, judging by my page-proofs.

[. . .] Above and beyond the copies put aside for requests from your subscribers, [. . .] from the number of copies that I will request of you, which will depend on the number printed, I would like to be able to have my booklet sent to a few friends [. . .]. I'd also like to keep four or five copies for when it is out of print, for I can't yet tell just how my life will go; but it is quite possible that I will never publish. I even want it to be that way. And if it can't be that way, at any rate, these pages would never be published again [. . .].   A.S.L.

1. Reference to Gide's play, *Le Roi Candaule* (1901).

2. Didymus Chalcenterus, Alexandrian grammarian, contemporary of Cicero at the beginning of the Christian Era. Théobald Fix (1802-1874), French Hellenist.

103

To Monsieur André Gide   [*Bordeaux, July 1911*]
[Paris]

Bordeaux—a hotel-room—and the clock's stopped: please excuse me [. . .].

Let me answer your letter, if I dare, more precisely: 150 copies? but that's more than enough! For me that's a huge printing (when I inquired of Verbecke it was for 50, 75, or 100). It isn't worth the trouble, I assure you, even thinking about a de luxe printing on Holland paper. I would never have dared consider such a thing myself. I don't know what paper is used in your books, but the paper on which they print the review strikes me as very good.

Yes, the first *Eloges* ahead of the rest. (I'll indicate to Verbecke what the order, numbering, and subtitles are to be when he sends me the proofs of what he is resetting.) Something greatly intrigues me: how did your letter to Verbecke about this get to him before my letter expressing the same wish?

If you really think that I don't run the risk, with the poem "à l'éloge d'une Reine,"[1] of making too many enemies, I'm quite ready to have it included.

The proofs that were sent are still in Pau. I'll take care of them as soon as I get back to my mother's. (I'm here to regularize my standing with a Law School where I can't take any more courses.) I'll take the liberty of making a few more corrections that should have been made on the first proofs and even of revising a few lines that a friend of mine pointed out as being easily misinterpreted.

And now I have to bring it up—excuse me and please don't be angry with me [. . .]—I have—after hesitating for two days and in spite of my extreme uneasiness (I don't want to tear up still another letter)—to speak to you finally about something. —Here is what it is: You say "all this at 'my' expense," and before, you said, "at 'our' expense." Have the arrangements been changed? —please tell me—and aren't you speaking any longer as a representative of the *N.R.F.*? Good Heavens, I wish I were a more skillful writer! How can I ask you to clear this up? —You see, M. Verbecke's letter, which I received a day before yours, said in so many words: "at the expense of the *N.R.F.* and on M. Schlumberger's orders." Please tell me, if you will be so kind, what I am to understand by that "my," to which I didn't pay any attention at first.

I want to close my letter by telling you once more of all my affection [. . .].

Most cordially.   A. Saint-Leger Leger

I can't manage to find out where Claudel is at the moment. In Paris, I think. If he comes anywhere near you these days, please tell him that I am proud of, and grateful for, all that he says to me about my *Eloges*. I'll get hold of his address, or else write to him, in care of you.

1. "Récitation à l'éloge d'une reine," later included in the series "La Gloire des Rois."

104

To Monsieur André Gide   *La Rochelle,*
London   *August 2* [*1911*]

I haven't forgotten that somewhere there is an André Gide.

[. . .] Summer is a wonderful thing, and heat is healthy, provided that these three months of the French year can be something other than literature.

[. . .] My mother was able to forward your letter from England to me. What role did you play there? If Valery Larbaud is still around, please tell him that my friendship for him is great and uncomplicated.

I ran into a nice fellow here, captain of a freighter that was loading up for England; he offered me passage on board his ship [. . .]. But some dreary business obliged me to give up the idea. I'll be going back to Pau.

A.S.L.

I don't know how my little book of poems is coming along. My last letter to Verbecke dates from at least a month ago—oh yes, longer than that. I had understood that he was to send me second proofs. But maybe he thought my last corrections were sufficient and has gone ahead with the printing. I'll inquire about it when I'm back at my mother's, [. . .].

Please excuse the impoliteness of my writing in pencil; there's no ink in these parts, or nothing that deserves the name of ink—they probably haven't any oak-galls!

105

To Monsieur André Gide   [*Pau, August 1911*]
Paris

Dear Sir . . . friend,

I am one up on you by a missing conjunction. My age authorizes it, since there is no such thing as a lapse in tone at my age.

[. . .] I've been in touch with Verbecke. I think the question of the proofs will soon be settled, and he'll be able to go to press before the week is out.

I had told him not to print the title pages until the very last minute, because I'd thought of publishing under a name other than my own. But Claudel writes me from somewhere in the Ain, urging me to publish under my own name. I'll do that. So there's nothing to change.

But tell me if this would be possible: that the outside cover bear only the word *Eloges* devoid of any author's name, which would appear only on the inner title page. If you thought this were really too contrary to publishing practices, I would immediately withdraw the directions I gave Verbecke. But it would really be nice if that were possible. Please don't think I'm a crank. It's just that it seems to me that poems should always preserve something of the sudden, anonymous way they come into being.

[. . .] In regard to the de luxe printing, please tell me if the following combination would in any way complicate things: the kind of paper used seems to me less important than the format in a small book, so wouldn't it be simpler to substitute a printing on ordinary paper, but with wider margins, for the printing on de luxe paper?—something more or less like the format of the two proofs that I received? [. . .] But—and I insist on this point—I'm really completely ignorant about typographical matters [. . .].

From the farthest seas of affection.   A. Saint-Leger

106

To Monsieur André Gide   *Saint-Sauveur (H.-P.),*
Criquetot-l'Esneval (S.-I.)   *August 19, 1911*

Dear friend,

Yes, that is the word I used—friend; I have taken the liberty of addressing you that way. —May you always be a little bit partial to me, should you ever happen to think of me. For there's nothing I like more than partiality in this world, where I hate the iniquity of a justice cold as winter, or as Kantian postulates, or as fine verse.

You have written me a letter for which I am grateful.

I didn't have the courage to reply because my life is burdensome at the moment; I have great responsibilities that I have to bear alone.

Since you tell me the news of the poems' having appeared, I can now tell you what I've been waiting to tell you. I could not allow myself the pleasure, nor the pride, of dedicating them to you. I was afraid you might be somewhat embarrassed. And even if you had had nothing to do with this publication, these pages were too far from satisfying me to give me any pleasure in dedicating them to you.

But since they were not worthy of bearing your name, they could not bear any other, and even though it is not done, I insisted on eliminating a name—the only name[1] that occurred on any of the reprinted pages. I'm eager to see if Verbecke did indeed notice and make the correction.

I'm going to write to Monsieur J. Schlumberger, who has written to ask me about the number of copies he should send me. May I ask for four copies on Holland paper for four persons whose names occur to me? And may I ask the review to do a little favor for me where other reviews are concerned—I mean the few reviews that regularly receive the *N.R.F.*, or were receiving it at the time these poems appeared in it? [. . .] It would be a great help to me, as I understand nothing at all about what they call "press service," and the only address I know is the *Mercure*'s.[2]

I hope you'll let me personally send you your copy [. . .].

Affectionately.   A.S.L.

I am very concerned about Rivière's present state of anxiety.

1. N. W. Bede-Bronte, to whom "Récitation à l'éloge d'une reine" was originally dedicated.

2. The periodical, *Le Mercure de France.*

107

To Monsieur André Gide   *Paris; 10, avenue Victor-Hugo*
Villa Montmorency   [*November 1911*]
Auteuil

I have seen Arthur Fontaine;[1] I thank you.

I want to see André Gide again,[2] to see you—tell me when [. . .].

Come with me to see The Fishes, the advertisements on the Metro walls announce an "aquaculture" exposition; may we expect to see you there?   Leger

1. See above, letter 65, note 1.

2. In the interim between this letter and the preceding one, AL had met Gide in person at the Gide residence in Auteuil. An account of this first meeting is given by AL in his obituary tribute to Gide, written in 1951 and entitled "Face aux Lettres françaises, 1909." Reproduced in OC pp. 472-482.

108

To Monsieur André Gide   *Tuesday*
Villa Montmorency   [*November 1911*]
Paris (Auteuil)

I greatly appreciate your fine long letter and the friendly concern that prompts you to write it.

But that is not my way of looking at things.

I do not harbor the sadness you thought you noticed—sadness at having to cut myself off from literary life for which I am really not at all suited. And perhaps there's something more. If there really is sadness, it stems from having to achieve, in the outward organization of my life, enough material independence to reserve a place in that life for the poet that I have to be in order to live—to live without offending life itself.

It is in pursuit of that achievement that I must walk alone.

I was glad to sit at your family table, and I carry with me a very vivid remembrance of the charming reception Mme. Gide accorded me.[1] Please transmit my best wishes to her again; and you, dear friend, must believe that it was not as a stranger that I stopped in.

Saint-Leger Leger

1. See AL's tribute, listed in the preceding note, for his impressions of Madeleine Gide.

109

To Monsieur André Gide   *Pau [January 26, 1912]*
Villa Montmorency
Auteuil

I've been at work for ages. And my affection for you is at least that old.

Have affection for me, who make wishes for you—great good wishes for your life and your work, since you did tell me, didn't you?—that they are one and the same.

I especially appreciated your card from Clermont.

My heartfelt wishes are with you.

A.S.L.

Stored away now in my memory, the huge fresco filled with vegetation[1] that I saw in your house is a marvelous thing—a healthy, prodigious thing.

1. It is hard to say whether this "great fresco of vegetation" is a metaphorical way of referring to the verdure of the Villa Montmorency or a reference to a painting that decorated the interior of the Gide house—perhaps the fresco "Le Parfum des Nymphes," by Piot.

110

To Monsieur André Gide   *London,*
Paris   *Clifford Residential Hotel*
                                           3 Templeton Place—S.W.
                                           July 1912

Maybe you'll be coming this way for a bit. You'll let
me know, won't you?

If not, I'll try to see you when I come down again next
winter, if I happen to pass through Paris.

I had to pass very close by you, two months ago.

I don't know anyone here [. . .]. This address is good
for twelve days more. After that, via Paris, care of Mme.
A. Dormoy, 176, bd Malesherbes.

Affectionately.   A.S.L.

111

To Monsieur André Gide   *London, July 16, 1912*
Paris   *Clifford Residential Hotel*
                                           3 Templeton Place S.W.

Dear friend, I thank you. Miss Tobin is indeed most
amiable.[1] I was on "the river," and I received both your
letters at the same time.

Miss Tobin talks about you a lot, about a mysterious
and very great influence that you have upon her, and
about the childish joy she felt at wanting you to come
here. She asks me quite seriously to tell you this, quite
seriously; and also to say that you alone can cure her!
You do know, don't you?, that Miss Tobin was bed-
ridden for almost five months, and that she probably
hasn't seen a blade of grass in longer than that? She's
reading *Les Dieux ont soif!*[2]

There, I've done my duty. Let Miss Tobin know,

please, that I did it as best I could. And be assured that
I most sincerely join my best wishes to hers.

A.S.L.

I'll undoubtedly be back on the water beginning next
week, but I'll still have an address c/o Miss Tobin, if
Paris or Pau isn't advisable.

1. Agnes Tobin (1864-1939), an American lady from a well-
known Californian family, was a frequent resident in England,
where she became an intimate of the literary group that gathered
around Alice and Wilfred Meynell. Through Francis Jammes,
she came to know Gide and Larbaud, and then AL. It was
through Agnes Tobin that AL came to know Joseph Conrad. See
letter to Larbaud of Aug. 1913 (137), and letter to Conrad of
26 Feb. 1921. (181)

2. Novel by Anatole France published in 1912.

112

To Monsieur André Gide   [*London, October 1912*]
Paris   *Clifford Residential Hotel*
                                3 Templeton Place

In answer to everything in your letter, which questions
me in a friendly way:

I take no "interest" in publishing poems; or, better
said, no "pleasure."

Decidedly, not to be a dupe in the period in which I
live and in which I have a life—maybe even several lives
—to lead. In addition, just plain circumstances have thus
far made my life what it is, and they will do as much
tomorrow—a life that is solitary enough so that there is
no serious difficulty whatsoever about this "no." Absolutely none. And that cancels at one stroke any right to
feel regrets, doesn't it?

Please don't consider this brief note as mere rudeness,
for I do thank you for your friendly thought. But in

Paris I may have spoken to you as I certainly would not now speak to you; at that moment I was burdened with more sadness and silliness than I ever was in my life—during which, God knows, I have accumulated enough unwanted fat.

Affectionately still, and with best wishes.   A.S.L.

113

To Monsieur André Gide   *London, October 23, 1912*
Paris   *Clifford Residential Hotel*
                                           3 Templeton Place S.W.

Dear friend,

I hope more than anything in the world that you are in the process of completing, in France, a work of the highest order.

I thought you would be coming this way this summer, without Edm. Gosse,[1] the "Alabama," and all "the really interesting people" knowing it! That way, wouldn't you have come to know, all at once, all the people—the others—that it took me so much time, and so many benign gods, to come to know little by little?—The Antichrist, who lives in the flesh here in London, right in the middle of Mayfair; the ethnographer, Sir Edward Ainley, and his friend who is the inventor of the use of dynamite in land-cultivation; MacDonald Rutherland, the court tattooer; Ramsami Leti, the Magnificent, who would have lent you one of his three mutton-fed horses; Luzac the orientalist; and Father Jensen, who lost one of his agents, a naturalist, in New Guinea, where he went in search of the great butterfly of the mountaintops, *Queen Alexandra* (his violin is now suspended above the specimen of the female of the species); J. G., the senior member of the "Sarawak Financiers," who outdistances

by a long shot Crisp (of the Chinese loan association)[2]
and Claudel's Thomas Pollock Nageoire;[3] Samuel Chu-
Chong (to whom I took one of Jammes' relatives); M.
and Mme. Gustave; the "AeRated Bread Co.," and so
many more. . . .

Miss Tobin is now in America, still pursuing you in
her dreams with great tenderness. (If you saw the way
she has your books bound!) [. . .]

Please remember me affectionately to Rivière.

                                                A. Saint-Leger

The *Nlle Revue Française*, instead of serving Arnold
Bennett[4] up to us, would do better to be the first review
in Europe to give us the work of Rabindranath Tagore.[5]
The English translation of his work, which he himself
made, and which is to appear within a fortnight, is the
only really poetic English-language work to have appeared in a long time (at least for those who don't believe in Coventry Patmore or Francis Thompson[6] himself, who is already quite "incestuous").

1. Sir Edmund Gosse (1849-1928), the English critic and
literary historian.

2. Of the persons mentioned in this fascinating list of London
eccentrics, at least one occurs elsewhere in the writings of AL.
Rutherland, the Court Tattooer, is mentioned in the poem *Vents*:

> . . . Avec tous hommes de douceur, avec tous hommes
> de sourire sur les chemins de la tristesse,
>> Les tatoueurs de Reines en exil. . . .
>
>   (III, 4)
> [. . . With all men of gentleness, with all men who
> smile on the paths of sorrow,
>> Tattooers of exiled Queens. . . . (Chisholm trans.)]

3. Thomas Pollock Nageoire is the American hero of Claudel's
verse play, *L'Echange* (1893).

4. Arnold Bennett (1867-1931), the English writer, author of
The Old Wives' Tale (1908) and many other novels. He was a
friend of Gide and Larbaud.

5. Rabindrananth Tagore (1891-1941), the Indian writer and

philosopher, whose English version of *Gitanjali* ("Lyrical Offering") was first published in 1912 in London. AL was instrumental in recruiting Gide as French translator of *Gitanjali*, as the succeeding letters to Gide reveal.

6. Coventry Patmore (1823-1896) and Francis Thompson (1859-1907) were two English religious poets much in favor with Claudel and Larbaud. (Claudel actually translated Patmore into French; Larbaud wrote an essay on him.) They were both "sponsored" by the Meynells and thus very familiar to Agnes Tobin.

114

To Monsieur André Gide   *Paris, December 7, 1912*
Paris

Dear friend,

Unfortunately I won't be in London when you pass through.

I haven't been able to get hold of the book here that you want to read. But drop me a line telling me whether you are in Paris, and I'll at least send you, even though it happens to be my own, a copy that I'll look for here in one of my trunks.

Great as my "critical" admiration for Tagore's work may be, the thought never crossed my mind of actually "recommending" a book. If I ever did take the liberty of citing what is to my liking or taste, I would recommend no one but Edward Lear,[1] the only poet of a breed that seems to me the poetic breed par excellence.

As for Rabindranath Tagore, whom a very great fame awaits in England, before we go any farther, I'll bring him around to visit you this summer, or take the liberty of sending him to you—this great, aged pilgrim of such delicate charm and unerring distinction. Tagore must be in the United States at the moment, on the western route to Japan. He probably doesn't make much of a distinction between France and Europe, and he doesn't understand a word of French; but he may learn a little between now and next summer.

Keep the book as long as you like. But do hold on to it for me, as it's my personal copy.

And here is my affection, along with my sincerest wishes—for your work and for yourself, and wishes, too, against the pernicious boredom that exudes from all the intelligent voices with which, out of laziness, we surround ourselves.

Yrs. truly[2]   A.S.L.

1. Edward Lear (1812-1888), the well-known author of *The Book of Nonsense*.
2. English in original.

115

To Monsieur André Gide   [*Paris, January 28, 1913*]
Villa Montmorency   *13, rue de Bruxelles*
Auteuil

Dear friend, Tagore's work is beautiful [. . .]. You are quite surely the only person in France at this time to be familiar with this little book, and I am going to write to Tagore on your behalf. He had not yet, when we parted in London, given his rights to any publisher. Please tell me, though, whether I should talk to him about a translation in a review or in book form. You won't be getting a reply for some time, because Tagore must be in Japan at the present moment. But it seems to me the thing will be quite simple. Keep my copy as long as you like [. . .].

I was terribly disappointed on finding your visiting card here. I was away from Paris for a few days without leaving any word. Here's a new address: 13, rue de Bruxelles. Would you let me know, at this address, whether I would find you at home next Monday, and at about what time? Please excuse me for choosing the day; I'm preparing for a competitive examination.[1]

Thank you for being so kind as to remember the few pages that I published.[2] If you could help me succeed in gaining an *entrée* into a diplomatic and consular career, I would give you poems with which you could do anything you like! This is my last try at reconciling the two. If it fails, the remedy would be all too clear: never again to encounter the poem.

Affectionately.   A.S.L.

1. The Foreign Service Examination.
2. Unidentifiable. Possibly the book edition of *Eloges*.

116

To Monsieur André Gide   [*Paris, February 9, 1913*]
Paris

I will always treasure this book,[1] coming from you. I thank you.

The fame that your French work will acquire is something, in its kind, that makes me profoundly happy. But it doesn't keep me from thinking about you personally, dear friend, you who play such a vital part in this present year of my life and who are good enough to think of me still.   Alexis Saint-Leger Leger

1. Gide's novelette, *Isabelle*.

117

To Monsieur André Gide   [*London, July 1913*]
Paris

Dear friend,

[. . .] I'm delighted that you want to keep the volume that revealed Tagore to you. (Memory: an optical science.) My apologies for having, even for a minute, thought of asking for the book back.

I wish you great pleasure, soon, in translating these poems: [. . .] a long season, pure and timeless.

Please simply remember that my joy is assured by my having been able to make certain that a work I wanted above all to see well treated, and capably, too, would, in France, have the benefit of your art and your name. So I'm the one who remains grateful to you. [. . .]

A dedication, dear friend?[1] It would be a signal honor to me [. . .]. But mightn't that be too great an honor if, perchance, my life took an abrupt turn within ten months and didn't even leave me worthy of it, as a friend?

Affectionately, with my best wishes for the work you are completing.   A.S.L.

1. The following is a translation of the entire text of Gide's dedication:

Dedicatory Epistle to Saint-Leger Leger

It is only natural that I inscribe your name here, dear friend. Thanks to you, I was perhaps the first person in France to come to know the work of Rabindranath Tagore, when very few literary people, even in England, as yet knew of him.

Gitanjali had only just appeared in the big white edition that is already so rare and that, in a few years, will very probably become as exaggeratedly valuable a collector's item as the first editions of the *Rubaiyat* of Omar Khayyam.

I shall never forget that, for me, you parted with your own copy, pretending that you didn't quite understand my bibliophile's scruples so you could make the gift more simply and exquisitely.

It is also thanks to you that I was granted the translation rights, which I thought exclusively mine—until the appearance in a review of an enthusiastic study of the Hindu poet, including a hasty translation of a little more than half the volume.

You know how unhappy I was about this over-eager defloration and how it was only upon the insistence of Tagore's friends that I again took up the work. For I had abandoned it, leaving it to cleverer persons than myself, fully aware that I could do a good piece of work only if I went at it slowly. I am convinced that I had a great deal more difficulty and took a much longer time in translating certain of the poems than Tagore did in writing them. And I might add that no other piece of writing ever gave me so much trouble. Of course, it is quite natural that translating should involve more revisions, more second thoughts and deletions, than something that is spontaneously inspired; and then, too, one dares translate one's own thought much more cavalierly than the thought of the person one has agreed to serve. It seemed to me that no present-day thought deserved more respect—I almost said devotion—than Tagore's, and I took pleasure in humbling myself in its presence, just as he had humbled himself in order to sing before God.   André Gide

118

To Monsieur André Gide   *[July 26, 1913]*
Villa Montmorency   *On board*[1] *Las Bodas de Oro*
Auteuil

Dear friend,

Just received your note this instant, via Royan.

I'm still on the high seas.

I'll write immediately to Tagore and at the same time to his attorney and to Larbaud.

Will you be good enough to excuse all this apparent neglect? In the same packet there was a letter from London explaining that William Hornell,[2] the friend to whom I chose to entrust this whole matter and from whom I'd had no answer, disappeared three months ago, en route to India.

If you have to drop me a line, address it:

> Cernay-Ermont (S.-et-O.)
> Villa Georgianah
> Route du Général-Decaen
> c/o Mme A. Dormoy

There will be two more packets of mail from my sister at Santander and Cadiz.

With friendly regards.   A.S.L.

1. English in original.
2. Probably Sir William Woodward Hornell (1878-1950), who eventually settled in Hong Kong.

119

To Monsieur André Gide   *Friday [August 1913],*
Cuverville, Normandie   *Villa Georgianah*
                                 Route du Général-Decaen,
                                 Cernay-Ermont (S.-et-O.)

Dear friend,

I've scarcely got back, via Dieppe, and I was so eager to know what was what regarding the translation rights for you—I've been so preoccupied with it ever since we last touched the shores of Europe that I thought of wiring you from Rouen to find out, if I could, whether I might see you at Cuverville without being importunate [. . .].

You tell me that everything has been arranged [. . .]. I never doubted, once we reached Tagore himself, that we could salvage the whole project for you. And I must also thank you no end for having notified me in time of his return to London.

When I met Tagore—who knew nothing not only of French literature, but also of the French language—he asked me right off, "not as an appropriate bit of advice," but "absolutely as I really felt," to select the names of a few Frenchmen; and I left a scrap of paper with him bearing your name and Claudel's. Whatever may have been his confidence in me at that precise moment, I could have wagered, simply by the way he treated that little scrap of paper, that he wouldn't forget it. As for Fox-Strangways,[1] who in London had a good piano and a small French clavichord, we knew each other only as music-lovers, and talking to him about Baudelaire and Gérard de Nerval in the history of the art of translation in France couldn't have meant much to him; but at least I wrote to him as severely as I could, which was the only ruse possible where he was concerned. When I met him, he had not yet received any authorization from Tagore. At that time he was music critic for the *Times* and secretary of the India Society, which he will surely invite you to join.

Should it be necessary to write any further, in any way you may deem fitting, and about any detail whatsoever, do let me know, please.

Claudel, with whom I was supposed to spend the last days of July before going down into Temesvar and Transylvania, writes me that he is leaving Frankfurt (the performances of his play have been put off until September); so my address for all the rest of this month is right here.

I send along my wishes for the fortunes of your latest work, and for the work itself; they are very special wishes.

And I hope that nothing comes up to deprive you of that trip to Syria.[2] —In Port Said, [. . .], if all that hasn't been changed too much, go and while away an hour in the curio shop of Mme. Fioraventi; everybody on the terrace of the Eastern will be able to tell you where it is. And nothing could be finer than the hall of mirrors of Coucouyamos (Tobacco). And above all, go and spend a night in that extraordinary Ismailia (a prodigy of immutability)—one hour by train, or an hour and a half by motorboat across Lake Timsah. —Early in the morning, the pools of water-birds, and all the profligacy of the strange fish that are taken at Port Tewfick, at the en-

trance to the Red Sea. —And then return in the evening
to that frightful, incomparable and nourishing city, Port
Said.

With friendly regards to you.   A.S.L.

1. Arthur Henry Fox-Strangways (1859-1948), music critic.
Author of *Music of Hindostan* (1914), *Cecil Sharp* (1933), etc.
2. Gide never made the projected trip.

120

To Monsieur André Gide   [*Paris, January 30, 1914*]
Villa Montmorency
Auteuil

Dear friend, I prize at its true worth, which I put very
high, the little book and the number it bears.[1]

Continue to be a friend to me, who think of you affectionately. You realize that it would be easier for me to
see you in Hamburg, Trieste, or Genoa.[2] And I think
I told you that I am preparing for a competitive examination—a minimal chance; a throw of the dice, after
which I don't know what sort of fate awaits me, and
whether I'll be raising cattle or poems—surely not the
one *and* the other [. . .].

Most cordially.   Saint-Leger Leger

I am so mightily bored. . . . Recite with me these two
lines of verse, which are beautiful:

> *For God's sake let us sit down upon the ground*
> *And tell sad stories of the deaths of kings.*[3]

—I'm sorry I can't show you, in an engraving received
from London, the real "Thomas Pollock."[4]

1. This copy of Gide's translation of *Gitanjali* bore the number
2. Number 1 had been reserved for Gide's wife.
2. . . . than in Paris.
3. Shakespeare, *Richard II* (Act II, sc. 2). Quoted in English
in the original.
4. See above, letter 113, note 3.

121

To Monsieur Valery Larbaud   *Pau, June 30* [*1911*]
[England]

A thoughtful gesture that pleases me, dear friend—
your sending me that souvenir of an "Isle". . . .[1]

And I, what nice thing could I do for you?

I'll wish you a fine summer, throughout the English
countryside.

Here are two lines of verse I like—and it would make
me happy if they gave you pleasure—for the silken alliterations of the first, the inflated diction that establishes
the final mood of the second, and then, too, that delightful "coquit":

En quid agis? Sīccās īnsānă Cănīcŭlă mēssēs
Jamdudum coquit, ēt pătŭlā pĕcŭs ōmne sŭb ūlmo ēst.

They are from a much maligned poet—from Persius,
who was too protectively brought up by a woman, but
who was a friend of Lucan, whom you like.

Cordially.   Leger

1. This island souvenir remains unidentified. Perhaps it was
a postcard from the Isle of Man, which Larbaud visited in June
1911.

2. From Persius, Satire III:
"And what do you do? The rabid dog-days dry out the har-
vests and have cooked them for long already, and all the
flocks are under the broad cover of the elms."

122

To Monsieur Valery Larbaud   *Pau, route de Bordeaux*
[Chelsea]   [*July 1911*]

My friend, how the simplicity of your letter goes straight to my heart!

I'd like to answer you more fully, and I still have to put off doing that, so taken up am I, until July 30, with preparing for one last law examination [. . .].

There is a real flavor of literalness in the pages of Landor that you're translating for *La Nouvelle Revue française*;[1] they merited an art like yours that, in a mysterious way, is capable of taking delight in what our 18th century called "miracles of phrase-turning."

I have sent along to you the June issue with the corrections that my contribution required.[2] I'll send you a copy of the little volume that André Gide wants to have printed at his expense, without there being any way for me to avoid acceptance of such disconcerting generosity. In this whole review business, Gide has been of an absolutely patrician delicacy [. . .].

I was deeply touched, let me tell you, by your offer to take care of a printing abroad for me. It must be a painful business. Yet that might have made things so much easier for me, I think. —Thank you.

Please allow me, as I take leave of you—and since you spoke to me about your health—to urge you to consent, most conscientiously, to every sacrifice that it demands of you. At your age,[3] looking after one's health requires something of a conscious effort, or "long patience" [. . .].

Cordially.   L.

1. A fragment of Landor's *High and Low Life in Italy*, published under the title, "Hautes et basses classes en Italie," in NRF of June 1911.

2. The faulty text of "Éloges." See above, letter 28, note 2.

3. Larbaud was thirty years old.

123

To Monsieur Valery Larbaud   *August 4 [1911],*
Chelsea   *La Rochelle*

My mother has sent along to me here your card from Harwich. I deeply appreciate your and Gide's thinking of me.

Please believe that when I think of you, I do it only with affection.   A. S.-L.

124

To Monsieur Valery Larbaud   *Esquièze (via Luz) (H.-P.)*
                                  September 22 [1911]

Dear friend,

I'm appealing to Gide's kindness to forward this letter to you. There's no other way I can reach you, since I let a month and more slip by, I think, beyond the last date you indicated for your Chelsea address[1] [. . .].

Don't think I've simply forgotten about you. I liked your independent spirit, which I spoke about to you, too much to do that. And I also recall that I was terribly embarrassed, after your visit to Pau,[2] to think of the very impolite way I went on questioning you all the time. Maybe you thought I'd totally lost touch with things under the deforming pressures of solitude.

Excuse me if you have not yet received your copy of my little book. I haven't yet obtained one. And the fault is entirely mine. But I wrote recently and expect to have the copies I asked for very soon now. Please let me have your present address.

I would be happy to have news from you, and happy also if you were willing to tell me about your writing—

the work that now commands your attention or that very soon will. I've reread your *Fermina*[3] and enjoyed it more than ever. Did I really tell you adequately, when I saw you, how much I like and admire that secret delight you take in knowing how to tell a story—a thankless art, hence a French one. A fine thing, in my eyes; for pure delight in form (let's say an almost sensual pleasure), is, in France, Lesage's *Gil Blas*,[4] which can be read surficially, the way a blind person does, so delightful are the turns and ornaments of an anonymous language.

And won't you also let me read the poems of *Barnabooth*?[5]

·From your friend Fargue,[6] whom you spoke to me about, I've never received the work he promised.

I want very much not to leave France without seeing you again. Will you be in Paris this fall? I have to be there some time between October 10 and November 10. Dreary formalities at the Colonial Ministry and the Ministry of Foreign Affairs, where I know no one. [. . .]

Claudel keeps insisting that I should prepare for a career in the consulates. And indeed, I couldn't wish for anything better; but I'm afraid, since I can't prepare myself in Paris as one should, that all I'll have to show for a year of solitary labor[7] will be a failure. And I'm afraid that Claudel can't realize very clearly what my family situation is.

In short, I'm going to Paris in order to get oriented and come to a decision. Above all, I have to make some arrangement with a relative who used to be my legal guardian. If I fail, I'll go off next spring, just anywhere; maybe to Guinea. If I succeed and feel I can take on the necessary preparation for the very difficult and not very fair Foreign Service examination, I'll be in France two years more, and I'll figure out some way to spend another month or two, next spring, in England—where it would be a very great pleasure to meet you.

—I learned, from a letter, that your study on Patmore[8] had appeared, but I haven't yet received this month's issue of the *N.R.F.* I spent some time rather high up in a mountain "refuge," and letters that my mother entrusted to a peasant haven't all reached me. (I was told there was one with a foreign postage-stamp on it; if by chance that was something from you, if only a postcard, I would be very disappointed not to receive it.) [. . .] I read Patmore very casually four or five years ago. I liked it then. I don't like it now. There was a sort of Great-Sunday-before-the-calendar-was-invented odor about the whole thing that I'd just as soon not come across again. Titles like "Eros and Psyche," if I remember correctly, put me off immediately. But I do remember a human odor about them. And there was also, accentuated by a sort of dignity that is Patmore's alone, that essential purity which makes of an Edgar Poe, "potentially," such a fine figure of a poet that one doesn't have to have his (written) work to know that he is a poet.

It was "movement" above all that I did not find in Patmore's art. I say this to you, because I distinctly remember, in regard to a Latin author, the importance you rightly attributed, as I did, to this thing: movement, which, after all is said and done, is the purest form to which we can finally reduce our taste for the things of this world.

You see, dear friend, "I do remember."

And you, Larbaud, I beg of you—though I don't really know just why—don't forget that doll dressed in red woolens,[9] on a little upright piece of furniture in that hotel, which, staring fixedly behind us, was a prodigious little thing. —Taking leave of you, I wanted to find something between us that was really a stroke of good fortune, and I was unaware there already was such a thing—affection.

With friendly regards. Leger

1. Larbaud had already returned to his home in Vichy.

2. AL and Larbaud had met, in Pau, for the first time, in Apr. 1911. See above, letter 95, note 1.

3. Larbaud's short novel, *Fermina Márquez*, which had been published in Jan. 1911.

4. Alain René Lesage (1668-1747), whose long picaresque tale, *Histoire de Gil Blas de Santillane*, published in three installments (1714, 1724, 1735), is usually considered the outstanding example of the picaresque genre in French.

5. A. O. Barnabooth, the rich globe-trotter and amateur *littérateur* dreamed up by Larbaud, was not to become widely known until 1913, when the NRF published *A. O. Barnabooth, Ses Œuvres Complètes, c'est-à-dire un Conte, ses Poésies et son Journal Intime*. Larbaud's close friends, however, were already familiar with a very limited earlier edition published in 1908 by Messein at the author's own expense. It is undoubtedly that edition, which contains considerably less material than the later 1913 one, that AL refers to here.

6. The "promised" work was Fargue's little book of poems, *Tancrède*, published by Larbaud in 1911.

7. In Pau.

8. "Coventry Patmore," in the NRF of Sept. and Oct. 1911.

9. A reference to a detail of the first meeting of AL and Larbaud in the dining room of a Pau hotel in Apr. 1911.

125

To Monsieur Valery Larbaud *Pau, October 17, 1911*
[London]

Dear friend,

I take a train for Paris in an hour. I am requesting that your copy of my little book be mailed to you. It was impossible for me to send you a copy on Holland paper; I had asked for four, and the rain ruined two of them on me while the bundle was lying around in some rural railway station.

I received L.-P. Fargue's *Tancrède*[1] and thank you for it.

[. . .] I'm not entirely my own master in orienting my life according to my choice; you really must believe that, and also that I would never be able to dabble in any "literature." To be sure, I am just as convinced as you that I'll regret it for the rest of my life if I have to give up the career in the consulates, for only there would I find the guarantees that I still hope to have in life.

I'd be happy to see you again at the end of November if you pass through Pau. Drop me a line when you are in Paris, on the chance that I might still be there—in care of M. Monnerot-Dumaine, 10, avenue Victor-Hugo.

I'll read Lesage's *Beauchêne*.[2] Thank you. I have often thought, in disagreement with all the biographies, that this Frenchman, who in his solitude kept himself amused by exercising his mysterious gift for the French language, must have been a very secretive and disdainful fellow. One never really knows anything but falsehoods about men of that ilk.

With friendly regards to you.   A. Saint-Leger

1. See above, letter 124, note 6.
2. See above, letter 124, note 4. Lesage was a prolific adapter and translator (from the Spanish). The work here referred to is *Les Aventures de Monsieur Robert, chevalier, dit de Beauchêne, capitaine de flibustiers dans la Nouvelle-France*, first published in 1732.

126

To Monsieur Valery Larbaud   *Paris, 10, avenue Victor-Hugo,*
[Paris]   *at the home of M. Monnerot-*
                                 Dumaine, [November 1911]

Dear friend,

I learned from Gide, incidentally, that you had published something in the *N.R.F.* for the month of November [. . .] and you told me nothing about it [. . .].

I don't know whether I'll be back in Pau when you
go to see Jammes. I definitely won't be there before next
Friday. If you should go down there before then, please
stop by to see my mother on my behalf. Don't talk to
her about me in literary terms; tell her simply that you
saw me in Paris.

Affectionately.   A.S.L.

127

To Monsieur Valery Larbaud   *Paris, 10, avenue Victor-Hugo,*
Vichy   *at the home of M. Monnerot-*
                                 Dumaine, [late November 1911]

My dear friend,

I went to see Léon Hennique again. He gave me his
formal promise to cast his vote for you on the first ballot.
He assures me that you can also count on Mirbeau's
vote. Yet I don't really think you can win this Goncourt Prize.[1]

I saw Gide, who says you are in London. I think it is
surer to write to you in Vichy, though.

I am your friend, affectionately.   A.S.L.

Don't think that you owe Léon Hennique's vote to
me; he has great admiration for your work.

1. Larbaud was being considered for the prestigious literary prize offered yearly by a group of ten writers who constituted the Académie Goncourt, which was founded in 1900 in compliance with the wishes of the naturalistic novelist and writer of memoirs, Edmond de Goncourt (1822-1896). He did not receive the prize. Léon Hennique (see above, letter 14, note 2) and Octave Mirbeau (1850-1917), were both members of the Académie Goncourt at the time.

128

To Monsieur Valery Larbaud   *Pau [end of] December*
Vichy   *1911*

My dear friend,

Only yesterday did I receive the too-generous pages that you were good enough to devote to my little book.[1] It really took all that friendship and affection can offer to make me accept such a token of literary esteem. So let me thank you "in the sunlight of the instant."

Believe me, I do not come anywhere near thinking as highly of those poems as you do. I know that I will not have pleasant memories of their publication and that I'll now have to find the time, if not the inclination, to make up somewhat for this thing I leave behind, by publishing other things. But our very sorrows, lying there before us, keep making sudden tremendous leaps—opossum leaps!—so long as we have not stripped ourselves of the exacting need for the absolute of our childhood, I mean its despotism and its conscience.

I thank you above all else for having thought to defend me, on the literary plane, against the charge of "exoticism." Any localization strikes me as odious, just as does any precise dating, for our poor little feasts of the mind. I have always craved liberation from spatial ties as much as I have craved freedom from what

is merely contemporary; and if I still cling, for simple
reasons of lighting, to a certain degree of latitude encir-
cling our globe, I cordially detest all longitudes. Antilleans themselves might think—not about my poems,
which are quite simply French, nor about my themes,
which I have always lived in the strictest sense—but
about my attitude as a human being prior to the dream
of life—that this attitude has in it more of the oceanic,
Asiatic, or African, or anything else whatever, than it
has of the Antillean.

And may I put your mind still more at rest by admitting that the "herbe à Mme Lalie" and the "oiseau Annaô"[2] and many other plant and animal names (real and
scientifically accurate as they may be) appeal to me solely
by the way they seem to mimic what is imaginary. Not,
of course, that I spurn familiar words, but I have always
felt that there is in us, along with a taste for going back
into ages and races in their semi-anonymity, an instinctive horror of naming things too specifically in accord
with science or custom. I have never enjoyed naming
things for any other reason than the joy, very childish
and primitive, of feeling that I am the creator of the
name. Just think for a minute of the radical difference
there is between a "word" and a "name." I recall a long
poem about sea birds[3] (which I withdrew from the
N.R.F. last year when proofs of it had already been
pulled) which would have struck me as the outpouring
of some ornithological crank or pedant, if most of these
birds had not received from me, without any deception
on my part, the baptism of their names. Yet I was thoroughly familiar with all of them, with the real birds as
well as with their scientific nomenclature and classification.

All this hatred of the relative, and of the abstract, in

poetry, is undoubtedly more evident in many of my un-published poems.

Hatred of estheticism too! —Can you understand how delighted I was by the uncanny intuition that leads you, a poet, to proffer, at the end of your article, a simple sentence like this, sweeping clean, to my delight, the poet's whole primitive domain: ". . . the four elements, the animals, plants, stones; hunting, war, and the passions of men . . .?"

I thank you also, dear friend, for having called my poems "the fruits of a perfect humility." "Humility" is the only word that can express the pure, proud way a poet has of *submitting*. And isn't there also a sort of pride in humility?

With friendliest greetings.   A.S.L.

I have just now received your copy of Lesage's *Beauchêne*—which, to me, is something infinitely French, and how far removed from exoticism in the way it recounts adventures! I'll take good care of it and send it back to you.

1. This was Larbaud's review of *Eloges*, which appeared in *La Phalange* of 20 Dec. 1911 under the "Mois du poète" rubric. This first public recognition of AL as a poet was reproduced many years later at AL's specific request in the special SJP number of *Les Cahiers de la Pléiade*, Summer-Autumn 1950, since Larbaud's tragic illness had, from 1935 on, made it impossible for him to do any writing. See letter to Jean-Aubry of 17 June 1949 and 17 Nov. 1949, (319, 320), and above, letter 38, note 1.

2. "L'herbe-à-Madame-Lalie" occurs in "Eloge xv": "Nos mères vont descendre, parfumées avec l'herbe-à-Madame-Lalie." The "oiseau Annaô" occurs in the poem "Pour fêter une enfance," Sec. iii: "ici les fouets, et là le cri de l'oiseau Annaô. . . ." For details on the Annaô bird, see letters to Caillois of 26 Jan. 1953 and Feb. 1953. (253, 254)

3. "Cohorte." See letter to Rivière of 21 Dec. 1910. (25)

129

To Monsieur Valery Larbaud   *Pau, February 11, 1912*
[Vichy]

Dear friend,

I don't know where my letter will find you. Tell me
if it's Vichy, Paris or London where I should send, with
my thanks once again, your copy of *Beauchêne*; for I'm
afraid you've given up the idea of coming through here,
as you had thought of doing.

Affectionately yours.   A.S.L.

130

To Monsieur Valery Larbaud   *Pau, March 2, 1912*
Cannes

Dear friend,

Can you, by chance, tell me anything about Mr. Algar
Thorold,[1] an English writer whose usual residence is in
Chelsea (Sun House, 6 Ch. Embankment) and who has
published at Constable's, a book of criticism, *Six Masters
in Disillusion?* [. . .]

I was glad to have news from you. I suspect that you're
working. Tell me that nothing in the way of a health
problem made you choose to spend time in Cannes.

Affectionately.   A.S.L.

Unfortunately I won't be in Pau when you come
through, though I don't yet know just where I will be.

1. Algar Labouchere Thorold (1866-1936), British writer on
theological subjects and eventually English translator of the
French Catholic religious historian and critic, Henri Bremond.
Six Masters in Disillusion appeared in 1909. The six masters
were Fontenelle, Mérimée, Ferdinand Fabre, Huysmans, Maeterlinck, Anatole France.

131

To Monsieur Valery Larbaud   *Madrid, April 28, 1912*
[Italy]

[. . .] Please, dear friend, share an affectionate thought with Gide,[1] if he is still with you.

I'm going to the south of Spain and then will pass close by where you are, for on the 9th or 11th I'm going to take a freighter from Malaga to Genoa; and from there I'll go to Hungary.

Let me hear from you occasionally, dear friend, always using my Pau address [. . .].

Excuse the impoliteness of this pencil.

Affectionately.   A.S.L.

1. Gide was Larbaud's guest at Vichy early in 1912.

132

To Monsieur Valery Larbaud   *Paris, Saturday,*
[Paris]   [*May 1912*]

Mi querido amigo[1]

I had to come back to France on urgent business. On the chance that you may be in Paris, I am sending you this letter. I beg you to let me hear from you. I would like very much to see you, as soon as you are so good as to tell me your whereabouts in Paris. If you have had to move on already—which I would deeply regret—at least I hope that I shall meet you the next time I go to London.

For the time being, my address is the following, which is my mother's house:

                13, rue de Bruxelles [Paris]
at other times, usually c/o my sister:
                176, bd Malesherbes [Paris]

I can't remember all the Malagueñian things one puts at the close of Spanish letters; but don't forget that I am your good friend   A.S.L.

> *Dicen que los albañiles*
> *Llevan el alma en un hilo.*
> *La lleven ó no la lleven,*
> *Vivo hace tiempo en el mundo!*[2]

1. This entire letter is in Spanish in the original.
2. A verse from a *cantar popular*. AL knew that Larbaud was very fond of Spanish popular songs. The text in English reads:
   They say that stonemasons
   Have a soul that hangs by a thread.
   Whether they do or not,
   I've been living for quite a while in this world!

133

To Monsieur Valery Larbaud   [*Paris*] *Monday*, [*May 1912*]
[Paris]   *13, rue de Bruxelles*

My dear friend,

I've learned by chance that you are passing through Paris, and I've just expressed, to one of your friends, Gaston Gallimard,[1] my desire to see you again. But I'm also thinking of how little time you'll have. Here's what I especially wanted to tell you: go and see Arthur Fontaine.[2]

Maybe my last letter addressed to the rue Octave-Feuillet arrived soon enough for you to go see Claudel. I very much hope so.

If you're on your way to Vichy by now, please remember to transmit my respects to Madame Larbaud.[3]

Yours in friendship.   A.S.L.

1. See above, letter 37, note 2.
2. In 1911 Arthur Fontaine was Secretary General of the

French Ministry of Labor. Along with Philippe Berthelot (see above, letter 58, note 1), Fontaine persuaded AL to continue his pursuit of a career in diplomacy.

3. Larbaud's mother.

134

To Monsieur Valery Larbaud   *London, June 8, 1912*
Paris

Dear friend, I don't know anyone in this town, where I'll be staying for six months and where I can't even give you a more or less permanent address [. . .]. You may be sure I am very disappointed to learn that you are not here. [. . .]

With a friendly handshake.   A.S.L.

135

To Monsieur Valery Larbaud   *London, October 23, 1912*
[Paris]

My dear friend,[1]

I am so sorry, I owe you an apology for not having answered your long and so kind letter of June last. It is indeed good of you to have written me in the way you did. I trust you will excuse my long silence. Perhaps it is lamentable that one who loves politeness above all things in the world is now having to make it a principle of hygiene not to write at all.

Although I have roamed a little through the country, and at sea (Western waters) on a sailing ship, I must beg your pardon for having "settled" in London instead of following your advice. You know, I am awfully fond of this town, and between London and Petrea Arabia I don't really think there is any middle place to be tolerated in the world. Moreover, if you knew how very happy I have been here! Circumstances here have made my life so extraordinarily happy that I wonder whether the future may ever prove the same. Henceforth, far from accepting the first things that come along, I will expect a great deal more.

It is ages since I last heard from anyone in France except my people. However, I never ceased thinking of your literary work with great confidence and best wishes for you. Many times I have wished that you would come to London, but now I see that I must renounce all hope of this.

I trust that this world is using you well, and that you are enjoying the best of health. And always I hope, my dear friend, that your name will not cease being that of a friend.

Yrs. most sincerely.   Saint-Leger

I heard that you saw Jammes at Vichy. So doubtless you chatted a great deal about literature, for J. is so very keen on talking about it now.

Chesterton,[2] from his village full of rabbits and from the crossing of his two roads, apologizes to you for that hurried reception in his motor car.

1. The entire text of the original letter is written in English and reproduced here without alteration.

2. Gilbert Keith Chesterton (1874-1936), the English journalist, story-writer, and Catholic polemist.

136

To Monsieur Valery Larbaud   *Paris, April 14, 1913*
[Vichy]

My dear Larbaud,[1]

I was wondering what had become of you; I have not heard from you for ever so long! I know you are not an over-talkative man, but rather the sort of one to carry out, secretly, the project of a most entertaining book.

And such a one is your "Journal d'un Milliardaire":[2] awfully good and "certain"! (if this word has its same meaning in my bad English). An authentic, thorough-bred thing, with the right stuff in it—a thing that I much admire. From the very beginning I simply loved it, and understood you were going to play, there, the very good game. My thanks are warm for it.

I hope to see you again. Do write me and let me know when you are in Paris. Perhaps I shall be back in time. I am just leaving for some days at sea, with friends. Don't imagine any big Ocean liner with the well-equipped tables, the damask, the silver and other ac-companiments, the oriental waiters in spotless white and all the sort of thing I am fond of, but only an uncom-fortable small boat, a lovely little schooner, which I am no less fond of. We don't intend landing except at Bris-tol. I remember you had great liking for that town, hadn't you? And so have I.

By Jammes, by Rivière, I heard of you in Paris, where I have been studying for nearly five months!

Best greetings of A.S.L.

       c/o Mme. A. Dormoy, Paris
       176, bd Malesherbes

 1. The entire text of the original letter is written in English and is reproduced here without alteration.

 2. Probably refers to the first three installments of "Journal de A. O. Barnabooth," which was published serially in five suc-cessive issues of the NRF, beginning with Feb. 1913 and con-tinuing through June 1913.

137

To Monsieur Valery Larbaud   *Paris [August 1913]*
London

Dear friend,

I've just thought it over: I accept.[1]

It is really too funny![2] A Franco-British John Donne Club under American patronage, founded in the midst of mid-Victorian England, by a Californian lady of Petrarchan tastes, in honor of an Elizabethan! . . . How could I turn that down? The very fact that I lack qualifications is itself a qualification! And we so desperately like a poet who hasn't yet had time enough to disappoint us!

So you can notify our three English confreres and our Presiding Grand Electress, Agnes Tobin, of my official acceptance, along with yours and Gide's.

In regard to this club, I like first of all that its headquarters are in London, yet it does not require one's presence there. . . . I also like that its six members, by turn, have no other obligation to fulfill beyond publishing once a year an edifying study on the work of John Donne, poet and "metaphysician." And above all else I like it that my situation as the junior member exempts me from the responsibility of writing until the very last, that is, not before six years are past, or even longer—and between now and then! . . . (Even longer, if your dean and first contributor, the most worthy and scrupulous Sir Edmund Gosse, with the same compunction as M. de Buffon[3] in lace cuffs, is obliged to approach his task in the waistcoat and top hat of the Librarian of the House of Lords, as I have always seen him, I do not doubt that the prescribed dates of expiration of term may be considerably postponed, on his initiative.

Which means just so much more time gained by Gide for the improvement of his English!)

And then, I like to think that, where Gide, you, and I are concerned, this vaccination that we are undergoing may assure us immunity against all future risks of being enrolled in other academies, such as the one founded in Paris by Armand du Plessis de Richelieu.[4]

So, lets go![5]

I am with you, in friendship.   A. S.-L.

1. Larbaud had been asked by Agnes Tobin (see above, letter III, note 1) to persuade AL to be a member of the "John Donne Club" described in this letter. Agnes Tobin had published English translations of Petrarch's poetry.

2. English in original.

3. Georges-Louis de Buffon (1707-1788), the celebrated naturalist who directed the compilation, and wrote much of the text, of a monumental *Histoire naturelle* (1749-1804).

4. The Académie Française (the "Forty Immortals") established by Cardinal Richelieu in 1635.

5. English in original.

138

To Monsieur Valery Larbaud   *London, Tuesday,*
[Vichy]   *[September 1913]*
                                           28a Baron's Court Road,
                                           West Kensington

Dear friend,

Let me hear from you. The human smell is an old one along our solitary roads [. . .].

Not much news here. The business of translation rights for Gide grows more and more complicated day by day and is becoming endlessly embarrassing.[1] But don't let him know that, please.

I was sorry to lose you here so soon; if I fail the Foreign Service examination in April I won't come back to

Europe for ten years or so. And I would so like to have welcomed you for a day or two, on the Solent,[2] in this prodigious old European dwelling where I sometimes live all by myself, and where I turn on the lights in the upper storeys, not as you light a candle in a death's head, but just to be doing something alive and aggressive. (Have you noticed to what a great extent electricity is at once joyous *and unconcerned*[3] in England?)

If I see you again before you take off for Spain, I'll lend you my little pocket edition of Cervantes, which one of my sisters has just sent to me here in London.

I was in Eastbourne for a time, whence the Gide business twice summoned me here. I'm going to return to the coast along the Solent. Hold on to my London address so you can send me news of yourself. I send along my best wishes for your literary work and for the ordering of your life; hold a friendly thought for me.

And then, keep feeding your harsh foolish virgins. A man's heart in a collar-box isn't much as extra baggage, but it can be singularly poisonous. And its strange brother, the sex organ, can be slipped into the hatbox until God has found something better.

Non tanta Oebalios junxit concordia fratres
quos peperit summo candida Leda Jovi.[4]

[. . .] Cordially.   A.S.L.

[. . .] The Binghams, after your visit here, asked me to tell them what name you published under. Naturally, I said, "Romain Rolland!" . . .

1. For Tagore's *Gitanjali*. See letters to Gide of 23 Oct. 1912, 7 Dec. 1912, 28 Jan. 1913, Aug. 1913. (113, 114, 115, 119)
2. The channel separating the Isle of Wight from the Hampshire coast, much used for regattas.
3. English in original.
4.   "Such concord did not unite the brothers Œbalios whom shining Leda conceived with great Jupiter."

This problematic Latin quotation from an unidentified source —Could it be of AL's own composition?—obviously has something to do with the equally problematic sexual references preceding it. OC has *fumno*, surely a typographical error for *summo*.

139

To Monsieur Valery Larbaud   *Paris, Friday,*
[Paris]   [*December 1913*]

My dear friend,

I admire your work[1] the way, in the street, we admire one breed of horse above another; or the way one recognizes at sea the vessel born in Glasgow.

I thank you from the bottom of my heart and send you wishes selected among my very best—lofty wishes for your work and for yourself. You can wager, my dear friend, that the quality of this work will secretly cause you to lose as many friends as your material independence has done up to now.

I believe you're in Paris. But please pardon me for playing dead. I feel compelled to do so at the moment, and really out of politeness; for some time now I've let myself slide into a boorish moroseness, and my boredom has a way of growing so fast that the first thing I have to do is to slough it off like a snake at the zoo.

Above all, present my excuses to Madame Larbaud,[2] whose warm welcome I have not forgotten [. . .].

Affectionately yours.   A.S.L.

—More than once I've had occasion to talk about you to Claudel, in Hamburg.

—You have honored my copy of *Barnabooth* with an inscription[3] that makes it impossible for me to show it to anyone; I'll get hold of another copy.

1. Undoubtedly the 1913 edition of *A. O. Barnabooth . . .* , referred to in the postscript to this letter.

2. Larbaud's mother.

3. The inscription was the Italian phrase: "Come a maestro."

140

To Monsieur Valery Larbaud   *Paris, May 29, 1914*
[London]

My dear friend,

[. . .] I occasionally had news of you, in Paris, from mutual friends [. . .]. And now and then I would also hear, in the English families, of some of our London friends. Are you there at the moment, or at Vichy, or Paris? Tell me, please, and give me news of yourself.

I read your *Rachel Frutiger* (in which there was a very fine gold cross filled with ether),[1] but I don't know anything more about you.

I thank you most sincerely for your sympathetic interest in my success in the examination;[2] I have mastered what it was my intention to master in life. I was not duped by my dreams nor by the opinions of others. I am quite simply happy at having found inside myself enough dislike and distaste for the usual cowardice and disgusting smugness of imaginative people, who really look upon their lives with the attitudes and hopes of beggars. Perhaps it's still better to take hold and lead one's life like a real woman, rather than follow it like a streetwalker. In addition, I had invested such a quantity of willpower in it, that failing it would have robbed me of all moral reward. *So, glad I won that!*[3]

If you're in London, give me news of O'Connor's[4] health. I couldn't get to see him during my last visits. And also give me, if you can, Miss Tobin's present address.

Here, ran into Montgomery at Mrs. Phelps'. He told me the latest Wells[5] scandal, along with the sad and

comical adventure of the young fellow from Edinburgh
—to whom Lady S—— supplied Greek epigraphs for
his poems. (It appears that there are still men in London
—and women—who can decipher Greek on occasion.)

Au revoir, my dear friend; see you soon, I hope [. . .].

A. Saint-Leger Leger

1. The story, "Rachel Frutiger," was first published in the
NRF of May 1914, pp. 745-756. It was later included by Larbaud
in the collection, *Enfantines* (1918). At the beginning of the
story, one of the girls at the aristocratic school drops the gold
cross she wears on a chain around her neck. It turns out to be
hollow and filled with ether.

2. The Foreign Service Examination.

3. English in original.

4. Daniel O'Connor was a British friend of Larbaud's, born
on the island of Mauritius. Sée Jean-Aubry, *Valery Larbaud. Sa
vie et son oeuvre.* 1, p. 108 and *passim*.

5. H. G. Wells, the science-fiction writer.

141

To Monsieur Valery Larbaud   [*Ministry of*] *Foreign Affairs,*
Paris   *Office of the Minister,*
                               June 23, 1914

Dear friend,

I don't forget to think of you [. . .].

What's become of you? You are lonely, I imagine, the
way we've been here in Europe for the last three thousand years [. . .].

Let me hear from you.   St.-L. Leger

142

To Monsieur Valery Larbaud   *Foreign Affairs,*
[Paris]   *Bureau of Political*
                                      and Commercial Affairs
                                      September 20, 1923[1]

Dear friend,

I keep my promise—on the date indicated.[2] Friendship does not cancel gambling debts.

I recalled that you had liked, in one little poem,[3] the amount of *space* that was assimilated in it; as a result, I chose these pages for you.

I certainly did take *pleasure* in welcoming these poems as they welled up, since I did just that; but what a job when, finally, one has to produce a manuscript! If you derive some little pleasure from it, I'll be sufficiently rewarded for my boredom and trouble.

These poems were never intended for publication. But if you persist in wanting to submit them to a review, it's agreed that I allow you a free hand to do so. The conditions: my approval of the choice of review, publication of the whole text in one issue, use of a pseudonym, printing in italics, and the proofs to be submitted to me [. . .].

I was glad to have word from you from Belle-Isle and Nantes. I hope you saw, at the Palace,[4] the Vauban Gate (Bangor Gate). I no longer, alas!, have any need for the pennant you offer me; my little sailboat has been put out of commission. . . .

If you are not going on to Italy right away, get in touch with me one day and come have lunch with me.

With friendly regards.   Saint-Leger Leger

1. Note the nine-year hiatus between this and the preceding letter.

2. AL had promised to send Larbaud the manuscript of the poem *Anabase*.

3. The "one little poem" was the "Chanson liminaire" of *Anabase*, which had been published already in the Apr. 1922 issue of NRF.

4. The ducal palace at Nantes.

143

To Monsieur Valery Larbaud   *Foreign Affairs,*
[Paris]   *Bureau of Political and*
                                     Commercial Affairs
                                     October 13, 1923

Dear friend,

I've been very busy these last few days, and troubled at not being able to have first-hand news from you. I've wanted repeatedly to toss your address to a chauffeur, but I gave up the idea; I recalled that when I, myself, have the least touch of flu, I lock myself in with a lamp and can't tolerate anyone's presence [. . .]. If these scruples fall wide of the mark, believe me, I am all the more mortified for it.

I read the second part of *Mon plus secret conseil*;[1] it has even more substance in it than the first part and gives no less pleasure. What I admire and like in these pages —where all the inflections of the French "voice," even more than of the French "language," are set down, and where the poet comes across a running spring at every step—is that their author knows how to defend his integrity, to be demanding enough, and to maintain enough mastery and instinct to reject every facile melodic effect (the most unpardonable defect in thoroughbred prose). Not a single noticeable hemistich, or even octosyllable, to sully the purity of your prose—never the least anticipatory effect for the ear—an articulated language, a language constantly renewed in all its attributes, through the play of its "inequalities" (if you will permit this horrible expression). It is here, I believe, that the prose-writer's art may require more care than the poet's; the area of uncertainty increases as his resources increase; his risks are multiplied along with his temptations; and by the very fact of his freedom, he must all the more urgently seek guarantees against what crops up fortuitously.

We'll see each other soon, dear friend. I'd like to be sure that you know how to deal with your indisposition somewhat methodically and persistently.

You were nice to write me as you did (about *Anabase*). You said everything to me that could give me pleasure. I even accept the partiality that stems from your friendship as the finest expression of approval that I could wish for these poems. I accept without cavil.

[...] Gallimard[2] is lunching with me on Tuesday. His insistence embarrasses me somewhat, because what he now asks on advice from you I have already refused to two other publishers and to him. Before considering any proposal for a new edition, it is my intention, since *Anabase* is to be published,[3] to utilize that text as rapidly as possible for a separate edition, adding four poems in the same series, three of which are unpublished.[4] If Gallimard could promise me a good large-format edition with fine, full-sized italic type, I'd reserve this publication in book form for him. But on that point I'd like to clear the ground right away; that's why I'd like to know definitely what Rivière intends to do, since the publication in book form must come after the periodical publication [...].

Take care of yourself, dear friend. I send you my friendliest wishes.   A. Saint-Leger Leger

—Fargue has just this minute given me news of you by telephone.

I'm going to reply to Adrienne Monnier.[5]

1. *Mon plus secret conseil* was first published in two installments in the Sept. and Oct. 1923 issues of the NRF. This story, dedicated by Larbaud to Edouard Dujardin, is written in the "stream of consciousness" form that Dujardin had first used in *Les Lauriers sont coupés* (1887) and that Joyce was to use in *Ulysses*.

2. Gaston Gallimard was urging AL to publish a new edition of *Eloges*. AL finally did authorize the edition, which appeared in 1925 under the pseudonym of St-J. Perse (*sic*). See letter to Gallimard of 23 Apr. 1924. (146)

3. In a review.

4. It is not possible to say just which four poems AL here refers to. The published one is undoubtedly "Amitié du Prince," which had already appeared under the pseudonym of St-J. Perse in the Summer 1924 issue of *Commerce*. The three unpublished ones may possibly be among those that remained in manuscript and were confiscated from AL's Paris apartment by the Gestapo in June 1940.

5. Adrienne Monnier (1892-1955) was the proprietress of the lending-library and bookstore, La Maison des Amis des Livres, in the Rue de l'Odéon, directly across from the shop in which her American friend, Sylvia Beach, was to establish her Anglo-American lending-library and bookstore, Shakespeare and Co. See letters to Adrienne Monnier. (289, 290)

144

To Monsieur Valery Larbaud
Paris

Foreign Affairs,
Bureau of Political and
Commercial Affairs
November 22, 1924

Dear friend,

My heartfelt excuses for not having replied to you yet [. . .].

I think of you often, and of the pleasure that it would be to have a leisurely chat with you about all the things you are doing that I no longer know about: your work, your life, your studies, and yourself. My professional enslavement gets worse every day, and friendship suffices to make that quite clear to me. I'll be going through another period of rather heavy work. But be nice and call me up next week and we'll pick out a day when you can lunch alone with me, preferably at the beginning of the week after that. Phone me at Foreign Affairs around 8 in the evening; or else at my apartment, PAssy 73-63, either late in the evening or in the morning before 7 o'clock.

I'll be seeing you soon at any rate, with friendliest best wishes, your   A. Saint-Leger Leger

145

To Monsieur Valery Larbaud   *Foreign Affairs,*
[Paris]   *Office of the Minister*
                                      May 14, 1925

Dear friend,

I claim my place next to you this evening[1]—the place that belongs to one of your earliest readers and admirers, the place of an old friend, and now of a "colleague," since I hold you to be one of our best plenipotentiaries to foreign countries.

All that remains to be done is for us to find, for your mission *in partibus*, one of those fine Low Latin names of the sort you find designating the dioceses of itinerant bishops.

I am thinking, dear friend, of all that you will go on loving in this world, of all that we will continue to love in your work, and I borrow John Donne's language to greet with all my best wishes *"that unripe side of earth . . . ."*[2]

With friendly regards, your   A. Saint-Leger Leger

1. Larbaud was made a Chevalier de la Légion d'honneur in Mar. 1925. A dinner honoring this event was organized by his friends at the Restaurant Marguery in Paris on the night of May 14.

2. English in original. First words of Donne's verse letter, "To the Countesse of Huntingdon."

LETTER TO GASTON GALLIMARD
(1924)

146

To Monsieur Gaston Gallimard[1]   *Paris, April 23, 1924*
Paris

Dear friend,

Under this same cover, the contract, which I have examined.[2] I had to modify article x. I am not a writer; and you know how hard I find it to tie myself down in publishing matters. I was determined to reserve the right for myself of putting an end to the career of this little book if I should one day feel it incumbent upon me to make such a decision. You've always shown me much too much friendly understanding not to accept this reservation, which I make on principle.

And I am asking you, in addition, for twenty author's copies instead of ten. This personal courtesy, for some twenty friends, both French and foreign, is what constitutes the whole interest of this re-edition for me. And besides, you don't have much of a burden by way of copies to the press. (There wouldn't be any at all if it were up to me alone, since I'd prefer to have as few readers as possible. But I must let you do as you wish on this point—do whatever best serves your interests and obligations as a publisher.)

Only one request, but an urgent one, concerning your publicity procedures—in your publisher's advertisements, refrain from all comment on the work and on its author.

Cordially yours.   Alexis Leger

1. Letter printed on p. 547 of OC and not included in the "Lettres" section.

2. The contract for a new edition of *Eloges*. See above, letter 143, note 2.

LETTERS FROM ASIA

LETTER TO PHILIPPE BERTHELOT

147

To Monsieur Philippe Berthelot   *Peking, January 3, 1917*
Paris

Dear friend,

This is not yet the beginning of the regular correspondence[1] between us that I promised you, for your
private information, about the political situation in
China. For that, I shall wait until I have a little better
perspective and on-the-spot discernment. This is just a
preliminary letter, written in haste on arriving here, to
let you know how I am getting along and to give you
my first impressions as a traveler.

A terribly slow voyage, with lots of unscheduled stops,
on the old *Polynésien* of fond memory, which you know
so well, with its legendary fauna of old Far East hands.
But she doesn't skirt the Laccadive Islands any more
the way Levet's *Armand Béhic*[2] did. And the stopovers
were much longer than usual: at Djibouti (where the
coal ran out), at Colombo (where the ritual evening at
Mount Lavinia made me think of the Claudel of *Connaissance de l'Est*),[3] at Singapore (where the Chinese
junks—the first I saw—flaunt their indifference to the
war), at Saigon and Haiphong (where they still talk
about your trip up to Yünnan), and finally at Hong
Kong (where the elite of the Shanghai adventuresses
came aboard, seeking out the traveler a long way from
port, the way a harbor-pilot does). Every day of the trip I
felt that by degrees I was becoming a different man,
and every day I had an ever-stronger feeling of how
relative are all things in this world.

Shanghai is still the prodigious crossroads whose activity no world-shaking event can slow down. I'm told that the anecdotal side of things doesn't change there either—Anna Ballard,[4] now a millionairess, still rules with the same authority, having brazenly acquired respectability through her war-work. The head bursar of the Jesuits continues to astound the big businessmen with his genius as a financier. The scientists at Zi Ka Wei[5] continue to argue about the capriciousness of the monsoon. And there's always some old Scandinavian explorer from Central Asia hanging around town waiting for the packetboat that will take him home.

I managed to meet your friend, Bons d'Anty,[6] who is quite seriously ill with dysentery and who, like the others, is waiting for the return boat from Yokohama. He's a man with a wide-ranging mind and mordant wit, and the tang of real originality, always quick to rise above the most painful events of his life with a word of sarcasm. His memory is filled with unexpected items, as are those huge Chinese camphorwood trunks of his that clutter up the Overseas Shipping Office. His long years of experience in the Chinese Interior and his knowledge of old Chinese traditions were to me a first and most invaluable revelation.

Naggiar[7] still has things well in hand, asserting the authority of his post intelligently and fairly over all the people in the French Concession, who are not exactly an easy lot to get along with.

In Peking I found Martel[8] firmly in the saddle and undeserving of all the criticism showered on him in Paris. He lacks neither common sense nor good judgment, and he has a very realistic way of looking at things, avoiding too much abstractness, yet achieving the necessary simplifications. He has the great asset of a sound nervous system, which is indispensable in China in the face of events like the present ones. He knows, as one would expect him to, how to handle things in a jovial, forthright way, without seeking to dramatize anything or without ever yielding to sudden impulses. His apparent apathy is not inertia; it is genuine cleverness. When all is said and done, all of this really isn't bad.

Shall I share with you my first impressions of a world that is new to me and that, as you can well imagine, leaves me very wide-eyed?

For the immediate present: There is the Franco-Chinese crisis[9] that precipitated my being brought here to help out a chargé d'affaires short of personnel. It can, I think, be settled without too badly compromising future Franco-Chinese relations or leaving any lasting scars. The trouble at Tientsin, which is already subsiding, can certainly be kept within local bounds—it's a question of being firm but patient and of holding on to the reins of authority without too much recourse to force or to any sort of ostentation (so as to let the Chinese "save face"). One must not be too quick to react to the collective outbursts of so hysterical, volatile, and gregarious a people as the Chinese, since violence leads them to every sort of madness. You bide your time until the somnambulistic behavior and histrionics, however misplaced they may be, have run their course. You wait for the moment when the satisfaction derived from the first outburst has begun to make the participants lose sight of the initial aims of their first reaction. (Even in medicine one does not fully treat an epileptic seizure until the initial automatic reaction has spent itself.)

At the Wai Chiao Pu[10] the old Chinese Minister of Foreign Affairs,[11] whom Martel and I have seen several times, seems to me quite wise and certainly in a position to assert his moral authority against the fanaticism of his

"Young China" entourage (especially one son who is very ambitious and demagogic). We must give him enough time to handle the first demands of public opinion in his own way. Naturally, he's not hoping for the worst and is privately concerned, just as we are, to safeguard the future of the special entente that exists between France and China. In this country, with its age-old communal tradition that makes it impossible to handle things in any other way but collectively, the problem for both Chinese and foreigner is to find a competent person to deal with. Neither logic nor reason has any place here in the search for conciliation, and forceps and Caesarean surgery even less. Psychiatry would be more effective in China than European-style diplomacy. The Russians know this, and their Slavic or semi-Asiatic instinct leads them, at the present time, to practice only a politics of osmosis.

For the future: Henceforward, we must keep our sights on the far horizon, without worrying too much about the past or even the present. In any case, such a view is totally beyond the Peking Diplomatic Corps, which has created for the last fifteen years, within the confines of the Diplomatic Quarter, its own very special, cocoon-like mode of life. On the private level, this may titillate the snobbery of its inhabitants, but it remains totally unrelated to China. Whence the isolation, inattentiveness, and mental indolence of the older Chiefs of Mission, whose corps of interpreters is totally useless, politically speaking. They will always be overtaken by events, looking back, as they do in their dilettantish way, to an ancient China whose foundations seem to them changeless. I forever hear them theorizing about the rural tradition that has shaped the Chinese people, finding in it an assurance of social stability that will be a guarantee against all future change. It is at the meetings of the Diplomatic Corps that one realizes what illusions are entertained on this subject. And even we French are inclined to count too heavily on the influence exercised in China by the philosophy of the French Enlightenment or the outworn positivism of Auguste Comte. All of that is much more *passé* than we think. And the China of the intellectuals and academics, such as our friends Li Yu-Yin[12] and Tsaï Yüan-Pei, who are more politically than socially minded—even *that* China is slipping sadly into apprehension and nostalgia, if not yet disaffection.

As a newcomer to the country, I see before me a China in full social ferment; and no matter how slow and laborious, no matter how confused and spasmodic this mutation may be, it is none the less absolutely certain within the historical determinism of a far broader Hegelian evolutionary movement. A whole future is here at stake, completely committed to a new form of civilization, in search of social institutions more suitable to China than to imitations of institutions and regimes suitable to the great Western democracies. The ideas of Karl Marx and of Engels already exert their subtle attraction on all the young Chinese intellectuals; and in the long run, after any number of subversions and transitional experiments, but perhaps even before the unification of China is achieved, nothing will stop the march of the Chinese community towards a collectivism very close to the most orthodox Leninist communism. The cliché of the age-old rural structure of China no longer holds. That structure is as good preparation as any other for a vast social collectivism; and the Chinese people above all others have, by their very nature, the most ancient sense of reciprocity. Perhaps nothing is really being altered in the depths of the human being who is Chinese, but it is those very depths, by their nature, that provide no immunization against anything. They are a people open to every influence, thanks to their capacity for assimilation and to the very existence of reactions jaded by long usage.

I landed here shortly after the death of Yüan Shih-kai[13] and his last attempt at restoring the monarchy, and not for a single moment did I doubt this new evolution sweeping China toward a destiny completely contrary to all our European predictions. One day in the Chinese countryside I saw with what placid unconcern and lack of surprise a peasant stopped a moment to gaze at the first airplane to appear in Chinese skies, as though it were just another kite. That was enough to make me understand how ready this very ancient—and very pliable—people would be to adapt themselves to every form of modern syncretism—technical or scientific as well as social, even though they are unaware of everything that makes up such a syncretism. I am convinced, moreover, contrary to all prevailing opinion, and without the slightest desire for paradox, that it is the peasantry itself that will one day furnish the basic element of great revolutions in China, so that it will be the Chinese rural masses, in this immense area of the planet, who will ultimately determine which path the whole of Asia, massively, will follow in the geopolitics of the future.

And that is the spectacle that already excites me—this transformation before my very eyes of an ancient human society ready for all the adaptations history may require. Wherever there is movement, there my interest is aroused. For so long, people have been saying that China is a civilization rather than a nation; but it is no longer possible to deny that China is by way of becoming a nation, unaware only of what future role it will be called upon to play in international politics.

It is of the utmost importance not to be misled about this any longer. That would be to underestimate, for the future, the assimilative powers of this people in scientific and technical, as well as social, matters; to underestimate, on the international scene as it unfolds, the prodigious natural resources of this immense country—resources that may one day turn it into an industrial power with all the physical advantages now enjoyed by America. At this, so to speak, equinoctial moment in its history, it is not a matter of indifference to know in what direction such an expanding mass of humanity may be led to move politically. Our share of responsibility, here again, may one day be great. It sometimes takes only the smallest object to determine which slope a river will run down.

If at this point we could persuade China to break with Germany and join the war on the side of the Allies by making her see the advantages that would accrue to her once a peace treaty is signed, that would obviously be the best means of drawing her, for the future, into the orbit and family of the great Occidental Powers, helping to bring about a single great international political under-standing—provided, however, that we would not expose her to a disappointment that would have immediate consequences of the gravest and most decisive sort for the West, consequences in which the Russians alone could find a momentary advantage.

The whole immense drama that will one day be gen-erated by the "Yellow Wind" has every chance, unfor-tunately, of escaping the attention of French politicians like Clemenceau or even Poincaré,[14] who think they are being Bismarckian when they take no interest in any-thing outside Europe. For the moment, the game seems to have been forfeited to England, and the alliance with England will be cynically exploited by Japan against

China, especially where the Shantung question is concerned. It is up to us French to pick up the cards after our present difficulties with China have been settled.

I think of you a great deal, dear friend, and I want to tell you affectionately, at the end of this long letter, how much I hope to be worthy of the confidence you have placed in me by having me sent here in the present circumstances. You were right in telling me that no professional or human education is complete without a sojourn in the Far East; and for that, too, I am grateful to you.

With heartfelt greetings to you and Hélène.

Alexis Leger

1. See above, letter 58, note 1. During World War I, Philippe Berthelot was in charge of Political Affairs in the French Ministry of Foreign Affairs, a post he held until 1920, when he was promoted to the office of Secretary General. He was, however, promptly forced to resign because of the affair of the Banque Industrielle de Chine. He was reappointed Secretary General in 1924 by Aristide Briand and served in that capacity through 1932. He was succeeded by AL, who was appointed Secretary General in 1933. Berthelot had been on a study-mission in the Far East from 1902 to 1904 and was appointed Assistant Director for Asiatic Affairs in 1907. He therefore had an abiding interest in Far Eastern affairs.

The following is a translation of a note printed in OC (p. 1238) in connection with the present letter: "It has been impossible to find any trace of this political correspondence. The personal correspondence likewise seems not to have been preserved after Philippe Berthelot's death. In his *Journal d'un attaché d'ambassade, 1916-1917*, Paul Morand quotes the following brief extract from a letter [from AL] that Berthelot had shown him: '. . . Peking is a city that is becoming more and more Belgian—couples that do not copulate, adventurers who shun adventure, and society folk who still believe there is such a thing as high society. A delightful immorality reigns here, and nothing comes of it; whereas everywhere else, especially in Europe, it is so amusing to see people struggling desperately against their fundamental moralness in order to live a little, in spite of everything. It's even more amusing to see people here, with all their basic lack of morality, make nothing of it.'"

2. Henry J.-M. Levet (1874-1906), a forerunner of the "globe-trotter" poets of a later generation, had been a friend of Berthelot, who liked to quote Levet's poem, "Outwards," which contains the verses:

L'*Armand Béhic* (des Messageries Maritimes)
File quatorze noeuds sur l'Océan Indien.

. . .

Miss Roseway, hélas, n'a cure de mon spleen,
Sa lorgnette sur les Laquedives au loin. . . .
   "Sonnets torrides" in *Cartes postales*

[The *Armand Béhic* of the Maritime Transport Lines
does fourteen knots through the Indian Ocean.

. . .

Miss Roseway, alas, pays no heed to my spleen;
her spyglass is focussed on the Laccadive Isles
   in the distance. . . .]

3. The opening text of Paul Claudel's album of Far Eastern sketches, *Connaissance de l'Est* (1900) is "Le Cocotier" ("The Coconut Palm"), which describes a stopover in Ceylon and a visit to the already "touristic" Mount Lavinia.

4. Anna Ballard was a well-known "madam" in Shanghai during the pre-World War I years.

5. Zi Ka Wei, some six miles from Shanghai, had long been an important center of the Society of Jesus. The meteorological and magnetic station (Zo-Se Observatory) was established there by the Jesuits in 1872 and was destined to become one of the most important meteorological centers of the whole China coast.

6. Pierre-Remi Bons d'Anty (1859-1917), French diplomat and explorer who spent most of his professional life in consular posts in China and Korea. Author of several travel-books and geographical reports, he died very shortly after AL's visit.

7. Paul-Emile Naggiar (b. 1883), French Consul in Shanghai at the time.

8. Count Damien de Martel (1878-1940), career diplomat who had been appointed Second Secretary of the French Legation in Peking in Sept. 1916.

9. The Franco-Chinese crisis referred to is the "Tientsin incident" of 1916. A Chinese mob invaded the French concession in Tientsin and stormed the offices of the French diplomatic

mission. AL was sent to China for the express purpose of giving temporary assistance to a chargé d'affaires whose work had been immensely increased and complicated by the troubles in Tientsin. On arriving in Peking, AL was appointed Third Secretary of the French Embassy; later, he was promoted to the rank of Second Secretary. (See his letter to his mother of 10 Jan. 1917 [154], and letter to Jules Damour of 28 Nov. 1917. [153])

10. Wai Chiao Pu: The Chinese Ministry of Foreign Affairs.

11. Wu Ting-fang (b. 1842), who was appointed Minister of Foreign Affairs immediately after the death of Yüan Shih-kai (see note 13, below). Wu Ting-fang was to be replaced by Lu Cheng-hsiang late in 1917. See letter 169, note 1.

12. Probably Li Yu-Ying (b. 1882), who later became an advisor to Chiang Kai-Shek. T'saï Yüan-pei (1867-1940), Minister of Education in the first Republican Cabinet and subsequently Chancellor of the National University of Peking.

13. Yüan Shih-kai (1859-1916), the famous military chief who became the first Provisional President of the Republic of China and then regular President. He was a virtual dictator from the time of the fall of the Manchu dynasty in 1911 until 1916, when he died under mysterious circumstances shortly before the arrival of AL. See AL's letter to his mother of 4 Apr. 1917. (158)

14. Georges Clemenceau (1841-1929), the "Tiger of France," and Raymond Poincaré (1860-1934).

LETTERS TO ALEXANDRE CONTY

148

To His Excellency,
Monsieur Alexandre Conty[1]
Minister of France in Peking
Personal and confidential.

"Temple of Tao-Yu,"
near Peking
July 13, 1917

Monsieur le Ministre,

I am really worn out and need the two-day leave that you promised me, after all the "Late Empire" events we have just lived through and after all of the petty back-stage Chinese intrigue in which, like an old-time Venetian diplomat, I had to become involved on your behalf.

Our diplomatic pouch doesn't leave for five days yet, and I shall be back in two days. Rest assured that you will have the official report and the account of mission that you are expecting from me, in time to send to Paris. Meanwhile, for you alone, *off the record,*[2] as a purely personal and confidential gesture, here is an informal account of the facts, which will tell you more than any official version about the accomplishment of the singular assignment that was mine of going to rescue a presidential family in the midst of a full-scale restoration of the Empire.

Moreover, the mission as such is of very little interest to the Quai.[3] And in addition, for everything pertaining to the political crisis and to urgent telegraphic communications or coded messages, you already have the official notes for public distribution and the wording of the telegrams, all of which I left in a large envelope for you at the Secretariat of the Legation.

Be assured that I am always your respectful and devoted   Alexis Leger

A RESPECTFUL RELATION[4]

ADDRESSED BY THE SECRETARY LEI HI-NGAI TO HIS
EXCELLENCY, MINISTER KANG-TE,[5] CONCERNING
THE SECRETARY'S MISSION OF COMING TO
THE AID OF THE FAMILY OF PRESIDENT
LI, AND THE CIRCUMSTANCES AC-
COMPANYING THE EXODUS OF
SAID FAMILY TOWARDS
A PLACE OF
REFUGE

I have the honor to report to you the mission, which you so graciously entrusted to me during the disorders that followed upon the heels of the restoration of the Empire, of assisting Mr. Po Leang-ts'ai,[6] First Interpreter of the Legation, in the measures taken to facilitate the flight of the presidential family to the Diplomatic Quarter.

To tell the truth, the mission was accomplished with such ease that, if I did not report every detail, however negligible, there might well be no report at all.

On the fifth of this month—which was also the fifth day of the Restoration of the Empire, and the Year Nine of the reign of Hsüan T'ung[7]—Marshal Tuan Chi-jui[8] and General Chang Hsun,[9] having sized up each other's supposedly inferior strength, no longer entertained any doubt that they would have to come to blows, and they began to observe each other with utmost caution, as Messieurs de Turenne and Montecuccoli[10] once did. Panic immediately spread through Peking, and the people of quality vied with each other in betaking themselves to every gate of the city that was not in the hands of the men of war. Those who were not able to follow this exodus suddenly recalled the inviolability of the Diplomatic Quarter. President Li Yuan-Hung,[11] who had already taken refuge in the Japanese Legation three days before, appealed for French protection and hospitality for his wife and children, who had been left behind in a private residence in the middle of the Tartar City. In his haste to choose between the honor of suicide and the advantages of flight, the President had paid little heed to the fate of a family that, up to that time, he seems to have held dear to his heart, at least so far as its illegitimate members were concerned.

As a matter of fact, the requested protection was not so easy to provide as it appeared to be. Was not General Chang Hsun already exercising his protection, in the most imperious manner imaginable, assuring the Japanese Minister that he would assume personal responsibility for the safety of said presidential family, his last hostages? Had he not deployed on every side a show of troops and policemen which, though they looked every bit like a gang of jailors, nevertheless constituted a guard, and a very imposing guard at that? Any attempt at escape planned without his knowledge was destined to failure; in addition, such action would only have resulted in turning the general against his protégés by revealing to him the doubts they entertained about his given word.

The first thing that had to be done, thus, was to obtain General Chang Hsun's consent, at least in principle. Baron Hayashi,[12] whom I saw upon your request, Monsieur le Minstre, was quite willing to use his good offices on my behalf in this matter and, without waiting to see what the results of the baron's intervention would be, but counting rather on the magnanimity that the writers of history customarily attribute to great captains, we proceeded forthwith, Mr. Po Leang-ts'ai and I, to the execution of our plan.

The police troops responsible for guarding the presidential abode were drawn for the most part from the forces of the Prefect of the Peking Police, General Wu Ping-Hsiang, a general who was ostensibly neutral but who had secretly participated in the preparation of the *coup d'état*. Forcing our way past the sentries of that part of the city, we went straight to General Wu Ping-Hsiang in order to wrest from him the orders that would allow us complete freedom of action among his men. This led to a discussion—learned, unyielding, courteous —in which the use of prevarication alternated with that of honesty. The skillfulness exhibited by Mr. Po Leang-ts'ai was great, the heat was extreme, and the crickets excessive; the general capitulated. We were authorized to take along with us in our automobile, on agreeing to assume full responsibility, the legitimate portion of the presidential family represented by Mrs. Li, her two daughters and her son but lately born; as for the illegitimate portions, we did not pursue our disputations on that score—not that any prudish Western reticence held us back at this point, but the number of the president's concubines was not known to us; the number of seats in our car was, however.

As we approached the presidential abode we had great difficulty in having our claims recognized as valid. In spite of the assurances given by General Wu Ping-Hsiang, the affair was not advanced without considerable discussion. After a painstaking verification of the identity of each of our persons, the officers of the Prefecture of Police hinted, in what they said, that they were not the sole party responsible for the guarding of the residence, but that, if all had to be told, they were operating quite passively under the tight and despotic surveillance of Chang Hsun's henchmen. And indeed it was doubtless quite necessary for the guards to guard each other, for we were able to distinguish in the nearby narrow streets, mingling with and neutralizing each other, men from every imaginable organization and background.

So, all along the line we renewed our parleying; and while a battery of couriers, emissaries, spies, and counter-spies were dispatched in every direction to check on the veracity of what we said, we were led by an escort into a guardhouse where Mr. Po Leang-ts'ai continued his most skillful fencing, while tea was graciously offered to me by the hands, rather disquieting, of syphilitics, sufferers from eczema, and consumptives. These men had good manners and, in spite of their rags, showed themselves to be of high rank. They kept us company in a most amiable way and were, upon my faith, of most agreeable converse until the couriers, emissaries, spies, and counter-spies returned.

When the officers and policemen designated to guard the president's family finally authorized us to take charge of their prisoners, it was Mrs. Li's turn to let us know how great was her mistrust of us. Fearing a trap, she would not consent to receive us or to go with us until she had exchanged missives with President Li. An old retainer, a faithful servant who, thanks to his mask of stupidity, Mr. Po Leang-ts'ai recognized immediately as a man from Hopeh—that is, from President Li's province, was dispatched forthwith to the president and was not long in returning from the Japanese Legation. The seals were finally broken and the doors thrown open, and courtyards piled high with miscellaneous furniture eventually led us to a Hall of Honor.

In a setting consisting of a Nile-green spittoon of the sort given away at carnival-lotteries, a more than life-sized portrait of President Li, and an autographed photo of Kaiser Wilhelm surrounded by his marshals—and in the company of a harmless old man held in leash by a bird and a young man of good family whose job it was to keep in motion a fan of such dimensions as we had never seen anywhere in the world—we waited. The furniture was upholstered in rep and the clock came from Bavaria. A man came up and stood beside us, dressed like one of the lowly but betraying by his gold tooth that he was the neighborhood police commissioner. We waited. . . . The Bavarian clock was slow. Certainly this waiting-room had about it the respectable and unassuming air associated with a provincial house of ill-fame. It was quite clear that all the really precious objects had already been removed. Except for a *sang de boeuf* vase, there was nothing in all the miscellaneous bric-a-brac that might catch the eye, inflamed with covetousness, of the police commissioner.

Meanwhile officers bearing the most extraordinary arms came and went through the rooms, numerous servants busied themselves, and fowl fluttered about in a frightened way. Suddenly, as the Bavarian clock struck an unreasonable hour, the full-length portrait of President Li, bigger than life, was manipulated from the other side and unexpectedly came swinging toward us like a shutter, and in the unobstructed framework of a huge glass window flooded with light, under the Haitian splendor of a history-making afternoon, a courtyard was revealed, through which, hierarchic and scared, a silent procession, whose order was dictated by invisible protocol, advanced. At the head, clinging with one hand to the arm of a lady of high birth and with the other leaning on a small European cane of black wood, was a goat-footed creature dressed in bronze-green whom we recognized, from having presented our respects to her in less troublous times, as Madame President Li. Next came her daughters, in light-colored tunics, followed by concubines in plum-colored silk, followed in turn by a number of female and male servants of every rank, house and stable boys, old retainers and laborers, chambermaids and stewards, roast-cooks and confectioners, healers, policemen and porters—yesterday privileged ones, and tomorrow beggars, in this land of China where the everyday business of living is more complicated than in any other land. Dominating the crowd, half naked and carried at arm's length by a giant wearing a beige-colored bowler hat, was a dirty child wearing silver bracelets, the last-born of the President's sons. In the background was the chorus of supernumeraries; and, amid the clamor of crickets, jackdaws, guinea-fowl, and magpies, the cawing of crows, the barking of thorough-bred dogs, the murmur of a treeful of neighbors, and the irregular sobbing of a numerous clientele, there was suddenly heard the unexpected rumble of two purple automobiles that no one had ever mentioned and that were being driven out of the court garages without warning. . . . Before we were able to take charge of the operation, and because of the general turmoil and hubbub, the two supplementary cars, stormed by the concubines and any number of persons whose names we shall never know, took off with a flourish at the head of the procession, while Mr. Po Leang-ts'ai and I, arms flailing, brushing off the clusters of humanity that clung to our car, had very great difficulty in keeping close to those who were our specific responsibility—namely, Mrs. Li, her two daughters, and her son.

The number of persons who were thus given a chance to fly the coop remains blessedly unknown to us. A rough estimate can be made by the capacity of three limousines filled to overflowing in a way that only Chinese spurred on by fear can achieve—meaning about three times the normal capacity of such a car in Europe, given the same circumstances and the same prevailing emotions.

It did not appear to us that the troops on guard

realized exactly what was going on so rapidly before their eyes. Being in doubt, they were careful not to neglect the usual amenities; so military honors were paid to us for a stretch of more than three hundred meters, just in case—though we were not sure for whom they were intended—the ex-president's family, the officers who rode off, clinging to the sides of our car, or your collaborators, Monsieur le Ministre.

The trip was made without incident. No firearms were put to use against us. Nor were we the target of unseemly gibes, threats, or garbage of any sort. Nor were we forced to suffer anything more humiliating than the total indifference of the public, and at no time did we have the feeling that our lives were exposed to any danger beyond that occasioned by the panic of our native chauffeur. The city, fortunately, did not present its usual aspect—that is, we did not have to jostle camels or rickshaws, funeral or bridal processions. Silent and most tactful, the troops we encountered at street-intersections might have been stationed there in our honor. The presidential family, had they had a bit more wit, might have claimed a certain advantage from this circumstance. They did nothing of the sort. Mrs. Li's daughters said not a word, concentrating instead on showing by their demeanor the equanimity of spirit that befits the mighty of this world who have suffered misfortune. The First Lady herself, hiding her face from the crowd behind a fan, and in the measure that two green cloth patches pressed against her temples because of a splitting headache permitted, fixed her gaze steadfastly on the nonexistent threat of death. Only the dirty child with silver bracelets, with that unconcern which the anecdotists of every clime and time attribute to the heir apparent in the midst of flight, seemed to be enjoying the adventure.

Driving through the diplomatic quarter was much less

to our taste. The number of queer persons of every aspect and class—military, civilian, servants and retainers—who clung to every protuberance of our car, left no room for doubt about the nature of this kidnapping expedition, which, perforce, could not have resembled anything less than it did an *affaire galante*.

Shortly before seven o'clock we arrived at the entrance to the French Legation where we had the satisfaction of delivering safe and sound: Madame President Li, the Misses Li, and the dirty child with the silver bracelets.

We found out later that the President's concubines, borne without incident in their purple cars, found refuge in the diplomatic quarter, at the Hôtel des Wagons-Lits, where President Li lost no time in paying them a discreet visit.

Thinking back today over this brief foray, I find it still impossible to say, Monsieur le Ministre, which is more worthy of praise in the conduct of its principal participants: the dignity of those who had nothing to stifle but their fear, or the correctness of those who had to stifle their laughter?

1. Alexandre-Robert Conty (1864-1943), French Ambassador to China from 1912 to 1917.

2. English in original.

3. The Quai d'Orsay, where the French Ministry of Foreign Affairs is situated.

4. This purely personal account, written in a style that parodies diplomatic "officialese," was intended exclusively for the perusal of Ambassador Conty. Twenty years after it was written, one of AL's successors, the diplomat Henri Hoppenot, ran across the document in the Legation files in Peking and had it printed by the Lazarist press there in a very limited edition (ten copies only). At that date, 1937, Hoppenot was Secretary of the Embassy in Peking. He was an old friend of AL and, much later, became a French delegate to the United Nations. (See letter to Mina Curtiss of June 1955. [339])

5. French transliterations of the Chinese equivalents of Leger ("Lei Hi-Ngai") and Conty ("Kang-te").

6. French transliteration of the Chinese equivalent of the name Beauvais ("Po Leang-ts'ai"). Maurice Beauvais was the chief interpreter of the French Legation at the time.

7. Pu-Yi, the Hsüan T'ung emperor (1906-1967), was the last of the Manchu dynasty. He was the nephew of emperor Kuang-Siu and succeeded to the imperial throne at the age of two, under a regency. In 1912, his abdication was forced by Yüan Shih-kai. Then, in 1917, the warlord Chang Hsun sought to restore the eleven-year-old boy to the throne, thus reviving the Manchu dynasty. The attempt was short-lived. See following note.

In 1932 Pu-Yi was declared regent of Manchukuo by the Japanese, and then emperor in 1934. His reign ended in 1945, when Japan surrendered to the Allies. He died in Japan in 1967.

8. Tuan Chi-jui (1865-1936), warlord appointed Premier of the Republic of China in 1916 and then removed by President Li Yüan-hung in May 1917, only to regain power in August of the same year, after the abortive attempt of his rival, General Chang Hsun, at restoring the boy-emperor to the throne. (See preceding note.) Tuan resigned his premiership in Oct. 1918.

9. Chang Hsun (1854-1923), an old-line military man summoned by President Li Yüan-hung in June 1917, when Chang attempted the coup of restoring the Manchu dynasty. That abortive coup forced Chang Hsun to take refuge in the Dutch Legation in Peking 12 July 1917. See AL's letter to his mother of 2 Aug. 1917. (162)

10. Turenne (1611-1675) and Montecuccoli (1609-1680) were rival generals during the reign of Louis XIV. In 1673 the imperial armies under the command of the Italian marshal Montecuccoli, forced back the French army in the Saar under the command of Turenne.

11. Li Yüan-hung (1864-1928), "President Li," was president of the Republic of China from June 1916 until July 1917. See above, note 8.

12. Baron Gonsuke Hayashi (1861-1943), Japanese ambassador to China in 1917.

149

To His Excellency,   *"Temple of Tao-Yu,"*
Monsieur Alexandre Conty   *near Peking*
Minister of France in Peking   *September 27, 1917*

My dear Minister,

I'll be at my desk three days from now; you can count on it.

The letter that you had delivered to me here was indeed from Philippe Berthelot. It confirms my being kept on in Peking, just as I had wished, and does not seem to express any obvious resentment over what at first seemed to him a sort of desertion on my part. As you know, there's nothing I wanted more than this extension of my stay in China, from the moment you became my chief. And there is no risk, as Berthelot knows, of my becoming "Asianized" while working closely with you.

What else is there to tell, of a more personal nature? The indulgence and discreet sympathy you have always shown in regard to what you have imagined going on in the byways of my private life would, today, be pointless. I am really alone here in my little Taoist hermitage, and my nights are more chaste than you seem to believe. My only nocturnal dialogues are with the wild geese that are now flying very low over these mountains of North China.

Such diversions do not make me forget the pleasant evenings devoted to your play-readings that we spent together at the Legation. (We'll take up *Cinna* again when I return.) My present diversions are simply a welcome change from the relentless nightly clamor of the Chinese theaters in the city and the official gossip of Diplomatic Quarter dinners. Here I am in "my" Asia, getting the feel of Chinese "time." And what is "time" in China but a clear violation of that Gregorian calendar from which neither our European Chancelleries nor our Diplomatic Pouch Service will ever be freed?

I am not sending you any note for Paris. One can't really wield an administrative pen here. You'll agree, I'm sure, when you do me the honor of paying me a little weekend visit in my Chinese "sanctuary," which is more ascetic and bare than a lama's skull. You are familiar with the spot and all you can see from here— the westward extension of Asia's first great geological folds stretching towards Outer Mongolia and the marches of Sinkiang. (All this, moreover, rather tantalizing to me.) You would not have committed the slightest indiscretion if you had dropped in on me yesterday, if it is true that, as I was told, you rode through these parts on that friend of mine, your big anthracite-colored horse that I once treated for cataract. Nothing could be more unpretentious, as you could have seen for yourself, nor less well-equipped, than my guest quarters. But we'd have shared many an agreeable moment here.

I beg you to believe, *mon cher Ministre*, in my sentiments of sincere attachment.   Alexis Leger

LETTERS TO PAUL VALÉRY

150

To Monsieur Paul Valéry
40, rue de Villejust
Paris

Peking, French Legation
in China
September 2, 1917

Dear friend,

I'm entrusting this letter for you to the English mails via Canada. It will be forwarded to you from London by the French Embassy, with the instructions that you are to be notified to pick it up at the Diplomatic Pouch Service at the Quai d'Orsay as soon as it arrives there. (At the moment, our letters run much less risk of getting lost that way than in the French mails via Suez.)

I have received *La Jeune Parque*, and I want so much to tell you of the profound admiration it has aroused in me, a joy that penetrates to the very depths of my being. You have developed the main theme much more elaborately than you had led me to expect; but it never really strays from the essentials. What a magnificent return to literature for you, and what a portentous event in the history of French letters!

I still vividly recall the poignant conversation we had on a bench in the Champs-Elysées in the deserted Paris of a mid-July afternoon only a few days before my departure for China.[1] The confidences we were able to exchange then about so many different things, human and intellectual, didn't exactly fit into the usual pattern of the intellectual life of Paris. My thoughts will often revert to all that with the utmost affection, believe me. And I think too of a few words we exchanged at your door, on the stair-landing of the Rue de Villejust.

I would like so much to hear from you: a few lines now and then through the Diplomatic Pouch (to be entrusted to Philippe Berthelot for me). You should now be able to do a lot of things that will help lighten your family responsibilities. May you, in spite of the times, find enough peace of mind to permit you to take up your literary pursuits once again. They mean so much to us.

I don't know what you would think of China, where I now live. I have never heard you say anything about Asia beyond your memories of a book read in childhood—*La Horde d'or* by old Cahun (?).[2] And that was only about Mongolia.

New China would surprise you because of its preoccupation with French philosophical thought of the Eighteenth Century and with the dreary positivism of Auguste Comte as well. But that is all borrowed finery that will be replaced by Karl Marx and Engels before long. The successive guises under which the old Chinese rationalism appears do not at all affect the special and peculiar way the Chinese mind works. You would certainly find its divergence-factors and refraction-indices most interesting. The mental processes of the Old Chinese and their sudden discontinuities in thought always strike us as somewhat "devious"—attractive and stimulating to us by that very fact. Their logic is not ours, and their categories are not based on the same premises as ours. Their mathematics is different, and their computations and arithmetical tables entirely different, as is their musical system or their system of perspective in painting. Their dialectic is utterly illogical and leads them instinctively to avoid all forms of dogmatism. A universal skepticism is the only hard-and-fast principle in their thinking, and contradiction is almost second nature to them. It really seems that, for them, obverse and reverse are the same in all fields of knowledge. At any rate, they are rather good humored and don't bore me.

There is something in the aberrant cast of mind of the Chinese that goes beyond its lack of discipline and its inconsistency, and it sometimes delights me: a natural receptivity to all promptings of the subconscious, a receptivity that turns these natural-born rationalists into first-line practitioners of a sort of super-rationalism. Even a taste for the absurd seems to them a legitimate mental stimulus. The ever-present "Why not?" seems to be the last word of these "possibilists." For them, even science, which is held in high esteem, forms a kind of fugue and counterpoint with the wildest fancies; geodesy, for example, very quickly becomes geomancy.

Above all else, the handling of money is their chief concern. With no care for spirituality, and being indifferent to all metaphysics, this eminently sociable people is undoubtedly the only one in the world that never seems to have felt the need for religion—with the result that it is the most superstitious of all peoples.

As for what poetry is to the Chinese, we might as well not talk about it. Our old quarrels about the poetic principle would here be out of place. Chinese concepts of poetry, which are always subordinated to the requirements of the most academic kind of conformity, never touch upon the true source of the mystery of poetry.

What might here surprise you the most, you, the lover of beautiful marble columns, is the Chinese contempt for raw materials, even when used in the most imperious and permanent of great historical edifices. The theme or idea becomes the great enduring abstraction to be perpetuated through the ages by constant refurbishment and restoration. So there remains only the framework, forever repeated, like a huge Chinese ideogram—established once and for all and fixed in the mind to withstand the vicissitudes of time. The rest is simply fill-in, always perishable and replaceable—in a word, an accessory like clay or sand under repeatedly fresh coatings of painted mortar. Perhaps the whole thing may be explained quite simply by the scarcity of fine stone in China, or by the early influence of the building concepts of the great nomads (stylizations of the tent). In any case, mere building material is here magnificently scorned, to the advantage of the idea. What is to endure is always invested in the pattern.

I sometimes wonder what sort of gift I could send you from China. The only things I can think of are those magnificent armillary spheres, and other astronomical instruments, carved out of bronze for a seventeenth-century Chinese emperor. At present they are still in Potsdam, but they are to be restored to China by Germany after the signing of a peace treaty.

Meanwhile, dear friend, what I can offer you whole-heartedly, along with my wishes for your whole family, is the affectionate and live concern of your faithful

Saint-Leger Leger

1. Paul Valéry's famous poem, *La Jeune Parque*, was published at the end of Apr. 1917. AL had advance knowledge of Valéry's intentions in composing the poem. In OC ("Biographie," p. xvii) we are told, "Shortly before his [AL's] departure from Paris, he had a long conversation with Valéry, who confided to him the purely human reasons (he was again to become a father) that were forcing him to take up his pen once more and to make a place for himself in French letters. (On that occasion, he supplied [AL] with details about the way *La Jeune Parque* was shaping up.)"

2. The question mark is AL's, and the doubt it expresses was apparently well founded, since no book by Léon Cahun (1841-1900) bears the title *La Horde d'Or,* though the Golden Horde figures in a number of Cahun's historical novels—*La Bannière bleue* (1877), among others.

151

To Monsieur Paul Valéry[1]   *Paris, November 26, 1922*
[Paris]

Dear friend,

Only last night I read your "Note and Digressions" on the Introduction to Leonardo da Vinci's Method.[2] Let me express to you my profound admiration for the uncompromising way you have pursued your spiritual quest to the very limits of strict intellectual consistency.

In literature, I know of no purer, more noble testimonial to the human spirit.

And I think of the incomparable chasteness of the language (so much fidelity and so much "modesty"—in the Latin sense of the word).

I wish it were possible to present the most beautiful artifact I have ever seen in this world to you as a gift: the crystal skull, reduced to almond-shape, that has reigned for ever so long now in London (British Museum, Aztec Room). That would mean treating you, at least, to the grammatical delight of reading, in the English newspapers, "French Poet *presented with* crystal marvel."[3]

Most sincerely yours,   A. Saint-Leger Leger

1. Letter printed on p. 463 of OC and not included in "Lettres" section.
2. AL had finally received the 1919 edition of Valéry's *Introduction à la Méthode de Léonard de Vinci*, which included a prefatory "Note et digressions," (pp. 8-41), written in 1919, along with the original 1894 essay (pp. 45-100).
3. English in original.

LETTER TO DOCTOR BUSSIÈRE

152

To Monsieur le Docteur Bussière[1]
Medical Attaché to the
French Legation
Diplomatic Quarter, Peking

"Temple of Tao-Yu,"
September 22, 1917

Dear friend,

This message is for you alone—an unabashed appeal to your friendship.

I need your help in defending my retreat here for a few days more against all comers, male and female. You alone have my address and could always reach me here if there were need to alert me about anything or anyone whatsoever. My trusty François[2] will stand by to assure communications with you. There's no point in forwarding any mail to me here.

Once upon a time on the high plateaus of Iran, you too enjoyed moments of withdrawal and real solitude, before the hour when the great nocturnal caravans arrive and the "cool stars" suddenly appear; so you will have no trouble understanding what I have come to seek here: a break with the endless stream of nightly distractions that engulfs Peking—the Chinese city and the diplomatic quarter—that incessant stream of noise that goes on until dawn, punctuated by the insomniac and frenetic chirp of the cricket like the Chinese theater's one-tone, one-stringed fiddle rising above the stone-drum bass.

Out here the nights are immense and empty, and the deafening frenzy is that of the compelling pervasiveness of absence and void that allow one to dream until dawn. Here I become a waking sleeper with eyes devoid of lids or lashes. And all around me there is that strange persi-flage of the void in which the Chinese soul makes light of its not really being a soul, and the Tao itself devours its own tail.

By day it is a great nameless country devoid of men and cattle. At my feet, the only human touch is a shallow valley with a sandy river, and rising from it I hear only the sound of small stone-drums, calling to the ferryman at the ford or engaging a dialogue from one bank to the other between invisible rural communities. Beyond are the terraced uplands, the first great open western spaces, stretching towards Mongolia and Sinkiang, where the earliest caravan-routes have their vague beginnings. Still farther on, at last, absence, the unreal, and the earthly horizon that only a timeless contemplation may obscure. And over all this, the unchanging time of the Asian high-lands; and far off the vanishing traces of the old nomadic empire and its marches where the roads have no markers. The Asia of Buddhism, lamas, tantric rites, striding off far from Confucian platitudes.

Some day I shall set out in that direction myself—I am sure of it—and perhaps with you, who love all this as I do, boundlessly.

Affectionately yours.   Alexis Leger

1. Dr. Bussière, medical officer in the French Colonial Troops, had been sent on special assignment to serve as Medical Attaché to the French Legation in Peking and also as chief director of the French Hospital in the diplomatic quarter. He and AL became close friends and were eventually to go on a trek through the Gobi Desert in company with Gustave-Charles Toussaint. See AL's letters to his mother of 21 Apr. 1920 (175), 5 June 1920 (177), and letter to Toussaint of 29 Mar. 1921. (185)

2. AL's chief "boy." See letter to his mother of 15 Sept. 1918. (168)

LETTER TO JULES DAMOUR

153

To Monsieur Jules Damour[1]　　　*French Legation in China*
16, rue de Lisbonne　　　　　　*Peking, November 28, 1917*
Paris

My dear Uncle,

Already a whole year has gone by in this very ancient land.

My thoughts turn affectionately toward you—you who helped me once to face up to my most pressing obligations.

I was sent out from Paris in an emergency and under rather exceptional circumstances to fulfill certain functions in Peking usually performed by officers of higher rank. My immediate responsibility was to assist a chargé d'affaires overtaken by events, working with a totally inadequate legation staff, and confronted with a rather serious outbreak of Chinese hysteria (the so-called Tientsin incident, involving riots and demonstrations in the French Concession). It really wasn't such a bad way to approach my first assignment—completely ignorant as I was of the milieu, and looking at everything for the first time with an entirely new eye. The challenge, met with no time for preparation, has been a fascinating one. My superior, who has been unduly criticized, lacked neither judgment nor skill, but the way Paris viewed things was rather unfortunate. The trouble is that the psychological and physiological approach of our superiors in Europe never corresponds at all to the Chinese approach; conceptions of time, on both sides, are not at all alike. And by trying to force things by a too-obvious show of authority, we only aggravate and prolong the inflammation in China. I knew instinctively that nothing must ever be dealt with here in the heat of the moment, but only when things have cooled off—which means, after a certain lapse of time and without losing patience. I feel that the crisis would have been briefer and easier to settle had we been able, from the outset, to take control of the situation with more flexibility and less ostentation.

I don't know how my modest role in all this has been judged at the higher echelons, but I do know that my position here has been made much more secure on orders from Paris, and with the complete approval of my Chief of Mission. I accept this permanent arrangement most willingly, as I am fascinated by the new China and all that I forsee in its future evolution. And I infinitely prefer this active life in China to a life in the offices of the Quai d'Orsay or in the big European embassies.

The legation is still seriously lacking in personnel. My official assignment is that of interim Second Secretary, but in reality I've had to do the work of a First Secretary and, for several months, even of Chief Counsellor upon occasion.

Naturally, I would be entirely happy in these conditions, were it not for the fact that my responsibilities are greatly increased without any corresponding increase in salary for my interim functions. And even that salary, already seriously reduced by all sorts of deductions, is here reduced still further in the most intolerable way by the state, which obliges us to put up with an almost sixty percent reduction in the local rate of exchange of francs into "Mexican dollars."[2] Confronted as we are by our foreign colleagues who are so generously reimbursed for losses in currency exchanges and even for rises in the local cost of living, and especially in the face of German and Austrian diplomats whose salaries in China are considered operational expenses, no one will ever know what ingenious lengths we've sometimes had to go to in order to maintain our standing respectably. Those of us who, like me, have no personal means, have had to accept the most onerous arrangements with local banks. And you know, dear Uncle, that I simply can not bring myself to live with the least indebtedness, no matter how favorable the conditions!

Will I some day have to abandon this career? I really don't know.

I often think of those distant days—distant because pre-war!—when I was all alone in Paris and started on my own personal study-plan, against the advice of my guardian, in preparation for the big Foreign Service examination—days when I would sometimes stay with you in the rue de Lisbonne. The dear face of Aunt Clélie still smiles down on me with all its French grace and Antillean charm. At that time Paris struck me as a conundrum that I had to work out, but the harshness of the battle was at least softened a little by the glow of a family hearth. I recall the chats with you before the wood fire in the library, and the confidence and smiling welcome I found there.

From now on my life will be that of the wanderer, the absent one. At least here, for the moment, my job is wholly French, and its broad outlines are dictated by a policy of sufficient scope to captivate the imagination.

I have far less leisure than I expected. But I still manage to make direct contact with much of the real China. I see many more Chinese than is considered advisable here, especially by our English friends. (You know their long-standing prejudice: "*Don't associate with natives!*")[3] The foreign diplomats prefer to live among themselves within the confines of the diplomatic quarter, with the same old petty concerns they have everywhere else.

The Chinese politicians, with whom I play Chinese chess in the evenings, are of great good humor, and as they are not stand-offish with me and do not mistrust me, they quite incidentally reveal many more things to me about what I am really after, here in China, than I learn from the legation interpreters. At any rate, they never bore me and always let me glimpse, without their realizing it, something of the old, underlying human substratum that, no matter what we say, is infinitely variable. Their logic is not ours.

[. . .] But there is in the Chinese mind something more than its inconsistencies, something that often delights me.

Didn't you tell me that your father, my "great-grand-uncle," loved to upset his old colleagues at the Institute by reminding them most politely that nature itself can be "aberrant," even in the realm of crystallography? (Thanks to you, I possess a singular colorless ruby that came from his collection of "*freak*" gems that he delighted in offering to the young ladies in the family.) [. . .] Thinking further about your father, who was a great geologist and mineralogist, and also, I believe, something of a vulcanologist, I keep wondering what he would think of the soil I ride over daily on horseback in and around Peking—a soil made up entirely of loess without any igneous rock or the slightest volcanic trace, even though it occasionally indulges in the unexpected luxury of a few very mild earthquake-shocks. Because I lack the necessary scientific knowledge, my chances of finding scaly "damourite"[4] here—the aluminum silicate that your father identified when he found it mixed in with the beautiful "Muscovite" micas—are slim, but there will be plenty of other occasions that will make me think of that Alexis Damour who abandoned diplomacy for scientific research in mineralogy.

Of course, I see a lot of the personalities of the diplomatic world here, since, in addition to my functions at the legation, I also perform those of "Secretary of the Conference of Allies" and "Secretary of the Diplomatic Corps." I don't find that coming to know all the Chiefs of Mission on an intimate personal basis makes me like them any better. Too much mental inertia, too much snobbish preoccupation with the old Imperial China of the curio-merchants [. . .]. The old missionaries from the interior, who come through here all too seldom, could surely tell me a great deal more about what is really stirring in the basic mentality of today's Chinese.

But what does all this mean to us on the scale of history as it is presently being made in Europe? Aren't we living in the moon out here? For us, the greatest crises of the West never take up more than a few lines in a news-sheet from the Reuters Agency. And it takes two months or more for newspapers to reach us, if they reach us at all.

My very dear Uncle, this is a long letter, and yet I now live in the part of the world where silence is the rule, where, seemingly, one's only right is the right to keep silent. All I ask, quite simply, is that you may always feel in your heart the enduring affection I have for you. After all, haven't you been intimately associated— and for so long a time—with those of my family who are dearest to me—my mother and my three sisters? It is a source of joy for me to know that your presence and good counsel are always with them. All four love you deeply.

Season's greetings?. . . It's time for them; but when will they reach you from here?

I embrace you warmly, my dear Uncle.

Alexis St.-L. Leger

1. Jules Damour (1836-1925) was AL's great-uncle on his mother's side. He was a mining engineer and industrialist, son of an eminent mineralogist, Alexis Damour (1808-1902). The latter's analyses of rare and "freak" minerals had fascinated AL during his university days in Bordeaux, when he had studied geology.

2. The American clipper ships of the nineteenth century "with their furs and ginseng [. . .] crossed the Pacific to China, taking with them also silver dollars which they had acquired in Mexico on the way up the Pacific Coast [. . .] and this practice incidentally accounts for the fact that the silver dollar in China came to be known as the 'Mexican dollar.'" Owen and Eleanor Lattimore *China: A Short History* (1944), pp. 113, 114.

3. English in original.

4. Damourite: hydromica, a variety of muscovite with a rather pearly luster. See above, note 1.

LETTERS TO
MADAME AMÉDÉE SAINT-LEGER LEGER
(1917-1921)

154

To Madame Amédée Saint-Leger Leger
Paris

*French Legation
in China, Peking,
January 10, 1917*

Dearest Mother, what vast spaces separate us, and how hard it is for me to forget that fact!

The old *Polynésien* of the Messageries Maritimes, sailing at eleven knots per hour in order to economize on coal, took me to China ever so slowly. Each day it seemed to measure off, with its old-fashioned masts and its cruciform yards, as if with outstretched arms, a little of the distance that had increased during the night and that, in the waking hours, added to the space separating us from each other—so much space between us becoming "time" that somehow had to be spent!

God knows that this need for space, which everyone has teased me about since childhood, this space that I have always coveted as the greatest luxury, is still my first requirement for any sort of life. But I didn't want space to come between us; and so, for the moment, the whole thing turns against me. When I was a child playing on some wide sunlit savanna or running off on the sly for a sail, space was simply the light-flooded embrace that held everything. Space was my innocence then.

Do you remember the Creole nickname that the black stable-keeper at Bois-Debout[1] bestowed on me? How that name amused my two uncles when they first set me on a horse, and Father too when he taught me to

sail! "Ban-moin-le," "Give-me-air, give-me-room!" . . .
Can you believe that Uncle Aemilio still called me that,
with feeling, when he picked me up at Port Said to take
me to spend the night with him at Port Tewfik while
we waited for the steamer to leave the canal and enter
the Red Sea? (The next day he was to put me on board
my ship in great haste, taking me in the high-speed
motorboat that he had as the company's Chief Engineer.)

I'll never forget that night spent with my uncle on his
verandah facing the canal. I keep going back to all the
things we talked over, all the intimate, moving things. It
was a final link for me between two worlds, between two
ages, at a turning-point in my destiny. And I'll always
hear with the same emotion the short sentence he spoke
almost timidly in the night at the close of our long man-
to-man conversation: "So, don't worry too much about
your mother and your sisters; I'll always be available if
I'm needed."

The present slowness and, even more, the present un-
reliability of communications throughout the northern
hemisphere makes even sharper the impression I have of
the distance between us. This time I'm taking advantage
of a special mailing from the British Legation to get my
letter to you in thirty days or so instead of five or six
weeks.

All this remoteness in time and space seems only to
increase your mysterious gift of telepathic vision between
us. The very day that I had to take to bed here on account of a minor upset (simple food-poisoning), your
motherly telegram astounded the Legation doctor, even
though he has no interest in "metapsychic" phenomena,
to use dear old Professor Richet's[2] language.

The situation here seems to be relaxing. It was actually
never very serious—rest assured of that—except in its
implications for general Sino-French policy, but it never

threatened the personal safety of foreigners. There is no longer any xenophobia in China; but there will be a rekindling of it much later, and it will be the Occidental Powers' own fault. Besides, the events you refer to broke out in Tientsin, not Peking.

The Minister to China who is my superior[3] is still away. He had to give up his regular leave in France and catch a boat back to China, in haste and without his family, to resume his post as Chief of Mission. He may arrive here in a week or so. I don't know him personally and have no idea what my relations with him may turn out to be. My only thought is that I'll have less to do at the Legation, unless the First Counsellor, who is presently the chargé d'affaires, wants to return to France immediately.

It is atrociously cold here: thirty or thirty-one degrees below zero[4] every night, and every night we have to go to a full-dress dinner somewhere. But, my dear Creole mother, don't be alarmed about your son's health; it is excellent and will be better than ever for having endured these Chinese winters. Don't forget the theory I've reminded you about so often, which is taken for granted in genetics and maintains that every living species, whether animal or vegetable, taken outside its native habitat, inevitably reinforces the qualities of its strain by a simple organic defensive reaction against transplanting. And you are fully aware of what our family strain was like, after three centuries of adaptation to the Islands.

Besides, the severity of the cold is made up for by the absolute dryness. The light is dazzling from dawn to dusk. I'm able to go horseback-riding every day—a welcome change from the social life typical of Peking's diplomatic quarter, which even the war hasn't managed to alter in the least.

I love my Mongolian horse "Allan," who has made

friends with me. A strange beast that you would not approve of and that baffles everyone here because he is able to get along so well with me. My stable-boys are still a little afraid of him, and my English friends at the club insist that at the mounting-block he should have a sack pulled over his head. But he comes to me with childlike eyes, and his young-brute roughness turns into a strange gentleness as soon as I can get near enough to whisper into his ear the name "Allan," which you used to call me when I was a child.

About the country itself, what can I tell you that might interest you?

I'll go into all that at greater length in another letter. What I most want is to hear more from you.

Give my sisters a warm hug for me and remember that I'm your grown-up son, clasped to your heart.

A.

P.S. Under the heading "Requests"—

Send me through the mails a batch of large pocket notebooks, and through the diplomatic pouch the last book Joseph Conrad inscribed for me, *Some Reminiscences*.[5] (He's the only old friend with whom I'd like to renew contact at the moment.)

1. One of the two main residences of the Leger family in Guadeloupe. See above, letter 73, note 4. The actual dwelling is still in use. It is a spacious, colonial-style wooden house.

2. Charles Richet (1850-1935), an eminent French physiologist, one of whose interests was the physiological aspects of "occult" phenomena. He coined the term "metapsychic."

3. Alexandre Conty. See above, letter 148, note 1.

4. Celsius units.

5. See letter to Conrad of 26 Feb. 1921. (181)

155

Peking, January 27, 1917

Dearest Mother,

[. . .]

Reaching out toward you, as I do, and toward France still at war, I don't feel very much like talking about China in our private correspondence. But I promised you I would.

How can I give you a preliminary bird's-eye view of this country that has momentarily taken hold of your imagination?—a country that you can imagine only through memories of books read long ago—old accounts and old pictures that have been out-of-date for such a long time now.

China—thank God!—is no longer an album to be pored over dreamily, filled with the time-honored plates based on old engravings and intended for young ladies' magazines—red-lacquer cabinets that still clutter Parisian boudoirs, paintings on silk, and colored prints that, even when they appeared on the lids of tea-boxes, used to delight my sisters. (Didn't you yourself, when I was a child in the Islands, love to explore the old family attics with me in search of leftovers from old Chinese collections—scraps of rare cloth and big blue-porcelain India Company plates?) Present-day China has nothing to do with the writings of Hervey de Saint-Denis[1] that so enchanted our great-grandmothers and that still enchant Jammes. For me it is simply, in all its rawness, a vast human fresco straining toward modernity, the living, convulsive history of a very great people worn down by a submissiveness that has gone on too long, a people now at last on the road to complete social, political, and moral transformation, with all the agony and rending of its slow emancipation, with all the mimicry and aping of a Western parliamentary democratic regime to which it can adapt only with the greatest difficulty, and for which nothing in its make-up or history could possibly have prepared it.

No, there is really nothing esthetic or picturesque in all this. But for me it is the most fascinating spectacle possible, this spectacle of the evolution, before my very eyes, of an old human society in full mutation. Wherever there is movement, my interest is aroused.

What shall I tell you about the physical appearance of the country?

Against a backdrop of age-old attrition, China, at first sight, seems nothing but dust. A soil overworked and worn down since time immemorial, which the slightest gust could transform into a "fifth element." (I've always wanted to write a book about dust. Well, I'm getting my fill of it here!) Under a dazzling sky, the whole of north China where I now live leaves the newcomer feeling totally alien. It's hard to say just what gives everything a certain spectral quality, even in broad daylight. And yet a little of the true majesty of Asia still reaches down into the cinder-choked main arteries of the Chinese city. A spectral sight, as I said. And yet, beneath this veil of unreality circulates the most flesh-and-blood, the most loquacious and lively mass of humanity—perhaps also the most adventurous and even the gayest, though it is hard to say just what gives rise to this gaiety. It is life itself, running about in felt boots among all the accumulated ash.

The constant activity of the Chinese is really prodigious, and its object utterly elusive. A feverish community on the march, though it is hard to say toward what. The individual Chinese, vain and grasping, harbors only two passions: money and the achieving of social status.

On the land, cleared and deforested by market-gardeners, I have yet to see anything non-utilitarian. For me, whom you have always chided for not liking flowers, it is in this respect, a sort of land of heart's desire.

All China lives to the sound of its coin, changing hands day and night behind the little grillwork booths of its counters, shops, and banks. Chinese cities are perhaps the only ones in the world that are totally insomniac. The noise of adding machines—abacuses and ball-counters—provides accompaniment to this frenzy. A whole people, from north to south, practices its scales on counting-instruments, and the song of its metal currency is the best expression of its soul.

A very old Chinese chronicle asserts that the emperor, coming back one day in his sacerdotal robes from a ritual performed in the Temple of Heaven, was crossing the very section of town through which I often pass when I come back from my horseback rides. The emperor suddenly ordered the imperial procession to halt so that he could descend from his lofty pontifical seat to pick up a coin he had spied in the dust, from his elevated position. Climbing back with the copper coin in his fingers, he held it up to the crowd for a moment, symbolically. The penny, sacramental copper host of China, the Usurious! I can think of no better illustration of Chinese materialism—which would be so distasteful to you, were you here.

What other image can I pick from all this heathen dust for you? By nature impervious to anything spiritual, the Chinese never experiences any religious welling-up, beyond the incredible jumble of superstitions that assail the dark depths of his subconscious. The incursions of Buddhism don't amount to much here, and Taoism is the exception that proves the rule. There is not even a true paganism, which would still be a form of religion.

The very philosophers of China are really only social educators. How you would dislike the basic existential-ism of these opportunists! Their social sense is so highly developed that they must still surround themselves with the innumerable company of their dead. Crowded to-gether in public, they seem constantly on the verge of sedition, whereas in private life they are the most sub-missive creatures imaginable. A nation of hysterics, which means one has always to avoid dealing with them in the heat of crisis. Nothing appears more conscious of what it wants, and at the same time more somnambu-listic, than a Chinese crowd that is suddenly aroused.

But may I finish this very long letter with something more pleasing for your Christian heart? Here, straight out of ancient, obsolete China, is the last page of a diplomatic ritual worthy of our Second Empire: the ritual of France, the steadfast Protector of Christendom.

The most beautiful French ceremony I have had to attend in full official uniform has been the New Year's Day "Diplomatic Vespers" at the Pei-Thang cathedral in the very heart of the Tartar section of the city. Yellow silks everywhere in the nave. A European bishop (a Lazarist) surrounded by his numerous Chinese clergy decked out in ample Asiatic mantles and extraordinary insect-like coiffures said to be in sixteenth-century style. The choir-movements were executed quite differently from the way they are in the West, and there was a special ceremonial for the crowd of little Chinese choir-boys. A marvelously skillful adaptation of plain-song, which, basically, requires a technique very like that of the Chinese theater. Finally, a Chinese tenor at the or-gan, with singing by the whole crowd massed in the nave and the side aisles. Since France still officially as-sumes the protection of Catholicism in the Far East, on that day the whole Legation, with its complete personnel and all their attachés, goes with great pomp to kneel with the French Minister or chargé d'affaires in a kind of "Field of the Cloth of Gold" set up in the heart of the cathedral. The representative of France, the Protector, is there obliged to submit to a series of incensings and carefully regulated ecclesiastical greetings, while the crowd of the faithful intone as best they can, in Church Latin, a *Domine, Salve Rem Publicam*, whose implications largely escape them. Afterwards, champagne in the sacristy offered by Monsignor Jarlin, a former officer of the Chasseurs d'Afrique, who loves his Chinese quite as much as his Frenchmen, and who has been my friend here for a long time.

All this contrasts very greatly with what goes on at the Legation on the same day: in the morning, a reception for the French colony and the reading of a fulsome patriotic speech—a piece of official eloquence, a set piece that would make all the stuffed shirts in the world weep onto their starched fronts—the work of the First Secretary, naturally—to my own chagrin this year! (If my literary friends in Paris or anywhere else ever get wind of this!) Dress for this occasion is not the uniform, but the frock-coat ("Prince Albert"). . . .

Monsignor Jarlin always talks privately with me about the evolution of present-day China and the cloudy future of the missions. He speaks with indulgence, but not without sadness, of the irreligious nature of the Chinese and confesses to me that what he finds hardest in his Catholic apostolate is the impossibility of effecting a lasting conversion among the Chinese. But at least that circumstance leads them to baptize as soon as possible all the Chinese children to whom they give asylum. He has a fund of personal memories that give me great human insight into the Chinese mentality. When I come back from my early morning horseback ride, I sometimes make a detour to his little Pei-Thang garden for a few moments' informal chat. As he sees me to the gate, he stops me with a smile before some unexpected tombstone, such as the one of an old French nun who was Henry Bordeaux's[2] sister.

[. . .]

1. Hervey de Saint-Denis (1823-1892), French sinologist who translated a number of classical Chinese poems in *Poésies de l'époque des Thang* (1862) and other books.

2. Henry Bordeaux (1870-1963), ultra-conservative Catholic novelist. *Le Pays natal* (1900), *Les Roquevillard* (1906), *Histoire d'une vie* (1946-1963), etc.

156

Peking, February 12, 1917

Dearest Mother,

[. . .]

I still have that "feel" of the distance that separates us and, all around me, of space—so much space turning into something dense, becoming duration. . . . I think about all this in spite of myself as I go riding, all alone, over the great loess plains around Peking that are now depopulated by winter. Perhaps the notion of space eventually gets mixed up with the notion of insularity, which, for one born in the Antilles, embraces every kind of loneliness.

[. . .]

I have no idea how my letters are getting through to you. Our official mail, coming by the northern route, is constantly getting lost, and we'll soon be reduced, if we aren't already, to limiting ourselves to the sea route via Suez. That's the longest route by far (forty days instead of thirty), and even it carries no guarantee against

the unpleasant surprises of submarine warfare. The best
we can do is to write each other as often as possible,
even though only briefly. So, from now on, do number
your letters. (This one is my tenth to you.)

The Minister who is my chief[1] has been here now for
a week. I turned over his quarters to him in the Legation residence but am still obliged to stay on in the
official dwelling while repairs are in progress on the
pavilion reserved for the Second Secretary. The Third
Secretary is housed there for the present and has to be
dislodged—always a delicate matter between colleagues,
and all the more so in this instance because the Third
Secretary is much older than I am.

The Minister returned here without his family, and
I had to agree to share his board, for he is such a sociable man, so overflowing with vitality and so accustomed to family life on a large scale that he can not
get used to being alone. The situation is in no way embarrassing for me, because he makes it amply clear that
he feels indebted to me. He's a nervous man, restless
and irritable, who once upon a time came a cropper at
the Quai d'Orsay in spite of all his qualifications. We
have very little in common, but he's basically a very
decent chap who knows his business and acts with authority, so I really have no trouble getting along with
him. And I like it that he's a strong personality, be it
good or bad. I even find rather amusing and attractive
what his colleagues find intolerable. In short, I'm coming to have a real liking for him. I like his gaiety, which
comes through even in his outbursts of ill humor.

His coming hasn't yet freed me from my interim duties as much as I'd hoped. The Chargé d'Affaires, who
is once again First Secretary, is taking a leave that he
wants to spend with his wife in Indo-China. I had hopes
of going there myself before too long, because, in addi-

tion to my regular work, I took it upon myself to give special attention here to questions relative to Indo-China, and I ought to go and discuss them with the new Governor General, Albert Sarraut.[2] I sometimes feel so bogged down in the day-to-day routine that I am very eager to get back into my traveling clothes.

The first few months that I spent here under the exceptional conditions you know about made it possible for me to gain entrée promptly into the main official circles, from the Presidency of the Republic down to the various Ministries; and that way I've been able to make many personal friends among the top-flight Chinese personalities. Unfortunately, it has meant that my obligations have been greatly increased, and the rate of exchange continues to climb in a disastrous way. For the moment, I have lost almost half of my meager salary. I was already losing a third of it just two months ago.

But I've been able to handle the expense occasioned by a new summer wardrobe bought right here on the spot, and I'm boarding my horse at the Legation stables. My friend Allan, whom I myself ride in the races, had the inspiration of paying me back almost his whole purchase-price by winning a race for me even before I'd entirely paid for him. A good Mongolian horse costs much less here than a good European saddle ordered from Paris or London; but there's always the chance of falling heir to good English saddles from among all the horsemen, English and American officers, polo-players, and diplomats who are constantly being transferred from one post to another.

[. . .]

The long letter you promised will doubtless tell me about Jammes' visit and his bitterness toward me. It's true that I've never written him, any more than I have to Claudel, Gide, Larbaud, Rivière, or any other of my literary friends. I don't want to hear any more about literary goings-on. I did write to Valéry to thank him for sending me his *Jeune Parque*, because there is a whole little human drama behind the publication of the book, of which I had personal knowledge.[3] And besides, for a long time Jammes has been a terrible disappointment to me, as poet, man, and friend. I hardly recognized the man I had known, once circumstances made me lose personal contact with him. But the four of you, mother and sisters, should nurture your affection for him, because he surely deserves it from you. I am particularly touched by the personal correspondence he has kept up with Eliane.

[. . .]

1. Alexandre Conty. See above, letter 148, note 1.
2. Albert Sarraut (1872-1962), the French statesman who was governor-general of French Indochina from 1911-1914 and 1916-1919.
3. See letter to Valéry of 2 Sept. 1917. (150)

157

Peking, March 14, 1917

Dearest Mother,

Please keep on writing me as you do, at length and often, and especially with the same intimacy. And may the news from all of you, at least the part of it over which you have some control, always be as good as my filial and brotherly heart desperately wants it to be.

[. . .]

My regrets at having to write you so hastily once again.

I am all alone with my Minister for the moment, temporarily fulfilling the functions of the First Advisory Secretary, who has taken two months off.

We've just come through a strenuous period of hard work that ended but an hour ago with the breaking off of diplomatic relations between China and Germany. A declaration of war shouldn't be long in coming. We had a terrible time, in the midst of the internal crisis here in China, making the Peking Government understand the advantages that would accrue from its entry into the war on the side of the Allies, once the peace treaty was drawn up, and to make it aware of the possibility, once peace is reestablished, of a general integration of China, as a new world power, into the orbit and political family of the Western Powers. If only we can avoid exposing China to a serious disappointment that would have disastrous consequences for its future development, with the unavoidable risk that China will again become the champion of an Asia in open opposition to the West.[1]

I keep Berthelot abreast of all this, but his personal influence does not seem great enough at this time to be exercised on China's behalf. Everyone's attention is understandably concentrated on Europe; and England, so far as Asia is concerned, controls the game, and as an ally of Japan.

[. . .]

My thoughts are ever with you, dearest Mother. If life for you and my sisters could just become a little less precarious and care-laden, how my life here would be easy to bear in spite of its weight of loneliness! But you don't have to worry at all about me. I am the one, dearest Mother, who has to worry about you, because of all I hear about the rising cost of living in Paris and about the difficulty of even obtaining certain household necessities, not to mention expenses incurred for heating or health-care. Let me know by return mail, please, what might help out in the way of sugar, rice, paste products, and tea that I could send you.

With all my heart.　　　　　　　　　　　　　A.

Under the "Requests" heading: send me still another batch of pocket notebooks, large size.

1. See letter to his mother of 21 Apr. 1920. (175)

158

Peking, April 4, 1917

Dearest Mother,

You ask me for snapshots. Here are a few taken at Pao-Ma-Tchang, the Peking racetrack where I myself rode. I'm the rider, the second in the first group, wearing weird headgear as protection against cold and wind.

I think of you a great deal; you are so much on my mind in the midst of all my work.

My responsibilities at the Legation are still quite heavy; my colleague and senior, Martel, didn't much like becoming First Advisory Secretary again after having served as Chargé d'Affaires for six months, so he's now on a trip to Indo-China, Yünnan, and Siam. I'm the only one here whom the Minister can rely on for drawing up all the first drafts. My functions as Second Secretary have been temporarily assigned to an elderly consul who is being transferred elsewhere. For all the rest of the work there's no one but the corps of interpreters and a few well-meaning assistants, along with the chancellory agents, the military attaché, the Legation doctor, and the Minister's private secretary.

My health continues to be good in this climate, harsh but dry, which suits me perfectly. The Legation doctor,[1] who is a very attentive and affectionate friend, is, besides, the best European doctor in all the legations. He is much sought after in official Chinese circles, where he has often been of great personal service to me. He was called in as a consultant at the bedside of the dying Yüan Shih-kai, and he is almost the only person to know the historically important secret of that very mysterious and suspect death. (His medical report, sealed and confidential, is still locked in the Legation safe.) I keep up my early-morning rides in the outskirts of Peking and am now sufficiently used to, and familiar with, the country to be able to ride out alone on weekends in the wide-open semi-desert spaces northwest of the city. I've even been able to make a few brief incursions into the interior.

The only thing I begin to miss in the immense space that seems to surround me is, immensely, the sea. And I have a strange sensation, which I seem to share with my horse when we stop in some remote spot on the Chinese plain—a sensation of being stirred by some sort of mysterious waves that cause us both instinctively to turn—at first, only our heads, but then the entire axis of our bodies—in unison in the direction of the sea, as my little pocket-compass confirms.[2] I'm sure that you are familiar with the law of animal magnetism that is denied by our European scientists. But you probably never had a chance to feel its effect, as a horsewoman, because of your dislike for that old enemy of yours, the sea.

My Mongolian horse, a primitive beast, sometimes seems to be so completely one with me that it is I, the man, who feel I am becoming horse, and that my horse considers me his totem—a strange and eerie impression, it seems so real. I think it goes back to my childhood.

Other than the sea and all it means to me spiritually, the only thing that is dangerously lacking for me here is music. As for the rest, all the rest, especially the plastic arts, how easy it is to get along without it!

[. . .]

Please give me more details about the material needs of your life. Quite as much as the expenses that weigh so heavily on you at this time, it is the cold that you and my sisters have to put up with that I keep worrying about. I never open one of your letters without the fear of learning some bad news about your health, because of a chill.

Do take care of yourself, dear Mother. You are always in my heart, and it is you who keep it from becoming too gloomy and empty at times.

Your son,   A.

1. Dr. Bussière. See above, letter 152, note 1.
2. Cf. letter to Conrad of 26 Feb. 1921. (181)

159

Peking, April 25, 1917

Dearest Mother,

I'm writing to you from my office, without your last letters to look at.

In the absence of the First Secretary, I am still very much taken up with the routine work of the Legation; but most happily, and in the most natural way, an intimate, trusting relationship, almost a sort of camaraderie, has sprung up between the Minister and me, and it shows no sign of diminishing. We enjoy living in close proximity, and his extreme kindness to me makes me forget all the extra work I feel called upon to do, because of the confidence he has in me—not to mention the patience with which, in the evening under the lamplight, I have to listen to him read his favorite plays. (He is

haunted by the theater, and he secretly hankers for it
—the true calling that he missed.) Finally, the solicitude
and discretion he would like to exercise, in a very romantic way, as a distant observer of everything he imagines concerning my private life, is very touching.

[. . .]

Must I keep repeating that there is nothing for you
to worry about with regard to me and the Chinese situation? As the nationalistic awakening of the Chinese
people continues, they go on painfully pursuing a political transformation that was bound to take on a social
character. They pursue it through every kind of vicissi-
tude and torment. An unavoidably arduous, spasmodic,
and convulsive evolution. But no matter what the various
governmental troubles here that you read about in the
European newspapers, the difficulties are never anything
but internal Chinese ones that pose no serious threat to
the personal safety of foreigners. The very course of this
evolution is such that we seem to be shielded for a long
time yet from any real cataclysm, even one exclusively
Chinese in character. It might even be better for them to
have done with so many abortive attempts and postpone-
ments and actually to experience some real upheaval or
explosion in this march towards renewal. But that is not
at all the present state of affairs—which conforms in
every way to the time-honored processes of Chinese
history. Dare I reveal that on occasion, from my personal point of view and out of professional interest—
and also just to escape the eternal monotony—I secretly
wish there would be some sort of nice little upheaval
that would speed things up a bit? You know how much
I am instinctively fascinated in all spheres by the play
of natural forces and by the movement created by their
active intervention.

[. . .]

160

Peking, May 25, 1917

Dearest Mother,

I have been very discouraged these last few days because I learned that our last two lots of mail were sent back to us. The English now route all their letters through Canada. We are going back to the Suez route.

I'm entrusting a small box to our Pouch—a box that will bring you a very little something from your son: three small cloisonné objects of genuine old enamel from fifteenth-century China. The shading-off of their natural patina will remind you of certain little-known studies, which you liked, by my old friend Odilon Redon.[1]

[. . .]

I've been swamped here this past week with the organizing of a big official celebration in the Legation gardens for the benefit of the Red Cross: a theater to be constructed to accommodate six hundred persons, a comic opera to be put on complete with orchestra and chorus, stars and supers—all this with only amateurs to draw on and train. My dear old Minister, who is crazy about the theater, runs about on the stage during rehearsals with his glasses pushed up on his forehead, brandishing his stage-manager's cane. He's never had such a good time. It breaks your heart to think he doesn't dare act in the play himself because the audience may include the very highest Chinese dignitaries. For myself, naturally, I was able to plead all the work at the Legation to avoid once and for all having to make a stage appearance.

[. . .]

1. Odilon Redon. See above, letter 14, note 4.

161

Peking, June 13, 1917

Dearest Mother,

[. . .]

There's still so much to do here that I don't have any idea when I'll be able to set out for Indo-China.

The revolution that finally burst the dikes and created unrest among the masses in the provinces has just this morning been settled by a compromise (a very shaky one, as I see it). The dissolution of the Parliament in Peking has succeeded, in the nick of time, in stopping the march of the provincial armies on Peking. Only one year after the death of Yüan Shih-kai (which brought about the restoration of the Republican Constitution of 1912 and the calling up of the Parliament originally created in 1913), here we are, confronted with the dismissal of the Republican cabinet and an uprising of the war lords in the north, along with intervention by a powerful Manchurian military leader determined to restore the Manchu Dynasty.[1] And that, of course, will expose us one day to the counter-move of a new march on Peking by the Republican armies.

In complete disagreement with all the predictions of the foreign diplomats, and even with the interpreters of our own legation, I had all along predicted that we would have to go through this episodic phase. Everything will not be settled—far from it!—after this interlude. The crisis will go on for a very long time in this country where so many small regional military autocracies are still in existence. But in terms of any spectacular change, the most immediate danger seems to have been dispelled. So I am reduced to deploring once again the fact that I hear the storm subsiding in the distance—once more failing to materialize. Nothing is ever really settled in China. Chinese obstetrics is the sorriest kind of maieutics. I genuinely regret that events did not come to a head so that they would have produced their own solution. And I'm very disappointed too—must I admit it again? —that my professional duties are never livened up by anything even slightly out of the ordinary.

Foreign diplomats, meanwhile, have never enjoyed greater prestige. So little were they threatened that, during the course of these last few days when catastrophe seemed imminent, the Chinese high-ups who were fleeing Peking deposited all their most precious belongings in our banks or private residences. Important political leaders were preparing to ask us for asylum. The inviolability of the Diplomatic Quarter, guarded by military detachments of all the Great Powers (including Austria, with which China has not yet broken off diplomatic relations) guarantees special immunity to the personnel of the legations, where it is always a good idea for a Chinese to have maintained some sort of friendly relation. It's not at all, at it was in 1900, a xenophobic movement, but only a repercussion of internal Chinese politics that, for the moment, divides Republican China itself into two parties: a military party with secret monarchist leanings, and a parliamentary party made up of liberal republicans. The whole thing is as chaotic and sorry a mess as one could imagine, with everything falling apart but nothing being liquidated—somewhat like the old Latin American routine. But that doesn't in any way diminish my sympathy for the fate of such an ancient human society in search of its future destiny.

But there's nothing in all this that, on the purely Chinese side of things, will add to the difficulty of postal relations with Europe. How many of my letters will get

through to you at this time? I'm starting a new series
of numbers as of this date. Please do the same.

[. . .]

1. Chang Hsun. See above, letter 148, note 9.

162

Peking, August 2, 1917

Dearest Mother,

[. . .]

I am writing to you from the depths of a small Buddhist temple situated on a rocky eminence to the northwest of Peking, where I have found a few days' refuge
from fatigue and a merciless summer.[1]

At my feet are valleys flooded by the last of the heavy
rains; at eye-level I already have a view of the first
massive ranges formed by the Mongolian uplift. Every
two days a man on horseback brings me news, along
with a few provisions, and, if necessary, work from the
Legation. I have Allan with me here, as I myself have
to be prepared to jump into the saddle at the first sign
from the Minister, for everything is still very unpredictable in this period of great political instability.

I can't understand either the language or the mentality of the Buddhist priests who, in the most cere-
monious manner, have rented out to me for the whole
summer, at a very low figure, the most sacred and cool-
est part of their sanctuary, with its private chapels badly
run down but still intact, on the highest point of this
site [. . .]. Over the steep bluff, debris of painted statues
are thrown out along with household refuse. But my
camp bed is permanently set up at the foot of the platform of the gods, with all the big windows open to the

pure night: a whole grimacing, gesticulating theogony that, I was told, includes among its minor members, a goddess of childbirth long since abandoned by the rural populace. My old chief boy from Peking is with me here to look after things; rather clumsily, he prepares rudimentary meals of eggs, stewed fruit, vegetables, and scrawny chickens picked up hereabouts and served with a few of the millet pancakes common to this region.

There is immense peace for the spirit here—an immeasurable margin; and the nights are wholly restful, far from the noise of the Chinese section of Peking. It's as if you could actually hear the passage of time, of that special time that seems to pass so much more slowly here in China than elsewhere. The transpositions and transgressions are such, here, that I might even sometimes be tempted to take up my pen again, in spite of all my longstanding resolutions to the contrary.[2] A really strange and unassimilable country for a foreigner—a fact for which I am most grateful to it, moreover. In the distance the only thing visible is the pale yellow line of the first camel-routes that lead off into the northwest and into Central Asia. And at my feet, not far from a small river that is running very low and that will soon disappear beneath the sand, there is a tiny rural community that is in the process of dying out.

Dearest Mother, you may be without news from me for some time yet. Last month's *coup d'état*, and all the various events that accompanied this attempt by the military to restore the empire, have disrupted things sufficiently to interrupt postal connections for the time being.

And I had so many amusing things to tell you about all these events.[3] In the midst of the crisis, when a whole section of the population of Peking panicked and fled to the provinces, leaving the city at the mercy of the

savage hordes of General Chang Hsun (the old sup-
porter of the Manchus who for twelve days restored
the little eleven-year-old emperor Hsüan T'ung to the
throne), my personal friendship with some members of
Chinese society resulted in my being entrusted with the
strangest mission: I was chosen to go by automobile
and pick up the wife, daughters, son, and concubines
of the President of the Republic, all of whom were
being held as hostages by the imperialist dictator. (President Li Yüan-hung himself had already found asylum
in the French Hospital in the diplomatic quarter.) The
whole affair was very amusing; and I am convinced,
contrary to the belief of my Minister, that I was never
personally in any real danger during the three strenuous
hours I spent aided by one of our legation interpreters,
in the heart of the Tartar City amid the general panic
that preceded the arrival of the Republican troops. My
wards, however, had every reason to be afraid; and they
really weren't sure they would come out alive until we
entered the Legation compound, protected by the European bayonets of the diplomatic quarter. The First Lady,
whom I had seen only in the pomp of official receptions,
was a pitiful sight as she sat, with eyes closed, in the
rear seat of my uncurtained automobile. They were all
housed in my lodgings for weeks, and my draperies
still bear the jam-smears made by the little hands of a
Chinese child.

A few days later we were awakened at four in the
morning by the general bombardment carried out by
the Republican army (cannon, machine-guns, and ri-
fles) which went on until three in the afternoon. But it
seems to have been so badly organized that in spite of
the enormous amount of munitions used up, the number
killed was negligible. We sustained very little damage
from it. Some shells landed in a Catholic church, and

a few stray bullets hit our Legation windows. Much ado
about nothing! Among the Europeans there were only
eight wounded, who were victims of their own curiosity: they were hit by bullets not intended for them.
Since the part of the city that was attacked is very close
to the Diplomatic Quarter, the projectiles whizzed over
our roofs, which were festooned with spectators, as were
the walls of the city. Stretching out back of us, the sight
of that immense empty city was to me one of the most
startling things; all the Chinese had disappeared like so
many insects burrowing out of sight into the sea-sand.
The contrast with the turmoil of the preceding days,
with rickshaws dashing about everywhere, loaded down
with the belongings of the fleeing populace—all under
the amused gaze of tall soldiers from the north, who
were once brigands. They still wear the pigtail, and at
the city gates they forced the inhabitants to comb them,
just as Xerxes' Persians once did. The next day, after
the flight of the dictator-for-a-day (who in his turn took
refuge in a foreign Legation), and after the surrender
of the troops he left behind, the Third Republic was
proclaimed. Then we went en masse to inspect the city,
lying in its smoking ruins. Stinking corpses still lying
about, brains crawling with flies, decapitated bodies of
the wounded, horses that had died "naturally" or whose
remains were charred; and, among other things, the
tiny corpse of a Chinese child in blue cotton breeches
who had been used by the soldiers of the imperialist
general to carry ammunition back and forth between the
trenches. The whole agonizing business swept through
and passed on, like a squall, and politics has already
taken up again where it left off, with all the governmental complications of a republican regime in the
frightened throes of its first experiment in democracy.

General Chang Hsun's Imperial Restoration lasted just twelve days.

[. . .]

Throughout this attempt at restoration, the upstart dictator used the person of the little Emperor, not at all as a symbol of legitimacy, but as the very vessel or incarnation of temporal power. In short, he used him as he would an imperial seal, wherein true power resides. The Chinese mind is by nature so concrete and so incapable of dealing in abstractions (a fact that may perhaps be attributed to the influence of ideographic writing), that the signs at its command finally end up by merging with, and totally embodying, the reality they designate. A Minister who flees with the seal of public authority in his possession remains, in China, the true repository of power. The printed character actually becomes the thing it signifies, and among the common people it sometimes happens that superstitious folk will paper their room entirely with printed sheets of paper as a magic substance that will ward off evil spirits.

[. . .]

1. The "Temple of Tao-Yu." See letters to Conty of 13 July 1917 (148), and to Bussière of 22 Sept. 1917. (152)

2. AL was not long in succumbing to the temptation. Among other poems, *Anabase* was written in the temple of Tao-Yu.

3. See letter to Conty of 13 July 1917 and the "Respectful Relation" attached to it. (148)

163

Peking, October 10, 1917

Dearest Mother,

[. . .]

I felt sure, during these recent days, that we were entering a new phase of the revolution as a result of the disagreements between the Northern and Southern Republicans. A President of the Republic resigns and flees to Tientsin, making a public avowal of his incompetence in an official manifesto in the purest conventional Chinese style. "Modest as the bean-pod beneath the leaf, I accuse myself of unworthiness and confess my remorse before all the people of China. . . ." Then came the arrival at Peking of a provisional Chief of State. This is followed by a quarrel between the political factions of the North and the South over the validity of the provisional Constitution and the last Parliament. Then there was the formation, in the South, of a military government elected by the Parliament Extraordinary of Canton, with Sun Yat-sen as generalissimo. In the North a new Parliament is called up, with a provisional Senate assigned to amend the electoral law with a view of ultimately drawing up a National Constitution. Thereupon civil war starts up again in one of the provinces of Southern China, followed by a battle in the government circles of Peking concerning the declaration of war against Germany. Then, in both the North and South, outcries against the signing of foreign loans, etc. Those are the facts. But the tornado will once again stop prematurely, and poor China will resume its slow gestation, its labor pains and inner rendings, when, for so long, nothing has prepared it for the responsibilities of representative government. Such is the normal course for this sort of evolution.

[. . .]

Yes, my health is as good as ever, and I never conceal anything about it from you. But what about you, dearest Mother? Why do you look so ailing in that last family snapshot of you and my sisters taken at Vernon? Yet you must have been fairly satisfied with how you looked at that moment, since you felt you could safely send the photo to your son beyond the seas. Please reassure me promptly. How can I scold you when you look so unwell?

Under the heading of "requests": Please send a hundred more visiting cards, which can be picked up at my printer's in the rue Vignon. Some small pencils with threaded tip for my pocket pencil-holder. My Abbé Crampon Bible; a portfolio of engravings from the British Museum, along with some of my papers from London, which I left with you, in the library. And finally, the first phrase of Satie's third *Gymnopédie*,[1] which was copied for me by the hand of my sister Paule.

I've managed to receive news from Conrad through an American friend;[2] please send my autographed photograph of him, which should be among the papers that I gave Eliane for safekeeping.

1. Erik Satie (1866-1925), French composer most often remembered for his score for the ballet *Parade*. *Gymnopédie* is one of his most familiar compositions.
2. Agnes Tobin. See above, letter 111, note 1.

164

Peking, November 4, 1917

Dearest Mother,

[. . .]

My work has been rather heavy these days, with all that is going on, and for five months now I have been Secretary of the Diplomatic Corps as well as Secretary of the Association of Allied Ministers. And at the Legation I'm once again alone, holding down the job of First Secretary, since Martel has again taken up his post as Chargé d'Affaires. The Minister, Monsieur Conty, has been recalled—a real falling out of favor, the exact cause or occasion of which escapes me. Perhaps it was some over-assertiveness in his official correspondence, or some plot against him by the Chinese in Paris. In any case, under the Ribot[1] ministry, he seems to have been the victim of one of those backstage enmities that are so frequent in this pitfall-strewn career. Most luckily for him, he'll find a new Ministry awaiting him in Paris, which will undoubtedly make a point of compensating its predecessor's victim. Pichon[2] himself has been Minister to China and knows the rules of the game thoroughly.

Poor Conty leaves behind, here in China, nothing but ingrates who detested his frankness, his authoritarianism, his rough tone, and his independent judgment. I really believe I was the only person who always got along perfectly, and quite sincerely, with this very decent man who wore his hair very short and had a robust intelligence and rare vitality—but who suffered from a lack of self-control and a tactlessness toward others the like of which I have never seen. But I much preferred that to the apathy or customary indifference, the world-weary tone and affected skepticism, all the false distinction and false elegance of manner of the "old career hands" who are never eager to do anything but repeat to each other their favorite maxim: "Urgent. For immediate inaction." In any case, as a man, Conty was a strong personality. To be sure, he sometimes did appear a little vulgar and brusque, and his cast of mind was not very refined or subtle and lacked psychological insight and intuition. But the way he got things done was really something remarkable, and so was his unfailing courage. Nor, in his way, was he devoid of a certain human kindness. In personal matters I always found him extremely tactful and uncommonly discreet —to the point of something like timidity at times. In spite of his *pater familias* self-centeredness, he often let me catch glimpses of a genuine sensitivity. At all events, he put such a great trust in me that I genuinely miss him. His active participation in things, and his prestige among the Chinese, as well as among the foreign Chiefs of Mission, will not be easy to replace.

As for Damien de Martel, you know that, at his instigation, I have always shared an open, easygoing, cordial camaraderie with him. Our relations, official or personal, will never be blemished by a single disagreeable moment. On the personal as well as on the professional level, I am heartbroken that he is obliged to leave soon —immediately upon the arrival of the new Minister, in fact. I do not know Monsieur Boppe personally, nor do I know much about him. I fear he may be a poor, rather empty-headed fellow, or at least, that he may have an "old career man" mentality. I don't know whom he may have requested in Paris as official replacement for Martel in the post of First Secretary. Nor do I know whether he intends to ask that I be replaced in my job here by someone of his own choosing.

Since I am at last freed from having my quarters and taking my meals in the Ministerial Residence, I am now living all by myself in my own completely remodeled house. I'm especially happy—for my off-duty freedom of movement, as well as for my personal life—about a private gate at the rear of my garden, cut right in the very wall of the Legation compound.

1. Alexandre Ribot (1842-1923), toward the end of a very long political career, was Président du Conseil from Mar. to Sept. 1917, and then Minister of Foreign Affairs until late October of that same year.

2. Stephen Pichon (1857-1933) became Minister of Foreign Affairs in Nov. 1917 and held the post until Jan. 1921. He had been French Ambassador to China from 1898 to 1900 and was thus present during the Boxer Rebellion.

165

Peking, February 2, 1918

Dearest Mother,

This year, winter has been much, much milder; the thermometer has never sunk lower than twenty degrees[1] below zero. I haven't suffered at all, and I've been able to continue my horseback rides except during the very rare snowfalls. It rains here only in summer. During the rest of the year the absolute purity of the air is altered only by dust-storms, or rather, loess-storms, from Central Asia, which are here referred to as the "yellow wind"— which is my delight.

My horseback outings do me a world of good, physically and morally. My chest is still expanding, at my age, so much so that I can't button the first button of my sports jacket. By now Allan and I are complete friends; he is as accustomed to my voice as to that of a close friend. I've become very attached to this wild animal whose twitching ear always seems to expect an intelligible word from me. But how sad it is, after all, to find in his look only that eternal subjugation to human magnetism. To me it's the same old story, the same old feeling of loneliness. They bring mounts newly arrived from Mongolia, still wild; and no sooner do I approach them than they react to the magnetism of gaze and gesture, even before their forehead feels the first stroke of my hand. After that, how can you be moved by what is simply an automatic response?

At first, like any self-respecting Central Asiatic horse, Allan couldn't abide the smell of foreigners; and even after he had established magnetic contact with me, looking me straight in the eye and quivering at the touch of my hand on his neck, he still seemed bothered by the smell of my Scotch tweeds. He now comes up to me with childlike eyes, oblivious of his ugliness and lack of manners. He comes right into the house, slipping around on the tile floor of the reception room, though I have to be careful to cover up a mirror that terrifies him. My "mafou" or Chinese stable-boy doesn't know what to make of it, nor does the acupuncturist who once tried, unsuccessfully, to treat Allan for sciatica. Once I'm in the saddle, I can make him do things quite willingly that he wouldn't do for anyone else. I'm the only one who has ever been able to ride him in a race or hunt him. If I went in for polo, I'd have no trouble acclimating him to the game, unsociable though he may be. But his very ugliness is a safeguard for him against all snobbish games.

The first time I climbed into the saddle, some Chinese trainers wanted to witness the scene and see me operate without the slightest technique or even very much instruction. The Chinese are all much too passively receptive themselves to conceive of any other way of breaking in an animal than by force and threats. For my part, I understood the temperament of this "unapproachable monster" when I noticed, in the stables, the amused and gentle way he put up with the worst kind of teasing from a very small Chinese boy who had slipped under his belly. Long after the miracle of our physical rapport took place, my "boys" still thought it necessary to give the "mafou" stable-boy a pyjama-top that had already been worn, or an old pair of jodhpurs, to hang up in the horse's stall during the night in order to get him accustomed to a European. Yet he was already nosing about my pockets in search of his carrot or his lump of sugar. At any rate, the animal is sure-footed enough never to have thrown me once, even though we do a lot of cross-country jumping out here.

My getting the feel of Asiatic horses has, all things considered, been easy to come by, even though these animals are already six years old by the time they are brought to China, hardly yet severed from the life of the steppes, where they are still caught with the lasso. I've often mounted other Asiatic horses than my own, and I've never had but one accident, not a serious one, during a "hunt," on a bad jumper who refused the obstacle because his English trainers had ruined his natural, wild-animal reflexes.

Allan isn't the only beast who approaches me affectionately. A huge foreign dog, a magnificent Australian beast that is the terror of the Chinese quarter, has decided to live with me more than with his English masters, whom I don't know personally. Every morning I find him at my door waiting for me to come down in "riding-coat" as Satie[2] says, and he tags along faithfully on my rides in the open country to the consternation of the native Chinese dogs.

Another one of my friends—don't laugh!—is a mere mosquito that holes up during the day in the little tunnel formed by the back-binding of a Petit Larousse dictionary that I never open. He then comes out in the evening to visit me on my desk without at all bothering me. We've been exchanging greetings for a long time already, and I've succeeded in putting a red ink-mark on him, like a Chinese actor, so I can identify him. Dr. Bussière can't believe his eyes. My Chinese "boys" think it's magic. The little tyke is named Ulysses—I'm not sure just why; and, out of regard for it, Bussière[3] has given up prescribing for me—as he wanted to—the company of a small cat or small dog in order to keep me from bolting my solitary meals.

I don't go out nearly as much in the evening now,

since I've really paid my dues, as a newcomer (a "griffin," as they say here), to all the foreign legations and all the drawing-rooms of important international functionaries. I've managed, little by little, to reserve a few evenings for myself or for a few close friends.

The political situation here is somewhat less tense, thanks largely to the confused state of things. Here's how events have shaped up since my last letter: At Peking, the inauguration of a provisional Senate; the third resignation, tendered and then withdrawn, then tendered again, by the only capable governmental chief, Republican General Tuan Chi-jui,[4] for whom I have a great deal of personal regard. And then lastly, an armistice decreed between North and South, with a military conference at Tientsin; in the South, the organizing of a Southwest Confederation with its seat at Canton; renewal of hostilities, and still another apology from a President of the Republic publicly confessing his incompetence; etc.—always the same style and the same rhythm.

[. . .]

1. Celsius units.
2. See above, letter 163, note 1.
3. See above, letter 152, note 1.
4. See above, letter 148, note 8.

166

Peking, March 5, 1918

What is wrong, dearest Mother? Never have you left me without news from you for so long a time. It's not that I fear something serious has happened, because bad news always travels fastest. Rather, it's that I fear you've been in one of those periods of prolonged depression, worry, and preoccupation of every sort; and that would be quite enough to upset me deeply. I have a foreboding of some sorrow that has befallen our house. I think, too, of my sister Marguerite's house, of the room there I sometimes slept in when I went through Paris before the war; it must now contain a cradle.

There's no better way to give you an idea of the slowness of communications than to tell you about the wild goose chase of our still-awaited new Minister. He left Marseilles on the 15th of December and hasn't yet been able to get any further than Colombo! First he had to stop over in Port Said, where he was obliged to wait for a message for I don't know how long. Next he was dumped in India by another steamer that had had to change course and then return post haste on orders from the French Government. At last he embarked on an English boat heading for Ceylon, and there he is waiting for a passage on the next French steamer.

It seems that there hasn't been a French steamer for more than three months. Here we've been without a diplomatic pouch for four months. There is only one reasonable channel, and I beg you to use it—that is, America. (Mark your letters "Via America," or even better, "Via Canada.") One of the advantages of this English line is that mail which is lost is reported to the public with very exact date indications.

I don't think my new Minister, Monsieur Boppe, can get here before another month has gone by. He's arriving with his wife and child. I haven't the slightest word from Paris, and I'm completely in the dark about what may happen to me in the shake-up of our diplomatic mission in China. But that's really my fault, as I don't write to anyone, at the Quai d'Orsay or anywhere else. I found out quite by chance that Claudel was Minister to Brazil[1] (a new Brazilian representative to China told me). I haven't answered his letters either.

[. . .]

1. Paul Claudel served as French Ambassador to Brazil from Jan. 1917 until Nov. 1918.

167

Peking, April 9, 1918

I very much hope, dearest Mother, that you have not been unduly worried about the plague epidemic that has been raging in northern China these last few months.[1] I have told you quite accurately what the situation is, and I've never wanted to hide anything from you, even if that had been possible. I just hope the European newspapers don't print too many preposterous tales.

The ravages continue in the western provinces and in the area around Peking; but there have still been only very few cases in Peking proper; and things could even get much more serious in Peking without greatly endangering the Diplomatic Quarter. All proper precautions were already taken four months ago, under my own supervision and control, since I have been—did I tell you?—the mayor or syndic of the Peking diplomatic quarter for a year already—more precisely, I am the elected president of the "International Administrative Commission of the Diplomatic Quarter"—with a large budget and excellent collaborators.

I had already—as discreetly as possible, so as not to cause a panic, but also as effectively as possible and with all the good humor and enthusiasm called for in such circumstances—seen to all the steps that could be taken ahead of time: hospitals and barracks, arrangements of every sort; isolation, quarantine, and disinfection camps;

doctors, nurses, and qualified assistants; pharmaceutical supplies and stores of masks. At the first sign of a serious alert, the Diplomatic Quarter, under the medical care of its own Legation doctors, would isolate itself from the rest of the world as if it were a Noah's Ark.

On the outside, I gave the Chinese Ministry of the Interior assurances of the collaboration between the Legation doctors and the "Chinese Commission for Defense against the Epidemic" with regard to official measures to be taken in the surrounding territory: regulation of means of communication, the closing of railway stations to travelers, the isolation of centers of infection, sanitary inspection and inspection of quarantine stations, etc. For the missions in the interior, which are often hard pressed, I made arrangements for sending out medical advice from our French doctor, along with special instructions and pharmaceutical supplies (the poor missionaries give us dreadful reports of the situation of their Christian communities, wherein whole families, even whole blocks of houses, are stricken).

The threat to Peking is now definitely subsiding; the battle of the Diplomatic Quarter may be considered won, and we'll come through with only four casualties, three of them fatal: three Russian travelers who were put up without inspection at the Hôtel des Wagons-Lits. The non-fatal case was especially moving to me, because he was a personal friend, the Spanish Minister,[2] a hardened old Basque who was living all alone and uncared-for in his diplomatic residence. I couldn't tear him away from the place, but alcoholism, contrary to all medical lore, miraculously saved him. (Pneumonic plague is here considered incurable and usually fatal within forty-eight hours, though sometimes even within a very few hours.) My friend Pastor waited all alone for death; his revolver was within reach, and he had surrounded himself with twenty or so portraits of women—who all appeared to me to be the same person.

As a matter of fact, this pulmonary plague, which is the most serious, is also the easiest to avoid individually. By simply wearing a mask you can avoid catching it even in a particularly infected area. Real danger exists only for the poor teeming masses plodding along the roads. Surely the Chinese authorities could have done more for them, since foreign loans had been guaranteed them. But there is nothing more atavistic than the fatalism of these people, for whom great natural cataclysms never are anything but the result of a mysterious lack of harmony between earth and heaven. Human life, moreover, counts so little to them that they feel nature must be left free to solve the demographic problem in its own way. Doesn't it seem that the simplest way out, for the local authorities, is to wait for the hot season to arrive, the coming of summer that infallibly destroys the plague germ? (It is, as a matter of fact, the most fragile of germs and can not survive desiccation.)

I can't forget how amused I was, shortly after my arrival in China, by an official visit in which I acted as secretary, accompanying the dean of the Diplomatic Corps—at that time, the Minister of Great Britain[3]—who went to offer financial assistance from the Great Powers after one of those natural disasters so frequent in China: floods followed by famine, refugee peasants fleeing, eating treebark and selling their children for a pittance. The poor British Minister, even though he was an old China hand, couldn't get over the placidity with which the Chinese statesman (who was perhaps also apprehensive about the risk of a foreign political takeover) told us, first, that it did not seem imperative to him to get mixed up in all this, running counter, as it did, to the higher laws of natural harmony that, unaided, take care of the demographic equilibrium of China.

The battle against the plague has now been won. No longer will the wrists of persons who have been inspected be marked with a red or blue stamp at the gates of the Chinese City or in the last railway stations still open around Peking. Very soon I'll be folding up the huge map of my Medical General Staff, bristling with little red flags. I'll be giving back to the polo-players the military glacis that I had to requisition for my sanitary sheds. And all that will remain to be done will be to audit the rather sizable account of expenses incurred; and once more I'll hear myself be accused of over-zealousness by the whole unthinking community of the Diplomatic Quarter, who will never suspect what they have been exposed to.

(When I was elected Syndic of the Diplomatic Quarter for the first time, my predecessor, a skeptical and non-chalant dilettante who was a Counsellor of the Italian Legation, smilingly passed along his functions to me with only one recommendation: "Above all, no over-zealousness!" And my first official act was a strict pro-hibition of opium in the Diplomatic Quarter! Well, within twenty-four hours, to my great amusement, it was in the cellar of my own house that my chief of police discovered a clandestine opium den, set up without my realizing it by my own "boys"! . . .)

Basically—dare I admit it to you?—in spite of the added fatigue that accrued, under the circumstances, from the job of being President of the Administrative Commission of the Diplomatic Quarter on top of my duties as Secretary of the Conference of Ministers of the Allied Powers, I really enjoyed this whole battle against the plague. I threw myself passionately into it, as into a great adventure—one that broke up much of the prevailing dullness for me. Dare I go even further in admitting the inadmissible? I am unable, I've always been unable, to keep from being fascinated, any time and in any clime, by this play of great natural forces: floods, typhoons, earthquakes, volcanic eruptions, great epidemics, and various other upheavals—they all cause a breakdown of equilibrium that tends to renew the vital thrust of the great, continuing movement throughout the world. (You should never, most Christian Mother, have entrusted my Antillean childhood to the pagan hands of a Hindu servant who was too beautiful—and also a secret disciple of the god Shiva.)[4]

[. . .]

My new Minister, Monsieur Boppe, is expected at Peking on the 17th of this month.

I've just learned of the imminent arrival of a new First Secretary appointed to replace Martel. I know who he is—an "old school" career officer who harbors only antipathy for me. But that's really of no importance. I may get under the skin of a man working in the same room with me; no one can get under my skin. You've long been aware of this basic principle of my behavior as a human being: Never react violently against a person, so as not to be dependent upon him, even if it be only for the brief moment while the reaction lasts. It's a question of hygiene—a defense of my oxygen supply against the carbon dioxide exhaled by others.

I shall very much miss, both as a man and a colleague, my senior and superior, Damien de Martel, who has been unfailingly the friendliest, most cordial, and easiest person to get along with of all my colleagues here abroad; a real "comrade," even when he found himself in the position of being my chief of mission. Though self-centered and skeptical, even cynical on occasion, he had a broad and very receptive turn of mind. He was not very well liked usually, but he always treated me with solicitude and delicacy and was absolutely discreet in his support of me. As chief, whenever he took over as Chargé d'Affaires, he allowed me so large a share in the undertaking and planning of his diplomatic activities that I ended up taking a very personal interest in them, as if they concerned me in a most personal way.

[. . .]

I think constantly of you, dearest Mother, and sometimes it seems to me that that is really the only thing I have to say, in the silence of my heart. I embrace you in all simplicity. May you, with the help of my sisters, be somewhat shielded from all the sorrows and worries that I am always afraid are casting a shadow on your brow.

Your grown son,   A.

Did my sister Marguerite receive the boxes of old tea from Hankow that I had sent to her several months ago? If possible, drink only weak Chinese tea and not the heavy Ceylon tea that coats the lining of the stomach with tannin.

1. An epidemic of pneumonic plague broke out in Mongolia in mid-December 1917 and spread south and east during the first three and a half months of 1918. According to *The China Year Book 1919-20*, the epidemic took a toll of some 15,000 lives but was not nearly so severe in Peking as in more northerly centers. The epidemic was stamped out by mid-April—that is, shortly after AL wrote this letter.

2. Don Luis Pastor (d. 1921) served as Spanish Ambassador to China from 1906 to 1921.

3. Sir John Newell Jordan (1852-1925), British Ambassador to China from 1906 to 1920.

4. Cf. letter to MacLeish of 23 Dec. 1941. (224)

168

Peking, September 15, 1918

Dearest Mother,

I really feel rather reluctant to talk to you about the political situation in China, for its basic elements continue to be so tedious. The curiosity that you show in this regard is a real surprise to me; but then, you never cease to surprise me.

What has been worthy of note since my last letter in all this sorry confusion between the North and the South? There was the publication, in Peking, of a decree prescribing the organization of the Parliament and the election of members to both Chambers; then there was the organizing of a Bureau for Participation in the World War. Then the embarrassment of a President of the Republic who doesn't know to whom to tender his resignation, since Parliament no longer exists, and who finally turns to the provinces, asking them to find a replacement for him within ten days. Individual undertakings by war-lords in the provinces; the formation by my great friend, the Republican General Tuan Chi-jui, of his third Republican Cabinet since the re-instatement of the third Republic; a military conference at Tientsin and then one at Hankow; then again at Tientsin, and still another time at Tientsin. Concurrently, in the South, the nomination of members of a "Southwest Directorate," including Sun Yat-sen; and finally in Peking the calling up of newly elected members of the two Chambers, the opening of Parliament, the closing of the Provisional National Council, and the election of the new President of the Republic.

And that still is, for the time being, the national

Chinese imbroglio, to which it's hard to find any real key.

[. . .]

And you keep asking, dearest Mother, for details about my living quarters and the way my staff of servants is organized.

I am very simply installed for a diplomat of my rank, and maybe I am the only one not acutely aware of the fact, for you know how little I require in the way of comfort and luxuries. The hardest problem for me to solve in this large two-story house, in which I live all alone, is warding off the cold. I've only halfway managed to do it by using four large Russian stoves that are fuel-devouring maws requiring almost the full-time attention of a special boy. In particular, there's an entrance-hall and stairway that are my despair when I have guests to dinner. When I'm alone I sometimes take my meals in a little orangery-hothouse adjacent to the salon and dining-room. There I have warmth, light, and plants— and a few insects to make up for a lack of fishes and birds, also a very tame little lizard, and a little tree-frog who is utterly delightful, but hard on my favorite crickets and moths.

Servants? —When I arrived here and realized how much of my salary, and of my paltry savings as well, I would lose because of the exchange rate, I got rid of a large part of the staff inherited from my peacetime predecessors, keeping only the head boy, who acts as my chief steward, personal valet, and butler all in one, along with a cook and his assistant (hidden away in the base-ment and never seen), a coolie porter for the heavy house-work (cleaning, floor-polishing, stove-tending, carrying hot water for washing and bathing), another one for er-rands in town and household purchases, and no one for the garden or wash-house. My laundry is done in town. An old Chinese woman, more or less related to my head boy, comes once in a while to look after the linen. There is just no way I can keep an eye on everything that goes on, but I don't think they take too much advantage of me. I've also managed to dispense with a "mafou" (stable-boy) by making an arrangement with the stablemaster of the Legation, and also to do without a rickshaw boy as well, by using rickshaw-rentals or ones that I pick up by chance in the street. When I entertain, I hire a few supplementary waiters at two or three dollars a head, to whom, though, I have to supply livery. The nearness of the club makes a lot of things easier for me.

The Chinese boys, products of a long tradition of serv-ice in the Diplomatic Quarter, and already inherently very refined, very shrewd, and naturally tactful, know surprisingly well how to facilitate things and how to im-provise prompt solutions to problems, in case of unex-pected gatherings, even going so far as to borrow table-services or even supplies from each other, to the great amusement of all interested parties. The firm courteous-ness with which they formulate their requests for a raise is always justified by the news of one's own promotion in rank, which they've read about in the newspaper or picked up at table.

I think I've already told you how lucky I was in my chief boy, "François" (a surname that is the only thing he seems to have retained from his childhood in the missions—a name that sounds vaguely Christian to him). He's a "good" man, but who rather gives the appearance of a "good" woman. He's slow, not very clever, far less nimble-witted than a Chinese usually is, but decent and trustworthy and with real dignity, full of tact and discre-tion in all matters concerning his master's private life; and, finally, he's well organized, quiet and dependable, always very well mannered, dignified, and perfectly clean and neat. I think he's quite honest, though I can't be absolutely sure. His wife and children, whom I do not know, live far off, in Tientsin; and while he is here he hardly ever goes out, except at night to slake his passion for the Chinese theater. If I were to get sick, he'd look after me rather stupidly, but in a kindly way, with a passive good will and patient assiduity that you could momentarily take for genuine attachment, were it possible for such a feeling really to exist in a Chinese. I shall never really know what he thinks of me as a man, independent of his consideration for the official figure I cut.

Indifference is the most basic Chinese trait, even among themselves; and that, in the eyes of the old missionaries, is the most hopeless obstacle that they have to overcome in their apostolate. Beneath the calm and patient gentleness of my good François, I have never found the least trace of perfidy or secret hostility, but not the slightest glimmer of real affection either. And then, he's already served so many Frenchmen in the life of the Diplomatic Quarter that he has become a rather special and very honorable type of old legation servant, only very little realizing, I think, what goes on outside; vaguely conservative and, on principle, faithful to his pigtail, which goes back to the Empire, in spite of all the police regulations of the Republic. I even find myself being a little proud of having in my house one of the only three surviving pigtails of the old Diplomatic Quarter servant corps.

[. . .]

169

Peking, December 1918

Dearest Mother,

[. . .]

The governments of the North and the South have managed to agree on the make-up of a joint delegation that is to represent China at the Peace Conference: two delegates to be named by the North and two by the South, under the guidance of a chief delegate who will be the present Minister of Foreign Affairs in Peking, Mister Lu Cheng-hsiang. The union of the two Chinas will thus be realized for the first time—in the field of foreign policy.

The Chinese delegation should be in Paris next month. I'll give Lu Cheng-hsiang[1] a private letter for you. He was so good as to ask me for your address. He is a personal friend of mine, rather exceptionally in these circles of Chinese officialdom, where so many things usually stand in the way of intimacy in personal relations. For a long time already he has shown me the greatest confidence and sympathy, oblivious of the difference in our ages or of the least consideration for protocol. He really is a most unusual figure, in such a period, on the Chinese political scene; and he owes much of his moral authority to his independence, rising above parties and factions of every kind.

As a career diplomat he served Imperial China in Europe when he was very young—at the court in Saint Petersburg, then at the first Peace Conferences at The Hague and at the Chinese legation in the Netherlands. After the abdication of the Manchu dynasty in 1912, he served the government of Yüan Shih-kai as Minister of Foreign Affairs and President of the Council of Ministers. Since 1917 he has continuously occupied, in Peking, the post of Minister of Foreign Affairs of the Republic of China, infusing a genuinely new spirit into Chinese diplomacy, a spirit compounded of method, clarity, broad humanism—completely transforming the organization of his administration and making every effort, above and beyond the internal strife and the increasingly complicated situation abroad, to raise Chinese national awareness to the level of a New China that may one day play its part in the international concert. His task remains an extremely difficult one in the present state of affairs, but his moral authority has always been recognized or accepted by everyone. His clearsightedness, even prescience, regarding events has had to be brought into play in the nick of time to overcome Chinese reluctance to declaring war against Germany. The patience, persistence, and indefatigable mastery of his patriotism have often made a true martyr of him in the face of Japanese intrigues in his country and also in the face of short-term objectives of certain factions in the South. His overriding preoccupation is, first of all, to arouse a patriotic feeling that has never really existed in China, for, to this day, the very idea of a fatherland, for a Chinese, is more racial than national. He leaves here entertaining high hopes of France's understanding the necessity of China's being given her rightful due at the Peace Conference. I am terribly fearful about what the consequences may be of the disappointment that he may bring back with him from Paris. Up to now, he has been quite an important trump card in Franco-Chinese policy.

Lu is, in his way, a highly civilized and literate man, having translated several French works (including a very refined one by Paul-Louis Couchoud, *Poètes et Sages d'Asie*,[2] and a bad play by Clemenceau, *Le Voile du Bonheur*).[3] He will surprise you with the delicacy and refinement of his French, by his distinguished manners, and even by his ease in wearing European attire. His elegance and his mastery of European languages were already very surprising when, as a young Chinese arriving from old Imperial China at twenty-eight years of age, he landed in Marseilles in 1912 wearing his silken robe and long braid.

Another item that will please you: This good Chinese who admires Confucius, is a Catholic—a really unheard-of thing in Chinese officialdom. A genuine practicing Catholic. He is even, to my knowledge, the only Chinese to betray any sign of a real spiritual life. I have no trouble imagining him, in adversity or solitude, ending his days in some European monastery.

Yet Lu is married, and happily married at that, to a European, a Belgian lady who is extremely devoted to him and who has always been an incomparable and most worthy companion to him. She is a very charitable soul, founder of many good works, for which France awarded her, two years ago, the Gold Medal of National Recognition, and for whom, that same year, the President of the Republic of China created a "Medal for Service." You will undoubtedly see her, too. When one sees her present state of fleshiness and overweight, it is hard to imagine what an attractive woman she once may have been. Once when I was making a rather heated defense of Lu Cheng-hsiang to Baron Hayashi, the Japanese Minister, who can not abide him, the old Japanese aristocrat smilingly let drop these few words: "I cannot follow him in his conjugal appreciation."[4]

[. . .]

1. Lu Cheng-hsiang (b. 1870) was Minister of Foreign Affairs from Jan. 1915 to May 1916 and then once more from Dec. 1917 to Aug. 1920. From Jan. 1919 to Dec. 1919 he served

as chief of the Chinese Delegation to the Paris Peace Conference. In 1927 he retired to the Abbaye de Saint André at Loppem-lez-Bruges, Belgium, and became a Benedictine monk.

2. Paul-Louis Couchoud's *Sages et Poètes d'Asie*, first published in 1916, is devoted mostly to Japanese literature and culture but also contains a section on Confucius.

3. *Le Voile du Bonheur* ("The Veil of Happiness") is a one-act play by Georges Clemenceau, first performed in 1901. The action of the play is set in Peking during the last years of the Manchu dynasty and presents a blind Mandarin *pater familias* whose sight is restored but who longs to be blind once again, since his restored sight has revealed to him nothing but treachery and evil.

4. English in original.

170

Peking, December 27, 1918

Dearest Mother,

I forgot to tell you about another Chinese personality who wishes to bring you news from me and to whom I was also obliged to entrust a few personal letters for friends in Paris—for Arthur Fontaine[1] among others, at the Ministry of Labor, and Philippe Berthelot[2] in Foreign Affairs. He is Liang Ch'i-ch'ao,[3] a writer admired for his work in several literary genres, a politician upon occasion, and an animator of Chinese youth. He is one of the Chinese figures I have found most congenial. He will astonish you a little in his Chinese clothes, which he alone still insists on wearing when abroad.

Here he has been nicknamed the "Prince of the Intellectuals"; but this brilliant writer, animated by a sense of civic duty and patriotism, has felt obliged to abandon his purely literary work momentarily to participate in a public campaign, between North and South, of general conciliation and national revitalization. Using the spoken and written word, he now makes himself heard only as a social reformer, economist, and jurist—like a French writer of the eighteenth century. He has never been willing to consider the political example of Europe entirely applicable to the new China; he demands for her the establishment of wholly original institutions. In the midst of the present crisis, his views still seem too theoretical and too much oriented toward the immediate future—but he has perceived very clearly, as it also appears to me, that the democratic Chinese community, experiencing for the first time the liberty it has won, must look to itself for inspiration and utilize the characteristics inherent in the Chinese race if it is to develop truly representative rule. Parliamentarianism of the European type seems to him unadaptable to the very nature of the Chinese people, and any confusion in this regard can only deflect or retard the evolution of the Chinese crisis of adjustment, with the most serious consequences for Chinese society and its relations with the Western world. New China ought to borrow from Western society only the purely technological conceptions of large-scale international modernism, reserving for itself the right to treat all social and political matters in its own way.

The study of ways to teach this technology is to be the first concern of the official mission that has been entrusted to Liang Ch'i-ch'ao ("economic, industrial, and scientific re-education of China under new institutions").

For a Liang Ch'i-ch'ao the very bases of Western civilization differ radically from those of Chinese civilization. He feels that the old sense of mutual assistance among the Chinese people would instinctively lead it toward the political idea of government by popular opinion, but in ways very different from those championed in the twentieth century by the Western hemisphere, because the gradation of classes along competitive lines does not exist in Chinese society, any more than do the ideas of capital and labor, as developed in Europe by scientific materialism. At the present time the whole country of China still depends entirely on a system of small-scale farmers—and that, moreover, would constitute for its future the best natural mode of collective organization, easy to readjust and readapt to the requirements of a modern society with considerable natural resources at its disposal.

Apart from his study-mission, Liang Ch'i-ch'ao, as a propagandist, will make every effort to enlighten foreign opinion about the national demands of China after its entry into the war against Germany (progressive abolition of capitulations, suppression of territorial leasing, revision of customs tariffs, and, above all, the direct surrender to China of the leased territories of Shantung recovered from Germany by the Allies).

On each of these counts, I greatly fear that China will be immensely disappointed,[4] so great is the incomprehension (or merely the heedlessness and inattention) in Paris about everything concerning Asia as a whole—and also about everything that a fundamentally misguided orientation of China with regard to Europe and America would imply in the way of future threats on a more or less long-term basis. The destiny of New China has less mystery about it than we think; but there is an extreme mental inertia prevalent in Europe with respect to all that concerns that future which prevents any consideration that anticipates anything beyond a five- or ten-year period. Yet every mistaken view in which we persist infallibly exposes us to irreparable damage. France, at the moment, no longer really seems to have a Far Eastern policy, and the game is too often dominated by short-sighted and conservative England, to the immediate profit of her Japanese ally. In fact, even here, my Minister is far from sharing my view of the future.

[. . .]

1. See above, letter 65, note 1.
2. See above, letter 147, note 1.
3. Liang Ch'i-ch'ao (1873-1929).
4. See AL's letter to his mother of 21 Apr. 1920. (175)

171

Peking, February 1919

Dearest Mother,

[. . .]

I wouldn't have believed it possible that you would be so amused by my telling you so often about the friendship of my horses. You want more details about these Mongolian animals, but there's really little to tell of interest.

When I think how, as a child, I admired the fine, noble figure you cut as a horsewoman on your big black mare, Tzigane, I ask myself what you would think today on seeing your son in the saddle on such ugly little creatures. And what would your American friend, Laura, think?—she who used to ride, dressed in white piqué, such a fine chestnut from Alabama—Laura, who presented me with my first child-size silver-headed riding crop.

These Mongolian horses, inadequately broken in and hard to groom, are really very ugly and common-looking. At first glance they look like some misshapen offspring of the equine family, but they are actually of a pure Kirghiz stock that, through direct cross-breeding, is descended from the famous Central Asiatic horse known as "Prjevalsky's horse," which is the ancestor of all our horses. (An animal that fascinates me and that I've never been able to see outside a zoo; but that I dream of running into one day, in some desert region, on the projected incursion into Mongolia and Chinese Turkestan that haunts me as a possibility for my first long triennial leave.)

They are squat, stocky beasts with a front leg-set that is too open and a hard rigid back without the slightest saddle-curve or bend of neck. They carry their gross, heavy heads very low, straight out from the withers. The jowls are too thick, the forehead too broad, and the lower jaw almost invisible. The hindquarters are ill-formed, and the chest is concave like that of a broken-winded horse. The whole animal is of a piece; and when it runs, it looks, in silhouette, like a large rat on wheels. But under their forelocks of matted hair, what wonderful eyes!—like a hummingbird's or a poodle's, really the most endearing you've ever seen. In open country they run like hunting dogs, head to the ground, since, by heredity, they are used to looking out for marmot-holes in the desert—which makes them admirable polo-ponies, but very bad companions for people who like to lean forward, as I do, over the ears of their mount. And they're also dangerous in the way they shy because of so much speed for their size. They tend to bolt, as if from intoxication, on the open plains. You have the feeling that you're mounted on a headless animal surviving for a moment after its decapitation. Fortunately, they are very sure-footed, although they're never altogether "broken in." Obviously they don't resemble those magnificent highly trained beasts that impressed me so in my youth at the horse shows in Pau.

On the credit side, one has to recognize a number of good qualities: robustness, endurance, sobriety, and courage proceeding from an astonishing vitality that maintains in them a sort of gaiety, playfulness, and zest. It has been scientifically proven that of all the world's horses, this one gives the greatest return in terms of the ratio of speed to size. Its resistance to cold is also very high. When, in polar exploration, there was a search for a better mode of traction than dog-teams, a famous English explorer had a lot of Mongolian ponies delivered to him through the intermediary of the Hong Kong and Shanghai Bank. Spending six months a year in a desert region where they have to live off the old stubble that persists in winter and that has to be extracted from under a thick layer of snow (which accounts for their chin-whiskers), they acquire unusual resistance, which is favored, moreover, by a very slow growth-rate. (They cannot be exported for sale outside Mongolia until they are at least six years old.) Their courage in every circumstance is famous, and their victorious resistance to wolves is so greatly prized that Chinese horse-traders sometimes present them for sale with cleverly simulated scars on their chest. I don't know whether they have anything in common with the horses of the ancient Cossacks, but I do know that the Russians still use them for their mounted combat-troops in southern Siberia, on the borders of the Manchurian plateau and the upper Amur River; for there is nothing like them for charging in desert or mountain regions, and their rear-guard raids are incomparable for inciting panic in any enemy reserve formation. They also make up the only mounted force in the Chinese army. To this day they are vastly preferred, for all units in Asia, to other breeds, seemingly handsomer but less spirited and heavier, such as the Polish breed, which produces only excellent beasts of burden and dray-horses.

It is certain that, as saddle horses, these little Mongol

steeds, which are excellent jumpers, have an astonishing aptitude for getting around in the worst terrain of the Chinese countryside. I myself have been able to mount a few animals imported from abroad belonging to friends (especially two fine Tarbes mounts that were presented to Yüan Shih-kai and that, since his death, are in the hands of an officer of the Chinese General Staff who was trained at Saumur). I prefer a hundred times, and in all circumstances, to use a Mongolian horse here. Of course, there are also big ceremonial horses in this country, of a breed known as the Ili, from Dzungaria; but they are dray-horses, gangling and awkward, with a stilted gait, good only in my eyes for ceremonial teams and dowagers' town-carriages. They would stumble about dangerously on the first ridges or ruts of a Chinese arroyo.

Our Mongolian animals, unfortunately, arrive in Peking with mouths that are already badly damaged because of the harshness of the bit and the brutality of the Mongol horseman. Contrary to general belief, the nomad riders of all countries are bad horsemen; they bear down on their mounts brutally, with no regard or care for the beast, often standing upright in the stirrups and pulling too hard on the bit. No lightness of touch with the reins or the beam of the bit, no play of the weight, no knee-control. The Mongolian beasts are, in addition, cruelly forced to speed, in keeping with the ancient tradition of the nomad couriers. I have seen some that still have their nostrils split so as to increase their breathing capacity— a procedure that would be enough to produce emphysematous or cardiac beasts in any other breed.

A Chinese acupuncturist who treats their attacks of neuritis or sciatica with reflexotherapy, tells me, anatomical chart in hand, that their motor innervation presents certain characteristics that are peculiar to the breed. This neural or medullary complexity may perhaps explain, in beasts as primitive as these, their strange susceptibility to the magnetic influence of man—as I've observed for a long time already in my relations with Allan: reactions to the simple suggestion of a glance, to the way certain gestures are made, to the way one approaches them, to the alternate shift from one shoulder to the other, to the placing of the right or left hand, etc.—not to mention the voice. I intend to carry on this experimentation more methodically with Allan, and I don't think it impossible that I may one day be able to induce a magnetic half-sleep in him.

[. . .]

172

Peking, April 20, 1919

Dearest Mother,

How happy I am at all you tell me about my two sisters, and how good it is to know you can once more find time for music in the midst of all the terrible day-by-day worries of your life.

No cause to worry about me. My health is as satisfactory as ever.

[. . .]

You mentioned the question of animal magnetism again, which you were always aware of in me and which has nothing to do with hypnotism. (Besides, here I experiment with it only on animals, my horse Allan, for example.) And you remind me of things in my childhood and adolescence—studies of the magnetic power of my childish hand which were undertaken by Dr. Damany.

Yes, I do remember that excellent navy doctor who, at Matouba,[1] saved me from a bad typhoid attack; and I've forgotten nothing of all his experiments. I also remember a lot of other occasions, in various countries and in my adult years, when this same power was studied, and even utilized through me for the benefit of others. Haven't I even helped all of you at times, within the family circle, in allaying physical suffering or certain organic discomforts? But what you don't know about is the secret sadness that I have harbored as a result of all this. You are wrong in thinking that there is in this power something special that may be put to advantageous use in a man's life. It would really be too disappointing, apart from all moral considerations, to have to think that every gesture of human sympathy, every confidence, every affection and every attraction—even of a passionate sort—that one might arouse were only an automatic result of the determinism that is animal magnetism. What sadness and what cumulative loneliness in the depths of a man's heart, in that case! Does mother-love alone escape from such a law?

The good doctor of my childhood never suspected all the loneliness that was sealed up within me because of this. So great is the sadness caused by this purely physical power, that I have always forbidden myself to use it voluntarily for the purpose of controlling men or in any way imposing myself on women. I have never used it except on myself or to assuage physical pain in those close to me, when they asked me to do it.

The professional Chinese magnetizers—who are very rare in this country where one commonly finds mediums (that is, the exact opposite of a magnetizer)—are, to my knowledge, the only Chinese who are devoid of gaiety.

[. . .]

1. Matouba, in Guadeloupe, on the western slope of Basse-Terre, not far from the volcano La Soufrière, was the site of a plantation belonging to the Dormoys, the maternal branch of AL's family. Because of its altitude, it was ideal for summer

habitation and for growing coffee-beans. The main dwelling at Matouba was La Joséphine, which was swept away much later (1964) by a hurricane.

173

Peking, May 17, 1919

Dearest Mother,

I am giving a letter for you to a Chinese lady, a friend of mine, who wishes at all costs to reach you and give you first-hand news of me—of all the things that your grown son couldn't tell you himself or that were told in letters that never reached you.

Madame Tan Pao-chao, wife of General Tan Pao-chao,[1] is going to join her husband for a time in Paris, where he is on mission as a deputy to the official Chinese delegation to the Peace Conference and future military attaché to the Chinese legation in London.

Madame Tan comes from an old and important Manchu family, and her heart is still faithful to her ancestors. Her father,[2] who was a high dignitary of the Imperial Court, was Chinese Ambassador to Paris in 1900 at the time of the Boxer Rebellion. His three children, two little girls and a boy, received a French education there; and he himself, in such a difficult diplomatic position, managed to carry off the situation successfully with all the intellectual refinement, moral elegance, and tact of an old Asian aristocrat who was remarkably open to the psychology of the Parisian milieu. Unofficially, he devoted all his private activity to artistic and literary personalities who at that time exerted a certain influence on the Parisian avant-garde; and he turned his Legation into a private center of culture whose influence contributed a great deal to making orientalism fashionable at a time of very hostile feelings toward China. His private relations with the whole Goncourt entourage did a great deal in this connection, and it was his son, a translator of Chinese works into French, who was actually the discreet co-author of a famous work by Judith Gautier.[3] Upon their return to China, the two daughters joined the Imperial Court, where they were the two youngest maids of honor of the old Dowager Empress and Regent of China, the famous Tz'u-hsi[4] of notorious and sinister memory, whose extraordinary personality and implacable despotism succeeded in prolonging the absolutist regime for quite a long time. Madame Tan's memories of all the mysteries of the old Imperial Court are fascinating. When the Ch'ing dynasty collapsed at the time of the 1911 revolution, she, a Manchu, managed to find safety by finally agreeing to marry a Chinese, a young officer in the army of the South, who had been in France at the same time she had, as a student at Saint-Cyr and Saumur, but whom the old Manchurian ambassador had never deigned to consider as a possible suitor for his daughter's hand. The marriage has been childless. . . . (Madame Tan's sister, Princess Der-Ling,[5] in the same historical circumstances, married an American. Indeed, both women have American blood in their veins through a maternal grandmother.)

At the present time, as Mistress of Ceremonies at the Presidential Residence of the Chinese Republic, she is managing, with good taste—that is, with a great deal of style, elegance, and tact, not devoid of humor at times —to establish some fitting continuity between the present and the past in Chinese state etiquette. She seeks always to use her personal influence in the service of her deep pro-French sympathies. She does this with a delicacy and a warmth of heart that the sisters of our Mission Schools and many of our charitable works have benefited from. She has helped me personally a great deal in my professional life by facilitating access to Chinese circles, both private and official, that are usually rather closed to foreigners, and in which it is always difficult to find your way about.

She has made it possible for me to understand a lot of things in my contacts with a very complex, frequently even a very hidden, China, and she has always been able to broaden the areas of my curiosity about it in a most intelligent way.

So do be kind and welcoming to her. You can trust her completely and question her about many things in my day-to-day life. Give her your best advice on shopping in Paris—on purchases for her wardrobe and on all the unexpected problems she might face as a foreigner in Paris. You'll notice right away the extreme simplicity of her bearing in private, so naturally resulting from the inborn distinction of her race. And her delicate mastery of French will make things easier for you. (She also speaks English and Russian with the same kind of mastery.)

I am giving General Tan's wife several personal letters to friends in Paris, the Berthelots among them. She will also deliver a few small souvenirs to you from me, which I hope to add to in the next pouch. She herself picked out for me the present I am sending to my sister Paule for her wedding; it is an authentic and very ancient robe of the sort that was formerly worn by great ladies at the Chinese Imperial Court in ritual festivals and great official ceremonies. I saw one of them in London that an English friend had made into an evening gown. Madame Tan is also bringing a ceremonial costume of ancient style worn by Manchu children—this for my god-son at my sister Marguerite's.

My heart is moved, dearest Mother, at the thought that a human being arriving from China will soon be telling you, "I saw your son, who loves you, and who talked about you."

I press all of you to my heart, you and my sisters, and especially my big Ysan,[6] whom I think of a great deal at this moment and to whom I want to write at very great length.

Your son,   A.

1. Dates on General Tan were unavailable.

2. Yü Keng, of the Manchu White Banner Corps, was appointed Chinese Ambassador to France in 1899 and remained at that post for four years. He died in 1905.

3. Judith Gautier (1850-1917), daughter of Théophile Gautier and an author in her own right, early in life developed an interest in Far Eastern culture. Her first book, *Le Livre de jade* (1867), published under the pseudonym "Judith Walter," was an adaptation of Chinese poems. She continued to exploit the Chinese and Japanese veins in subsequent works, including a play, *La Fille du Ciel* (1911), written in collaboration with Pierre Loti.

4. Tz'u-hsi (1834-1908), Empress and then Regent of China.

5. Princess Der-Ling married an American, Thaddeus C. White, in 1907. She is the author of several memoirs, the best-known of which is *Two Years in the Forbidden City* (1911).

6. "My big Ysan" refers to AL's sister Eliane.

174

Peking, January 3, 1920

Dearest Mother,

Is this the end of the Chinese torture that I've endured for such a long time—that is, the continued uncertainty of our postal communications? It will have taken more than the end of the war, the recent abolition of inter-Allied censorship in the Far East, and the overdue revelation of a postal scandal in Japan to clear up any number of the unexpected aspects of this whole question. But there's no point in telling you more about it. At last it's over! Even French censorship has been discontinued in China, Chinese censorship is going to be completely discontinued, and then the Japanese—the worst of all. Naturally, I will say no more about the route through Russia. I'll send this letter via the United States or Canada, which means via Japan.

A letter that my sister Paule, in Italy, had managed to get into the Italian diplomatic pouch for me, actually did get here, bearing the address of the Italian Minister, Garbasso; but *he* had just been recalled from Peking to take charge of Tittoni's diplomatic bureau in Rome, so my sister's letter was duly forwarded from Peking to Rome, and from there it has been sent back to me by Garbasso himself.

All that you tell me about the long silence between us that resulted is very discouraging. I just don't know where or how to pick up where I left off, even if I summarize, and tell you all the things I wanted to but wasn't able to.

Here is, however, what is the most important or essential: Upon the personal insistence, in Paris, of the Chinese Minister of Foreign Affairs, Lu Cheng-hsiang, and on my own insistence as well, Philippe Berthelot finally relented and backed up my acceptance of a position as political counselor to the presidency of the Republic of China, a post to be created especially for me and offered to me under exceptional conditions. I readily understood his personal reticence, even disapproval, friendly though it was; and I was quite upset about it, for he had already, quite a while ago, led me to understand in a very friendly way his disappointment, as a senior officer, at seeing me stay on so long in China and turn a deaf ear to calls from Paris. I wonder if he has finally understood the material considerations that forced me, against my wishes, to accept such a change in my long-range plans? Did he fear, finally, that he might see me one day forced to accept something worse—namely, outside the sphere of all diplomatic activity, one of those financial posts as counselor in the field that several large European banks have already offered me? The project is now being studied by Paris and Peking. To judge its merits, I'll have to wait for the return to Peking of Minister Lu Cheng-hsiang, who is being delayed in Paris by his functions as chairman of the Chinese delegation to the Peace Conference.

However unusual the proposed post may be, it would have the exceptional advantage for me of reconciling my availability to the Chinese government and my maintenance of a "detached status" in the French administration of Foreign Affairs in which I would retain my seniority rights and the possibility of resuming service in French diplomacy at any time. And my work in such a special post would still be a diplomatic activity and most suitable to my taste and aptitudes.

I certainly would not, today, lightly throw over the traditional French diplomatic career, in which I have thus far been given privileged treatment. But I might very well have to resign myself to doing so, if I am—as I intend—to take control of my life as a man with a sufficiently firm hand so as to assure myself material independence against all future contingencies and, possibly, even give myself the right to act with a certain insolent disdain towards events as they occur.

I'll keep you informed about the final outcome of the project under study.[1]

[. . .]

There is something, dearest Mother, that you never talk to me about and that sometimes torments me whole nights through. How do you manage to live in Paris, materially, under present conditions? What I hear about the difficulties and the cost of living makes me terribly afraid for you, even though you are sure to have the good counsel and, if need be, the actual assistance of my banker brother-in-law. The cost of living, according to the statistics of the Ministry of Labor, has gone up one hundred per cent.

Please tell me what the status of your meager portfolio is, and what the state of your present resources is, approximately. You had shares in the Russian holdings of the 1913 Chinese Reorganization Loan. I am looking into that right now and will tell you more about it presently. And what about your Mexican securities?

[. . .]

1. See final paragraphs of following letter. (175)

175

Peking, April 21, 1920

Dearest Mother,

[. . .]

Everything I feared for poor, unhappy China has now come to pass. Her humiliation at the Peace Conference has been complete, and entering the war on the side of the Allied Powers has been of no benefit whatever to her.

More than the rejection of any other of her national demands, the refusal, at Versailles, to restore the province of Shantung, taken back from Germany, directly to Allied China and, instead, turning it over to Japan as a reward for war services, is an ignominious slap in the face to China. Worse—it is a political blunder whose consequences we shall pay for dearly. From now on, the whole pro-Western school here can only find itself disparaged and discredited.

The Chinese Delegation was obliged to leave the Conference without signing the Peace Treaty. Lu Cheng-hsiang, back in Peking, yesterday turned in his resignation as Minister of Foreign Affairs. I have no doubt that, in spite of all the friendly urgings of his friend, President Hsü Shih-ch'ang, he will retire definitively from public life, giving some question of health as the reason. Now his one and only concern is to preach the re-awakening of Chinese patriotism, and he is preparing some sort of national homage to the memory of Confucius, who was born in Shantung—the laying of an expiatory palm-branch in the cypress forest known as "The Forest of Confucius," on Taïchan Mountain. This is a grandiose national shrine devoted to the cult of pilgrims faithful to the teachings of the great Chinese sage, the place always selected in times of mourning to perpetuate loyalty to the sacred soil, faith pledged to the future of the country, and confidence in the precepts of reason and justice that have ruled the Chinese soul for more than four thousand years.

Shantung has always been considered the cradle of Chinese civilization and in fact remains the holy land of the Chinese people. The eyes of the whole Chinese world remain fixed on this province.

It is inconceivable that no one at the Peace Conference was able to realize for a moment the inescapable consequences of this iniquitous settling of accounts in the Shantung affair. Before ten years are out, the full extent of these consequences will be felt. A splendid opportunity has here been lost to assure China's future orientation toward the concert of Western Powers. Only Soviet Russia will gain any immediate advantage from all this. To come to this pass it took all the short-term stupidity of conservative British policy, faithful to its past in China and to its present alliance with Japan, and it also took the indifference of a Clemenceau in regard to Asia, and, finally and inexplicably, the total eclipse of the Wilsonian spirit.

Liang Ch'i-ch'ao,[1] more than ever, is reiterating his theme of the opposition between Chinese and Western civilizations, denouncing the imitation of Western methods as one of the principal causes of all the internal strife in China since the 1911 revolution. China, according to him, should no longer look for help or justice from the other Powers, and instead should work alone, fiercely, on its own recovery, political and social.

The hour of China's nationalistic awakening is bound to come, with a really explosive outburst against the Western world and complete abolition of the regime of "Capitulations."

Meanwhile, the political crisis between North and South has been revived by the South's criticism of the North, which it accuses of weakness in the face of the Allied Powers and even of suspected acquiescence towards Japan. The result is violent demonstrations of patriotic students against the central government. The South has always been hostile to entry into the war on the Allied side.

Here is how things were before this last turn of events in the Shantung affair: A peace conference between the North and the South had to be suspended because of the extreme demands from the South. The President of the Republic in Peking vainly offered his resignation without finding anyone to replace him. Sun Yat-sen at Canton had resigned as a member of the Southwest Confederation, and, fearing a meeting of minds between the militarists of the North and the South, had gone to Shanghai to preach another revolution; meanwhile the

Canton Parliament had launched a new project for a Permanent Constitution, contrary to the views of the central government.

[. . .]

I hardly need tell you that I have now abandoned any thought of taking a position as diplomatic counselor working in concert with the presidency of the Chinese Republic. It no longer makes any sense, offers no interest or possibility for useful action, would be very precarious, and could only, being inopportune and inappropriate, arouse the suspicion here that I am a mere parasite.

My conception of future developments in China, however personal it may be, is now so clear to me that I can not ignore it. So I am studying the possibilities of a return to France. The time has come for me to leave China. My one remaining desire is, before I leave Asia for good, to realize a few projects that I've nurtured for a long time, such as a little expedition into Central Asia. I'll tell you more about it when I've had a chance to think all this through.

[. . .]

1. See above, letter to his mother of 27 Dec. 1918. (170)

176

Peking, May 4, 1920

Dearest Mother,

It is settled, and everything is arranged: I'll be leaving for Kalgan[1] in five days, and from there I'll start off on my trek into Outer Mongolia. That will take me across the Gobi Desert to Urga, the very hypothetical capital of that country of nomads, not far from the Russian frontier. From there I intend to strike out a little way toward the west, as far as possible on horseback, with the object of studying the eventual possibility of returning to Europe via the old caravan trails through Sinkiang and Chinese Turkestan.

Don't be alarmed, I'll be very careful on this first expedition and in regard to any future plans as well.

For this first trip into Mongolia, everything has been methodically prepared, and the Chinese government has made special arrangements for me with the Mongolian authorities and the Living Buddha of Urga. Besides, I'm not going off by myself nor traveling on horseback. I'll cross the desert in an automobile (a huge American Buick) with two choice companions: my friend Dr. Bussière,[2] the Legation doctor who's already been on this sort of expedition in Iran, and my old friend Gustave-Charles Toussaint,[3] an orientalist specializing in Tibet who has an insatiable appetite for covering long distances and who is 'an old hand at traveling alone through Central Asia.

So everything is shaping up for the best, and I'm jubilant at finally being able to realize the dream that has haunted me for so long, the dream of living a bit of life as it really is, in the midst of a real desert. I used to talk about it as a child with Uncle Aemilio, planning an excursion to Sinai with a return trip through Thor and Arabia. And right here in Peking, during my hours of solitude, these desert expanses that extend through the west and northwest of China have exerted a hold on my thoughts, a fascination that approaches hallucination. The bits of the African desert that I glimpsed on the edges of the Red Sea never stirred my imagination nearly as much as these high Central Asiatic expanses. And quite apart from the mysterious physical attraction that this sort of thing always has for me, I am boundlessly curious about the repercussions on my inner self that may be set off by such a complete involvement of my whole being and by all the unknown ultra-human elements that may be revealed to me.

On my return, if I am forced to give up all thought of a projected return to Europe through Central Asia, I'll use up part of the long leave that is due me after almost five years in China by living on the high seas among the islands of the South Pacific. Then I'll go home via America, not Suez, as the French Administration of Foreign Affairs ordinarily forces us to do. So, during my absence, my mail will be held for me at the French Consulate General in San Francisco. At any rate, I don't think I'll ever be going back to China.

So, dearest Mother, you will soon have news from me about the Mongolian trip. No need at all to worry about this modest little jaunt.

With all my heart.   A.

1. Kalgan, about 125 miles northwest of Peking near a gate in the Great Wall, was the most important Chinese-Mongolian trading center of this period.

2. See above, letter 152, note 1.

3. See letter to Toussaint of 29 Mar. 1921. (185)

177

Peking, June 5, 1920

Dearest Mother,

Just got back from Mongolia. A marvelous trip! The expedition was a complete success from every point of view, always interesting, and frequently even fascinating. I'm still full of enthusiasm about it. And the "human experience" carried me, in spiritual terms, even further than I expected, to the very frontiers of the mind. My memories of all this will never fade.[1]

On the animal plane, I ran into wolves and met up with big wild dogs whose innocent ways were more instructive to me than those of the gazelles. As for a possible return to Europe through Sinkiang, the investigation was conclusive—there's not the slightest possibility. So now I am going to get to work arranging for my leave at sea, in the South Pacific, and, first of all, discussing with Paris the conditions of my return to the Quai.[2]

But I'll tell you all about this in another letter. Now I have to get busy on my regular routine at the Legation, with all the work that has accumulated during my absence.

[. . .]

1. This trip was to furnish much of the raw material of AL's celebrated poem, *Anabase* (1924). See letters to Larbaud of 20 Sept. 1923 (142), and 13 Oct. 1923. (143)
2. The Quai d'Orsay.

178

Peking, March 20, 1921

Dearest Mother,

The time has come; I am getting ready to leave China for good. I leave for Japan the second of April and will embark on the fourteenth at Yokohama for Honolulu, where I'll be able to pick up some sort of passage to Samoa, and from there to the South Sea Islands. I'll go back to France via America, not via Suez. I'll telegraph you from San Francisco and New York.

In California I'll undoubtedly stop over for a few days to see, if possible, my old London friend Agnes Tobin,[1] in her family place where she is still ailing. After that

I'll head straight for Washington where my official mail from Paris will be waiting for me. Then straight to Le Havre, on the French line.

I'll say no more. It's not a time for words, but for the emotion that grips me at the thought of clasping all four of you to my heart this year.   A.

It turns out that my decision to leave China for good came at just the right moment, because Berthelot, since he has been appointed Secretary General of Foreign Affairs, replacing that colorless and lazy Paléologue,[2] has privately made it very clear that he wants to see me return to Paris.

There's even a possibility of my having to sacrifice a part of my leave and cut short my escapade into Oceania, because there is talk of a projected International Conference that would be held soon in Washington, and the French Delegation would need a political expert on Chinese and Far Eastern questions.[3]

1. See above, letter 111, note 1. Apparently AL was not able to see Agnes Tobin, as he had hoped he would.

2. Maurice Paléologue (1859-1944), French diplomat who was Secretary General of the Ministry of Foreign Affairs briefly in 1920.

3. AL was, in fact, named to that very post. See above, *Introduction*, p. xii.

179

*On board the S.S. Manoa
(Matson Line) at sea,
May 17, 1921*

Dearest Mother,

I had to return to Honolulu in order to find a suitable ship to take me to San Francisco.

I'm writing to you on the high seas, in heavy weather,

having all the trouble in the world holding on to my little sheet of ship's paper, which seems impatient to fly off towards you.

My South Sea cruise went very well: Samoa, Fiji, Tonga, etc. Not the least incident nor the slightest disappointment in this marvelous cruise, except for being a little tired. When I landed in Honolulu the first time, I was rather sick with some sort of gastric upset or food-poisoning resulting from the bad food on the Japanese ship. An American doctor mistakenly treated me for typhoid, but I had the satisfaction of seeing my illness end suddenly after five days; and what really put me back on my feet completely was the fact that I was just in time to jump aboard the first ship in the harbor that was about to leave for the islands. The sea did the rest. Do you recall that good old family doctor who, when I was a child, used to say of me, "If anything ever happens to that one, all you have to do is to take him down to the sea, and he'll be on his feet in no time!" My dear Mother, you who hate the sea so much, it is not blood that you put in my veins, but sea-water.

I am traveling, on this boat, with a very good friend from China, whom I ran into in Honolulu. She's returning to her family in Chicago, after losing a small child whom I myself saw buried in Peking. (I can think of nothing sadder than what will become of that poor little body in the Chinese earth of a military cemetery where adults are buried after a salvo from the "Marines" or the "Sikhs" of the Legation detachments.) I'll be stopping in Chicago for a few days. After that, Washington and New York; and then the French steamer *Lorraine*, on which I've already booked passage by telegraph. That will be my seventh and last boat.

[. . .]

180

San Francisco, Stewart Hotel
May 19, 1921

Dearest Mother,

There's nothing from you in my mail.

The Consul confirms that they've been looking for me everywhere and that a telegram from Foreign Affairs is waiting for me in Washington, along with some official mail.

So I have to hurry off to Washington, and after that, to New York, to take the first available French boat. I'll telegraph you my sailing-date from New York. Through your cousin John Dal Piaz, the director-general of "Transat," you will have no trouble finding out the exact date and time of the boat-train's arrival in Paris. Tell my brother-in-law to meet me alone at the station, to embrace me and give me the first news about all of you, man to man.

I don't know what sort of life awaits me in Paris. I may have to put up quite a battle. I'll fight with such weapons as I have and will manage to make up for those I don't have. I now know what men are worth, and life has hardened me. My greatest strength, though no one suspects it, lies, as a matter of fact, in my personal detachment and total lack of ambition—contrary to what people think, and will always think, about me. So don't worry yourself about my future. Life will always provide me, in spite of myself, with what I do not ask of it. It's the way of the world.

For you, I'm eager to find better ways of organizing your family resources. The important thing at the moment, though, is the reunion of our five hearts.

I embrace you, my dear Mother, with deep emotion. Your grown son,   A.

Behind me—two bits of bad news in my mail from China:

—My Minister in Peking died shortly after my departure. Poor Madame Boppe is terribly alone with her tragedy.

—Young Chabanne-La Palice, nephew of Monsignor de Guébriant,[1] was killed in a race, riding a horse that he got from me, a remarkable beast, much finer than Allan, which had been given to me and of which I was particularly fond. I offered it to Chabanne-La Palice before I left, because there are some animals that one simply does not sell—because I loved this one and was sure it would be happy in the hands of such an excellent horseman, younger and lighter than I am, an officer, fresh from the African light cavalry. My only condition was to make its new master swear never to retrain this Asiatic animal in the European manner. He probably did not keep his promise and spoiled the animal's natural reflexes.

1. Monsignor Jean-Baptiste de Guébriant (1860-1935).

LETTER TO JOSEPH CONRAD

181

To Mr. Joseph Conrad
"Oswalds," Bishopsbourne,
via Canterbury
England

French Legation in China
Peking, February 26, 1921

Dear friend,

I have received your message through Agnes Tobin.
Our friend is still in California, and her health will
not permit her to come all the way out here; but from
California, thanks to her, I have more than once had
news of you in England.[1] I am replying to you by way
of the same intermediary.

I am very touched by your recalling my first visit to
Ashford in Kent, in the company of Agnes, before the
war—as I am by all your reminders of the friendly conversations we had in those days. Nor have I forgotten
anything that I carried away from visits with you; many
a scrap of those first informal chats we had in the evening, in the little downstairs apartment where a terrible
attack of gout confined you, recurs to me in the most
unexpected way.

I am still with you, poring over the old family album
that contains all of your Polish childhood. I still hear
you reciting the first stanzas of Edward Lear's "Jum-
blies," and assuring me that you found in them far more
of "the spirit of great adventures" than in the best sea-
authors, such as Melville. I still hear you becoming irritated at my passion for Dostoievsky and my distaste for
Turgenieff. And you surprise me again in confiding to
me that the French authors you know best are Molière

and Zola. And finally, you still show your annoyance when I repeat that for me you are the only real poet of the sea, whereas you claim that it is only the ship itself that you wanted to exalt—man's work against the sea like the bow bent against destiny or the fiddle rigged against the night.

I don't think you ever took my obsession with the sea seriously; it struck you as a literary affectation when, in fact, because of my birth, childhood, and ancient insular atavism on a small Caribbean island, the sea is to me something absolutely basic, mingled with my very blood; and without my noticing, it has spread to every part of my being.

There is nothing metaphysical in all this. When I was still very young, I heard a grown-up peremptorily state that woman was the fifth element. I countered bluntly, saying that it was the sea, which, in my mind, was quite distinct from water and air.

Dear, great, friend, to me you will always be the most humane man of letters I have ever met. Do you know what I admire most about you? Your abiding inability to pass judgment on those whom fate places in your path as friends.

Do you bring the same fatalism to your judgment of a whole period? The one in which I met you cast a lovely radiance on the earth. It was a golden age that still had about it, without our realizing it, much of the glorious leisure that once reigned over the empire of the Four Seas. The war has blighted all that and severed many a thread. But you are not one ever to be caught unawares by destiny; and the past disappears so suddenly into the depths of the sea that it forces us to confront our future masks with a sharper awareness. As long as there is still movement, there is no cause to despair of the morrow. The important thing is to live, with our strength intact, coiled close at hand like fine rope rolled upon the deck.

I was somewhat surprised by the curiosity you expressed about present-day China. I wonder if fate didn't do exactly the right thing in forever keeping you away from here? To every man his forbidden territory; China is yours, and you must not regret it!

China is surely the country least suited to a seaman. It is a land of peasantry and small artisans, and its immensely long coastline in no way affects its hostility to the sea. The individual Chinese, who does not like the sea, can live or work on the water only the way a peasant lives on the land, with his family and *lares* and all his land-gear. He constructs his finest high-decked junks like a Noah's ark to ride out the Flood, and he makes them of the same "eaglewood"[2] from which state coffins are made. When he fancies he is modernizing things, he goes about enthusiastically constructing ships of reinforced concrete! The last great families of Chinese lacquerers hated having to live at sea, off the coast of Petchili, so as to avoid the dust blown by the "yellow wind." (Ultimate easement imposed by a land-habitat upon the sea.)[3]

The whole of China is nothing but dust, an ocean of wind-blown dust, a rather poor imitation, in this, of the sea itself—that other mass of continental proportions, which at least preserves its cohesion, consistency, and integrity without ever lapsing into inertia.

I really can't imagine what I could offer you of interest here, unless it might be, from among the cosmopolitan fauna of Shanghai, a few fine specimens of the European adventurer; and beautiful adventuresses as well, transplanted from America or White Russia, arrogantly flaunting the respectability they have won. I might also throw in the astonishing corps of estuary pilots, comfortably supplied with bank accounts and extensive maritime connections, all of them from Europe, recruited among the Scots. And finally, in the Shanghai club, where the bar is the longest specimen of the cabinet-maker's art in the world ("long as an ocean-front"), you might casually pick up many a salty tale, and the confirmation of many tales already heard. You might even run into a few of your old shipmates. For sooner or later they all end up in Shanghai; and Shanghai is the only place between Java Head and Vladivostok that is still the prodigious crossroads of adventurers, an inexhaustible haunt of tough men, untamed and carved in one piece out of that rare material we call energy. For my part, I was immediately attracted by the western regions, looking towards the Chinese interior with its high central Asiatic rampart. But I could offer you nothing from that part of the world but a few very ancient land routes, worn down almost beyond use and memory, and, trudging these monotonous trails, a vast human community, perfectly anonymous and uniform, and infinitely gregarious—an undifferentiated mass forever impervious to individualism's happiest mutations.

For me, the feeling of being in a completely alien world comes in the western, and not in the eastern, regions of China—the same alienation that is produced in us by the strange anonymity of certain seas. Something, in short, rather extraplanetary.

Here the boundless earth is the most perfect imaginable simulacrum of the sea—a mirror image, like the very ghost of the sea. The obsessive memory of the sea makes itself strangely felt here. A mystery that I myself can attest to is that, in the Asiatic highlands and in the very heart of the desert, horse and rider still instinctively turn toward the east, where lies the invisible table of

the sea and the source of salt. The silent countryside
seems, at that moment, to awaken a distant sea-murmur
in one's ears. And in all the Mongolian or Tibetan
lamaseries, where no man has ever seen the sea, the
whole liturgy is based on an evocation of the sea; conch
shells are part of the cult; coral and mother of pearl are
altar ornaments; and the long, deep-sounding horns
mounted on the corner terraces of the temples are used
during the morning prayers to supply the distant rumble of the ocean.

In the expression of the faces of camel-drivers encountered in the Gobi Desert, I sometimes thought I caught
a glimpse of something like a seafarer's glance. And on
the approaches to the desert I have even run across nomad carts rigged with a sail as though they were at sea.
The gulls and terns of the Gobi (which I would some
day like to discuss with your friend Hudson) give the
same illusion.[4] (Actually, they fly down from the Arctic
Sea along the fluvial basins of northern Russia.)

There are in all these flat expanses in the interior
Chinese highlands, vast depressions or basins embedded
like ancient sea-floors. To the mind it is like the sea
turned inside out—land seeking to become sea, or sea,
out of mockery, becoming sediment—unity regained,
restlessness dispelled.

Does this marine transposition, so familiar to the geologist, explain why ancient astronomers bent over their
huge lenses, were unconsciously led to baptize as "seas"
the vast depressions on the surface crust of the moon
and other planets? Some day I'll put the question to the
new school of American astronomers. As for the spasm
of that gigantic medusa, the sea—the only thing really
comparable to it that I have ever known is the aurora
borealis.

Thus, the Chinese land-mass, quite unparadoxically,

has made me more aware than ever of my passion for the sea, which here tends to become an obsession. Never have I understood so clearly, here, far from the sea, how much the sea is part of us, and that one does not stray far from her without sacrificing part of oneself.

Besides, I am preparing to leave forever this country where I have lived for five years as a diplomat. I am going to spend a few months leave sailing among the South Sea isles. I'll return to France, afterwards, by way of America, where I shall see Agnes[5] once more.

I hope very much to see you again in England at your new address. I won't ask you about the book you are presently working on, for one must never do that. But I think about you a great deal, dear friend, and I hope that the old arthritis you suffered from now gives you enough respite to go on working with complete peace of mind. I have had with me here in China, along with the fine portrait you gave me, the last book you inscribed for me, *Some Reminiscences*, which reveals to us your most human side. You should know that, in this part of the world, you are the most widely read of English writers—much more than Kipling or Wells, whose human understanding and psychological insight seem really too rudimentary or superficial.

My very best wishes to you and yours—wishes chosen from those I deem most worthy of everything I esteem in you.

Cordially.   Saint-Leger Leger

1. See above, letter III, note I.
2. Eaglewood: the soft, resinous wood of a Southeast Asian tree, the agalloch (*Aquilaria agallocha*).
3. AL was to mention these lacquerers many years later in the poem *Exil* (1941). In that poem there is a long catalogue of "princes of exile," including "celui qui laque en haute mer avec ses filles, et ses brus, et c'en était assez des cendres de la terre"

(Canto vi). ["he who does the lacquering on the high seas with his daughters and his sons' wives, and they have had enough of the ashes floating above the land." (Devlin trans.)]

4. William Henry Hudson (1841-1922), the British naturalist and novelist (*Green Mansions*, 1904), friend of Conrad. Cf. a passage from *Anabase*: "Et quelques grands oiseaux de terre, naviguant en Ouest, sont de bons mimes de nos oiseaux de mer." (Canto vii.) ["And several great land birds, voyaging westwards, make good likeness of our seabirds." (T. S. Eliot trans.)]

5. Agnes Tobin. See above, letter iii, note i.

LETTER TO A EUROPEAN LADY[1]

182

Peking, March 17, 1921

No, dear friend, you must not come here. There's very little for you here. Your friends in London would all tell you that present-day China is no longer a country where one can travel in any kind of style.

As for me, I have only this to say to you: You are far too brimming with vitality and demand far too much of life for this worn-out land. China is nothing but dust, powdery loess blown in by the west wind, a land worn down to the bone by age. Don't come here and exchange the good + sign of Europe for the — sign of Asia. And above all don't slacken the grip on the reins of your marvelous vitality—reins you held so high. It's a question of breed, race, and blood; a loyalty in all things to the fine onward movement that carries us men and women of the Occident along with it. You are no more fit than I am for opium or day-long dreaming over Chinese silks. Too healthy and strong for all this negation, apathy, or amnesia—the real name of which is resignation or desertion. Nor is Chinese "time" made for you, nor its space without conflicts, nor its all-pervasive neutrality.

Believe me, there is nothing Byronic to be found in this country without margins, in all this flatness without relay or relief.

Besides, circulating in and around Peking is rather difficult at the moment. And the wonderful animals you ride in Ireland would inspire nothing but pity in you for the little short-legged mounts that are the only ones that can be used here.

As for tracking down really fine objets d'art, should you by some misfortune still have a taste for that sort of thing, they are far more available at the moment right in London. What remains here is just trinkets, not even real jewelry. And I can't imagine you're the kind of woman to become ecstatic over cricket cages, ivories, or jades. China hasn't had a place in the boudoirs or alcoves of our European women for a long time now. Leave all that curiosity about the usual Chinese things to the beautiful itinerant American women who arrive with letters of introduction to the Manchu family of the little deposed Emperor, with ready-made ideas about Taoism or Zen Buddhism, who want to smoke opium, and who swathe themselves in beautiful riding veils for protection against the evil smells of Peking.

No, dear friend, the amnesiac stare that China turns on us really has nothing invigorating in it for an Occidental woman of your kind. And should I add that China is very hard on the beauty of European women? They age ten years in one, right before our eyes, and the "yellow wind" has a way of ruining their skin, to the delight of the Chinese ladies.

Instead, go horseback-riding in Morocco, or motoring in the Spanish highlands.

Besides, I wouldn't be here to welcome you. I'm preparing to leave China, never to return. One has to know how to start afresh at the right moment, and the time is more than ripe for me after five years of diplomatic life in Peking. Everything here is showing its "seamy" side, and one fine day you long to see the "right" side. You feel you've had enough of China spread out so thinly across this cramped, half-fossilized planet. China, like its women, has hips too narrow ever to conceive any-

thing ample in life. Its very eroticism, a kind of accul-
turated product, merely tends to substitute a narrow
nervous exacerbation for fullness of being, both physical
and moral.

I am leaving because I have not yet made my peace
with the wild odor of this world, which is vast, somber,
and strong. And I am leaving also because I have exhausted the professional interest of the job that was entrusted to me here.

I'm going off to spend a few months living on the
high seas (the South Pacific) before returning by way
of America. Necessity to experience once again a little
of the living reality of the sea, which you love as much
as I do. And also, so much of the dust of Asia to be
washed out of one's mind, as one washes behind the
ears of a dirty child!

I'll be without a foreseeable address for some time to
come. You can write me care of the French Embassy in
Washington. I enjoy your letters; they are you, and not
London, Rome, or Paris.

I would have liked to accompany you on the trip to
Spain that I've recommended. With a good car, you can
reach many astonishing places in the high country of
northern Spain, where I myself once laid out an itinerary
for you.[2] Besides, it's the place in Europe that most resembles certain parts of China—the same stripped, deforested, flayed land, but with more bite, flavor, and
individuality. And the same dust, red or yellow, color
of human clay; and the same naked highlands of a big
country—a whole kingdom! The Russian composers
made no mistake when they chose Spain as the place
to develop their great Central Asian themes.

Go, go steep yourself in all that. And reach out to
anything that strikes your fancy. There is never anything hateful in this world—where it is important not

to make a mistake—except life going inert in our hands, "habit," "respite," "torpor," and especially forgetting, or simply not caring, to press onward.

Take care to avoid all that, and believe me as ever close to you.   Alexis Saint-Leger Leger

1. Recipient unidentified.

2. AL had traveled in Spain in 1911, visiting Aragon, Catalonia, both the Castiles, and the Asturias, and again in 1912. See letters to Larbaud of 28 Apr. 1912 (131), and May 1912. (132)

LETTER TO GUSTAVE-ADOLPHE MONOD[1]

183

To Gustave-Adolphe Monod   *French Legation in China*
Paris   *Peking (February 1921)*

Dear friend,

I recognized your handwriting, and my heart warmed just as it did fifteen years ago. I know nothing about you any more—except the most important thing of all, which is that you are you. I have lived for a long time in countries where one forgets all notions of time. Life is made up of a single, long, undifferentiated day; and during that day I came to know your friendship. I still prize it unreservedly. My affection is as real and deep as ever. It would be wonderful to see you again, and I say it to you unabashedly.

With the hope of seeing you very soon.

Alexis Leger

1. AL's schoolmate and friend in Pau. See earlier letters to Monod. (1-16)

LETTER TO JACQUES RIVIÈRE[1]

184

To Monsieur Jacques Rivière   *French Legation in China,*
Paris   *Peking, February 25, 1921*

Dear friend,

I am terribly ashamed of my very long silence. But please don't doubt my affection; that would pain me deeply.

I received your letter from Switzerland. All I could do was remain silent. A year is made of a single day; life is made of one year. It was yesterday that I was conversing with you in closest friendship.

I am returning. I'll be seeing you again. I am sailing any day now, but I don't think I'll be in Paris before the end of May at the earliest.

Embrace Jacqueline for me, and be sure to remember me to Madame Rivière.

Affectionately.   A. Saint-Leger

I've read everything of yours that found its way to me here: happy to know that your voice commands increasing respect.

1. See earlier letters to Rivière. (17-49)

LETTER TO GUSTAVE-CHARLES TOUSSAINT[1]

185

To Monsieur Gustave-Charles Toussaint   [*Peking*]
Legal Counsel to   *March 29, 1921*
the French Legation in China
High Consular Judge
presiding at Shanghai

Dear friend, I am leaving.

I'm deeply disappointed at leaving without being able to shake your hands warmly.

I am leaving China with no idea of ever returning. It is wrong to become accustomed to any one place, especially in Asia. I'm a man of the Occident and have never smoked opium. I'll always have an English saddle in my baggage, along with a mariner's compass. Both of us have had enough experience of China to have the right to quote that Ptolemaic maxim we used to enjoy repeating to each other in the midst of the Gobi Desert: "Give me running water to drink!" And we now know enough of life and death not to be any longer obliged to listen, in China, to "what the weights of a clock say in secret converse with each other." (That's one of your own verses, dear friend.)

So let's hasten to make a new start. "On to new horizons!" is the order of the day. You understand all this—who were such a good companion in adventure to me in Mongolia. I regret infinitely that events in Russia didn't permit us to go through with the expedition to Kamchatka that we had already gone to such lengths to prepare. Disconsolate also at the thought that I couldn't join you at Feng-chen last fall to go galloping off on "a wolf-colored horse" over the four hundred and fifty kilometers of muddy, flooded wilderness trails leading to the great yellow tent where the silver coffin of Genghis Khan is enshrined. You are, unless I am mistaken, the third Frenchman—after Bonin and Lesden[2]—ever to have accomplished that feat, which was certainly worth your thirty days on a nomad diet of sorghum pancakes and sour milk. A lost chance that I will never cease to regret.

I'm not taking anything along from Asia except the horse's skull we brought back from the Gobi[3] and the shaman's thunder-stone that we picked up near the Tolgoit of Urga.

I am eager to get away from Peking. "Satiety" is an all-powerful word when once spoken. I suddenly have enough of the rationalistic grand style of a China that exists only in the imagination, enough of the paper processions in the streets of China, enough of the clay-whistle pigeons in the Peking sky, enough of the bowing of that friendly hoopoe on the sheet-iron roof of the legation.

China has sufficiently enlarged for me the field of my earthly vision on this narrow planet. At the moment I dream only of life on the high seas and of sailing between the isles of Oceania. I'm going to use up, there, the accumulated leave I have coming to me, and which I couldn't devote to my cherished project of returning to Europe via Central Asia. I'm sailing from Tientsin on a little Japanese steamer that will give me a chance to become better acquainted with the small islands of the Korean straits and the Inland Sea of Japan. At Yokahama I'll take the *Shinyu Maru* to the Hawaiian Islands, and at Honolulu I'll find some "tramp steamer" headed for the South Seas. Your Padma Sambava[4] danced his skull-dance long enough for me on the agate terraces of the Gobi; now I must have the bare tables of the sea.

Later I'll return home through America, after I've managed to build up enough skin and bones again to be able to present a flesh-and-blood man, and not a wraith, to the Quai d'Orsay.

Dear friend, dear Great Shaman, we shall surely see each other again somewhere. In the meantime, you must continue the publication of your great Tibetan text, because the *Padma Tanguig*[5] is a fine and important thing. Pelliot[6] promised me he would help you to interest the big scientific publishers in it. And you must also—I insist on it—publish the verse of Gustave-Charles Toussaint.[7]

If you reach Europe before I do, salute your native Brittany for me. Brittany has always been a holy land to those who, like myself, count three centuries of "men of the Atlantic" in their Antillean ancestry.

Yours most cordially.   Alexis Leger

1. Gustave-Charles Toussaint (1869-1938), an orientalist specializing in Tibetan studies. Along with Dr. Bussière, he was AL's other traveling companion on the trip to the Gobi Desert. (See AL's letters to his mother of 4 May 1920 [176], and 5 June 1920 [177].) At the time of AL's residence in Peking, Toussaint was legal counsellor to the French Legation. He was associated with Staël-Holstein, Pelliot, Granet, and Bacot—all of whom were acquaintances of AL.

2. Charles Eudes Bonin (1865-1929), was a French explorer who followed the Marco Polo route from east to west around 1900. Comte Jacques Bouly de Lesdain was another French explorer who traveled widely in Asia and published several books about his travels, including *En Mongolie* (1903) and *Voyage au Thibet* (1908).

3. Another detail incorporated into the poem, *Anabase*: "—Mais dis au Prince qu'il se taise! à bout de lance parmi nous/ ce crâne de cheval!" (Canto III.) ["—But say to the prince to be still: on the point of a lance, amongst us,/ this horse's skull!" (T. S. Eliot trans.)]

4. The Tibetan guru Padmasambhava, founder of lamaism.

5. At the lamasery of Lithang on 3 Apr. 1911, Toussaint had

acquired an excellently preserved manuscript of the Tibetan liturgical work, *Padma Thang Yig*, which recounts the successive existences of Padmasambhava (see preceding note). Toussaint's translation appeared fragmentarily in 1923 and 1925 but was not published in its entirety until 1933, when the Institut des Hautes Etudes Chinoises in Paris published *Le Dict de Padma. Padma Thang Yig, Ms de Lithang*, in Vol. III of the *Bibliothèque de l'Institut des Hautes Etudes Chinoises*.

6. Paul Pelliot (1878-1945), the eminent French sinologist who, in 1904-1906, along with Sir Aurel Stein, exploited the treasure trove of manuscripts, imprints, and other articles discovered in 1900 by a Tibetan monk in one of the Touen-Huang grottoes of Kaman on the edge of the Gobi Desert. AL came to know Pelliot in Peking and remained in touch with him after AL's departure in 1921. See letter to Le Gallais of 1 Feb. 1957. (355)

7. Toussaint had already published two books of verse in his younger days: *Stupeur, poèmes* (1891) and *Le Cœur qui tremble* (1892). In 1935, in a very limited private edition, he published *Miroirs de goules*, a book of poems that contains one piece (No. XXXV: "J'ai marché") bearing an epigraph taken from AL's *Anabase*: "L'été plus vaste que l'Empire suspend aux tables de l'espace plusieurs étages de climats" (Canto VII). The first stanzas of this rather long poem read:

> J'ai marché tout autour de toi
> O terre, pour t'étreindre, ô terre!
>
> Au cœur froid de la Haute Asie
> Parcouru royaumes déserts;
> Salué tes jeux sur le steppe,
> Givre étincelant du matin!
>
> Par au delà du Grand Gobi
> Jonché d'agate et de squelettes,
> Au Tolgoït d'Ourga surpris
> Les bêtes déchirant les corps;
>
> Sur un coursier couleur de loup,
> Atteint par sables en tourmente
> La yourte royale où s'appendent
> L'arc et le glaive de Gengis; . . .

[I have walked all around you, to embrace you, O Earth!
In the cold heart of the Asian highlands I have wandered

through desert kingdoms, greeted, upon the steppe, the play
of hoarfrost sparkling in the morning light!

Beyond the Great Gobi Desert strewn with agate and
skeletons, to the Tolgoit of Urga, where I suddenly came
upon beasts tearing bodies asunder;

On a wolf-colored charger, whipped by whirling sands,
I visited the royal yurt where hang the bow and blade of
Genghis; . . .]

LETTER TO ANDRÉ GIDE[1]

186

To Monsieur André Gide   *Honolulu (Hawaii),*
Villa Montmorency, Auteuil   *Waikiki Beach*
Paris   *May 10, 1921*

Dear friend,

I know what friendship is—its reticence, its scruples, its right to silence. I never doubted your friendship; I ask you simply to believe in my affection.

[. . .] I'll no longer be in China when you get there. You will like that anonymous and lunar land, where space takes on a value all its own, like that of time. You'll especially like Peking, the astronomical capital of the world, beyond place and time, ruled by the Absolute. Hurry and go before the "Tartar City" ceases to be what it is—a beautiful abstraction, a stone encampment for the mind's ultimate maneuvers, the last "geometrical locus" in this world.

I really believed that you would be coming. You couldn't have returned by way of Turkestan, because the Marco Polo route is once again closed; but I could have taken you to the Gobi Desert, where I lived for a whole month. Nothing is more prodigious than the logic of the landscape on the approaches to Central Asia.

I expect to be in Paris around mid-June. It's painful to have to take that road again. But I'll be happy to see you, and I'll certainly make every effort to do so, even if you're in the country. I won't have much time left to decide, on the professional plane, what new country I want to be stationed in, because I've already used up most of my leave along the way, and I still have several foreign countries to visit. I'm getting a few days rest here after wandering around the South Seas (Fiji, Samoa, Tonga, Tahiti, etc.) preceded by a short stay in Japan.

I was happy to run across your works sometimes in the most unexpected ways. In this part of the world they don't read much beyond the brochures put out by travel agencies and steamship companies. Which is really not literature to be disdained. I can't think of more fitting traveling companions for the works that I admire and love.

You must believe, dear friend, that my very best wishes have always been with you. I've read everything by you that has reached me here. And I have only myself to blame for not having heard the sound of your voice more often. I know you are not the man to misjudge my silence. Life is made of one day only. There's nothing more to say. But affection has nothing to do with time, and the heart of man keeps its same clairvoyance wherever it may be.

Please pay my respects to Madame Gide, whose charming welcome I have never forgotten.

I'll see you soon, I hope. I am about to sail for America.

St.-L. Leger

My temporary address in Paris:
c/o M. A. Dormoy
5, avenue Alphonse, XIII

1. This letter is out of order in OC, where it is printed on pp. 893-894, preceding the letter to Toussaint of 29 Mar. 1921. See earlier letters to Gide. (93-120) Gide never made the proposed trip to China here alluded to.

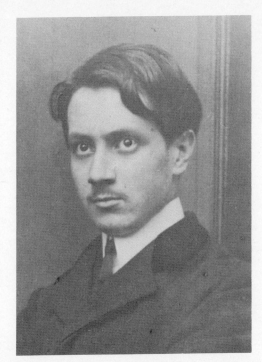

1. Leger at the age of seventeen, Bordeaux, 1904

2. The Habitation du Bois-Debout, the Dormoy house at Capesterre, Guadeloupe, 1899 or earlier

3. Valery Larbaud, about 1910
(top left)

4. Gabriel Frizeau, Bordeau about
1910 (?) (top right)

5. Jacques Rivière in 1922 (bottom)

6. André Gide in 1910 (top left)
7. Francis Jammes in 1904 (top right)
8. Paul Claudel in 1905 (bottom)

9. Leger in China, at temple of Tao Yu, about 1918 (top)

10. Leger in Peking, about 1918 (bottom left)

11. Leger and Chinese dignitaries in front of the Ministry of Foreign Affairs in Peking, about 1917 (bottom right)

12. Francis Biddle at the War Crimes Trials, Nüremberg, 1946 (top left)
13. Katherine Biddle, about 1949 (top right) 14. Allen Tate, about 1942(?)
(bottom left) 15. Leger with Katherine and Francis Biddle, near Savannah,
Georgia, 1942 (bottom right)

16. Leger in his study in Washington, D.C., about 1947 (top) 17. Georges Braque and Alexis Leger, Paris, 1962 (bottom)

18. Leger in front of his house, Les Vigneaux, France, about 1958

LETTERS FROM EXILE

LETTERS TO MRS. FRANCIS BIDDLE
(1940-1957)

To Mrs. Francis Biddle[1]   *Shelton Hotel, New York*
Washington, D.C.   *August 27, 1940*

Chère Madame,

Through the good offices of a foreign diplomat I have received an undated letter from your sister, Marguerite de Bassiano,[2] which brings me news of my family in Europe and speaks of her family in America.

I do not know how long my stay in the United States will be, but I very much hope that I shall have the opportunity of meeting you here.

Mme. de Bassiano, who thinks I am in Washington at the present time, asks me to give you news of her. At the time when she wrote me, she was staying near the Italian-Swiss border, ready to leave for Geneva. Concerning you, she repeated all the affectionate things that I have often heard her say when she was living in France, in Paris or Versailles.

And this, *chère Madame,* is what I would have liked to say to you in person, along with all those other things that belong to the gods.

Please accept, along with my profoundest respects, my very special good wishes.   Alexis Leger

1. Mrs. Biddle, née Katherine Garrison Chapin, was the wife of Francis Biddle, who in 1940 was Solicitor General of the United States. He was to be appointed Attorney General in 1941. The Biddles had always had a great interest in literature and the arts.

2. Marguerite de Bassiano, Princess Caetani (1880-1964), née Marguerite Chapin, was Mrs. Biddle's half-sister. She married

Roffredo de Bassiano, later Prince Caetani and Duke of Ser-
moneta. The Caetanis had a home in Versailles, the Villa Ro-
maine, which became an important meeting-place for artists and
writers of all nationalities and persuasions. Marguerite Caetani
established the steadfastly non-commercial literary review, *Commerce*, in Paris in 1924. Its official editorial staff was made up
of Valery Larbaud, Léon-Paul Fargue, and Paul Valéry, with AL
as an unlisted "silent partner." AL's friendship with Marguerite
Caetani dates from those years. *Commerce* continued publication
until 1932.

The Caetanis were obliged to stay in Italy during World War
II. After the war, Marguerite founded another international
literary review, this time based in Rome and bearing the name
of the street on which the Palazzo Caetani is situated, *Botteghe
Oscure*.

188

To Mrs. Francis Biddle   *New York, Shelton Hotel*
Philadelphia   *September 13, 1940*

Chère Madame,

There was so much kindness and delicate tact in your
welcome[1] that I felt for the first time a softening of that
inner hardness which I force myself to maintain here
in the solitude of my exile. In spite of the fear I sometimes feel that I might let my sadness appear too openly,
and of the qualms I might have at doing so amongst
friends, I would not have resisted the temptation of
seeing you again this week and of sharing with you and
your husband, in the "family weekend" atmosphere in
Philadelphia, a few hours that would have meant more
to me than you can imagine.

Unfortunately, I shall not be free to leave New York
tomorrow. I have with me at the moment a French
diplomat-friend[2] whom I am trying to help as best I can.
He used to be one of my most trusted associates in Paris,

and I have to discuss a certain number of questions with him before he embarks for France [. . .].

Would you be so kind as to tell your husband, until such time as I shall have the pleasure of meeting him in person, with what great interest I followed the evolution of the debate at the American Bar Association convention in which his great moral authority came into play so propitiously? That discussion allowed Francis Biddle, by elevating the debate, before the Criminal Law Section, to bring up one of the most urgent needs of the moment—which is likewise one of the most basic for any democratic regime—the safeguarding, in fact, even the strengthening, of executive authority—entirely compatible with respect for institutions which, more than any others, really demand it.

Please accept, along with my profoundest respect, my best wishes, to be shared by you with Francis Biddle.

Alexis Leger

1. On receipt of the preceding letter, Mrs. Biddle made a special trip to New York to meet AL and offer him the hospitality of her home in Washington and Philadelphia.
2. Unidentified.

189

To Mrs. Francis Biddle   *Shelton Hotel, New York*
Washington, D.C.   *November 6, 1940*

Chère Madame and dear friend,

In this very moving phase of American national life, I was so overjoyed for your country by the outcome of the presidential elections[1] that I instinctively look for a sympathetic friend toward whom I can turn, in mind and heart.

I had followed with interest everything your husband did as he took part in the presidential campaign, and I had always admired the high level on which his participation exerted its moral authority.

I had also heard Mr. Roosevelt at Madison Square Garden. It was the first time I ever saw him; and sizing up this fine new breed of elected chief with an unprejudiced eye, I was deeply impressed by the fact that, in our time, a democracy had the good fortune to be embodied in a true aristocrat of the mind and spirit. Up to that moment I had been able to judge only the statesman, whom it is easy to admire; and I was fearful that I might be disappointed by something in his platform on domestic issues. Well, in a completely sober and unadorned speech, I had the profound satisfaction of never catching any hint of facile self-indulgence or of his giving in to either rhetoric or demagoguery—the two usual temptations of the political orator.

The man I heard speak is not "cheap."[2] His supreme right on the personal level resides precisely in the way he manages never to sacrifice his deepest inner demands, his most secret demands, to the indispensable political adroitness. In reality, the true human drama is that of a secret solitude in the midst of the crowd, the solitude of every leader of men who has a mission to fulfill in this world.

I have thought about you so often since I received your last letter. You have no idea how someone like yourself can make one love your country. Won't you let me read some of your poems?[3] I really don't deserve to, it's true, because of my silence, which I can't explain even to myself. How have I been able to go on for so long without thanking you for your delightful letters? I was beset with so many personal worries here that I finally lost all notion of time. I am only just emerging from that Gobi Desert where remaining silent struck me as my first social obligation [. . .].

It won't be long before I take the train to Washington in order to study some of the problems that my present situation has created. I recently learned through the newspapers that the Vichy Government, immediately after the Franco-German talks in Paris, had taken the most extreme measure against me—that of depriving me of my French nationality. Certain consequences of this act, especially in material matters, tragically affect my poor mother, with whom I can not even communicate.[4]

If I did not have to endure that torture—the only one that can touch me to the quick—I would really, so far as I myself am concerned, scarcely deserve to be pitied. For, do I not now have the same status as my friends, the squirrels in Central Park and the seagulls along the East River, for whom my exile's budget will always provide enough "peanuts" and "crackers?"[5] As for exile itself, is it not everywhere in this world, beginning in the heart of a woman? In any event, I find it in the eyes of the little black boy who shines my shoes and, even more, in the eye of the policeman's horse who, every night, with the same gentleness, refuses the lump of sugar I offer him out in the street.

A bientôt, chère Madame, dear friend. I'll be so happy to see you again and to meet your husband at long last.

Please believe in the constancy of the homage and good wishes I place at your feet. And in that word "constancy" may you find the sense, as I do, of a friendship much older than its actual age.

Alexis St.-L. Leger

I've just this moment received a telegram from Rome from your sister, who was able to obtain—I have no idea how—more news of my mother in Paris, as of October 18.

1. This letter was written immediately after the presidential election of 1940, in which Franklin Roosevelt was elected for an unprecedented third term, defeating Wendell Willkie. The portions of this letter relative to Roosevelt's behavior during the electoral campaign were communicated, presumably by Francis Biddle, to President Roosevelt, who thereafter took a personal interest in AL. At this date Roosevelt had known of AL for several years already, since William Bullitt had repeatedly spoken about AL in his private correspondence with Roosevelt from 1933 on. See letter 191, note 4; and *For the President Personal and Secret: Correspondence between Franklin D. Roosevelt and William C. Bullitt*, Orville H. Bullitt, ed. (Boston: Houghton Mifflin, 1972), *passim*.

2. English in original.

3. Under her maiden name of Katherine Garrison Chapin, Mrs. Biddle had already published several volumes of verse, including *Outside of the World* (1930), *Time Has No Shadow* (1936), and *Plain Chant for America* (1942).

4. The Vichy government stripped AL of his French nationality in Oct. 1940, at the same time confiscating his property and revoking all official honors that had been bestowed upon him. AL's mother and two of his sisters were living in Occupied France, so that any direct communication with them was impossible.

5. English in original.

190

To Mrs. Francis Biddle   *Shelton Hotel, New York*
Washington, D.C.   *December 10, 1940*

Dear friend,

The delicacy of your welcome and the charm of your hospitality were such a precious thing to me that I have gone on living, in my thoughts, in that warmly human atmosphere that, for an instant, was once again mine.

Having once more donned my exile's armor—which resembles too closely the outfit of a deep-sea diver—I feel that I now discern more clearly, across the depths of silence, the quality of those friendly voices that I can still hear in your house. In this world where words are everywhere so suspect, it is rare that one can do so well without them as one can in your presence. Your husband, man of letters that he is, must sometimes be tempted to address you as a character in Shakespeare (Coriolanus, I believe) addressed his wife: "My gracious silence. . . ."[1]

Please be sure to tell him what a happy memory I keep of the hours I was able to share with him in the intimacy of your family circle. Without his knowing it, his conversation enlightened me in human terms about any number of things in America that strike me as so very essential. I like it that so free an intelligence never cuts itself off from its living source, and that such a fine independent judgment always goes hand in hand with so much humanity.

On returning here I found news from France that has stunned me. It is easy for a man to accept a personal ordeal, to welcome it even, as one does a stranger who crosses one's threshold. But how can we endure, at a distance, the ordeal of those who are dear to us and for whom we can do nothing? The worst suffering a man can endure, as a man, is it not having to fail others? [. . .]

I've had to put off my departure for Chicago because of a cold I caught here that has worn me out.

At any event, I intend to settle down in Washington, come January. I am going to write MacLeish, confirming without further delay my acceptance of the position that he has been good enough to reserve for me in the Library of Congress.[2] I wouldn't want him to think for a moment that I have ever underestimated the interest

of that position or failed to recognize the trouble he
went to so as to be sure that all the arrangements were
just right for me.

Since I've come back here, I have noticed quite a
number of blunders committed in Washington. Concerning the two basic questions on which the outcome
of the war, and of the world, depends, the first question
—the Mediterranean business, is turning out far better
than one could have predicted two months ago. But the
second question—material aid to England (aircraft and
ships)—is turning out much less well than one had
hoped two months ago[3] [. . .].

With my most faithful thoughts, please find here a
host of good wishes to be shared with my sympathetic
co-admirer of Montesquieu and Daumier, Francis Biddle
of Philadelphia, who had the impertinence to be born
in Paris.[4]   Alexis St.-L. Leger

1. Coriolanus to Virgilia in *Coriolanus*, II, I.
2. Archibald MacLeish (b. 1892), the poet, playwright, and
lawyer, was Librarian of Congress at this date and a close friend
of the Francis Biddles. Though MacLeish had spent a good deal
of time in France and had been an admirer of AL's *Anabase* ever
since 1925, he had never met AL. On learning of AL's presence
in New York and of his personal plight, he invited him to join
the staff of the Library of Congress as a consultant on the Library's French acquisitions. AL refused to accept any post that
would be paid for out of the treasury of a foreign power, no
matter how friendly to France. MacLeish was able to "tap" a
privately endowed fund that was under the Library's jurisdiction,
thus overcoming AL's major objection. MacLeish obtained a
similar arrangement for the German writer Thomas Mann, also
a refugee in the United States at that time. See the letters to
MacLeish. (221-245)
3. The British had successfully stymied Italian plans to dom-
inate the Mediterranean by destroying a good part of the Italian
navy at Taranto in Nov. 1940. At this same date, however, the
U.S. Congress still balked at giving all-out aid to Great Britain.

The Lend-Lease bill was not introduced into Congress until 10 Jan. 1941 and finally passed only in Mar. 1941.

4. Francis Biddle was born in Paris on 9 May 1886, while his parents were on a cruise to Europe.

191

To Mrs. Francis Biddle   *Washington, D.C.,*
Harvey Cedars,[1]   *July 18, 1942*
Long Beach Island
Ocean County (New Jersey)

My dear Katherine,

Nothing could have touched me more than the delicate way you thought of me in the midst of the sadness I have felt during these past hours that have been devoted to France [. . .].

But I wasn't able to take part personally in the events of this French week in New York after all, because I was detained here—and am still detained—in constant anguished expectation of receiving a telephone call which the Red Cross informed me might possibly be made between the 10th and 20th of July. Once more, thanks to your intercession, I received, from Unoccupied France, a telegram from a friend asking me to cable my telephone number for an immediate call "from a person very close to me who is looking after my mother." I just wonder from what country anyone might attempt to telephone me, since it isn't possible from France. I am consumed with fear of receiving bad news. And the waiting is interminable. For fear of missing this unpredictable phone call, I leave my apartment as little as possible. And I keep wondering whether my telegram actually reached its destination, through all the present censorship barriers [. . .].

I'm back again with my faithful insomnia, made worse by the exhausting ordeal of tropical nights in Washington at this season. One doesn't even have the energy to go out to get something to eat. My French friends of the Resistance must not have understood my being away from New York on the 14th of July. All I could do was send a message that was published in the French newspaper *Pour la Victoire*,[2] where I had the pleasant surprise of finding a very beautiful and noble message bearing the autograph signature of President Roosevelt, along with messages from Halifax, Litvinoff,[3] etc.

I find the American arrangement with de Gaulle well-conceived and well-balanced.

Bullitt,[4] about to leave for London, told me he had been ordered by Hull[5] to make unofficial inquiries for him about the exact situation and personal leanings or covert aims of those in the "Free French" circles [. . .].

I've just received a third appeal from Churchill[6] which embarrasses and bothers me, after everything that we said face-to-face to each other on this subject.

I think of you, dear Katherine, and of Harvey Cedars. If you sleep where I slept, in the upstairs room that faces the Atlantic, just remember that I never opened my eyes there at dawn, or saw the sun framed in my window, without thinking gratefully of all that I owe you and Francis. Ever since I have entered upon my ordeal as a refugee, I have never really been able to breathe freely, far from my loved ones, anywhere but with the two of you, under your roof.

Think a little about yourself as you do about others, being careful to do everything necessary to make the most, physically and morally, of what one can, and should, derive from Long Beach Island.

Faithfully.   Alexis

1. Harvey Cedars was the site of a summer house on Long Beach Island, New Jersey, belonging to Mrs. Biddle. It was there that the Biddles had offered a solitary refuge to AL in the summer of 1941 when AL's anguish over the situation of France, and of his relatives stranded there, was extreme. The poem *Exil* was written at that time. See letter to MacLeish of 9 Sept. 1941. (223) The house at Harvey Cedars was later completely demolished by the hurricane of 1958.

2. The text, headed "An III de l'Exil," is reproduced in OC, pp. 615, 616.

3. Lindley Wood, viscount Halifax (1881-1959), British Ambassador to the United States from 1941 to 1946; Maxim Litvinoff (1876-1951), Soviet Ambassador to the United States from 1941 to 1943.

4. William Bullitt (1891-1967), American Ambassador to France from 1936 to 1940, had also been American Ambassador to the U.S.S.R. from 1933 to 1936.

5. Cordell Hull (1871-1955), Secretary of State from 1933 to 1944.

6. Winston Churchill (1874-1965) had come to know AL at various international conferences that occurred between 1935 and 1940. He had seen Churchill in England in 1940 on his way to America and was to see him again, in the United States, at the occasion of one of Churchill's visits to Washington during the war.

192

To Mrs. Francis Biddle   *Seven Hundred Acre Island*
Washington, D.C.   *off Dark Harbor, Maine*
          Sunday, September 20, [*1942*]

Dear Katherine,

It's been almost a month now that I've abandoned myself alone to the enchantment of this wild, and yet privately owned, island where the affectionate solicitude of an old friend from France, Beatrice Chanler,[1] has made possible for me a complete retreat from the world. I'm gaining new strength, physical and moral, in this

marvelous Maine climate—to enable me to take up my
activities in Washington again.

I had to leave Georgetown hurriedly one day when I
was in very low spirits, without having had the time to
scribble a few lines to you [. . .]. Since then, here on
this island, I haven't been able to surmount the material
difficulties that stand in the way of getting a letter to
the mainland[2] addressed to you. Today I'm taking advantage of an exceptional opportunity—an unexpected
visit by a war-time volunteer in the Maine Coast Guards.[2]

I would never have dared dream of an isolation such
as this island affords—augmented, to be sure, by the war
being on: all the summer houses on the neighboring
islands closed down, the yachts laid up, fishermen
drafted, gasoline rationed, navigation forbidden after
certain hours, etc. What a reward to have the mystery
of this island restored—now that it is closed in upon
itself like a strong, silent being, sure of itself, in whose
intimacy I daily find some new revelation.

Here I lead the spacious physical life of a trailblazer,
woodsman, beachcomber, cold-water swimmer, imaginary landscape gardener,[2] and amateur naturalist, half
poacher, and passionate entomologist, botanist, and geologist.

I'll owe a great deal to this island where I have already
drunk such large draughts of solitude and walked, day
after day, in dreams more richly endowed than now
seems healthy to me. In order to explore all the woods,
all the coves and peat-bogs of this jungle, reverted to its
virgin state, where my unexpected footsteps scarcely
frighten off the animal life of land and shore, I sometimes have to advance, hatchet in hand, as in the great
days when the French made their first incursions into
Indian country.

For company, only a huge red dog, an Irish setter, whose look goes to my heart. For all household chores, the wife and sister-in-law of the island's keeper—two strange tall girls, daughters of a Penobscot squaw and a Danish sailor, who teach me the name and use of the "simples" of this countryside. (They also teach me the ancestral rites: never pull a plant out of the ground without offering it something in exchange—a little tobacco, if possible. Finally, they keep a close watch on all the anomalies of the night sky for me, as they are to awaken me at the first premonitory sign of a display of Northern Lights.) My daytime visitors: a pair of ospreys,[2] whose nest I've spotted on a little uninhabited island nearby, accessible by row boat;[2] a great blue heron who haunts my cove during the twilight hours, and a solitary old seal who is fascinated by my friend, the dog, and who follows us, swimming parallel to the shore where we walk along. There are also, very early in the morning, a few old lobster-fishermen, who are the only beings I talk to. They tell me about the time when the Holy Rollers[2] held their meetings of convulsionaries on this island, when the elks of Maine, which they call moose, would swim out to the islands along with the deer, and when the winters were so cold that over the solidly frozen sea the islanders had to push their boats on sledges all the way to the coast, toward Camden or Rockland. My only other friends are an assortment of cormorants, loons,[2] and guillemots. . . .

But soon I'll have to break this magic spell. I'm just waiting for the first calm in a series of windstorms, fog-banks, and mad barometric gyrations that completely cut off this island during the period of the equinox [. . .]. I hope that Francis has been able, in spite of everything, to steal a few days of rest at Harvey Cedars after his being so mercilessly overworked as Attorney General.[3] I have a hard time keeping up with the news here on a little radio set.

I embrace you, dear Katherine. I hope to hear, when I return, that you have been able to get a little work done this month.

Lots of affectionate thoughts from me to Francis, who, as always, has been so kind in giving his personal attention as Attorney General to a number of petitions that I had recommended on behalf of French friends of mine in the Resistance.

Warmly.   Alexis

1. Mrs. Beatrice Chanler, née Minnie Ashley (died 1966), was the wife of the diplomat and explorer, William Astor Chanler (1867-1934). She had spent a great deal of time in Paris during and after the years of World War I, when she came to know AL. On learning of AL's presence in New York in 1940, she set about doing what she could to help him and thereafter offered him residence almost every summer on an island she owned in Penobscot Bay, Maine, Seven Hundred Acre Island.

2. English in original.

3. In mid-1941 Francis Biddle was promoted to the post of Attorney General by Franklin Roosevelt and remained in that post until Roosevelt's death in 1945.

193

To Mrs. Francis Biddle   *Washington,*
Harvey Cedars,   *July 20, 1944*
Long Beach Island
Ocean County, New Jersey

Dearest Katherine,

The same veil of sadness still descends each day on my Washington solitude. My years of trial do not seem to be nearing their end.

I was alerted last Saturday about a telephone-call from Paris which came through on Sunday, and I'm expecting another next Sunday, from Switzerland.

The news of a personal nature is rather reassuring; the news of public matters is not so good.

If you know to whom, in the American Embassy, the latest parcels for my mother and sisters might have been entrusted, please let me know. I have some other packages being prepared for them. The "Bermuda wool" and the other woolens will be especially valuable to them for the coming autumn and winter.

I'm told that Bullitt[1] is expected here any day now. I hope he will be bringing me a letter or some message from my family [. . .].

Most warmly.   Alexis

1. See above, letter 191, note 4.

194

To Mrs. Francis Biddle   *Seven Hundred Acre Island*
Washington, D.C.   *near Dark Harbor, Maine*
                                      September 13, 1945

Dearest Katherine,

You have known how to anticipate, in your presentiments, the most hidden movements of my sadness, which I try in vain to conceal from those I love.

You will certainly find me unchanged in my affections, but in spirit, where I myself am concerned, an entirely different man—for it is a strange work indeed that I have come here to finish in solitude: the annihilation of the poet in me.

Even to you, dear Katherine, I can say no more, for a Frenchman always hates the bad taste involved in dramatizing anything. I'd prefer to smile at having had to admit to myself that it is more difficult to destroy than to build. The rather somber, and very Nordic, island where I am staying for a while longer, in order to accomplish this task, is a great help, thanks to the severity of its cold waters. (I swim twice a day in all weather.) You must believe that it is not out of pleasure or affectation that I am compelled to stifle within me the only being who is really entirely natural to me and whom I have had to struggle against all my life. I no longer had any choice; for that being, waiting for its freedom, or freed, was becoming too much of a hindrance in the practical measures I must take in preparing for a new life, a life for which, materially, I find I am the most ill-adapted of men. I'm quite aware of the fact that the problems I'll have to face in providing for the members of my family will not be as easy to master as were, for me, those of my former professional calling as a diplomat. Having said that, I really have no cause to rail against the gods, who have facilitated this final sacrifice by the very way they ordered my previous life.

It has been wonderful for me to feel your heart beat at the news from France. On my side, a song of thanksgiving wells up in every part of me for this America where I came, four years ago, in search of the assurance of such a final outcome. I am happy to see expressed enthusiastically in all the press reports, even in the papers with the greatest partisan bias, the irrepressible pro-Americanism of the true people of France. And I am profoundly happy to note the legitimate and increasing authority that is devolving upon America in Europe, thanks to the dazzling prestige of its arms and to the magnificent strategical and tactical intelligence that capped the miracle of the war industries that had prepared the way. I hope that Roosevelt and his associates will reap the moral benefit of all this in the approaching elections. I also hope their influence will be increased, as a result of those elections, in determining the great international settlements in which my country, above all others, has the greatest interest [. . .].

I was deeply touched by your concern for my mother. How can I say anything about that except face to face? I expect to be back before the end of the month. I am very conscientiously arming myself with the greatest possible measure of good health in order to meet all the challenges that will arise [. . .].

I have received up here, after endless delays, a letter from Charlton Ogburn[1] which I have not yet answered. I can't think of anything more appealing than the tact-fulness, both intellectual and moral, of such a personality. He has all sorts of illusions about my future role in France; but it's his very idealism that I like so much— a "parfit gentle knight."[2]

I don't know what MacLeish will think of the way I am prolonging my stay here. I was supposed to spend a few days with him at Cricket Hill[3] in September. And he surely has no inkling of the somber matters that keep me here.

I hope to hear, on my return, that the accumulated obligations of your official life in Washington will not have distracted you too much from your own concerns and from your work as a poet.

Lots of affectionate thoughts to Francis from me. I still think about Harvey Cedars and that last summer we spent there together in the glass house with the wood panelling that smells so good [. . .].   Alexis

1. Charlton Ogburn (1882-1962), American lawyer and scholar, friend of the Biddles. In 1942 he accompanied AL and the Biddles on a trip through South Carolina and Georgia, during which AL composed the poem *Pluies* (*Rains*). Ogburn wrote an

article about the trip and the composition of the poem that has
been published in French translation in *Honneur à Saint-John
Perse* (pp. 273-279) under the title "Comment fut écrit *Pluies*."
   2. Original text reads "un parfait galant homme."
   3. Cricket Hill is the site of the MacLeishes' Uphill Farm.

195

To Mrs. Francis Biddle   *700 Acre Island*
Washington, D.C.   *near Dark Harbor, Maine*
                                August 20, 1946

Dear Katherine,

   [. . .] My stay on this island, forever veiled for me in
the grief of a bereavement and in my early memories
of exile, will at least end well in physical terms. I'll be
back in Washington by the beginning of September.

   A telegram from MacLeish inviting me to Cricket
Hill didn't reach me here in time.

   The Bollingen Foundation[1] is offering me a literary
contract involving a "grant in aid."[2] Unfortunately, it's
not enough to allow me to make any long-term commitment at this present stage of my life [. . .]. Will I
have to reconsider some of the solutions suggested in
Paris? The prospects they offer are even less to my personal liking, in view of what I feel is in store for the
political future of my country at this time.

   Francis writes me letters from Nuremberg[3] of a sort
that just are not being written any more; they radiate
that enthusiasm, good humor, and mental vigor that is
the surest proof of health. I like it that the "High Judge
of Nuremberg" so seldom wears a wig.

   To you, dear Katherine, my deep affection.   A.

   1. The Bollingen Foundation, established by Paul and Mary
Mellon in 1945, had as one of its principal objectives assistance
to individual scholars and writers through support for research

and publication. AL was awarded a Bollingen Fellowship in Oct. 1946. It was renewed regularly thereafter until Oct. 1966, and was AL's chief source of income during those years. The Bollingen Foundation published bilingual editions of all AL's poems from *Exil* (1941) on, as well as a St.-John Perse *Collected Poems* (1971) and several miscellaneous pieces by AL.

2. English in original.

3. In Sept. 1945 President Harry Truman appointed Francis Biddle chief American member of the International Military Tribunal to try the major German war criminals (the Nuremberg Trials). The trials went on until Oct. 1946.

196

To Mrs. Francis Biddle   *Washington, June 21, 1949*
Harvey Cedars,
Long Beach Island
Ocean County, New Jersey

Dear Katherine,

[. . .] The foreign delegates to the "Goethe Bicentennial Convocation and Festival"[1] at Aspen, Colorado, are beginning to arrive from all different countries. My friends just can't seem to understand, once more, why I refuse to represent France literarily and to speak at an international gathering. They make much of the delights of this meeting of "Great Men," when all I want is the wide sands of your dunes, the "perfect no use"[2] that you alone do not chide me for, the uninhibited laughter and human warmth of a fine summer shared along the Atlantic—far from the scholars and their wives! . . . You are sages at this moment, you and Francis; and sages, to our way of thinking, will always have the advantage of staying the most youthful. Nevertheless, try to reserve, if you can manage, a little energy for work; and then, throughout the coming year, you will enjoy the lovely wake that summer leaves behind it.   A.

I have had a visit from the German, Curtius, who is a great friend of Thornton Wilder.[3]

1. The Goethe Bicentennial Convocation and Festival was held in Aspen, Colorado, from 27 June to 16 July 1949, and was attended by such notable literary figures as Ernst Curtius, Ortega y Gasset, and Thornton Wilder. See letters to Gide of 28 May 1949 (294), and 20 June 1949. (296)

2. English in original.

3. Ernst Robert Curtius (1886-1956), the eminent German scholar and critic. Thornton Wilder (1897-1975), the American novelist and playwright. See above, note 1.

197

To Mrs. Francis Biddle   *700 Acre Island*
Bound Brook Island,   *near Dark Harbor, Maine*
near Wellfleet   *August 28, 1949*
Cape Cod, Massachusetts

Dear Katherine,

The days pass here outside all reality, and my voluntary exile is being prolonged without making me feel the urge to take up my pen again.

I was sad, that evening, to watch the beautiful, big yacht disappear across the waters—that yacht owned by your friends to whom I owe the happy surprise of your visit to my northern waters. You probably watched me, at the oars of my little rowboat,[1] returning alone at the hour when the evening light gives a faraway tinge to so many things in the hearts of old Maine sailors. The next morning I had to confront all alone the fearful beauty of this rainless summer—a summer that begins to have the disquieting look of a face that will never again feel the solace of tears. In my thoughts I was able to anticipate every place where you dropped anchor for the night, for I know them all. I wanted so much to conjure up for you so many lucent things that my Tibetan magic somehow couldn't guarantee you: Northern Lights,[1] phosphorescent seas, electric storms. . . .[1] I hope you were able to prolong your cruise a bit—a few days or so—in the neighborhood of Cape Cod. You must now have faces so tanned that you could all disembark naked without fear of being recognized—Francis, like a true Biddle or Randolph, has probably regained a bit of the Pocahontas "blend"[1] of his ancestral mask.[2]

What kind of weather are you having on the Cape now? Enough fog to dampen the ardor of the bob-whites[1] and crickets? Enough morning dew to be shared by the ghost-horses of your moors[1] and Michael's bees?[3] Have your white maidservants found peace of body and soul, and will they stay on?

Here, all you hear is talk of an apocalyptic drought and of forest-fires on the mainland.[1] Canada sends us the marvelous smells of its flaming forests. The pine-clad islands are fragrant with resin. And all this is a bit too much for the lonely asceticism of a Frenchman from the Islands[4] who has to plunge three times a day into the icy waters of Penobscot Bay! . . . And this is the moment chosen by a clergyman from a neighboring island to come over in a dinghy and tell me that an article on "Monsieur Perse" had appeared in the *New York Herald Tribune*! . . .

Before going on to New York, I am to stay a while at Guilford, in Connecticut, with friends arriving from France who bring me news of my family. I won't return by sea this time, as I have no taste for return voyages and for that end-of-the-summer state of mind. So, down your way, I won't be seeing my little "sea-captain's"[5] cottage.

To both of you, most warmly.   A.

1. English in original.

2. One of Francis Biddle's ancestors, a grandson of William Randolph of Virginia, had married a granddaughter of Pocahontas.

3. Michael was a gardener employed by the Biddles at Wellfleet.

4. AL, of pure French stock, was born on the island of Guadeloupe in the French Antilles.

5. English in original. The cottage was a small house on the Biddle property at Wellfleet where AL did a good deal of writing.

198

To Mrs. Francis Biddle   *Hotel Manger, Boston*
Bound Brook Island,   *September 13, [1950]*
near Wellfleet
Cape Cod, Massachusetts

Dearest Katherine,

[. . .] The need to steel myself comes over me once more—at this moment in the depths of the most hideous imaginable hotel in which an evening's human solitude was ever stranded.

[. . .] I leave tomorrow morning for Greenfield and Conway, and from there I'll go directly to Washington by way of New York. What a shame I couldn't take that horseback trip in the New Mexico Sierras with Francis! I still dream about it!

Boston has been in a state of excitement in expectation of the cyclone from the south, announced every hour on the hour, which finally turned away and lost itself in the night. The cab-drivers scurried to their garages, the hotel lobbies suddenly came to life in a hysterical way, just as they did in the great days of the blackouts.[1] All I could think of was the wild grapevines at Wellfleet, undoubtedy torn to pieces, after all the trouble I've given myself, so devotedly, these last two years to rescue them from their wild state! Compared to that, what indeed were all the trifling little bourgeois catastrophes along the coast, which the radio kept announcing? Your lovely barefooted neighbor, Priscilla, must have found her tall house invaded by sand, since she could not ask the wind, as she does her guests, including me, to take its sandals off. The three wandering horses most probably took refuge in my cottage. And your cook, the lady from Trieste, undoubtedly let a few exile's tears drop into her excellent watercress soups.

My drive with D., who was in high spirits, went off uneventfully. After Plymouth, Melville's New Bedford (Old Whaling Museum)[1] and the historical little port of Mystic, with its two great retired sailing-ships (the old whaler, *Charles Morgan*, from my childhood in the Islands, and the clipper, *Joseph Conrad*). I brought my series of nautical reminiscences to a close with another visit to the old frigate, *Constitution* (*Old Ironsides*), now one hundred and fifty years old. [. . .]   A.

With you, warmly.

1. English in original.

199

Mrs. Francis Biddle   *Washington,*
Bound Brook Island,   *June 27, 1951*
near Wellfleet
Cape Cod, Massachusetts

Dear Katherine,

My thoughts rejoin you at Bound Brook Island, where I still have such a lot of weeds to cut down, so many suffering trees to amputate, while I listen to the folk-chronicle of Cape Cod.

I hope that the winter storms at your place did not get the better of that last dead branch, near the house, that I always spared in my pruning labors so it could serve as a perch for your birds (eastern kingbirds and eastern peewees),[1] and also as an antenna for your secret thoughts (as yet unborn poems by Katherine Garrison Chapin).[2]

I hope to be arriving around the 26th or 27th of July. Between now and then, I'll have wandered about the north and northwest, following itineraries as yet ill-defined—for my Canadian friends, and some others from Boston, unable to arrange things for me in the Canadian Northwest, have decided to organize something else ("a real 'mule-packing' affair")[1] to the Canadian-American border. *Roughing it*[3] will be the motto. Unfortunately, I already deflowered a part of that circuit during my solitary wanderings last summer. I don't know if I'll have the chance, this year, to reserve myself a few days' retreat in some fairly nicely situated log cabin[1] come upon by chance.

Washington is becoming empty. At the French Embassy I dined alone, *tête-à-tête*, with the ambassador[4] on a terrace haunted by the cries of screech-owls! . . . At least I, for my part, have nothing more to fear from the political screech-owls.

When will I be able to take off for the Peruvian highlands? I've again been invited there, with everything arranged to my convenience.

Affectionately, to you and Francis.   A.

1. English in original.

2. Maiden name of Mrs. Biddle. See above, letter 189, note 3.

3. English in original. The title of Mark Twain's Gold Rush book.

4. Henri Bonnet (b. 1888), French Ambassador to the United States, 1944-1955.

200

To Mrs. Francis Biddle
Washington, D.C.

*700 Acre Island
near Dark Harbor, Maine
August 27, 1951*

Dearest Katherine,

The days fly by, bringing the hour of your departure for Europe ever nearer.

I can't think of a single interesting personality to whom I could send you in Paris at the end of summer, either in the world of letters or of politics. I did not think I should propose to Francis a letter of introduction to the French jurists who worked with me at the Quai d'Orsay. Nor did I bring up Herriot[1] again, who is now old and sick and who will surely be at Lyons when you pass through Paris. The other politicians, in the present mêlée, are passing figures of small stature with whom my relations are not at all close. As for England, I enclose a friendly letter to Vansittart.[2] You will relish the way he and his wife, Sarita, will welcome you. They have, near London, a very beautiful place where I stayed on my emigrant's route between France and America [. . .].

Yes, I did indeed receive the proofs from the magazine *Poetry* (my French text of *Et vous, mers*),[3] which I immediately corrected and returned.

Up here I've been fog-bound, almost without interruption, since my arrival. I go swimming nevertheless, like a blind man, in icy water. I keep dreaming of Labrador and cut down lightning-struck fir trees with my hatchet.

I think of you, dear Katherine, dear Francis, and am, with all my heart, yours.

A.

1. Edouard Herriot (1872-1957), the French statesman, was a friend of AL.

2. Robert Gilbert Vansittart (1881-1957), British diplomat who occupied the post of Permanent Undersecretary of State in the British Foreign Office from 1929 to 1938. He thus held the post "equivalent" to the one held by AL in France from 1933 to 1940.

3. The first section of the long poem, *Amers*, under the title "Et vous, mers," was published in the Oct. 1951 issue of *Poetry*, along with an English translation of the text by Wallace Fowlie, under the title, "And you, Seas."

201

Mrs. Francis Biddle　　　　　　　　　　　　　*Washington,*
Bound Brook Island,　　　　　　　　　　　　　*June 26, 1952*
near Wellfleet
Cape Cod, Massachusetts

Dearest Katherine,

My thoughts go winging down to you among your winged guests at Bound Brook Island. I hear that the bobwhite[1] and partridge couples are very amorous, but that the mateless peregrine duck-hawks[1] are reduced to cracking their heads against the window-panes during your cocktail parties,[1] at the risk of being drenched with whisky!

Here there is less romanticism in the air, and the champagne of the aged hostesses[1] doesn't manage to liven things up very much in the face of the merciless humid heat that comes after these subtropical downpours.

I spent ten days with friends on Long Island. There's nothing drearier than these big luxurious estates, already run down, as if in mourning for past glories, where you're dragged for tea or dinner, from neighbor to neighbor, all to the accompaniment of the usual seasonal chatter.

My plans for a ranch and for a life on horseback in the west appeared to me to be too expensive this time. And as for my friends in California, they themselves are coming east and prefer to meet me once more at the Canadian border, in northern Maine, with its coastline and rivers, which I explored last year. So in August I'll still be staying on the same island in Penobscot Bay— unless I find some new island between now and then, way out at sea, more to my taste and humor of the moment. I've also asked D., always so understanding, to make inquiries for me about the possibility of finding some kind of rudimentary lodging at some wild spot along the coast.

I embrace you, dear Katherine, and seek out, for the two of you, wishes that come from what is best in me.

A.

1. English in original.

202

To Mrs. Francis Biddle
Bound Brook Island,
near Wellfleet
Cape Cod, Massachusetts

Seven Hundred Acre Island
near Dark Harbor, Maine
July 31, 1953

Dearest Katherine,

I have no doubt that the good air of the Cape and the favorable state of mind that goes along with Wellfleet have promptly restored Francis and you. I like to picture the two of you gardening or clearing brush, roaming about your domain and dunes, swimming, reading, rest- ing, "wasting time like water,"[1] or each of you working, on his own, in the twin cells of the garden-house studio [. . .].

I spent a week with Mina Curtiss[2] in upstate Massa- chusetts (at Chapelbrook). At Conway, our friends the MacLeishes had a full house.[3] Mina is ever the attentive high-spirited hostess, who, nevertheless, knows perfectly how to let her guests alone. Her summer seems to have organized itself under the sign of music. A composer, Marc Blitzstein, was working under her roof. She had me to lunch with two other composers, the American, Copland, and the Mexican, Chavez; and she took me to Tanglewood to hear a Bach Festival conducted by Munch.[4] She also wanted to take me to Bennington to meet my American translator Wallace Fowlie.[5]

I don't know just how long I'll stay this year, on this Maine island. It will depend on arrangements, which are still vague, either for a campaign on the high seas off the Great Banks,[6] with my hardy Canadian fishermen, or for a jaunt to Anticosti Island, or less ambitiously, a stay on the outermost little island of the American high seas, Monhegan Island or Mattinicus Rock.

D. is in Paris, where she has won the hearts of my whole family.

Life isn't the same here this year. The yachting season is in full swing at the moment throughout the archipelago, and deck hands are scarce everywhere. For the Fourth of July, Dark Harbor is preparing to entertain, along with the usual sailing guests, the big cruise of the New York Yacht Club—sixty-five yachts to be welcomed in the open roadstead where you once saw me, all alone in my little dinghy,[1] rowing before the storm over lonely waters. I manage to have a little solitude only by getting up very early and going over to the nearby uninhabited islets in my rowboat[1] to eat the wild raspberries there. There I can at least swim, in beautiful water, with no other companion than the old bell-buoy that has been my friend and confidant through so many years of exile.

With you and Francis, warmly, at Wellfleet.

Alexis

1. English in original.
2. Mrs. Mina Curtiss. See letters to her. (327-346)

3. Archibald MacLeish's country house, Uphill Farm, at Conway, Massachusetts.

4. Marc Blitzstein (1905-1964), American composer. Aaron Copland, American composer. Carlos Chavez (1899-1947), Mexican composer and conductor. Charles Munch (1891-1968), the French musician who was conductor of the Boston Symphony Orchestra at this time.

5. Wallace Fowlie, American scholar and critic, translator of AL's *Amers*.

6. Inadvertence for Grand Bank, off the coast of New Foundland.

203

To Mrs. Francis Biddle
Bound Brook Island
near Wellfleet
Cape Cod, Massachusetts

700 Acre Island
near Dark Harbor, Maine
August 11, 1953

Dear Katherine,

You'll soon be with Mina Curtiss at Chapelbrook. Embrace her for me, and scratch the spine, please, of Monkey, my little friend, the double-masked cat with the Picasso face.

The very cold, but very clear, weather here has suddenly given way to the cycle of Maine fogs [. . .]. The sixty-some luxury yachts, which brought us the hysteria of beautiful divorcees drunk on bourbon, gossip,[1] and childishness, had to beat a hasty retreat in the face of bad weather, and had to cut short the official program by one day. Sensuality is now represented (and for me alone, out on the water, for everybody now sleeps in the summer-houses that are already half boarded up) only in the belated self-indulgence of a few female porpoises[1] rolling their flanks not far from my ascetic skiff. I no longer see the old seal, my friend of the other late summers.

I'm thinking of going to Boston when the season here is over. I'll embark from there in a sailing-yacht with friends who are going up the American coast and can let me off, finally, at Monhegan Island or Mattinicus Rock. No other address during that time but General Delivery, Waldoboro, Maine.

Yes, I'll be delighted to join the two of you after September 15th.

D. will soon be returning to us from France. I do hope that this year, all by herself at the steering-wheel of her car, she won't have to come to my rescue again or pull me through some illness or other. Her departure from Paris was delayed, but the news from her is excellent; and about my family, thank God, she had only good things to tell me.

I open my arms to both of you, dear Katherine and dear Francis.

A.

1. English in original.

204

To Mrs. Francis Biddle   *Chapelbrook, Ashfield Road*
Bound Brook Island,   *Williamsburg, Mass.*
near Wellfleet   *July 14, 1954*
Cape Cod, Massachusetts

Dear Katherine,

Is there a little sea-breeze blowing through your lilacs and choke-cherries?[1] Here it is surprisingly cool; you have to wear woolens, and the nights are almost cold [. . .].

I was able to accompany D. from Washington to Darien,[2] to her sister's house, so she wouldn't be driving all alone in her car.

I'll be here until the end of the month. After that I'll be all alone for a month at sea, in the waters of northern Maine and Canada, and maybe even toward New-foundland, aboard a very fine Canadian fishing schooner. I don't know yet what my mailing addresses may be.

At Conway I was able to see the MacLeishes several times. And I'll soon be seeing Dean Acheson[3] again at their house.

Mina continues to open her house as generously as ever to all her friends and to all her friends' friends. Anne Lindbergh, the daughter of my old friend Dwight Mor-row,[4] was here for a few days. At the moment she's writing a novel to distract her thoughts from something that depresses her; but the saddest thing, in my eyes, is that she wants to sell, in France, her Breton island that I have always loved, the Île Iliec.[5]

I manage to get a little work done, in spite of the generalized disenchantment that I tend to feel in any happy surroundings that I frequent in my exile. Yet I'd like to see a lot of other things before my literary con-tract in this country expires.

I've abandoned the little cottage here—too dark and damp—for the big north bedroom that looks out on the beautiful Lachaise[6] nude that the hummingbirds seem to be investigating. The enclosed garden there that Mina keeps up herself is so nostalgic with its tree-peonies and roses of old-fashioned varieties. At night I hear the wood owl and the squeals of hedgehogs tearing each oth-er to pieces in the apple trees. The water that awaits me in the morning for a swim in the river is fast-running and clear. The rocky escarpments form a beautiful en-closure for this dream-hallowed spot.

My heart is with you, my dear Katherine, my dear Francis.

Alexis

1. English in original.

2. Darien is a town in Connecticut.

3. Dean Acheson (1893-1971), Secretary of State under President Harry Truman, 1949-1953.

4. Dwight W. Morrow (1873-1931), American banker and diplomat, father of Anne Morrow, who became Mrs. Charles A. Lindbergh in 1929. AL had come to know Morrow in the '20's during negotiations leading to the ratifying of the Briand-Kellogg Pact.

5. The Lindberghs had bought Iliec in 1938 through the good offices of Dr. Alexis Carrel.

6. Gaston Lachaise (b. 1886), French sculptor.

205

To Mrs. Francis Biddle   *Washington,*
Bound Brook Island,   *October 30, 1954*
Wellfleet
Cape Cod, Massachusetts

Dear Katherine,

The dejection and depression that always lie in wait for me when I return to Washington made my incurable forgetfulness of dates even worse than usual this time.

If, contrary to my expectations, your stay in Wellfleet were to continue until the end of November, I would certainly arrange things so I could join you there after Mendès-France's visit.[1]

I was able to get here just in time to meet three French personalities[2] who were waiting to see me before boarding the New York-Paris plane.

Not much news for you from here. I didn't go out until yesterday—for a concert at Dumbarton Oaks,[3] after a little dinner at D.'s. A full and, as always, mummified house. Never has high-society Byzantinism seemed to me so close to the catacombs. (Byzantium, in my early days in London, was already a subject of dispute between me and W. B. Yeats.)[4] My consolation for a few days yet is the beauty of the trees, which are flaming shamelessly before they shed their finery. If you arrived in time, we should have to rush off by auto to Big Meadows, on the Skyline ridge, to see once more the Virginian autumn aflame.

Don't forget to remind Francis of his promise to order a second Mugho pine[5] for me from our timid, gentle neighborhood nurseryman, for the spot I indicated. It shall be named "Edna," and the first one "Carol," in memory of this year's two fine hurricanes.[5]

And don't forget either, if there are still grapes to be gathered beyond the dune, to cut back, all the way to the second "eye" from the bottom, the branches that have borne fruit.

I embrace you both.   A.

I haven't yet been able to do anything about Waldo Frank's[6] case. What a warm-hearted man, our good Waldo! His letters are disarming.

1. Pierre Mendès-France, the French statesman who became Prime Minister in June 1954, visited the United States in Nov. 1954.

2. Unidentified.

3. Dumbarton Oaks, the estate in Washington, D.C. that was deeded by the owners, Mr. and Mrs. Robert Woods Bliss, to Harvard University. See letters to Mrs. Bliss. (217-220)

4. AL met the poet William Butler Yeats (1865-1939) in 1912, when AL spent six months in England. See letters to Gide and to Larbaud.

5. English in original.

6. Waldo Frank (1889-1967), American novelist, social critic, and Latin American specialist.

206

To Mrs. Francis Biddle   *Chapelbrook, Ashfield Road*
Bound Brook Island,   *Williamsburg, Mass.*
near Wellfleet   *September 5, 1955*
Cape Cod, Massachusetts

Dear Katherine,

I'll head once more, joyously, as always, toward Wellfleet and expect to be with you by Tuesday the thirteenth.

Mina Curtiss has to make arrangements, in New York, for her departure for Europe; she'll put me on a train headed for Boston in some nearby railway-station. (There's still some uncertainty about train routes because of the repairs that are still going on as a result of the last hurricane.)[1]

I'm happy to learn that this cyclone treated Wellfleet with a certain considerateness, as I was quite worried about you. In the environs, though not right here, the thing seems to have been quite serious. I fear that I greatly shocked people by taking too obvious delight in this unleashing of the elements. What a curious idea, giving the name of Diana, the huntress, to a New World hurricane! We were served right![1]

I'm eager to hear, from Francis and you, all your impressions, good and bad, of Europe.

From me, nothing of interest. My summer at sea was uneventful, since not one of the first three hurricanes deigned to get as far as Canadian waters or even to those of northern Maine. The final stage of my itinerary was, nevertheless, somewhat affected by the precautions that finally had to be taken (refuge north of Anticosti).[2]

I've been here since August 18th. I've done a lot of work, in spite of the visitors.

Cordially.   A.

1. English in original.
2. Anticosti, Canadian island in the St. Lawrence estuary.

207

To Mrs. Francis Biddle   *Washington,*
Bound Brook Island, Wellfleet   *October 28, 1955*
Cape Cod, Massachusetts

Dear Katherine,

The various personalities that are assembled within you and go to make up such a complex and sensitive being may of themselves give rise to a great wealth of hidden torments.

I thank you for writing me as you did. I'm the one who ought to wonder whether I shouldn't chide myself for remaining too silent with close friends. In my somber moments, I was simply preoccupied by the way things are going in France.[1]

I couldn't stay on with you and Francis, as I would like to have, for the end of the season, when I like the Cape the most. I had to meet a number of personalities in New York and Washington after the U.N. session [. . .].

It won't be long, I presume, before you'll be coming back for the deliberations of your Yale Literary Prize Committee.[2] You'll have to fight to see that it is awarded to the right person. There shouldn't be any hesitation in favoring Conrad Aiken,[3] for, after the death of Wallace Stevens,[4] the moment has come to let the star of a poet of Aiken's stature and age shine brightly. Give him my friendliest greetings [. . .].

See you very soon.   A.

1. The summer and fall of 1955 were marked by the increasing Gaullist opposition to Mendès-France's North African policy and by the rise of the populist neo-fascist Poujade movement.

2. Mrs. Biddle was a member of the jury that awarded the Bollingen Prize in Poetry of the Yale University Library.

3. Conrad Aiken (1889-1973), the American poet, novelist, and critic. Aiken actually did receive the 1955 Bollingen Prize. AL

continued to hold Aiken in very great esteem. See letter to Francis Biddle of Sept. 1957. (214)

4. Wallace Stevens (1879-1955), the celebrated American poet who was also an insurance company executive.

208

To Mrs. Francis Biddle   *Washington,*
Washington, D.C.   *December 12, 1955*

No, dear Katherine, you can't be indiscreet where I am concerned. Your questions yesterday were perfectly natural and most pertinent.[1] Here, on one particular point, is what I might have been able to tell you a little more precisely—

It is very important not to make any mistake, where French poetry is concerned, about the basic impulse that leads to the expansiveness of inclusive poems like *Vents* or *Amers*. It would be erroneous to see verbal amplification or oratorical self-indulgence in them when, in fact, such elaborations, strictly imposed by the theme itself, are still a vast linking-together of ellipses, shortcuts, contractions, and even, on occasion, of simple flashes devoid of all transitional material.

The situation, in poetic creation, as I see it—the very function of the poet—is to integrate the thing evoked or to integrate himself into the thing, identifying himself with it to the point of becoming that thing and confusing himself with it—living it, miming it, incarnating it, in a word—or taking possession of it, always in a very *active* way, in its innermost movement and very substance. Whence the necessity of expanding and extending, when the poem is the wind, when the poem is the sea—just as the exact opposite would be called for—that is, extreme brevity—if the poem were the thunderbolt, the lightning flash, the sword blade.

Nothing could be further from English poetry, from its form of initiation and its method of elaboration, even when it seeks to be experimental—a poetry of "statements,"[2] of commentaries and evaluations, all more or less discursive, belonging more or less to the logician or the moralist and carried on at a certain intellectual remove by the poet, who remains apart, always outside his poem and always refusing to grant any share of autonomy to the poem itself.

But all that is in itself of minor importance. The important thing, in no matter what frame of reference or in what dimension (third? fourth?), will always be the "biological" situation of the poet in a "symbiosis" (horrible word!) with the independent life of the poem. The primary justification of a poem will always reside in its inner vitality,[3] in the thing that necessitates its composition—in every language and every discipline. And isn't that, after all, what you yourself had in mind, in your study, when you spoke "of such great poems which, through their vast exploration, can move centrifugally while pursuing a central ideal, and emotion, with final and complete integration. . ."?[2]

Some other time we'll talk about the question of internal metrics, strictly observed in the general distribution and articulation of large prosodic units (in which all the separate elements are grouped, in stanzas or *laisses*,[4] into one vast contraction, dictated by the same inevitability—separate elements, all of them, that are treated like regular verse forms—which, in fact, they are). It is, of course, very easy for a foreign reader to misjudge this overall economy of a precise, albeit unapparent, versification—which has absolutely nothing to do with current conceptions of "free verse" or "prose poems" or elaborate "poetic prose." As a matter of fact, it's the exact opposite of these. And once again, it seemed to me that you yourself had grasped this better than any other American critic by contrasting with the poetic art of a Walt Whitman the rhythmical requirements "of such a rigorous metrique: an internal metrique so exacting and precise, although kept inapparent in its enclosed order, that not one syllable of the text could be changed or displaced without serious damage. . . ."[2]

(Whence still one more difficulty for the foreign translator.)

Most affectionately yours, dear Katherine. When do I get your next question?

A.

1. Mrs. Biddle, under her maiden-name, had already published four articles on AL's poetry and was to publish at least a half dozen more, including the very revealing personal sketch of AL in America that appeared in the Washington, D.C. *Sunday Star* (26 Feb. 1961) a few months after he had been awarded the Nobel Prize for Literature. At the time of the present letter Mrs. Biddle had mustered enough courage to ask AL a number of "indiscreet" questions in connection with an article she must have been writing at that date, submitting to him a draft of it from which he quotes in this letter. The quoted passages, though very similar to any number of passages in Mrs. Biddle's various published articles, do not seem to be verbatim from any one of them. Much of what AL says in the present letter was expanded into a "letter-article" he sent to the ephemeral little magazine, *The Berkeley Review*, on 10 Aug. 1956. See OC, pp. 564-568.

2. English in original.

3. The original French reads *élan vital*.

4. *Laisse*: The French term for a stanza of varying length in which each verse ends with the same assonating vowel. This is the typical verse form of the medieval French epic. AL here uses the term somewhat more freely.

209

To Mrs. Francis Biddle   *Chapelbrook,*
Bound Brook Island,   *August 30, 1956*
Wellfleet
Cape Cod, Massachusetts

Dear Katherine,

I've been away for a month and a half at sea, roughing it, in the Canadian far north, without the slightest fore-seeable forwarding address for mail or without even the slightest possibility of sitting down at a table. I got your two letters, very late, here at Mina's, each forwarded to me twice from Washington.

My eye is now turned toward Bound Brook Island with a true "homing-pigeon feeling."[1] I'd like to get under way around the 14th or 15th, as planned. Mina is sailing off to France on September 22nd.

The disturbances of every kind that it is fashionable to attribute to sunspots have not, I hope, had too much effect on your staff of servants this year. . . . What I wish is that, in all things, I could be sure that you have enough peace of mind to be available for the solicitations of poetry. And here we are, almost at the door of Indian Summer![1]

As for me, I've lived through this high summer cut off from everything. It's only thanks to Mina that, very belatedly, the issue of the *N.R.F.* in which my last poem appeared[2] was delivered to me. But D. writes me from Darien that she was able to get a copy of it for you in New York. Her last letter is from North East Harbor, Maine, and I am very eager to see her after such a long absence. If she is able to visit you around the end of September, I'll return by automobile with her so that she won't be traveling all alone between New York and Washington.

Dearest Katherine, the years go by and the shadow lengthens under my footsteps, but my affection for my two friends of Harvey Cedars, Washington, Dennis Bay,[3] and Bound Brook Island keeps growing [. . .].

Yours warmly.   Alexis

1. English in original.

2. The NRF had published the section of *Amers* beginning "Etroits sont les vaisseaux," in its July 1956 issue. This was to become Canto IX of the "Strophe" of *Amers*.

3. Dennis Bay: a plantation on Saint John Island (Virgin Islands) that the Biddles had once rented.

210

To Mrs. Francis Biddle   *Les Vigneaux,*
Bound Brook Island,   *Presqu'île de Giens (Var)*
Wellfleet   *September 30, 1957*
Cape Cod, Massachusetts

Dear Katherine,

How moving, to think that you and Francis were contemplating another trip to Europe to come all the way to see me here in maritime Provence where I have withdrawn for a few more days yet!

I have lived a rather unreal life here, an almost somnambulistic life, and I've hardly been able to get back in touch with reality. Five months on French soil, and it's already time to pack the suitcases for a return to America![1] That means pulling myself out of my dream suddenly—a dream suffused, in spite of myself, with some sort of vague apprehension. And, believe me, this has nothing to do with dissatisfaction with fate, which has been more than generous to me! But dreaming always gives rise to some sort of uneasiness. A little undisclosed insolence will put to rest in me these unreasoning worries that are sometimes kept alive by the demon of the Absurd. Mediterranean sunlight, bright as ever I could wish, will do the rest. Never insist on questioning our nights too much, even in so bright a region. (A land of archaisms and mythology—myrtles, cypresses, asphodels—under the too-well-known sign of Athena's little owl.)[2]

Will I ever, though, become accustomed to the Mediterranean as a sea? "We who are of the Atlantic. . ." was an expression used constantly throughout three centuries by my ancestors.

My health, at any rate, seems to me quite privileged in such a climate, or rather, more particularly, on this peninsula-tip, so well ventilated. I haven't missed swimming in the sea for a single day up to now, and I'm sure I can continue to swim until the end of November or even December. Very steep coves at the base of my cliff plunge me rather rudely into open water. It's not at all, far from it, your fine gently sloping beaches of Cape Cod; but the water here is of rare quality, almost tropical in its clearness, but more tonic than in the tropics. All I have to do is exchange the trades for the *mistral*.[3] I'll get used to it; they're both wind, after all.

My life during the summer, here at Les Vigneaux, still remains tied to the rhythm of life at Bound Brook Island. When I lay down my spade and unwind my garden-hose here, or when I doggedly stick into the ground some modest wild plant that I pulled out of the brush, I think to myself, "Francis is now doing the same thing on his 'moors.'"[4] And when I pick up my pen in a tentative way, I think that Katherine and Francis are in their separate studies, heads bent over their big tablets of yellow paper. And at the hour when you whistle up your dogs to go for a walk along the crest of your dunes, Francis with his hawthorn cane and Katherine with her Basque beret, I whistle for my promptest thoughts to go along with me for a turn (the customs officer's path) atop my Provençal *calanques*.[5]

Dearest Katherine, dearest Francis, I'm so eager to receive you here one day with open arms. Over and against my monstrous silence at times, you will always know, won't you?, what is in your friend's heart.   A.

1. AL and his wife spent six months of each year at Les Vigneaux and six months in their Washington residence in Georgetown. See letter to Mrs. Curtiss, 9 Sept. 1959. (346)

2. A small owl, said by some classical scholars to be the European Little Owl (*Athena noctua*), that was sacred to the votaries of Athena.

3. The *mistral*: the cold wind that blows off the Alps down the Rhone Valley.

4. English in original.

5. *Calanque*: Provençal term for a small rocky sea-cove.

LETTERS TO FRANCIS BIDDLE
(1942-1965)

To the Hon. Francis Biddle[1]   *Washington, January 1942*
Attorney General,   *Library of Congress*
Department of Justice
Washington, D.C.

Dear friend,

Have I really made you understand how interested I am in all the things you tell me about the times in your younger days that you spent with Justice Holmes[2] and about the eminent jurist's philosophical thought and his personal influence in shaping the great concepts of public law in America?

You have no idea how attractive American public law, arising out of a creative transformation of natural laws, can be to a French mind that was brought up to respect the imperatives of Roman law, but that revolts instinctively against the systematic dogmatism of the Latin judicial system.

American pragmatism—which on another plane has always profoundly shocked me as a general philosophy excluding all metaphysics—here, for me, finds its best justification: in a special philosophy of law that is subordinated, socially, to the empiricism of life itself.

Continuing our conversation of a few nights ago about Montesquieu, here, in the exact text, are the three quotations from *L'Esprit des lois* that you found particularly attractive:

"Custom makes better citizens than laws do."
"When one wishes to change customs and manners,

430   LETTERS FROM EXILE

it is not the laws that should be changed."
"Useless laws weaken necessary laws."[3]

Holmes surely took delight in such aphorisms, if he was familiar with them—which is more than likely.

From a very different standpoint, the great gentleman and wit that you described your former master and friend—the "Magnificent Yankee"[4]—as being, and in such a human way, would have liked the other Montesquieu no less—the man of the world who, in order to express himself succinctly concerning his philosophy of marriage has recourse, in his *Notebooks*, to psychological shortcuts such as "All husbands are ugly."[5]

Dear friend, may we soon resume our friendly chats.

A. S.-L.

1. Francis Biddle (1886-1968), Attorney General of the United States from mid-1941 to Apr. 1945, first met AL some time between 6 Nov. and 10 Dec. 1940 (see the letters of those dates, [189] and [190] to Mrs. Biddle), while he was still Solicitor General. The two men seem to have taken immediately to one another and became very close friends—in fact, AL came to regard Francis Biddle as his closest American friend.

2. Francis Biddle had been a secretary of Justice of the Supreme Court Oliver Wendell Holmes (1841-1935) in 1911-1912 and became one of the Justice's closest friends and warmest admirers. Biddle later wrote two books about his former "boss": *Mr. Justice Holmes* (1942) and *Justice Holmes, Natural Law, and the Supreme Court* (1961).

3. The first two quotations from Montesquieu's *Spirit of the Laws* come from Bk. XIX, chap. 14 (wording slightly altered), the third from Bk. XXIX, chap. 16.

4. Holmes.

5. The notation is no. 1260 in the Bordeaux edition of Montesquieu's notebooks entitled *Mes Pensées*.

212

To the Hon. Francis Biddle   *Washington,*
Bound Brook Island,   *July 31, 1945*
near Wellfleet
Cape Cod, Massachusetts

My dear Francis,

Nothing could have touched me more than your taking the trouble, in the midst of vacation, to look over the
legal forms of these testamentary matters for me, and
then your taking pen in hand immediately to make sure,
personally, that I get things straight, and giving me
further guidance as you do. I know what that means
when you've scarcely put off the yoke of governmental
life[1] and can at last breathe freely in the open air, with
every right to forget about all else. I thank you from
the bottom of my heart for your warm solicitude.

I've had so much to worry about these last few days
(not to mention the enervating effect of this tropical
summer), that I haven't yet got around to straightening
out this simple little matter of a will drawn up in
America. But God knows you made the thing much
simpler for me!

Where are the good old days when the only assistance
one had to give friends was in amusing "affairs of
honor"?. . . I can't even offer you that in my exile!
The old Emigrés certainly had a lot more style.

I expect to leave for Maine day after tomorrow (700
Acre Island near Dark Harbor, Maine). I'm expecting
another telephone call from Europe tomorrow that was
supposed to come through today, but the storm deprived
me of that [. . .].

How good it is to see your magnificent freedom of
spirit come flooding in on you again the moment you
are released!—that freedom of spirit which is your real

fountain of youth. There's no better safeguard against fossilization, and no better assurance that you have remained fully yourself in spite of high public office. It is rare that a governmental career, or even a simply professional one, leaves us completely intact.

Always stay so completely human, my dear Francis— I mean so free of limits—and you will always be a joy to your arteries and to your friends.

Lots of affectionate thoughts to be shared with Katherine, and do keep me informed about the unexpected things that may shape your life. I just can't get used to the idea that the end of summer won't bring you back to Washington. I still hear talk of your being appointed Ambassador to Paris, but in my solitude I can't tell how serious this rumor is.

As for myself, if I had enough to live on, I'd certainly be ripe for a hermitage on Cumberland Island or at Taos![2] [. . .]

Warmly yours.   A.

1. Francis Biddle, at the request of President Truman, resigned as Attorney General in June 1945, to be replaced by Tom Clark, then head of the Department of Justice's Criminal Division.

2. Cumberland Island, off the coast of Georgia. Taos, New Mexico.

213

To Francis Biddle   *Washington,*
Paris   *[April] 1946*

My dear Francis,

Your visit to my mother![1] . . . I'm still very moved at the thought, and your telegram is the most wonderful New Year's gift I've had in a long, long time.

You give the lie to the French eighteenth-century tradition that maintained that a man of wit could not also have a generous heart.

I often think of you, dear friend, and I follow you in all your marvelous public activities. But that doesn't stop me from rather selfishly feeling how much I miss you here in Washington. You were, in a way, the salt of America for me; so don't stay away too long, or it will go rather flat.

Warmly, with wishes chosen from among my best and most worthy of our already long-standing affection.

Alexis

1. The Nuremberg War Crimes Trials were still in session at this date, and Biddle, as chief American representative, was still in Europe. During the Christmas recess, Biddle went to England and spent two nights in Paris on the way back to Nuremberg. (See Biddle, *In Brief Authority*, p. 430.) This was probably the occasion of his visit to AL's mother.

214

To the Hon. Francis Biddle   *Les Vigneaux,*
Bound Brook Island,   *Presqu'île de Giens (Var)*
near Wellfleet   *September 1957*
Cape Cod, Massachusetts

My very dear Francis,

I have never felt more keenly, now that I am far from you, all the brotherly ties that life has established between us. My thoughts go out to you across the seas and never cease to associate you here to the rhythm of my summer life, which was close to yours for such a long time. I still feel I'm striding over the dunes or beaches of the Cape where we talked so often and so freely about everything, the way friends do for whom words no longer have any very great meaning beyond the simplicity of affection.

Katherine tells me you are working very hard on your memoirs[1] at the moment. I'm curious about them, thinking, as I do, of all that I had the privilege of getting to know about you, on a person-to-person basis—your human, profoundly human, qualities and your fundamental indifference to the world's prevailing values. For as free and independent a spirit as yours, what fine material you have to work with in these memoirs, covering such a wide field of vision! Maybe you could read me a few parts of them when I get back to Washington at the end of October [. . .].

To my friends at Cape Cod a faithful and very cordial handshake. Above all, to Conrad Aiken,[2] for I was especially affected by the generosity of a literary testimonial he gave on my behalf and published a few months ago in a Paris newspaper. It had an elegance and nobility of tone about it that corresponded completely to what I always felt about him in America. Testifying in someone else's favor, even extravagantly, always gives the finest and surest measure of what an author has the right to think about himself [. . .].

How I liked your letter, dear Francis, and everything it told me, so sensitively and vividly, of the atmosphere of Bound Brook Island to which I remain so firmly attached, with you by my side. Yes, I would indeed have liked, as you so thoughtfully suggested, to run up to Cape Cod before going to Washington. But I won't be arriving soon enough to be able to do that.

Here, renewing contact with France has been a real shock and leaves me in great sadness. Not that there is anything to worry about so far as the future fate of my country or the vitality of its people is concerned, for it is still what it always was, with the same resources and rare human qualities. But what poverty, what lack of coordination, and what disintegration in its political life! —and, what is much more serious, what a pernicious gap between its national life and its political life! That political life was compromised and stricken with paralysis throughout the final days of the legislature, as a result of a parliamentary dissolution that was hurriedly brought about in an underhand way before changes could be made in the election laws, and before a bad constitution could be revised.[3]

Think of me, dear Francis, during the moments of relaxation from your intellectual labors, in the incomparable light of your autumn strolls. That way you will be, in your thoughts, with a friend who is fond of you and who seeks along with you, in affection and in the outdoors, the true secret of youth.

See you soon in Georgetown.   Alexis

1. More than eleven years separate this letter from the preceding one. The memoirs referred to were eventually published in two consecutive volumes entitled, respectively, *A Casual Past* (1961) and *In Brief Authority* (1962).

2. See above, letter 206, note 3. Aiken had contributed a brief but heartfelt tribute to AL in a 1957 issue of the Paris newspaper, *Combat*, on the occasion of the publication of AL's poem *Amers*. The note is reproduced in OC, p. 1253.

3. The summer of 1957 was marked by debate on the Common Market and Euratom, as well as by heated controversy over French public education. After bitter debate over a "special powers act" in July 1957, Bourgès-Maunoury, who was Premier at the time, dissolved Parliament, as the special powers act permitted him to do. Unrest was such that he was forced to call it back into session a week earlier than he had intended, and his government promptly fell, on Sept. 30.

215

To Mr. Francis Biddle   *Hotel Westminster, Nice*
Washington   *November 3, 1959*

My dear Francis,

It's hard for me to realize that so much time has already gone by under this Mediterranean light! The

suddenness of departure awakens me as if I were a som-
nambulist [. . .].

Tomorrow the plane to Paris, then twelve days or so
there to be devoted to my family before taking off for
America. (My sister, Paule, is making a special trip
from Italy, since, for health reasons, she wasn't able to
join my sister Eliane this summer at Les Vigneaux.)

You must be in the midst of the battle for the Roosevelt Memorial Project there in Washington.[1]

A telegram from the Blisses[2] desperately urges us to
attend a dinner in Washington on the 24th, without even
telling us what or whom it is all about. They must at
the very least be expecting Charles de Gaulle himself at
Q Street, or maybe even the queen of Raratonga or the
comte de Paris.

Here the most honored guest is the fine weather,
which is really pushing its arrogance to scandalous extremes.

Just the same, I'm longing to be back with you one of
these days in the streets of Georgetown, where the violets
still grow wild.

I'm delighted to hear from Katherine that you're
about ready to send your memoirs off to the publisher.
Delighted, too, to know that Katherine is back in the
poetic vein and ready to correct the proofs of her new
collection[3] [. . .].

I embrace you both.   A.

1. President Eisenhower, in Nov. 1955, appointed Biddle chairman of the Franklin Delano Roosevelt Memorial Commission.
The particular design for the monument that was championed
by Biddle gave rise to fierce controversy, and nothing ever came
of the project.

2. Mr. and Mrs. Robert Woods Bliss, at Dumbarton Oaks, on
Q Street in the Georgetown section of Washington, D.C. See
above, letter 205, note 3.

3. *The Other Journey: Poems New and Selected* (University
of Minnesota Press, 1959).

216

To Francis Biddle   *Les Vigneaux,*
Washington   *Presqu'île de Giens (Var)*
                                   January 2, 1965

My dear Francis,

In a few days we'll be back in Georgetown, to which I am still so attached; but I have my heart set on letting you know from this end, before I pack my suitcases, what live connections there still are between my life at Les Vigneaux and the life I shared with you in America. I love the Atlantic alliance as much as Charles de Gaulle hates it!

Diane[1] and I were disappointed at not having you here on your return trip from Italy. But I'm glad to know that everything turned out well, the voyage and the cure, for Katherine and you. Basically, you need to move about in order to realize in what good physical shape you are. I was very much aware, during our last escapades on Cumberland Island and Eleuthera, how much physical renewal restores you to your real self again [. . .].

Francis, I keep thinking of all that we still expect from your literary pen—things that you alone in America can supply: a real memoir-writer's work. It would be a work bringing to life—as you know how to, in essential terms and always in a lively and very human way that is at once sensitive and psychologically very perceptive, and in a completely casual manner that is entirely your own, magnificently disdainful of accumulated erudition —a series or gallery of American portraits that academic historiographers have never been able to bring to life under the weighty paraphernalia of their compilations. Only the English strike me as having preserved, between the 18th and 19th centuries, that impertinent, irreverent strain of independent-minded memoir-writers that in

France we classify, paradoxically, under the heading of "moralists."[2]

The success of your memoirs, taking the public of the moment by surprise, has already given rise in America to something of that quickening of pace that I keep so wholeheartedly wishing for. And your monographs on Holmes and Randolph of Roanoke[3] could take their place in a more inclusive showcase. You'd be presenting a veritable panorama of American Society, as it seems never yet to have been understood; it would come to life there, step by step in the course of its human un-folding. You have all the requisite talents, and perhaps you are alone in having them, through intellectual af-finities as well as personal experience. The advantage, moreover, of this sort of writing, especially for as free a spirit as you, is that it can be taken up whenever you please, like a real pastime (a rare thing!), with the as-surance of getting real personal pleasure out of it (an essential condition for success in anything).

During the hours or longer periods when you didn't feel in the "mood"[4]—which is essential to that state of grace and which can't be forced—there is a marginal work, a voluntary work that you could set yourself as an immediate task to be accomplished. That would be a little book written as a historical document about—and a personal reminiscence of—the Nuremberg Trials.[5] Judging by the present extraordinary vogue for historical reminiscences about the war and the years immediately after, and judging too by the swarms of partisan pub-lications here in Europe and the dearth of American correctives to them, I can guarantee you—at least where France is concerned—a real sales success, which couldn't help being of interest to your American publishers. And for this sort of methodical work, quite apart from your own first-hand knowledge in these matters, you already

have at your disposal a vast, first-class body of documentation.

We'll talk all this over when we resume those good
hours of intimacy where we left off. Today I want simply
to embrace you both, Katherine and you, and to tell
you how close you are to me at the moment.

A.

1. Mrs. Leger's "French" name. See letter to Mrs. Curtiss of
9 Sept. 1958. (346)

2. See above, letter 214, note 1.

3. See above, letter 211, note 2.

4. English in original.

5. "Book Four: The Nürnberg Trial," of *In Brief Authority*,
is a very interesting personal account of the trial. AL apparently
had a more "detached" historical account in mind.

LETTERS TO MRS. ROBERT WOODS BLISS
(1948-1953)

217

Washington,
August 1, [1945]

Dear friend,[1]

Need I tell you of my emotion on learning of your sudden departure for Europe,[2] at the very moment when I was locking my suitcases to leave for the north? (I'd been struggling with a difficult telephone connection with Europe—a heartbreaking call that was broken off four different times by the bad storm conditions.)

In haste, I am entrusting two letters to you. The telephone number for my mother is the number of one of my sisters (Mme. Abel Dormoy: WAGram 39-49).

Dear friend, your nobility, fervor, and mute tenderness send you winging on toward my poor country; it is a heavenly favor that sends you on your way today, with no thought for yourself and all your weariness— smiling with the smile that is reserved exclusively for moral elegance, that ultimate expression of impertinence!

And you must know that I, in the ever-increasing loneliness I feel here, am smiling from afar at something you approach without my being along.

My wishes and thoughts go with you.

Alexis St.-L. Leger

1. Mrs. Mildred Barnes Bliss (d. 1969) was the wife of Robert Woods Bliss (1875-1962), who had been attached to the American Embassy in Paris during World War I. The Blisses had remained strong Francophiles.
2. Mrs. Bliss made a hasty flight to Europe in the summer of

1945, picking up a supply of penicillin in London which she took to AL's ailing mother in Paris. In OC (p. 932) this letter bears the date 1948, an obvious misprint.

218

Washington,
October 25, [1948]

Dear friend,

Only you, here, are able to realize what a weight of sorrow and loneliness I have to shake off to bring myself to confide in you the news that my mother died yesterday morning in Paris.

I am telling you this so promptly, not only because I owe it to you as a personal debt, but because you were so kind and attentive to her, fully aware of *who* this human being really was.

I embrace you, dear Mildred.   Alexis

219

Washington,
July 8, [1949]

Dear Mildred,

I'm so sorry that I have to leave Washington in such a hurry without being able to see you once more or even reach you by telephone.

I would so like to have told you about all that I came away with from those easy, intimate hours we shared yesterday at Dumbarton Oaks.[1]

Until the end of July I'll be with Francis and Katherine,[2] at Wellfleet, Cape Cod; then in August, in Maine —on that island of Beatrice's[3] where so much sorrow awaits me (that's where I lived all alone through a whole summer's end, on tenterhooks as news of my mother's health came through).

Au revoir, dear Mildred. Wherever you go during my absence, always keep that delicate, pretty little head alert and clear-eyed as it surveys the heavy seas of our time—a head so full of so many things, and such precious ones.

Affectionately yours.   Alexis

1. The Bliss residence in Georgetown. See above, letter 215, note 2.
2. Francis and Katherine Biddle.
3. Beatrice Chanler's Seven Hundred Acre Island. See above, letter 192, note 1.

220

Hobe Sound
January 15, [1953]

My very dear Mildred,

What excuses can I make for such a tardy letter? . . . I went wandering around the far reaches of the south (Everglades, the chain of keys, even did a bit of sea-faring) after I left my hosts at Hobe Sound [. . .].

You'll never know how close to me the thought of you was, here in this climate that, for me, links so much of your country to the Old France of the Islands. I return, once again, marveling at the wealth of large birds in the Everglades, a fauna that is really more flora than fauna. Your little pocket spyglass, which at first delighted me as a sort of scientific plaything, turned out, in the wilds, to be of an astonishing precision, and now it never leaves my pocket. It flatters my worst longing —my frustrated desire to become a naturalist. [. . .]

Dear Mildred, you who think of others with such intuition, I think of the hours of genuine leisure that we have never shared, of the trips that we never have taken together. The water was very beautiful throughout this southern area (Atlantic, Caribbean, and "Gulf"), and I swam a great deal. I know both you and Robert[1] would have loved it.

I am with you both, affectionately,   Alexis

1. Mr. Bliss.

LETTERS TO ARCHIBALD MACLEISH
(1940-1960)

221

To Mr. Archibald MacLeish,[1]   *October 18, 1940*
The Librarian of Congress   *Shelton Hotel,*
Washington, D.C.   *New York, N.Y.*

Dear friend,

You have been so close to me as a living personality
for such a long time already that I can not address you
in any other way. In any case, my authorization for
taking this liberty is the exquisitely tactful concern that
you have shown on my behalf ever since you learned
that I was in your country.

I can't forgive myself for having let your second letter
arrive before I answered the first. And now I'm even
more embarrassed at having been so slow in replying
to the second.

I have been waiting, with regard to my immediate
future in France, for indications that I thought would
be forthcoming from the political trials at Riom,[2] indications that might themselves determine my freedom of
action in this country. And, to tell the whole truth, I
had just sunk into one of those abysmal states of loneliness and silence that are very hard to shake off, simply
because one loses all notion of time in such a state.

I was deeply moved by your two letters, and I don't
know how to thank you for the delicate way you showed
your friendly concern in your October 8th letter.

The idea[3] you so kindly put forward has very much
aroused my interest. It is in some such terms that I can
envisage activity here that would be best suited to my

special situation as well as to my personal principles and private tastes. It is also the only way I might have the moral satisfaction of being employed, however modestly, in the country that has extended its hospitality to me. The only thing I still have to think over is to what extent the arrangement that so kindly accompanies your suggestion may be acceptable to me at this moment, considering that it is not purely honorary. I am studying the matter and will let you know about it at the earliest possible moment. Even if *that* turned out to be a moral impossibility, I wouldn't be any the less grateful to you for any opportunity you could offer me of being associated, simply on an informal, friendly basis, with the studies being made relative to acquisitions in French literature at the Library of Congress.

We can talk all of this over more satisfactorily when I'm able to get down to Washington [. . .].

With the hope of seeing you soon, I am, in mind and heart, yours truly,   Alexis St-L. Leger

1. See above, letter 190, note 2.

2. On 30 July 1940 a "Supreme Court of Justice" was established by the Vichy government for the purpose of bringing to trial those leaders of the Third French Republic held responsible for the defeat of France. In actual fact, it was not until Feb. 1942 that the trial actually got started in the town of Riom. It was cut short in Apr. 1942 because the proceedings did not develop favorably for the Vichy regime and because Hitler was dissatisfied with the trial.

3. Through an intermediary—probably Mrs. Biddle—MacLeish had offered AL a post as Consultant on French Literature at the Library. See above, letter 190, note 2.

222

To Mr. Archibald MacLeish,   *Shelton Hotel,*
The Librarian of Congress   *New York, N.Y.*
Washington, D.C.   *December 4, 1940*

Dear friend,
   [. . .]

All my apologies for having been so slow in confirming my acceptance of the situation that you are so kindly
reserving for me. On returning from Washington, I was
quite stunned by the news that awaited me here about
the fate of my family in the occupied region of France,
and I was also very worn out as the result of a cold that
I didn't look after properly. But I have already notified
my friends in Argentina[1] that I have given up all thought
of leaving the United States, and I'm making all necessary arrangements for settling down in Washington as
of the beginning of January.

I intend to devote myself fully, and as best I can, to
the Library of Congress. I can assure you that the work
itself interests me greatly. I don't take it on in appearance only, nor simply paying it lip service, but rather
with real moral satisfaction. And above all, dear friend,
let me say quite simply how highly I prize the opportunity of being closely associated with you so long as I
live in America [. . .].

I shall always remain deeply touched by the extreme
tactfulness that has constantly dictated your friendly
concern for me, in spite of all the seemingly discouraging reactions on my part [. . .].

Don't bother to go on looking for lecture possibilities
in America. I prefer, so long as I am able, to limit myself
to my activities at the Library of Congress [. . .]. My
most pressing concern, at the moment, is to preserve

the greatest possible measure of solitude, silence, and withdrawal in my retreat.

I'll be seeing you soon, dear friend. Please, when you present my respects to Mrs. MacLeish, tell her how much her singing moved me, in a musical program that strangely resembled a "taking of the veil" for France.

Most cordially yours, Alexis St.-L. Leger

1. Chiefly Victoria Ocampo. See letter to Caillois of 1 Apr. 1944. (249)

223

To Archibald MacLeish,[1] *Washington*
The Librarian of Congress *The Library of Congress,*
Washington, D.C.   *Consultant Service*
         September 9, 1941

My dear Archie,

Here's my poem on exile.[2] It is yours. Do whatever you want with it. It has at least afforded me the opportunity of making this gesture of confidence towards a poet I admire and a man I love.

If you could get it typed, would you please give me the copies so I could correct them? I'd keep one or two, as I myself have only a crude rough draft, and I really owe it to our friend Katherine to let her see this poem before it comes out in print, since it was written in her house.

Besides, I don't know whether this sort of work can be published in French in the United States. And it's quite untranslatable—not so much where intellectual content is concerned, with its abstractions, ellipses, and intentional "ambiguities," as in its physical aspects—its alliterations, assonances, and incantations (sometimes dictated by the rhythm of waves)—and in literal terms, too, because of the etymological content of certain of the words—the most immaterial and simplest of them.

Among the concrete words of the poem there is a single rare or exotic word, for which I apologize— *azalaïe*,[3] which you won't find in standard dictionaries, is the name given to the great annual salt caravan in the African deserts. I needed the word for a transposition.

Affectionately.   A.S.L.

1. Letter printed on p. 548 of OC and not included in the "Lettres" section.

2. *Exil*, composed at Harvey Cedars, on Long Beach Island, New Jersey. (See above, letter 191, note 1.) The composition of this poem marks AL's "return" to poetry. It was published, in French, in the Mar. 1942 issue of *Poetry*, along with an article on AL by MacLeish, wherein MacLeish quoted long sections of the letter immediately following this one (23 Dec. 1941).

3. The word occurs in *Exil*, canto v: "Le ciel est un Sahel où va l'azalaïe en quête de sel gemme." ["The sky is a Sahel desert where the holy caravan goes in search of rocksalt." Devlin trans.]

224

To Mr. Archibald MacLeish[1]   *Washington,*
Washington, D.C.   *December 23, 1941*

My dear Archie,

I really couldn't bring myself, these days, to talk to you about anything literary. I've lived too close to you in spirit through these, your first hours of war,[2] which increase the already heavy burden that falls upon your shoulders even more. You know that close by my free Frenchman's heart there will always be an American heart beating in me.

Yet I must make up my mnd to answer a letter from you that goes back quite a long way already.[3]

You wanted a few personal items of information for a study of me that you over-generously let yourself be inveigled into doing. Unfortunately, I can't reconcile myself to the idea that the reader has to know anything about the author's person, at least on the absolute plane for which, I feel, a poetic work should always strive. It is out of neither affectation nor deliberate calculation that I have always adhered so strictly to the separation of my two personalities.

In Malaya, once, I was told about a belief held by an aboriginal tribe in Borneo. Every night man sets his "double" free in the very honorable form of a monkey, who goes about all night perpetrating the most outrageous and amazing exploits, which are quite beyond the abilities of the poor daytime slave. But in broad daylight it is forbidden to mention the slightest connection between the two beings. I subscribe wholeheartedly to such an act of faith.

And then, where memories are concerned, you know how few of them are likely to remain after a man goes his way—especially one who believes he is more French, the more universal he is. The true voyagers were perhaps those eighteenth-century French missionaries whose "Edifying Letters" never let any personal concerns come between the outside world and a craving for human knowledge.

And you are already quite familiar with my fierce hatred of literary exoticism.

Of Asia, especially Central Asia, the extraplanetary and extratemporal, I could say to you, like a pedant, that it gratified my need for a broader gauge of space and time. But I prefer to tell you this recollection that, for me, obliterates so many others. At the entrance of a Mongol yurt in the middle of the Gobi Desert, just as I was climbing back into the saddle, I asked for the translation of a wonderfully guttural sentence pronounced by a migrant high lama of the Red Sect: "Man is born in a house, but dies in the desert. . . ." For days and days, during the long, silent hours on horseback, I kept ruminating this sentence, so delectable to the palate of an Occidental who can never be sure of having his mouth sufficiently rinsed of all romantic aftertaste. Until the day, in a lamasery, on the edge of the desert, I was given this trivial explanation: "A dying man must be exposed outside the tent so as not to infect the dwelling-place of the living."

A nice slap in the face for the incurable associations of ideas of literary culture!

Yet my hostility to culture has something homeopathic about it—I feel it should be carried to such an extreme that, on its own, it recoils, and by an act of self-betrayal is voided.

Of all the museums of Europe I have visited out of courtesy (and isn't politeness still the surest way of preserving one's freedom?), I have retained very few impressions. In London, at the British Museum, the crystal skull in the pre-Columbian collection,[4] and in the South Kensington Museum, a little child's boat (now gone) that Lord Brassey picked up in the Indian Ocean; in the Kremlin, a woman's bracelet around the rough hock of a stuffed horse, weighted down by the crude harness of a nomad conqueror; in the Armeria of Madrid, a suit of armor for a child; in Warsaw, a beautiful letter from a prince on a leaf of beaten gold; in the Vatican, a similar letter on goatskin; in Bremen, an historic collection of fanciful engravings for the linings of cigar boxes.

About France there is nothing to say. It is myself and all of myself. For me it is something sacred, uniquely so—the only medium through which I can communicate with anything basic in this world. Even if I were not an essentially French animal, made of essentially French clay (and my last breath, like my first, will be chemically French), the French language would still be for me my only home, the shelter and refuge par excellence, the armor and the arms par excellence, the only "geometrical locus" in the world where I can station myself in order to understand, desire, or renounce anything.

(On a little Polynesian island under English protectorate, where the French flag had not been seen since the time of Louis Philippe, I was invited to hear a scene from *Esther*, in French. The verses of the scene had been patiently rehearsed for a week by young Tongan girls under the guidance of a very old French nun of the Order of Saint Paul of Chartres. The girls could not understand a single word of what they were reciting. Never has Racine been less betrayed, and never have I better understood the miracle of the French language, whose magic power is too often obscured by its genius for precise analysis.)

Nor have I anything to say to you about the Antilles, which, even though they steeped my childhood in the animal and plant life of the tropics, are to me of the very oldest French essence.

There, my dear Archie, and only because you are you, is all I can manage, and with great effort, by way of a personal confession.

As for literary doctrine, I have none to formulate. I have never found "scientific" cooking edible.

With all my Christmas wishes for you and yours. Affectionately.   Alexis St-L. Leger

1. Letter printed on pp. 549-551 of OC and not included in "Lettres" section.

2. The Japanese attack on Pearl Harbor had taken place on

7 Dec. 1941, and the United States entered the war on the next day.

3. MacLeish probably wrote requesting information some time in October or November.

4. This is the same crystal skull that AL "presented" to Paul Valéry. See letter to Valéry of 26 Nov. 1922. (151)

225

Memo to Mr. MacLeish,   *Library of Congress*
Librarian of Congress   *Washington, May 4, 1942*

Re: A search, in America, for the earliest German translations of the works of Saint-John Perse.

At your request, I received Mr. Herbert Steiner[1] of Zürich, whom I had never met in Europe. He struck me as very interesting, extremely well-informed about literary activity in France, and trustworthy. He reminded me that long ago he had been personally recommended to me by Paul Valéry and Valery Larbaud but had been unable to reach me in Paris. We exchanged all information available here concerning that bibliography of the German translations of my works, which is of particular interest to him and to a number of researchers who have asked him for assistance [. . .].

Here is how things now stand, if the matter is, indeed, worthy of even the slightest consideration:

In a general way, I am at the present time unable to furnish any personal information concerning the final outcome of any *German* translations I may once have authorized. I never had either the taste nor the time to take any interest in the matter; and, harried by the hectic pace of my diplomatic pursuits, I let my private secretaries handle all literary mail written in German, without their even showing it to me. The bibliography that was cited for possible publication in *Poetry*[2] in Chicago was compiled in France by Valery Larbaud, who was extremely painstaking in such matters. A sizable portion of it was printed by the publisher, Gallimard, in his *Anthologie des poètes de la Nouvelle Revue Française* (available at the Library of Congress).

1. *A translation of* ANABASE *by Groethuysen and Benjamin, with a preface by Hugo von Hofmannsthal*:

The typewritten text was submitted to me. I was informed of negotiations with the publisher (Insel Verlag, Leipzig); and Hugo von Hofmannsthal's preface was reprinted, in German, in the *Neue Schweizer Rundschau* (Zurich, Jahrgang XXII, Heft 5, mai 1929) under the title: "Einige worte als vorrede zu St. J. Perse Anabase," and in French in *Commerce* (Paris, Giraud-Badin, été 1929, no 20) under the title, "Emancipation du lyrisme français." The German publication in the *Neue Schweizer Rundschau*, which one of my friends tracked down in the New York Public Library (Room 303: Rare Books—File K.P.) in Karl Jacoby's bibliography of Hugo von Hofmannsthal (p. 95), contains a footnote, as a final indication: "The German version of *Anabasis* is being published by Insel Verlag, Leipzig."[3] Nevertheless, Mr. Herbert Steiner, whom I have every reason to trust fully, tells me that at the last minute, upon his own request and that of a few of his friends, the publication of that particular translation was suspended to make way for a better-qualified translator, a German poet whose name escapes me.[4] At the present time, Groethuysen and Benjamin's translation, announced by Insel Verlag of Leipzig, is said to be in a trunk in Zürich that belongs to Mr. Herbert Steiner.

2. *The translation of* ELOGES *by Kassner*.[5]

Mr. Herbert Steiner is also familiar with the existence of this one, but in 1938 he had seen in print only a few fragments, which he himself published in *Corona* (a Swiss literary review printed in Germany) [VIII-3].

Although I twice met Kassner in Paris, the authoriza-

tion for translation in a private edition that he requested
was taken care of through the intermediary of a friend.
I didn't follow up the matter on my own.

3. *A translation of* IMAGES À CRUSOÉ *by Rilke.*[6]

So far as I can remember, it was around 1924 that
Rilke, in Paris, showed me his translation for the first
time (based on a very faulty text of the poem, published
for the first time by the *N.R.F.*). At first I refused to
authorize publication, as I was not permitting myself, at
that time, any contact with literary life and was even less
inclined to consider any possible reprinting of these
pages from my very early youth, dated 1904.

After the accidental publication of fragments of *Anabase* in *La Nouvelle Revue française* (1924), Rilke once
more insisted, in a letter to me, on authorization for a
limited edition of his translation of *Images à Crusoé*
(First Version), of which he sent me a revised text.
Following the publication of *Anabase* and the announce-
ment of a new edition of *Eloges* (1925), I gave a favorable answer, through a friend, to Rilke's third request.
Even though it was only a *private* edition, my acceptance
of this German publication obliged me to add, *in extremis*, to the revised edition of *Eloges*, a greatly revised
text of *Images à Crusoé*.

I really don't know whether Rilke's revised translations finally took into account my own revision of the
text. I had resolved never to formulate any judgment of
a translation by a poet of Rilke's stature. All I remember is the external appearance of his typed manuscript.
I have no personal memory of the printed text. I knew
what was going on only through what friends told me.
As I was completely absorbed, from 1925 on, by the direction of Briand's Staff, I lost all direct contact, by my
own fault, with Rilke. It was through a lady—a mutual
friend—and through Valery Larbaud that I subsequently

heard several times about his private translation, which was said to be already in print, or in the process of being printed. It's possible that this information was erroneous, because inquiries, made by some Frenchmen in New York, of Austrian collectors residing in America have produced no results. A friend in New York wrote me last February that a Swiss publisher, expert in matters of German imprints, and now living in America—but whose name he failed to indicate (might it not have been Mr. Herbert Steiner himself?)—had put out a flier on this subject, alerting more than 800 American book-dealers.

As for myself, my ignorance of the German language and the conditions of my professional life in Paris combined to keep me much too far removed from such questions to have any personal memories about them that might be sufficiently valid.   A. L.

May 4, 1942

1. Herbert Steiner (1892-1966), Austrian writer who founded the literary review *Corona*, based in Zürich. He came to the United States during World War II, devoting his energies to academic and literary pursuits, the principal of which was the editing and publication of the complete works of the Austrian poet Hugo von Hofmannsthal.

2. Presumably the "St.-J. Perse: Bibliography," that was actually published in *Poetry* (Mar. 1942), immediately following MacLeish's article, "A Note on Alexis Saint Léger Léger."

3. German in original.

4. The "better qualified translator" remains unidentified. The Groethuysen-Benjamin translation was finally printed, after being revised by Steiner, in the Oct. 1950 issue of *Das Lot*, published in Berlin under the auspices of the Conseil de contrôle interallié.

5. The complete translation of *Eloges* by Rudolf Kassner and Herbert Steiner was subsequently published in the 1952 issue of *Das Lot*.

6. Rainer Maria Rilke (1875-1926), the celebrated German-language poet of Bohemian extraction.

226

[*Library of Congress*],
August 15, 1942

My dear Archie,

Jameson passed along the letter from Mr. Roditi, which I am returning to you.[1] I think that the simplest way to handle it would be to reply that permission for the translation in question has been, and is still being, withheld by the author.

You know that as long as there is the slightest chance, no matter how remote, that you might one day translate this poem, nothing else will be of interest to me; and the mere *thought* of this is enough, in my eyes—by virtue of all the comradeship that such a thought symbolizes for me—to exonerate you from having to realize it in the midst of all your public responsibilities.

I take this occasion to send along a manuscript[2] at the same time. I have no way of getting it typed. If you could ask one of your secretaries to do me that favor, I would be most grateful, because I want to send this poem, without delay, to some Frenchmen who are founding a review of pure poetry(!) in New York and who ask me to help them out with their first issue. (I don't like this sort of thing much, but *here* in the U.S. I like even less the inelegance of a refusal.)

I have tried, dear Proteus, to get in touch with you outside your own home, but I had to give up [. . .].

Affectionately.   Alexis L.

1. R. D. Jameson was one of MacLeish's assistants at the Library of Congress. Edouard Roditi, an American essayist and poet born in Paris, had written to MacLeish inquiring about the possibility of obtaining AL's authorization for an English translation of *Exil*.

2. The manuscript of *Poème à l'étrangère*, originally entitled,

"V Street," with the subtitle "Poème à l'Emigrée." The poem was published in the first issue of Yvan Goll's short-lived bilingual review, *Hémisphères*, Summer 1943.

227

To Mr. Archibald MacLeish   *Georgetown,*
Georgetown, Washington, D.C.   *Washington, D.C.*
                                             August 19, 1942

My dear Archie,

What a refinement of delicacy! (It's so like you!) My poem was first of all for you.[1] What more could I wish than to have you as my first, or even my only, reader? And this poem, in spite of my horror of any kind of direct or "personal" poetry, is, in spite of myself, in its transposition, steeped in this Georgetown where I live, not far from you, and where your presence takes on its full human value for me.

Affectionately.   A.

1. MacLeish, in his answer to AL's letter of 15 Aug. 1942, had indicated that he did not feel free to read the new poem (*Poème à l'étrangère*) without AL's express permission.

228

February 24, 1943

My dear Archie,

A thousand apologies for such a tardy reply. But my first reaction to all stationery with a publisher's letterhead is to look for an excuse to ignore it.

1. About the bilingual edition of *Eloges*: I didn't acknowledge the last offer from New Directions,[1] but you can tell the Norton people I accept their offer. For I really feel very guilty about the way I treated Mrs.

Varèse,[2] who went to such a lot of trouble over the translation.

2. As for the introduction, you know perfectly well, my dear Archie, that you are the only person by whom I would be happy to be "presented." But you shouldn't be taken advantage of this way at every turn. And it occurs to me that, if you ever find the leisure to do the translation of *Exil* that is reserved for you, you might want, at that time, to supply a few lines of introduction the way Eliot felt obliged to do for *Anabase*.

You'll have to be the judge. Your decision, whatever it may be, is accepted in advance with the same confidence and the same affectionate understanding as ever.

If you feel you can do something, this time all reference to Alexis S.-L. should be avoided in order to preserve intact among Frenchmen the pseudonym St-J. Perse; for, since I long ago strictly forbade all reprinting of my work in France, the bilingual American editions will for a very long time remain the only definitive ones, even for France.

With the hope of seeing you soon, my dear Archie, and always most fraternally yours.

Alexis S.-L. L.

1. The New Directions Publishing Corporation of New York.
2. Louise McCutcheon Varèse, wife of the composer, Edgar Varèse (1885-1965). Louise Varèse's translation of *Eloges* was published the next year (1944) by W. W. Norton and Co.

229

To Mr. Archibald. MacLeish   *Georgetown,*
Alexandria, Va.,   *(Washington, D.C.)*
(Washington, D.C.)   *Saturday, August 21, 1943*

My dear Archie,

I've just notified your office that I am leaving for a vacation.

It's a source of great regret to me, not having been able to share a few full summer days with you. When I return, I'll get you to hire me one Sunday to help harvest the corn and pile the firewood for the winter in the cellar.

I'm sending back to you a photostat copy of *Eloges* that was borrowed by the Norton people for use in the publication of that text, which they are working on. I think it would be a good idea to have this photostat entered in the Library catalogue, since the other copies have evaporated.

As for the typescript of *Pluies*, which I wasn't in a hurry about—when you get it, you would be very kind to take personal charge of it until I get back.

Lots of affectionate thoughts, my dear Archie, for you and yours.   Alexis

230

To Mr. Archibald MacLeish   *Georgetown,*
Alexandria, Va.,   *(Washington, D.C.)*
(Washington, D.C.)   *Tuesday, August 2, 1944*

My dear Archie,

I'm not feeling well and must leave for Maine sooner than anticipated (W. Astor Chanler's 700 Acre Island near Dark Harbor, Maine).

I am completely worn out with insomnia, and for ten days now I have been suffering from the worst blows I have yet received in my solitude: bad news about my mother, a brother-in-law in jeopardy, another one who has disappeared, nephews interned God only knows where, new deprivations inflicted on the one sister about whom we were still able to get news, and the deportation to Germany of someone very dear to me who had the courage to look after my mother for me and help out all the members of my family whom, as a man, I have had to abandon. I pound my head against every wall futilely searching for ways out. The worst torture a man can know is, surely, to be unable to do anything in a practical way for the persons, especially women, who are entirely dependent on him, but whose very name can bring harm to them.[1]

For you, dear Archie, and for Ada, my most affectionate thoughts. Take care of yourselves. People such as the two of you will be only too rare, after the war, as links between France and America [. . .].

Yours,

A.

1. AL's name was high on the official Nazi blacklist.

231

To Mr. Archibald MacLeish   *Georgetown,*
Alexandria, Va.,   *(Washington, D.C.)*
(Washington, D.C.)   *November 5, 1944*

A red-letter day, my dear Archie![1]

I give you a bear hug for your country, my country, and for heaps of other reasons!

The view from here is so filled with the things we all have cause to rejoice about that I haven't had a minute, not even a second—believe me—to devote to the thought that I'm losing your protective wing at the Library of Congress [. . .]. The important thing is your acceding to a position of importance[2] at the appointed time for the end of the war and after [. . .].

With all my heart.

A.

And I embrace you too, Ada!

1. On 4 Nov. 1944, Franklin D. Roosevelt was elected to his fourth term as President of the United States. Abroad, Allied victories continued unabated in the European theater of war.

2. MacLeish served as Librarian of Congress from 1939 to 1944 and, simultaneously, as head of the Office of Facts and

Figures (1941-1942). In the reorganization following the 1944 election, Roosevelt appointed MacLeish Assistant Secretary of State for Public and Cultural Affairs—a post MacLeish occupied from Dec. 1944 to Aug. 1945.

232

To Mr. Archibald MacLeish   *Washington, March 24, 1946*
                                 3120 R Street, N.W.

My dear Archie,

I don't know where my letter will catch up with you. They tell me you've become a southerner for a few months, even a sailor. In reality, it has been more than a year since the "perils of the sea" carried you off, and the Gulf Stream that swept up your shell seems every day to carry it a little farther away from your friend.

How can I tell you what this loss of contact with my "brother-in-arms" means to me? [. . .] So long as you breathed somewhere nearby—even in Alexandria[1]—it didn't make any difference that I didn't see you and that I dared not interfere with a life so filled with obligations. I knew you were there, and that meant so much [. . .].

But I won't insist. I don't want there to be the least shadow on your sails. I want only to think of the brilliant flood of light of the extended vacation that has been coming to you for such a long time already. Gorge yourself on it, dear friend, with the soul of a child and a poet, of a dolphin[2] and an osprey,[2] with all your athletic vigor restored—a vigor that will link you once again with the mysterious forces of this world. And out of all this, may you have a clearer vision of the way the next phase of your life must shape up, whatever the choice you make.

For the moment I want to confide only messages of joy for you to the seagulls. I'll only say briefly, so you won't be wondering about my long silence, that I've had to endure a series of paralyzing ordeals—preoccupations of every sort, sadness and worry that I've had to face, powerless, in the midst of fatigue and insomnia bequeathed to me by a bout of good old Washingtonian flu.

I heard that you were concerned about my situation at the Library of Congress. Please don't worry about me on that score! But don't ask me about the cast of my thoughts, each day, in my little glassed-in cell, now that I realize you aren't there. No more buzzards[2] on the dome of the old building, and the Angel of the Absurd has let no more horse-droppings fall on the top of the aerial stairway to the dome.[3] At least I am still grateful to the pure and consoling waters of the little drinking fountains in the hallways, which, as if they were in the greenhouses and aviaries of a zoological garden, are still offered up to the dove-breasted stenographers, the lizard-throated Chinese women students, and the turtle-chested old scholars.[2] And isn't this guarantee of pure water, after all, one of the best gifts of American democracy? [. . .]

I hope with all my heart that the freedom from care that you are enjoying at the moment will profit you, even on a long-term basis, and in every conceivable way. The main thing for you was to have a period of "fasting." The benefit of this sort of fast is a delayed-action benefit, as is the case with hot-spring cures.

I would so like to have let *you* read a very long poem[4] which is quite important to me, and in which, in a new conception, I have pushed my own demands upon myself further than I ever have before. But, in order to take advantage of an available messenger, I had to speed up the delivery of the text to the Paris publisher (Gallimard), and I didn't keep a typed copy of it.

Tell Ada for me that I'd give a lot to hear her sing and laugh in the prow of your sailboat. Tell me if she knows the tune of the French "chanty" *Les Filles de La Ro-chelle*.[5] If she does, I'll send her, from memory, all the words to it—for your pleasure as a poet, sailor, and Frenchman by adoption.

To both of you, warmly.   A.

1. Alexandria: the town in Virginia directly across the Potomac from Washington, D.C.

2. English in original.

3. The presence of fresh horse-droppings each morning at the top of the dome of the Library of Congress baffled and irritated the security guards of the Library. The mystery was never explained, though AL was of the opinion that the droppings were carried there daily by a pair of vultures (the "buzzards" referred to) that were seeking to establish their eyrie on the library dome.

4. *Vents* ("*Winds*"), first published in a limited edition in Paris by Gallimard later in 1946.

5. A traditional French sea-chanty. "Chanty" is English in original.

233

To Mr. Archibald MacLeish   *Washington,*
Uphill Farm, Conway, Massachusetts   *June 26,* [*1947?*]

My dear Archie,

Your good letter restored calm to your friend's heart. I liked its very human truthfulness, and though it made me ever more aware of the moral ordeal you have just come through[1] (because, for you, everything always assumes its reality in the moral sphere, and its echo in the spiritual sphere), it made me happy to feel that life is flowing back into you, along with all the uneasiness occasioned by life's new demands. It's this very interrogation and sudden feeling of being unsatisfied, this voluntary remove from everything usual, that reveals to us—by breaking continuity and giving rise to a precious kind of disaffection—the renewal of our life at a higher level of true being.

I very much want to see you before too long, and under your own roof. I deeply appreciate your invitation.

I expect to arrive around the 17th or 18th of August, very probably by way of Boston, after a cruise in Canadian waters. I'm leaving tomorrow morning to set sail from Halifax (that sinister port where I disembarked as a refugee).[2]

I've learned that you were already up and about enough to resume your usual activities and that you had been seen, looking very fit, with your complete "aura," at important public functions. So I'm leaving with heart and mind at peace, where you are concerned.

My heart goes out to you and to Ada, whom I embrace affectionately.   Alexis

1. The "ordeal" has not been identified.
2. AL's first port of call on the American continent in July 1940 was Halifax, Nova Scotia.

234

To Mr. Archibald MacLeish   *Washington,*
                                 November 12, 1948
                                 2800 Woodley Road, N.W.

My dear Archie, what a joy it is for me, on reading over your latest book of poems[1] with all the objectivity and critical severity I owe you, to feel once more the same pleasure and sense the same mastery.

Let the critics say what they will—your book is beautiful and good and the worthy product of a complete poetic maturity. By its stripped quality, its nudity, it satisfies in a most harmonious way the requirements of classical art—the very requirements that assure its apparent artlessness. You've managed to reconcile thought and song without transgressing the inherent laws, that is, the very mystery, of poetic creation. Your art, and some sort of heaven-sent felicity, triumphed over my prejudices—which have always been very strong—against the use of current events or political morality as major themes. Undoubtedly because of that well-spring of humanity, that primal source you have managed to keep flowing deep within you, the man and the artist share equally in your poetic process. And the voice I hear is your own true voice. Modesty and mastery, are they not far better than pride? Step out onto your threshold and breathe freely, my dear friend—you who were born, like the best among men, marked by the sign of dissatisfaction with one's own performance.

I'm not only thinking of the successful way your long poem[2] unfolds—though you thereby won a risky wager that will always be to your credit. I've already told you how much I like the pure modulations, the free movement and the "wordless inception" of certain of your short lyric poems. The most elusive, most sensitive of your latest musical notations, reduced to the bare essentials yet rich in "tactile" quality, enchanted me with their suppression of all "intellectual" matter. Finally, I would like to tell you more particularly how much I was interested and delighted by your treatment of the intellectual theme in poems made up of *laisses* or verses [. . .]. One has there the "sensitized intelligence" taking its complete revenge, as it leagues up with a bit of magic, in order to light its own way on the frontiers of what is beyond our grasp.

And now, if I have to give you an earnest against all friendly partiality, I'll look for a poem I can't entirely accept. I find only one—the last one, which will undoubtedly get you the greatest number of admirers. I

don't like that one—maybe bcause I too much liked the
one that precedes it.[3]

My dear Archie, I wanted to write to you much
sooner. I just wasn't able to pull myself out of the de-
spondent depths of a sleepless, heavy heart. My mother
died two weeks ago without my ever having been able
to reach her. . . I won't talk about it. It is a profound
sorrow that I bury in my heart, and my loneliness, in
consequence, is enormously increased. To her motherly
heart I owed all that I have been able to preserve of faith
in human nature. I am glad that she had known you.[4]

For you and for Ada, my affectionate thoughts.

Your friend   Alexis

1. *Actfive and Other Poems.*

2. The "long poem" is the title poem: "Actfive."

3. The poem "Brave New World" is the last in the book. The
one that precedes it is "The Young Dead Soldiers."

4. AL's mother died 24 Oct. 1948. See letter to Mrs. Bliss of
25 Oct. 1948. (218)

235

To Mr. Archibald MacLeish   *Washington, D.C.,*
                                   June 18, 1949
                                   2800 Woodley Road, N.W.

My dear Archie, where are you, anyhow?

I learned, very tardily, through a press notice, that I
could rejoice with you in a very happy event—your appointment to that important chair at Harvard,[1] which
strikes me as solving so many problems for you. At that
special level which, historically, goes far beyond that of
university life and restores you somewhat, morally speaking, to national life (isn't it the chair that was once occupied by John Quincy Adams?) your intellectual au-

thority is given official recognition, to the benefit of everyone, in a way that may satisfy your patriotic concerns; and your literary influence is thereby increased, at the same time, without in any way altering the demands you make upon yourself—and without your freedom being in any way impaired, I believe. Nothing at all like the administrative bondage of the Library of Congress. And finally, I think of what a material advantage it is for you not to be too far away from Conway. At any rate, you'll be living there among people very warmly and fervently devoted to you.

You must have received, from an American publisher (Pantheon Press—Bollingen Series) a book by me[2] that I regret not having been able to inscribe for you. Your copy, without my knowing, had been sent to you ahead of time, even before I received my author's copies. The publisher, it's true, owed you at least that, after having exploited you by reproducing your introductory note to *Eloges* in an appendix.

I am counting on a stay at Cape Cod in July, and I'll then spend the month of August in Maine. I have lots to do to complete a very long work,[3] the most ambitious I've ever contemplated, but one I've had to put down too often. As a matter of fact, I've forbidden myself to work at it so long as sorrows or cares weigh me down; for I have sworn, in defiance of our time, to take nothing from it but joy, unfettered and freely given.[4]

Affectionately yours, my dear Archie, with faithful thoughts for Ada, whose bright gaiety is sadly lacking on the Washington scene.   Alexis

1. The chair of Boylston Professor of Rhetoric, which MacLeish held from 1949 to 1962.

2. *Exile and other Poems*, the first book by AL to be published in the Bollingen Series. It is a bilingual, de luxe edition contain-

ing *Exil, Pluies, Neiges,* and *Poème à l'Etrangère,* with English
translations by Denis Devlin.

3. *Amers (Seamarks).*

4. This sentence was quoted by MacLeish in his essay.

236

To Mr. Archibald MacLeish   *Wellfleet, Cape Cod*
Conway, Massachusetts   *July 23, 1949*

My dear Archie,

I am always moved by the noble way you do things![1]
Is there still, in our time, one writer—and a poet at that
—who is able to take pen in hand to defend the living?
[. . .] From you I can accept a partiality that dictates a
judgment illumined as much by the heart as by the head.
For that matter, I have long since learned to like only
partiality, the only mode of knowledge that nature
teaches us.

You are too modest—or too demanding—in the way
you underestimate the literary repercussions of your fine
article. Quite apart from its perfect appropriateness to its
object and audience, I liked its high literary tone and
implications, which you project harmoniously into the
true realm of the spirit, where you always manage to
take your stand, evoking everything that should be
evoked—I mean *what is really at stake*[2] there—but in an
incidental way! I won't even mention your language,
always my delight, which here gives your book reviews
the dignity of the true essay.

As a friend my thanks go out to you, even though you
may not want to hear this from me.

Yes, of course, I'd love to see you at Conway. I can't
arrange that very easily at the moment, but, when I'm
in Maine, where I'll be in August, I'll inquire about

chances of seeing you in September, on the way back to Washington—I don't yet know exactly when.

Give my friendly regards to Bullitt,[3] at whom I would gladly have thrown eggs, not hens' or turkeys', but dinosaurs', to teach him not to leave friendship in the lurch.

If your children are with you, line them all up in a circle to form a living wreath around their mother, whom I embrace.   Alexis

1. MacLeish had just published an article on AL's poetry, with special attention to the four "exile" poems (see above, letter 235, note 2), entitled "The Living Spring," in *The Saturday Review of Literature*, 16 July 1949.

2. English in original.

3. William Bullitt. See above, letter 191, note 4.

237

To Mr. Archibald MacLeish   *Washington, April 10, 1950*
Harvard University   *2800 Woodley Road, N.W.*

My dear Archie,

What have you gone and thought up again[1] for your friend, and managed to bring off?—with that refinement of discretion that I've come to know so well.

I know you're laughing up your sleeve at everything your powers of sorcery were able to accomplish this time. There is so much moral elegance in what you did, and in the friendly way you did it, that this moral elegance alone, in my worst hours, will ward off the temptations of pessimism.

Naturally, I was far too moved by the thought that I owe the decision of the American Academy to you personally, to think for a minute, this time, of turning it down. And too moved also by your being designated as my sponsor to refuse to participate in the May 25th ceremony.

I clasp you in my arms, my dear Archie, and Ada too.

A.

1. The American Academy of Arts and Letters, of which Mac-Leish was a long-standing member and later president (1953-1956), voted to bestow its Award of Merit Medal on AL. The award was presented at the Academy's "Ceremonial" of 25 May 1950, at which time William Faulkner received a similar award.

238

To Mr. Archibald MacLeish   *Washington, February 15, 1952*
Harvard University   *2800 Woodley Road, N.W.*

My dear Archie,

You'll always manage to find twenty different ways of going straight to your friend's heart.

You know quite well that I know that you are the sole responsible party in this latest initiative of the Charles Eliot Norton Committee.[1] And it is you only I have in mind when I feel uneasy about being once again obliged to notify the Provost of Harvard of my refusal.

I remember your last words at Ashfield last September; I remember the look of affectionate concern that you gave me then. Today I can gauge all the worrying you have done over the fate of your difficult friend [. . .].

Do I need to tell you that, this time, I did not turn down Harvard's official invitation without hesitation? But the Bollingen Foundation[2] has just supplied me with the assurance of a renewal of my contract; and even though that will bring in less over a period of three years than the two thirds of the Harvard endowment for three months, at least it still guarantees me, for the immediate future, a peace of mind that I still so much

need in order to complete the poem I am presently working on.

I hope I haven't put you, personally, in too awkward
a situation with the Ch. Eliot Norton Committee by
refusing this second time.

I think affectionately of you, dear friend, whom I
would like to see more often. The only attraction a stay
in Cambridge might have offered me would have been
your and Ada's presence.

Will my letter find you still at Harvard? I've heard
that Ada was already in the vanguard at Antigua, your
"Désirade."[3] Embrace her for me as soon as you can,
and, as a friend, please don't harbor any resentment at
my turning down the Harvard offer.

Cordially.   A.

1. In Oct. 1947 AL had been invited to occupy the Charles
Eliot Norton Chair of Poetics at Harvard University and had
declined the honor. The invitation was extended a second time,
in 1952, undoubtedly upon the suggestion of MacLeish, who
had been Boylston Professor of Rhetoric at Harvard. (See above,
letter 234, note 1.) AL declined a second time.

2. The Bollingen Foundation had just renewed AL's fellowship
for another three years.

3. La Désirade is a small island off the eastern tip of Guadeloupe. The MacLeishes had a winter residence on the British
Antillean island of Antigua.

239

To Mr. Archibald MacLeish   *Washington,*
"Uphill Farm,"   *June 30, 1953*
Conway, Massachusetts

My dear Archie,

Your letter still moves me. You are, in everything, so
nobly the poet, from the depths of the heart and mind!
And in the voice that is uniquely yours, I always recog-

nize so many familiar notes that I want to stop and listen to again, echoing them, without pessimism or weariness.

I wanted to make absolutely sure, this year, that I could share a little of the intimacy of your family circle. So I unceremoniously altered my summer plans in order to schedule my visit to Conway before my stay in Maine and on Cape Cod, for fear of missing you at the end of the season. I am to be at Ashfield-Chapelbrook on the Fourth of July, and I'll inquire about life at Uphill Farm right away.

I had to pay my tribute to an insidious case of summer flu that has left me worn out; but the good air of your "high places" will quickly restore my walking legs.

I'm so eager, my dear Archie, to be with you and Ada again, to share for a moment, under your vine with the still green bunches of grapes, a little peace of mind and warm intimacy.

With the hope of soon being among you.

Alexis

240

To Mr. Archibald MacLeish　　　　*New York,*
Harvard University　　　　*May 31,* [*1956?*]

In haste, my dear Archie, before I take the train to Washington.

I'll soon have the joy of seeing you once again in our old Conway intimacy.

What you express in *Life* about the moral crisis in America is a fine, good thing, which broadens, in a human way, the implications of Stevenson's[1] political analysis.

Affectionately.　　　　A.

1. *Life* magazine ran a four-part series, beginning in the 23 May 1960 issue, on "The National Purpose." In the 30 May 1960 issue, the two major contributions to the series were by Archibald MacLeish and Adlai Stevenson, whose articles appear side by side, beginning on pp. 86 and 87. Reference to these articles seems to indicate that the conjectural date in OC is off by four years.

241

To Mr. Archibald MacLeish   *Washington, April 25, 1958*
Antigua (British West Indies)

Archie, never have I so deeply regretted that you and Ada are so far away. I would like to have opened my heart to you in person at this moment when an important event in my life is taking place. I'm getting married tomorrow; and tomorrow in my thoughts you will be at my side, because I would like to have had you as a witness along with Francis.[1]

I'm marrying Dorothy Milburn (Mrs. Russell), whom you already know slightly, and who, for her part, already finds the two of you so congenial. I am thus fulfilling a wish that was dear to my mother's heart, for the person who is linking her fate to mine brings rare human qualities with her. My sisters, who love her, are preparing to welcome her to France, where I now have a roof. But I'm not snatching her away from America, because I'll come back here with her seven months out of every year, and my official residence will still be here [. . .].

To both of you, with all my heart.   Alexis

1. AL married Mrs. Russell, née Dorothy Milburn, in Georgetown, with Francis Biddle as one of the witnesses.

242

To Mr. Archibald MacLeish   *Washington,*
New York   *May 14, 1958*

Archie, my brother,

Your letter was so moving that I can't keep from telling you so, and also from telling you how much Dorothy appreciates the expression of your warm feelings toward her. She has already brought a great deal of moral elegance into my life, and now she fills my cup to overflowing by so spontaneously sharing some of the warmest affections I feel.

For the moment, I've had to put off our flight to France. I must first have a somewhat clearer picture of the outcome of the crisis that is building up there. I'll never bring myself to accept the possibility of a dictatorship in my country.[1]

I am happy for you about all I hear concerning the increasing success of your play.[2] You have revived the notion in literature of a work of art—a notion that tends to be forgotten in these days of literary fragmentation. And it seems to me that your mastery of language has here overcome the most serious difficulties of movement, action, and density posed by the metrics of poetic language in the contemporary theater.

Most affectionately yours, my dear Archie. . . . What anguish I feel over what is happening in my country!

A.

1. The spring of 1958 was a climactic period in the Algerian crisis. On 13 May, General Salan in Algiers spoke out against French policy in North Africa and called for the return of de Gaulle to power. This marked the end of the Fourth Republic. The Fifth Republic began on 1 June 1958, when de Gaulle again took over the reins of the French government.

2. MacLeish's play, *J. B.*, performed in New York in 1958.

243

To Mr. Archibald MacLeish   *Washington,*
Antigua (British West Indies)   *February 8, 1960*

My dear Archie,

A lucky chance brought me news of you through a
friend who had seen you in Antigua. He told me what
a good impression he had got of your convalescence. I
conclude from this that you've managed to behave and
to be patient, and that you'll be able to see it through
this way until all this is over. My friend was enthusiastic
about the spot you've chosen for your retreat and about
the miracles Ada has been able to accomplish with your
tropical setting. Get a good rest, and drift happily along
to the rhythm of your surroundings, as when the sap
rises; and, especially, don't be afraid to "fast," literarily
speaking, as long as you feel like doing so. At certain
moments, that's the best way for the creative instinct to
store up a reserve and lie coiled in readiness to strike
(all of which in no way resembles the boa constrictor[1] of
the Romantics).

I won't ask you about the new dramatic work you
were thinking about and that you may be working on
at this moment. We should never talk about what we
are holding our breath for, or even what we simply have
our hearts set on, during the incubation period.

I think affectionately of you and Ada, whom I embrace most cordially.   A.

The death of poor Camus[2] was a terrible shock to a
whole group of my literary friends in Paris. I was in the
process of finishing a letter to him when I heard the
frightful news on the radio. He had asked me for a play
for the Théâtre Nouveau which had just been entrusted
to him. Once again, I had to answer him in the vein that

you can imagine. But while refusing on my own behalf, I took advantage of the opportunity to tell him about you.

1. English in original.
2. Albert Camus (1913-1960) was killed in an automobile accident in which the driver of the car, Michel Gallimard, was also killed, on 4 Jan. 1960 at Villeblevin. During the last year of his life Camus had been offered the directorship of the Comédie Française but had indicated he would be more interested in a less traditional state-supported theater. The offer had come from the then Minister of Culture, André Malraux.

244

To Mr. Archibald MacLeish   *Washington,*
Antigua (British West Indies)   *February 26, 1960*

My dear Archie,

A most unexpected letter signed by Douglas Moore and Glenway Wescott[1] officially informs me of my election to the American Academy of Arts and Letters and to the National Institute of Arts and Letters.

Even though you are no longer actively president, I can't help thinking you had a hand in this. I can't forget the way you received me at the American Academy when I was awarded its quinquennial prize, nor can I forget so many other things that have happened since I arrived all alone in America—the most recent being the offer of the Charles Eliot Norton Chair,[2] which would at least have given me the chance to tread the sacred flagstones of Harvard in your company!

The official notification I have just received mentions a "formal induction," "taking place at the annual ceremonial to be held on Wednesday, May 25."[3] Although they offer to mail the insignia and official citation to me, should I prefer that, I suppose it would be rather inelegant of me not to be there. Will you, at least, be there?

I won't be going to France before mid-June. Next week I'm taking off for Argentina, where I have accepted—in my literary capacity this time—an official invitation from the Argentine government.[4] I'll return by way of Chile and Peru.

I want to hear good news from you when I get back. See that you regard your health in the same light that M. de Buffon regarded genius—as "a long patience."[5]

Affectionately with you and Ada.   A.

1. Douglas Moore (1893-1969) and Glenway Wescott (b. 1901) were, respectively, Chancellor of the American Academy of Arts and Letters and President of the "mother organization," the National Institute of Arts and Letters. MacLeish had been president of the Academy from 1953 to 1956. (See letter to MacLeish of 10 Apr. 1950. [237])

2. See above, letter 237, note 1, and letter 238, note 1.

3. English in original.

4. AL's trip to Argentina was to have been for twelve days but turned out to be a month and a half in length. Nor did he return by way of Chile and Peru; he came directly back to Washington instead. See letter to Maria Martins of Apr. 1960. (362)

5. "Le génie est une longue patience," is the commonly abbreviated form of a sentence attributed to the eminent 18th-century naturalist, Buffon (1707-1788), by Hérault de Séchelles in his book, *Visite à M. de Buffon* (1785).

245

To Mr. Archibald MacLeish   *New York, May 16, 1960*
Antigua (British West Indies)   *156 East 71st Street*

My dear Archie,

Your last letter still warms your friend's heart.

I'm here in New York for a few days, where I finally agreed to attend the ceremony of the American Academy on May 25. I'll be back in Washington by the 27th or 28th of May in order to prepare for my yearly flight to France. I'll be most unhappy to leave without good news about your health, and I'd like to get that news straight from you or Ada. If either of you happens to be going through New York between now and the 27th, be sure to get in touch with me, please, so I can have the pleasure of visiting with you, even if only by telephone [. . .].

My wanderings in Argentina kept me down there more than a month and a half. The extraordinary good will of the Argentine government fulfilled my fondest wishes by finally arranging a trip to Patagonia, the Straits of Magellan, Tierra del Fuego, the Beagle Channel, and the Cape Horn archipelago—with the aid of Navy planes and a gunboat from the Antarctic bases. When I got back, I found an invitation from the Brazilian government, which I unfortunately had to decline. But this year I'm homesick for the sea of the Antilles. I hope to learn that its effects on you were beneficial.

Very affectionately yours. Embrace Ada for me.

A.

LETTERS TO ROGER CAILLOIS
(1942-1955)

246

To Monsieur Roger Caillois[1]   *Washington, July 2, 1942*
Director of *Lettres françaises*   *3120 R Street, N.W.*
Buenos Aires

Cher Monsieur,

I thank you for your letters; they mean a great deal to me [. . .].

I have read only the first two issues of *Lettres françaises*—one of them, thanks to you; the other, thanks to Denis de Rougemont.[2] That was enough to let me form some idea of the quality and merit of your undertaking in Argentina. But your name alone was really guarantee enough.

If I have not been able to reserve for you my first available text,[3] that is because some friends had disposed of it elsewhere—friends to whom I had *given* my manuscript outright. At that time I hadn't given any thought to possible publication [. . .].

The pages of your own[4] that you sent for me to read are beautiful [. . .]. I like their sobriety, their timelessness—in a word, the irreducible element they contain. What I liked most of all was that mastery of a language that is wholly self-contained and makes no concessions to facility. Underlying your very modern view of things is a live discipline that manages to prolong the French tradition in ways other than by simply indulging in purely cultural games. It would be a shame if such well-written pages did not appear in France. Here, I don't know of any really good exclusively literary review that might publish them in French [. . .]. In France, I can't think of anything beyond the *Cahiers du Sud*, *Fontaine*, and *Poésie 41*[5] that would be worthy of your consideration, to judge by the few issues that get through to me here, thanks to anonymous intermediaries unknown to me. I have also received from time to time, and in just as mysterious a fashion, a few new Swiss reviews that might be of interest to you [. . .].

Monsieur Marcel Raymond, author of a book that was once published long ago by Corti—*De Baudelaire au surréalisme*,[6] has asked me from Switzerland, through an unexpected emissary (a representative of the International Red Cross whom you will undoubtedly see when he passes through Argentina), for permission to publish *Exil* in book form, for Switzerland and France. I'm refusing, so that it won't encroach on your publication of it; and I'm authorizing only such printings of it as may possibly appear in periodicals. [. . .]

My wishes, most attentive and sympathetic, for the completion of your own work.   Alexis St-L. Leger

Thank you for the bibliographical information. I myself had never heard of that already aged translation of *Anabase* into Spanish (in Mexico).[7]

1. Roger Caillois, translator and essayist who lived in Buenos Aires during World War II, where he founded the review, *Lettres françaises*, in 1941 and remained its editor until the Liberation of France in 1945, when he took over the editorship of the London-based review, *La France libre*.

2. Denis de Rougemont, French critic, author of *La Part du diable* (1944) and other works.

3. The poem, *Exil* (1941). See letter to MacLeish of 9 Sept. 1941. (223)

4. Probably the text of either or both of Caillois's descriptive essays, "La Pampa" and "Patagonie," which were later combined in a large-format book published under the single title *Patagonie* in 1942.

5. The *Cahiers du Sud*, a literary review published in Marseilles, founded in 1913. *Fontaine*, a literary review published originally in Algiers from 1939 to 1948 under the direction of Max-Pol Fouchet. *Poésie*, a review of French poetry issued yearly by Pierre Seghers from 1940 to 1948.

6. Marcel Raymond (b. 1897), Swiss critic and professor of literature, published his *De Baudelaire au surréalisme* in 1933.

7. *Anabasis*, Spanish translation by Octavio J. Barreda, originally published in the Mexican review, *Contemporaneos*, Jan. 1931.

247

To Monsieur Roger Caillois   *Washington,*
Director of *Lettres Françaises*   *August 8, 1943*
Buenos Aires   *3120 R Street, N.W.*

Dear Roger Caillois,

[. . .] Thank you for your magnificent edition of *Exil*,[1] a real achievement! And I'm not speaking solely of all that had to go into such an undertaking: typography, paper, etc.; I know in addition all I owe you for the accuracy of the text, and I am boundlessly grateful to you for your personal vigilance on my behalf, which you guaranteed to me at such a far remove. Everything was impeccable and perfect.

Thank you for the very fine study you gave to the *Nación*[2] and for the French text of it that you are putting at my disposal. It is so penetrating and broadly comprehensive a study that, had I been able to speak to you in person, I would have had nothing to add to it. The prose, moreover, is so patrician and of such rare quality, in my view, that of itself it has the greatest interest, quite apart from the subject treated. Whence my misgivings about exposing it right off to the betrayals of an English translation. So I've taken the liberty, without first seeking your approval, of granting the privilege of its publication to a modest Franco-American review (*Hémisphères*) that has just been launched in New York and that was in need of a little collective French support to set it afloat.

[. . .] I must point out to you the one liberty I took with your text, since you authorized my making changes. It was the suppression of half a sentence about my use of dictionaries, which might seem to imply that I resort to an intellectual device which you surely consider, as I do, contrary to the very essence of poetic creation, which is a sudden flash that occurs when synthesis is achieved and an elliptical discharge is given off—an event that, in a kind of unyieldingly fanatical way, permits no interference with its accomplishment, even in what may seem to be extensive amplifications of it.

Thank you for whatever it is you say you wrote about me in an issue of *Lettres Françaises* of last February.[3] (I never received the issue in question.) [. . .]

And finally, thank you for the pleasure I derived from your *Patagonie*,[4] in a format that is worthy of its content. You know what I think of the masterly way you handle language—the purity, propriety, and tact of it, as well as its sensitivity and its etymological accuracy. It is a rare thing, these days, to find writing that has a texture of such high quality that it may be felt with the fingertips, like Braille.

To all these thanks I have nothing to add but a manuscript for your review.[5] I've been withholding it a long time so that you would have first chance at it, but I had no way of getting it typed. You'll find it in this same envelope. I once more entrust to your care the whole matter of the correctness of the text.

[. . .]   Alexis St.-L. Leger

1. This was the first authorized edition of *Exil* in book form, published in July 1942 by the Editions des *Lettres françaises*.

2. Caillois's study was originally printed in Spanish in the 28 Feb. 1943 issue of the Buenos Aires newspaper, *La Nación.* The French text of the article was published in *Hémisphères,* where it appeared in the first issue, Summer 1943, under the title, "Sur l'art de Saint-John Perse." See letter to Tate of 26 Nov. 1944. (263)

3. "Situation de la poésie," in *Lettres françaises,* Feb. 1943, pp. 7-8.

4. See above, letter 246, note 4.

5. The poem, *Pluies* (*Rains*), which had its first printing in *Les Lettres françaises,* Oct. 1943.

248

Monsieur Roger Caillois   *Washington,*
Publisher of *Lettres Françaises*   *October 18, 1943*
Buenos Aires   *3120 R Street, N.W.*

Dear Roger Caillois,

Very hastily, between trains. Your letter's been here a long time already; it couldn't be forwarded to me. (A month and a half of solitude on a little northern island, two hours out to sea, where I was cut off from everything.)

Yes, I can authorize your publishing *Pluies* in book form; it gives me pleasure to be able to reserve it for you [. . .]. I'll arrange things, as I did for *Exil,* so that any American publication of it will be put off until the Buenos Aires edition is out of print. My only stipulation is that the Argentine edition be a physical replica (format and type) of the edition of *Exil.* The two poems are part of the same series and ought to be printed in a way that would permit them to be bound together.

[. . .] I'm going off to sea again, but only for a few days. Thereafter I'll be staying permanently in Washington.

Your study of me has been given to *Poetry* by Archibald MacLeish, where it will presently appear.[1] I do hope they haven't forgotten to send you the issue of *Hémisphères* in which your study appeared for the first time.[2]

People ask about you here more than you would suspect, but nobody knows how to get hold of your *Patagonie*. I think it might be wise, in connection with your publications,[3] to consider the possibility of setting up some sort of material arrangement that would assure your having a correspondent in publishing circles here[4] [. . .]. I don't even know, physically, how to go about getting hold of a few copies of *Exil* for myself, so I just give up, out of sheer laziness.

I hope we'll meet soon. Most cordially yours.

Alexis St-L. Leger

1. The article, in English translation, finally appeared, not in *Poetry*, but in the Spring 1945 issue of *The Sewanee Review*.
2. See above, letter 247, note 2.
3. In Buenos Aires.
4. In the United States.

249

To Monsieur Roger Caillois   *Washington, April 1, 1944*
Buenos Aires   *3120 R Street, N.W.*

Dear friend,

I'm loyal to *Lettres françaises*: under the same cover as this letter, a new and yet unpublished poem, which is reserved for you.[1] Please see that it gets the same italic type in your review as the preceding poems did. The printing of them was perfect [. . .].

I liked "L'Héritage de la Pythie"[2] in your October issue. I consider your conception absolutely right. What it so rightly asserts might even deserve to be more soberly expressed. The propriety and beauty of your lan-

guage so naturally tend to be sufficient unto themselves
[. . .] that they lead you, without your being aware of
it, to put too great an emphasis on scrupulousness, to the
detriment of authoritativeness. Because these pages must
be preserved, I am sure that your own severe critical
sense will demand that they be more elliptical, when you
redo them for publication. There's no better way that
I can express my great liking for your writings than by
taking this sort of liberty with you [. . .].

You're wrong in thinking that *Patagonie*[3] has not
caught on with those you might have wished to interest.
You'll see this when you're a bit further removed from
the present. In my own experience, I've always had the
same reaction from the persons I've given it to. Rougemont, to whom I talked about it recently, would tell
you the same thing.

Would you tell Victoria Ocampo[4] for me how guilty
I feel at not having written her yet. So many things
that she and I experienced together—or that I experienced through her—have quite simply become a part of
me, so much so that my thoughts go out to her much
more readily than she suspects, in her familiar setting
of San Isidro (I keep thinking of its river, its trees, and
its vast stretches of sky).

[. . .] Maria-Rosa Oliver[5] has confirmed the postpone-
ment of your plans for a trip to America,[6] and also of
Victoria's plans. But we still have much more time before us than we think . . . "as a large expanse of water."[7]

I shake your hand most cordially.

Alexis St-L. Leger

1. *Neiges* (*Snows*), which was to be published for the first
time in Caillois's review, *Les Lettres françaises*, July 1944.

2. Appeared in the Oct. 1943 issue of *Les Lettres françaises*.

3. See above, letter 246, note 4.

4. Victoria Ocampo (b. 1891), editor of the Argentinian re-

view, *Sur*, and *grande dame* of Latin American letters, long-time friend of many European writers and artists.

5. Maria-Rosa Oliver, a friend of Victoria Ocampo.

6. I.e., the United States.

7. English in original.

250

To Monsieur Roger Caillois   *Washington,*
Buenos Aires   *August 2, 1944*

Very hurriedly, dear friend, from between two suit-cases that have to be closed. (I'm leaving sooner than expected for a little island off the Maine coast; I'll try to get a better letter off to you from there.)

Your telegram about the printing of the *Quatre Poèmes*[1] took forever to get here, no doubt held up by some censorship or other. Your proposal appealed to me, and I wouldn't want you to think that I had any hesitations. On the contrary, as soon as I learned of it, I went about turning down three other proposals—from Algiers, New York, and Switzerland—in favor of yours.

(Speaking of Algiers, I must tell you that I had no part in the reprinting of *Pluies* in *Fontaine*[2] [. . .]. I was neither informed nor consulted. I was not even treated to a copy of the issue.) [. . .]

My address for one month:

Seven Hundred Acre Island

Dark Harbor, Maine

Very cordially yours,   A. St-L. Leger

1. *Quatre Poèmes: 1941-1944,* a collective edition of *Exil, Pluies, Neiges,* and *Poème à l'étrangère,* with an introductory piece by MacLeish, was actually published by the Editions des *Lettres françaises* in Buenos Aires in 1944.

2. *Pluies* was published without AL's authorization in the Mar. 1944 issue of *Fontaine* in Algiers.

251

To Monsieur Roger Caillois   *Cape Cod,*
In care of UNESCO,[1] Paris   *September 29, 1952*

Dear friend,

[. . .] I appreciated receiving all the things you have written, and I am delighted to see ever more positive signs of the widening horizon, the basic self-demands, and the mastery that I've always confidently expected of you. Never has such a discipline seemed to me more desirable than at the present time, and I would like to know something about the possible role you may be playing in French letters at the moment, quite apart from the international sphere of UNESCO [. . .].

Tell me what your projects are at the moment. What are you working on, or what do you have in view? Quite by chance, I recently ran across a very intelligent piece by you on the crisis in language,[2] which is tied in with an even more profound crisis of the spirit [. . .].

I can't forgive myself for not having managed to tell you how greatly I appreciate the remarkable study you were kind enough to devote to me in an issue of the *Cahiers de la Pléiade* put out in my honor.[3] Your two studies, in my eyes, are so understanding and penetrating that, in themselves, they would quite suffice as an introduction to my work and would act as a safeguard against many absurd interpretations. Paulhan,[4] two years ago, told me he had urged you to combine them into a little book, which, with only very slight additions, would form an organic and complete whole. Interesting as that suggestion was to me, I couldn't bring myself to say anything about it to you. I would have felt that it was indiscreet of me to do that, since I always feel uneasy about taking a writer away from his own work to my advantage.

[. . .] I had occasion to tell Gaston Gallimard that I wouldn't feel happy about any study of my work to be published in book form at the moment, unless it came from your pen. Whereupon he told me, in two letters, of the wish he had expressed to you on this matter and of the favorable reply he received from you. I was very touched by that [. . .]. On an entirely impersonal level, and independent of all biographical elements, your little book would continue to serve as a reliable intermediary in the interpretation of my conceptions,[5] not only abroad, where critics are always paralyzed with uneasiness and timidity when confronting the real content of a French work, but in France as well, where you would shield me from the damage of certain false and tendentious interpretations. (I've received word that the *Editions du Mercure de France* has announced for this fall the publication in book form of a study on me. Do you know if it's still that deplorable "thesis" of Saillet's that appeared in the review *Critique?*)[6]

Tell me all about yourself, dear friend, and let me know if there is any chance of seeing you again soon on your way through America. Should that be the case, you must let me know in advance, for I am often away, far from Washington, and I'd make it a point not to miss you when you are on this side of the water.

I hear lots of good things here about the group of Latin American writers that you are sponsoring for presentation in Paris [. . .].

With an affectionate handclasp.

Alexis Leger

1. Caillois began his duties at UNESCO in 1948. He was to become head of the Department of Cultural Activities in UNESCO's Division of Letters in 1970.

2. Probably the essay *Babel* (1948), or an extract from it.

3. Caillois's contribution to the Summer-Autumn 1950 issue of

the *Cahiers de la Pléiade* was "Une Poésie encyclopédique." The other article referred to is undoubtedly the study, "Sur l'art de Saint-John Perse." See above, letter 247, note 2.

4. Jean Paulhan (1884-1968), essayist and critic who took over the editorship of the NRF in 1925, after the death of Rivière. He continued in that post until 1940 and then, after the war, resumed the editorship in 1953.

The project eventually did succeed. Caillois published his *Poétique de Saint-John Perse* in 1954. See letters to Caillois of 25 Nov. 1953 (256); 15 Jan. 1954, 20 Jan. 1954, 30 Jan. 1954. (257, 258, 259)

5. I.e., literary conceptions.

6. It was. See next letter, and letter to Adrienne Monnier of 26 Mar. 1948. (289)

252

To Monsieur Roger Caillois
Paris

Jupiter Island (Florida)
January 26, 1953

Dear friend,

[. . .] I wish I could have told you sooner how deeply I appreciate your devoting so much of your time and energy to me, and how often my thoughts have gone out to you—you who only let me guess at the extent of the responsibilities and constraints imposed on you by your intellectual pursuits.[1]

[. . .] A month and a half of vagabondage has kept me far from Washington, without much possibility of having mail forwarded. In the company of some naturalist friends, I visited the last wildlife reserves of the extreme southern tip of Florida, and then I did a little sailing between the first chains of small islands (anonymous or almost so) of the Gulf of Mexico and the Caribbean Sea. And now I'm loitering on this island off the Atlantic coast, very civilized, but where one can still forget modern America in the shade of an abandoned coconut grove [. . .].

—S[. . .]?[2] Yes, you are right in not mentioning him or giving any reference to him. Through some friends, I got hold of his little book, which he did not even have the courtesy to send me (Was he thereby passing judgment on himself?)—any more than he had the courtesy to send me his articles in the review *Critique* (now augmented with a "biography" in which the gratuitous allegations and errors of fact never appear absolutely inadvertent). Moreover, I know nothing at all about the man. I can't even say whether or not it's just a case of simple failure to recognize the poetic principle itself (quite a natural thing for a critical mind) and the role of the imaginary in artistic creation.

[. . .] I'm delighted to hear that the *N.R.F.* is assured of your collaboration. Paulhan has confirmed your participation in one of the very first issues [. . .].

Affectionately yours, dear friend,

Alexis Leger

2800 Woodley Road, Washington, D.C.

—The Nobel Prize? Absurd. I'm not a candidate for it.

1. 1952 had been a particularly busy year for Caillois, involving missions to Iran and Iraq, founding and editing the interdisciplinary review, *Diogène*, and various literary collaborations and translations.

2. See above, letter 251, note 6.

253

To Monsieur Roger Caillois[1]   *Jupiter Island (Florida)*
Paris   *January 26, 1953*

Dear friend,

[. . .] Here is my answer to your questions:

1. The "Anhinga" bird (*Vents*, II, 4), to my great regret, does exist scientifically under that very name

(*Anhinga anhinga*), long ago portrayed by Audubon. Its popular name is water turkey or snake bird.[2] So far as I know, it is mentioned only in Indian legends and the folklore of the blacks. It is found in abundance in the Everglades and on the Keys of subtropical Florida. I'll see it again tomorrow, a few hours from here, on the swampy confines of big Lake Okeechobee. I accepted it by that name not, indeed, because of a taste for erudition, which has nothing to do with poetic creation, but because of the very unlikeliness of the name (poetic reality, even more than scientific reality, according to Marcelin Berthelot's[3] dictum, being inversely proportional to literal exactness).

2. The "Annaô" bird (*Eloges*, "Pour fêter une enfance," III)[4] also really exists, but under a scientific name that is entirely different from this purely fictitious one, which I made up, and which has for me an exactness that is far more precise and absolute. (In reality it is an ox-pecker or tick-eater of the *Icterid* family, a *Cassidix* related to the "Cassidix mexicanus" and mistakenly called "blackbird" in the tropics, that follows cattle on the savannas near the edge of the forest—a bird of high noon.)

3. The *Cocculus indien* (*Anabase*, VIII),[5] like the Anhinga, does, alas! really exist under that scientific name, and I accepted it by that name for the same reasons of unlikelihood or more-than-likelihood. (I believe that, ever since Linnaeus, it has been so listed in the botanical terminology of the European school, with absolutely no relationship to the "Cannabis Indica." French missionaries in the Far East used to mention it to me frequently. I wish I had invented the name!)

4. "The Scarface" (*Vents*, IV, 3)[6] does not refer to any known figure, any human personage of ancient or contemporary history. (Good Lord! How could such poetic

conceptions ever have been attributed to me? We're not still living in the age of Dante!)[7] There was nothing in this Scarface but a simple physical apparition or supernatural presence, with no more interest or pertinence than that of being a premonitory sign: the stunning blow of the Thunderbolt, along with the lightning-flash, across the Traveler's path. It is just as absurd to seek the faintest rational reference or correspondence in it as it is to see a Hitlerian swastika in the simple visual image of the sun shining across the sea and casting its glitter on my exile's threshold![8]

My entire work, which is one of re-creation, has always moved in regions beyond place and time. Allusive and full of recollections as it may be for me in its final form, it seeks to avoid all historical, and likewise geographical, points of reference. And however "lived" it may have been for me in its avoidance of abstractness, it seeks to transcend all personal allusions. In this respect, the second part of my published work[9] tends, no less than the first part, toward transpositions, stylizations, and creations on an absolute plane. (And *that* is precisely what I would like to see recognized, if there is really anything at all that should be recognized.)

Nothing, moreover, strikes me as more surprising, as a contradiction, than the desire to explain a "poet" in terms of his cultural acquisitions. And as for what concerns me in a more personal way, I am astonished to see favorable critics finding my art an art of crystallizations, when poetry, to me, is, above all, movement—in its inception, as well as in its development and final liberation. It seems to me that the philosophical concept "poet" may be, in its essence, brought back to the old and elemental "rheism" of ancient thought—like the rheism, in Occidental thought, of our pre-Socratics. And the metrics of poetry, too, which is ascribed to rhetoric,

is motivated only by movement, in all its living manifestations, which are the most unpredictable ones. Whence
the importance in all things, for the poet, of the sea.
[. . .]
Affectionately yours, dear friend.   Alexis Leger

1. Letter printed on pp. 561-563 of OC and not included in
"Lettres" section. Much of the information in this and the following letter was utilized by Caillois in his article, "Contestation
d'une contestation," published first in the *Nouvelle* NRF of 1
Feb. 1954 and then incorporated as an appendix into *Poétique
de St.-John Perse.*

2. The passage in question is:

"Et l'Oiseau Anhinga, la dinde d'eau des fables, dont
l'existence n'est point fable, dont la présence m'est délice et
ravissement de vivre—et c'est assez pour moi qu'il vive—

"A quelle page encore de prodiges, sur quelles tables
d'eaux rousses et de rosettes blanches, aux chambres d'or
des grands sauriens, apposera-t-il ce soir l'absurde paraphe
de son col?" (*Vents*, ii, 4.)

["And Anhinga, the Bird, fabled water-turkey whose existence is no fable, whose presence is my delight, my rapture
of living—it is enough for me that he lives—

"To which page of prodigies again, on what tables of
russet waters and white rosettes, in the golden rooms of the
great saurians, will he affix tonight the absurd paraph of his
neck?" (Chisholm trans.)]

See next letter to Caillois.

3. Marcelin Berthelot (1827-1907), the celebrated French chem-
ist, father of Daniel and Philippe Berthelot. See above, letter 147,
note 1.

4. ". . . ici les fouets, et là le cri de l'oiseau Annaô—" ("Pour
fêter une enfance.")

[". . . here the whips, and there the cry of the bird Annaô—"
(Varèse trans.)]

See next letter.

5. "O Voyageur dans le vent jaune, goût de l'âme! . . . et la
graine, dis-tu, du cocculus indien possède, qu'on la broie! des
vertus enivrantes." (*Anabase*, viii.)

["O Traveller in the yellow wind, lust of the soul! . . . and the seed (so you say) of the Indian cocculus possesses (if you mash it!) intoxicating properties." (T. S. Eliot trans.)]

6. "C'est en ce point de ta rêverie que la chose survint: l'éclair soudain, comme un Croisé!—le Balafré sur ton chemin, en travers de la route,

"Comme l'Inconnu surgi hors du fossé qui fait cabrer la bête du Voyageur." (*Vents*, IV, 3.)

["It is at this point in your reverie that the thing occurred: the sudden flash of light, like a Crusader!—the Scarface on your path, athwart the road,

"Like the Unknown One arisen fom the ditch, who causes the Traveller's animal to rear." (Chisholm trans.)]

7. AL was to insist on this difference between medieval and modern conceptions of poetry in his speech on Dante ("Pour Dante") delivered at the opening of the seventh centennial celebation of Dante's birth, held in Florence in Apr. 1965. See OC, pp. 449-459.

8. AL here refers to a passage in Saillet's *Saint-John Perse, Poète de Gloire*. See letter 290, note 4. This is a misinterpretation of:

"Les clés aux gens du phare, et l'astre roué vif sur la pierre du scuil." (*Exil*, 1.)

["The keys with the lighthouse keepers, and sun spread-eagled on the threshold stone." (Devlin trans.)]

9. That is, the long poems, of which *Exil* (1941) is the first by date.

254

To Monsieur Roger Caillois   [*Washington, February 1953*]
Paris

For a little more exact information about the "Anhinga," the "Annaô Bird," and the "Indian cocculus," here are a few supplementary notes.

               A. L.

ANHINGA

This is Linnaeus' *Anhinga anhinga* (family: *Anhingidae*) which the American ornithologists—under the name of "Anhinga" or the popular name of "water turkey"—also class among the "darters." (Another popular name: "snake bird.")

The bird is well known in the tropical and sub-tropical regions of America, from North Carolina to Argentina. (Its popular names in Spanish: "marbella," "corúa rela.")

Along with other "Pelecaniformes" and several families of large wading birds, it frequents the vast wooded inland swamps and the shoreline stands of mangroves. While it is a long-flight bird and high-altitude glider, it also swims under water or at the surface, with only its head and its very long neck emerging, whence the popular name of "snake bird." Perching on a low branch, it then dries its wings spread out like a cross in the sun, as does the cormorant, which it resembles by its size and shiny green-black coat. Its nuptial dance is famous.

It was popularized by Audubon's illustrations (*The Birds of America*, 1827-30), where it is labelled as follows: "Black-bellied Darter, Plotus Anhinga, Linn.").

You can see it at two hours' distance from Palm Beach or Miami!

THE "ANNAÔ" BIRD

This one is really the *Quiscalus lugubris* or Lesser Antillean grackle, under an alias. (Fam: *Troupiales* in the old French nomenclature—*Icteridae* in Anglo-American ornithology.)

Mistakenly called "merle"[1] in the French Antilles and "blackbird" in the English Antilles, the bird in question is about midway between the Florida grackle, or *Quiscalus quiscula quiscula* of Linnaeus, and the boat-tailed grackle, or *Cassidix mexicanus major* of Vieillot.

About the size of a large European blackbird, and with a purplish-black coat, it is a bird that likes full daylight, and its strident voice may be heard over the savannas and cultivated lands. It lives in loose colonies and flies down from the palms or tall border-trees, where it nests, to follow the pasturing herds or the ox-teams at work (in search of ticks and worms).

Its name "Annaô" brings back a tropical childhood and, for me, the bird came by that name through a song of an oxherder—a song that always seemed to me directed at the special bird that accompanied the herds, even though I never found out the literal meaning of the word. (It was not from the patois of the black Antilleans, which we white children could understand, but a leftover from ancient Bambara, I was told—unless it might be from the Congolese?) Here are a few snatches of the invocation which I still remember:

> Ann'naô! . . . Ann'naô! . . .
> Mâ-tchápri, mâ-tcháki!
> Kô-gnári, kô-gnára!
> T'Ann'nahi! T'Ann'nao
> T'Ann' . . . nâ-oulo-oulo!

INDIAN COCCULUS

Cocculus indicus in the nomenclature of the old French botanists; *Annamirta cocculus* to the English botanists. (Fam: *Menispermaceae*.)

It's a tall climbing shrub, native to India and well-known to Asiatic travelers. Its seed, when cracked, has a strange bitterness, at once very harsh and very arresting, repulsive and, at the same time, engaging. It contains a toxic ingredient that has been isolated in Occidental pharmacopeia under the name of "picrotoxin." Since time immemorial it has been utilized by the Hindu mountaineers and caravan drivers (as a stimulant) and by the shamans of central Asia (as a euphoria-inducer), and also in Malaysia (as a stupefacient for fish). Its properties, at once irritating and anesthetic, are very different from those of "hashish" or "Indian hemp" (*Cannabis indica*), and in no way, thank God!, like those of the very literary "dawamesk," dear to the old Parisian "Hashishins" of the Hôtel Pimodan (Baudelaire, Gautier, etc.).[2]

The plant is sufficiently well-known today to be listed in the *Encyclopedia Britannica*. (Its effectiveness in counteracting tubercular night-sweats is mentioned there, I believe!)

1. Merle (Fr.): Eng. "blackbird."
2. The Club des Haschichins was an informal group that convened, around 1843, in the Hôtel Pimodan (formerly and presently the Hôtel de Lauzun) on the Ile Saint-Louis in Paris. Baudelaire and the painter Boissard de Boisdenier were tenants in the Hôtel Pimodan at the time, and Théophile Gautier, Balzac, and others were frequent visitors.

255

To Monsieur Roger Caillois   *Dark Harbor,*
Paris   *July 25, 1953*

Dear friend,

[. . .] I still have a very vivid memory of your stopover in Washington [. . .]. The hell of my silence is paved with good intentions [. . .].

Thanks to your good letter of four months ago, I was able to follow you to some extent in Martinique and Saint Lucia. You have understood very well the dark side of all that tropical brilliance, along with the disquieting shimmer of all that reflected splendor. You will often think back to the "cannas." And take special care of the Brazilian seed that you showed me. A Frenchman, more than anyone else, should seek out such a charm so as to insure some secret contact with mysterious natural forces. You yourself could have picked up these seeds on some Antillean shore; it's the "Burning Mucuna"[1] (*Mucuna urens*)—from the Brazilian *mucuna*—which is called "œil de bourrique" in the French Antilles, and in Creole patois "zieu à bourrique" (Linnaeus' *Dolichos* and Tussac's *Negretia*). As a child, I loved this seed of the shoreline, and I never run across it now without a twinge of emotion. It comes from a huge liana that bears clusters of yellow flowers and beautiful pods, fifteen or so centimeters long. It is very bitter but would make good eating when roasted, if the Blacks weren't afraid of its magic properties. That astonishing Nicolas de Jacquin,[2] at the end of the 18th century, pompously named it *Mucuna altissima* (and popularly "canicroc") in his *Selectarum Stirpium Americanarum Historia*. Take a good look at its strange grooving between two brown stripes, which almost completely encircles the seed that is set in a funicle. The Blacks used it to hypnotize others and themselves.

Thank you for taking care of matters at Gallimard's [. . .].

Emilie Noulet,[3] whom you mention to me, did not send me a copy of her study.

Yes, Bosquet's study[4] is intelligent and deserved to be published in something better than a popularization series [. . .]. I agree with you that his theory of imagery [. . .] does not fit my case; but I decided, when he insisted on sending me his manuscript, that I would refrain from making the slightest remark about anything he said in regard to me. What he says about the "translatability" (is there such a word in French?) of my work also seemed to me rather unjustified, for you can't really be any more untranslatable—and from French!—than I am, giving such importance, as I do, to the language itself, to its internal metrics, to its es-

sence, to the very substance of the word or to its deriva-
tion. If I have tempted some translators (and I've never
been able to figure out why), that is certainly in spite
of the difficulties of translation. But for the rest, Bosquet's analysis was always interesting, and, in a general
way, I accept his interpretation, which I never had to
clear up or guide for him.

Gallimard, on his own initiative, is putting aside a
quantity of "special offprints" of the text of *Amers* that
appeared in the *N.R.F.*, even though it is only a fragment of an organic whole. I hope they remembered to
reserve a copy for you. (I, of course, had no way of
checking up.) If you didn't receive the offprint, you
could ask for it, in my name, at the Gallimard offices.

[. . .] My good wishes for you, dear friend, are much
more than just an epistolary formality. Rest assured that
they contain my affectionate regards.

Alexis Leger

I'll be at sea for two months, with few forwarding
addresses, but I'll be back in Washington by October.

1. The plant is mentioned in "Eloge xv":
   "Le vieillard même m'envierait une paire de crécelles et de
bruire par les mains comme une liane à pois, la guilandine
ou le mucune."

   ["Even the old man would envy me a pair of rattles and
being able to make a noise with my hands like a wild pea
vine, the guilandina or the mucuna." (Varèse trans.)]

2. Nikolaus von Jacquin (1727-1817), Austrian botanist, pupil
of Jussieu.

3. Emilie Noulet, "Saint-John Perse, poète d'aujourd'hui," in
Revue de l'Université de Bruxelles, Mar.-Apr. 1953.

4. Alain Bosquet, *Saint-John Perse* (Pierre Seghers, 1953) in
the "Poètes d'aujourd'hui" series. See letters to Bosquet. (347-
351)

256

To Monsieur Roger Caillois   *Washington, November 25, 1953*
Paris

Dear friend,

[. . .] After all the extra interim work you had to put up with at UNESCO, I like to think about what your stay in the Balearic Islands must have meant to you. (I know that whole area quite well; I used to go sailing there, but I usually docked at Ibiza.) Has the island-obsession infected you in the course of your travels, as the Patagonia obsession once did? It's a malady against which your Brazilian sorcerer's charm will be of no help whatever. I'm trying to pinpoint you somewhere on that slope of Palma, which smells of goats and Raymond Lull,[1] not of sheep.

And will you allow me to say how sincerely embarrassed I feel, as a friend, when I think of the way you have been tied down, all through your vacation, by a literary study devoted to my work?[2] [. . .]

Your summary interested me greatly, and I see in it nothing that isn't excellent. Your essay, in itself, quite apart from its subject matter, can't fail to be something of a surprise; and the method that you apply in it will undoubtedly lay you open to quite a few comments. Provoking them, at the present time, is your most useful role, since literary criticism, out of incompetence even more than out of smugness or false precision, sinks so easily to mere impressionism [. . .].

With an affectionate handclasp—and the assurance that I keep thinking of new things to add to the friendly thoughts that go out to you.

Alexis Leger

1. Ramon Llull (ca. 1233-1315), the Catalonian theologian and mystic, was born at Palma.

2. Caillois was working on the book-length essay, *Poétique de St.-John Perse*. See above, letter 251, note 4.

257

To Monsieur Roger Caillois   *Washington, January 15, 1954*
Paris   *2800 Woodley Road, N.W.*

Dear friend,

Your scruples touch me infinitely, and your misgivings indicate the full measure of the demands you make upon yourself. Nothing could show more clearly the quality of the study you are so good as to devote to me [. . .].

You told me that you had incorporated into your essay—and you were right in so doing—the study that you contributed to the homage number of the *Cahiers de la Pléiade*. I hope that you will not hesitate to incorporate into it also the first general study that you did in Argentina—the numerous reprintings of that piece notwithstanding. Nothing has ever been written that better explains the true medium in which, for me, a poem exists and, in one form or another, in one place or another (as preamble, conclusion, or even as an incidental elaboration), a reprise of that development (or envelopment) will furnish a wide-angle perspective that will make even more evident to the reader the preciseness of your formal study [. . .].

I didn't know that your little book was to include a bibliography. It would be easy for me, especially where foreign criticism is concerned, to help you bring it up to date; two young American graduate students are presently working on revising and completing a critical bibliography (foreign and French)[1] on my work. (You surely know that the mania for bibliographies is a real

obsession here, inherited from the German tradition.)
[. . .]

Yes, I've been shown the article in the review *Preuves*,[2]
which is received here. I know nothing about its author,
and even less about its illustrator [. . .].

I know nothing about the study by René Girard that
you mention.[3]

I select my wishes for you, dear friend, from my very
best stock. I keep thinking of all the good things I would
make happen to you, if only I had a bit of the mysterious
power of your Brazilian "*quimbois*."[4] But above all else,
take care of your health as a first condition in preserving
peace of mind and assuring a casual attitude towards life.

With an affectionate handclasp.   Alexis Leger

1. The two students remain unidentified. No critical bibliography of AL's works appeared around this time.

2. "Saint-John Perse ou les pleins pouvoirs de la poésie,"
Preuves, Nov. 1953. On the first page of the article (p. 58),
there is a small, very neat lithograph in which a good likeness
of AL's head in profile is accompanied by horse, leaf, and heron
motifs. The tiny signature is, unfortunately, illegible. *Preuves*
was an international magazine begun in 1951 and published
under the auspices of the Congrès pour la Liberté de la Culture,
with Denis de Rougemont in charge.

3. René Girard, "L'Histoire dans l'Œuvre de Saint-John Perse,"
The Romanic Review, 11 Feb. 1953.

4. "Quimbois"—a Creole word designating a magical remedy.
AL here applies it to the mucuna seed. See above, letter to Caillois of 25 July 1953.

258

To Monsieur Roger Caillois   *Washington, January 20, 1954*
Paris   *2800 Woodley Road, N.W.*

Dear friend,

I've just this morning received the galley-proofs from
Gallimard [. . .]. Right off, I discover, in its general

economy of expression and in the way it is put together, how extraordinarily comprehensive this little 200-page book is [. . .].

Your "Avertissement"[1] is, in itself, a very nice item, first-class and really masterly. I hope people will appreciate its style as much as they do its content. The modernity of what they say notwithstanding, those three pages could have been written toward the end of the 18th century.

I also turn immediately to the appendices [. . .]. I espouse your thesis completely: poetry, a heightening of reality . . . and I like the felicitous sentence that sums up your conclusion.[2] I find nothing to object to in the body of the chapter except the reference to Saint-Pol Roux and his daughter,[3] which should be deleted. The association of ideas here can not be modernized, for, to me, it goes back to 16th-century Spain, with its traditions of court assistance for the daughters of great and honored poets (an assistance that was, later on, vainly solicited for Cervantes' poor unmarried sisters) [. . .].

Affectionately yours.   Alexis Leger

Would you pardon my taking the liberty, in the interest of your "Avertissement," of entering a formal protest against a word that seems to me out of place in it: "*exhaustif*"? Not that it isn't the exact word, entirely naturalized and now fully accredited in its essential Frenchness, but because, in this case, it is not in the style of the period suggested by that whole marvelous page.

—And, in actual content, at the end of the paragraph that follows, is "*érudition*"[4] the word you really want?

—Thank you, infinitely, for the whole second paragraph. [. . .]

1. The "Avertissement" is a three-page preface (pp. 7-9 of *Poétique de St.-John Perse*) dated "3 novembre 1953."

2. The reference is undoubtedly to the last sentences of "Appendice II: Contestation d'une contestation," which reads, in translation: "He [Saint-John Perse] is the poet of truth and reality. He is, moreover, the poet of every civilization, that is, of every patient and carefully thought-out attempt to achieve some sort of excellence; the poet of institutions, moral systems, ceremonies, rites, procedures, rhetorics, of all the age-old ruses that man has employed to impose some sort of order, some sort of style, upon nature and instinct, which are always, alas, refractory; always, fortunately, inexhaustible and vigorously alive."

3. The reference was deleted in the final version. Saint Pol Roux (1861-1940) was a symbolist poet belatedly admired by the surrealists.

4. Both words were deleted in the final version and replaced by others. "Exhaustif" became "complet," "érudition" became "vaine curiosité."

259

To Monsieur Roger Caillois   *Washington, January 30, 1954*
Paris   *2800 Woodley Road, N.W.*

Dear friend,

I sent back your galley-proofs yesterday by air mail[1] [. . .].

The work is remarkable in every way and impeccable in its tact. It is extremely well-constructed and always very intelligent, and it maintains its class to the very end without ever ceasing to illuminate its main thesis—which is right, as I see it—in the happiest way. Finally, it is, like everything of yours I've read, always very well written—a rare thing these days in analytical or critical literature [. . .].

Your little book [. . .] is of and by itself a success— a lovely, very patrician thing [. . .]. It will certainly attract attention, as it speaks for your own talents quite apart from the subject treated.

Affectionately yours.   Alexis Leger

1. English in original.

260

To Monsieur Roger Caillois[1]   *Washington, February 10, 1954*
Paris   *2800 Woodley Road*

Still more answers for you, dear friend.

Concerning the "*red* clay of the abyssal depths" (*Exil*, VI),[2] it is a genuine correction, not simply a "variant reading"—a factual rectification imposed by oceanography. (Surely a most unexpected rectification, as an association of red with abyssal darkness does not at all occur naturally to one's imagination. —With my own eyes I have seen only the *mauve* clay of lesser depths, brought up on the sounding lines or anchor-prongs of an amateur sailor's moorings along the coast. Whence the unconscious mechanism of a false association.)

Your question was quite natural. The revised edition of my *Œuvre poétique* put out by Gallimard involved a few rare "corrections" (notably, in *Anabase*, "the feathering of *arrows*" substituted for "the feathering of *bows*") but there are no real "variant reading," so far as I can recall.

Luck was always with me in that no metrical dissonance resulted from the corrections (same number of syllables and same accent); otherwise I would have had to modify the whole text, as you know!

My reply only goes to show the general correctness of your thesis about poetry's preoccupation with an underlying reality.

Have no fear—no fear at all!—about the effect of what you maintain. Your little book, within its chosen limits, has nothing "provocative" about it. All it does is to give very precise answers to occasional general or fundamental questions. [. . .]

At any rate, have no scruples where I am concerned. Everything that can broaden the scope of your essay beyond its immediate and particular subject can only be

all to the good. One can wish nothing better for a monograph of which one is beneficiary. Old Huxley, devoting
a book to the crayfish,[3] came up with happy discoveries
for all of biology. May I congratulate myself on both the
fate and the role of the crayfish!

Cordially.　　　　　　　　　　　　　　　　　　　　A.L.

1. Letter printed on pp. 563-564 of OC and not included in
"Lettres" section.

2. The first printed version of *Exil* (in *Poetry*, Mar. 1942) has
"l'argile mauve des grands fonds," which becomes, in subsequent
printings, "l'argile rouge des grands fonds." See Caillois *op.
cit.*, p. 113.

3. Thomas Henry Huxley, *The Crayfish. An Introduction to
the Study of Zoology* (1880).

261

To Monsieur Roger Caillois[1]　　*In the harbor of Port-of-Spain*
Paris (17c)　　　　　　　　　　　　*March 24, 1955*

I think fondly of you, dear friend, and reproach myself
for too long a silence. I've been wandering about so
much lately! I'm just now on the return leg of a long
sailing trip that took me from island to island all the
way to the coast of Venezuela.

I picked up—on more than one beach—those floating
seeds that you and I alone count among our friends.
They came to me, doubtless, from the Orinoco.

Know that I am always near to you.

Alexis Leger

1. This message was written on a postcard sent from Port of
Spain, Trinidad, during a sailing cruise in the Caribbean.

LETTERS TO ALLEN TATE
(1944-1960)

262

To Mr. Allen Tate[1]   *Washington, April 5, 1944*
Washington   *3120 R Street, N.W.*

With pleasure, dear friend, next Sunday evening.[2]

I'll be delighted to see you again. I want to tell you in person how much I admired and liked the very pure, very lofty, and very rare demands of your art in that beautiful sequence of poems *Seasons of the Soul.*[3] Elegance of mind can not be more discreetly combined with elegance of "soul." Cruelty towards oneself and rejection of all compromise are carried to such a point here that nakedness almost seems to become invisibility.

With cordial thanks.   A. S. Leger

1. Allen Tate, critic, poet, and novelist who was one of the co-founders in 1922 of the regionalist review, *The Fugitive,* then Southern editor of *Hound and Horn* (1932-1934), and finally editor of *The Sewanee Review* (1944-1946). AL met Tate at the Library of Congress where Tate occupied the Chair of Poetry, 1943-1944.

2. Presumably an acceptance of an invitation from Tate. The specific occasion has not been identified.

3. "Seasons of the Soul" was first printed in the Winter 1944 issue of *The Kenyon Review* and then as the first poem in *The Winter Sea,* published also in 1944.

263

To Mr. Allen Tate[1]   *Washington, November 26, 1944*
                                        3120 R Street, N.W.

My dear Allen,

I've thought over your friendly suggestions.

My answer is *yes* for the printing of the French text of *Pluies*,[2] with the English translation *en regard*, to be sent to the readers of the *Sewanee Review*. (My only request is that I be allowed to correct the final proofs of the French text myself, as I am very concerned that it should be absolutely correct in France, since you have so kindly assured me that there is a possibility of its being sent there.)

Yes likewise for the publication of *Neiges*,[3] both French text and English text, in the *Sewanee* (with the same request about the correcting of the French text).

I would, upon reflection, set very great store by a publication in English—should you be able to make room for it in your review—of the study by Caillois that was published last year in French in the very precarious review, *Hémisphères*.[4] It is really the only true introduction available in America at the moment to enlighten and guide the American reader—a really interpretive study, intelligent and penetrating, and very well written to boot. It discusses the work itself, and the poetic vision from which the work proceeds, in general terms—not in terms of what concerns the author's own person. (American critics, where I am concerned, will always be a little reluctant to venture beyond studies that present only externals—studies drawing more or less exclusively on personal, anecdotal, or bibliographical references—that is, studies belonging more to literary history than to literary criticism properly speaking.) Roger Caillois' text first appeared in Spanish in *La Nación* of Buenos Aires, February 28, 1943. I sent the French manuscript of it, which had been sent to me by the author, to Yvan Goll to help out in launching his first issue of *Hémisphères* [. . .].

As for a series of studies on contemporary French literature that might be published right away, I really can't think of a single name of anyone here in America that I might recommend to you. The best thing you could do is to get Roger Caillois to collaborate on such a project from Buenos Aires [. . .].

I wish I were able, dear friend, to talk with you about more human matters. Suffice it here to tell you once again, quite simply, as a friend, how happy I was to see you in Washington and how much I regret that your stay here was of such short duration. Do keep me informed about all the things that really matter to you in the conduct of your work or of your life, and rest assured that I am always with you in my thoughts.

Affectionately yours.   Alexis St.-L. Leger

1. No place-indication given.

2. *Pluies*, which had been published for the first time in *Les Lettres françaises* of Oct. 1943, in Buenos Aires, had not yet appeared in the United States. It appeared, along with an English translation by Denis Devlin, in the Oct. 1944 issue of *The Sewanee Review* and then, as anticipated in this letter, in a special bilingual edition put out by the same review in 1945. See letter to Tate of 31 Jan. 1945. (265)

3. *Neiges*, also published in Buenos Aires for the first time in *Les Lettres françaises* (July 1944), was then published, with an English translation by Devlin, in the Apr. 1944 issue of *The Sewanee Review* and in a subsequent special edition put out by the same review in June 1945. See letters to Tate of 6 Dec. 1944, 31 Jan. 1945, and 5 Feb. 1945. (264-266)

4. See above, letter 247, note 2.

264

To Mr. Allen Tate   [*Washington*], *December 6, 1944*
Sewanee, Tennessee

My dear Allen,

I must tell you frankly that October would be much too late for publishing *Neiges* in your review. First of all, it is highly improbable that I will still be in America after next spring, and I insist on correcting the proofs of the French text myself. Second, the poem will already have been published a long time in America, in a bilingual edition that will appear soon. (I'd even gone so far as to make an agreement about it with the publisher for this autumn.) An exclusively French edition of the collection is appearing at the present time in Argentina, and similar ones are being prepared in Switzerland and in France. The poem in question will be published independently in a French review[1] [. . .]. I'm in a very antiliterary mood at the moment, and that's really one of the reasons why I want to get all publications now in process out of the way *rapidly*, the way one liquidates accounts.

Au revoir, my dear Allen. I wish you all the peace of mind one can wish a friend, and tell you once again what a pleasure it would be to resume sometime, far removed from all cares, our friendly conversations.

Affectionately.   Alexis St-L. Leger

1. Either *Fontaine* (Algiers), in which the poem was printed in 1945 or, more probably, the London-based French review, *Choix*, Jan. 1945.

265

To Mr. Allen Tate   *Washington, January 31, 1945*
Sewanee, Tennessee

My dear Allen,

I have just now received your edition of *Rains* (*Pluies*).[1] I want to tell you right off how attractive I find it and how grateful I am to you for all the tact and care, all the elegance and taste, that you have brought to bear upon it.

I don't know whether women will have their clothes fashioned in New York after the war, but, for poets, it would be most desirable to have themselves decked out at Sewanee, under your supervision.

I carried my respect for your edition to shameful lengths: I reread myself. I didn't find a single misprint[2] [. . .], but one word got omitted in one sentence: "BIEN" —in the repetition: ". . . la taie sur l'homme de bien, sur l'oeil de l'homme BIEN-pensant"[3] (in the third stanza of the VIIth canto) [. . .]. May I ask you, if there is still time enough, to be so good as to make that correction by hand on the copies already printed for delivery by the review? I'd be especially grateful if the correction could at least be made on the batch destined for the Gotham bookshop.[4]

I'm expecting Denis Devlin[5] tomorrow; we'll be going over his translation of *Neiges*.

Affectionately.   A. S.-L.

1. See above, letter 263, note 2.
2. There were two very minor ones. See next letter.
3. "The film from the eye of the upright man, from the eye of the right-thinking man" (Devlin trans.).
4. Undoubtedly the Gotham Book Mart in New York.
5. Denis Devlin (1908-1959), translator of *Exil*, *Pluies*, *Neiges*, and *Poème à l'étrangère*, and a poet in his own right, was an Irish diplomat attached to the Irish Embassy in Washington at this date. For his description of working with AL on the translations, see his "Saint-John Perse in Washington," in the *Cahiers de la Pléiade*, Summer-Autumn 1950.

266

Mr. Allen Tate   [*Washington*], *February 5, 1945*
Sewanee, Tennessee

My dear Allen,

Nothing could touch me more—I'm still smiling over it—than to see you so terribly upset about those two insignificant printer's errors,[1] trifling, both of them. These tricks of fate are inevitable; they are the devil's due.

I'm sending the second proofs of *Neiges* back to you.

Devlin is still sick, and I've still not been able to get in touch with him again, neither for the revision of his translation nor for his signing of the special edition of *Pluies.*

Thanks for such a lot of things. Dear friend, you possess every elegance of mind and heart.

Affectionately.   Alexis St-L. Leger

1. See above, letter 265, note 2.

267

To Mr. Allen Tate   *Seven Hundred Acre Island*
New York   *via Dark Harbor, Maine*
                           August 22, 1946

My dear Allen,

[. . .] Around the 16th or 17th of July, when I was passing through New York, all I could get (from James Sweeney)[1] was your telephone number at the Holt publishing house, and you weren't in.

I'd like to have chatted with you a bit, to have heard all sorts of things about you, both literary and personal. I think I understood that you have now worked out a satisfactory formula for having material independence, thus leaving yourself enough spare time and peace of mind to do all those things that still beckon, in pursuit of your own work as well as in your activity on the American literary scene. I rejoice for you, in mind and heart [. . .].

As for me, my preoccupations are the same as ever, becoming even more urgent at this critical juncture I have reached. I have to hurry up and decide immediately between two different and mutually exclusive possibilities: setting up an independent literary life based, I had hoped, in America (staying on indefinitely in this country with a yearly return voyage to France) or harnessing myself once again, in France, to public life, from which, at my age,[2] I had hoped to be freed once and for all. Here, I had already accepted the intervention on my behalf of a number of friends (James Sweeney, Monroe Wheeler,[3] Katherine Biddle) to go ahead and try to obtain an annual allocation, for several years, from the Bollingen Foundation[4] [. . .]. Might you, on your own, have some way of discreetly forming an opinion of such an arrangement? The person with the final say-so in the matter is Huntington Cairns, Consulting Editor of the Foundation (the founder, Mrs. Paul Mellon, is its Editor), and I think I recall that he was one of your friends in Washington.

A bientôt.   Alexis St-L. Leger

1. James Johnson Sweeney, a long-time director of the Museum of Modern Art in New York, later to become Director of the Museum of Fine Arts in Houston, Texas.

2. AL was fifty-nine at this date.

3. Monroe Wheeler, head of Publications and Exhibitions at the Museum of Modern Art in New York.

4. The Bollingen Foundation was established in 1945 by Mr. Paul Mellon (b. 1907) and his first wife, Mary Conover Mellon (1904-1946). Huntington Cairns (b. 1904) was a trustee of the foundation and is himself a man of letters. Allen Tate, in his turn, was to be a beneficiary of the Bollingen Foundation some years later (1952).

268

To Mr. Allen Tate   *Washington, June 10, 1949*
Chicago   *2800 Woodley Road*

My dear Allen,

I've no idea where this letter will catch up with you. I've put off writing it much too long. You were supposed, so I am told, to leave Chicago around the beginning of this month. So where might you be after that? Where can I reach you, at least in thought? [. . .]

[. . .] How great is the intellectual loneliness, in this country, for those who, like yourself, keep such a warm human presence alive, behind the writer! For me, who have accepted the same loneliness, there is no justification for any recrimination since it was an outsider's choice. But you, my dear Allen, in your own country, and so gifted for literary activity, what a force going to waste! I keep thinking of all you could do by way of encouraging, enlightening, and guiding, in a society or time less subjugated than the present one to a respect for immediate values, surface values that bind it with the chains of the most sterilizing—and by that I mean the most "dehumanizing"—mechanization and materialism.

I've never picked up your selected essays (*On the Limits of Poetry*)[1] without clearly realizing all that your mission could be—indeed, ought to be—in more favorable circumstances or times—not only in American or Anglo-Saxon[2] letters, but in the wider scope of Western civilization. In those few hundred pages there is so much lucid mastery of judgment, so much genuine authority replete with intelligence, and even better, with "knowledge" or with hidden instinct, that I would so like to see a French translator extract the essential parts of it, so as to make available all the lively suggestions, useful distinctions, and irresistible directives that well up in it (of the sort that we are always so fond of in France and that your beloved Edgar Poe wanted to acclimatize here).

Speaking of Poe, dare I ask how your book[3] is coming along? You know that over against Eliot, I continue to be fond of Poe for all the potential that he still contains.

Will I see you before winter, in Washington or New York? What will be your new address?

I'll be gone from Washington at the end of this month (July at Wellfleet, Cape Cod, with the Biddles; and August on that little island off Maine near Dark Harbor, where I used to receive a yearly visit from our poor Ted Spencer).[4]

You may be getting a letter from Jean Paulhan about a special issue of the *Cahiers de la Pléiade* that is to be put out in my honor, under the patronage of Gide and Claudel. I accepted, on condition that it would be concerned with the work more than the man. The main idea is, precisely, to consider a number of the literary problems of the present moment as they seem to arise in relation to my poetic works. In France, at least. But they would also like, on another level, to extend the scope of this study or inquiry to foreign literatures and, in that regard, to make sure of the collaboration of a representative from each country: homage from a poet or testimonial from a critic. For England, Paulhan has called on T. S. Eliot [. . .].

[. . .] If you don't have the time to do this for Paulhan, a simple page of friendly greeting would be enough for me. It's your presence as a personal friend that is most important to me—even a mere token presence in the abstract collection that I'll be surrounded with. An act of solidarity that stems from the heart, in the life of the spirit, is the ultimate luxury and sole elegance in these sad literary times. I keep thinking [. . .] of all that you have constantly tried to do, as a friend, to stir up enthusiasm for my work, ever since I have here enshrouded myself in the solitude of a foreign land, and of all the things you have told me, with such extraordinary tact, to make me believe that there exists some vital connection between me and the American literary scene [. . .]. Nor, finally, do I forget the period of the *Sewanee Review*,[5] under your personal leadership, more effective than any other review in creating Franco-American understanding [. . .].

My best wishes, most attentively, to you.   Alexis L.

1. A collection of critical essays Tate published in 1948.

2. AL's usual designation for all English-language literature.

3. Possibly a reference to an address Tate was preparing for delivery at the Poe Society of Baltimore, entitled "Our Cousin, Mr. Poe," which actually was delivered there 7 Oct. 1949, and eventually included in *The Forlorn Demon: Didactic and Critical Essays* (Chicago: Regnery, 1953).

4. Theodore Spencer (1902-1949), American poet and critic who was Boylston Professor of Rhetoric at Harvard just prior to MacLeish.

5. Tate had been editor of *The Sewanee Review* from the fall of 1943 to 1945.

269

To Mr. Allen Tate   *Washington, October 4, 1949*
Princeton   *2800 Woodley Road, N.W.*

My dear Allen,

[. . .] I never did receive the publication by you[1] that you said would be sent to me, and that I awaited with interest [. . .].

With the help of word from our excellent Huntington Cairns, I try to imagine you in Princeton at this moment, with Caroline,[2] in the circumstances that your letter described to me. May you find there, dear friend, that peace of mind that it is so difficult to come by these days, and that one would so like you to have, because you have earned it—perhaps more than anyone in this country—earned it because of the use you could put it to on behalf of all the best writers.

I greatly appreciated your willingness to contribute to the special number of the *Cahiers de la Pléiade* in my honor. Paulhan confirmed your participation—about which he was particularly happy, in view of the special character he is trying to give this assemblage [. . .]. Above all things, though, it must not be a literary "chore" for you that might distract you from your own work in any way. Just let us be sure of *your presence*, no matter how brief nor in what form—even were it to be a simple "message" [. . .].

In this friendly country where my fate can only be that of a foreigner, you are to me, my dear Allen, somewhat like the obliging gentleman of your southern states that one felt could be called upon as a second in affairs of honor.

Affectionately yours, with wishes that are to be shared with those around you.   Alexis L.

1. Perhaps *The Hovering Fly and Other Essays* (1949).
2. Tate's first wife, Caroline Gordon, from whom he was later divorced.

270

To Mr. Allen Tate   *Washington, November 12, 1949*
Princeton   *2800 Woodley Road*

My dear Allen,

The pages you've given to Paulhan have real quality;[1] and I especially liked, needless to say, their warmly human, as well as intellectual, elegance. What was meant to be simply an easygoing conversational piece rises, with rare ease, from the personal plane to the plane of ideas. You've managed, as you always do, to "raise the level of the debate," and your observations are rich in suggestions for those who are stimulated, in all things, by that aroma of intelligence that one always breathes where you are concerned. In any case, don't worry about the effect your digressions may have on the French reader; you've hit upon the ones best fitted to spark him, bring him to life, and wake him up to his own potentialities. Thank you for that final bit of bowing.[2]

I've read Vivienne Koch's[3] long study of your art as a poet. It's an analysis of rare intellectual integrity, but one that struck me as sticking more to the letter than to the spirit of your poetic work. There is in the very essence of your work, throughout all its phases, something special and irreducible, something constant and personal that eludes this analysis—fortunately, moreover! (You will tell me, won't you? if you still need that copy of the *Kenyon Review*.)

And now, dear friend, let me tell you what an enchantment the reading of *The Fathers*[4] was for me. Need I confess to you that I had never read *The Fathers*? I haven't the slightest doubt that, with this book, you will strike all the responsive "harmonics" of the French ear. In your way of telling a story there is something that, in its delicacy and poetic flavor, seems to have been lost since Stevenson; but along with that are all the complexities of modern psychology, or even psychiatry. All the nostalgia, all the incurable human nostalgia that you have succeeded in capturing in this young boy's recital— the magic of it is to be found only in that "state of grace" created by your art in the deepest, remotest climes of childhood.

Affectionately yours, with my respects and good wishes for Caroline.　　　　　　　　　　　　　　　　A. L.

Yes, I did notice occasional negligence or stylistic awkwardness, and even a few very minor outright mistakes, in the French of your translator, but all that is unimportant. What is more remarkable, and infinitely precious, is the intimate understanding, the sensitivity, and the taste, the perfect tact with which her transposition is made. In the really essential things you have never been betrayed—no false note—a woman's intuition and magic are discreetly put to use in re-creating, without self-indulgence, that "state of grace" I've been talking to you about.

1. The text published under the French title, "Mystérieux Perse," which appeared in the *Cahiers de la Pléiade*, Summer-Autumn 1950, in both French and English.

2. I.e., violin-bowing. Tate is a very competent violinist.

3. Vivienne Koch, "The Poetry of Allen Tate," *The Kenyon Review*, Summer 1949.

4. Tate's Civil War novel, published in 1938 and subsequently translated into French by Maria Canavaggia under the title *Les Ancêtres* (Gallimard, 1948).

271

To Mr. Allen Tate   *Washington, May 20, 1950*
New York

My dear Allen,

Time goes by without bringing our paths very much closer together. I was terribly disappointed at missing you the last time you passed this way (I was away from Washington), and I haven't heard about anything that might bring you back here before vacation sends us on our separate ways.

I'm to be in New York on the 25th and will stay on there for three days [. . .]. I've taken the liberty, just in case, of including your name among those few friends whom I would like to meet at a small private dinner on Saturday, the 27th, at the home of a friend—the home of one of my former coworkers in Paris who is presently French Delegate to the United Nations, Ambassador Jean Chauvel.[1]

[. . .] I liked the last thing of yours that you sent me to read—the lecture on Edgar Poe,[2] in which your fine human sense has finally produced for us, as a sort of reparation, that very fair evaluation, which omits nothing about Poe's exceptional gifts (even the ones that remained latent), without glossing over his weaknesses and the limits of what he actually achieved.

And I've also thought about you throughout all the activities you have initiated here during the past year[3] to stimulate and defend the life of the mind, with all due respect for its limits. May you not come away from it with too much skepticism or lassitude, after so much selfless devotion! [. . .]

Finally, I'd like to ask your advice about the following matter: Claudel has devoted to my poem *Vents*, as yet unpublished in America, a long and important study in last November's *Revue de Paris*.[4] Do you think any American review might be interested in reproducing this rather exceptional study? If so, which review? And to whom might I entrust the job of translating it? [. . .]

The friendly testimonial you so kindly contributed to the issue of the *Cahiers de la Pléiade* in my honor—and that you wisely had published here in *Poetry*, continues to command attention. An Italian poet recommended by Ungaretti would like to use it for an Italian review in an issue it is supposed to publish in my honor [. . .].

My respects to Mrs. Tate, and all the best to you.

A. L.

1. Jean Chauvel, diplomat who was the French representative on the United Nations Security Council from 1949 to 1952.

2. Probably the text of "Our Cousin, Mr. Poe." See above, letter 286, note 3.

3. Besides his teaching at the University of Chicago, Tate, who had supported Ezra Pound's *Pisan Cantos* for the 1949 Bollingen Prize in Poetry, was in the thick of the controversy that followed the award.

4. Paul Claudel (see above, letter 52, note 1), from his retirement at Brangues, had written an extended study of AL's *Vents*, entitled simply, "Un Poème de Saint-John Perse," that deeply affected AL. See letter to Claudel of 7 Jan. 1950. (305)

272

To Mr. Allen Tate   *Washington, June 8, 1950*
New York   *2800 Woodley Road, N.W.*

My dear Allen,

I am sending you, as promised, the study by Claudel—with corrections and excisions indicated.[1]

The excisions needed to be made in order to divest the study of a few unnecessary digressions and notes, or to restore the meaning of the text where it had been mutilated in the printed version. The corrections—alas, numerous—mostly restore the quotations, which were terribly deformed or truncated. (Claudel, at eighty-three, was no longer able to correct his proofs very carefully.)

Besides, all of the excisions and corrections have already been approved by the author in connection with a partial reprinting of his study in the homage issue of the *Cahiers de la Pléiade.*

I would be quite ready, in any event, to help the American translator in correcting his proofs, especially where the exactness of the quotations is concerned. (You once spoke to me of Wallace Fowlie[2] and his mastery of French; do you think he might be interested in the translation job?)

Your friend Van Doren,[3] whom I've always found

congenial ever since we met at your place in Washington some eight years ago, pleased me so much yesterday by the refinement of mind and heart with which he spoke of you.

Stay in good health, my dear Allen, and also in good humor. The American literary scene needs the gad-fly of a mind like yours.

Affectionately.   Alexis L.

1. The original printing of Claudel's article in *La Revue de Paris* of Nov. 1949 contained a host of errors and minor omissions, especially in the lengthy quotations from the actual text of *Vents*. An English translation of the article, done by Hugh Chisholm, was eventually published in the Autumn 1951 issue of *The Hudson Review*, along with Chisholm's translation of Canto 1 of *Vents*.

2. See above, letter 202, note 5.

3. Mark Van Doren (1894-1972), American poet and scholar. See AL's letter to him of 29 Apr. 1959. (360)

273

To Mr. Allen Tate   *Washington, May 14, 1951*
Princeton

Dear friend,

[. . .] Good luck for your *Poe*;[1] and likewise for your task as moderator, even should it be at the cost of still more battles.

[. . .] Yes, I will try to see you some day at Princeton and will let you know in advance when there is such a possibility. All of us live in a far too inhuman way outside the gate of friendship.

Affectionately.   Alexis L.

1. Exact reference unidentified. Tate had already written about Poe. See above, letter 268, note 3. The reference in the following clause to Tate's functions as moderator is likewise unexplained.

274

To Mr. Allen Tate[1]   *Washington, May 15, 1958*
                                    1621 34th Street, N.W.

Dear friend,

I would like to have told you in person the news of my marriage, [. . .] Along with Archie,[2] you were the first among men of letters to welcome me to this country, and quite beyond that meeting of minds, I have come to know the warmth of your heart. Your friendship has become a live, human thing to me, in spite of all the silence and all the distances that have increasingly come between us. After almost eighteen years of moral solitude far from my own country, I know quite simply that your friendly attitude has not changed, and your handclasp is among those I am always happy to feel once again [. . .].

I was about to fly off to France, where I have three sisters who are eager to receive her who now becomes part of my family life. The seriousness of the developing crisis in France,[3] though, obliges me to put off, maybe even to cancel, any flight plans for this summer. In any case, I'll maintain my residence in America at the address indicated at the beginning of my letter. Now you will never pass through Washington without knowing that there is a place for you in my house. A modest house, as a matter of fact, but one where you will be welcomed by the One with whom I have chosen to spend my life [. . .].

With friendly regards.   Alexis Leger

1. No destination indicated.
2. Archibald MacLeish.
3. The Algerian crisis was becoming more and more acute. See above, letter 242, note 1.

275

To Mr. Allen Tate[1]   *La Polynésie, Giens (Var)*
                                        October 12, 1959

My dear Allen,

I've thought too much about you since your marriage[2] not to want, with all my heart, to make you a little bit aware of my affectionate presence.

It's a wonderful thing that is happening to you at this moment, in your life as a man and as a poet—and those two beings that inhabit you cannot, thank God! be separated [. . .].

My dear Allen, we've come a long way together along friendship's road; our paths were the same paths, and we are not of those who expect from life, either as poets or as men, any other enrichment than the broadening of the human being within us [. . .].

I'll be back in America in November. I hope you'll be passing through Washington this winter.

My wishes for you, my dear friend, are chosen from the best of yourself, from all that, up to the present, has gone to make up the elegance and disinterestedness of your intellectual integrity. It is from that source alone that we can expect, in the midst of the materialism of these times, whatever makes living, growing, and creating worth while for us [. . .].

A thousand thoughts for the two of you.   Alexis

1. No destination indicated.

2. Tate married his second wife, Isabella Gardner, on 27 Aug. 1959.

276

Mr. Allen Tate[1]   *1621 34th Street, N.W.,*
                                      Washington 7, D.C.
                                      February 13, 1960

My dear Allen,

Once more, I am deeply touched by a letter from you
[. . .].

As far back as I can go in my long solitude in this
country, I always find your moral support no whit less
forthright and sensitive than your intellectual support.
Believe me, I value all this at its full worth.

I'm thinking of what you so kindly told me about the
study you are currently writing about me.[2] Aren't you
being too painstaking? Aren't you worrying yourself too
much about it? [. . .] I could never forgive myself for
weighing you down with the slightest friendly obligation
[. . .].

Affectionately yours, my dear Allen, along with my
best wishes to Isabelle.[3]   A. L.

I'm sending you, under separate cover, an issue of a
French review[4] containing my latest poem, which will
be published in book form presently. With the title of
Chronique, taken in its etymological sense, it is a song
to the earth and to time, which, for me, merge into a
single intemporal conception [. . .]. The work will appear in two different French editions, put out by Gallimard, and in a bilingual edition in Germany. I have
authorized its translation in Italy and Latin America,
but not, as yet, in either the United States or England
[. . .].

In the same mailing, also an issue of the Swedish review *BLM*,[5] where you will find, under the title "Thé-
matique d'*Amers*," a note bearing my signature, in re-

sponse to a request for clarification of my last published work (request from my Swedish translator, the poet Erik Lindegren) [. . .]. This note was reprinted as an appendix to the bilingual edition of *Amers*[6] published last year in Germany by Hermann Luchterhand Verlag —German translation by Friedhelm Kemp.

1. No destination indicated.

2. No study of AL's poetry by Tate of this date or later has been published as yet.

3. Tate's wife. See above, letter 275, note 2.

4. The first edition of *Chronique*, in a special printing in the *Cahiers du Sud* of Oct. 1959.

5. *BLM* is the usual designation for the Swedish literary review, *Bonniers Literära Magasin*. The note in question was sent to Lindegren after he had inquired of Dag Hammarskjöld whether he, Lindegren, had correctly interpreted *Amers*. Hammarskjöld transmitted Lindegren's question to AL, who then wrote a lengthy reply. The original note and Lindegren's Swedish translation of it were then published, with AL's consent, in the Jan. 1959 issue of *BLM*.

6. Edition published under the title *See Marken*.

LETTERS TO MAX-POL FOUCHET
(1947-1948)

277

To Monsieur Max-Pol Fouchet[1] *Washington, December 12, 1947*
Paris   *2800 Woodley Road*

Dear Max-Pol Fouchet,

Ever since I received your last communication long
ago from Algiers,[2] though I never told you so, I have
often thought of your milieu and of all your own activities in it. I like the quality of what you are striving for,
and the quality of your success; and I'm always happy to
spread the word about them, here abroad. What I like
most of all is the way your free spirit manages to guard
your review from the crystallizing effect of success and
from the automatic adoption of accepted standards—
yet without ever sacrificing to false eclecticism. [. . .]

But I mustn't let this hasty note become a letter. I
simply want to request, since you are good enough to
have your review sent to me regularly, that you note on
your mailing list a change of address for my Washington
residence: 2800 Woodley Road, N.W. (and no longer
3120 R Street), Washington, D.C.

May I add that I'd like to know a bit more about *you*
personally? Don't keep me in the dark about what you
yourself are presently working on.

My good wishes to you, Max-Pol Fouchet.

                                                    Alexis Leger

1. Max-Pol Fouchet, poet, art historian, and critic. In 1939 he
took over the review, *Mithra*, in Algiers, which continued publication under the title *Fontaine* until Jan. 1948, when it was
discontinued. See letter to Fouchet of 16 June 1948. (282)

2. There is no indication as to whether this "communication" was a personal letter, a copy of a review, or something else.

278

To Monsieur Max-Pol Fouchet   *Washington, January 7, 1948*
Paris   *2800 Woodley Road, N.W.*

Dear friend,

I appreciated what you said in your letter. I like your "France au cœur,"[1] and the way you are running *Fontaine* gave me at least some idea of "the length of the shadow you cast."

From you, Max-Pol Fouchet, and your review *Fontaine*—and I like to hear you say that it is your whole life—I accept the projected homage[2] that has been offered with so much tact [. . .].

I would, personally, be especially pleased if the opening statement were by you. I admire Rougemont's[3] talent, and I often took note of Gaëtan Picon's critical articles in the old *Confluences*.[4]

I'll stop asking you about yourself. Time and friendship will little by little bring out all that is essential about you. And it's not a matter of indifference to me that you've devoted a thesis to Vouet.[5] Don't abandon your *Poésie et langage*.[6] The theme is important and the title demanding. So many silly things are still being written these days on that subject.

May you sense here, dear friend, everything live that one transmits in a sincere handclasp.   Alexis Leger

1. *La France au Cœur* (Algiers: Charlot, 1944), reissued by *Fontaine* in 1945.

2. The remaining letters to Fouchet largely concern this proposed tribute, which *Fontaine* was never able to publish, but which was taken over by Jean Paulhan and finally published in the *Cahiers de la Pléiade*, Summer-Autumn 1950. See letter to Gide of 28 May 1949.

3. Denis de Rougemont. See above, letter 246, note 2.

4. Gaëtan Picon (1915-1976), French critic. *Confluences*, literary review published in Paris, 1941 to 1947.

5. Simon Vouet (1590-1649), French baroque painter employed by Louis XIII and Richelieu.

6. No work by Max-Pol Fouchet was ever published under this title.

279

To Monsieur Max-Pol Fouchet   *Washington, February 3, 1948*
Paris   *2800 Woodley Road, N.W.*

Dear friend,

André Gide is quite ready, he writes me, to give your review a literary tribute to me for the special number you have in mind.

Will you please get in touch with him about this and give him all the practical information concerning your arrangements?

His present address: Evole 15, Neuchatel, Switzerland.

Very cordially yours.   Alexis Leger

280

To Monsieur Max-Pol Fouchet   *Washington, March 27, 1948*
Paris   *2800 Woodley Road, N.W.*

Dear friend,

I'm still waiting for a sign from you to send, in time for it to be of use, the unpublished text that you wanted for your "homage" issue. (It will fill about 12 to 14 typewritten pages.)

How is your project coming along? I have no idea just how you conceive it.

Insofar as you may be able to influence or orient the persons you are calling upon, I have only one request to make: Have them consider my work, leaving out as completely as possible any mention of my personal life, which is not the reader's concern. Above all, may I be spared any references to my diplomatic life. I haven't gone to all the trouble of adopting a literary pseudonym, and of always keeping the two aspects of my personality strictly separate, just for nothing. It's not simply a matter of taste or conventional behavior; as a matter of actual fact, any connection established between St.-J. Perse and Alexis Leger inevitably ends up by deforming the reader's view and basically vitiating his poetic interpretation. I have once more been subjected to such a betrayal in a long study[1] that abusively exploits both my personalities —resulting in an utterly false interpretation of my later poems, which are linked to temporal or personal events that have nothing to do with them.

And that brings me to a rather delicate question: Marcel Raymond,[2] a Canadian, whom I scarcely knew, and only through letters, took the precaution, in a most courteous way, of sending me the study that he had sent to you. I found the man of such extreme tact, of such fundamental decency and probity, that I felt I simply must not, or could not, speak out against the inopportuneness of the biographical part of his study (which, at least, seeks to be painstakingly accurate). Do you think it would still be possible, without hurting his feelings in any way (which I want to avoid at all costs), to ask him, or suggest to him, that he lighten his study by making it a bit more "impersonal," at least when it comes to the political life of its subject?

But I don't want to insist too much, and I leave it up to your own feelings in the matter, especially since I don't remember very well any more just how extensive the biographical part is.

I hope, dear friend, that you don't have to wrestle with

too many difficulties (for *Fontaine*). You've already over-come the most perilous obstacles; the "growing pains" are over, and the vitality of your review is now too well-established to give you cause for being discouraged by any dark clouds of the present moment or the immediate future. There again, you have an obligation "beyond time."

Don't fail to let me read whatever you find worth-while by the younger generation of writers. They're the ones who interest me more than all the rest, and it is precisely in that area that I have no direct human con-tact. If I were better acquainted, on a personal basis, with present-day literary groups, it would be the contribution of a young writer—or at least one younger than myself—given of his own accord to your "homage" issue, that would please me the most.

All my best wishes, dear friend; and continue to main-tain your high standards for *Fontaine*. It is thanks to *Fontaine*'s selection that I've come to know, before they are published in book form, the best of your thorough-breds—among them, René Char[3]—whom I've already told what I think of his art.

Cordially yours.   Alexis Leger

—You were right in welcoming the pure poetic voice of Schehadé,[4] whom I encouraged with my best wishes.
—What's become of Guillevic?[5] I don't see anything of his anywhere.

1. Maurice Saillet, *Saint-John Perse: Poète de Gloire*. See letter 290, note 2.
2. Louis-Marcel Raymond, French-Canadian botanist who be-came the director of the Jardin Botanique de Montréal. See let-ters to Raymond. (284-288) The study in question first appeared in a 1948 issue (14th year, no. 3) of *L'Action universitaire* in Montreal under the title "Lecture de Saint-John Perse." It was eventually published in the special Saint-John Perse issue of the

Cahiers de la Pléiade, Summer-Autumn 1950, under the title "Humanité de Saint-John Perse."

3. René Char, French poet associated with the surrealists in his earlier work, active in the Resistance during World War II, and a close friend of Albert Camus.

4. Georges Schehadé, poet and playwright writing in French, of Lebanese origins. AL came to know his poems in 1938 and remained one of his great admirers. See "Poète, Schehadé," in OC, p. 482.

5. Guillevic, French poet of Breton origins.

281

To Monsieur Max-Pol Fouchet   *Washington, May 2, 1948*
Paris   *2800 Woodley Road, N.W.*

No, dear friend, *Fontaine* could not go under! . . . But how moving your letter is in its simplicity. I have no trouble at all understanding what you must have gone through, in the most solitary depths of your being. I admire how, in spite of everything—I admire how, in the face of everyone's opposition—you managed to keep alive within you courage enough not to despair. Every intellectual undertaking has a hard time of it when it comes to material necessities. I just hope that you've at least been able to find a little genuine human support in Paris among all the people who are interested in seeing your undertaking continue [. . .]. On this side of the ocean, I'll do my best to stir up as much interest in your project as I can, and, if possible, active support as well. The whole French cause is involved here—I wish people could understand that.

I am deeply moved by the thought that in the midst of all your worries you can still be concerned about the "homage" issue that you once again mentioned. Here, without more ado, are my answers to your letter:

1. Under this same cover is the text by me that you've been expecting—its title: *Et vous, mers . . .* (opening section of a poem).[1] —Print it in italics (rather large italics, if possible) and, above all, be sure I am sent the proofs so I can correct them myself. (I absolutely insist on this point, because I've always been plagued with trouble in this area—"typos" have a special taste for my texts the way certain snails have a special taste for seaside plants.) But you needn't send my manuscript back with the proofs.

2. The pages on Briand that Rougemont told you about[2] don't belong in an issue intended as a literary tribute. They are simply the text of a speech for a special occasion that I had to deliver at a public commemoration held in a foreign country. I managed to find them, and I am sending them along to you as friend to friend, since you mention them to me—but solely for your own perusal, not for publication. There should be nothing by me or about me that is outside the area of literature. Protect me, as much as it is in your power, from any merging of St.-J. Perse with Alexis Leger. I've already told you what I think of the sins committed in the name of such a merger between my absolute role as poet and the contingencies of a professional career. My private life, moreover, is not the public's business, and I appreciate your tactfulness in not asking me for a picture of myself. If you feel that Marcel Raymond's study should be left just as it is, so be it, since he showed the greatest tact in my regard and since I did not, as a matter of fact, express any reservations to him. But there shouldn't be any other exception of this sort.

3. I've asked Breton and Paulhan[3] to submit something to you. Their testimonials would make me happy as both an intellectual and friendly gesture. But I don't know whether they've been informed of the resurrection

of *Fontaine* and of your project. Would you get in touch with them directly about this?

In the later generations, which I don't know very well, Michaux and Char are the only ones whose literary approval would have any meaning for me. But I have never met Michaux;[4] and with Char,[5] whom I consider a real poet, I've never had any contact other than a brief exchange of letters.

I'm delighted to hear you mention Béguin.[6] I'm counting on Rougemont to even up scores a bit in the matter of absurd literal interpretations, as he has spoken so intelligently about the domain of the "fabulous" in his recent very fine book.[7] Along with my warmest regards, please transmit this reproach to him from me: he still has not sent me his address in Europe [. . .].

[. . .] Again, all my best wishes.   Alexis Leger

1. This was the text of what became the entire first section ("Invocation") of the poem *Amers*. It was first printed as the lead-piece in the homage issue of the *Cahiers de la Pléiade* under the title "Et vous, mers. . . ."

2. This was a speech in commemoration of the eightieth birthday of Aristide Briand, who had died in 1932 at the age of seventy. AL delivered the speech at New York University on 28 Mar. 1942. It was published in a special brochure in 1943, in Aurora, New York. An English translation of it had already appeared in 1942 at the University of New York, at the request of President Franklin Roosevelt. See OC, pp. 605-614.

3. André Breton (1896-1966), chief instigator of the surrealist movement, contributed a text, "Le Donateur," to the special issue of the *Cahiers de la Pléiade*, which Jean Paulhan had taken over from Max-Pol Fouchet.

4. Henri Michaux, the Belgian poet, prose writer, and painter whose work AL had come to know in the days when it first appeared in *Commerce*. See above, letter 187, note 2.

5. See above, letter 280, note 3.

6. Albert Béguin (1901-1957), Swiss scholar and critic, director of the review, *Esprit*.

7. Denis de Rougemont, *Doctrine fabuleuse* (1947).

282

To Monsieur Max-Pol Fouchet   *Washington, June 16, 1948*
Paris   *2800 Woodley Road, N.W.*

Dear friend,

Please don't misunderstand my reasons for writing this letter. It is, quite simply, dictated by uneasiness about the difficulties I fear you are struggling with at the moment [. . .].

Last April you thought you had surmounted the grave crisis that was threatening all French literary publications. You announced the reappearance of *Fontaine* for May 15 and thought that July 15 would be the date of publication of the "homage" issue, about which you kept me so carefully informed in a way that I especially appreciated. On May 2nd I sent the text I had promised you, adding only that I wanted very much to correct the final proofs myself. And now, just a few weeks away from the projected date of publication, I still have no word from you. Nor have I received any issue of the review since the date announced for resuming publication [. . .]. What fatal obstacle has cropped up in your path, and what is the sad state in which I must picture you, after the collapse of your latest hopes?

Could you enlighten me by dropping a line about what has befallen you? It would grieve me greatly to have the mere fact of distance exclude me from your preoccupations. What could one do to help you?

Believe me, I am with you, my dear Fouchet, and as ever, your friend,   Alexis St-L. Leger

283

To Monsieur Max-Pol Fouchet *Washington, September 15, 1948*
Paris   *2800 Woodley Road, N.W.*

Dear friend,

Your silence since my letter of May 2nd, along with its enclosures, is more than eloquent in telling me the fate of your review [. . .].

Paulhan wrote, late in June, that, on his own initiative, he had offered to put the *Cahiers de la Pléiade* at your disposal for a "homage" number that would be presented by you, but that the resumption of *Fontaine* was once more in prospect. Then, two months ago, Gide seemed to feel that it was doomed to disappear, and he very much deplored the fact [. . .].

Do let me have word from you, please, no matter how brief, hasty, or tentative. That will at least let me know what has become of you. And then I would also know —as I need to at the moment—if I could use the text I gave you in some other way. (In that event, I would appreciate your sending the text back to me, as I have no other typed copy of it.)

But above all, I want you to know how concerned I am at this time, above and beyond all literary considerations, for your personal well-being.

Most cordially, with the wish that you be of good courage and have confidence in the future.

                                          Alexis St-L. Leger

LETTERS TO LOUIS-MARCEL RAYMOND
(1947-1966)

284

To Monsieur Louis-Marcel Raymond[1]
Jardin Botanique de Montréal,
Canada

Washington,
September 12, 1947
2800 Woodley
Road, N.W.

Dear Marcel Raymond,

I deeply regret that you have had to remain without answers to your letters for so long a time. I was on a little island, not very far from your country, in the coastal waters off Maine, and there was no way of having mail forwarded there.

I continue to be very appreciative of all the thought that you have so generously devoted to me. Your study is very fine,[2] and laudatory though it be, I accept it, man-to-man, for all the human warmth it contains [. . .].

I would some day like to receive you here in person, for abstractness must be avoided in all things, even in intellectual exchanges [. . .].

With attentive wishes, most cordially yours—

Alexis Leger

1. See above, letter 280, note 2.
2. "Lecture de Saint-John Perse." See above, letter 280, note 2.

285

To Monsieur Louis-Marcel Raymond   *Washington,*
Jardin Botanique de Montréal,   *December 1, 1947*
Canada   *2800 Woodley Road*
                              (Telephone: Decatur 5682)

My dear Marcel Raymond,

I'd be delighted to see you on Monday, December 8th, at whatever time best suits you and for as long as you wish, [. . .].

I can't forgive myself, and I ask your pardon, for having left your last letter unanswered. I've had to do a great deal of running around these days, and also to deal with many annoyances. I was fascinated even by the very little you told me of your botanical field trip into the depression at Coney Hill.[1]

To our prompt meeting, most cordially.

Alexis Leger

1. Unidentified.

286

To Monsieur Louis-Marcel Raymond   *Washington,*
Jardin Botanique à Montréal,   *April 30, 1948*
Canada   *2800 Woodley*
                                          Road, N.W.

Dear friend,

I often see you in my mind's eye with great affection, ever since you became a real, live presence to me.

I never did thank you for the copy of *Exil* (the Swiss edition) that I received from you. It was good of you to think of me, and it is thanks to you that I know what this separate little edition looks like. Your friendly gesture somewhat resembled that of a botanist bringing back a wayward plant. When will I be reading a fine study on "tramp seeds"[1] by you? When I was in my twenties, knowing as little then as I do now, I took an interest in them on the London docks—at the warehouses for wool and colonial products, and also at Bremen and in the last remaining ports serving long-distance sailing vessels.

Your parcel of offprints[2] delighted me, and I can't thank you enough for them. Don't fail to keep me informed about your work. I envy you the eager anticipation that your last letter conveyed; and I try to picture you, hot on the trail of discovery, amidst all your scattered documentation on the "Carex."[3] You've got hold of a magnificent subject! When I think about it, it reminds me of the way I became secretly excited— around 1926, I believe—over the wonderful investigations by the Russian botanists of the Cyperacea and the evolution of the "wild wheats" from the Orient of Biblical times all the way to contemporary Abyssinia.

You've given me a most valuable lead about shore-plants, and I'm having that particular memorandum of the Biogeographical Society looked up in Paris.

Could you recommend a work to me, even a very sketchy one, about New World flora, that is in French and uses French terminology? American terminology disgusts me both by its inaccuracy and by the grossness of its popular nomenclature, which simply blots out any sort of scientific classification.

Thank you also for Stehlé's address.[4] I'd like very much to see his monograph.

About Father Düss,[5] truth demands that I rectify a note you added to your *Lecture de Saint-John Perse*: My family—I am sorry to say—did not "count among its members" in Guadeloupe, but merely "welcomed as a friend of the family," the botanist of Antillean flora.

Finally, I must tell you, dear friend, how pleased I am on rereading your study of my literary work—leaving aside the material concerning my personal life—pleased with it as an independent work revealing your own art and yourself. It is this integral kind of criticism that seems to be threatened these days, even in France, by the "scientific" mechanism of German criticism now become Anglo-American. Your kind is the only truly "comprehensive" criticism, in the etymological sense of that word.

Your letter gave me the first definite news concerning the calamities that have befallen the various French literary undertakings, the review *Fontaine* among them. A few days later a letter from Max-Pol Fouchet gave me the whole story, including the rescue and refloating of *Fontaine*, no longer connected with the former publishing house and financially backed by a new publisher. Resumption of publication is slated for May 15 (64th issue). The issue in my honor is scheduled for July 15 (number 66). You are among the contributors whose inclusion is a certainty, and Max-Pol Fouchet tells me that he is especially counting on your study, as it will be the only one accepted in which biographical elements will be permitted [. . .].

Have you given up all thought of your spring trip to Washington? If you still think of coming, let me know somewhat ahead of time, for I'd hate to miss you; and I myself have plans for moving around a bit.

I explored the Arizona deserts thoroughly for almost a whole month. They fascinated me in every way, and I would have stayed on much longer, had I been able to afford it. Now I'd like to see, in the Great Smokies, what is left of a few virgin forests that are still intact in those latitudes [. . .].[6]

Please remember me to that specialist in mosses, sphag-
nums, and lichens who was your traveling companion!
Very cordially yours.   Alexis Leger

1. English in original.
2. Offprints of his botanical studies.
3. *Carex*, a genus of the sedge family.
4. Henri Stehlé, botanist specializing in Antillean flora.
5. The R. P. Antoine Düss. See above, letter 98, note 1.
6. See letter to Fouchet of 27 Mar. 1948 (280), and 2 May 1948.
(281)

287

To Monsieur Louis-Marcel Raymond   *Washington,*
Jardin Botanique de Montréal,   *December 15, 1949*
Canada   *2800 Woodley Road*

Dear friend,

Knowing you are so nearby and yet out of reach only
makes me feel even worse, where you are concerned,
about the silence I couldn't seem to break. Yet there
were so many things I wanted to tell you, and so many
things I wanted to hear about from you. I wanted to
ask the botanist part of you a number of questions about
fascinating finds that greatly puzzled me during my
recent peregrinations along the southern coast of America[1] [. . .].

Dear friend, I wish you all sorts of happy surprises
in Paris. My mother, whom I would like to have asked
you to go see, is no longer there[2] [. . .]. Let me have
news of France, and share your impressions of it with
me.

Will you go to the Museum?[3] Will you see your old
Jardin des Plantes once again? Is anything still left of
that beautiful Chinese-red coloring that graced the fa-
çade of the building on the left, which took the form of

an Orangery (the one that had a few sorry meteorites lined up in front of it)?

If you hear of any good studies by French botanists on arenicolous flora, of any latitude whatsoever, let me know of them. You've already given me one very valuable reference on the subject [. . .].

Affectionately yours, dear friend. And please don't forget to keep me informed about your scientific works [. . .].   A.S.L.

1. Late in 1949 AL had spent a month at Cape Hatteras on the North Carolina coast. See next letter.

2. AL's mother had died in Oct. 1948.

3. The Muséum d' Histoire Naturelle, situated on the grounds of the Jardin des Plantes in Paris.

288

To Louis-Marcel Raymond   *Les Vigneaux,*
Jardin Botanique, Montréal   *Presqu'île de Giens (Var)*
Canada   *November 4, 1966*

Dear friend,

You have often been in my thoughts, without your knowing it, ever since the time you helped me, in Washington, to identify the "spartines"[1] that I brought back from Cape Hatteras. . . . I am more annoyed with myself than you can imagine for having allowed so much space to grow between us, but I have only myself to blame for the regret I feel at having done so. How many times you would have been able to come to my rescue, in my wanderings, in every latitude, when I came across neritic flora, and those giant "sand-sedges" that still haunt me and play havoc with my paltry knowledge of botany. (Are you still as devoted as ever to the study of them, and are you publishing anything on the subject?) [. . .]

How is your scientific work coming along? and your literary activities? Are you publishing anything that you haven't told me about? And what news from your naturalist and botanist friends whose monographs you had me read? Is anyone in your entourage interested in geology?—and anthropology?

From now on I'll be spending six months in France (June-November) and six in America, which is still my official place of residence. I'll be in Washington two weeks from now. Won't you be passing through there again one of these days? And won't we ever have a chance to examine the graminates growing on the slopes alongside the zoo? And won't you ever again have occasion to tell me all about the extraordinary characteristics, the Asiatic affinities, of the flora of Anticosti?[2] And who else will be able to tell me more about the Canadian caribou? And the old ethnographic studies made in your country? And the amazing voyage of Michaux[3] into the Canadian far north? (A really touchy subject between us, for, as you know, I've never forgiven you, and still don't, for not having written the book that I want you to write, for the French, about that fascinating unknown figure! Could you tell me if he figures among the old French botanists whose statues are lined up at Montpellier?)

It's with a sincere *au revoir*, my dear Marcel Raymond, that I affectionately shake your hand.

Alexis Leger

1. *Spartina,* genus of grasses that grow in salt marshes.

2. Anticosti Island, in the St. Lawrence estuary, forms part of the province of Quebec.

3. André Michaux (1746-1803), botanist and explorer, pupil of Jussieu.

LETTERS TO ADRIENNE MONNIER
(1948)

289

To Mlle Adrienne Monnier[1]   *2800 Woodley Road, N.W.,*
Paris   *Washington,*
                                  March 26, 1948

Dear friend,

I've often thought of you with an affection that is troubled by the lack of any word about what has become of you—about your problems of day-to-day living, about your health, about your possibilities for literary work, about the difficulties of every kind that the present moment strews in your pathway. Only the MacLeishes[2] (who don't live in Washington any more) were able to give me news of you once—always with the same heartfelt loyalty, but without being able to tell me much about the things that worried me. I don't even know where to write to you. I've heard in a roundabout way that you wrote a few pages on Fargue for the *Mercure de France,*[3] so that's where I'm sending this letter.

(I'd like very much to see your article; Valéry, Fargue, Larbaud, made up, between us, the living strands of an unbroken web of friendship.)

Let me hear from you, dear Adrienne, and as "unabstractly" as possible, and tell me something of your present occupations. You have a book within you that you owe us; I've always been expecting it to burst upon the scene, radiant with health—a book that is your own and bears your own unmistakable stamp—which means a very French one, manifest with that free and independent spirit that we so like in you. And tell me about

Sylvia;[4] I'd so like to be assured that both of you are enjoying enough immediate security and peace of mind to be able to go on with all the projects that the two of you used to keep alive. What new generation of young men and young women are you helping to find themselves? You are a very live presence here for many friends, known and unknown to you; and some of them were ready to give me really effective aid when there was talk, around 1941-1942, of setting up the possibility for Sylvia, and possibly for you too, of taking refuge in America.

Can you tell me anything about Larbaud? of the possibility of getting in touch with him, in person?

As for myself, there's little to say that you haven't already imagined. Intellectual solitude, but good health, and moral freedom. No connections any more with the Library of Congress. I travel around as much as I possibly can—as much as I can materially afford—and I keep silently pacing off the length and breadth of this continent, which has a "planetary" interest for me. I'm not returning to France for quite humble, simple reasons that have nothing to do with the reasons imputed to me. There's no way I could subsist in France—no roof, no bed, no table, no private resources—and I refuse once and for all ever to hold any public office again. The little—very little—that the state still owes me must be reserved for my family (my mother and one of my sisters, unmarried).

All this is far removed from the political or Byronic "hostility" of the cheapest romantic sort, that people insist on reading into my most recent writings [. . .].

Take good care of yourself, dear friend; and within you, take good care for your friends of that open, healthy, good humor, that wonderful human instinct, that were as generously cut from whole cloth, at your birth, as you yourself, like the true Girondine you are, used to cut your own ample skirts from those huge woolen bolts.

Affectionate regards to you and to Sylvia.

Alexis Leger

1. See above, letter 143, note 5. From 1915 to 1940 Adrienne Monnier's lending library and bookshop, La Maison des Amis des Livres, was a veritable clearing house for many of the most celebrated writers of the period—Gide, Valéry, Fargue, Larbaud, among others. In 1955, the year of Adrienne Monnier's death, AL wrote a tribute to her for a special issue of the *Mercure de France* (Jan. 1956) dedicated to her memory. The piece is reproduced in OC, pp. 486-487.

2. Archibald and Ada MacLeish. MacLeish had frequented Adrienne Monnier's shop during his stays in Paris between the two Wars.

3. "Premières Rencontres," in *Mercure de France*, Feb. 1948.

4. Sylvia Beach (1887-1962). See above, letter 143, note 5.

290

To Mademoiselle Adrienne Monnier[1]   *Washington,*
Paris   *March 26, 1948*
                                              2800 Woodley
                                              Road, N.W.

Dear friend,

[. . .] Some American friends have passed along to me a lengthy study about myself; it is dedicated to you and appears in the French review, *Critique*.[2] It is basically unfavorable to me—and not always in a sufficiently forthright way—and, when all is said and done, is suffused with a deep personal antipathy to me. This leaves me without any hope of appealing to the author himself—not, of course, to seek in any way to soften the severity of his literary reservations and suspicions, nor even to correct the fundamental error of his poetic interpretation—but merely to have one simple assurance, which I would like to see forthcoming from him, out of courtesy, since any sympathetic understanding from him is out of the question. The assurance: That no picture of me be published in the book he intends to make out of his articles. (There are still a few pictures of me lying around somewhere in Paris from the old days of my administrative life.) All I can do is confide this wish to you and hope you will act as a friendly go-between.

In the study, which is written as a kind of "thesis," there is already a certain abuse of details from my personal life, both diplomatic and literary. Neither the use of a pseudonym, nor the strict separation of the two aspects of my personal life, nor the determined effort of the poet to be only an abstract presence behind his work, have deterred the critic (who is totally wrong, may I say in passing, about the last verse of *Exil*).[3]

The poet's personality in itself is none of the reader's concern; *he* has a right only to the completed work, severed like a fruit from its tree. Still more absurd, infinitely, is this systematic search for a political personality, along with the arbitrary intrusion of contemporary history, with all its moral, patriotic, or social implications, in poems that can not be pigeon-holed in any temporal framework—poems bound to no special time or place, and always conceived, on their ideal or absolute plane, as a violent reaction against any notion (even of the most indirect sort) of "committed" literature. Behind these unrestricted stylizations of a purely poetic sort, there is no more place for the mythical personality of a Saint-John Perse than there is for the real personality of an Alexis Leger, diplomat or private citizen. If the critic who claims to give such a "personal" analysis of me had never known anything about my personal life, I have no doubt that he would have read me in an entirely different way. A less conditioned reflex, free of all associations of ideas, would have kept him from the unlikely temptation of seeing a swastika in an ordinary sunset on a deserted beach, the transmission of a moral directive to political émigrés in the simple act of depositing the key to an isolated house for safekeeping with a neighbor,[4] and I-don't-know-what-all literary allusions in purely imaginary images and themes that belong to all times and cultures (without pinning them to the "iron grill" of the Escurial), a political and redemptive purification in the purely physical fact of being exposed to heavy downpours of rain that so strikingly suggest a ritual of material release; and, finally, an inner struggle between renunciation and a demand for political redress in a simple generalized depiction of all the cosmic violence and organic renewal, all the unleashing of vital forces, of the Wind[5] that is implied in a "Shivan" concept.

There is not the slightest concern for political current events or personal circumstances in the poem *Exil* (which is simply about human exile, terrestrial exile in all its forms), any more than there is in the poem *Pluies* (which is solely about the general feeling of discontent with the human condition and its material limitations), or in the poem *Vents* (which is about the general impatience that is felt in the face of all consummated things, of all ashen remains and accumulated acquisitions of the human habitat). But the critic was already obsessed with the preconceived notion of a former Secretary General of Foreign Affairs—an obsession that, right off, leads him to find the theme of political ambition and I-don't-quite-know-what extraordinary psychopathology of "failure" (?). He himself arbitrarily introduces biographical references which he interprets after his own fashion; and then, to fit the needs of his thesis, casually postulates the collusion of the writer and the public servant. Alexis Leger is, from that point on, used as a "guide-rope"[6] to Saint-John Perse. Whence this constant return to the same base, which invalidates any poetic interpretation of a purely imaginative work. All one has to do, from that point on, is to follow this guide-line systematically and come up with the discovery of an invalid and parasitic aspect of the work, the so-called public-service aspect, that the critic himself has dreamed up.

And then, too, maybe the logical turn of mind of the analyst, when he had to leave the beaten track, was misled by a terminology or play of associations between images that tends to integrate the characteristics of modernity into purely poetic syntheses. The same rationalistic turn of mind misled him woefully in his exegesis of sources (all of them wrong), as it also did in his search (a sterile one) for historical or geographical points of reference. As for the pointless biography—and you already know what I think of that—it is, naturally, replete with factual errors. But on that score I will say nothing, since that is precisely the part that I would like to see completely eliminated.

But I've really let myself go on at length [. . .]. Please don't consider this, dear friend, as anything but the free expression between us of my lasting trust in you, of that spontaneousness that I hope we will always share.

Alexis Leger

1. Letter printed on pp. 552-554 of OC and not included in "Lettres" section.

2. Maurice Saillet's study, *Saint-John Perse, Poète de Gloire*, first appeared serially in the review *Critique* Oct., Nov., Dec. 1947 and Feb. 1948. It was published as a book, in considerably modified form, under the same title, in 1952.

3. The passage in Saillet's study reads, in English translation:
First of all, let us separate, in these poems, what is inspired

less by the event than by a certain pretension at directing the event, such as, in *Exil*, these exhortations to patriotic propriety:

"Voilez la face de nos femmes; levez la face de nos fils; et la consigne est de laver la pierre de vos seuils. . . . Je vous dirai tout bas le nom des sources où, demain, nous baignerons un pur courroux."

["Veiled be the faces of our women; raised be the faces of our sons; and the order is: wash the stone of your sills. . . . I shall whisper low the name of the springs in which tomorrow we shall plunge a pure wrath." Devlin trans.]

Mercure de France, Feb. 1948, p. 109.

4. The passage in Saillet reads:

The enemy is referred to in transparent fashion at the beginning of the poem: "l'astre roué vif sur la pierre du seuil" ["the sun spread-eagled on the threshold stone" Devlin trans.] designates, not without magnificence, the swastika that reigns from one end of the country to the other. And at the same stroke one learns that the safeguarding of France—"les clés aux gens du phare" ["the keys with the lighthouse keepers" Devlin trans.] —is the business of those who have withdrawn beyond the sea, beyond the ocean."

5. Saillet's comments on *Pluies* may be found in the same issue, pp. 109-111, 112-113, and the comments on *Vents* on pp. 114-116.

6. English in original. The mention of failure in this same paragraph refers to declarations made by Saillet in his original text (*Mercure de France*, Feb. 1948) p. 110 and especially in his concluding sentence on p. 126, quoted from an unnamed source, in which AL is compared to Retz, the *"grand cardinal de l'échec."* (Saillet's italics.) The sentence was not retained by Saillet in the 1952 book-version of his study.

LETTERS TO ANDRÉ GIDE
(1948-1949)

291

To Monsieur André Gide   *Washington, January 2, 1948*
Rue Vaneau, Paris   *2800 Woodley Road, N.W.*

Dear friend,

Must we give up all hope of seeing you here this winter? I've been wishing so hard that we would be seeing you, and I've been keeping this hope alive among those around me for a long time already. The Baltimore idea[1] was first brought up by a group of friends. Long before that occasion, and long before your Nobel Prize, there was a great deal of interest in you here worthy of your consideration. Eliot Coleman, the first messenger who was sent to you last year, was quite ready to go over and pick you up in order to make the trip easier for you. And in order better to satisfy your personal needs, provision was made, as you know, for someone close to you to make the trip with you. And I can give you my personal guarantee that the utmost delicacy would be exercised in regard to all the arrangements attendant upon your staying in the private residence that has been offered you in Florida under the best possible conditions and in a climate that would be most reassuring to your doctors. My friend Huntington Cairns[2] told me about the telephone call that it was possible to get through to your entourage. We still have hopes that between now and the end of April all possibilities will not have been cut off.

I won't bother to tell you how happy I would be, now that I am free, to enjoy your live, friendly presence here.

I've thought about it often, ever since your letters from Algeria. But my silence is a cancer that is aggravated by solitude.

Ever since my arrival in America, I've done my best to extol you and your work in this country. I didn't do it just out of friendship or as an expression of my own intellectual preferences; I did it because, living abroad as I do, one comes to have a clearer idea of what is really representative of French thought in its most intrinsic and universal aspects. It was in that way that you were able, in accepting the Nobel Prize, to be sure of "serving the French cause." The Man from Ferney would also have accepted it. There have been times when I thought about sending you the principal articles that have been devoted to you here during these last years; but I was always assured that they were sent to you directly by their authors. And I'm impressed that they knew of ways to get in touch with so elusive a man as you [. . .].

I wasn't able to send you, personally, two books that Gallimard published for me: *Exil* and *Vents*; but I did receive assurances that you had received the copies reserved for you.

I had suspended the publication of my new works and abandoned an offer from Blum[3] to have a search made in Germany for the works in manuscript that were taken from my Paris apartment by the Germans.[4] And then the director of the review *Fontaine*[5] announces that a special number of the review devoted to me is being prepared [. . .]. I really can't separate thought from sentiment when I think back in a friendly way to that whole French geological cross-section, so badly eroded by now, to which I belong by virtue of our mutual friends. Valéry, Fargue, Larbaud, Rivière are the ones who would have waved a greeting to me in a way that would still make me smile. The hands that wave to me from the review *Fontaine* are those of strangers.

But my letter is going off on a tangent, when all I wanted to do was inquire about you, now that the American newspapers have spoken of your health. Let me hear from you when you are able; and if the trip here is still a possibility, feel free to ask me for any information you might want.

Along with my best wishes, dear friend, I send a faithful thought. Alexis Leger

1. An International Symposium on literary criticism was eventually held in Apr. 1948 at Johns Hopkins University in Baltimore. Elliott Coleman was the moving spirit in this project and actually edited the symposium lectures for the Bollingen Series, which published them under the title *Lectures in Criticism* (by R. P. Blackmur, Benedetto Croce, Henri Peyre, John Crowe Ransom, Herbert Read, and Allen Tate) in 1949.

André Gide had been awarded the Nobel Prize for Literature in 1947.

2. See above, letter 267, note 4. Cairns presided over the Johns Hopkins symposium and later wrote an introduction for the book. See preceding note.

3. Léon Blum (1872-1950), the French statesman who headed the Popular Front (1936-1937) and who was a friend of AL.

4. When the Nazis plundered AL's Paris apartment in the rue Camoëns in June 1940, they confiscated many objects and papers, including bound manuscripts comprising five unpublished poems, a play, and a political testament.

5. Max-Pol Fouchet. See above, letter 278, note 2.

292

To Monsieur André Gide
Paris

Washington,
February 1, 1948

Dear friend,

I've been away, traveling. I received both your letters at the same time [. . .]. Such a separation, in time and space, brings us at last to a clearer realization of what really matters to us, simply by making us feel what we have been deprived of. With you, after rejecting so many things, and after all the events that I was caught up in, I would now like to share a little peace of mind.

So you will understand how I cling to the good news in your last letter. What a relief to know you are better, and how good it is already to think about the kind of revitalization that you could derive from simply planning a trip. It's your best resource, your surest medical guarantee, provided that all the proper precautions are taken, of course. Need I tell you how happy I'll be to help you out a little, here, to make sure you will not miss the best of all that you may expect from a sojourn in America?

I've received your *Poétique*[1] along with your letters. I'll write to you about it at greater length. The essentials are there—with that elegance, very French, of seeming to be there only in an incidental way, and without insisting—because those essentials are part of you.

Nothing could please me more than your thinking of me in connection with your *Anthologie*.[2] Over and above the honor you thereby do me, I feel once again the emotion that is inspired by that connection, still very live, with everything that your crucial presence on the literary scene meant to me, in our day. It's the same feeling that has now dissipated any lingering hesitation I may have felt about asking you to participate in the special issue of *Fontaine*. Whatever thoughts you may wish to express about me I shall cherish—and you offer them in such a friendly way! So I've come around to accepting this whole business, which now appears to me in a new—and attractive—light. I'll write to Max-Pol Fouchet, who will tell you how he has organized the thing. My thanks to you, my heartfelt thanks.

Here, now, are some practical suggestions that I want to make right away for your trip to America and your participation in the Baltimore Conference:

[. . .] The papers will be on the art of criticism, with illustrative examples, in its traditional roles as well as in its contemporary evolution and present-day tendencies. (A subject that interests the Anglo-American world much more than the fate of actual works of literature!) [. . .].

You might bring up, in general terms, the whole question of European or, more properly, French humanism. (Anglo-American criticism—once again very close to German criticism—is concerned with the letter much more than the spirit, with chronology and bibliography much more than with living history, and has come to believe in its autonomy, insofar as it lets its automatic, that is, "scientific," pretensions take over, in much the same way that so-called "technical" medicine has turned its back on clinical medicine, and self-styled "team" physics has repudiated the synthesizing and personal role of the imagination—that is, of the "artistic" intuition that is dear to the heart of even the soberest mathematician.) This development afflicts a whole industrial society that is not yet mature enough in human terms. Things are made even worse by very bad education in which hasty preparation for specialization and, more and more, for so-called technical careers—to the detriment of general culture—takes precedence over the human shaping of character and personality. This means that such criticism can never adopt the "dominating view" of the essayist, moralist, or esthete.

However that may be, and whatever you may be tempted to expatiate on here, as the great European and great intellectual that above all else you represent to your American admirers, at this very special Baltimore conference you will be operating on such a level that you need have no misgivings about the least necessity for any precautions dictated by psychological or political considerations. The milieu is quite closed to the general American public and takes little heed of what is written about you in the big newspapers. It is assumed that you will take a stand dictated solely by your own intellectual requirements, oblivious of current fashions. Choose what is easiest and most agreeable for you, and you'll be surer than ever to please.

[. . .] But the important thing for you, on this whole trip, is to avoid being imprudent, medically speaking. The heart is a very finely adjusted bit of clockwork whose whims may take us a very, very long way, provided we know how to treat it with a similar delicacy. You must practice the same sort of courtesy in regard to yourself. A man who carries as little excess weight as you do and who has such physiological adaptability —protected by his medullary and nervous reserves, and perhaps even by his low blood-pressure; a man whose very fatigue is sometimes his best ally—must know what all the chances are, as well as all the obligations they entail.

Take good care of yourself, dear friend, and we'll be seeing each other in America, tomorrow or the day after.[3]

Affectionately.   Alexis Leger

Thanks for your good suggestion on how to track down my manuscripts in Germany.

1. André Gide *Poétique* (1947).

2. Gide had compiled an anthology of French poetry which Gallimard published the next year (1949) under the title *Anthologie de la poésie française*. The selections in it were limited to poets who had already died; AL was, therefore, automatically excluded. Gide, however, concluded the "Préface" of his anthology by quoting the very last strophe of AL's *Vents*, thus circumventing the imposed limitation.

3. Gide never did make the trip to America, nor was AL ever to see him before his death in 1951.

293

To Monsieur André Gide   *Washington, May 11, 1948*
Rue Vaneau, Paris

Dear friend,

I would like to have reassured you sooner. (I had, once again, left hastily, for a trip out west.) Everything went off well at Baltimore, judging by what was reported to me about it. Your invisible presence was felt by many of those who attended. Still the same concern for the state of your health, and without the slightest sign of anything that your extreme tact may have led you to fear. Everyone understood perfectly why you gave up all thought of sending a written contribution; they know that you had very sincerely wanted to make the effort, and all they remember with emotion is the way you responded to the invitation from Johns Hopkins. I had no trouble in seeing to it that your final decision elicited the kind of psychological response that you were so concerned about. There is a freshness of feeling in these American intellectual circles that is hardly conceivable in France. Your intuition told you so, and that made you all the more concerned. They were ready to free you of all obligations. Don't let all this bother you in any way; and don't have the slightest regret, for the time being, about putting the whole matter off to a later date [. . .].

But having said this, dear friend, tell me what other sadness lurks between your lines? [. . .] Yes, I can easily imagine how inactivity must be hard on a temperament like yours. But I persist in believing that the fatigue you are suffering, in this instance, is the best natural safe-guard for, and the best guarantee of, recuperation. Nature itself has its periods of fasting and remission. And all through this "leave of absence," the basic rhythm is being restored.

I'd like to hear from you—even though only briefly and from someone in your entourage. Are you at least permitted to read enough so you don't lose all patience?

I had news of you recently from Gallimard.[1] Some friends spoke to me only yesterday about you—friends who had heard you twice in Cairo[2] without being able to get near you.

Max-Pol Fouchet, the director of *Fontaine*, writes me that he "got after you" for your contribution to his issue[3] planned for July 15th. I don't much like that. You are sufficiently aware of the great value I place on anything you would write so that you will understand when I ask you, affectionately, to lay down your fountain-pen or pencil rather than impose the slightest fatigue on yourself for such a purpose. Above all, don't be in the least upset about it. I'll always remember the terms you used in telling me you would participate in the project.

Take good care of yourself, dear friend, and be a good "patient." We all have to be good patients in one way or another. I would so like to see you in Paris once again before some day welcoming you in America.

Affectionately.   Alexis Leger

1. Gaston Gallimard. See above, letter 143, note 2.
2. Gide had spent several months in Egypt in 1946.
3. The "homage to Saint-John Perse" issue. See next letter and above, letter 278, note 2.

294

To Monsieur André Gide   *Washington, May 28, 1949*
Rue Vaneau, Paris   *2800 Woodley Road, N.W.*

Dear friend,

How often, far from you as I am, I have sought to rejoin you in my imagination, [. . .]. Judging by this faraway feeling, I realize more and more why you have never become a mere abstraction to me. I've had so little to do with the literary life.

I would like to hear that by now you are free of all health worries that might affect your humor and peace of mind in any way.

[. . .] In the intellectual realm, I imagine that it won't mean much to you if I tell you what great interest is aroused here at the mention of your name.

Paulhan tells me that he wrote to you regarding a special issue of the *Cahiers de la Pléiade* that is to be dedicated to me. (A project taken over from the old *Fontaine* review and from the *Cahiers du Sud*.)[1] [. . .] You know how much, in both human and intellectual terms, your participation in such a venture would mean to me; but I also recall all the trouble you went to, so kindly, a year ago, to assure me of your participation, with no thought for your health. And today, in the absence of any news about the state of your health, I want to avoid any indiscretion whatever where you, my friend, are concerned.

Repeated communications from Chicago—the most recent, by telephone—about possible French representatives at the "Goethe Bicentennial Convocation"[2] at Aspen, Colorado—have taken into account the medical reasons that make it impossible for you to come to America at this time. I trust that this simply refers to the same reasons, dictated by a very wise cautiousness, that last year

led you to forego all the special kinds of fatigue attendant upon any trip to America. I myself mentioned your
name to the organizers of the Chicago affair, and to their
secretary, Sims Carter,[3] but only "for the principle of the
thing" (as I always do); for, when it came down to it,
I'd have been the first to advise you not to take the trip
—the elevation of the gathering-place alone would be
sufficient reason.

Having said that, I ask you to keep tucked away in
your thoughts the certainty that, if ever the measures
your health requires were sufficiently in accord with your
tastes and desires to make you welcome an opportunity
to spend some time in America agreeably and free of
obligations, I wouldn't have much trouble in finding the
best possible pretext for you, however fictitious it had to
be.

I followed your advice and am having a search made
in Germany for my stolen manuscripts. What would
console me for their loss is the fact that, in a life so late
in coming around to literary interests as mine—a life
that bears the mark of solitude—one has neither the time
nor desire to follow the vicissitudes of works once written. One has real enthusiasm and eagerness only for the
nascent, living work. I already have a devil of a time,
when so many new things beckon, managing to give
a work its final polish, or merely to put it into acceptable
shape for publication—from which I expect no return.

Could you suggest anything that might guide me in
regard to our poor Larbaud?[4] Apart from the aphasia,
does he still have any intellectual perception, any possibility of engaging in a human exchange? Can he read a
letter? And if, as friends, we can still come to his aid
this way, can one write to him freely?—or must it be to
another, a totally different Larbaud? And would we
really be doing him a service?

I read the "Histoire des *Nourritures terrestres*" with interest. Yvonne Davet[5] has come up with an intelligent piece of work. Useful also in more than one way to the younger generations.

Gallimard sent along your correspondence with Jammes.[6] How sad it is to discover in it such a Jammes, so different from the man I thought I knew from 1900 to 1912!

Affectionately yours, dear friend, and with all the good wishes that a friend's thought can convey.

Alexis Leger

1. Gide finally did contribute a very interesting piece to the *Cahiers de la Pléiade* homage: "Don d'un arbre" (pp. 23-26).

2. See above, letter 196, note 1.

3. The Goethe convocation was sponsored by the "Goethe Bi-centennial Foundation" based in Chicago, of which Sims Carter was secretary.

4. Valery Larbaud had been stricken with aphasia as the result of a cerebral hemorrhage in 1935 and was never to regain his speech or any real independent movement. He died early in 1957. See letter to Jean-Aubry of 17 June 1949. (319)

5. Yvonne Davet, *Autour des* Nourritures terrestres, *histoire d'un livre* (Gallimard, 1949), a book about this influential early work by Gide, which first appeared in 1897, passing almost un-noticed at that date.

6. Francis Jammes and André Gide, *Correspondance 1893-1938*. Préface et notes par Robert Mallet. (Paris: Gallimard, 1948.)

295

To Monsieur André Gide   *Washington, June 6, 1949*
Saint-Paul-de-Vence   *2800 Woodley Road, N.W.*

Dear friend,

How moving your letter is! And how touched I am by all the trouble you went to, just to write me, in such circumstances![1] I was still completely in the dark about them, as I hadn't heard a thing from Paulhan.

The foreign press pictured you, to the contrary, as being in the midst of resuming full activity, surrounded by motion picture people near the Italian border.

[. . .] I'm glad to know you're at Saint-Paul-de-Vence, which should be beneficial to you at this particular time. I know the spot where I must picture you. I once walked to the site all alone, during an unavoidable delay in the course of a cruise. The air is of rather a special quality there—less enervating and humid than right along the coast. You can relax completely there to restore your strength, which will come back to you completely before the summer equinox; meanwhile, you've earned the right to all the serenity that can be drawn from that delightful and invigorating clear air. Give things a real chance to run their course; put all your trust in this. If your doctors are at all intelligent, they must already have explained to you how, in your case, all the spells of apparent weakness are in reality a sort of lightening of the body's labors and, by that very fact, they help nature along. Then too, by virtue of your own physical predisposition and medical age, you have the advantage of already having gone beyond the stage of the most usual, and uncontrollable, organic disorders. The surest guarantee of all that you have a "well-tuned" motor! Do be a bit indulgent with yourself, dear friend; let the instinctive "naturism" so deeply ingrained in you take over. I suspect you have simply had to pay the usual dues that immunized healthy European constitutions have to pay: too much sedimentation and calcareous deposits in the organism [. . .].

When you are well along in your convalescence, let me have news of yourself, in very few words [. . .].

Above all, don't give the slightest second thought, even when you're feeling much better, to the piece that you had intended to devote to me [. . .].

I'd like to send you a few books from over here just

to divert you and while away the time. But I don't know whether reading, especially in a foreign language, would appeal to you very much at the moment.

I'm looking forward eargerly to your *Anthologie,*[2] which has already been announced abroad, and which will provoke another wave of Anglo-American enthusiasm for you.

Affectionately, and with the most confident best wishes.

Alexis Leger

1. Gide's health was very precarious. He had been hospitalized in Nice for over a month and had finally moved to Saint-Paul-de-Vence only at the very end of May.

2. See above, letter 292, note 2.

296

To Monsieur André Gide   *Washington, June 20, 1949*
Saint-Paul-de-Vence   *2800 Woodley Road, N.W.*

Dear friend,

This is not a letter and requires no reply. I keep thinking of you and your convalescence and want to send you my best wishes [. . .]. I am happy you were able to avoid an operation, and happy at the thought of the reserves of strength the medicos must have discovered in you.

Your absence from the Goethe Bicentennial—which you have no cause to regret missing, indeed, far from it —only enhances your "Goethean" halo here at the present time [. . .]. So great, at the present moment, is the premium placed by everyone on all that is "human."

I declined to accept this convocation, for which I was neither qualified nor had any taste; but many of the foreign representatives who attended have come to see me en route to Aspen, Colorado; and all of them tell me how much it would have meant to them to have had

the meeting called in your name. I haven't yet had a visit
from Ortega y Gasset; I am told he is one of those, along
with your friends Thomas Mann and Curtius and my
friend Thornton Wilder,[1] who express themselves most
warmly about you.

Your work in translation continues to make the most
astonishing headway here in a way that would oblige the
subtlest of French criticism to simplify radically its way
of looking at you. Even the big newspapers are beginning to carry excerpts from your *Journal* as their "quotation for the day." You'll see from the attached clipping[2]
that it is always what is "human" that sparks things.

Rest your eyes at length, dear friend, on the beautiful
serene lines of the landscape that is so beneficial to you
at the moment, and please accept all the affection that
my friendly thought contains.

                                            Alexis Leger

1. See above, letter 196, notes 1 and 3.
2. Unidentified.

297

To Monsieur André Gide   *Washington, July 3, 1949*
Saint-Paul-de-Vence   *2800 Woodley Road, N.W.*

Your valuable *Anthologie* just arrived.

You do me honor in it, dear friend. And you know
how highly I prize a testimonial from André Gide.[1] But
more than even the literary honor, I think of the elegance of your friendly thought; I am endlessly appreciative of it. I thank you. I'll say no more in this letter. I'm
hoping to hear very soon, from Paris, that you are much
better.

Affectionately.   Alexis Leger

1. See above, letter 292, note 2.

298

To Monsieur André Gide   *Cape Cod, Massachusetts*
Saint-Paul-de-Vence   *July 26, 1949*

An affectionate thought goes out to you, dear friend, from this tip of America that juts out toward Europe.

I hear that the summer in France is exceptionally fine this year. I'm delighted at the thought of how much it will do you good.

I've learned that a book by you (*Feuillets d'automne*) has arrived in Washington for me, but there hasn't been time yet to forward it to me here.

Dear friend, you don't have to answer my letter; instead, you must take the greatest care in your convalescence, filling it with patience, indolence, and confident complicity.

Friendly greetings.   Alexis Leger

299

To Monsieur André Gide   [*Dark Harbor, Maine*]
Saint-Paul-de-Vence   *August 1949*

Dear friend,

[. . .] I've brought your *Anthologie* along with me here. I've decided I was wrong about that first impression I told you I had,[1] feeling that the tone of your preface was too casual and familiar. After all, the very flexibility and ostensible casualness of your "approach,"[2] as they say here, is what makes the inflexions of the human voice ring truest.

As for your choice, except for Casimir Delavigne and your last three poets,[3] it seems to be essentially right. Read, in England, has just done a similar winnowing job for the traditional *Oxford Book of English Verse*,[4]

but without the sensitive play of "antennae" that is yours alone in perceiving the truly poetic.

And I may add that I understand only too well the feeling of sadness and detachment that you had on closing the blighted herbal of our poetic heritage.

[. . .]

A. L.

1. The letter in which AL's first impression was given is missing.

2. English in original.

3. The last three poets Gide included were Jean-Marc Bernard (1881-1915), Catherine Pozzi (1882-1934), and Raymond Radiguet (1903-1923). Casimir Delavigne (1793-1843) was a minor French romantic poet.

4. Herbert Read (1893-1968), British poet and critic, who, in collaboration with Bonamy Dobrée, compiled *The London Book of English Verse* (1949).

300

To Monsieur André Gide   *Dark Harbor, Maine*
Rue Vaneau, Paris   *August 29, 1949*

Dear friend,

A letter from Paulhan, incidentally and briefly, gives me news of you. —A letter dated July 22. But since that date, I've been roaming the sea a great deal.

You were planning a return to Paris. Did you already feel you'd had enough of the Midi, in spite of the ordeal of the torrid summer that prevailed throughout our hemisphere? Or might it be that you went through Paris on the way to finish up your convalescence in Switzerland? At all events, I'm taking all this as a favorable sign for your projects.

Paulhan tried to convey to me—and those three lines

of his still move me deeply—that in spite of the state of your health, you had still not entirely given up the literary testimonial you thought about devoting to me.[1] He went so far as to say that you'd wanted to find, in Paris, a study that you had already sketched out. How acutely I am aware, in such circumstances, of the extent of your human elegance!

[. . .] Valéry's[2] absence will grieve me greatly. His last letters (shortly before his death) bore the stamp, in a very human way, of an astonishing and moving frankness. To you, I will one day confide two of his most unexpected intellectual confessions.

Claudel preferred to reserve for *La Revue de Paris* the independence of a long study of the single poem, *Vents*.[3]

I thought about you a great deal, and about the way your name is inseparable from so many Franco-English ties, while reading Aubry's *Valery Larbaud*, after his *Joseph Conrad*.[4] Don't forget that I was one of your colleagues in Agnes Tobin's John Donne Club![5] (The poor lady died in San Francisco shortly after I arrived in America.)

Your overseas friends, ever more numerous, continue to ask about the possibilities of welcoming you one day on this side of the Atlantic. Here or anywhere else, I would like to see you again. For you, from the American far north, an affectionate and lively concern.

Alexis Leger

1. In the special number of the *Cahiers de la Pléiade*.
2. Paul Valéry had died in July 1945.
3. See above, letter 271, note 4, and letter 272, note 1.
4. G. Jean-Aubry, *Valery Larbaud: Sa vie et son œuvre. La Jeunesse (1881-1920)* (1949). This volume was to have been completed by a second one on Larbaud's maturity, but Jean-Aubry himself died (1951) before being able to write it. His edition of Conrad's letters written in French had appeared in 1930.

5. See letter to Larbaud of Aug. 1913 (137), and above, letter III, note 1. AL erred slightly with respect to the date of Agnes Tobin's death. She died in 1939, a year before his arrival in the United States.

301

To Monsieur André Gide   *Washington, December 6, 1949*
Rue Vaneau, Paris   *2800 Woodley Road, N.W.*

Here, dear friend, is something[1] that in itself is sufficient to damn any creative art that requires the intermediary of performance: music, theater, or poetry readings!

The article really doesn't do you any harm—far from it—since it reveals you to the great American public as a sufficiently serious musician, on both levels, to trigger such a reflex from one of the princes of professional virtuosity, and to make him lose all sense of the ridiculous. Your position is flattering and "ultra-Goethean."

I hope against hope that this missive will find you installed in the Rue Vaneau, that is, re-installed in, what for want of a more accurate term, we call good health.

Affectionately.   A. L.

1. Artur Rubenstein, "Celebrating the Genius of Chopin," *The New York Times Book Review*, 16 Oct. 1949. The article is a very unfavorable review of the English translation of Gide's *Notes sur Chopin* (1948).

LETTERS TO PAUL CLAUDEL
(1948-1950)

To Monsieur Paul Claudel
Paris

Washington, January 3, 1948
2800 Woodley Road, N.W.

Dear friend,

It's a hideous cancer, this silence that takes hold of a solitude like mine. But this time I will not let your son Henri[1] go off without entrusting him with an affectionate thought for you. Without your knowing it, my thoughts have often turned toward you, and it was not simply an instinctive mental orientation. In the depths of my heart there is still that living store of all we have shared as human beings. And I like it that for me the man Paul Claudel has always had the same stature as the writer. After so many years of being tied down by administrative duties—years during which I lived in a deep-sea diving suit even more than in a coat of mail—freed of all that, I would now like to find again a bit of our old affectionate give and take, under your trees at Brangues or sitting close to a wood-burning stove in Paris.

From over here I have kept an eye on the advancing careers of your grown sons, secretly grieved at not being able to extend more of a helping hand to them. I've watched your grandchildren grow up and detected on more than one brow that gleam which emanates from you. I am happy for you at such a show of moral robustness in the midst of the general depravity in which we live. And their confidence in me went beyond just talking about you—I was able to leaf through the albums of photographs that told me even more, ranging from your accustomed walk along the water's edge to the bench where you rested in front of your granddaughter's grave, surrounded by its white fence.

From other sources you have surely learned with what friendly interest I have kept an eye, from a distance, on the luxuriant production that marks your wide-ranging maturity. It's the splendid old age of Sophocles. And the very integration of your fame into our national heritage[2] is sufficiently exceptional to be appropriate to you, since that integration, far from being the result of any concession or literary compromising, of itself enriches the French heritage. Is there really any other way that a creative writer can "serve?"—any other way he can "commit himself" in literature? France will be beholden to you, before all the world, for a new upheaval in its orographic mass, like that great, strong, and most "rhythmical" entity that you were able to describe in those admirable pages you devoted to the country of Ramuz.[3]

The most recent lines by you that I have read are those you devoted to our poor old Fargue.[4] It was so good that you devoted them to the memory of so pure a poet. Only men of your stature know how to "testify" with grace and do it generously.

I would like, dear friend, to have word from you and to hear something about the ambience in which you live. The crisis in France is still serious,[5] very serious, in fact, but even more serious potentially because of all the ways it may distort our national and international position. I am among those who firmly believe that such a crisis calls for therapy, but not surgery. But the price of such patience is, unfortunately, an erosion of moral values.

You expressed friendly regret at not seeing me back in France. Believe me when I say that there is where I would like to be at a time like this, in spite of my total uselessness because of circumstances beyond my control. As a private citizen, at least, I would like to breathe the air of France right now; and it's there that all my human ties are: an eighty-five-year-old mother and other near ones whose fate worries me. I can't return yet, for quite simple material reasons: no room I could call my own, and not the slightest means of subsistence, even though I know how to live very simply—retirement pay of 15,000 francs a month (and for how much longer?), considerably reduced by taxes, put at the disposal of my mother and an unmarried sister.

You can imagine that my life here is not a bed of roses. All by myself, wandering about this continent, which interests me only in a "planetary" way and holds nothing for me in human terms, I feel so personally cut off from things that I am sometimes forced to consider what the first accident or serious health problem would mean for me: disappearance without help or without a trace left behind.

I won't say anything about my literary work. Once again I'm losing all taste for publishing what I write. What future can still be expected in favor of lyricism, which alone interests me? And, in human terms, what can I expect from a literary milieu[6] where all the faces are strange to me and whose very faint echo, never really caught, must remain for me something abstract?

But what I've just said is frightful, since I was able to have you read *Exil* and *Vents*, and your two letters were my reward—my only reward, but how completely adequate!

The director of the review *Fontaine*, Max-Pol Fouchet, whom I do not know personally, has informed me about a special issue of his review that is to be devoted to me

[. . .]. The friends who might have waved a friendly hand to me can no longer do so; they were Larbaud, Fargue, Rivière, Valéry, Jammes [. . .].

But my letter is taking too personal a turn. And all I wanted to do was to send you best wishes for the New Year while they are still more or less fresh. I choose them for you among those I feel most deeply; and please share with Madame Claudel my most faithful and live concern.

Affectionately.   Alexis Leger

1. Henri Claudel (b. 1912).
2. Paul Claudel was elected to the French Academy in 1946.
3. Switzerland, the country of the writer Charles Ferdinand Ramuz (1878-1947). The text here referred to is undoubtedly Claudel's *Du côté de chez Ramuz*, a tribute made up of fragments dating from 1925, 1937, and 1947 and published in booklet form by the Editions Ides et Calendes in 1947, several months after Ramuz's death.
4. A tribute to Léon-Paul Fargue that first appeared in *Le Figaro littéraire*, 29 Nov. 1947, later reprinted under the title "Le maître du Tumulte."
5. In 1947 labor unrest increased alarmingly in France, coming to a climax in December, when the Schuman government took vigorous steps to head off a general strike.
6. The literary milieu in France.

303

To Monsieur Paul Claudel   *Washington, June 23, 1949*
Brangues   *2800 Woodley Road, N.W.*

Dear friend,

I have learned, through our friend Marthe de Fels,[1] that you wanted to write something about me. I was deeply touched. I continue to occupy a place in your heart as a friend, and along with that I enjoy your generosity as a poet.

You are quite aware how much this handclasp means to me. What you may not know is the psychological consequences this gesture of solidarity may have for me—at this particular moment when I am submerged in total solitude—by way of orienting my life, or what is left of it.

On hearing of your friendly· intention, but without knowing anything about what you have in mind, I took the liberty, just in case, of mentioning it to Jean Paulhan who, just now, was telling me about preparations for a homage number of the *Cahiers de la Pléiade*. The former director of the *N.R.F.*[2] took the occasion to talk to me about bringing together a group of writers devoted, intellectually and morally, to the basic conceptions that have determined my own work and that, in my eyes, you exemplify above all others. It occurred to me that this coincidence might be opportune, and that you might be favorably disposed toward a review to which you contributed not long ago—a review, moreover, that is the official organ of your publisher. But, of course, I am much too much in the dark about what is going on in Paris to surmise what your feelings may be in this case. And although Paulhan is naturally quite ready to wait as long as may be necessary for whatever you may give him, I will always second whatever your own choice of outlet for it may be.

The scant literary news I am able to receive from France, which is of necessity of a very general national scope, seems to prove to the eyes of foreigners the amazing way that a work as exceptional as yours has inspired the public to rise to its level. How magnificent that you have been able to endow our country with this literary miracle right under your very eyes! And in what a period of platitudes and intellectual poverty! Amidst what disaffection for all the seats of greatness! It's the greatest of all privileges for France—that overly moderate coun-

try—that an immoderate and seemingly alien contribution, at the very moment when moderation seems at its
most stultifying, should swell its flood tide. Right now,
when things seem completely becalmed, your own works
are the immense surge that carries along even those who
are unworthy. One would have to be really petty, and a
miserable sort of Frenchman, not to grant joyful recognition to all that so ennobles us.

All your children are with you now, and I keep thinking about the many fine family reunions that you may be
holding at Brangues this summer [. . .]. Remember once
in a while that my thoughts are with you. They are the
thoughts of a man who has shed all things except what
is dear to him, and what he holds dearer than himself
as a result of that affection.

Faithfully yours.   A. L.

1. Comtesse de Fels, née Marthe de Cumont, wife of Comte
André de Fels, director of *La Revue de Paris* for many years.
2. Paulhan had been director of the NRF from 1925 to 1943
and was to resume the directorship, along with Marcel Arland,
in 1953.

304

To Monsieur Paul Claudel   *Wellfleet, Cape Cod, Mass.*
Brangues   *August 1, 1949*

Dear friend,

How your generosity moves me, and how my loneliness draws warmth from your friendly embrace! I had
reached the point where I expected nothing more from
the literary life, at so late an hour and for a work so
often disowned—with fate, moreover, keeping me from
the community of Frenchmen at the very time when one
should be among them. I owe to your good-heartedness,
while I am still among the living, the first genuine

justification of my literary work, the only one that really matters to me.

I understand perfectly—and I thank you for the thought—all that you say to the effect that a detailed study such as you wish to write about me might be better presented in some other way [. . .]. There is something false and discomfiting in the very conception of these "Special Tributes" which are always open to the suspicion of sycophancy [. . .].

I have more misgiving than you may think about letting you consume, on my behalf, hours that you might devote to your own work. Yet I accept this quite simply, because of all the good I derive from it, morally as well as intellectually [. . .].

What I find most moving is the thought of all that you are giving me of your own self, in spite of what you call my "agnosticism." I am fully aware, believe me, of what this gulf between us means to you; and, as a result, I realize even more the full extent of your kindness. I know that this very judgment on the intellectual plane opens your heart even more to me. What is more wretched, more tragic even, in its absurd contradiction, than this unending call of a spirituality without any religious object or aim; where everything about a human being, in the impatience imposed by the human condition, is merely a pointless incursion, an attempt at raiding something beyond human limits? The very function of the poet, in terms of human knowledge, is, for me, simply a way of organizing life which keeps us more alive, even more painfully alert, to the far side of mere appearances. But what a bitter undertaking, on the far reaches of the mind, is this exploration without "reconnaissance," and these endless evasions, this "issuing forth" without issue! There is no possible retreat nor resignation for anyone who hates intensely, and with all his being, the surrender to material things. Far better that fatality in all things, imposed by a "divine" impregnation that forbids all access and appeal. (Need I tell you how much I loathe all "existentialist" philosophy—just as in art I loathe all "naturalistic" esthetics?)

What is saddest to me in such a state is that everything must always be done consciously. A hatred of letting go, in all things! Art itself, to my way of thinking, is only a kind of incest between instinct and will. (The poet, for centuries in France, was but a horseman without a mount; and then one fine day he wanted to be a horse without a rider. It is high time we make the irrational and the rational come to terms.) Another sad development is the refusal to recognize that poetic creation has no other object than the liberating of joy, or rather, more precisely, of "pleasure" in its very essence—the most mysterious, most useless, and by that very fact, the most sacred of pleasures. Whence the taking refuge, on the part of the agnostic, in a kind of blind and, as it were, vital reverence, which must be, alas! quite close to that of primitive man.

I often think of you, dear friend, and try to picture you in the setting of our French milieu. For us, you give sharper relief and greater mass to the "French phenomenon" in a magnificent way. A theatrical season like the one just over, marked by your triple presence,[1] has done a great deal, in the eyes of foreigners, to enhance the literary prestige of France. You could not have served in a more distinguished way. And God knows that the times go begging!

I'd like to join you now, under one of the big trees at Brangues, in the midst of your family holidays and of that fine human order on which you have so spaciously built. When shall I have occasion to pay you an affectionate call? I am working to overcome the material difficulties that still keep me from reappearing in France. In the prolongation of my stay over here there has never been any of the standoffishness or sulking pride that you have imagined. (I do not like the dupery of false romanticism, and I recall having often pointed out to Philippe[2] all the sterility and negativeness there is in the rigid posturing of Stoicism—and also the inconsistency in the automatism of its servitude.) I'll be really delighted to see you again.

[. . .] Affectionately yours, along with all the very best wishes I can muster for you and the family that surrounds you.

Alexis Leger

1. Three of Claudel's verse plays had had successful runs in Paris in 1948-1949: *Partage de Midi*, *Le Pain dur*, and, most important of all, *Le Soulier de Satin* presented by Jean-Louis Barrault.

2. Philippe Berthelot.

305

To Monsieur Paul Claudel   *Washington, January 7, 1950*
Paris   *2800 Woodley Road, N.W.*

Dear friend,

I was traveling through the snows of the west—and getting away from the end-of-the-year celebrations, in one of the unhappiest phases of my life (with no other reason for this unhappiness than simply being a man living his life). What an emotion, on my return, to find you waiting for me, so simply and so warmly, back of those magnificent pages in *La Revue de Paris*![1] Beyond all literary gratitude, how my heart, on the purely human level, went out to you [. . .]—a heart still enshrouded in an indefinable kind of sadness and silence.

(One of the abnormalities brought on by extreme loneliness is that it finally leads us to imagine that our private
monologue can be sensed, wordlessly, at a distance.)

Very dear friend, you who extended a helping hand
to me on the threshold of my adult life, it is a joy to me
to feel that same friendly embrace on the belatedly
crossed threshold of a literary life.

From you, the only real "great" of my time, and the
only one invested in my eyes with the true lyric power,
I have received, literarily, the highest recognition I could
have wished for—the only honor worth anything and the
only one that really moves me.

I have measured fully, believe me, everything I have
there received from you. It is a great thing for anyone to
know how to bear witness; but for you to do it as you
did, and in the way that you insisted on doing it, with
all the attention and care that you take in my regard—
that to me is the incomparable thing.

And entirely on its own merits, the study you have
devoted to me is done in the grand style and is a beautiful thing—extremely penetrating in its "comprehension" and always generous in its interpretation. The
vitality that runs through the whole article amplifies
its sweep. You've put a great deal of your own vitality
into it.

I liked everything about this piece of writing, down
to its digressions and its personal asides—everything of
your own that spurts out, in every direction. You alone,
on the theme of the Wind, were capable of elevating the
discussion in the way you did, giving it the dimensions
of your own ample rhythms. And only you could illu-
mine as you did the "dominating view" of the American
scene. For, in everything, you seize upon the greatness,
and likewise "invest" each thing with greatness, always
hastening toward the heights. The immense scope is

what I like in your pages, and the movement carries everything along with it, right down to your summaries of quotations.

[. . .] So many things in me were stirred by your gesture. But beyond all the literary benefit I derive from it, I am thinking of all that, morally, I owe to a friend's heart. And could I find its measure anywhere any better than in the very thought that dictates your conclusion?[2]

Yes, I anticipated such a conclusion. It is no more than what I expected; and, as such, it contains nothing that could offend me. Thank you for the word "religiously," that your understanding led you to insert there. It is only too true that I am obliged to avoid, scrupulously, misuse of a word that today carries with it a confessional acceptance—obliged to avoid it so long as the metaphysical notions of the absolute, of eternity or infinity, cannot for me be combined with the moral and personal notion that is the basis of revealed religions. The search in all things for the "divine," which has been the hidden mainspring of my whole pagan life, along with that intolerance, in all things, of human limitations—an intolerance that continues to spread in me like a cancer—can qualify me for nothing beyond my own striving. You alone, assuredly, were able to grasp in my poem the wide implications of that "Sea beyond the Sea,"[3] forever extending the line of my horizon into the distance. And yet, even to you, quite honestly, I would rather not talk about it. Too many people have made a great show before you of some sort of "religious crisis," genuine or feigned. That sort of thing is utterly foreign to me. It is, quite simply, my whole life that has never ceased to bear the ever-increasing tragic sense of its spiritual frustration, at grips, in all humility, with the most elementary need for an Absolute.[4]

In the face of all that, what does the physical space that

separates us really matter, even though it must be overcome? I'm working at it as best I can. The material difficulties are still great.

Let me embrace you, dear friend—expressing once more, affectionately, that gratefulness of mind and heart that resides within my deepest self.

A. L.

Jean Paulhan writes me that you have kindly authorized the reproduction of some extracts from your study in his special number of the *Cahiers de la Pléiade*. Still one more obligation I have to you; and I thank you very, very much. I wanted so much to have a bit of your presence, of the "shadow that you cast," wherever I have to appear in public view.

1. "Un poème de Saint-John Perse: *Vents*," in the Nov. 1949 issue of *La Revue de Paris*.

2. Claudel had written, at the very end of his article: "But God is a word that Saint-John Perse avoids, shall I say religiously?—and that, even were he promised an empire—isn't it so, Leger?—he would not let escape from his lips. And yet, led on by the sun against this gust, by turns violent, perfidious, and meditative—what was he seeking beyond all barriers, what did he ask of the vast reserves of the incommensurable?"

3. Possibly an allusion to the second half of Canto 2 of Section IV of *Vents*. The exact phrase, "Mer au dessus de la Mer," does not occur in the poem.

4. This paragraph is, in a sense, the last word in a debate between Claudel and AL that began at their first meeting in 1905, when Claudel immediately set about trying to convert the "adolescent in search of himself" that AL then was.

LETTER TO JULES SUPERVIELLE
(1949)

306

To Monsieur Jules Supervielle   *Cape Cod (Mass.)*
Paris   *July 29, 1949*

Dear friend,

How much I appreciated your letter! [. . .] I have
never known you to be anything but morally elegant.[1]
So I am all the more vexed with myself for not having
managed to break my silence for a few persons like
yourself. Yet, my friendship is very much alive, and the
years, in spite of my absence, have only made it more
affectionate. And since I have as little sense of time as
you have, one of these days, in Paris, it will seem to me
that I cover only a very short distance as I make my
way to your door.

Thank you for the last things you sent. The poems[2]
you gave me to read are of the sort that you alone could
write. I like the self-discipline and secret pride of your
art. There is no better way of renewing the purest tradition while at the same time losing nothing that has
been gained by our modern plunge into the great swells
of the subconscious. It's almost as if you had made a
wager to revive, with all its risks, the psychological, or
even philosophical, poem. You win, thanks to a sensitized intelligence and a very personal music, helped
along by your very human compassion and your sense
of the universal.

I try in vain to imagine how the Parisian ambience
must strike you at the moment. I know that you carry
your own private world along with you. But in human

terms, at least, I very much hope that life for you there is worthy of what you are—in both heart and mind.

In what corner of France will my letter find you? What you tell me of those close to you means a great deal to me. I shall never forget the welcome I received at Port-Cros:[3] that lovely, bright face alongside yours, your young bathers who are today mothers, and the little girl's hands clinging to my portholes and, very early in the morning, hoisting a little basket of fruit for me that the child had swum out with [. . .].

I am delighted to see that you are gaining more and more literary recognition in France at the moment. No one deserves it more, for the quality of his work as well as for its disinterestedness.

Stay in good health, my friend, and defend your peace of mind.

With yet one more affectionate thought, I send wishes chosen from among my very best, for you and for all your gracious entourage.

Alexis Leger
(2800 Woodley Road, N.W.
Washington, D.C.)

1. Jules Supervielle (1884-1960), born in Montevideo, Uruguay, spent about equal portions of his life in South America and France. AL had known him personally in France and had then lost contact with him. In 1949 Supervielle composed a poem addressed to AL, which was incorporated the next year into the *Cahiers de la Pléiade* tribute and entitled simply "Hommage."

2. Perhaps the poems of Supervielle's collection, *Oublieuse memoire*, which was published in 1949.

3. One of the Iles d'Hyères, not far from the Presqu'île de Giens where AL settled in 1957. See letter to Paulhan of 28 June 1966.

LETTERS TO JEAN PAULHAN
(1949-1966)

307

To Monsieur Jean Paulhan   *Washington, May 3, 1949*
Paris

Dear friend,

What a pleasure it was to pick up your little book
again![1] I haven't told you how much I liked it. Literarily speaking, I liked the "chaff" as much as the "grain"
—I mean the letter as much as the spirit. That so rarely
occurs these days; so how could I resist indulging myself right off?

Yes, a real luxury, that constant "appropriation," that
taste for "propriety" always pushed to such extremes, in
the handling both of the language and of the idea. Fugue
and counterpoint; attacks, slip-aways, parries; syntax!
[. . .]. The unpredictable felicity of "passes" accepted
or provoked for their own sake [. . .]. Your special skill
is to carry as far as it can be carried, and with the sup-
plest of movements devoid of the least foil-clicking, the
liveliest and most exquisite kind of fencing with side
arms. And then there's your elegance in seeming always
to use only buttoned foils. Such beautiful passes force
us to smile every time there is a pause.

But tell me, please, why must you "commit" all this,
and yourself (if it is really you in question), on the level
of immediate political actuality? Doesn't that mean ex-
celling in an irrelevant way, and at your own expense
and counter to your own instincts? It's a double shame,
in any case, to substitute mistakenly for the legitimate
simplifications of public life the equally legitimate de-

mands—but requirements that are here out of place—
of a literary life. Will public controversy not lead you
into a false, extra-literary position precisely through the
very pressure of your own literary demands? [. . .] and
at a time when the literary work of art is already being
sacrificed far too much to literary action, itself considered to be dependent on political action.

Watch out, for this may also entail an enslavement to
freedom, just as one may be enslaved to cleverness and
contradiction. (A reflex mechanism in the play of human
reactions and counter-reactions.) These are tricks that
"freedom of spirit" is quite capable of playing on you.
In order to have the moral satisfaction of being intellectually right, and because we end up savoring our
illustrations as if they were grammatical examples, you
find yourself, as the director of a review, doing violence
to your *literary* standards. And isn't that, indirectly, also
a form of "commitment?"

May such writing at least have the effect of rekindling
in France a taste for freedom of thought. —That is
devoutly to be wished. But in the present case it was a
matter of freedom of action, and on a very high national
level.

But here I go letting myself be carried away . . . or
is it simply that, being far from France, I am out of
touch with the Parisian way of looking at things?

With friendly regards.   A. L.

1. See above, letter 251, note 4. In addition to his editorship
of the NRF in the twenties, Paulhan had also been active in an
advisory capacity in the editing of *Commerce*, and it was during
those years that he became a friend of AL. (See next letter.)
The little book here referred to is Paulhan's *Lettre aux Direc-
teurs de la Résistance* (1951).

308

To Monsieur Jean Paulhan   *Washington, June 21, 1949*
Paris

Dear friend,

[. . .] (I refer to your "homage" project for the *Cahiers de la Pléiade*.)

I was glad to hear you talk about a literary "grouping" or "regrouping." Not, to be sure, around me, but simply in company with me, for the occasion. Because what will mean the most to me in this "homage" is whatever will make of me the "occasion" for it. Yes, it's a fine assemblage[1]—one that still takes a certain pride in the basic attitude shared by all its participants. A reunion of very different families, but all of good stock, neither bastard nor "servile" (by which I mean "serving-class"); and all their works, at the very least, refuse to be harnessed with the team of so-called "committed" literature [. . .]. An assemblage of men who are intransigent where their art is concerned and who, basically, "know what it's all about." Isn't that already sufficient to make it a rallying place at a time like the present? It's somewhat the sort of thing that—in a very clandestine way, you may recall —I strove for in the *Commerce*[2] era (and our efforts then were already joined secretly).

[. . .] But there I am, my dear Paulhan, going far beyond the "thanks" I wanted my letter to express.

Most sincerely yours.   A. L.

1. The *Pléiade* tribute eventually included pieces by the following French-language writers: Gide, Fargue, Char, Supervielle, Schehadé, Larbaud, Blaise Allan, Jouve, Claudel, Breton, Picon, Renéville, Béguin, Caillois, Bounoure, Lefebvre, L.-M. Raymond, de Rougemont, and Fouchet. The non-French contributors were T. S. Eliot, Herbert Steiner, Jorge Guillén, J.-G. Cruchaga, Ungaretti, Denis Devlin, Jorge Zalamea, MacLeish, Spender, Poggioli, Kemp, and Tate.

2. See above, letter 187, note 2.

309

To Monsieur Jean Paulhan   *Washington, September 29, 1949*
Paris

Dear friend,

[. . .]

I have, of course, never read *The Book of the Dead*,[1] in spite of all the learning I am supposed to possess (and that is just the kind of reading that, instinctively, I would not indulge in). Nor are any of the elements of ethnography and folklore that are constantly being pointed out in my works attributable to any concern with any special sort of erudition. And when it happens that, in spite of myself, I let myself use—all too naturally—nautical, equestrian, botanical, or naturalist terms, simply because they make up part of my everyday vocabulary, and when—as was bound to happen—I unconsciously use technical terms of the most unlikely sort: "Anhinga," "Cocculus," . . . the critic considers them a hoax![2]

(As a present for you, this authentic picture of the Anhinga, a bird that always fascinates me when I'm in the southern tip of Florida. Don't bother showing it to S. . . . He has much too firm a faith in the prerogatives of culture ever to savor the laws of transposition. He will never understand how much "deviation," or even "desertion"—even more than stripping down to bare essentials—is required to recreate "verisimilitude," which is the very essence of an *absolute* "reality." At the farthest limits of consciousness, poetic creation or re-creation, in its proper context, can, at a distant remove, assure the perpetuation of life without recourse to "scissiparity." Fugue and counterpoint, as we confront life, have formed the basis of all art since the earliest days of the caveman.)

Affectionately.   A. L.

Heartsick at reading the pages Dr. Alajouanine[3] has written about our poor Larbaud.

—Bacot?[4] The last survivor among my "Chinese" friends. A gifted French writer, but without his realizing it, because he devoted himself too exclusively to Sanskrit.

1. The Egyptian *Book of the Dead*, which Saillet had cited as a possible source of AL's poetry. See Saillet, *Saint-John Perse: Poète de Gloire* (1952), pp. 106-109.

2. See letter to Caillois of 26 Jan. 1953. (252) Saillet had accused AL of fabricating these items from whole cloth, on pp. 121-122 of his book. See preceding note.

3. Théophile Alajouanine, "Valery Larbaud et la maladie," in his *Valery Larbaud sous divers visages*, pp. 137-151. See letter to Jean-Aubry of 17 Nov. 1949. (320)

4. Jacques Bacot (1877-1965), French orientalist who specialized in Tibetan studies. Translated *Milarepa* and wrote several travel books, including *Le Tibet révolté*, of which AL was particularly fond.

310

To Monsieur Jean Paulhan   *Washington, January 22, 1950*
Paris

Dear friend,

[...] Your *"Causes célèbres"*[1] disconcerted me at first. The cruelty of such lucidity, presented in so masterly a style, struck me as too often alternating between the modesty of heroism and the cynicism of curiosity. Later, I better understood the human significance that dominates these pages, and from then on enjoyed it, even in its reticences. The essential content finally appeared worthy of all the intellectual interplay. And I was able to surrender without reservation to the joy that your language always gives me. Isn't style, when all is said and done, the only measure of freedom? —A nice lesson for the "Existentialists," who seem to me so little worthy of the absurd, whose theoreticians they fancy themselves as being, and who are much too much dupes of their own rationalism ever to let style overcome it. I especially like the natural refinement of your syntax [. . .].

[. . .]

A. L.

1. Paulhan's essay had just been published (1950).

311

To Monsieur Jean Paulhan   *Washington,*
Paris   *2800 Woodley Road, N.W.*
                               February 23, 1956

My very dear friend,

How touched I was by your letter written entirely in block letters, and how deeply I appreciate the trouble you went to in writing to me [. . .]. I am much relieved to know that it is only an accidental thing.[1] I'm familiar, medically, with the extraordinary resilience of the human eye, which is really beyond all imagining. Do be patient and well-behaved, so your recovery will be prompt. The way to master this lies in that "considerateness" we most often lack only toward ourselves.

Glad to know you are resting up a long way from Paris, not far from those Iles d'Hyères[2] that you used to visit. But I can't help thinking, too, about everything that may be making you feel depressed at the moment, and about the fact that peace of mind, for a man of your moral cast, is easy to preserve only when that mind vies with another mind. I wish I could say I'll be seeing you soon and could stop by to shake your hand.

Above all, don't worry about the "homage" number of the *Cahiers de la Pléiade* [. . .].

With you, most affectionately.   A. L.

I much appreciated what you told me about André Breton.[3]

1. Details regarding Paulhan's eye trouble at this period are lacking.

2. Islands off the Mediterranean coast of France, some of which are visible from the very house in which AL settled scarcely a year later.

3. The "Pope of surrealism" had reaffirmed to Paulhan his admiration for AL's work. Breton had already contributed to the 1950 *Cahiers de la Pléiade* tribute. See above, letter 281, note 3.

312

To Monsieur Jean Paulhan   *Les Vigneaux*
Paris   *Presqu'île de Giens (Var)*
                                            July 19, 1960

Dear friend,

Your letter traveled around for a long time before it was finally forwarded to me here. When I returned from Latin America,[1] where my wanderings went on much longer than planned, I indulged myself once more in a few "fugues" that I just couldn't resist, and I ended up by landing, in the most unexpected way (so I could do a bit of horseback riding), in a rather remote part of the American northwest.

Since I landed here (without stopping over in Paris), all I've been doing is clearing away, without looking up, a year's accumulation of responsibilities of every sort: material, household, administrative, and fiscal. What a horrible business it is to own anything! and how ill-adapted I would have been to Xenophon's *Economics*![2] I take my revenge on all this by being my self-appointed handyman, all alone, for three miserable hectares of *garrigue*[3] worn down to the very bone: digging, brush-clearing, masonry, woodwork, planting. Fortunately, growing flowers, that ultimate abomination, is out of the question! And no real sea-temptations, other than a daily, bourgeois swim in the unrelieved scandal of this fine Mediterranean weather. (All I had here was a wretched canoe, and it was promptly stolen from me. No point in replacing it, for it would be just as promptly stolen again) [. . .].

A lady who is an art-editor and a friend of yours whom I received in Washington, felt she could say positively that you would be staying at Port-Cros this summer. However that may be, a guest room awaits you here. (Just give me a little advance notice about your plans and your itinerary in the Midi. We can pick you up easily at Toulon, three-quarters of an hour from here.)

[. . .] I like it that you wrote to me as you did. What you were good enough to tell me about the large-scale work[4] you are preparing, or meditating, pleased me very much. —Yes, I've thought about it; that's the book you could now give us, that you *must* give us [. . .]. You will give it to us because it is worthy of you and worthy of the torments it will put you to. This very dissatisfaction that has such a hold on you is, for me, the best guarantee of the "scope" of such a work. And who, in these days of fragmentation and facileness, is up to the requirements of a real "work"? It's time for you to gather up the reins, just as it is time for our era to determine what its "coordinates" are. I don't think that the conception I seemed to glimpse in your few lines is in any way arbitrary or far-fetched. "Synthesis," in our time, is what always seems rather discouraging, at first glance—not that it involves more of our being as humans, or makes greater demands on it—it's simply that a synthesis is effected on a greater number of levels. Our friend Valéry even went beyond eluding, beyond abdicating; he privately admitted his own limitations, to himself.[5] Whenever I reproached him, in a friendly way, for being content (always fortuitously and in a very fragmentary way) with mere reactions to the thought of others, and for always refusing, in spite of all his Cartesianism, to set his own thoughts in order with a view to some definitive statement of them (for lack of the constructive work for which he had such distaste), he would answer me, as Gide the Evader might have done, that even *that* was too much for him, insofar as it put a limit upon his intellectual availability —any "precipitate" seemed to him suspiciously like a limiting, rather than a refracting; every construction or simple coordination suspiciously like imprisonment. A very strange inconsistency on the part of someone so fond of mathematics. This "definition-maker" par excellence would quite readily have taken refuge behind the *Determinatio negatio est* of Spinoza or the Ούδεν Ορίζω[6] of a Sextus Empiricus. I was always afraid that, alas! behind all this was something even sadder!

But for you, dear friend, the difficulty stems only from waiting too long and being too unavailable—considering all you have already grasped, defined, pointed out, and discovered. It will simply be a work of elucidation, and the important thing is to get at it; because in cases like this, getting started is everything. It's the first step in settting up a "method." Take heart and go at it day by day, without waiting any longer for that complete remove—which you will never have. And take a bold delight in your dissatisfaction!

Let me hear from you, and tell me that we'll be seeing each other again this summer, before my brief stopover in Paris at the end of October. I think of you affectionately.   A. L.

—No, I don't know those three verses from Lucretius with which you seek to whet my appetite. You undoubtedly did it on purpose, knowing how little taste I have for that Latin, who was a sorry poet and a sorry thinker. I don't have him within reach. You'll have to bring me a copy.

—Do you know anything, at the publishing house, about what has been decided on as a publication date for the most recent of my works now in press (*Chronique*) or being reprinted (*Œuvre poétique* in two volumes)?

1. From Argentina. See above, letter 244, note 4 and letter of Apr. 1960 to Maria Martins. (362)

2. The *Œkonomikos* (ca. 355 B.C.) of Xenophon, a short treatise on revenues for improving the economic situation of Athens.

3. *Garrigue*: the arid, stony brush-country along the Mediterranean coast of France.

4. This large-scale work was apparently never completed.

5. Cf. letter to Gide of 29 Aug. 1949 (300), and letter to Paulhan of June 5, 1966. (317)

6. "I determine nothing"—a basic adage of the Greek skeptic philosopher, Sextus Empiricus, who lived at the end of the Second and the beginning of the Third century.

313

To Monsieur Jean Paulhan   *Presqu'île de Giens (Var)*
Paris   *July 25, 1961*

Dear friend,

[. . .] The uneasiness you may feel in writing about me[1] strikes me as perfectly natural. I'd feel the same way, were I writing about you—perhaps even a great deal more so. But you are undoubtedly making far too many demands on yourself in all this, especially since these demands are already complicated by an excess of friendly solicitude toward me.

There is just one thing that surprises me, and that is the uneasiness you feel at "the disparity between the man you know as a friend and the man whose work you are trying to sound out."[2] Isn't this sort of slippage a perfectly natural thing, involving no real break in continuity? From one term to the other of the relationship, which extends from the relative to the absolute, the same fundamentals are present. By concentrating on what strikes you as still very consciously arranged on the absolute level of the work, you lose sight of the fact that whatever may be "consciously arranged" there has first been organically, physiologically, and, so to speak, unconsciously ordered, that is, more "naturally" ordered than is supposed.

I'm too fond of all your geologically illustrated literary references, and too fond also, in Provence, of the Moustier-Sainte-Marie fault,[3] not to savor your comparison. Yet it is not an accurate one. The fascinating iron-bearing stratum in that instance does no more than join together two equal sections, originally on the same level and belonging to the same mass and the same age, made up of the same materials and structures.

But I have to admit that, after all, I'm not really very good at any sort of self-analysis [. . .].

Affectionately.   A. L.

1. Paulhan was writing the articles on AL that were to be published under the title, "Enigmes de Perse," in the Nov. 1962, Jan. and Mar. 1963, and Jan. 1964 issues of the NRF.

2. In a letter to AL dated 30 June 1961, Paulhan had written: "I'll try to tell you briefly what bothers me. It's a contrast, where you are concerned, that I can't manage to explain to myself. Because, on one hand there is the simplicity of your manner and your speech that strikes me. [. . .]

"Well, your work has all the qualities that you personally do not seek, and the least one can say is that your work dazzles us from the outset, and not like just a momentary flash: [. . .] The result is that, on reading your work, we think less of a series of lightning-flashes than of a chain of mountains."

3. Immediately following the passage quoted in the preceding note, Paulhan continued: "At Moustiers in the Lower Alps, one sees a chain three hundred meters long that links two rocky points—thanks to some vow or other made by a certain Chevalier de Blacas. In a like manner you talk to us as if you were pledging something.

"But a poetry that is votive is *likewise* an organized, willed poetry. Whence my perplexity. . . ."

314

To Monsieur Jean Paulhan   *Les Vigneaux,*
Paris   *Presqu'île de Giens*
                                  October 12, 1962

Dear friend,

How did it come about that there was such a long delay in notifying me about the introductory note that they had the temerity to request of you for the exposition at La Hune?[1]—and of which you made something very fine. I've only today received it; Gueerbrandt thought I'd already received it from Gadilhe, and Gadilhe thought I'd received it from you. The surprise is a pleasant one, and your text goes far beyond the usual occasional piece. I liked everything about it, content and form—and the tone, as usual [. . .].

Not only do your slightest articles tend imperceptibly towards the heights, my dear Nicholas da Cusa;[2] on the literary level as well, your exegesis prolongs the actual evolution of the poem as it was created [. . .].

Affectionately.   A. L.

—No, not "L'Ordre des Oiseaux," which was the title of my joint publication with Braque,[3] but simply
"Oiseaux," which is the title of my text, printed independently. [. . .] the publisher proposed that I change
Braque's title, which had been agreed upon before they
knew whether I would accept the hoped-for collaboration. I turned down the suggestion out of deference to
Braque, as the original title seemed to me most fitting
for his part of the publication; but I insisted on reserving the right[4] of using my own title, which was more
appropriate to my text (originally conceived, moreover,
quite independently; for the references to Braque were
added as an afterthought). I was all the more eager to
do this for Braque because of the great tact with which
I was treated—an insistence on the entirely unconditional
bringing together of our two contributions, without any
reference from one to the other being required. You
know my feelings toward your friend.[5]

1. A Paris bookshop and gallery very close to Saint-Germain-
des-Prés. The monumental de luxe edition of *Amers* with color
lithographs by André Marchand, published by Les Bibliophiles de
Provence, was first exhibited there in Oct. 1962, and Paulhan
wrote an explanatory note for the exhibition.

2. Nicholas da Cusa (1401-1464), a very learned and subtle
German theologian.

3. *L'Ordre des Oiseaux*, a collaboration work for which AL
supplied the text and Georges Braque, twelve original color
etchings. It was published, in a large de luxe edition that appeared in 1962, "Au Vent d'Arles," by La Société d'Editions d'art

4. I.e., the right for any separate publication of AL's text.

5. Braque was a friend of Paulhan.

315

To Monsieur Jean Paulhan[1]   *Washington, June 12, 1963*
Paris

Dear friend,

[. . .] There's been a lot of misunderstanding, thus far, about the study you're working on.[2] I hope you're not the man to give it a second thought, either on my account or your own. By making excessive demands on yourself, you may have disconcerted some by the very refinements of your subtlety. It's the grammarian's privilege to be suspected of deviousness when all he wants is to say something relevant. As far as I am concerned, believe me, it simply makes me realize all the more, as friend to friend, all that I owe you for the trouble and extreme care you have taken on my behalf.

Before saying anything more, I'll wait until I've been able to read your whole article. Here are simply a few marginal comments—on points that are really not very important—that I owe you in response to your last letter:

> And preceding the master works in linguistics, we clear our new ways to those unheard-of locutions where the aspiration withdraws behind its vowels (*Snows*, IV, 3). [Devlin trans.]

There's no hint here of a spoken language or pre-language, as yet unarticulated. I thought only of the initial aspiration, which is still indicated by a special sign in many languages that are still spoken to this day in the Near and Far East, and that are highly articulated and even highly evolved—languages wherein the emission or ejection of the word under the pressure of its initial consonant is triggered or formed by more than a mere intonation—there is an actual backward accentuation of the breath—just the reverse of sound-disappearance.

Like those Dravidian languages which had no distinct words for "yesterday" and "tomorrow" (*Snows*, IV, 3). [Devlin trans.]

Here my authority was Pelliot, who, along with Staël-Holstein and Granet,[3] had discussed this question in my presence with a Japanese, in Peking, in 1918. Recalling the interest that I had seemed to attach to the question, Pelliot spoke to me about it again in Paris once, and then, passing through Washington after World War II, he gave me an article on the subject to read in a journal for Orientalists, a scientific paper whose author I could probably find out again. But the interest this has for me is not a scholarly one, but rather the fact that a human language, any human language whatever, could incorporate, simultaneously, such an extension and such a contraction of mental concepts.

"Man is born in a house, but he dies in the desert."[4]

I really don't know whether the same sort of maxim could be found among non-nomadic peoples such as the South Chinese, who know nothing about the use of the tent. What I can guarantee you is that the human being I met in Inner Mongolia was quite incapable of ever proceeding from the concrete to the abstract.

I speak in esteem. (*Eloges*, "Pour fêter une enfance," III).

"Esteem." —No, there's nothing here derived from the language of the sea.[5] The word, used with its primary meaning, is merely intended to indicate, in a kind of aura of lyric outpouring, a yielding to praise and approval, an exaltation of participating and admiring, in a state of ecstasy and wonder much like a state of grace and reverence.

(The Argentine poet, Ricardo Güiraldes, the first one to translate *Eloges* into Spanish, understood very well what I meant—and the generalized invocation of the title sufficed to guide him—when he wrote to Valery Larbaud in 1925: "Do you know that one phrase of *Eloges* here exerted a sort of tyrannical power, for a time, over the minds of the young people who think and write?— 'I speak in esteem.' It was a sort of capsule poetics, even a whole definition of poetry, that was cited as a standard of judgment and lyric exaltation, as a sort of rule to go by. It was no longer a question of classical or modern art, but simply of things felt and written down in this state of 'esteem' . . .")

Let us be left, the two of us, to this speech without words which is yours to speak, O you all presence, O you all patience! . . . (*Snows*, III, 2). [Devlin trans.]

A simple silent communing between two human beings: "*langage*," and not "*langue*," between son and mother.

I don't believe I have ever anywhere suggested the absurdity that maintains that the poet, in writing, can express himself without "words." I simply wanted to suggest that he combined spirit and letter, the "language" and the "word," in a single flash, at once unconscious and conscious, discharged by the whole of our "being."

1. Letter printed on pp. 580-582 of OC and not included in the "Lettres" section.

2. "Enigmes de Perse." See above, letter 313, note 1.

3. Three well-known French orientalists. See above, letter 185, notes 1 and 6, and letter to Le Gallais of 1 Feb. 1957. (355)

4. See letter to MacLeish of 23 Dec. 1941. (224)

5. Fr. *estime*, besides meaning "esteem," "regard," "opinion," also has a technical, nautical meaning: "reckoning" as in "dead reckoning" (Fr. *navigation à l'estime*).

316

To Monsieur Jean Paulhan   *New York, March 22, 1965*
Paris

Dear friend,

Yesterday in Washington I received the last three issues of the *N.R.F.*, and I find there something of your own way of thinking in the orientation given to the review [. . .].

I'm leaving for Italy on April 14th. I am to deliver, in Florence on the 20th of April, the opening speech at the International Congress on the Seventh Centenary of Dante.[1] Obligation finally accepted, contrary to all my tastes and principles, since, had I persisted in my refusal, it would have meant the abandoning of a long-established French-language tradition. (It was Hugo, in 1865, who delivered the inaugural address.) I had also hoped that this trip would give me a chance to spend a little time in Milan with one of my older sisters[2] whom I could never have with me at Les Vigneaux because of the state of her health. Alas, she has just passed away, of heart failure; and the profound sadness that I have to endure silently casts a great shadow over the very thought of this trip.

After Italy, I'll be spending some time in a corner of the Belgian countryside, in Wallonia, and won't be in Paris until around May 15, for one or two weeks, before settling down for my regular summer and autumn stay on the Presqu'île de Giens.

I would like to hear good news from you—about your

health, your literary activities, and your day-by-day life. Believe me, dear friend, I am ever affectionately and faithfully yours.   A. L.

1. AL accepted this invitation, not as an official representative of France or as a Dante specialist, but as a contemporary poet speaking for the whole international community of poets. The text of this speech was published in 1965 by Gallimard under the title *Sur Dante* and again, with English translation by Robert Fitzgerald *en regard*, in the Bollingen series, *Two Addresses* (1965).

2. Paule (Mrs. Ubaldo Sommaruga), (1886-1966).

317

To Monsieur Jean Paulhan   *Washington, June 5, 1966*
Paris

Dear friend,

[. . .] Your last letter was written in a fine, clear hand, which, right off, brought me good tidings about the state of your health.

But nothing could have been more reassuring to me than your remarkable "Note sur la pensée à l'état brut."[1] I've never seen you, in so few lines, achieve so easily, which means so regally, such mastery of thought and composition.

Here at last, in a fine condensation, is the introduction to that "discourse on method" that I have so long kept hoping you would write. I already sense in it something of that reduction to bare essentials that will determine your conclusions, observations, and questions. A concentrated work, and not one that is haphazardly scattered, almost anecdotally, like Valéry's, in which he dissipated his gifts, for lack of real control and of ability to follow through, and also for lack of a really demanding vitality.[2]

I'm so very eager to hear a few words from you about how your work is going. At the present moment, you couldn't find a better way to fire your enthusiasm, to get into a healthier, more impertinent frame of mind with which to confront life than in gathering up the reins of your thought in this way [. . .].

With the hope of seeing you soon, dear friend.

A. L.

1. Text unidentified.
2. See letter to Gide of 29 Aug. 1949 (300), and letter to Paulhan of 19 July 1960. (312)

318

To Monsieur Jean Paulhan   *Les Vigneaux,*
Boissy-le-Bertrand   *Presqu'île de Giens (Var)*
                                  June 28, 1966

Dear friend,

[. . .] I was disappointed at having to leave Paris last Friday without having been able to manage to see you again at Boissy-le-Bertrand.[1] I had my heart set on it, and I would so like to have had an hour or two of friendly tête-à-tête. What makes me even sorrier is that I dare not hope to see you in the Midi this summer, and I won't be passing through Paris again before flying off to America in December.

Absurd, those luncheons in Paris where one meets only oneself, and the very worst of oneself at that! At least I deeply appreciated all the trouble you went to in coming that far; and even though I wasn't able to converse with you as I would have liked, I was glad to find you at your friends' in such good form, and so at ease in town—glad to see you moving about without the slightest trouble, approaching cut flowers to teach one of the ladies that they are called "larkspurs!"

[. . .] I keep thinking of you, dear friend, and of that luminous bit of French sky under which I left you the other day, among friends, protected by your lovely enclosed meadow. Diane[2] and I are still talking about the excellent dinner that was prepared for us with the condiments from Africa and Guiana. And, for my part, I am especially indebted to you for having come face to face, in your little courtyard, with that Turkestan knot-grass that the German botanists have martyrized with the name *Polygonum Boldschuanicum*!

Here, the shade of our good Marceline, the "Lady of Port-Cros,"[3] for whom Diane developed such an attachment, saddens the whole atmosphere of our first hours in Maritime Provence [. . .].

Take good care of yourself, dear friend, and be careful to live without impatience and without disturbing the harmonious flow of things—in short, live prudently. There is an art of living on good terms with one's body that is quite compatible with the wildest excesses of the mind. And above all, don't do as Gide did; he never managed to give physical fatigue its due—nature's golden rule.

Most sincerely yours.   A. L.

1. Actually Boissise-la-Bertrand, a small town not far from Melun in Seine-et-Marne.

2. I.e., Mrs. Leger.

3. Madame Marcel Henry, "la Dame de Port-Cros," owner of a large portion of the island of Port-Cros not far from the Presqu'île de Giens. She bequeathed her portion of the island to France, as a national park. Madame Henry was the friend of many French writers, musicians, and artists.

LETTERS TO G.-JEAN AUBRY
(1949)

319

To Monsieur G.-Jean Aubry[1]   *Washington, June 17, 1949*
Paris

My dear Aubry,

[. . .] A final word about our poor Larbaud.[2]

I have always insisted, as Gallimard knows, that everything of mine that may be published in Paris be sent to him. I make of this, alas! simply a ritual, as it can't be much else, since the very sight of printed matter, I am told, means nothing to him any more. But I insist, for my own sake, on the perpetuation of this gesture, this friendly fiction.

For the same reason I would find it distressing if our friend, who is still "alive," could not be included in the drawing up of a homage number that is to be devoted to me in the *Cahiers de la Pléiade*. Jean Paulhan, who has taken over its preparation, would like it to be an occasion for a real "reunion." And what "presence" more than Larbaud's—even though only nominal—could better fulfill my wishes, in a sentimental way, in presenting a kind of united front to the French literary world? Could you assist me in reserving a place for him indirectly, on some pretext or other, in this reunion?

Please understand, above all, that it is our friend's moral presence that I am seeking to preserve in this way, out of a sense of personal loyalty that becomes *my* tribute to him. Larbaud, as I told you, was the first person ever to write about me, and ever after he never failed to express himself on my behalf, either by means of the written or the spoken word, and in several languages, with that serene audacity familiar to you, along with the massive simplicity of his affirmations. I have never known any other literary figure who could raise a hand in favor of others with so much easy grace— whether one was or was not among his friends. And then, I actually did become a friend of his.

A particularly moving incident for me, among many, was the following: At the time of the founding of the Académie Mallarmé,[3] to which I always refused to belong, Edouard Dujardin,[4] whom I did not know personally, sought to inveigle me into accepting membership by having recourse, at one time, to an argument he knew would affect me more than any other. He reported to me, in heartrending terms, on a visit he had paid Larbaud, who had already indicated his own acceptance of membership (I don't know in just what way) and who, from the wheelchair to which his paralysis and aphasia confined him, kept trying, in a pathetic way, to make himself heard and understood, urging that I accept membership. He was incapable of articulating even so much as a fragmentary phrase, and I was told in vivid terms about his physical struggle, about the way he gripped his chair, and how his face was agonizingly contorted, straining painfully toward his visitor, and how he finally managed to utter, after terrible, totally exhausting efforts, a single cry—my name. Larbaud was the first to speak my name publicly—a name that may also have been the last one he spoke, judging by what I was told about his state at that time. After I had accompanied my visitor to the door, (we were in the office I had as Secretary General at the Quai d'Orsay), I recall what a time I had trying to concentrate sufficiently to go on with my work. The same feeling still comes over me when I now think of our poor friend.

To conclude on a less gloomy note, may I at least make you smile by telling you that in London, around 1912, I was elected—I can't recall just how it came about —along with Larbaud and Gide, to a singular "Academy" which you have surely never heard of—the John Donne Club,[5] presided over by the most worthy Hon. Edmund Gosse. (Agnes Tobin, an American lady who was more or less the instigator and moving spirit of the whole business, died in California a year after my arrival[6] in America.) Naturally, I never fulfilled the duties imposed on elected members, which involved the publication by each of us, first an Englishman, then a Frenchman, alternately, of an essay on John Donne. The first in order, Edmund Gosse, at one stroke filled the entire bill, amply! But don't you think that was a nice form of immunization against academies of every sort?

So I ask you, dear friend, nay, I beg you, to see what could be selected for Jean Paulhan from among the things that Larbaud had occasion to write about me. (I recall an article in *La Phalange*, in 1911,[7] because it was the first thing he ever wrote about me and because it provoked some sharp reactions; and I also recall his preface to a Russian translation of *Anabase*.)

Nor would it be devoid of interest for you to recreate incidentally, in a note of your own writing, something of the Franco-English atmosphere of pre-1914 London, where I met Larbaud during two long and leisurely stays in England. Chesterton, Belloc, Conrad, Bennett, Arthur Symons, and Edmund Gosse were, more or less, our friends in common. This special atmosphere that Larbaud liked pervades many of my poems of that period, which were never published, and which he alone knew about. (A little poem from that London series was published later, without a signature, in an issue, in honor of Larbaud, of the review *Intentions*, in 1922).[8]

To me, cosmopolitan London was simply a transfer-point in knocking about, and I always used to say to our friend, whenever we met—rather rarely, as it turned out—that I greatly preferred the huge bronze cricket atop Lloyd's to all these tales of the Meynells[9] and the other well-known families that figured so largely in his literary interests.

[. . .]

Cordially yours.   Alexis St-L. Leger

1. G. Jean-Aubry (1882-1950), friend and biographer of Valery Larbaud, and also an art and music critic and translator. See above, letter 300, note 4.

2. Larbaud, who did not die until 1957, was already an almost total invalid. See above, letter 294, note 4.

3. The Académie Mallarmé, founded in 1937 by a group of writers, including Edouard Dujardin, as a living tribute to the author of "L'Après-midi d'un faune." AL was once more invited to join the Académie Mallarmé in 1951, two years after Dujardin's death, but he once more courteously refused. See OC, p. 557.

4. Edouard Dujardin (1861-1949), novelist, poet, and critic of the Symbolist era, chiefly remembered today for his novel, *Les Lauriers sont coupés*. See above, letter 143, note 1.

5. See letter to Larbaud of Aug. 1913. (137)

6. AL errs by a year. See above, letter 111, note 1.

7. See letter to Larbaud of Dec. 1911. (128) The introduction to the Russian translation of *Anabase* appeared in 1926.

8. The little poem is the "Poème pour Valery Larbaud," reproduced in OC, p. 464. It is an extract from a series of poems AL wrote in London in 1912 but never published. AL had shown a number of them to Larbaud, who was in London at the time. Larbaud had been particularly fond of one of these poems, and AL subsequently allowed it to be published in Larbaud's honor in the Nov. 1922 issue of *Intentions*.

9. The well-known family of English writers of the Victorian era, Alice and Wilfred Meynell and their seven children.

320

To Monsieur G.-Jean Aubry   *Washington,*
Paris   *November 17, 1949*

My dear Aubry,

[...] I have received the first volume of your *Valery Larbaud (1880-1920)*.[1] More than just a competent piece of work, it is a very fine piece of work that we are indebted to you for. Honesty could be carried no further. I feared, at first, that this honesty was too painstaking, and that by dint of utilizing every bit of documentation it might risk becoming heavy, to the detriment of whatever light it might otherwise shed. But that is not at all the case, for this massive and wholly chronological presentation, relentlessly based on time-sequences, at least has the advantage of integrating Larbaud, in a masterly way, as a humanist and a man of his period, into the great living fresco in which, above and beyond his works, his attitude as a living person stands out—a helping hand extended to all things, as to all creatures, of his choosing. And thus, your book, in itself, becomes a testimonial to the period it covers. The way you have conceived it— so different from your life of Conrad[2]—nevertheless required, but in a different way, the same self-effacement on the author's part.

I haven't yet been able to bring myself to write to our friend. Something paralyzes me that I can't readily explain to you, but that arises, as you can well imagine, out of consideration for him—a kind of bashfulness where he is concerned, when I think of what my own reactions would be, were I in the state he is in. Nor can I at all imagine the tone that one should take when writing to him, or what may be the limits of what he can perceive. The medical study by Dr. Alajouanine[3] published in the

Cahiers de la Pléiade upset me terribly without enlightening me. I know of nothing more poignant, nor more pointless [. . .].

Let me hear from you, dear friend, and know that I remain faithfully yours.   Alexis St-L. Leger

1. G. Jean-Aubry's biography of his friend, Larbaud, was originally intended to be a two-volume work. See above, letter 300, note 4.

2. G. Jean-Aubry, *Vie de Conrad* (Paris: Gallimard, 1947).

3. See above, letter 309, note 3.

LETTERS TO T. S. ELIOT
(1949-1958)

321

To Mr. T. S. Eliot   *Washington,*
24 Russell Square   *2800 Woodley Road, N.W.*
London W.C. 1   *September 28, 1949*

Dear friend,

Harcourt and Brace, in New York, is pressing for a November publication date of the new bilingual edition of *Anabase*.[1] I took it upon myself to read the proofs carefully, making sure that they stuck faithfully to your new revision. Robert Giroux,[2] who is one of your most faithful admirers, is most obliging in every way. He seems to take a great personal interest in this edition, which will be a good one, and a definitive one.

In order to avoid all further delay, which has been worrying our publisher very much, I felt that I simply had to sign the contract, in haste, just as it was submitted to me; but I must emphasize that this contract would imply abandoning your share of the royalties,[3] as Giroux made a great point of what he said were your express wishes in this matter. I don't know what to tell you in this regard, dear friend. I have become accustomed to so much elegance on your part, but this latest gesture is of such a nature that I can, for my part, neither accept it tacitly nor ignore it in a formal manner. In both cases I would be woefully misrepresenting my feeling about it. So all I can do, as a token of affection between friends, is leave the decision up to you [. . .].

From the far sidelines where I stand, and at my age, which is the same as yours, you can easily imagine how much a few such expressions of friendly support mean to me, intellectually and morally. Your support will always be of the highest importance to me [. . .].

I am delighted to see your French audience grow ever larger, especially at this time when literature, in Paris, bewildered by its new agents, is only too taken with a taste for disintegration; for the cult of the inorganic involves much more than contempt for art; it entails the complete desertion of the "work of art" as such, in the interest of self-affirmation.

In that area, your influence continues to act as a leaven. Lately, there has been a general outcry against everything that your name represents or is represented by— a massive reaction of a whole body of bad literature against good literature. Nothing could be more natural; in economics, we know how bad money drives out good. A weekly magazine devoted to literary popularization, the most bastard and hypocritical of them all, [. . .] briefly became the platform for your attackers[4]—the ultimate tribute to your role as a reagent in the still conventional literary life of England and America. Take care never to indulge in the slightest personal recrimination or to let them goad you into the slightest reflex action.

Affectionately yours, dear friend. When and where will I be seeing you in a more casually human setting? The years go by for both of us,[5] and they have not inculcated in me any taste at all for things in the abstract.

Saint-John Perse

1. T. S. Eliot (1888-1965) was the first translator of *Anabase* into English. He began work on the translation in 1925, but, with characteristic scrupulousness, he did not wish to publish it until he had AL's revisions and commentaries. Because of the pressure of work at the Quai d'Orsay, AL was slow in responding. Eliot's translation, with the French text *en regard*, finally

appeared in 1930 under the title *Anabasis* (London: Faber and Faber). A revised edition of it was published in the United States by Harcourt, Brace and Co. in 1938. The edition here referred to involved still further revision and appeared soon after the present letter was written.

2. Robert Giroux was editor-in-chief of Harcourt, Brace and Co. at this date.

3. English in original.

4. Probably the article by Delmore Schwartz, "The Literary Dictatorship of T. S. Eliot," in *The Partisan Review*, Feb. 1949.

5. AL was sixty-two; T. S. Eliot sixty-one.

322

To Mr. T. S. Eliot
24 Russell Square,
London W.C. 1

Washington,
2800 Woodley Road, N.W.
May 7, 1953

Dear friend,

I asked Jean Paulhan, at the time when the *Nouvelle N.R.F.* was being launched, to have copies of the first two issues (January and February) put aside for you, as I had to contribute to them. I never did find out whether that was done for you, as the whole printing was sold out immediately, leaving the publisher empty-handed, [. . .]. Would you please let me know if you have those issues by now? I hope very much you have, as the texts I was obliged to publish in them constitute an important fragment of a work in progress,[1] and even though this premature publication breaks up the construction as a whole and destroys its unity, as friend to friend I don't like it when anything I authorize for publication does not find its way to you.

You already have, from another source,[2] your copy of *Vents* ("*Winds*") [. . .].

My life here is what it should be, and with my full consent. Loneliness is a threat only to physical health. Being a foreigner in this country and separated from my own, I must accept with good grace the limitations of a literary life. Yet, I would like to have had more contact here with the English milieu, in which I spent a good part of my youth, and which I have always enjoyed. At all events, it is to you that I, and English letters, owe that enduring and most exceptional tie—a translation that does me honor.[3]

Will you be reconsidering, before late in the year, your plans for a return to America? Will I never have the chance to hear once more, from friends, about our long-standing project of going down the Mississippi in what Madame de Sévigné, of whom Mark Twain was unaware, called the "water-coach"?[4] And when can we expect your prodigal son's return to Maine?[5]

Affectionately.   Saint-John Perse

1. The NRF was made an organ of the Nazis for three years (1940-1943) under the Occupation, with Drieu la Rochelle as editor. In 1953, Jean Paulhan and Marcel Arland re-established the magazine and, in order to distinguish it from Drieu's collaborationist publication, gave it the awkward title of *La Nouvelle Nouvelle Revue française*; it reverted to its original title in Feb. 1959. AL had published the first seven cantos of the "Strophe" of *Amers*, under the title "Amers," in the Jan. 1953 issue of the *Nouvelle* NRF, and the "Choeur" section of *Amers* in the Feb. 1953 issue, again simply under the title "Amers."

2. Probably the first English-French edition put out by Pantheon Books of New York for the Bollingen Series in 1953.

3. Eliot's translation of *Anabase*. See above, letter 321, note 1.

4. Fr. *coche d'eau*: actually an archaic term for a river-barge drawn by men or horses. The Marquise de Sévigné (1626-1696) is the most celebrated letter-writer of the reign of Louis XIV. Eliot was born and spent his boyhood in St. Louis, Missouri, within sight of the Mississippi River.

5. As a boy, Eliot usually spent his summer vacations at a family place in New England and later studied at Harvard.

323

To Mr. T. S. Eliot   *Washington,*
24 Russell Square,   *1621 34th Street, N.W.*
London W.C. 1   *May 21, [1958]*

Dear friend,

I have just now received the new edition[1] of *Anabase*. It is perfect, and I know how much it owes to your friendly vigilance. I hope that too much of your own time did not have to be spent correcting proofs.

It pleases me, after all these years, to resume this literary companionship that has meant so much to me. Here, the prestige of your name will continue to favor the fortunes of this book. I am still moved by the fraternal thought it inspires. I say it unabashedly.

There are better things for friends to share than the literary life, and circumstances seem to prevent our paths from crossing. I would so like to meet Mrs. Eliot, at your side, and to introduce both of you to the lady who now shares my life.[2] If your summer or fall travels ever bring you down toward the Mediterranean, remember that there is always a guest room awaiting you at my house on the Presqu'île de Giens, where I spend every summer, now that I am married. Address: Les Vigneaux, Giens via Hyères (Var). The house is mine, on a cape, quite well protected against everybody and everything, except the mistral. I'll be there next June 12th until the end of October, when I return to Washington. (We could easily have someone meet you at either Toulon or Marseille, or even Nice.) Our friend Valéry used to spend his vacations on this Presqu'île de Giens, as a guest of Madame Behague in a house close to my present one.

If that wish is not to be fulfilled, I can then only hope to see you on your way through America next winter.

But our meetings there are always so much a matter of chance, so artificial and brief!

My most cordial wishes, dear friend, selected from among the best.   Saint-John Perse

Could you ask Faber and Faber to send me, at my Washington address, a few more copies of the new *Anabase*? I received only two.

1. Eliot still further revised his translation of *Anabase*, and Faber and Faber published that final revision in 1959.

2. Eliot married his second wife, Valerie Fletcher, in 1957; AL had married Dorothy Milburn Russell in 1958.

LETTER TO E. E. CUMMINGS
(1949)

To Mr. E. E. Cummings[1]   *Washington,*
4 Patchin Place,   *1621 34th Street, N.W.*
New York City 11   *December 1949*

My very dear Cummings,

What can I say about your work, to a poet of your pedigree and rank, that won't make you shrink away in horror? Well then, simply accept my thanks, proferred in a very friendly way, for the friendly gesture that brought me your latest work.[2]

It delights me to receive from you, a born poet of a most princely sort, this precious little book, disdainfully "paperbacked."[3] It goes so well with your charming informality.

I won't make too many excuses for my silence, for you know how it is between us. But I would at least like to run into you more often—the flesh-and-blood you—and to share a lot of things we both like, not forgetting that one of them is laughter. I'm fond enough of your poems, in all their freshness and true essence, to feel absolutely sure of the great worth of their creator. And I also value highly, in a human way, your friendly handshake.

Take care of yourself, my dear Cummings, and look after your health. You, more than anyone else, need peace of mind. Tell Marion[4] that I haven't forgotten how we chatted one day, way up there in her studio. Don't ever pass nearby, whenever you are in this part of Washington, without letting me know. And believe that I always remain, dear friend, most warmly yours.

                                  Saint-John Perse

1. E. E. Cummings (1894-1962), American poet and novelist.

2. The volume Cummings sent AL has not been identified. Cummings wrote a poem, which he dedicated especially to AL, for the special number of the *Cahiers de la Pléiade*, but it arrived too late for inclusion. The text of the poem, published for the first time in OC, pp. 1328-1329, reads as follows:

> being to timelessness as it's to time,
> love did no more begin than love will end;
> where nothing is to breathe to stroll to swim
> love is the air the ocean and the land.
>
> (do lovers suffer? all divinities
> proudly descending put on deathful flesh:
> are lovers glad? only their smallest joy's
> a universe emerging from a wish)
>
> love is the voice under all silences
> the hope which has no opposite in fear;
> the strength so strong mere force seems feebleness
> the truth more first than sun more last than star.
>
> —do lovers love? why then to heaven with hell.
> whatever sages say and fools, all's well.

3. English in original.

4. Mrs. Cummings, née Marion Morehouse (d. 1969), well-known model, actress, and photographer.

LETTERS TO W. H. AUDEN
(1949-1958)

325

To Mr. Wystan H. Auden   *Washington, November 12, 1949*
New York

My dear Auden,

What elegance there is in your gesture, and how greatly I appreciate it![1] [. . .]

Your contribution is princely, and Jean Paulhan will be delighted to be the first to welcome you, and on this footing, to the *Cahiers de la Pléiade*. As for me, I simply wish to thank you for the pleasure you have given me.

It is, in its own right, a beautiful meditation which you have taken time from your own work to devote to me. I particularly like the way—in the most organic fashion—you give us a beautiful lesson in control and lucidity, at a time when poetry, in its very essence and practice, has so many things to integrate and to order, in justifying its "all-embracingness." I am glad to find that I agree with you in your analysis.

Naturally, I saw to it without delay that the text you have entrusted to Jean Paulhan was sent off to him.[2]

I hope it won't be long before I have the pleasure of telling you in person all that I still have to say about your text and about the friendly thought to which I owe it.

Cordially.   Saint-John Perse

1. W. H. Auden (1907-1975) had written a long piece for inclusion in the *Cahiers de la Pléiade* tribute to AL; but, probably because of its length, it was not included.

2. For the special number of the *Cahiers de la Pléiade*.

326

To Mr. W. H. Auden   *Washington, 1958*
New York

Dear friend,

Here you are, close by at last; and I'm indeed delighted
about it, on my return from Europe. What a gift for
ubiquity you seem to have! England? America? Italy?
Austria? . . . It was impossible for me, this last summer,
to find out your exact address.

Is it still not too late for me to tell you a little of what
I so much wanted you to hear, about your generous and
remarkable article,[1] after its publication in the *New York
Times*? Let me just say that I prized it very highly.

My dear Auden, this gift you have for saying a good
word in others' behalf—you exercise it with so much
elegance and so effortlessly that it undoubtedly seems a
perfectly natural thing to you. You yourself can not
realize how exceptional it is [. . .]. And to me, much
more important than the intellectual stature is the human stature that is revealed in it.

Which is a way of telling you that, for me, it redoubles
my friendship for you.   Saint-John Perse

1. Auden had written a piece on AL's work at the time of the
publication of *Amers* in its bilingual edition (*Seamarks*, 1958).
The article was published in the *New York Times Book Review*
of 27 July 1958 under the title, "A Song of Life's Power to
Renew."

LETTERS TO
MRS. HENRY TOMLINSON CURTISS
(MINA CURTISS)
(1951-1959)

To Mrs. Henry Tomlinson Curtiss[1]
[New York]

Washington,
January 10, 1951

Dear friend,

What do we know about "monsters"?[2]—That they hold their tongue and that the only thing that might one evening loosen it is a little music. (Isn't every man worth his salt haunted by the memory of the *violon d'Ingres*,[3] which has finally to be smashed on our adolescent back?)

I did indeed receive your records. Thank you. They revive memories of many a scrap of our conversations at Chapelbrook[4] about "our" composers—always to the pizzicatto accompaniment of your cats sharpening their claws on the silk hangings and upholstery in the library. There is no quarrel between us about music. We'll always have your beloved Proust[5] to argue about [. . .].

Terribly embarrassed that I wasn't able to answer your questions sooner. *Bug Jargal* and *Le Dernier Jour d'un condamné* are indeed by Victor Hugo. *Le Dernier Jour d'un condamné* Hugo got almost word for word from the diary kept by the prisoner, Armand Barbès,[6] one of my fellow countrymen from Guadeloupe, whose moral figure has always struck me as more congenial, more candid and proud, than Blanqui's in the history of French revolutionary republicanism. A people's representative in 1848, imprisoned in 1849 and reprieved *in extremis* from the death penalty, he chose to remain in prison for five years rather than accept his personal freedom from the hands of Napoleon III. When he was a voluntary expatriate in London, he one day got up from his restaurant table to challenge an Englishman to a duel for making vulgar remarks about Empress Eugénie (though the Englishman said no more about her than what Barbès himself thought).

[. . .] I keep thinking, dear friend, about that piece of ironwork[7] wrought long ago in upper Burgundy which you were able to rescue for me, God only knows how. It bears the date of the first departure of a Saint-Leger Leger who, as the youngest son of the family, set out for the Leeward Isles, along with two missionaries of a religious order whose name escapes me at the moment [. . .].

Yours,   A.S.L.

1. Mrs. Henry Tomlinson Curtiss, née Mina Kirstein, sister of Lincoln Kirstein, the editor of *Hound and Horn* (1927-1934), a noncommercial literary review somewhat analagous to *Commerce* in Europe (see above, letter 187, note 2), and subsequently one of the founders of the New York City Ballet. Mrs. Curtiss is an author and scholar in her own right. See below, note 5, and letter 327, note 2.

2. Mrs. Curtiss apparently applied the term to AL chiefly because of his habit of never answering letters.

3. "Le violon d'Ingres" is a French way of designating a serious hobby or avocation, since the celebrated nineteenth-century painter, Ingres, was fond of playing the violin. The reference here is double, however, since AL, passionately fond of music from his earliest childhood, had had to forego the study of the violin at a very early age.

4. Chapelbrook was the name of the property of Mrs. Curtiss in upstate Massachusetts, near Ashfield.

5. Mrs. Curtiss was not only a great admirer of Marcel Proust's works; she had actually translated a copious selection of Proust's letters into English (*Letters of Marcel Proust,* 1948). AL's abiding dislike of Proust is well known, even though Proust had

gone out of his way to mention AL, very flatteringly, in *A la recherche du temps perdu* (in the *Sodome et Gomorrhe* volumes) and actually written a half-dozen letters to AL, none of which he ever acknowledged.

6. Armand Barbès (1809-1870), French revolutionary born in Guadeloupe, collaborated with the socialist activist Auguste Blanqui (1805-1881), and later broke with Blanqui. Barbès, after numerous imprisonments and pardons, died in exile at The Hague. The journal in question, *Deux jours de condamnation à mort*, was first published in 1849.

7. This piece of ironwork took on an almost talismanic char-acter for AL, who ultimately had it mounted on a leeward wall of his house at Les Vigneaux. See letter to Mrs. Curtiss of 27 July 1957. (344)

328

To Mrs. Henry T. Curtiss   *Washington, February 29, [1952]*
New York

I think of you, dear friend, of your solitude, which is no less great than mine, of your elegance—so human—in matters of friendship, of your indulgent attitude toward "monsters."

Need I say more? Sentimentality will never be our climate.

I'm delighted that your book is coming along so well.[1] The chapter I'm sending back to you is really very lively and straightforward; it conveys the atmosphere of a whole period without detracting from the main concern of your study in any way. I liked the sobriety of the lan-guage and tone. Your short, rapid sentences and the quo-tations, so felicitously worked in, keep the whole thing moving—which is surely the most difficult thing to main-tain in a documentary work. And your re-creation is in no way "fictionalized." (Easy makeshifts are as foreign to your writing as to your life.)

As for the subject matter, throughout I found that

psychological interest which is your specialty, and that feel for things human which, in your mind, is perhaps of a piece with what you call your taste for "the concrete."

My warmest thoughts will be with you, dear friend, when you are in Paris and Sweden searching for manuscripts and autographs. Right in Stockholm, other surprises, besides those of the collector, await you. Inquire about the musical life there. Stravinsky tells me very good things about it. In Paris you'll see my family [. . .].

A.S.L.

1. Mrs. Curtiss was working on her book, *Bizet and his World*, published in 1958 by Alfred A. Knopf.

329

To Mrs. Henry T. Curtiss   *Washington* [*September 1952*]
New York

Dear friend,

These two chapters are really very good, in spite of the abundance of quotations from letters which throw so much light on the moral, or simply human, make-up of your Bizet—his freedom of action and his independent spirit. Interest is kept up to the very end, thanks to the constant interweaving of the historical background, done so deftly and unobtrusively, without any loss of momentum [. . .].

Thank you for having gone to so much trouble for me in all this book-hunting.

Yes, in the Álfred W. Paine catalogue (Wolpits Road, Bethel, Connecticut) which really astonished me, there are three items you might inquire about for me:

No. 180: *Lettres édifiantes des Missions étrangères*, xviiie Recueil.

No. 176: Las Casas *Relation des Voyages et Décou-vertes des Espagnols dans les Indes Occidentales*.

No. 65: *Voyages du Capitaine Cook*, Paris, Le Rouge, 1811.

I think of you, dear Mina, more spontaneously and more often than you suspect.   A.

330

To Mrs. Henry T. Curtiss   *Washington, November 3, 1952*
Williamsburg, Massachusetts

I've been thinking, dear Mina, about your approaching flight to Europe.

Don't keep thinking about that long face I made the other night on the doorstep of your Washington hotel. I had too many things about France in my head—or maybe I was just tired out from a long series of sleepless nights. (It's stupid, the way life can become so outwardly complicated and take its revenge that way when one has mastered it too well inwardly.)

Your pills put me to sleep, and I thank you for them, but they leave one feeling logy, "sticky" as an "existentialist."

Yes, you can give me little Paul Reynaud's latest lies[1] to read, although they don't come from an enemy worthy of my wishes. ("There you go again, with your 'arrogance'", you will say, using that fine English word which conveys so much more than the same word in French.)

Keep up the good work, and finish up your book quickly so you may have the joy of renewal.

You've been through a hard year, and I've often gauged, and still do, what it means to a person of your moral constitution to have had to get so many things under control.

Preserve your vitality above all else. Along with me, it's your best friend. As for the former, grant him the confidence, in all matters and in spite of everything, that his heart deserves. And don't worry yourself about his future; it's not true that he absolutely must have a sea island [. . .].

Friendly regards to your Timothy, that adventurous big tomcat.

Yours,   A.

---

1. Paul Reynaud (1878-1966), the last Prime Minister and Minister of Foreign Affairs of the Third Republic, was responsible for the removal of AL from his post as Secretary General (18 May 1940). In 1951 Reynaud published his memoirs of the World War II years, *Au Cœur de la Mêlée*.

331

To Mrs. Henry T. Curtiss   *Dark Harbor, Maine*
Chapelbrook   *July 23, 1953*
Ashfield Road,
Williamsburg, Mass.

Dear friend,

This is not a "bread and butter letter." You wouldn't believe your eyes.

Our final hours together in Boston made me cherish more than ever that simple thing, nameless and ageless, we have between us: friendly confidence freely shared.

Neither the daily presence of the sea nor the sound of it in the night distracts my thoughts here from all I left behind in the closed circle of your heights, boulders, and woods. I love Chapelbrook—you know that. I have left much of myself in the very shady, very "moody"[1] heart of that little wooden cottage, close to your house, which was mine—almost too much so. It won't do any good for Belle, Grace, and Una, your three tall servant-girls, to sweep the ashes from my fireplace; I'm still there, and not one of your guests will ever be more there among your maple trees heavy with stars and your apple trees haunted by nocturnal hedgehogs.

Dear Mina, to whom my thoughts turn, you would shut me up if I said the least word about all your attentions, all your affectionate concern, and all your indulgent understanding of the "monster" that I am (Mina *dixit*!). Instead, let me embrace you warmly, sharing one of those kindly and genuine smiles that are our due.

A.

—Don't forget your promise to leave off your life in the fields this fall when you should. Too much solitude far from the city really makes me a little uneasy for you.

—Don't pamper Fluffy—my favorite of all your cats— by disguising her as a Chinese cat just for my benefit. She's nothing but a byproduct of the Goncourts![2] It's high time that I take her in hand and let her know what's what.

1. English in original.
2. The Goncourt brothers, Edmond (1822-1896) and Jules (1830-1870), the celebrated novelists and journal-writers, who collected Japanese and Chinese art objects.

332

To Mrs. Henry Tomlinson Curtiss   *Washington,*
153 East 74th Street, New York, N.Y.   *January 11, 1954*

Mina, could you find out for me, from your brother[1] or from one of your musician friends, what to think about the composer Alan Hovhaness, for whom I've been asked to grant permission for a musical setting of *Anabase*?[2] [. . .]

I've already had to turn down several proposals of the

same sort, especially one that was recommended by T. S. Eliot for a theatrical performance, in the form of a choral drama, by the "Forty-Eight Theatre Group"[3] of London. You know how little taste I have for these mixtures of two arts so completely independent, to my way of thinking, as poetry and music. To make me surmount such a prejudice, it would take a lot of esteem, and even more personal sympathy, for the composer, young or old. And I don't think that the present period, nor the present place, holds very many Stravinskys in reserve for us.

I think of you, dear friend, in all sorts of new ways.

S.-J. P. (The real one.)

1. Lincoln Kirstein. See above, letter 327, note 1.

2. Alan Hovhaness, American composer who in 1954, was commissioned by Broadcast Music, Inc. to do a musical setting for *Anabase*. Permission was granted, and Hovhaness' score, using the English translation by T. S. Eliot, was published in 1956 under the title *Anabasis*. See letter to Juan José Castro of 3 June 1960. (363)

3. A British theatrical troupe, under the direction of E. Martin Browne, that had produced Eliot's plays.

333

To Mrs. Henry Tomlinson Curtiss   *Nassau (Bahamas)*
153 East 74th Street, New York, N.Y.   *March 26, 1954*

I've just returned from a cruise, and I offer you, dear friend, a picture of this tiny uninhabitable island, which is not far from here—the tiniest I've ever set foot on! That means I'm offering you a great deal of myself— more of myself, in fact, than I myself possess or ever shall. In your mind's eye, treat the place generously; it doesn't think very highly of itself, and that's really its greatest charm.

I'm getting ready to return to Washington after a long

ramble around the isles and reefs of the Bahamian archipelago. First off, some friends of mine took me much
farther south to the little English island of Cat Key,[1] to
improve my state of health, and my state of mind. I still
haven't managed to get back my sleep, but I've redis-
covered the "monster" in me.   S.-J. P.

1. Cat Key, the nearest of the Bahamian islands to Florida.
For the "monster" reference, see above, letter 327, note 2.

334

To Mrs. Henry T. Curtiss   *Washington,*
Chapelbrook   *June 21, 1954*
Ashfield Road, Williamsburg, Mass.

Dear friend,

You must call a halt to the search you've undertaken
for living arrangements that would make it possible for
me to spend a summer in California. Material considerations make this faraway "country holiday" impossible,
since I'd have to resign myself more or less to some sort
of hotel life. What I would like on the Pacific coast is
not a sedentary retreat, but rather to move about freely
over that whole section of America so I could see the
southern California coast (which I'm not very familiar
with), a little of the Sierras maybe, and above all, more
to the north, the route of the giant sequoias—the thought
of them still fascinates me the way the thought of the
Grand Canyon did. All this to stow away in my baggage
before the end of a stay in America that, I feel, by more
than one sign, will soon be over for me.

At the moment I'm turning toward something else.

I am to spend the month of August on the high seas,
in Canadian waters, with an old friend of mine from the
Far East[1] who asks me to assist and advise him in the

choice and testing of a Canadian fishing schooner that is to be transformed into a yacht for the end of one man's life at sea. (Happy man, whom I envy—I who have never envied anyone!)

In September I'm expected by the Biddles at Cape Cod[2] after Labor Day. It would be infinitely more painful to me than you think to have to go back on the promise I made you. Let me know if, at Ashfield, you could have me visit you in July, and around what date.

Thank you again for all the trouble you have just gone to on my behalf.

I embrace you.   S.-J. P.

1. Unidentified. (Bacot, perhaps?)
2. Bound Brook Island, Wellfleet. See above, letter 197, note 12.

335

To Mrs. Henry Tomlinson Curtiss   *Washington,*
Hotel Ambassador, New York, N.Y.   *June 28, 1954*

Dear friend,

Terribly disappointed that I can't get to New York in time to see you. I'd have liked so much to drive up to Chapelbrook with you, with a stopover at your seafaring brother's place, and also to see our friend Anne Lindbergh.[1] I'll just have to forget about it; there are too many things to take care of before I leave Washington.

I can't be in New York before the evening of July 6th, so I'll take the train to your place on Wednesday the 7th. I'll regret infinitely that I won't be able to have my traveling companion for the drive on a fine summer night up to the great landswells of Massachusetts.

Most warmly.   S.-J. P.

1. See above, letter 204, note 4.

336

To Mrs. Henry Tomlinson Curtiss   *The Chatham,*
Chapelbrook   *New York, N.Y.*
Ashfield Road, Williamsburg, Mass.   *Friday, [July 1954]*

Just a brief note, dear friend [. . .].

To let you know that I am loyal to Chapelbrook and grateful for everything that I have received from it, or, unknowingly, taken from it. It was a happy and beneficent stopover along a route that no longer means very much to me. In spite of my discontentment with the literary life, at Chapelbrook I found the coolness of an oasis that momentarily revived in me the taste for writing.[1] I found many other things there too, of a more precious human sort. Thank you, Mina. I embrace you warmly.   S.-J. P.

Leaving day after tomorrow for Maine, twenty-four hours later than scheduled. . . . Everything is now in order, though. Embarcation at Portland.

1. AL was probably composing portions of *Amers* (*Seamarks*) at this date.

337

To Mrs. Henry T. Curtiss   *Washington,*
156 East 71st Street, New York, N.Y.   *April 13, [1955]*

No, dear friend, above all don't desert the concrete for the abstract; you'd lose too much in such an exchange.

And don't believe for a moment that you're a "domesticated" creature; that's not you at all, I assure you.

Warmly.   A.S.L.

—Do you know anything about an American learned journal called *P.M.L.A.* (*Publications of the Modern*

Language Association of America), in which there is said to be an intelligent study devoted to me by a Mr. Arthur Knodel, a professor at the University of Southern California, under the title of "The Imagery of Saint-John Perse" or something like that? Could you get hold of it for me without too much trouble?[1]

1. Arthur J. Knodel, "The Imagery of Saint-John Perse's *Neiges*," *PMLA*, Mar. 1955.

338

To Mrs. H. T. Curtiss   *Washington,*
Chapelbrook   *May 21, 1955*
Ashfield Road, Williamsburg, Mass.

Dear friend,

[. . .] I'm still trying to arrange my summer in Canadian waters. From July 15 to August 15 (end of the "Terre-Neuve"[1] fishing season). So it will be after August 15 that I can turn toward Chapelbrook. If that weren't possible, I would stop off, after my cruise in the north, in some little Maine port in order to get some work done, for I'm behind in so many things, and I'm beginning to have a terribly guilty conscience.

I follow you in my thoughts, dear Mina, and want you to feel them near you, powerless as they may be at the moment to lighten your hours of sadness and family worries. I don't like it, feeling you so alone, suffering insomnia and subject to the anxieties of your long nights in the country.

Let me hear from you. I embrace you and am quite simply there with you.   A.S.L.

How touching, dear friend, that in the midst of all your family cares, you still think, for me, of all those minute things in my Antillean family's past. Yes, you may inquire for me at Nantes about the fate of those three maps mentioned in the catalogue.[2]

Do you think I might find in New York, without going to too much trouble, the following books?—

W. Adolphe Roberts, *The French in the West Indies* (Bobbs-Merril and Co., Indianapolis, 1942);

Algernon Aspinall, *West Indian Tales of Old* (London, Duckworth and Co., 1912);

Lenis Blanche, *Histoire de la Guadeloupe* (Paris, 1938);

Nellis M. Crouse, *The French Struggle for the West Indies* (Columbia University Press, New York, 1943).

1. OC, p. 1052, has "Terre-Neuvas." Probably a misprint.
2. The three maps remain unidentified.

339

To Mrs. H. T. Curtiss   *Washington, Sunday*
Chapelbrook   *[June 1955]*
Ashfield Road, Williamsburg, Mass.

My poor friend, it makes me heartsick to hear you admit your weakness in such a family trial. (And weakness, to me, is so much more poignant when it engulfs a strong person's heart.) Now that the news is better, you are doubtless having to suffer the aftereffects of all that you have had to repress or surmount within yourself [. . .]. I like—and at the same time, I don't like—to think of you steeped in that peace, but likewise that isolation, which the up-country of Chapelbrook affords. Now is the moment I wish I could be with you.

Tomorrow I'll be in the north, where I'll embark from Halifax. I don't think I'll be back in Boston, to wend my way from there to your place, before August 18 [. . .]. I still don't have any definite information to give you about sending mail to me. I'll let my Washington apartment house know my main relay or general-delivery stops. I'll let you know, too.

I spent four days in New York with the Hoppenots,[1] and three days on Long Island with American friends. The French Delegation[2] passing through New York on its way to San Francisco has once more put me in touch with several of my former associates of the Quai d'Orsay, among whom was one of my last private secretaries,[3] whom I am still very fond of, and whom I was happy to see again.

Thanks for the books and magazine articles that you send me. Thanks especially for that old map of Saint Christopher (St. Kitts)—which some of my Island ancestors explored, or at least set foot on, in the 17th century under the governorship of M. de Poincy.[4]

I keep looking for the four-o'clock afternoon light at the edge of your big woods; I hear you calling out from the raspberry vines to your servants; I watch them shelling peas in the pantry as I go by; in the library I listen to Mozart's *Don Giovanni* and, just before midnight, I extend my hand to the Statue of the Commander; and I carry off, to read in bed, a few of your French archives from the Paris Commune. . . . The little screech-owl that nests in the barn is on the roof.   A.S.L.

1. Henri Hoppenot (b. 1891), French diplomat, friend of Paul Claudel and AL, Ambassador to Switzerland, 1945-1952 and to South Vietnam in 1955. See above, letter 148, note 4.

2. The French delegation to the United Nations General Assembly in 1955 consisted of Antoine Pinay, Pierre Henri Teitgen, Jules Moch, Yvon Delbos, and Hervé Alphand.

3. Probably Etienne de Crouy-Chanel.

4. Philippe de Lonvilliers de Poincy was the first governor of the French Antilles, a post he held from 1639 to 1660. His headquarters were on the island of Saint-Christophe (present-day St. Kitt's), which was then the "queen of the French Antilles." It was later shared with the British, and then completely taken over by the British in 1783.

340

To Mrs. Henry Tomlinson Curtiss   *Wellfleet,*
on Board the Cunard Line   *Cape Cod (Mass.)*
"S.S. Queen Mary"   *September 17, 1955*
(leaving New York on September 21), N.Y.

Dear Mina, I'm there with you.

With you on your beautiful English liner, impregnated through and through with the heavy smells of Europe— of a very ancient and now, for me, passé Europe (English woolens and Scotch tweeds).

Make the most of your fondness for old English liners, for their days are numbered, and we won't be saying for very much longer, with Kipling, "The Liner, she is a lady."[1]

May you travel free of care and get out of this trip everything zestful that it may have in store for you.

For me, it is still exile. Between France and me, there is only that horseshoe you brought back from your last trip for me—a horseshoe picked up for me in the Pyrenees on the road to Gavarnie! . . . There's nothing more to say.

I embrace you.   A.S.L.

1. English in original.

341

To Mrs. Henry Tomlinson Curtiss   *Washington,*
156 East 71st Street, New York, N.Y.   *December 30, 1955*

Mina, dates are not for us, and our calendar has nothing Gregorian about it. Yet we must recall that the other night it was Christmas,[1] and that tomorrow night, they tell us, the year is coming to an end. I will again be alone in this country, as I have always wanted to be on such dates. At midnight I won't be sharing in the ritual—a lugubrious one in any case—of "crossing the line" in gay celebration. But you, where will you be? With a few friends? —At Chapelbrook or in New York?

Because I am now a bit more familiar with the way your day is parceled out, I can gauge your inner solitude somewhat better—the moral strength that shields you and lets you face life, head high. I'll never again refer to you as a "natural force," I promise you. That's too easy, too unfair, and even rather graceless.

Just open your Chapelbrook gardener's hands (I don't say "sorceress' hands" any more), so that I may place in them, along with my wishes, the two seeds of wild heather that old tramps, in Brittany, offer their hosts as payment for being welcomed around the hearthfire.

With you, warmly.   A.

1. English in original.

342

Mrs. Henry T. Curtiss   *Washington,*
156 East 71st Street, New York, N.Y.   *January 25, 1956*

I should have told you much sooner how delighted I am for you by your decision about the purchase of Manet's letters.[1] Always look upon Manet as a *grand Monsieur*. As for the price, have no scruples, since you'll be drawing *life* from them for yourself, in the best sense of the word, and not just the futile satisfaction of a collector. Your own father[2] would have told you as much —money that is spent is worthless unless converted into what is really alive. And I especially like, as you know, your sense of the real, the live, which makes a "concrete" (your favorite word) being into something much closer to the poet than you think.

I clasp that being, in any case, to my heart.   A.

1. Mrs. Curtiss had decided to buy the autograph letters of the painter Edouard Manet (1832-1883), with the view of utilizing them as the basis of a book, as she had done for Bizet.

2. Louis Edward Kirstein (1876-1942), long-time vice-president of William Filene's Sons Co., the Boston department store.

343

To Mrs. Henry T. Curtiss   *Monhegan Island,*
Chapelbrook   *August 5, 1956*
Ashfield Road, Williamsburg, Mass.

Dear Mina,

This is the first chance I've had of getting a letter to the mainland. But even at that, I'll have to entrust it to some little fishing port or other along the nearby coast rather than to the postal station of an island as independent and casual as Monhegan, the farthest out in the North Atlantic.

Forced southwards by the northern fogs that keep rolling in, and by the evil doings of the sun-spots, we're wandering about somewhere between Georges Banks and Monhegan, and my plan is to have myself put ashore, at the proper moment, at Rockland, Portland, or Boston so I can join you on the 15th. I'll find some way before then of touching land somewhere so I can phone you and confirm that everything is going as planned—and also to ask you to go over practical details of route and timetable once more.

My navigation has thus far been as devoid of incident as of sunlight. I've been especially good—not once in the water, in these icy Labrador currents that I like so much!

Will I find you hard at work? I would like everything around you to be as salubrious, tonic, and generous as the trout streams of Chapelbrook always strike me as being!

Affectionately yours.   A.

Best regards to Ibsen, the best-named of your cats—
since it was I who named him!

344

To Mrs. Henry T. Curtiss   *Les Vigneaux,*[1]
156 East 71 Street, New York, N.Y.   *Presqu'île de Giens (Var)*
                                  July 27, 1957

I await you here, dear Mina [. . .].

Don't forget to bring me, from Chapelbrook, the
wrought-iron sign that was forged in upper Burgundy.
A place is already reserved for it on one of the outside
walls of the house, landward. I spoke about it yesterday
to a local master smith, a good man whom I like a lot
and who was formerly a "Companion of the Tour de
France."[2] (Nothing will be hung seaward, for the sea
is devoid of memory.)

Maritime Provence is bright and beautiful, rather
"pathetic" in the American sense of the word—yes,
desperately prodigal, towards me, in the way it tries so
hard to please, almost supplicating at times. . . . But
how far away I am here from the Atlantic, and how
many waves must I still send off which will always persistently and furtively roll back toward me. But all that
is a small matter compared to everything that has already taken hold of me.

Solitude that I must defend even on French soil!
[. . .]

What else is there to say about this new turning, on
the tip of a peninsula, and of France? The evenings,
strangely silent, with no animal yet beside me. Far off,
only the little screech-owl dear to Pallas.[3] At dawn, the
sea rising to the wide windows of the large empty salon
and spilling over into the study, right onto my work

table—high conscience satisfied, and one that still continues to remind me of the other side of the world.

For the moment, my thoughts are still with you in New York; and I am there to welcome you on your return from Chapelbrook, the good smell of hemlock and fern from upstate Massachusetts still clinging to you.

Warmly.   A.

1. Les Vigneaux is the name of the villa on the Presqu'île de Giens, on the Mediterranean coast of France near Hyères, which became AL's residence in 1957, and where he lived until his death in Sept. 1975. It was Mrs. Curtiss who found the villa for the group of American friends who presented it to AL as a tribute. See letter to Mrs. Curtiss of 9 Sept. 1959. (346)

2. See above, letter 327, note 7. A "Companion of the Tour de France" means that the craftsman had done his stint as a guild journeyman, traveling from place to place in order to perfect his trade. The tradition of *compagnonnage* dates back to the fifteenth century.

3. See above, letter 210, note 2.

345

To Mrs. Henry T. Curtiss   *Les Vigneaux,*
Chapelbrook   *Presqu'île de Giens (Var)*
Ashfield Road,   *September 9, 1958*
Williamsburg, Mass.

Dear Mina,

Might this be the end of an exile? Or only of a nomad's wanderings? . . .

So here I am on French soil, the sea still at my back. What is living but wandering? Nobody will ever be able to teach me how to draw a red line between those two columns in the same account book: land and sea. One single surge—land and sea—still enfurls my nightly dream. And what am I to do with this inner sea that dwells within me? Wring its neck, as one wrings the neck of "eloquence"?[1]—or submit to it as to one's destiny?

Though I still can't feel I've the soul of a landsman, and even less of a property-owner, here I am, a man of one place—but not yet entirely so, since I'm still poised between America and France. (And hasn't that always been my lot?—never to belong wholly in any one place? . . . It's been such a long time since I've trodden upon any soil still really unknown to me!)

And here I am, married, twice married, to Dorothy in America, to Diane in France (because that is what I call her here).

"*Almost happy!*"[2] I once read in New Orleans, scribbled at the bottom of a self-portrait in grease-paint of Audubon (bearing a London date, I believe, towards the end of his life)—an aged Audubon, bearded and grave, graying, but still as handsome as ever with his sweeping Creole glance. (And it was in the same curio-shop museum of the Vieux Carré—a Spanish-style barracks—that I first saw the original of that moving Pascalian mask of Napoleon made by Antomarchi on Saint Helena.)

Make my peace with the land? . . . Will I be living here long enough (six months out of the year) to puzzle out meaning and custom of a whole landbound mode of life that is foreign to me? Really a pointless question, under such an eternity of brilliant sun!

Provence, so-called Maritime Provence—and that here insists on being a peninsula, thank God! On this farthest extremity of the France of "Oc"[3] with no other frontier to the south than that very fictive dividing line between sky and water, I must confront this Latin sea, which is not the sea of my childhood nor of any of my ancestors. It makes me more aware than ever of the Celt in me, of that distant murmur that always comes from the north to my inner ear.

Here, the land will very gradually open its eyelids for me, and I'll be able to accept its charms. The discretion, here by the sea, of this ascetic earth, devoid of fat and flabbiness—and by that very fact more avid to live. A land that knows neither ploughshare nor spade and that, I think, would give way only to bulldozer or dynamite. (There isn't a single pocket of soft earth, Mina, that you could knead with your gardening hands, your lovely gardening hands.) Perhaps the day will come when I will take great delight in the beautiful, finely articulated body with the patrician bone-structure that is the soil of Provence. Haven't I always been fascinated by stone and its hidden energy? Seferis,[4] a Greek poet and a good one, when he dined with me one evening in Washington, tried to entice me into spending some time in Greece by promising me a stony place where there is nothing but stone, and the most beautiful stone in the world.

Don't worry, Mina, I'll take up my work as a poet again here. At night, maybe, so as not to lose any of the flaming daylight.

The whole countryside here, night and day, smells of essences, resin, and that aroma of yellow amber as it rises in the evening warmed by the bodies of women with mat skin. The dryness is that of a violin-bow rubbed with colophony. (When Paganini died, his body was exhibited under glass on one of the coastal islands. America's great instrument-makers come here and seek out the finest Provençal canebrake for making recorder and oboe reeds. And I even like to feel that sort of invisible threat of fire around me that rides the breath of the cistus bushes without grazing them.) A land teeming, like a sluice-grating, with bodies of cicadas and with white shells.

For me, that's all to the good! My horror of flowers will be well served here! But less so my passion for tree, leaf, and fruit.

In this Latin light where so much knowledge, I believe, and so much consciousness has been lost (I used to argue about this long ago, in a friendly way, with Paul Valéry!) I eat figs as Cato did, without forgetting Carthage and the lesson of the proximity of Africa. I've now made friends with my fig tree, a tamed monster that I have taught manners by pruning him way down so that he will learn how to flaunt his treasures where women's hands can reach them—Diane's and my sisters'. (I rather like, in spite of myself, its odor, warm and honeyed, like that of the cows that wander through the streets of Bombay.) Planted, in its honor, an African pomegranate (*Punica granatum*) and an Egyptian avocado (*Persea gratissima*). And I dream of also having a filao of the West Indies[5] (*Casuarina*); a Cape Verde dracena, an *Ombu* or *Belombra* of the Argentine pampas, and a jacaranda from Brazil. Since vetiver is unobtainable, I've ordered, from a good Toulon nurseryman, tufts of *Gynerium argenteum*[6] that my mother used to like in the Islands and that still stirs something in me.

Not that we lack exoticism here: "Phoenician broom" and "Mexican yuccas" keep a fine sense of ubiquity alive in me. "Argentine ants" besiege us on every side; big lizards play at being iguanas; tiny tortoises endlessly repeat the proud geometric pattern of fine sea-turtles; the black galley worms of my childhood inch along the rough-cast walls of my stone terraces; and the gecko or marbouya of the old Antillean plantations spies on us from the dining-room ceiling, perhaps in search of beautiful bare shoulders like those to whom Romuald, our old black family butler, on the evenings of formal dinners *en décolleté*, would hold up a pocket-mirror, so as to make the sticky-footed little monster let go. Finally, from the marshes of Camargue come Caspian or Black Sea birds. And a few gulls, Celtic-born, who know nothing about Homer and still speak to us of the Atlantic—feeling sufficiently out of place on these tide-less coasts so that they choose to mate only on my roof terrace. I flushed out with my rowboat yesterday, from the crevice of a neighboring islet, a mysterious little Arctic petrel that had undoubtedly strayed from its migratory route and had no business being in these parts.

The sudden manifestations of natural forces are no less surprising here, and strongly resemble something that has strayed off course—tropical tornadoes and fine electrical storms, such as one sees off the coast of Guinea or Mauritania; waterspouts moving across the sea like those that enchanted my Antillean childhood and that, I was told, would have to be broken up by carronade broadsides from the old gunboats riding at anchor in the roadstead. And the house itself, in its fine square style that is more colonial than Provençal—wasn't it built by an Englishman who perhaps remembered Aden, Colombo, or Nassau?

Hybridism, hybridism in all things. In the site, first of all, which is that of an island still not very firmly attached to the continental spine. On this crest between land and sea where I've planted my flagpole, only one key turns for me—the key of a single spatial continent at eye level. Is a new era opening up for me? Between the plebeian land and the patrician sea—those two flaps of the same packsaddle—I am quite ready to follow here the "customs officer's path,"[7] like an Andalusian muleteer between his load of carob beans and his baskets of seafood.

Faithful in this way to everything that the sea still moors at the tip of my peninsula, I have the whole sea before me—and behind me, the whole land; and at my side, in the distance, salt[8] and those salty lands where in my dreams I have always lived. Here are the Pesquiers Salt Flats to the left, toward the east; further on, to the right, are the Salt Flats of Hyères. According to Hugo von Hofmannsthal, the thought of salt haunts my poetic works—a sort of principle or residue of its action. (As a child, when I dreamed about France on reading La Fontaine, it was not of the Waters and Forests or of Tax Farmers or Masters of the Wolf-Hunt that I dreamed,[9] nor of a wonderful life in the fields with the wheat, the skylark, and the fox, heronries and fresh-water fish ponds, but of a simple career as Salt-Tax Collector.) With these pyramids of white salt now at my back in the distance, I count my blessings and take my stand, in these parts, against any threat of inordinate listlessness. The mistral helps me in this—the mistral of which everyone, including you, dear Mina, speaks ill, but which, as it suddenly blows up, always seems to me salutary. (An old wine-grower in the neighborhood, *père* Gauthier—at whose place Valéry, like the true southern Frenchman he was, liked to catch the smells of Provençal cooking—told me how one lick of the mistral sufficed to rid his vines promptly of all parasitic blights.)

Other friends in this region: a master ironsmith who forged my grillwork and fence posts and who tells me tales of his youth when he was a "Companion of the Tour de France."[10] There is also an old master bee-keeper, the dean of French apiculturists. I especially like it that he treats his rheumatism by having his own bees sting him. Otherwise this coast is today quite devoid of artisans—coopers and wheelwrights or others of the band who wear leather aprons and used to talk under the jutting roof. (One just cannot find here any point along the coast, as you can on the Atlantic shore of France, where seaman and farmer meet on the same threshold and around the same forge fire to have some chainlink or other mended.) As for literary folk, there are none, thank God! that I know of, but the ghosts are legion: Stevenson, and Conrad, and beloved Edward Lear; Vogüé, Edith Wharton; Lamartine and Michelet—even Tolstoy, would you believe it? and finally Valéry,[11] whom I wish I could still tease by reminding him that Mediterranean light blinds us and shuts the door on our metaphysical threshold.

My visitors and familiars?—two fine foxes in my *garrigue*,[12] a kestrel, and a few tame magpies; but still no big dog or little Sicilian donkey.

How I spend my time? —Very little on literature. Brush-clearing and terracing, by main force (my own!) and hand tools (marvelous ones!). (Can you think of anything more wildly fascinating than a huge country hardware store? —far richer in temptations than any cave of Saint Anthony.)

The day's events? —Installation, down in the cove, of an iron ladder and a platform for the diving board; setting up the rigging, at the lower end of the grounds, for the pretty pink-brick well under a coquettish pavilion; finally, the search for another well somewhere in the depths of a gully or thicket so that my domain of Les Vigneaux shall not be one-eyed like Hannibal.

I know that sooner or later I'll come across that old lost well,[13] which is shown on ancient notarized maps and whose praises are still sung by the old-timers who knew the place long ago before the underbrush of my jungle ran wild. And, for me, that will be quite an event, for the mystery of water, as you know, has always and everywhere deeply affected me. Through the magnetic eye of my uncovered well, I will here have access to the mystery, nay, to the very breath, of our terrestrial night. I won't put a stone pavilion over it, not being a stonemason like Churchill; but it will be quite enough for me just to bend over it. And I'll lower into it, on the end of a little rope, the silver mug from my childhood that has always served me, in every country, to sample, on land, the various "vintages" of water. And this is a way of telling you, dear Mina, how deeply I will be indebted, humanly speaking, to Les Vigneaux.

And there you have, Mina, the long, very long report that you've been waiting for—long enough, I imagine, to earn forgiveness for all my accumulated silences. And now it's your turn, from the other side of the water, to be nice and send me an equally long account of the way you spend the year's end, with a thousand details (*mil e tre*)[14] about your daily life at Chapelbrook and in New York—something like what was once called, in land-locked France, a day-book.

Yours, without further words, very faithfully and very affectionately.   A.L.

1. Reference to the oft-quoted verse from Paul Verlaine's "Art poétique":

> Prends l'éloquence et tords-lui son cou!

> [Take eloquence and wring its neck!]

2. English in original.

3. *Oc* is the word for "yes" in Provençal, which was spoken throughout southern France until the thirteenth century; it is traditionally opposed to the language of northern France (which became modern French), in which "yes" was *oïl* (later *oui*).

4. George Seferis (1900-1971), the Greek diplomat and poet who was to be awarded the Nobel Prize for literature in 1963. He had visited the United States in 1956 and 1957.

5. English in original.

6. *Gynerium argenteum* or uva grass.

7. This is a narrow path, almost completely hidden by brush, that skirts the rim of the cliffs of the Presqu'île de Giens and that forms part of a continuous "coast guard" path that skirts all the coasts of France.

8. Von Hofmannsthal had written, in an article intended as a preface to *Anabase* and first published in the *Neue Schweizer Rundschau* of May 1929: "Evocative of purity and severity, of domination and self-control, the following words occur again and again: scalebeam; pure salt; the pure idea; the cleansing and sanctifying qualities of salt—*les délices du sel*." (James Stern trans.)

9. The French fabulist La Fontaine (1621-1695), inherited the official post of Master of Waters and Forests. The Tax Farmers were the hated contractual tax-collectors of the Old Regime, while the Masters of the Wolf-Hunt were the officers of the state organization for the extermination of wolves first instituted by French kings long before the fourteenth century and subsisting, as a purely honorific title, even today. The Salt-Tax Collectors (or *gabelous*, from *gabelle*, the tax on salt) were as unpopular as the Tax Farmers, under the Old Regime.

10. See above, letter 344, note 2.

11. The nearby town of Hyères was a wintering spot frequented by Queen Victoria and by any number of English writers including Robert Louis Stevenson, Joseph Conrad, and Edward Lear, as well as such Anglophile American writers as Edith Wharton and her friend Henry James. The French writers mentioned are the poet and statesman, Alphonse Lamartine, the historian Jules Michelet (both of the Romantic Era), and the great popularizer of Russian literature in France, the Vicomte de Vogüé (1848-1910). AL's friend Paul Valéry had been a frequent visitor to the area, where he spent vacations at the villa of the Comtesse Behague, a stone's throw to the east of Les Vigneaux.

12. See above, letter 312, note 3.

13. See next letter.

14. Italian in original.

346

To Mrs. Henry T. Curtiss   *Les Vigneaux,*
Chapelbrook   *Presqu'île de Giens (Var)*
Ashfield Road,   *September 9, 1959*
Williamsburg, Mass.

Mina, my peace here is made, and the alliance consummated. Les Vigneaux has had its way with me! "For better or for worse," as you say in America before the person who performs the marriage ceremony. And I've found the second well; it shall be my wedding ring.

The more I circulate in this Mediterranean south of France, against which I've always had pronounced aversions and prejudices, the more I am convinced of the exceptional character of this peninsula of Giens, by virtue of its cliffs and rocky spit, with the best air circulation of the whole coast. On the day when the Lady of Chapelbrook, who had explored and searched on my behalf along all the coasts of France (islands being out of the question) set foot on this blessed spot, I know a magic finger pointed the way just as a water-diviner's rod does. May the gods who guided her still hold me in their favor! My old obsessions of sadness and precariousness now do a Pyrrhic war dance far from me, out on the steppes of forgetfulness and the sands of the past. The great shadows of exile will no longer be cast upon my terraces, now open to the future. Diane is happy here, and we laugh a lot. And here I am master, on French soil, of a hearth and home. And you, dear Mina, have the right to smile from afar at all the rather miraculous things that somehow favored me here.

Don't think for a minute that Diane and I might ever desert America, to which I owe so much. I shall keep my residence in Washington and will henceforward spend six months in France and six months in America. My years of exile in your country, and the wonderful welcome that was there assured me, increases for me the debt of gratitude that my grandparents had already incurred at the time of the first French Revolution.[1] And wasn't my birthplace, after all, geographically in the American Atlantic? All these are things which can not fail to mean a great deal, deep in the heart of me, a Frenchman from the Islands. So it is share and share alike, between my ties with Europe and with America.

In our thoughts Diane and I often join you on the other side of the water at Chapelbrook, which will forever be paired in some way for me with Les Vigneaux. Give us more details about your summer in Massachusetts.

Here I continue the work of fencing and brush-clearing—(work required by regulation to eliminate the fire hazard). And I'm going ahead with laying out of service paths in the big pine grove choked with gorse (and sometimes I bring back the fairylike sloughed-off skin of a beautiful grass snake). I've already made much more than just a start on the steps and cornices along the whole seaward side of my house. I've cleaned out my three copses of evergreen oaks[2] (which are really black oaks to me!); thinned out, at the bottom of the valley, my stand of wild acacias, and made the first inroads, on the hillside, for a few rugged paths around the upper mass, still impenetrable, of my thornbush thicket (domain reserved for the fox and for a stormy-weather brook).

We'd love to show you a little of all this. Diane has put aside for you a selection of the finest sandals in the region, as well as your Italian straw hat and the bathing suits which you left, rather than forgot, here. But will the spell of your princely roses and your mountain laurel,[3] and soon your autumn witch hazel,[3] be broken soon enough to leave you time to fly out our way?

And what lovely little trips there are to tempt you into the hinterland! Diane, who is a fine swimmer and canoeist, is also a wonderful companion to me at the steering wheel of her little car, and I am quite willing to be initiated along with her into all the high back country, which holds real surprises and endless attractions—distant glimpses of green expanses and of wild horizons wooded by only one species, the pine—which scarcely conceal from us the relief, and does not at all conceal the movement, of tremendous geological upheavals—all without prettiness or rhetoric, or as it is better put in the testament of M. de Saint-Simon, "without magnificence or modesty."[4] What unexpected authority there is in all these uplands of back-country Provence!—a land teeming, they say, with boars, and in whose skies still occasionally hover the last great raptors in France, doomed to extinction. . . . And then suddenly the rupture, or shattering, of all this green solitude for the unexpected appearance, in the open, of human habitations. And there before us is the magic of all this French concern for things human, a concern in which an assimilated clarity recovers its grace, measure, and vitality. You would love this chain of little communities happily perched on their bare eminences. Diane distributes the alms of her graciousness on ten stone villages with which she is on familiar terms, and the good folk of the place are all smiles for her; she transforms them all into the *Ravis* and other *Santons*[5] of the traditional Provençal Christmas manger.

Dear friend, come back to see us. This is my last letter from exile, or rather, from an exile that is almost over. Diane, here with me, opens her heart to France the way you do; and from France, dear Mina, we both open our arms to you.   A.

—At Chapelbrook, don't forget that clearing we decided on so as to make the view back of your new dwellings visible.

—I'm very sad over the news you give me of Cummings' health,[6] for he is quite as congenial to me as a human being as he is intellectually—a good writer and a born poet. Always remember me to him affectionately, and to Marion.[7]

—Yes, you guessed right. Accepting that Grand Prix National des Lettres[8] meant for me a sorry sacrifice of all my principles and tastes. I gave in, far away as I was, for purely moral, and very unliterary, reasons. Officially notified about the award by the French Ambassador in Washington, I felt that, being away from France, I must not do anything that might be interpreted as even the slightest slackening of my allegiance to France. The very national character of the literary prize, freely awarded by a committee of French writers, sufficed, in this instance, to force my decision, quite apart from all political considerations.

1. An ancestor in the collateral branch of AL's family who had been an officer in the king's army at the time of the French Revolution had emigrated and taken refuge on the island of Sapelo, off the coast of the state of Georgia. The ancestor, after painfully setting up a plantation on the island, died there.

2. The holm oak (*Quercus ilex*) native to southern Europe.

3. English in original.

4. See above, letter 49, note 2.

5. The *santons* are the figurines used in the Provençal Nativity groups displayed at Christmas. The *ravi* is the "happy man," the ecstatic beholder with uplifted arms who was always included in the Nativity group.

6. E. E. Cummings was crippled with arthritis during his later years. He died in 1962. See letter to Cummings, Dec. 1949. (324)

7. E. E. Cummings' wife.

8. AL was awarded the Grand Prix National des Lettres in 1959, along with the Grand Prix International de Poésie.

LETTERS TO ALAIN BOSQUET
(1951-1955)

347

To Monsieur Alain Bosquet[1]
Paris

Washington,
October 18, 1951

Dear friend,

[. . .] My answer to you is yes, finally.[2]

You yourself foresaw what my dislikes would be; you know my tastes, and one is not likely to change them at my age.[3] But neither can one, at my age, avoid certain things, and the *Cahiers de la Pléiade*[4] have indeed raised the portcullis. (As a matter of fact, they did it quite elegantly.) Still with some misgivings, I yield, chiefly because the thing has been entrusted to you.

So go ahead, and do your best. I know I'm in good hands [. . .].

Cordially.

Saint-John Perse

1. Alain Bosquet, poet and critic of Belgian origin. He was the co-founder, along with Yvan Goll, of the short-lived bilingual poetry magazine, *Hémisphères*, based in New York. It was in the first issue of that magazine that AL's *Poème à l'étrangère* was first printed (Summer 1943).

2. In answer to a request from Bosquet for permission to write and publish a study of AL in the "Poètes d'Aujourd'hui" series put out by Pierre Seghers. The volumes in this series are intended as popularizations and introductions. Each is made up of a long critical essay followed by selections from the poet's works, with photographic illustrations throughout.

3. AL was sixty-four at this date.

4. The special St.-John Perse issue published in 1950.

348

To Monsieur Alain Bosquet   *Washington,*
Paris   *November 30, 1951*

Dear friend,

I have written to Gallimard, asking him to grant the reproduction rights you desire.

I'm writing to a member of my family in Paris to assemble the little file of required snapshots.

For the biographical part, I request that you be as matter-of-fact as possible. You know how I feel about that. The author's personal life does not belong to the reader; only the published work is rightfully his, like a fruit picked off the tree. I've already seen enough tales circulated about me, stuff that belongs in newspaper feature-stories rather than in a literary analysis. Just stick to the mere vital statistics [. . .]. The pictures, since there seems no way around including them, will amply fulfill the requirements of this series for popular consumption.[1]

I think that, in a general way, it might be to your advantage to raise the level of this sort of publication by emphasizing the literary aspect, thereby turning it into a real essay. You are in a perfect position to do just that, and your scruples in this regard qualify you all the more for it. I am thinking of your own entrance upon the present Paris literary scene, where you will have to take your place with a certain show of authority, since every affirmation or development of your own work will be carefully scrutinized. I am, moreover, happy to see that your liking for my work and for its author should not be a drawback in any way in the present situation, for your own works owe nothing to mine, and your voice is distinctively your own.

I'm in total disagreement with you when it comes to

any reference to the works that the Germans made off with.[2]—There is no point in drawing public attention to works that are lost, that the public will never read, and that can never be judged. It is in bad taste; and, above all, it's a psychological error that puts the writer in an unfavorable light, for he would inevitably be suspected of self-serving or literary posturing. In any event, there is a certain cheap romanticism about it. If you have to mention the fact incidentally, do it very summarily. Even the information I had to furnish you privately—as preliminary indicators and practical pointers, when I still entertained some hope of tracking things down in the American sector—would really be no longer relevant to your study.

Thanks for telling me about the German editions of *Anabase* and *Eloges*[3] [. . .].

I am happy for you about your settling down in Paris. This is the right moment for you to set yourself up there and take stock [. . .]. This new start, in any case, will do you a world of good. But aren't you too hard put, on the material side? What kind of arrangements are available to you? Above all, don't let your health suffer in any way, as it will always play a crucial part in your intellectual effectiveness. One must go through life, even the literary life, like a thoroughbred animal.

My very best wishes to you, dear friend.

Saint-John Perse

—I received *Langue morte*[4] only yesterday; it must have come by sea. I'll report to you about it in detail.

1. See above, letter 347, note 2.
2. The works in manuscript confiscated and presumably destroyed by the Nazis. See above, letter 291, note 4.
3. One cannot be sure just which German editions are here referred to.
4. A volume of poems by Bosquet published in 1951.

349

To Monsieur Alain Bosquet   *Washington,*
Paris   *December 9, [1952]*

Dear friend,

[. . .] For your study, I have no excisions to suggest, especially since I have forbidden myself to suggest anything that might seem to alter your own basic thinking. —Not even for the "Affinities" chapter,[1] though you must surely surmise what I thought about it here and there. But I am only following your own example when I advise suppressing the whole page of quotations from V. Segalen—who is brought up in only a very incidental and isolated way, quite outside the framework or main lines of your own argument, in a most anachronistic connection.

As for the question of the photographic illustrations, you'll have to decide on that for yourself; I'm sure you'll make the best of it. Since it has to be done, I think it might be wise to satisfy certain technical considerations. Remember just one thing: that, for the body of the book, I expressed only one wish, which is really a demand: the reproduction, no matter what the technical difficulties may be, of the page of decrees that were issued against me by the Vichy government.[2] And please take special care to reassemble the snapshots that are used and to return the whole album to the following address: Mlle. Eliane Saint-Leger Leger,[3] 22 bis, rue Jouffroy, Paris.

—One last answer: The poem, "Midi, ses fauves, ses famines . . ." (which I sent you for the first issue of your review *Exils*)[4] was a short fragment of the long poem *Amers*. No, in spite of all the support and cooperation I would like to extend at this time to your courageous enterprise as director of the review, I can't promise you a thing for your next issue, for the simple reason that I have nothing available that I could detach from any work in progress.

I'm still waiting for your first issue to arrive. I'll say good things about it in this country, and anywhere else I may have the chance. Don't lose confidence, in spite of the material difficulties that are already hard enough to overcome on the personal level in the Paris literary world. In every undertaking that we really get involved in, a mysterious and increasing force of "creative evolution" comes into play [. . .].

For yourself, your own work, and for *Exils*, my very best wishes.

Saint-John Perse

1. Bosquet's study contained a chapter (the first chapter of the second part of his study) entitled "Les affinités," in which he discussed real and supposed similarities between AL's poetry and a great variety of other works and documents. Among these is the book by Victor Segalen (1878-1919) entitled *Stèles* (published posthumously in 1922) from which Bosquet cites four passages (p. 97 of his *Saint-John Perse*).

2. This was done. The photograph of these documents appears between pp. 40 and 41 of Bosquet's study.

3. AL's unmarried sister.

4. *Exils*, a short-lived literary review launched by Bosquet in Paris in 1952. AL's text, "Midi, ses fauves, ses famines. . . ." actually did appear in the first number of the review (Oct. 1952). The text was to become the closing passage ("Dédicace") of *Amers* (*Seamarks*).

350

To Monsieur Alain Bosquet   *Washington, March 9, 1953*
Paris

Dear friend,

I have received the personal copy of your little book,[1] which you were so kind as to send me by air. I thank you for all the care and trouble you put into it, and I want to reassure you very promptly about those aspects of it over which you had no control. The material presentation is certainly better than usual for this popularizing series. It seems to have improved a bit in order to match the tone of what you wrote. And that is the important thing.

As friend to friend, I accept this tribute, partial to me though it may be, because in so doing I experience, quite simply, a double satisfaction: first, of finding something of my own thought in this projection for public consumption; and second, of feeling sure that your essay, in itself, apart from its subject, is very much to your credit—in its literary correctness and in its general appropriateness to the level for which it was intended. I like the intelligent insight that comprises its density, and certain incisive qualities that justify its stance.

As for what you tell me about the exposure to public view that I'll now have to put up with—at least your little book will counteract the worst "refraction indices," as they say in physics.

And above all, don't worry yourself over those minimal typographical errors that depress you so. Those that I myself noticed were unimportant (such as "March" instead of "May," in my birthdate).

As for copies to be sent out, I request only three of them, for relatives—my three sisters, to whom you are indebted for the preservation of a selection of personal snapshots: Mlle. Eliane Saint-Leger Leger, 22 bis, rue Jouffroy, in Paris; Mme. Abel Dormoy (same address); Mme. Ubaldo Sommaruga,[2] Via Sismondi, 62, Milan, Italy.

[. . .] But all that is very minor, compared to what I wish to express, right now, in my cordial handclasp.

Saint-John Perse

1. Bosquet's study of AL. See above, letter 347, note 2.
2. Mesdames Dormoy and Sommaruga, AL's two married sisters. For Eliane, see above, letter 349, note 3.

351

To Monsieur Alain Bosquet   *Washington,*
                                             October 30, 1955

Dear friend,

I follow the course of your literary activity in Paris as much as I can [. . .].

I liked quite a number of things in *Langue morte* that have the authentic ring of your voice and express the demands you make upon yourself. *Quel Royaume oublié?*[1] brings me still more—sharper, more basic, and swifter. Disdainful as you are of any sort of facile conformity, it is most reassuring to see you strike out, right from the start, for what is most elliptical, but without giving way too much to abstractness—a tendency that has dealt a mortal blow to so many excellent poets. The dangers posed by intelligence are always very great for those who, in poetry, are not intelligent enough or strong enough to put intelligence in its place. I've often caught glimpses in what you write of a real intellectual conflict. I think you win out, on the plane you have selected; and the very quality of the movement, in the quite apparent progression of your poetic work, seems to keep you from deincarnation (horrible word!).

When I think of you—a friend who has so many difficulties to overcome, in such a time as this, simply to insure the material necessities of a literary life—I am at least happy to think that the development, even the success, of your activities as a critic, obliges you to establish ever more radically this dual personality [. . .].

With friendly regards.   Saint-John Perse

1. Two collections of poems by Bosquet. *Langue morte* was published in 1951, *Quel Royaume oublié* in 1955.

LETTERS TO PIERRE GUERRE
(1956-1964)

352

To Monsieur Pierre Guerre[1]   *Monhegan Island (Maine)*
Marseilles   *August 17, 1956*

I think about you, dear friend, and chide myself for not writing more often.

I always seek out the notes in the *Cahiers du Sud* that bear your signature; it pleases me to find in them your broad and lively human curiosity. You are of the opinion that we will never meet, but *I* know that one day I will shake your hand, maybe even in Marseilles, or at least somewhere else in France. And to me it won't be the hand of a stranger that I clasp.

I'm returning, still completely befogged, from a long sailing cruise farther to the north (banks of Newfoundland and the coasts of Labrador). A month and a half at sea without a single day of dry sails, but affording me the chance to shake quite a number of Breton hands.

I keep thinking of all the anguish that weighs so heavily on our national life, of all the efforts that come to nought because of human error. I have no trouble at all imagining the zone of sadness in which my thought coincides with yours.

Cordially.   Alexis Leger

1. Pierre Guerre (1910-1978), a lawyer, writer, and scholar of Marseilles long associated with the review, *Cahiers du Sud*, published his *Saint-John Perse et l'homme* in 1955. He was the first visitor at Les Vigneaux when AL took possession of the villa in 1957. From then on, he and AL remained fast friends, and in 1974 he became the Director of the Fondation Saint-John Perse in Aix-en-Provence, a post he held until his death.

353

To Monsieur Pierre Guerre   *Harbor Island (Bahamas)*
Marseilles   *April 27, 1964*

We hear nothing from you any more, dear friend.

Of these isles, these hours, these waters I will say nothing. I'll simply throw this bottle into the sea for you, with the reading of my present position:

> —37¼ degrees west longitude
> —24½ degrees north latitude

Affectionately.   A. L.

LETTER TO HENRI PEYRE
(1956)

354

To Monsieur Henri Peyre[1]
Yale University, Dept. of French
New Haven, Connecticut

*Washington,
August 19, 1956*

Dear friend,

[...] I am happy about what you say concerning my latest published poem.[2] But I must ask you to excuse me from participating in plans for a public reading of it in Washington. You will understand when I tell you this: I am opposed, on principle, to all recitation of poetry, which seems to me—at least so far as French is concerned—to limit or deform the implications of the text as it leads one along its various pathways, whether they be concurrent or divergent. (Admirable duplicity—or multiplicity—of the French tongue, that can thank its very spareness for its power to liberate so many simultaneous or associated suggestions, since its individual words, as in monetary systems, play the role of fiduciary signs.) And still more particularly, where I am concerned, I have never been able to endure the idea of reading anything aloud, even to myself; and I am completely unaware of what my voice, as a poet, must sound like. Poetry seems to me fashioned only for the inner ear.

I would ask anyone but you, dear friend, not to see in this any affectation on my part. But you are not among those who have ever suspected me of oratorical facility, nor of being rhetorical in the unfavorable sense of the word.

I am, however, delighted at the prospect of seeing you again this winter in Washington [. . .]. May you find in America a bit more peace of mind for the furthering of your personal activities as well as of your French activities abroad. We'll talk some more about all that. I would also like to hear what you have to say, when you get back, about many things in France.[3] As you can imagine, I am haunted by all that hangs over our national life at the moment [. . .].

My cordial wishes to you.   Saint-John Perse

1. Henri Peyre (b. 1901), long-time chairman of the French department of Yale University and author of numerous works of literary criticism. Peyre was instrumental in persuading AL to accept an honorary Doctor of Letters degree from Yale University in 1959.

2. Probably "Etroits sont les vaisseaux" (incorporated into *Amers* as Canto ix of the "Strophe"), which appeared for the first time in the July 1956 issue of the NRF.

3. The looming cloud on the French political horizon in the summer of 1956 was the Suez crisis precipitated by President Nasser of Egypt's nationalization of the Suez Canal, 26 July 1956, which was to result in the abortive intervention of France and Great Britain in Egypt in November.

LETTER TO MONSIEUR HUGUES LE GALLAIS
(1957)

355

To Monsieur Hugues Le Gallais[1]
Ambassador of the Grand Duchy
  of Luxembourg
Washington

Washington,
February 1, 1957

Dear friend,

The spice of life is always to be found in its misunderstandings. And you always reserve for us the surprise of so many unexpected things.

You gave me no advance hint of the choice quality of your guests at the excellent dinner you invited me to the other night. You mustn't be surprised at my surprise at finding myself the only layman in a gathering of renowned orientalists of various nationalities; and please don't take it amiss that I so often refused to participate, in spite of the insistence of your guests, in the scientific controversy that later took up the better part of that long evening with you. It was certainly not out of lack of interest, but simply because I knew that I was not qualified enough to take part in the discussion and had nothing to contribute on the questions that were raised.

I have always protested against the way people insist on endowing me with real competence in matters of orientalism, but I've never been able to convince anyone— not even you, dear friend. I read neither Chinese nor Japanese, modern or ancient, and I can make nothing of the old Japanese Zen Buddhist calligraphy. During the five years I was in China, in constant contact with four or five of the world's greatest orientalists whom the events of the moment had thrown together there, I never made any real attempt to acquire from them, in any methodical way, any truly scientific knowledge. Life is at once too short and too vast to permit imposing such limitations.

Dare I go even further and confess to you that I would never really have acquired a taste for oriental studies? They strike me, in themselves, as another form of exile, which they simulate rather badly in their retroversion. They can even be, for fanatical adherents, a sort of deprivation or intoxication that transforms the living man into a kind of deserter, turning his back on the life of the present or future. I think that, in my own case, I have never lost my foothold in the present. My interest in oriental studies has always been in the spirit of those studies, not their letter—a kind of necromancer's or conjurer's art, turned exclusively to the timeless aspect of the past. Furthermore, my personal life in China steeped me in things Asiatic much less than people think. Even here, in my exile, in this country where the finest collections in the world are to be found—especially the most overwhelming of all to me—that is, the collections of sacred bronzes—I never go near a great museum without feeling a certain uneasiness or remorse, the way a deserter must feel.

Modern oriental studies seem to me to have evolved a great deal, preoccupied now, like all the other scientific disciplines, with the letter more than with the spirit. No longer does ancient Orient meet modern Occident, as it did in my youth, in London or Paris—but rather in New York or Chicago, in the German or Japanese schools of thought.

Now that I have said all this, and at too great length, please don't doubt for a moment the lively interest I took, the other night, in following the scientific discus-

sion at your dinner, even though I refused to be put on
the spot by your erudite guests from three different
countries. But don't expect me to put forward any personal conclusion concerning the various controversies,
which arose rather more from exegesis than from any
general interpretation.

In regard to what more particularly concerns the historical and epigraphic study of that marvelous Zen painting that graces your collection, and that we have both
talked about so often, it just seems to me that the dating
proposed by your renowned orientalists was not very
convincing. I'd some day like to know what Suzuki[2]
might say to you about it.

In answer to your letter, and since you insist, come
what may, on having something by me in the projected
brochure, I have no objection to your printing the four
lines that I left in your autograph album last night. By
the sheerest coincidence, they are a very free paraphrase
of the Zen priest's inscription on his enigmatic painting.
(But at your own risk and peril, dear friend, for getting
Saint-John Perse mixed up in all this will not add an
authoritative note to the public display of your collection
in Venice, where the painting in question is to be included, along with all its inscriptions.) All I ask is that
you restore the ritually accepted capitals for the five key
words in my bad quatrain (doesn't rhyme right): Passion, Flame, Thunder, Lightning, and Scythe. Their
visual presentation should, to the mind, fuse with the
total flash of the Japanese artist's magnificent brush-
stroke, in it fine flourish:

Preserve, O Passion, your Flame without smoke,
Thunderbolt! resume your paths consumed . . .
Drunk, the Scythe that cuts down all the straw
Does not cross the Lightning in my human night.[3]

No objection either to your utilizing, since you want so much to do it, this quotation from Saint-John Perse on your Christmas cards[4] as a literary motto.[4] (Which, moreover, was never my motto, as I've never had one.)

How much finer, infinitely, in its simplicity is the casual inscription of the Japanese monk:

> *The Kite says: Let the Wind blow!*
> *I have no desire for flowers.*

With warm regards, my friend, and with the prospect in the near future, I hope, of some new surprise at your house—maybe in your cellar, where your great French wines confer with each other. There, I would consent to speak up.

Alexis Saint-Leger Leger

1. Hugues Le Gallais (1896-1964) was Ambassador of Luxembourg to the United States from 1955 to 1958. He possessed a very fine collection of oriental art, including a seventeenth-century Zen Buddhist painting of a kite. The painting and a reduced facsimile of AL's French version of its inscription are reproduced in *Honneur à Saint-John Perse* following p. 807.

2. Daisetz T. Suzuki (1870-1966), Japanese authority on Zen Buddhism and author of several important books on the subject.

3. See above, note 1. The original reads:
> *Garde, ô Passion, ta flamme sans fumée,*
> *Foudre! reprends ta route consumée . . .*
> *Ivre, la faux qui tranche tous les chaumes*
> *Ne croise point l'éclair de ma nuit d'homme.*

4. English in original.

LETTERS TO DAG HAMMARSKJÖLD
(1958-1960)

356

To Monsieur
  Dag Hammarskjöld[1]
The Secretary General
The United Nations
New York

Les Vigneaux,
Presqu'île de Giens (Var)
September 1958

Dear friend,

I was just going to write to you. Our thoughts seem to attract each other by a kind of magnetism. I reply to your letter.

I wanted to tell you how I've been following, week by week, and then day by day, the blown spume of political currents from which you've emerged, every time, head above water—sometimes a scapegoat and then again a lifebuoy against cowardice, inconsistency, and confusion, each time to the final advantage of all parties concerned [. . .].

Here I'm wrestling with a new work[2] that suddenly begins of itself to gravitate in my orbit and that will once more have America as its setting. Life in France doesn't bring me the peace of mind I had hoped for. Not that I am abandoning my solitude in any way, for I haven't told anyone this year that I'm here, any more than I did last year. But everything I am able to sense at the moment about French public affairs worries me a good deal: political inertia, general passivity, even a slackening of the social reflex—they all deprive the country of its best chances for a great national revival [. . .]. In cases like this, even exceptional circumstances no longer act as a counterirritant [. . .].

Cordially.   Alexis Saint-Leger Leger

1. Dag Hammarskjöld (1905-1961), the Swedish statesman who was Secretary General of the United Nations from 1953 to 1961, when he was killed in an airplane crash over Rhodesia. This and the three following letters to Hammarskjöld are printed on pp. 634-637 of OC and are not included in the "Lettres" section.

2. The poem *Chronique*, which Hammarskjöld was to translate into Swedish: *Kronika*, a bilingual edition published by Alb. Bonniers Forlag, Stockholm, 1960.

357

To Monsieur Dag Hammarskjöld   *Washington,*
Secretary General,   *February 1959*
The United Nations
New York

Dear friend,

Ubiquity has become your most important prerogative, and one really gets out of breath trying, along with the press, to follow you around the planet. To speak as they do in the Orient, the wheel of the law turns in vain for you, since it finds you at its very center one moment, and then the next, on its rim. Even the press can't keep up with you.

Yet I must somehow manage to catch up with you somewhere, so I can tell you how much I liked that serious, firm speech you delivered at the end of January at the Rockefeller Institute on the occasion of the Atoms for Peace Award Ceremony.[1] What a striking, broad synthesis you managed to achieve in those three pages in depicting the ever-expanding dynamism of our time;

and how I like your pithy condensations! I sincerely believe that pages like these go far beyond giving official recognition as "judicial evidence"; they surely merit inclusion, literarily, in the collection of your public utterances that you must one day publish [. . .]. Your reflections, in the grand manner, capture the rhythm of an epoch [. . .].

I'd like to see you in New York before I fly off to the south of France this summer.

Most cordially yours.   Alexis Saint-Leger Leger

1. Address delivered at the Atoms for Peace Award Ceremony on 29 Jan. 1959 in the Rockefeller Institute, New York.

358

To Monsieur Dag Hammarskjöld   *Les Vigneaux,*
The Secretary General,   *Presqu'île de Giens (Var)*
The United Nations   *August 16, 1959*
New York

Dear friend,

Thinking of you, I was questioning your little bronze Anubis, who is the tutelary god of my Mediterranean study, when I heard over the radio one evening the news of your lightning trip to France [. . .]. But once again this is not the occasion for a stopover on my cliff; and I doubt very much that you were even able to get a fleeting glance of your own cliff, in the north—you, the man forever deprived of vacations and respite! [. . .]

How I'd love to go over all the current problems of the international situation with you! Your obligations at the U.N. are all so different, except for the importance of what is ultimately at stake each time [. . .].

Here, from my peninsular retreat, all I can discern, alas! is the massive paralysis in which French political thought is becoming locked—an increasingly negative and static body of thought that has adopted outward signs of just the opposite sort, which are mere rhetoric. There is more passivity in all this than we suspect, or at least more uncertainty and "insecurity complex,"[1] more of a dilatory and hesitant attitude, the elimination of more and more reflexes and a tacit giving up, in all the superficial stubbornness and all the temporizing, which are simply escapism[1] [. . .]. As a matter of fact—and at such a crucial turning point in history, so fraught with possibilities—the immobility of France may make us pay dearly for this pulling of the wheel of time off its axle [. . .].

Most cordially yours.   Alexis Saint-Leger Leger

1. English in original.

359

To Monsieur Dag Hammarskjöld   *Washington, June 3, 1960*
The Secretary General,
The United Nations
New York

Dear friend,
I like the speech you gave at the New Law Building in Chicago.[1] This "creative evolution" of international law, as you describe it, has always interested me passionately. Your aerial reconnaissance supplies an excellent photographic record for the future; and no matter how lofty your vision may be, it never loses sight of the earth. Biology and sociology, quite as much as political science, are the bases of any broad humanism.

I'm flying off to the south of France from New York on the 17th. Once more, not without misgivings. A feeling of disgust at all the "Jesuitism," all the "prima donnaism" prevailing at the moment, in contempt of all that, for me, constitutes the true spirit of France—its real soul, its source of humanizing influence. When its comes to renovation, we're really back into paleontology. We're paying the price for a basic flaw in the regime that was there at the outset [. . .].

I'll stay on at Giens until the end of October and will return[2] in November, after a brief stopover in Paris.

My best wishes go with you, as always, in your ceaseless activity; and my friendly thought will reach out toward you by way of all I can learn of your activities through the international press.

Cordially yours.

Alexis Saint-Leger Leger

1. Address delivered at the dedicatory celebration of the new Law Buildings of the University of Chicago Law School, 1 May 1960.

2. To Washington, D.C.

LETTER FOR MARK VAN DOREN[1]
(1959)

360

LETTER READ AT A BANQUET IN HONOR OF
MARK VAN DOREN HELD AT COLUMBIA UNIVERSITY,
NEW YORK, APRIL 29, 1959.

Friend, in every country the loneliness of the writer is great, but here on the immense reaches of this planetary America consumed by industrial fever, it is even greater.
. . .

During the nights of the long winter when we count our lamps, to think of Mark Van Doren is to seek, as far as eyesight can pierce, in the depths of the night and the forest, the fire, far off, of a bright hearth where a vigil flame is tended.

"Neighbor, we didn't see much of each other this season, but there was light in your house; you were there, and that was a great deal."

And indeed, all of us have to live, one day, our *Winter Diary*;[2] but who can be assured he will do it with enough humility of heart and enough secret pride to merit, as you do, the state of grace in which such a meditation takes shape?

And who, then, clinging so closely to his human surrounding and his time among men, could, in the same breath, be at one and the same time more wholly himself and more universal, more immediate and more timeless?

We praise you, very pure poet and smiling friend, for having kept alive, in your words as a writer and your presence as a man, this profound thought that, for us, is neither an abstraction nor an intellectual game, but that very thing you cherished so much in one who was close to you: "a subtle, delicate concern with whatever it is that we mean when we say human life, and a capacity for honoring that life whenever it is most gentle and generous. . . ."[3]

Thus, upon your living face, the poet's face is not a mask; a single truth unites for us the two equally authentic beings that we love in Mark Van Doren.

Saint-John Perse

1. Mark Van Doren (1894-1972), American poet, critic, and teacher, introduced to AL by Allen Tate in 1942. See letter to Tate of 8 June 1950. (272)

2. *A Winter Diary* (1935), one of Van Doren's books of poems.

3. Quotation unidentified.

LETTER TO ANDRÉ ROUSSEAUX
(1959)

361

To Monsieur André Rousseaux[1]
Paris

Les Vigneaux,
Presqu'île de Giens (Var)
July 30, 1959

Dear friend,

[. . .] How often my wife and I speak about the in-comparable trip through Provence we took with you on my return to France. I was already fond, as you were, of the fervor, the keenness, of that lively Haute Provence, devoid of self-indulgence. The beautiful stretch covered in one long haul in the uplands still trails its luminous wake within me. It is helping me to distinguish the basic lines of force of an invisible earthly power that I need in order decently to overcome my old anti-Mediterranean prejudices [. . .].

With a friendly handclasp.   Saint-John Perse

1. André Rousseaux (b. 1896), French critic and essayist, who was to contribute an article to a homage-to-AL issue of the *Cahiers du Sud* (Oct.-Nov. 1959) entitled "Dans l'empire des choses vraies."

LETTER TO MARIA MARTINS
(1960)

362

To "Maria" Martins[1]   *Washington, [April] 1960*
Rio de Janeiro

Dear "Maria,"

You can't imagine what it meant to me, flying over Brazil without being able to stop there! I was the guest of the Argentine Government, traveling officially in a jet of the Argentine airline that did not stop at Rio.

I am still filled with gratitude for the extraordinary invitation from the Brazilian government, which you undoubtedly had arranged for me. It meant not only putting a wonderful dream within reach—the possibility of at last getting to know your country, which, in so many ways, attracts me by its powerful vitality (the obsessive dream of Amazonia, of its river, of its disquieting forests)—it also meant seeing "Maria" once again, surrounded by all her pagan sculpture—"Maria" of Washington and New York, freed at last from her obligations as ambassadress, her own mistress once again, confronting her savage gods [. . .].

I missed a chance, three years ago, of going with some American friends to the dedication of the Museum of Modern Art in Rio de Janeiro. At that time I learned, through my friends, that you had succeeded in getting into China all by yourself, and that certainly must have been more interesting for you than any return to things Parisian might have been. I would love to have compared your impressions as a traveler with my old memories of that country, which I will never see again, as I never have any desire to revisit any place. What would have interested me would have been, from someone such as you, who knows how to approach things in her own way, your reactions as a human being.

I really dare not hope that the official invitation of the Brazilian Government will ever be renewed, unless there is some new earthshaking event like the dedication of Brasilia! I was fully aware of what I was missing when I had to turn down the Brazilian invitation upon my return from Buenos Aires. But at that moment I really had to get back to Washington at once, for the most pressing reasons. My wanderings in Argentina kept me down there much longer than I had ever intended. I had been officially invited for twelve days and finally had to stay on for a month and a half. For a Frenchman, the exquisite way one is welcomed in that country is such that he can't resist it. At the outset, quite jokingly, I mentioned that my most unrealizable dream, my oldest and most secret wish, was one day to come to know Patagonia, the Straits of Magellan, Tierra del Fuego, and the Cape Horn archipelago. To my happy astonishment, I was immediately taken at my word; and thanks to the great elegance of the Argentine Government, with Navy planes and a gunboat based in the Antarctic at my disposal, I was able to range widely around Ushuaya, all the way to the icy landscapes of that whole wild part of the world, which has always haunted me, and which will forever fascinate, even almost obsess, me, as one of the most magnetically attractive points in the world—the lordly domain of the Wind! I hadn't met with anything like it since the freedom of my horseback trips into the Gobi Desert and Central Asia.[2] What surprises might that prodigious contrast, the Brazilian selva, now hold for me? It's a confrontation I can look forward to some day.

Meanwhile, I want to hear from "Maria." Tell me what you are absorbed in at the moment. How is your sculpture work coming on? In an American illustrated magazine I saw a photo of your magnificent outdoor sculpture for one of the esplanades of Brasilia.[3] Keep faith with your art, always as close as possible to primitive sources—your special fief, and remember I am always with you, most affectionately.

Saint-John Perse

1. The wife of Carlos Martins Souza, Brazilian Ambassador to the United States from 1939 to 1948. Maria Martins (1900-1973) was a sculptress of abstract and "primitive" works.

2. See AL's letters to his mother of 4 May 1920 (176), and 5 June 1920. (177)

3. In *The National Geographic* of May 1960, p. 707.

LETTER TO JUAN JOSÉ CASTRO
(1960)

363

To Monsieur Juan José Castro   *Washington, June 3, 1960*
Director of the National
  Orchestra of Buenos Aires

Dear friend,

[. . .] I'm leaving for France in a few days. I just want
to tell you how I prize the memory of the evening I spent
at your house in Buenos Aires among true friends: it
revealed to me so much about you [. . .].

Don't be surprised to receive from "Broadcast Music
Inc." of New York, a fat score by the American composer, Alan Hovhaness,[1] based on one of my works,
Anabase. I was the one who requested that it be sent to
you, recalling what you said to me about it [. . .].

I put a stop, somewhat too brutally perhaps, to studies
and preparations being made for its presentation in the
theater. Stokowski[2] had visions of an elaborate scenic
presentation à la Diaghilev, to put on the road in Europe
after its American showing. The Maestro finally had to
resign himself to working it up, with his Texas orchestra,
as a simple oratorio, no matter how thankless and austere
listening to such a long work at a concert may be. All
this preparatory work was abandoned because of the turn
Stokowski's career took after his divorce—his leaving
Texas, and the resumption of his freelancing without an
orchestra of his own. There's nothing I really regret in
all this, except for certain scruples I have with regard
to Hovhaness, who is a composer of great probity and
complete artistic integrity, and a very congenial chap into

the bargain. He had great hopes for this creation—a rather exceptional one according to Stokowski himself and according to Varèse.[3] So, the fact is that I found myself bringing the career of such a work to an abrupt halt.

I would now like to hear something of your own personal appraisal of the score that is being sent to you. Hovhaness unfortunately had to use the English text of the T. S. Eliot translation, unlike Karl Blomdahl, the Swedish composer, who for the same work used the original French text word for word[4]—a text that Stravinsky told me one day ought to be treated, musically, as fugue and counterpoint!

For you, dear friend, my most cordial remembrance [. . .].

Saint-John Perse

1. See above, letter 332, note 2.
2. Leopold Stokowski (1882-1977), the long-time conductor of the Philadelphia Symphony Orchestra.
3. Edgar Varèse. See above, letter 228, note 2.
4. The Swedish composer, Karl Birger Blomdahl (1916-1968), composed an oratorio, *Anabase* (1956), utilizing AL's original French text, though not quite word for word, as AL indicates. For musical reasons, Blomdahl was obliged to make occasional omissions from the original text.

LETTER TO MADAME KUMAR NEHRU
(1961)

364

To Madame Braj Kumar Nehru, Ambassador   *Washington,*
Indian Embassy, Washington, D.C.   *March 1961*

Dear Madame,

I thank you for your kind thought.

The little book on Tagore[1] is very well written and of quite unusual quality for a work of popularization. I was especially interested in all the new things it told me—about the man as well as about the writer—of the last part of so generously full a life.

Reading such a book allowed me to resume, with the Sage of Santiniketan, a very ancient dialogue, already more than fifty years old! that I held with him when I was still very young, in London, before the first World War. . . .[2] And the book also prolonged a little the charm of your conversation, one evening, in the house of a Georgetown friend.

At your feet, dear Madame, this homage and these good wishes.

Alexis St-L. Leger

1. The "little book on Tagore" has not been identified with certainty.

2. See letters to Gide of 7 Dec. 1912, 28 Jan. 1913, July 1913, 26 July 1913, Aug. 1913. (114, 115, 117-119)

LETTERS TO IGOR STRAVINSKY
(1958-1962)

365

To Monsieur Igor Stravinsky[1]　　　*New York, March 2, 1958*
North Wetherly Drive
Los Angeles, California

Dear friend,

I have just come from St. Thomas' Church, Fifth Avenue.

There was grandeur in this Sunday solemnity presided over by you.

And in the stone nave of this local church, your grandiose work erected another nave, of universal implications.

The performance of the Symphony of Psalms was especially affecting. . . . I am still deeply moved as my thought turns toward you, with my wishes, always of the best when they are for you.

Cordially.　　　Alexis Saint-Leger Leger

1. Igor Stravinsky (1882-1971) was an old friend of AL, who had met him in Paris before World War I and actually attended the tumultuous premiere of *Le Sacre du Printemps* in 1913. This letter is printed on p. 499 of OC and not included in the "Lettres" section.

366

To Monsieur Igor Stravinsky　　　*Washington,*
1260 North Wetherly Drive　　　*1621 34th Street, N.W.*
Los Angeles, California　　　*January 25, 1962*

Dear friend,

So now you are done with your recent physical ordeal in Washington.[1] I was rather worried, out of friendly concern, seeing you give so generously of yourself. Need-lessly so. You are of the race that has nothing to gain by holding back. And I quite understand why you feel this need to pursue, physically, the destiny of your work, even to the ultimate *corps-à-corps* with conducting. So, go right on being prodigal. Artistic creation was not in-vented, as woman is said to have been, for the hero's repose. Artistic creation is war itself. And you are a warrior. And besides, wisdom was not invented for the wise, any more than madness for the mad [. . .].

I very much hope our paths will cross soon again. Tell Vera[2] how vividly she is a part of my thoughts of you [. . .].

Affectionately yours.   Saint-John Perse

1. Stravinsky had completed still another concert tour, in spite of his eighty years.
2. Vera: Igor Stravinsky's second wife.

INDEX

Library of Congress Cataloging in Publication Data

Leger, Alexis Saint-Leger, 1889-1975.
   Letters.

   (Bollingen series; 87, 2)
   Includes index.
   "The French text of the letters is taken from the Pléiade
edition of Oeuvres complètes of St.-John Perse published by
Editions Gallimard . . . 1972."
   1. Léger, Alexis Saint-Léger, 1889-1975—
Correspondence. 2. Poets, French—20th century—
Correspondence. I. Knodel, Arthur, 1916-
II. Series.
PQ2623.E386Z5313   1978   848'.9'1209   [B]   78-9080
ISBN 0-691-09868-9